The Ship
That
Stood
Still

Captain Stanley Lord of the Californian. *Picture taken in 1908 when he was in command of Leyland Line's* Louisianian.

The Ship That Stood Still

The Californian and her mysterious role in the Titanic disaster

Leslie Reade

Edited and updated by
EDWARD P. DE GROOT

Foreword by Titanic survivor
Miss Eva Hart MBE, JP

W·W·NORTON & COMPANY
New York   London

Copyright © 1993 by Leslie Reade Estate
First American Edition 1993

Printed in the United States of America

Manufacturing by The Maple-Vail Manufacturing Group

Library of Congress Cataloging-in-Publication Data

Reade, Leslie.
  The ship that stood still : The Californian and her mysterious
role in the Titanic disaster / Leslie Reade : edited and updated by
Edward P. de Groot.
      p.   cm.
  Includes bibliographical references and index.
    I. Titanic (Steamship) 2. Californian (Ship) 3. Shipwrecks—
–North Atlantic Ocean.   I. Groot, Edward P. de   II. Title.
G530.T6R43   1993
910′.9163′4—dc20   92–44376

ISBN 0-393-03537-9

W. W. Norton & Company, Inc., 500 Fifth Avenue, New York, N.Y. 10110
W. W. Norton & Company Ltd., 10 Coptic Street, London WC1A 1PU

1 2 3 4 5 6 7 8 9 0

To

JUDITH ASHE

or my "Madame Sans Qui . . ." who
in all innocence married the *Titanic*
and yet somehow survived.

And to

STELLA

who bravely held another fort.

With love and gratitude to both.

Contents

List of diagrams

All illustrations are from the collections of the author and editor unless otherwise stated.

Foreword

by Miss Eva Hart MBE, JP

How vividly I remember seeing the lights of a ship when I was in the lifeboat, that cold April night in 1912, and how hopeful everyone was that help was coming forward from it.

I was, as a seven year old girl, with my parents aboard the ill-fated *Titanic*, on our way to begin a new life in Canada, but what a different future lay before me after that night.

My mother, who was awake, felt the impact, but not very much, as we were on the port side of the ship. She immediately woke my father, and myself. Father went to investigate and mother began to dress me. Before she could do so, he came back and said we must go on deck, taking me in his arms.

There was no panic at this stage, and my mother and I were put into lifeboat No.14 by my father. He then stood back and I saw him helping other women and children. After the boats were all lowered, people began to realize that there were too few lifeboats, and as we rowed away, we could hear the panic.

I watched the dreadful sight of the ship sinking, and heard the screams of people drowning; something I shall never forget.

Like everyone else in our boat, I saw the lights of a ship, not just some lights on the horizon, but clearly the lights of a ship. It seemed fairly close and I never saw it move; how we all hoped that help would come from it — rockets having been fired from our sinking ship — but our hopes were in vain.

Two Official Investigations were held, and it was reported that the ship we had seen was the *Californian*. Not until some time in the 1960s did I become aware that this was disputed. I have been asked so many times, both at home and abroad, to confirm that it was NOT the *Californian* I had seen, but this I am unable to do, as I do not know. At no time was I, or anyone else in our boat, sure about the identity of that ship; we were simply not near enough to tell, and as a magistrate I am fully aware of the importance of weighing evidence.

Whatever the identity of the ship I saw so clearly, I still feel bitter that she did not come to help us, as I am sure more lives could have been saved.

This book is a carefully studied and remarkable work, I am sure it will be greatly appreciated by all who read it.

Eva Hart
London, 20 June 1992

Introduction

Many people who have no interest in the sea, but who read mystery or detective stories, either to wake them up or to lull them to sleep, are sure to be familiar with the names *Mary Celeste, Waratah, Cyclops, København*. They are all ships that either disappeared or never reached port, and left not a single survivor to say why. They are among the most famous mysteries of the sea.

The *Californian* was a British steamer, afloat between 1902 and 1915, which, although she certainly failed to appear on a particular occasion, did not actually disappear and indeed reached port quite safely, with all her crew aboard, fit and working. Nevertheless, her name belongs with the mysterious quartet above and others whose stories have aroused endless speculation and argument.

The *Californian* was, and still is, inextricably linked with the *Titanic* because of the part she played — or did not play — in the tragedy. The fact that she did make port undamaged, so that all the evidence from the ship and crew was available for investigation makes her unique in the catalogue of mystery ships. She was distinguished also in that the puzzle she presented was compounded at least as much by questions relating to human behaviour as those of nautical technicalities. Less sensational perhaps than any of the other four vessels mentioned, her story has a strange and bizarre quality of its own, even possibly with an occasional hint of comedy, and, without doubt, her case and the conduct of her master, Captain Stanley Lord, have caused more controversy than all the others combined.

I believe that the most probable solution to the case of the *Californian* will be found in what follows in this book.

Principal characters

Andrews, Thomas — Managing Director of Harland & Wolff.

Balfour, Gilbert William — Marconi travelling inspector in *Baltic*.

Barnish, Geoffrey — *Carpathia* 4th Officer.

Barnett, Captain Thomas W. — The 'Inspector' of the 1990-1992 Reappraisal.

Barrett, Frederick — Leading Stoker, *Titanic* No. 6 Boiler Room.

Bates, E.J.M. — Receiver of Wreck, Liverpool.

Beesley, Lawrence — *Titanic* 2nd Class passenger; important eyewitness.

Biles, Professor Sir John Harverd — Assessor at Mersey inquiry.

Binns, Jack — Marconi expert; examined *Californian's* set.

Bishop, Dickinson H. — *Titanic* 1st Class passenger; witness to times.

Bisset, James — *Carpathia* 2nd Officer. Witness to sighting of *Californian*.

Boxhall, Joseph Grove — *Titanic* 4th Officer. Reckoned SOS position. Fired rockets.

Bride, Harold S. — *Titanic* Junior, and surviving wireless operator.

Buley, Edward John — *Titanic* AB; perhaps first to see the other ship.

Buxton, Sydney — President of the Board of Trade.

Coverley, Captain James de — The Deputy Chief Inspector of Marine Accidents of the 1990-1992 Reappraisal.

Cottam, Harold Thomas — *Carpathia* wireless operator.

Cotton Powder Co. Ltd. — Manufacturer of *Titanic* rockets.

Crawford, Alfred — *Titanic* steward; told how other ship drifted.

Crosland, Rt. Hon. C.A.R. — President Board of Trade; dismissed second MMSA petition, July 1968.

Cunliffe, Sir R. Ellis — Board of Trade solicitor.

Dillon, Thomas Patrick — *Titanic* fireman; said ship steamed on after collision.

Dunlop, Charles Robertson — Counsel for Leyland Line and Captain Lord.

Durrant, John Oscar — *Mount Temple* wireless operator.

Evans, Cyril Furmston — *Californian* wireless operator.

Fleet, Frederick — *Titanic* lookout with Reginald R. Lee at time of collision.

Foweraker, Albert Moulton — Solicitor; wrote articles pro-Captain Lord.

Franklin, Philip A.S. — US head of IMM.

Fry, Captain — Marine Superintendent of Leyland Line, Liverpool.

Gambell, Captain G.J. — Master of *Virginian*. Told *Californian* of *Titanic*.

Gibson, James	*Californian* apprentice; on middle watch with Stone.
Gill, Ernest	*Californian* assistant donkeyman. Said ship ignored *Titanic* rockets.
Glenn, George	*Californian* fireman; uncalled witness.
Groves, Charles Victor	*Californian* 3rd Officer; said other ship was *Titanic*.
Haddock, Captain Herbert James	Master of *Olympic* sister ship of the *Titanic*. First mentioned *Californian*.
Hamilton, Thompson	Secretary to Tom Andrews and Edward Wilding; attended every session of Mersey inquiry.
Harrison, Leslie	General Secretary of MMSA. Led campaign for Captain Lord.
Howard, Roy Wilson	News Manager UP; his wrong dispatch led to first disclosure *Californian* had been near *Titanic*.
Isaacs, Sir Rufus	Attorney-General.
Ismay, Joseph Bruce	White Star and IMM chief; survived *Titanic*.
Jensen, Gerald J.G.	Civil engineer; drew Buxton's attention to *Californian*.
Kirk, Benjamin	*Californian* AB; coal-basket lookout.
Knapp, Captain John J.	Hydrographer of US Bureau of Navigation.
Latta, Sir John	Captain Lord's post-Leyland employer.
Lee, Reginald Robinson	*Titanic* lookout with Frederick Fleet at time of collision
Lightoller, Charles Herbert	*Titanic* 2nd, and senior surviving, Officer.
Lightoller, Sylvia	Wife of above; till her death in 1969, a repository of documents, photographs and memories; attended every session of Mersey inquiry.
Lindsay, Professor Robert Bruce	Physicist; rocket expert.
Little, D.A.S.	Technical director of Pains-Wessex Ltd., makers of fireworks.
Lord, Captain Stanley	Master of *Californian*.
Lowe, Harold Godfrey	*Titanic* 5th Officer; told of rockets' noise.
McGregor, W.F.	*Californian* ship's carpenter; broke rockets' story before Gill in Clinton, Massachusetts, newspaper.
McKenna, J.	*Virginian* wireless operator, told *Californian* of *Titanic*.
McNabb, J.D.	Senior Board of Trade examiner; attempted defence of Lord in 1912.
Mahan, W.S.A.	*Californian* Chief Engineer.
Marconi, Guglielmo	Inventor of wireless.
Marples, Ernest	Minister of Transport, released *Titanic* files in 1964.
Marriott, Captain Peter B.	Chief Inspector of Marine Accidents and the 1990-1992 Reappraisal.
Mason, Roy	Minister of Shipping, 1965; dismissed MMSA petition.
"Master Mariner (Retired)"	First publicized principle that origin of rockets was immaterial.
Mattinson, Miles Walker, K.C. later **Sir Miles Mattinson, K.C.**	A power in shipping; director of Leyland's, who threatened to resign if Lord remained.
Mersey, Lord	Presided over London Board of Trade Inquiry.

Moore, Captain James Henry	Master of *Mount Temple*.
Naess, Harald	Son of Captain Naess; denied father's journal was ever published.
Naess, Henrik Bergethon	1st Officer of *Samson*; later Captain.
Ogden, Louis M.	*Carpathia* passenger; took photos.
Olafsson, Johann Gunnar	Former Sheriff of Isafjordur, Iceland.
Olliver, Alfred	*Titanic* standby QM; said ship went half-speed ahead after collision.
Padfield, Peter	Author of *The* Titanic *and the* Californian.
Peuchen, Major Arthur Godfrey	*Titanic* 1st Class passenger; Chemist and yachtsman; implied *Titanic* heading was east soon after 1 a.m.
Phillips, John George (Jack)	*Titanic* senior wireless operator.
Pitman, Herbert John	*Titanic* 3rd Officer; said clocks were not put back.
Potter, E.	Assistant Solicitor Board of Trade; advised against prosecuting Captain Lord.
Rees, Eric	*Carpathia* 3rd Officer.
Reynolds, L.G.	Trinity House practical rocket expert.
Ring, Captain Carl Johann	Master of *Samson*.
Roberts, Mr	Manager of Leyland Line.
Ross, William	*Californian* AB, uncalled witness.
Rostron, Captain Arthur Henry	Master of *Carpathia*.
Rowe, George Thomas	*Titanic* QM, fired rockets.
Scanlan, Thomas	Counsel for National Sailors' and Firemen's Union; cross-examined Lord on failure to use his wireless.
Scott, Frederick	*Titanic* greaser; said *Titanic* went ahead after collision.
Smith, Captain Edward John	Master of *Titanic*.
Smith, Senator William Alden	Chairman Senate Subcommittee of Inquiry.
Sowerby, Captain C.F.G., RN	British Naval Attaché, Washington, DC.
Stengel, C.E. Henry	*Titanic* 1st Class passenger and engineer; said engines started again after collision.
Stephens, Dr R.W.B.	Imperial College of Science; acoustics expert.
Stewart, George Frederick	*Californian* Chief Officer.
Stone, Herbert	*Californian* 2nd Officer.
Stone, John A.	Son of above.
Strachan, Frank	Leyland agent in Brunswick Ga, USA; got Lord job with Lawther Latta
Stulping, Captain Ludwig	Master of *Birma*.
Swinson, Arthur	Author of *The Other Ship*.
Thomas, John H.	Boston, Mass., agent of IMM, including Leyland's.
Thomas, William	*Californian* greaser; uncalled witness.
Thompson, Captain Sir Ivan	Commodore of Cunard; ex-President MMSA.
Walters, Charles Edward	English journalist; wrote *Birma* story.
Wilding, Edward	Successor to Tom Andrews at Harland & Wolff.
Williamson, Stanley	BBC producer of *The Other Ship* and co-author.
Woolner, Hugh	*Titanic* 1st Class passenger; spoke of light at stern of *Titanic*.
Young, Captain A.H.F.	Professional Member, Marine Dept., Board of Trade; urged prosecution of Captain Lord.

General notes and sources

The system of references is intended primarily for the convenience of the reader, for which reason the references are placed at the end of each chapter, where practical experience has shown they are far easier to find than when all lumped together at the end of the book. Readers not interested in sources can easily skip those pages and go on to the chapter following. In the case of footnotes, the references are given directly within the footnotes.

References to the US transcript, briefly described as the "Hearings", are designated by 'US' with the page number. The Senate Committee's Report, which set out the findings and recommendations of the committee appointed to hold the inquiry, is separately paged and is cited as 'US Senate Report' with a page number.

The British transcript, described hereafter as the "Proceedings", conveniently assigns consecutive numbers to the questions asked of the witnesses and references to it are lettered 'B' with the question number. Other matters in the Proceedings, such as comment by the Commissioner, Lord Mersey, discussions between him and counsel and speeches by counsel are not numbered, and, when used as a source, are cited 'Mersey' with the page number. The report of the British inquiry, like that of the Senate, has its own pagination and is cited 'Mersey Report' with the page number.

Material quoted from the files of the PRO is cited according to the PRO's own method. For instance, '[MT 9/920/5] M 25810' consists of the "Group Letters" MT, "Class Number" 9/920 and "Piece Number" 5, without these particulars, the file number, M 25810, alone is useless.

One source, of which, for reasons to be stated, the author has been permitted to use only a minute part, is the tape of a two-hour conversation between Captain Lord and Mr Leslie Harrison in February 1961. Mr Harrison was then the General Secretary of the Mercantile Marine Service Association, and Captain Lord, near the end of his life.

In July 1964, Mr Harrison wrote to the author offering to make a copy of the recording available to him. The author accepted this offer and in due course heard the tape. Some 11 years later, in April 1975, Mr Harrison's solicitors wrote to the author that the tape recording was not to be used in this book. As a result of this veto, no part of the tape has been used in the book, with the exception of a few small extracts which had previously been disseminated in the national press, television or radio and Mr Harrison's own book *A Titanic Myth*.

Unpublished sources include much information privately acquired. The latter consists mostly of personal interviews and correspondence, which, for convenience is cited as 'P.I.' (Private Information). This designation is, as I am well aware, an ambiguous and even dubious authority. Yet, it may be the only exact, and certainly is the shortest, reference when, as frequently happened in my inquiries, some fact was finally obtained from a long search, involving much correspondence and also personal questioning of many people, whose very names were unknown at the beginning of the inquiry. P.I. may also represent the source of information easily obtained, but only on condition that the name of the informant be protected. Generally, I have tried to put readers in the position to check my statements, if they wished to do so; and when the P.I., for one reason or another, stands alone, I have, when possible, at least provided the date when I obtained it.

In addition to all that, I have also had the benefit of access to the papers of Mr Lawrence Beesley, 2nd Class passenger of the *Titanic,* Captain Sir Ivan Thompson, formerly Commodore of the Cunard Line and shipmate and friend of Captain Rostron, Captain Bisset and other officers of the *Carpathia,* Commander Charles Herbert Lightoller, 2nd Officer of the *Titanic,* Captain Charles Victor Groves, 3rd Officer of the *Californian.* The last included his unpublished typescript 'The Middle Watch', written in April 1957 and containing his recollections and interpretation of the events aboard the *Californian* on that fateful Sunday night in April 1912.

On this category of sources, it should perhaps be said its acceptance must depend on the judgement, and especially the good faith of the author. Little credence for it can, or should be, accorded to those who have manifestly shown themselves careless, or even unscrupulous, in their manipulation or even suppression of sources which can be checked, such as their use of the transcripts of the evidence. In my opinion, it would have been foolish, however, to have disregarded information of the highest importance, solely because it was imparted to me, without documentary corroboration, by anybody in whose veracity I had every reason to have complete faith.

Regarding the general Press, it has seemed to me essential for many obvious reasons, to read the 1912 dailies and periodicals both widely and selectively, but concentrating, of course, on *Californian* items. In those days, the Press was much larger than now, when it is but one medium of news and communication among several, and I have examined scores of newspapers and periodicals from Britain, the United States, Canada and Ireland, including some technical papers and the most important French and German newspapers. The reckless and totally false reports published in some of the American papers between the news of the sinking of the *Titanic* and the arrival of the truth in the *Carpathia* are notorious and an indelible stain on the profession; but, once the news came in with the arrival of the *Carpathia,* the *Californian* and the other ships involved, on the whole, both the accuracy of the reports and the quality of the writing in many of the popular, no less than the "class", papers, were a tribute to the individual journalists responsible and there certainly was no common hysteria in reporting. As regards the *Californian* in particular, it will be seen what history owes to the careful but fearless Press of Boston.

The names of newspapers, periodicals, books, etc., are italicized.

Quotations are mostly exact. Cuts are indicated by the usual dots of ellipsis (. . .), but where any matter appears within double quotation marks ("), there have been no changes in words, spelling, punctuation, emphasis (unless stated), use of capitals or lower case letters. Words appearing within single quotation marks ('– – –') represent the sense, but not necessarily the exact words, of a source, and often there is a change from the first, to the third person, or of tense.

Where no year is stated in dates of quotations from newspapers, etc., it should be taken as 1912.

Chapter 1

24 Shed, Royal Albert Dock, 'failed to join'

On New Year's Day, 1912, there was nobody on earth who was said to be responsible for the death of 1500 human beings. Before that year had advanced very far into its second half, that sombre distinction had been conferred on a previously unknown sea captain by the duly constituted authority of two nations.

The name of the captain, who is the chief character in this strange story, was Stanley Lord; his command, the SS *Californian*, and the voyage which unexpectedly carried him into history began in London, his intended destination being Boston, Massachusetts.

Lord was born in the prosperous north of England cotton-spinning town of Bolton in 1877.[1] His family had no connection with the sea, but from an early age he was so determined to make his living as a merchant seaman that, in spite of parental opposition, he was apprenticed to a Liverpool firm of sailing ship owners, and made his first voyage when he was only 13½ years old. In 1897, he went into steam, joining the West India and Pacific Steam Navigation Company as a second mate, and in 1901 at the early age of 24 Stanley Lord obtained both his Master's and Extra Master's certificates.

He then applied for a position with the White Star Line and was offered a berth, but only as a third or fourth officer. With his Extra Master's ticket already in his pocket, he refused the job.

At the time Captain Lord was getting the *Californian* ready for her fateful voyage to Boston, which began on 5 April 1912, the White Star were absorbed with the immensely greater task of preparing their new *Titanic* — the largest ship the world had ever known — for her maiden voyage, to start a few days later on 10 April. Under ordinary conditions, that would have required an enormous amount of work; but conditions were far from normal. British shipping was still crippled by a strike of the coal miners, which was to be settled on 6 April, and the New Dock (site of the modern Ocean Terminal) at Southampton, where the *Titanic* was berthed, was still crowded with delayed liners. Some had lent their coal to the *Titanic,* for it was a matter of national prestige that her sailing should not be interfered with by the activities of gangs of idle, though possibly underfed, miners, and that she should leave on time.

As a seaman, Lord earned, to the end of his professional career, the highest commendation from his different employers, and the chances are that had he joined the White Star at the outset of his career, he would have been regarded as among their best officers. In all probability, he would have been honoured by an appointment to their newest and largest ships including, in due

course, the *Titanic*. Had that been the play of fate, one thing at least seems
certain among these 'iffy' speculations, the *Californian,* under the command
of any other master on that April voyage, would never have attained notoriety.

This was Lord's 28th voyage as a Leyland Line master. He had been in
command of the *Californian* for a little more than a year, and this was his
sixth voyage in her.* Now, as her master, he was responsible at 35, for a crew
of nearly 50 and a ship and cargo worth many thousands of pounds, and he was
in receipt of a salary of £20 per month, plus an annual bonus of £50.[§][2] Lord,
who had a comfortable background and, unlike many seamen, understood
something about money, realized he was exploited.

In appearance, Stanley Lord was a lean man, of fine carriage, just under six
feet tall, with a stern, clean-shaven face of great distinction, dominated by a
Roman nose and with deep lines about the mouth — a veritable Caesar in a
sailor's suit. He was said to be quite devoid of humour, domineering, with a
high opinion of himself, and he would rarely speak, even when spoken to.[3] He
never drank at sea — he also said in fact that he was a teetotaller — and, at
best, his relations with his officers, other than those with his Chief, were
correct rather than companionable.

His Chief, a man by the name of Stewart, was born in 1877 in West Derby,
Liverpool, and had the then common Christian names 'George Frederick'.
He was 35 years old, had considerable experience in the Atlantic trade and held
a Master's certificate. Groves, the Third Officer, described him as "nearing
middle age".

Herbert Stone, Second Officer, 24, and with a First Mate's certificate, had
been eight years at sea.[4] It was a malign trick of fate that beneath the stolid
exterior of Herbert Stone there dwelt a sensitive spirit with little self-confidence
and, most regrettably, considerable fear of his imperious and Roman-visaged
skipper.

There was also an apprentice, James Gibson, born at Southport, Lancashire,
20 years old, and now three-and-a-half years past the signing of his Indentures.
He was an alert and willing youth, but rather inarticulate.

The *Californian* was equipped with wireless, and carried a single Marconi
operator, Cyril Furmston Evans, of whom more later.

Considerably different in most respects from his fellow officers was Charles
Victor Groves, who was serving as Third, but had a Second Mate's certificate.[5]
He was born in Cambridge, one of seven brothers. Groves, like Stone, was 24
years old. He had been educated at Perse Grammar School, which gave him
probably a better education than most seamen had. Then, apprenticeship with
Runciman's, and a sea experience which took him first to South America and
the Mediterranean. After three years in that trade, he joined the P. & O. Groves
had a lively mind, and, as it was said 'he couldn't stand the passengers', he
gave up the glamour of P. & O. for the prosaic passages of Frederick Leyland
& Co., whose employ he had entered only a few months previously. Groves
was interested in signalling (for which he held the Board of Trade's special
certificate) and electricity. He was teaching himself wireless telegraphy, and
even when at sea he made a point of keeping up with the news of the day by
regular visits to Evans's wireless cabin.

Of the remainder of this little band, now heading down Channel, the Chief
Engineer came — as one might anticipate — from Scotland; there was an

* See Appendix I.

§ In 1912, £1 = $4.87, or, as commonly reckoned for convenience, $5.

Austrian donkeyman, a German storekeeper and a Dutch cook.[6] They were all then, as they are now, no more than mere names on a list. The white beard of Captain Edward J. Smith of the *Titanic* was soon to be known around the world; but more than half a century later, only persistent and ingenious search can drag a few of the *Californian* men from the darkness into, at best, the shadows: George Glenn, fireman; William Ross, AB; W.F. McGregor, ship's carpenter; William Thomas, newly promoted from fireman to greaser, because somebody had "failed to join . . . ".

If these men from the lower deck are faceless now, they were little more to Captain Lord even at the time of his passage 'towards Boston'.

It is not meant to suggest that Captain Lord was a bully, or ever acted with deliberate harshness to his officers or men. There is no doubt that he was a strict disciplinarian, and one could hardly be surprised if his appearance and manner were not such as to encourage his seamen to come and tell their troubles to their 'old man'. One can go even further and say, with assurance, that evidently without trying, he aroused fear. But that Lord often frightened his men was more their fault than his. He clearly was a larger fact in each of their lives than they, together, were in his. This, though, did not affect his practice of fair dealing with them. So when Lord's crisis came, they were not waiting, ready to gang up on him. At the same time, it would be sentimental to believe that Captain Lord had any high regard or even respect for his crews as such, who as British seamen, were underpaid, underwashed, indifferently fed and over-worked.* That his natural manner was distant and even arrogant, merely served to emphasize the gap between him and them. He would do his job, and let them be careful to do theirs.

Before Lord was to see England again, he was asked about a long conver-sation he was reported to have had in his cabin with one of his quartermas-ters. His reply betrayed his opinion of familiar talks in his cabin with a man from the lower deck.

"No member of the crew," Captain Lord said scornfully, "has ever been in this room, and none of them come near the place except to clean up!"[7]

Far more than material or technical matters, it is the character of Stanley Lord himself, which explains, and was largely responsible for, the strange story of the *Californian*. It is in the deceptive personality of this one man, hitherto ignored or misjudged, that the solution to a famous mystery of the sea is to be sought — and, to a great extent, found.

The *Californian*, official number 115243, was a single screw steel vessel, whose final measurements were 6,223 tons gross, 447 feet long, 53 feet beam and a hull 30 feet deep. She was owned by Frederick Leyland & Co. Ltd., commonly called 'the Leyland Line'. This was a long-established British company, which in 1901, like the White Star Line and many other shipping lines, had become part of the Morgan-made and American-owned combine, the International Mercantile Marine. Leyland traded extensively in the North Atlantic, the West Indies and South America. Their cotton-carrying steamers were said to have the largest capacity of any which entered New Orleans.[8]

The *Californian* had four steel masts with fore and aft rig, a single funnel coloured salmon pink with a black top and seven large cargo hatches with double derricks at each. She had triple expansion engines with two large steel

---

*   Jack London, commenting on the many Americans then serving in British ships, presumably for lack of American, wrote: 'Their wages are low, their food is bad, and their treatment is worse'; but he also asserted that although everything else was better in American ships, work aboard them was even harder. The People of the Abyss, pp. 127, 235.

double-ended boilers, working at a pressure of 200 lb per square inch. Her propeller was of manganese bronze, and "a complete installation of electric light, consisting of about 260 electric lamps" was planned.

The crew were to be "comfortably housed below the shelter deck forward"; in other words, in the traditional forecastle.

After her launching, on 26 November 1901, the builders entertained some 150 guests, which was followed on 23 January 1902, by the trial trip, when she attained the satisfactory speed of 13½ knots.

The ship was, in fact, nothing more than an ordinary British cargo boat of her day, with, in the end, a certificate for 47 passengers. Her crew's quarters were as bad or indifferent as those for which British vessels had a tradition- ally evil reputation, going back beyond the 'limejuicers', and persisting, unpublicized but undeniably, at least to the time of, and including, the *Queen Mary* herself.[9] Save that the *Californian* usually wore the plain red original Leyland house flag* except when she was under charter to another company, she was similar to dozens and scores of others, and in spite of the notoriety she attained, in the 13 years of her career she seems to have been photographed only a very few times.[§]

By 1912, the Leyland Line offered a Second Class passage every Saturday, London to Boston, for £10, or Boston to London for $50;[10] but on this partic- ular voyage, beginning 5 April 1912, The *Californian's* accommodation for the 47 passengers permitted was unoccupied.[11]

Her appearance and her prosperously deep loading were so characteristic of Leyland ships that, in the days before wireless, vessels of the other owners often reported: 'Passed four masts and a funnel bound W, presumed Leyland's'. The *Californian,* although somewhat bigger, was just one of Kipling's cargo boats, which had 'got to do their business first, and make the most they can!'

The home port of the *Californian* was Liverpool, from which she had last sailed for New Orleans on 21 January; but on the return passage she went to London, where she had arrived back as recently as 30 March.[12] She was due to sail again in less than a week, for in those days of bustling prosperity British shipowners did not allow their ships to linger in port; and Leyland, with their hope of wiping out their debit balance that year, had even less use for idle ships than had the average owner. It was hard on masters and their crews who, even when they were in England, sometimes did not have time to visit their families at all, if their homes — as in the case of the *Californian* — were in a distant town.

At the Royal Albert Dock in London,[13] in the early days of that April, everything to do with the *Californian* was being done in a hurry. Young Evans, the Marconi operator, had mistakenly got himself the new wireless chart for the South instead of the North, Atlantic,[14] which he would need for the voyage to Boston.

It was 1.30 in the morning of Good Friday, 5 April 1912, when the *Californian,* her cargo and crew safely aboard, left her berth at No. 24 Shed in the Royal Albert Dock,[15] moved out into Gallions Reach and down the river. She had a crew of 47,[16] which included three 'substitutes', signed on at

---

* It was changed later, not for political reasons, but to distinguish it from that of the Bibby Line.

§ (a) Probably in April, 1902, in Dominion Line colours, when she was under charter to that line; (b) Peabody Museum, almost certainly the same picture as (a), but cleverly retouched with the ship in Leyland Line colours; (c) 15 April 1912, twice arriving on the scene of the Titanic disaster, taken from the *Carpathia*; (d) *Boston Herald*, 26 April 1912, p.9, at the Clyde Street pier; (e) National Maritime Museum, taken during the First World War, probably about 1915.

the last moment, because a mess room steward and three others had 'failed to join'. Such an offence as this was indeed the only blemish on the otherwise spotless record of Captain Stanley Lord himself. An Elephant-memoried Board of Trade official had scrawled across his papers: "Mr Stanley Lord is the holder of an OC Cert. No. 030740. He failed to join the "Barbadian" O.N. 102072 on 7/9/99 [7 September 1899] . . .".[17]

The passage of the *Californian* was normal and routine, the ideal passage, and the usual kind, so far as Captain Lord could control it. The ship made 11 knots as she steamed down Channel. Her speed 'depended on coal consumption', and on this trip the coal shortage resulting from the strike kept her from doing more than 11.

The strike and its settlement filled not only the Marconi news bulletins, which Groves read every night, but the Southampton docks as well. There, as the *Californian* passed the Isle of Wight, the *Titanic,* among many liners delayed by lack of coal, was lying, preparing for her first and only voyage. Before the *Californian,* too, made her solitary appearance on the stage of world notoriety, her name appeared only once in the shipping news, eight days after she had left the Royal Albert Dock, when it was reported that on 7 April she had been 100 miles SW of Brow Head.[18]

A week later, 14 April, which was a Sunday, she was on a westerly course, making her way at 11 knots on a calm sea and under a cloudless sky. It was very cold. Chief Officer Stewart was on the bridge, and at about 20 minutes past five in the afternoon, Groves came up to relieve him, so he could go below for his tea.[19] Groves found Lord also on the bridge talking to Stewart, while both men scanned the horizon. About five miles away to the south were three large flat-topped icebergs, and nothing else in sight. Within a few minutes, Lord and Stewart both went below to eat. Afterwards, Stewart came back to resume his watch and Groves went below.[20]

About half-past seven, ship's time, which was an hour and 55 minutes ahead of New York,[21] Lord wrote out a report about having seen the three icebergs, to be sent to another Leyland liner, the *Antillian.* Lord gave the position of the *Californian* at 6.30 when he saw the icebergs as Lat. 42.5°N, Long. 49.9°W.[22] During the early spring days of that year the shipping papers had been publishing reports of ice in the North Atlantic steamer tracks. Here was one more, and it would be remembered longer than many of the others, for according to Harold Bride, the *Titanic's* junior Marconi operator, the *Titanic* heard it too. . . .[23]

At eight o'clock, the beginning of the First Watch, Groves went back to the bridge to take over from Stewart[24] and was told by him that wireless messages had been received giving warning of ice ahead. Stewart stayed for about a quarter of an hour, for Groves to get his eyes 'in'.

Writing many years later, Groves confirmed that Lord came onto the bridge and warned him "to keep a sharp lookout for this ice". Lord had doubled the lookout, with an extra man on the forecastle head — the 'eyes of the ship' — in addition to the usual lookout in the crow's nest.[25]

"The night was dark," Groves went on, "brilliantly clear with not a breath of wind and the sea showed no signs of movement with the horizon only discernible by the fact that the stars could be seen disappearing below it." Time passed. The *Californian* had no clock on the upper bridge,[26] a fact to bear in mind. Lord himself made the obvious and sensible statement: "We didn't notice times much then." They were simple words of great significance. We know now from another source, as will be seen, that it was shortly before half-past ten when, according to the narrative in the third person written by

Groves: ". . . suddenly the Third Officer [Groves] perceived several white patches in the water ahead which he took to be a school of porpoises crossing the bows. Captain Lord evidently saw this at the same moment and as he was standing alongside the engine room telegraph he at once rang the engines Full Speed Astern."[27]

What Groves had seen was not a school of porpoises, but ice. Even before the ship had run her way off,* which took about three minutes, and stopped, she was surrounded by light field ice. Groves received orders from Lord[28] to go down and take in the log, but it had already gone, cut by the ice.[29]

When the ship had stopped Lord had spun the wheel round to port, and under the influence of the helm and the propeller going astern the *Californian* swung round. She had been steaming S89°W (true), said the captain, but after she had stopped she was heading ENE by compass or NE (true). Lord left the bridge then, and shortly afterwards calculated his position by dead reckoning[§] as 42°5'N, 50°7'W. He gave Groves instructions that he was to be informed if any ship was sighted, and told the Chief Engineer, W.S.A. Mahan, "to keep main steam handy in case we commenced to bump against the ice."

"Absolute peace and quietness now prevailed," according to Groves's recollections, "save for brief snatches of 'Annie Laurie' from an Irish voice which floated up through a stokehold ventilator."[30]

There were more sounds, never mentioned but nonetheless apparent on the bridge of the *Californian*; the faint bumping of the light field ice against the ship's sides, the hissing of her generator engine, the regular sound of shovelling coal into her boilers, the feeder pump to keep up the water level in her boilers and the regular whistling noise of the Weir (vacuum) pump to keep down the vacuum in the condenser, for the *Californian* kept up steam and these sounds were around and heard everywhere on the ship.

"About 11.10 ship's time," said Groves in his evidence in London exactly a month and a day after it had happened, "I made out a steamer coming up a little bit abaft our starboard beam."[31]

"It was a most peculiar night," Lord had said in Washington, "and we had been making mistakes all along with the stars, thinking they were signals."[32]

"It was very difficult at first," Groves agreed, "to distinguish between the stars and a light, they were so low down."[33]

So, when he first saw "one white light" he did not pay much attention, because he thought "it might have been a star rising."[34]

Five minutes later he began to pay attention,[35] and at 11.25, he made out "Two white masthead lights". There was now no longer any doubt that it was a ship. When he had first seen the one light, it was "10 to 12 miles away", but the ship was getting nearer and the lights clearer all the time.

In accordance with his orders, Groves then went below to report to Captain Lord. He knocked at the venetian door of the chart room and told him there was a steamer coming up on the starboard quarter.

"Can you make anything out of her lights?" Lord asked.

"Yes," Groves replied, "she is evidently a passenger steamer coming up on us."

The only passenger steamer known to be close by was the *Titanic*.

---

* *Run her way off* – The time and distance between the stopping or reversal (as here) of a ship's engines and the stopping of the ship herself (see Appendix A).

§ *Dead reckoning* – Approximate position of ship, based on mean of courses steered and distance steamed, or by log (see Appendix A).

Sources

1 P.I. and Affidavit of Captain Stanley Lord, 25 June 1959.
2 Official Log.
3 Press descriptions & P.I., including Groves, 'The Middle Watch'.
4 Press descriptions; P.I.; Somerset House, General Register office (Birth, Death and Marriage Registration).
5 P.I. for nearly all biographical material about Groves, mostly from his elder brother, Mr C.L.D. Groves, friends and professional colleagues.
6 Official Log.
7 *Boston Journal*, 26 April 1912.
8 *Lloyd's Register of Shipping*, 1912; 'Encyclopaedia of Ships and Shipping', 1908, p. 308; *Sea Breezes*, Vol. 16 (July–Dec 1953), p. 422.

9 Largely P.I.; [MT 9/920/5] M 25810.
10 'Encylopaedia of Ships and Shipping', p. 348; *Christian Science Monitor* (Boston, Mass.) advt., 11 April 1912, p. 4.
11 B 6679–82.
12 Board of Trade General Register & Record Office of Shipping and Seamen & *Lloyd's Weekly Index*, January–March, 1912.
13 *Shipping & Mercantile Gazette & Lloyd's List*, 1 April 1912, p. 11 ('London Dock Directory').
14 B 9183.
15 Official Log & *Shipping & Mercantile Gazette & Lloyd's List*, 6 April 1912, p. 6.
16 Official Log.
17 (MT 9/920/M6) M 23448.
18 *Shipping & Mercantile*

Gazette & Lloyd's List, 13 April 1912 p. 10.
19 'The Middle Watch'.
20 Ibid.
21 B 8935.
22 B 6694 & B 8943. The latter is from Evans's evidence. Testifying with his P.V. (Procès-Verbal or wireless log) in his hand, he put the Lat. as 42.3 N., two miles further South.
23 US 141.
24 B 8569.
25 'The Middle Watch'.
26 B 8141.
27 'The Middle Watch'.
28 Appendix D.
29 Capt. Lord's Affidavit, Appendix C.
30 'The Middle Watch'.
31 B 8135.
32 US 728.
33 B 8135.
34 B 8143.
35 B 8144-45, 8147, 8160, 8163-64, 8133, 8167, 8170-72.

Chapter 2

The *Titanic* breaks a record

Shipwrights, plumbers, painters, electricians and a host of others hammered and clattered on most of the nine decks of the *Titanic* at 44[1] Berth in the New Dock, Southampton. Though their only job was to give the ship some finishing touches — to put a polish on perfection — the ladders and paint pots, the rolls of carpets, pieces of furniture, boxes, wires, tools, stores and much more, so cluttered the alleyways, the cabins and public rooms that there was not a safe square yard for visitors.

"Sightseers Need Not Apply!" a local columnist[2] headed one of his paragraphs about the ship. "The officials," he wrote, "have had so much worry lately" — this being before the *Titanic* sailed and merely a reference to the coal strike — "that we gladly acceded to their request for our help in making it known that the *Titanic* will not be open for inspection."

On her arrival in Southampton, midnight 3 April, the *Titanic* encountered her first incident, caused by none other than Mrs Sylvia Lightoller, wife of Second Officer Charles Lightoller. Mrs Lightoller and her cousin had taken a small sailing dinghy out into Southampton Water to meet the new ship. They had got too close to the line of navigation for Captain Smith's taste and he had ordered 'to blow the whistle on them.' "Some idiot in a little boat was nearly run down by the ship, when coming up river to go to the dock," Lightoller told his wife the next morning at breakfast, still annoyed by the incident. "I said not a word and never told him it was us," Sylvia Lightoller admitted years later, "but, at the time, I thought it was great: I had made the mighty *Titanic* blow her whistle."[3]

"There was no cheering or hooting of steamers' whistles . . ." Lawrence Beesley wrote,[4] ". . . the whole scene was quiet and rather ordinary," when the *Titanic* began her maiden voyage.

Shortly after noon on Wednesday, 10 April 1912, the new ship cast off and moved slowly ahead. It was five days after the *Californian* had taken her own most ordinary departure from London. Coming out of the New Dock, the movement of the *Titanic* dragged the *New York* away from her moorings, and the famous old Atlantic flyer was drawn steadily, out of control, towards the departing vessel.

Many years later, Captain Follett, master of a Southampton tug, who had been a deckhand in the *Albert Edward*, one of the Red Funnel tugs attending the *Titanic*,* told me: "The *Vulcan* got a line aboard the *New York* and pulled her stern away from the *Titanic*."[5]

This action, and the stopping of the *Titanic's* engines, prevented a collision.

"Unfortunately, as it turned out," Captain Follett remarked.

The collision would certainly have damaged the *Titanic's* port quarter sufficiently to have compelled postponement of the sailing. But Lachesis had allotted her fate.

This is the first of the two mishaps the *Titanic* sustained; the second is better known.

Better known, probably than any other in modern maritime history is the voyage of the *Titanic* which followed that exciting departure. It is a tragedy in the classical tradition and a great story by any standard. It has often been told, and sometimes well and accurately. Those who may not know the details and have a taste for stories of the sea should read Lawrence Beesley's excellent book, *The Loss of the SS Titanic*, which gives a survivor's account, or Walter Lord's now famous *A Night to Remember* and its sequel *The Night Lives On*.

The *Titanic* was owned by the White Star Line and built by Harland & Wolff at Belfast. She was launched on 31 May 1911, did her short trials on 1 April 1912, and arrived at Southampton at midnight on 3 April. She was the largest ship in the world, being 46,328 gross tons (displacement, 52,310), but she was not, as frequently said, the fastest. She had never been run all out, though it had been intended to do so on the afternoon of Monday, 15 April,[6] by which time, however, she was at the bottom of the Atlantic. Her speed, nevertheless, was definitely exceeded only by the Cunard liners, *Mauretania* and *Lusitania* and it is probable that she might have reached about 23$\frac{1}{4}$ knots.[7] Her engines were a combination of reciprocating and turbine, the latter working only ahead. She was 882.5 feet long, 92.5 feet beam and 60.5 feet from the waterline to the boat deck.[8]

She was licensed to carry 2,603 passengers and a crew of 944 — 3,547 in all. On her voyage, she had some 2,200 persons aboard, but there was lifeboat accommodation for no more than 1,178, this being the total capacity of her 14 lifeboats, two emergency boats and four collapsibles. She was also equipped with 3,560 lifebelts or lifejackets and 48 lifebuoys. Her means of making distress signals, which later became a matter of controversy, included: 36 socket signals, in lieu of guns, made by the Cotton Powder Company Ltd, with two sockets, one on either side of the ship, 12 ordinary rockets, 2 Manwell Holmes deck flares, 12 blue lights, and 6 lifebuoy lights.[9] In addition to that, the *Titanic* was fitted out with the most powerful Marconi wireless equipment of the time; the 5kW rotary spark set.[10] §

In all her life-saving effects the *Titanic,* in fact, exceeded the official requirements of the Board of Trade at the time, but, even so, her boats provided no more than one place in three for her permitted carrying capacity, and gave a bit more than a fifty-fifty chance for the number she actually had on board. On the other hand, her First Class passengers were surrounded with splendour, her Second Class with comfort, and even the Steerage were carried without squalor. The living accommodation for her crew was the floating equivalent of servants' quarters in rich houses on land, or possibly slightly less disgraceful.

Outwardly, the *Titanic* was a beautiful ship, with four funnels, the aftermost

---

* According to the 'Journal' of the Southampton, Isle of Wight & South of England Royal Mail Steam Packet Company Limited (the 'Red Funnel Line'), these were the *Neptune, Hector, Hercules, Ajax, Vulcan* and *Albert Edward*. The same tugs had attended the *Titanic* at midnight on 3 April, when she entered her berth in the New Dock.

§   The actual transmitted power in the aerials was about 10% of the 5kW, or about half a kilowatt.

of which was used to carry fumes from the galleys, but was otherwise a dummy and added merely for the symmetry of her appearance. The smoke billowing from all four funnels so prominent in numerous pictures of her is pure fancy.

Her voyage was made in good weather and she had called at Cherbourg and Queenstown before starting her Atlantic crossing.

On Sunday, 14 April the weather became very cold, and several warnings of ice, in addition to that sent from the *Californian* in the late afternoon, had been received. Following the custom of the day, as the weather was clear, her speed was not reduced. Orders to keep a good lookout were issued, and in the dark but dazzlingly star-filled and bitterly cold night, with her hundreds of portholes and saloon windows brightly lit, steering a course of S86°W,* she steamed on at about 22 knots, or 25 miles — or 40 km — per hour.

In the Second Class saloon, the Reverend Mr Carter, who had been conducting hymn-singing, received a final request about 10 o'clock. It was *For Those in Peril on the Sea*. 'In this ship,' said Mr Carter, 'we're not in peril; but others may be. Let us sing the hymn for them.'[11] And they did. It was still about an hour and a half before the *Titanic* struck her iceberg. Mr Beesley, in his published account of the incident, omitted Mr Carter's remark, "because afterwards it might have seemed like a criticism of God."

Ninety-five feet above the waterline, the two lookouts in the crow's nest, Frederick Fleet and Reginald Robinson Lee,[12] came on duty at 10 o'clock, having had the order passed on from the men they relieved, Archie Jewell and George Symons, to keep a sharp lookout for ice, especially growlers. Symons, according to Second Officer Charles Herbert Lightoller, was the 'smartest' of the *Titanic's* six lookouts.[13]

Fleet had the port side and Lee the starboard. The crow's nest was equipped with a bell, to which a rope pull was attached, a telephone on the starboard side connected with the bridge, and, behind the two lookouts, said Fleet, "just two bits of screen," of "canvas", which, according to George Alfred Hogg, another lookout, could be lifted up.[14] The canvas shut out light from aft and as a weather cover also gave some protection.

Fleet was 24 years old and had been at sea five or six years, more than four of them spent as a lookout in the *Oceanic*. When he first gave evidence before the US Senate inquiry in Washington, DC, and was asked, and soon pressed, to give his estimate of distances and sizes, Fleet repeated, again and again, "I have no idea . . . I am no hand at guessing . . ."[15]

It was "just after seven bells," that is, after 11.30 p.m., when Fleet first saw the iceberg, "a black mass", right ahead.

"Who sighted the black mass first; you or Lee?" asked Senator William Alden Smith, of Michigan, chairman of the committee conducting the inquiry.

"I did," Fleet replied. "I say I did, but I think he was just as soon as me."

He had no idea of its size or of its distance from the ship. It wasn't "the size of an ordinary house" or as large as the room in which they were sitting.

"I reported it as soon as ever I seen it," he said "and struck three bells to signify an object right ahead. Then I went straight to the telephone and rang them up on the bridge."

It is at this point that it is worth recording something Fleet himself told me, which, although not directly concerned with the *Californian,* is of historical interest and, so far as I know, has never been published.[16]

It was more than 50 years after the sinking, when I had a long talk with

---

* Nowadays, with the introduction of the gyro compass, this would be a course of 266°.

the old man about his experience. He was then almost 77, a stocky man, with a rather square head thrust forward, and the deep-set eyes, that had been a feature of the 1912 photos, were now framed in yellow-rimmed glasses. He looked and spoke like an old-fashioned British working man, who had apparently missed the benefits of the Welfare State.

"It was the beautifullest night I ever seen," he began. "The stars were like lamps. I saw this black thing looming up; I didn't know what it was."

And here, he added something to the evidence he had given at the American and British inquiries, which, if true, was at least a vivid detail, and possibly of great significance.

"*I asked Lee if he knew what it was,*" said Fleet, "*He couldn't say.* I thought I better ring the bell. I rang it three times."

How long did this interval last while Fleet questioned Lee? Half a minute-? Only a few seconds-? Whatever it was, there had never previously been a hint of any pause between Fleet's sighting the iceberg and ringing the bell.

It seemed to me that he was telling the truth in this new, and slightly different, but perhaps important, version. He did not realize the possible significance of what he was saying, but the impression he made throughout was that of an honest man.

At Washington, Fleet had said: "Before I reported, I said, 'There is ice ahead' and then I put my hand over to the bell and rang it three times, and then I went to the phone."[17] And also: "I reported it as soon as ever I seen it."[18] And reported it as "an iceberg".

Fred Fleet, for his part, still had more than a clear memory of the terrifying seconds that had passed while he and Lee waited in the crow's nest after telephoning the bridge. He said the memory had haunted him for many years after the wreck.[19] He could not sleep at night, remembering the slow advance of that "black thing". Eventually, he had gone to a doctor for help. He thought that Lee also was shocked by the experience. Lee left the White Star and joined the Union-Castle, where he served in the *Kenilworth Castle*.

"Lee," said Fleet, "he died of drink many years ago."

I tried to bring the old man back to the approach of the iceberg.

"We watched the thing. It had a pointed top. We didn't like the look of this thing. I said to Lee, 'You better go down, there's no sense the two of us being up here, if we strike.' He didn't want to go. 'I can't do that,' he said. But I made him and he went down the ladder."

That, also, was new, though not important, I asked him if he was alone then up there when they hit the iceberg.

"No, he climbed up back. We was up there together."

When the iceberg was reported by Fleet to First Officer William McMaster Murdoch on the bridge, he "put her hard a-starboard and ran her engines full astern."[20] According to the helm order of that day, this meant he turned the ship to port.

Murdoch, who lost his life, was also reported as saying: "I intended to port around it,"[21] which meant that first having put her to port, he would turn her again to starboard, to get around the iceberg (see Diagram 1). To do this, he would have to give another order, 'Hard a-port'.

The standby-quartermaster on the bridge was Alfred Olliver. He had come off duty at 10 o'clock, and had remained on the bridge as a messenger.[22]

"I had just performed an errand," he said at Washington, "and was entering the bridge when the collision occurred."

He was too late to hear Murdoch's first order, 'Hard a-starboard', but arrived just in time to hear the second.

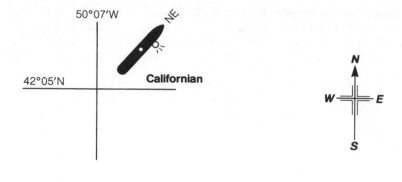

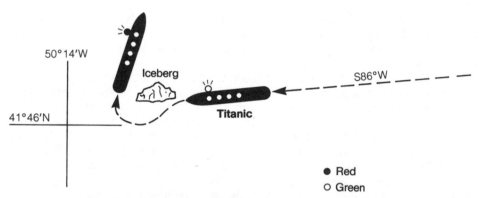

Diagram 1. 'Porting round the iceberg'
'Porting round the iceberg', of course, is what the Titanic *tried but failed to do, as the iceberg sliced open her starboard side on the way round. This diagram shows why the green light of the ship approaching from the south could be seen from the* Californian, *and later, after she stopped and swung to starboard, the only sidelight Lord, Groves, Stone and Gibson saw was red.*

"I heard hard a-port," he told Senator Theodore Elijah Burton of Ohio.[23] The Sixth Officer, James P. Moody, saw that the order was carried out.

Murdoch's efforts were in vain: the iceberg was too close. When she struck it, the *Titanic* was still turning to port and so, spurs or ledges of the berg methodically cut, foot after foot, a 300-foot, but non-continuous, gash, beginning about twenty feet aft of her bows, in the starboard side of her hull below the waterline. Her first five forward water-tight compartments were ruined and the *Titanic* was doomed.

Thirty-seven seconds passed[24] between Fleet's report to First Officer Murdoch and what Thomas Hardy in his poem called 'the convergence of the twain'. If Fleet had not asked Lee's opinion; if the *Titanic* had had, say, 30 seconds more to turn farther away and to slow down, she would not have completely escaped the collision, but the iceberg would have begun its deadly cutting farther aft and perhaps fewer compartments would have been opened to the sea — she could float with any two flooded.

Fleet's reaction to his first sight of the iceberg, his pause to stare and inquire, was not that of an automaton, but of a human being, however highly trained. So, too, was the reaction of First Officer Murdoch. It was said later at the Board of Trade inquiry by an expert witness, one who knew everything about the design and strength and weakness of the *Titanic*, and repeated afterwards by many others, who were far from being experts, but who understood the simple facts, that if Murdoch had done nothing at all but order the engines to be stopped or reversed and continued on course, the ship would have been saved. In other words, if the *Titanic*, in the time left, whether it was 37 seconds, or more than a minute, had moved on, but slowing all the time, and had crashed into the iceberg, head on, she would not have sunk. Scores of unfortunate firemen asleep in the forecastle would have been killed in their bunks; the bows of the ship would have been crumpled, and not a soul of the 2,201 aboard could have escaped knowing a serious accident had occurred; but probably only those firemen in the forward accommodation would have lost their lives.[25]

"I think it would have taken a very brave man to have kept his ship going straight on an iceberg," said Joseph Bruce Ismay, Chairman and Managing Director of the White Star Line.[26] "I think he would have endeavoured to avoid it." Murdoch did, and scientifically, it seems, he was wrong.

Possibly, a modern computer might have chosen the one correct move, which was no move, to save the *Titanic*; but it was against human nature to continue going full tilt into an obstruction, instead of trying to avoid a collision with it; and First Officer William Murdoch, a brave and efficient seaman, was at once more and less than a computer.

Many striking similes to describe their impression of the collision were used by passengers and members of the crew, but few of those below in the stokeholds and boiler rooms had need to think up any comparisons. In No. 6 Boiler Room, the farthest forward, the warning bell rang and the red light in the dial, meaning 'Stop', came on. Leading Stoker Frederick Barrett, who was talking to Junior Second Engineer James H. Hesketh, 'sang out': 'Shut all dampers!' — the doors to the furnaces, to cut off the draft — but even while it was being done there was a tremendous crash — "Just like thunder, the roar of thunder," said Fireman George William Beauchamp. The side of the ship might have been a sieve, and Barrett and Hesketh were standing in the swirling Atlantic Ocean, they leapt into the next 'section', boiler room No. 5.[27]

It was 11.40 p.m., Sunday night, 14 April, when the *Titanic* collided with the iceberg, and in doing so she broke a record. She was not out to break the Atlantic speed record, and if she had safely completed her voyage and arrived at New York on the Wednesday morning, she would have been some 12 hours behind the fastest voyage of her sister, the *Olympic*,[28] which in turn was a long way behind the record of the *Mauretania*, the world's fastest liner.

But no ship before the *Titanic* had ever struck an iceberg on her maiden voyage. The Guion Line's *Arizona*, 5,150 tons, had come closest to it, when in 1879, only five months after she entered the North Atlantic service, she ran head-on at full speed into an iceberg in mist off the Banks. More fortunate than the *Titanic*, she sustained only the concertina-crumpled bow. The *Arizona's* forward bulkhead held, nobody was seriously hurt and she was able to put in at St John's, Newfoundland, for temporary repairs. The *Titanic's* own singular record remained intact until January, 1959, when the small Danish ship *Hans Hedtoft*, 2,872 tons, on her maiden voyage, hit an iceberg off Greenland, and was ultimately lost with all aboard. But, as the *Hans Hedtoft* was on the homeward passage of her maiden voyage, the record of the *Titanic* may be regarded as still unbroken.

"We still take chances," a famous Cunard officer said to me one day, in the 1920's, aboard the *Aquitania* in New York harbour, "but not the way we did before the *Titanic*." Then he repeated reflectively: "But we still take chances."

After this digression, it must be explained that 11.40 p.m., when the *Titanic* collided, was ship's time which, according to different sources, was 1 hour and 50 minutes, or 1 hour and 55 minutes, ahead of New York. Harold Bride,[29] the junior and surviving Marconi operator, whose business it was to keep two clocks running, one giving ship's, the other, New York time, and who, therefore, was the most reliable witness on the matter, called the difference between ATS (Apparent Time of Ship) and New York time, as 'about two hours'. Today, of course, every ship, whether in the Pool of London, the Upper Bay of New York, or anywhere else in the world, keeps Universal Time, which is the equivalent of Greenwich Mean Time, as the standard for timing messages, etc. In 1912, however, when a westbound vessel reached 40°W she adopted New York time, which was, and is, five hours behind Greenwich.

ATS changes with the longitude, and clocks are set at midnight for the approximate noon position of the following day. The *Titanic's* clocks were to have been put back 22 minutes at midnight (and 25 in the next watch), but, said Third Officer Herbert John Pitman, "we had something else to think of,"[30] and the clocks were not put back. This would account for the apparent difference in *Titanic* time as stated, for instance, by Second Officer Lightoller, and that given by Bride.

Immediately after Pitman had given the Senate inquiry the time the *Titanic* sank, which was 2.20 a.m. according to his watch,[31] Senator Smith turned to Lightoller, and asked him: "What was the Greenwich time, compared with the ship's time?"

"5.47 - 2.20 - 5.47 Greenwich time; 2.20 apparent time of ship," said Lightoller.[32]

It is clear that Lightoller, in equating 2.20 *Titanic* time with 5.47 GMT, had stated the ship's time as if the clocks had been put back 22 minutes at midnight Sunday. Her time then would have been not about two hours ahead of New York, according to Bride, but only one hour and 33 minutes.

It is necessary to go into these details and to note both *Titanic* and *Californian* times, because there is an alleged difference in time between the two ships. As in the case of the *Titanic,* the most reliable evidence of *Californian* time comes from the wireless operator, Cyril Furmston Evans. At Washington, he told Senator Smith he had completed his ice message to the *Titanic* 'At 11 o'clock, approximately; 9.05 New York Time.'[33] In London, he was even more precise. The Solicitor-General, Sir John Simon, asked him: "What is the difference between New York time and ship's time at the place where you stopped?"[34]

"One hour and 55 minutes," said Evans.

In other words, according to their wireless operators, the time of the *Californian* and the *Titanic* was very close, if not absolutely identical.

Lord treated the time difference as one hour and 50 minutes, and we do not know if the *Californian's* clocks were retarded at midnight, and, if so, by how much. The implication in the evidence given by Evans is that they were not.

Among much else that is overlooked regarding the possible time differences between the two ships is, for example, a document, compiled by The Marconi International Marine Communication Co. Ltd., and headed, "Substitute for the *procès verbaux* [wireless logs] of the 'TITANIC', from the 12th April until her last signals were received; . . ." The *Titanic's* records having, of course, been lost, this table was made up from the documents of other ships and wireless stations, and its uncontradicted conclusion was that *Titanic* time was one hour and 50 minutes ahead of New York (incidentally, exactly Captain Lord's estimate of *Californian* time). This substitute P.V.* was dated 8 June, many weeks before Lord Mersey delivered the Report of his inquiry, which was read on 30 July. Apart from the evidence of the Marconi operators, mentioned above, it is therefore idle to assert that the decision of the British court on the time kept by the two ships was superficial. Realistically, the court could have come to no other conclusion.

The heart of the case against the *Californian* is that she saw the *Titanic's* distress rockets, and did nothing to help. Hence, the wider the time gap between the two ships, the better for the defence of the *Californian*. And thus her supporters insist that the times found by the British (and American) inquiries were wrong, and so far as the British, at least, were concerned, arbitrary, if not positively dishonest.

The broad truth of the matter is that there was no precise or split-second timing aboard either ship that night. On any showing, the time aboard the two ships was very close, with a possible difference of about 10 or 12 minutes, but no more; and, much more probably, the time was the same. The most important thing to remember about the time is that it was of much less importance than the events themselves and the sequence in which they happened.

To go on with the story of events, odd as it seems in the circumstances, even after the collision, Fleet and Lee remained in the crow's nest, continuing their watch. They had expected to do two hours and 20 minutes[35] because of the change in time, but as there was no change, they were actually relieved at midnight. Two fresh lookouts, George Alfred Hogg and Alfred Frank Evans, came on, just as if nothing had happened, although by midnight the decks below were filled with unusual activities, and Captain Smith and a few others already knew that the ship was fatally damaged.

A rather mysterious incident may conveniently be examined here. This is the movement of the *Titanic* after she had stopped as a result of the collision.

Third Officer Herbert John Pitman said bluntly: "She didn't move",[36] but there is abundant and convincing evidence that he was mistaken, and that she did steam on again after the accident.

QM Olliver, who was on the bridge, said: ". . . she went half speed ahead. . . . The Captain telegraphed half speed ahead."[37]

A fireman, Thomas Patrick Dillon, said that after the engines had stopped, they went ahead again "for about two minutes."[38] Then the order was given to 'Keep steam up', before they were finally ordered to draw the fires.[39]

Frederick Scott, a greaser, said that after the 'Stop', ". . . they rang down 'Slow Ahead'. For ten minutes she was going ahead."[40]

First Class passenger C.E. Henry Stengel, a Newark, NJ, leather manufacturer and familiar with machinery, said the engines "started again just slightly. I do not know why . . ."[41]

Colonel Archibald Gracie, another First Class passenger and amateur historian, also noticed the *Titanic* was still moving. Shortly after the collision he

* Wireless log.

had gone to the boat deck to discover what had struck the ship. He saw a middle-aged couple "promenading unconcernedly, arm in arm, *forward* on the starboard quarter, *against the wind*"[42] [emphasis added]. The absence of wind that night was testified to by many witnesses and thus the only 'wind' felt on the *Titanic's* decks could not have been anything else than the airflow created by the ship's own movement forward.

Mr Beesley gave a most vivid account of what he saw and did.[43] "The ship had now resumed her course," he wrote, describing what he saw from the open deck after he had dressed and gone up for the second time, "moving very slowly through the water with a little white line of foam on each side." Having seen an officer climb into No. 16 Boat and begin to throw the cover off, and noticing how the ship was tilting down towards the bows, he went below to D Deck. There, after some talk, he led three alarmed ladies to a bathroom and, by making them place their hands on the bath to feel the vibration, convinced them the engines were moving again. All of which strongly suggests that the *Titanic* must have steamed for longer than the two minutes of Dillon's estimate.

But, it may be asked, why trouble with all this detail? And, anyhow, why was the *Titanic* steaming after the collision?

It has been asserted that if there really had been a ship in sight when the *Titanic* struck, Captain Smith, before giving orders to lower the boats, would have steamed towards that ship; and one writer gracefully adds that he would have been 'an imbecile' not to have done so.[44]

Despite the preponderance of the evidence, it is maintained with emphasis by the supporters of Captain Lord that the *Titanic* did not move after the accident: "Because obviously there wasn't another ship to steam to. This completely disproves that the *Californian* was near the *Titanic*."[45]

The originator of this theory, Mr Leslie Harrison, at the time General Secretary of the Mercantile Marine Service Association (MMSA) who had taken up the task of clearing Captain Lord's name in 1958, maintained on more than one occasion that the damage to the *Titanic* "was really very limited", she 'remained' "an effective ship" and that "she could have continued steaming in any direction."[46]

It has been said that a philosopher could deduce the existence and shape of the earth from a single grain of sand; but to begin with the assertion that the *Titanic,* with her first five compartments torn open and enormous quantities of water pouring in (about 16,000 tons in the first 40 minutes[47]), 'remained' "an effective ship", and to leap from that rickety premise to the conclusion that this proved the *Californian* was nowhere near, is an item which at first glance bids for a high place in any anthology of illogicality.

The statement that the damage was "very limited" and in fact amounted to only "12 square feet" is a figure derived from the evidence of Edward Wilding, one of the ship's designers, while he was explaining to the British inquiry the fatal consequences of the non-continuous hole in the side of the *Titanic,* extending to about 300 feet.[48]

If any man on earth must have been aware of the 'lost opportunity' in the *Titanic* not steaming, after the collision, towards the tantalizing light of a ship on the horizon where help may have been at hand; and of her remaining capability as an 'effective ship', it was Edward Wilding.[49] His absorbing evidence at the Mersey inquiry was spread over three days. Yet nowhere does Edward Wilding, the alert and imaginative expert, give the slightest hint that he thought the *Titanic* herself could or should have taken her 2,000 and more passengers and crew to the *Californian*.

Wilding's failure even to mention that the *Titanic* had sustained 'only limited damage' and 'was able to steam in any direction' may, of course, have been due to sudden mental fatigue; but it seems far more probable that his silence was an expression of his unceasing mental acuteness, and that he would instantly have pointed out the fatal objection, if the notion of having used the *Titanic* as a ferryboat to the 'light' had been advanced by anybody else.

Quite independently of one another, this objection was expounded by three highly qualified seamen; an Admiralty assessor, a holder of an Extra Master's Certificate with special interests in shipbuilding, and a Board of Trade ship's surveyor.[50] Although the engines and engine room were not damaged by the collision, they would not have remained so for very long, if the *Titanic* had steamed, even slowly, in her damaged state. The pressure would inevitably have increased on the bulkheads in the already flooded compartments, and although the increase might not have been great, it was estimated what resistance was left would have been insufficient and the result catastrophic: those bulkheads would have collapsed abruptly, so that the remaining after compartments, which were slowly filling, would have flooded within seconds, and the ship sunk there and then.

It was also pointed out that if the foremost compartments had remained intact, it is barely conceivable that the ship might have steamed very slowly without materially worsening her condition: but in the actual state of damage to 'the casualty', any attempt to move her for long would have brought about almost instant foundering.

It is hardly surprising, after this, that practical seamen, much more experienced and learned than those who have embraced the 'effective ship' theory, have described it succinctly as 'reckless rubbish'. Sir Ivan Thompson, a former Cunard commodore, added: "Of course, if this suggestion had been followed . . . she would have sunk before any boats could be lowered, and all would have been lost."[51]

We do not know, nor can we discover, why Captain Smith ordered the *Titanic* to steam on, but that he did is clear from the evidence of QM Olliver and others quoted earlier. Olliver, in fact, said more than once that he had heard Captain Smith order 'half-speed ahead'.[52] Smith was lost, as were Chief Officer Henry Tingle Wilde and First Officer Murdoch, who were with him on the bridge. It is possible they did see the other ship at, or immediately after, the time of the collision and were trying to make for her, but it is clear that the brief period of steaming that did undoubtedly take place must have convinced the captain that to continue would have sunk his crippled ship within minutes, rather than hours. Captain Smith stopped her engines, forever, and gave the order to uncover the boats.

Almost at once, reports of 'a light' spread about the decks. How and where that report started is not known. If Captain Smith had in fact begun steaming towards the 'light', the bridge itself may have been its source.

Fleet and Lee both denied that they had seen the lights of any other ship from the crow's nest.

"There was no lights at all when we was up the crow's nest," said Fleet in Washington.[53]

"It must have been 1 o'clock" when he saw it, he said in London.[54]

And in 1964 he said the same thing.

"Did you see the lights of another ship when you collided?" I asked him then.

"No, sir, I must tell the truth. There was no light."

He was emphatic about this, repeating it more than once, and pleadingly, as if begging to be believed, although no word of contradiction was put to him. Having missed the iceberg until too late, he gave the impression that he knew he should have seen a light, but in fact he had not, and nothing would persuade him to change his story. He was obviously an honest man, though probably not the best lookout in the world.*

When I asked him directly if he had seen the *Californian* he promptly replied: "She was there all right. She seen us."

Fleet's denial of seeing the light of another ship when he was in the crow's nest inevitably made him an important witness for the *Californian;* but less weight has been attached to some other words of Frederick Fleet. Asked whether the 'one bright light' he did see, had moved or not, the old man answered: "No, it didn't move. It never moved." He was as positive about that as he had been earlier about having seen no light at the time of the collision. And he had said the same thing to Senator Burton in 1912: "It did not seem to be moving at all."[55]

Colonel Gracie was another one who did not see the light immediately, and he is also paraded as an important witness by the supporters of Captain Lord. "We [Colonel Gracie and a 'young lad' he had met on the boat deck] strained our eyes to discover what had struck us. . . . I swept the horizon near and far and discovered nothing."[56] It was an accurate account of his experience, but easily, and generally, misunderstood. Gracie could see a good deal around him, but he could not possibly see where he should have been looking; forward of the port bow where the light was seen. That part of the horizon was obscured from his vantage point on the boat deck by the bridge and the bridge wings. In a moment we shall see how he later had to lean out of a port window on A deck to see the light bright and clear.

Evidence of the time when the light or lights of another ship were first seen from the *Titanic* is not far to seek.

There is, first, that of Fourth Officer Joseph Grove Boxhall.[57] Boxhall was a Yorkshireman from Hull, 28 years old. Although only a junior officer in the *Titanic,* he already held an Extra Master's Certificate, the highest attainable. Boxhall had been 13 years at sea, and was a specialist in navigation, with 12 months' training at a navigation school in Hull. As his ability in this science was later to be bitterly criticized, this is a fact to be borne in mind.

At Washington, partly because of illness,[58] Boxhall gave his evidence before the Senate inquiry into the disaster in three instalments, and during the second, Senator Duncan Upshaw Fletcher (Florida) asked him: "I understood you to say that you saw a steamer ahead of you, or saw a light that night, about the time of the collision?"[59]

"Shortly afterwards; yes, sir."

One can find out what 'shortly afterwards' meant in clock time by looking at some of Boxhall's evidence in London, where he told what happened as he himself was beginning to help with clearing the boats.

"I was unlacing covers on the port side myself and I saw a lot of men come along — the watch I presume."[60]

This was the middle watch, 12.00 - 4.00 a.m. It will be remembered how

---

*   ". . . the *whole* blame should have been placed on the *bad lookout*." (Original emphasis in [Mt 9/920/6] M 12286.) So wrote Sir Alfred Chalmers, Professional Member of the Marine Department of the Board of Trade, until 1911, who firmly believed that the *Titanic* had too many boats, not too few, but occasionally was not manifestly absurd.

Fleet and Lee were relieved in the regular fashion at the end of their watch in the crow's nest; and now, on the Boat Deck, Boxhall noticed men coming up as they would ordinarily, though they were to be diverted immediately to getting the boats ready for lowering. The watch came on some minutes before the time they were due; hence this would be before midnight.

"Seeing all the men were well established with this work," [that is, taking off the boat covers] Boxhall continues, "I heard someone report a light, a light ahead."

Edward John Buley, AB, on his first trip in the merchant service, just after finishing 13 years in the Royal Navy, had this to say in Washington: "There was a ship of some description there *when she struck* [emphasis added] and she passed right by us. . . . You could see she was a steamer. She had her steamer lights burning. She was off our port bow when we struck, . . . we could not see anything of her in the morning when it was daylight. She was stationary all night; I am very positive for about three hours she was stationary, and then she made tracks. . . . I should judge she was about 3 miles [away] . . . I saw two masthead lights. . . ."[61]

Later, Senator Fletcher asked Buley: "When did you first see that boat on the bow? How long was it before you launched?"

"When we started turning the boats out. That was *about 10 minutes after she struck* [emphasis added]."[62]

The contradictions in Buley's evidence stand out. There is more to be said about this later; but here, Buley is quoted as evidence, in addition to that of Boxhall, to prove that, whatever time is taken as that of the first sighting of another ship, at the earliest, it was at 11.40, "when we struck"; at the latest, at 12.05.

The 'Digest of Testimony' to the transcript of evidence before the US Senate investigation has a heading "Ship Light In Distance", which enumerates 26 sightings at whatever time they occurred. Altogether, if the evidence given afterwards at the British inquiry and reports from other sources are included, there are even more. Together, they provide a variety of description, some contradictions, and much agreement. They mention 'a light' or 'lights', which came from a steamer or some kind of sailing vessel. One witness, QM Robert Hitchens, in fact described it, in Washington and London respectively, as both ". . . codbanker, a schooner that comes out on the Banks,"[63] and (somehow!), "We surmised it to be a steamboat."[64] But, with very few exceptions, all the observers (like Buley) saw the object somewhere on the port side of the *Titanic,* in which direction the *Californian* lay stopped in the ice (see Chapter 4). The overriding comment must still be made, and should be kept in mind: whatever it was the *Titanic* saw, and whenever it was, is important and interesting, but what is decisive is what the *Californian* saw.

Here, let us glance at the scene aboard the sinking ship: the engineers working far below the passenger decks to keep the lights and pumps going, realizing that they had little or no chance of escape, underpaid in life, after the fashion of their day, and dying to the last man; but all to be later compensated with their names on memorials here and there in the ports of the world, plus an unexpected bonus in the form of a precisely drafted tribute from the Attorney-General, who, measuring out his praise like drops from a medicine bottle, declared: ". . . on the whole, I do not think that one is saying a word too much when we say that the behaviour of these men was heroic;" the hundreds of men passengers standing back from the life-saving boats and doomed, the band playing its catchy popular music, perhaps ragtime, perhaps not, but certainly not the hymn, *Nearer, My God to Thee* which legend foisted on them from the beginning* — all this and more has passed into the folklore of many nations.

Less well known, in fact not known at all, are the stories of the shadowy hundreds in the steerage, almost as far below the Astors, the Strauses, the Thayers and such, in the physical bulk of the ship as in the social scale; the adventurers, the optimists, the oppressed. It was officially decided that on no account should it be thought that the Third Class were treated unfairly in any manner whatsoever, such as being prevented from going to the boats by locked doors or gates, of which there were none. Stewards showed Third Class passengers the way, and if most of them nevertheless were drowned, that was largely their own fault, because they tarried, not wanting to be separated from their luggage; and it was only a minor factor in the comparative failure of the attempts at rescue that there was an inadequate number of guides to lead the inordinate number of passengers to the inadequate number of boats.

A hundred and a thousand incidents of human behaviour on the rim of death showed the human animal coming through, most of them, with much dignity and almost no panic. The purpose and reassuring manner of individual members of the crew were at least partly responsible for the calm which filled the *Titanic*. The seamen of all categories had no time, and probably no inclination, for reflection on the irony and implications of their situation.

Boxhall, for instance, after hearing about the light, went on the bridge "and had a look to see what the light was." Whether or not he at once broke off his supervision of the work on the boats on the port side he does not say. In any event, he went onto the bridge and from there saw ". . . a steamer that was almost ahead of us."[65] He saw "The two masthead lights and the red light." This was soon after the order had been given to clear the boats, that is, soon after 12.05.

Meanwhile, still keeping his watch on the after bridge, stood QM Rowe. He had had a very close view of the iceberg, and had looked at his watch, when he felt "a slight jar". ". . . it was then 20 minutes to 12," said Rowe.[66] "I looked towards the starboard side of the ship and saw a mass of ice. I then remained on the after bridge to await orders through the telephone. No orders came down, and I remained until 25 minutes past 12, when I saw a boat on the starboard beam . . . I telephoned to the fore bridge to know if they knew there was a boat lowered. They replied, asking me if I was the third officer. I replied, 'No; I am the quartermaster.' They told me to bring over detonators, which are used in firing distress signals."

Some time after 12, Rowe was joined by his relief, QM Arthur John Bright, and each of them carried a box of detonators to the bridge.[67]

"What next happened?" Senator Burton asked Rowe.[68]

"I turned them over to the Fourth Officer . . ."

The Fourth Officer — Boxhall — had been watching the unknown steamer, which seemed to be coming towards the *Titanic*.

"I told the captain about this ship," said Boxhall.[69] "I saw the masthead lights first, the two steaming lights; and then, as she drew up closer, I saw

---

*   This became the most popular and enduring of all the legends about the *Titanic*. In the summer of 1912, an angry Paris crowd, shut out from the concert, through some ticket muddle, threatened violence until a quick-witted musician struck up *Auprés, mon Dieu, de Toi*, whereupon men reverently removed their hats and stood in silence while women wept. And, it was said, the murderer George Joseph Smith, of brides-in-the-bath infamy, adjourned to his harmonium in the next room to render the hymn while one of his victims lay drowning. Fifty years later, a lady warmly praised a BBC programme on the *Titanic*, her sole criticism being the failure to play the hymn, 'which had made it all worth while.'

her side lights through my glasses, and eventually I saw the red light. I had seen the green, but I saw the red most of the time. I saw the red light with my naked eye."[70]

"What kind of steamer was that which you saw," Senator Fletcher asked, when Boxhall was recalled to give further evidence, ". . . as to size and character?"[71]

"That is hard to state, but the lights were on masts which were fairly close together — the masthead lights."

"What would that indicate?"

"That the masts were pretty close together. She might have been a four-mast ship or might have been a three-mast ship, but she certainly was not a two-mast ship."

"Could you form any idea as to her size?"

"No; I could not."

"You know it was a steamer and not a sailing vessel?"

"Oh, yes; she was a steamer, carrying steaming lights — white lights."

Captain Smith had come and stood by Boxhall's side on the bridge; and, in yet a further instalment of his evidence, Boxhall said,[72] ". . . we both came to the conclusion that she was close enough to be signalled by the Morse lamp."

So Boxhall went over and started the Morse signal.[73]

"I called her up and got no answer.[74] The captain said, 'Tell him to come at once, we are sinking.' So I sent that signal out, 'Come at once, we are sinking.'"

When Rowe and Bright arrived on the bridge, bringing the detonators, a lot of stewards were standing around the bridge and boat deck.

"Of course," said Boxhall, "there were quite a lot of them quite interested in this ship, looking from the bridge, and some said she had shown a light in reply but I never saw it."[75]

Elsewhere, passengers were being reassured by other stewards, who pointed out the light and said another ship would soon come along to pick them up. Colonel Archibald Gracie, the amateur historian, leaned out through a window on the port side of A Deck to show three ladies "a bright white light".[76] On the starboard side of the Boat Deck, a crowd of passengers stood quietly waiting for orders, or pacing slowly up and down, watching the crew preparing lifeboats Nos. 9, 11, 13, and 15 for lowering.

Boxhall and Rowe and Bright were busy on the bridge.[77]

"Suddenly," Mr Beesley writes,[78] "a rush of light from the forward deck, a hissing roar that made us all turn from watching the boats, and a rocket leapt upwards to where the stars blinked and twinkled above us. Up it went, higher and higher, with a sea of faces upturned to watch it, and then an explosion that seemed to split the silent night in two, and a shower of stars sank slowly down and went out one by one. And with a gasping sigh one word escaped the lips of the crowd 'Rockets'!"

It was then about quarter to one.

Sources

1 Southampton press.
2 *Southampton Times*, 30 March 1912 – 'On Ship and Shore', p. 10.
3 P.I. From Mrs Sylvia Lightoller, 1964.
4 Lawrence Beesley, *The Loss of the SS Titanic*.
5 P.I., 4 June 1956.
6 US 3.
7 B 20923.
8 Mersey Report, p. 7.
9 Mersey Report, pp 19 amd [MT 9/920/2]
10 *The Marconigraph*, May, 1912.
11 P.I. from Mr Beesley.
12 B 2394.
13 US 428.
14 US 323, 578.
M 13495.

15 US 316, 320, 366.
16 P.I., 21 September
    1964.
17 US 321.
18 US 318.
19 P.I.
20 US 229.
21 US 230.
22 US 526-27.
23 US 527.
24 Mersey Report, pp. 30-
    31.
25 B 20279.
26 US 950.
27 US 1141; and
    Beauchamp's and
    Barrett's evidence in
    London, Mersey, p. 31
    seq. and p. 53 *seq.*
28 Mersey, p. 470; Harold
    Sanderson's evidence.
29 US 905, 906.
30 US 294.
31 Ibid.
32 US 295.
33 US 744.
34 B 8935.
35 US 317.

36 US 313.
37 US 531-32, 533.
38 B 3727-29.
39 B 3756-58.
40 B 5609.
41 US 975.
42 *The Truth About the
    Titanic*, by Col.
    Archibald Gracie, p. 16.
43 Beesley, Dover ed., p.
    30.
44 Peter Padfield, *The
    Titanic and the
    Californian*, p. 173.
45 BBC programme, *The
    Other Ship* , p. 8 of
    script.
46 Ibid.
47 B 20422.
48 Ibid.
49 *Who Was Who 1929-40,*
    and P.I.
50 P.I.
51 P.I.
52 US 531-32, 533.
53 US 328 and B 17429.
54 Ibid.
55 US 358.

56 *The Truth About the
    Titanic*, p. 15.
57 US 209.
58 US 259.
59 US 909.
60 B 15385.
61 US 611.
62 US 612.
63 US 451; B 1169.
64 Ibid.
65 US 235.
66 US 519.
67 US 832.
68 US 519.
69 US 235.
70 US 933.
71 US 911.
72 US 934.
73 US 235.
74 US 934.
75 Ibid.
76 *The Truth About the
    Titanic*, p. 21.
77 US 832.
78 Beesley, Dover ed., p.
    35.

Chapter 3

Sunday night at sea: black, cold and strangely still

". . . the extraordinary combination of circumstances . . . you would not meet again once in 100 years," Second Officer Lightoller said. There was no moon, no wind, "and most particular of all," he continued, ". . . there was not any swell. . . . I guarantee 99 men out of 100 could never call to mind actual proof of there having been such an absolutely smooth sea."[1]

On the other side of a strip of that black and phenomenally still Atlantic lay the *Californian,* where Third Officer Groves had just announced to Captain Lord that "a passenger steamer is coming up on us."[2] The width of that strip of icy water has been the subject of many estimates.

Captain Lord first calculated that it was 19½-20 miles.[3] Later, he widened it to the maximum estimate of "32 miles".[4] The British official inquiry decided it was at most "10 miles". If the ship seen from the *Titanic* was the *Californian,* and that seen from the *Californian* was the *Titanic,* it was, according to observers in either ship, possibly only five or seven miles.[5]

But whether the distance between the two was five, seven, ten, 19+, or even 32 miles, nobody has ever disputed that the *Californian* was much nearer the *Titanic* on the fatal night of 14/15 April than any other known vessel. The *Carpathia,* which ultimately saved every one of the 711 persons who were saved,[6] was 58 miles away.[7]

The different opinions about the distance between the two ships are more than matched by the contradictory evidence given by Third Officer Groves and Captain Lord about the first sighting of the approaching steamer.

Standing alone on the bridge and watching the ship, after some minutes Groves saw that it was a passenger ship which was approaching them.[8] "She had a lot of light," he later testified at the London inquiry, and he saw two mast-head lights.[9] 45 years later, in his memoirs of the middle watch, Groves mentioned only "a light"[10] and he was probably right then.

The *Titanic* had only one masthead light in her foremast. The misconception that she had two masthead lights may have arisen from an exchange between Lord Mersey and Sir Rufus Isaacs. Captain Lord had told the Attorney-General that he had seen only one masthead light, but he added: "The third officer said he saw two."[11]

"Now, that is important," Sir Rufus said.

"That is very important, because the *Titanic* would have two," Lord Mersey agreed.

"Yes, that is it — two masthead lights," Sir Rufus confirmed.[12]

The two learned gentlemen were wrong and were probably quickly informed that the *Titanic* had only one masthead light. The description of her 'Mast and Rigging' in the Mersey Report[13] and her 'Rigging Plan' do not mention or show a masthead light in her main (after) mast. On photographs of the *Titanic,* the masthead light in her foremast can, in some cases, be seen, but on none that has been closely inspected does her main mast reveal such a light.

In 1912 a steam vessel was to carry at least one masthead light in her foremast, but when under way was allowed to carry an additional white masthead light, at least 15 feet higher, in one of her other masts. It seems that in practice most two-masted ships would carry one masthead light, and three- or four-masted ships two, but this was not a set rule.[14]

The republication, in the 1950s, of a famous night picture of the *Titanic,* called; 'By Night — An Impression at Cherbourg', was credited as a 'heavily retouched photograph'. It reinforced again the belief that the *Titanic* had had more than one masthead light. In fact the picture is not a photograph, but a washed drawing — with white placard dots for the masthead lights, typical of the time and done for *The Sphere.* In 1912 it had been internationally very much in demand, and appeared in many illustrated magazines the world over. It shows the *Titanic* with one light in her foremast and two mast lights in her main mast, and smoke from all four of her funnels, both of these details are wrong and only a personal impression of the artist.

Anyway, Groves said about the approaching stranger:

"There was absolutely no doubt her being a passenger steamer, at least in my mind."[15]

So, following the orders Lord had given him, he went below to report. It was then about 11.30 p.m.,[16] and the steamer was getting nearer and her lights clearer all the time. She was very slowly changing her bearing.[17]

"I knocked at his [Captain Lord's] door," said Groves, "and told him there was a steamer approaching us, coming up on the starboard quarter."[18]

Lord said later he already knew about this steamer; but he did not trouble to tell Groves that.

"Can you make anything out of her lights?" was all he asked.[19]

And that was when Groves replied that she was evidently a passenger steamer.

"Call her up on the Morse lamp," said Lord.[20]

So Groves went up back to the bridge and called up the steamer by the Morse lamp.[21]

"I sent the word 'What?' meaning to ask what ship it was. When I sent 'What?' his light was flickering. I took up the glasses again and I came to the conclusion it could not have been a Morse lamp."[22]

In fact, he got no reply. But he continued signalling and watching the steamer, and at 11.40 she seemed to put her lights out.[23]

"What makes you fix the time 11.40," asked Mr S.A.T. Rowlatt, one of the junior counsel for the Board of Trade, "for her lights going out?"[24]

"Because that is the time we struck one bell to call the middle watch."

"Do you remember that bell was struck at that time?"[25]

"Most certainly."

It was at 11.40 the *Titanic* hit the iceberg and was turning to port when she did so.

Groves had recently been in the P. & O. service,[26] where it was the practice to put out the lights as a hint to passengers that it was time for bed. Hence, he was neither puzzled nor surprised that this unknown passenger ship should have put out her lights.

But something else was in Rowlatt's mind. Evidence had already been given of the *Titanic's* turn to port in a vain attempt to avoid the iceberg.

"I want to ask you a question. Supposing the steamer whose lights you saw turned two points to port at 11.40, would that account to you for her lights ceasing to be visible to you?"[27]

"I quite think it would," Groves answered.

Meantime, Captain Lord arrived on the bridge.

"He had not been on the bridge again," said Groves, "since about 10.25."[28]

The junior officer pointed out the ship, now stopped, and many years later Groves reported what Lord had said.

"That will be the *Titanic* on her maiden voyage."[29]

At the London inquiry, Groves's evidence was substantially, but not precisely, the same.

"When he [Captain Lord] came up on the bridge he said to me, 'That does not look like a passenger steamer.' I said, 'It is, sir. When she stopped, her lights seemed to go out, and I suppose they have been put out for the night.'"[30]

According to Groves's 1912 evidence, Lord then said: "Well, the only passenger steamer near us is the *Titanic*."[31]

Whatever were the exact words about the *Titanic,* which later became a matter of sharp dispute, there is no doubt that at the time they were uttered they seemed of no significance to either man. Lord said, more than once, that he had expressed the opinion that the unknown ship was "something like ourselves,"[32] i.e. about 6,000 tons.

Groves, of course, remained on the bridge, his watch not ending until midnight; but Lord, very sensibly on this freezing cold night, soon went below again to his steam-heated quarters.

"I do not think, Groves said, "he would have been up there for more than three minutes at the outside with me."[33]

Lord's version, or more exactly, versions, of the sighting of the steamer — there were four of them altogether — we shall examine in detail in Chapter 15. Meanwhile, it may be said briefly, the gist of his evidence about this was quite clear: he saw the steamer approaching from the East;[34] she was showing her green,[35] or starboard, light (see Diagram 2) and one masthead light.[36]

Groves, on the other hand, said clearly he saw two masthead lights,[37] but the remainder of his evidence about the direction from which the steamer approached is far from clear. He insisted she must be going "westward",[38] because he saw her red, or port light,[39] but, as he also said she was "three points abaft the beam', "S ½ W",[40] on the quarter of the *Californian,* which was heading north-east,[41] this, as Diagram 2 shows, is impossible. Nor can one even be sure whether Groves meant he saw her red light while she was approaching, or not until she had stopped.[42]

Groves was possessed of a powerful and incisive intellect, and his character was distinguished by exceptional candour. Hence, the confused quality of this phase of his testimony has always seemed inexplicable. It may be he was suffering from a common and passing mental aberration, in which the speaker says something almost the exact opposite of what he means, or thinks he is saying, and he corrects himself only if and when he hears what he is saying. What is certain is, his report of the approach of the steamer was an acute contradiction of Captain Lord's, but no one has ever asserted that he and Groves saw two different ships.

To resume the story: the air temperature at midnight, according to the log of the *Californian,* was no more than 30°F[-1°C].[43] The ice was bumping against the sides of the ship; the night was very dark. It is not hard to imagine that young Groves, or anybody in the same situation, was impatient for the end of his watch.

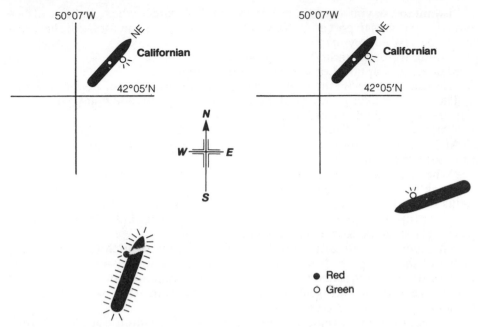

Diagram 2. Approach of the unknown steamer, as seen by the *Californian*
Groves saw her (above, left) coming up obliquely about 3¹/₂ points abaft the star-board beam with two masthead lights and 'brilliantly lit like a passenger ship'. Later, he saw her red sidelight, but throughout maintained she was heading west until she stopped at 11.40 p.m., when most of her lights seem to go out.

Captain Lord saw her (above, right) approaching from the east and heading west showing one masthead light, a broad green sidelight, and a few other lights. He thought her a tramp, a 'medium-size steamer', 'something like ourselves.'

After he had tried ineffectually to Morse to the steamer, he did not pay particular attention to her, but he certainly continued to notice her; it would have been difficult not to, if he paced from one side of the bridge to the other.

"We were swinging slowly to port," said Groves, "very slowly."[44] But he corrected this to "starboard" three questions later.[45]

The effect was as if the other steamer was working towards their head, and he could see her port light.[46]

"I stayed on the bridge till something between 12.10 and 12.15."[47] Then, the Second Officer, Herbert Stone, came up to relieve him.[48]

Lord had not returned to the bridge, but stopped Stone outside the wheel-house door and given him his orders for the watch. He pointed out the steamer, which was "a little abaft" their starboard beam and said she was stopped.[49] He also pointed out the loose field ice all around the *Californian* and a dense icefield to the south.

Stone saw the other steamer, from which he spotted "One masthead light and a red side-light and two or three small indistinct lights."[50]

Lord told him to keep an eye on her and let him know if she changed her bearing or got any closer to them.[51] At the time, Stone thought she was "approx-imately about five miles" away.[52] Lord also told him, Groves had been trying to get in touch with her by the Morse lamp but could get no reply.[53] Stone then went up to the bridge — "about eight minutes past 12". He later wrote[54] — and the captain said he was going to lie down on the chart-room settee.

"I pointed out the steamer to him," said Groves, describing Stone's arrival to relieve him, "and said: 'she has been stopped since 11.40"; and I said: "She is a passenger steamer. At about the moment she stopped she put her lights out'."[55]

Before the steamer stopped, Captain Lord saw her green sidelight. Groves also watched her going westward, but did not see her green light.[56] Then, she evidently turned to port, and, he said, seemed to put out her lights.[57] This, incidentally, to a layman, at least, is one of the puzzles in this part of Groves's evidence. As she was approaching "obliquely",[58] and then turned to port, it seems, she must "have opened up the longest broadside in the world", and have actually increased the amount of light she was showing. However, after she stopped, Groves certainly saw her red light, as Stone had seen it first from below. This meant the ship had then turned back again to starboard. It was as if she had moved in a kind of inverted question mark (see Diagrams 1 and 2).

When the *Titanic* met the iceberg, First Officer Murdoch tried to 'port around it'. First, he turned her to port, then back to starboard again. As QM Rowe had noticed her stern swinging to the south, her head would be towards the north.[59] She, would then be showing her red light to a ship north of her. She, too, would have moved in a kind of inverted question mark — curiously enough.

In London, Stone's evidence about what Groves said to him on the bridge was: "He told me the steamer had stopped at one bell and that he had called her on the Morse lamp and got no answer."[60]

Neither here, nor in his written statement to Lord, does Stone report that Groves had described the ship as 'a passenger steamship'. He does, however, confirm Groves's evidence about the time the vessel had stopped: 'one bell', which was 11.40. The *Titanic* also had stopped at 11.40.

The two young men chatted for a time, while Stone got his eyes in, after which Groves said 'Good night' and went below.[61] He did not go straight to his own cabin, but went along the deck to call on Evans, the Marconi operator, as he often did, to hear the news.

Cyril Furmston Evans, later known as 'Furmston-Evans',[62] 20 years old and born at Croydon on the outskirts of London, was a slim youth with glasses, who had had six months' experience as a wireless operator at sea. His training, like that of other young men in this new profession, had been obtained in a ten months' course at the Marconi school. He had had one trip in the *Cedric,* then joined the *Californian* in January 1912 when her wireless was installed.[63] He made the trip to New Orleans and back to London, and was now crossing the Atlantic in her for the third time.[64] The Marconi Company paid him £4 per month, and the Leyland Line had him down in the *Californian's* log as a 'telegraphist'[65] at the nominal wage of one shilling per month.

He was the sole operator aboard, which meant that when he was asleep — and it was conceded implicitly, if not in so many words, that he had to sleep some time — the ship would miss any messages, and would be as deaf and *incommunicado* as any ship in all the long centuries since man had first ventured out to sea.*

One wireless operator for most shipowners of any nationality was more

---

* In April 1912 perhaps a thousand of all 23,217 registered power-driven ships were equipped with wireless of one kind or another, of which 410 were British. (Estimate made up by Marconi, German Telefunken and American De Forest.)

than enough. The system used was not a good one, and on that Sunday night in mid-Atlantic, it blew up, and in no other place than aboard this unremarkable vessel *Californian,* property of Frederick Leyland & Co. Ltd., Liverpool, England.

As Groves went along the deck to visit Evans that night, although he was greatly interested in the still unusual means of communication, it was the news rather than the wireless which drew him, as he said: "to have a yarn with Evans, before turning in."

As it turned out, Groves was disappointed. Evans had been working for 16 hours, with a short time off for meals, and at 11.35, he had taken off his phones, got undressed and turned in. Groves found the wireless cabin in darkness, but he switched on the light and discovered Evans asleep in his bunk with a magazine in his hands.[66]

"What ships have you got, Sparks?" Groves asked his friend, waking him up.[67]

"Only the *Titanic,*"[68] Evans replied dreamily. "You know, the new boat on its maiden voyage. I got it this afternoon."

Evans also remembered Groves asking ". . . if I had got any news."[69] Groves had no recollection of that; but long afterwards he said that in response to Evans's information about the *Titanic,* he had remarked, she was "in sight on the starboard beam."[70] Evans, in turn, could only recall Groves asking what ships he had. He had only "a faint recollection" of the whole visit, and he was already "half asleep".[71]

"Almost mechanically",[72] Groves then picked up the phones, put them to his ears, and listened.

"Did you hear anything?"[73] he was asked at the London inquiry.

"Nothing at all."

"How long did you listen?"

"I do not suppose it would be more than 15 seconds at the outside — well, 15 to 30 seconds . . ."

It was then after a quarter past twelve, between 12.15 and 12.20.[74] In the *Titanic,* Jack Phillips, the senior Marconi operator, had just begun to send out his distress call: "CQD CQD CQD CQD CQD CQD, MGY. STRUCK ICEBERG. COME TO OUR ASSISTANCE AT ONCE. POSITION: LAT. 41.44N; LONG.50.24W" *

Groves was positive that he could read a distress call; but he heard nothing. To make signals audible in the apparatus used in the *Californian* and other ships at that time, a magnetic detector was used, and this was wound by clockwork. When Evans had hung up his phones, the clockwork had gradually run down. Groves put the phones to his ears without noticing that the clockwork needed winding.

"That fact," he wrote in remorse in later years,[75] "I am sure was the determining factor in the loss of all those lives. I *know* I was capable of reading a distress call and naturally would at once have passed the earphones to the wireless operator when Captain Lord would speedily have been made cognisant of the position and Mr Stewart also."[76]

Groves never forgot, and never recovered altogether from the wound those few minutes inflicted on him. It seemed as if this sensitive man blamed himself for the 1,500 deaths in the *Titanic,* and he was loath ever to talk about it.

Evans was almost asleep again. Groves laid down the phones on the table,

---

* This position was shortly altered by Boxhall to the celebrated, '41.46N 50.14W'.

switched off the light, closed Evans's door, and went straight to his own cabin.[77]

Up on the bridge, meanwhile, Stone was keeping the other steamer under observation the whole time.[78]

"Was there any reason for that?" he was asked.[79]

"None whatever, except that it was another ship stopped in ice the same as ourselves."

At quarter past twelve, James Gibson, the young apprentice, brought coffee up to the bridge and, with Second Officer Herbert Stone, began a watch which must forever linger in the imagination as one of the most mysterious of all sea stories.

After Groves left the bridge, Stone called up the steamer on the Morse lamp, and again there was no reply. Now, as he and Gibson stood drinking their coffee, Gibson asked him if there were any ships around. Stone said there was a ship on the starboard beam, and looking over the weather cloth, Gibson saw a white light flickering. At first, he took it to be a Morse lamp and he went to the keyboard and gave one long flash in answer. Her light still flickered and Gibson gave the calling up sign. He then turned his glasses on her, and what had seemed to be a Morse lamp, now seemed to be a masthead light flickering.[80] Gibson also saw her red port light[81] and "a glare of lights" on her afterdeck, "white lights," he said.[82]

"I then went over to the Second Officer," Gibson wrote a few days later in his report to Lord,[83] 'and remarked that she looked like a tramp steamer."

Why a tramp should have "a glare of lights" on the afterdeck Gibson never explained. In those days, the crew of a tramp or, as Lord said, a ship 'something like ourselves', 'a medium-size steamer', had their quarters in the fore-castle, from which, therefore, any 'glare of lights' might, if anywhere, have been expected, but a tramp Gibson always maintained was what the steamer was.

Stone agreed, and said she was burning oil lights. It is worth repeating that Stone makes no reference, even by way of disagreement, with Groves's statement to him, when he (Stone) took over the watch, that the steamer in sight was a passenger ship. Soon after, about 25 past 12, Stone sent Gibson below to get the gear ready to stream on a new log, to replace that carried away by the ice.

It must have been while Gibson was unsuccessfully searching below that Lord communicated with Stone. In his report to Lord of 18 April, Stone merely says: "At 12.35 you whistled up the speaking tube and asked if the other steamer had moved. I replied 'No' and that she was on the same bearing and also reported I had called him up and the result."

In Lord's Affidavit nearly 50 years later, he had a rather different version of the incident.[84]

"At ten minutes after midnight, it now being 15th April, the Second Officer came on to the saloon deck. I drew his attention to the fact that we were stopped in and surrounded by ice and that I intended to remain stopped until daylight. I pointed out the other steamer to him, told him that she was stopped and that he was to watch her and let me know if we drifted any closer to her. He then went on to the bridge to relieve the Third Officer, and I went into the chart-room." At the London inquiry, Lord's own evidence about this was much the same as Stone's.

". . . I was up and down off the bridge till 12 o'clock . . ."[85] ". . . I went into the chart room at a quarter past 12."[86]

Then, in corroboration of Stone, Lord's evidence was, he went from the chart-room into his cabin, and from there called up Stone on the speaking tube,[87] when he was told the news about the steamer. Lord put the time at "20 minutes to 1. . . . I told him I was going to lie down in the chart room then."[88]

This whole incident is a trifle, but it should be said, the whole tragedy was built of trifles, added one to another in the hours that followed.

Soon after Lord's talk with Stone, Gibson came back, having been unable to find a new log line. He asked Stone about it, and noticed that the steamer, which had previously been "right abeam",[89] was now "one point and a half before the beam",[90] that is, bearing closer to the bows of the *Californian.* Stone gave Gibson further information about the whereabouts of the log, and the lad went off again.

What had happened hitherto during this middle watch, drinking coffee on a freezing cold night, going to replace a log line, the skipper retiring to lie down, even the unanswered calls on the Morse lamp — all were ordinary incidents of a normal night at sea, uninteresting and unimportant trifles, not worth remembering; but they were recalled later as the tiny events which occupied the men of the *Californian,* before something new and in no way a trifle occurred.

Stone was now alone on the bridge, walking up and down. Evans was fast asleep, and probably Groves and Chief Officer Stewart as well. Gibson was below on the quartermaster's deck busy with the log; and Lord was in his steam-heated chart-room, with all his clothes on, including his boots and his cap, which shaded his eyes from the electric light. He was lying uncomfortably on the settee, as he was nearly six feet and the settee was not.

Captain Lord always insisted on the importance of these details, the implication being that he, although fast asleep, was also simultaneously fully alert, and ready throughout, at a moment's notice, for any emergency. In view of what happened when the gravest emergency did arise, Captain Lord might just as well have been not only comfortably pajama-ed and snugly tucked into his bunk, but even peacefully asleep far away at home in distant Liscard, Cheshire, England.

In the story of the *Californian,* all these men — Lord, Groves, Stewart, Stone, Gibson, Evans — are familiar names, and one other as well, Ernest Gill, assistant donkeyman, who was also below. But in the still and sleeping ship, with only the faint bumping of the light field ice against her sides and the regular shipboard sounds, there were other names too, not hitherto known, names of men who were watching silently, watching when Herbert Stone's moment came, the most shining and the most terrible in his whole life; so soon now and so unexpectedly.

"First of all," Stone said, "I was walking up and down on the bridge, and I saw one white flash in the sky immediately above this other steamer. I did not know what it was; I thought it might be a shooting star."[91]

He realized before long it was a white rocket.

It was then about quarter to one.[92]

Sources

1 B 14197-14200.	8 B 8178.	14 From 'The regulations
2 B 8172.	9 B 8147.	for preventing
3 US 718.	10 'The Middle Watch'.	Collisions at Sea'.
4 B 6823.	11 B 6806.	Under orders in Council
5 B 7819, B 17851.	12 B 6807.	issued in pursuance of
6 Mersey p. 716.	13 Mersey Report, p. 17-	the Merchant Shipping
7 B 25389.	18.	Act, 13 October 1910.

15 Ibid.
16 B 8169.
17 B 8165.
18 B 8170.
19 B 8172.
20 B 8182.
21 B 8185.
22 B 8189.
23 B 8197, 8213.
24 B 8217.
25 B 8218.
26 B 8265 & P.I.
27 B 8223.
28 B 8206.
29 Private letter from Groves.
30 B 8197.
31 B 8239.
32 B 6752.
33 B 8241.
34 B 6734.
35 B 6728.
36 B 6805.
37 B 6806.
38 B 8467-68.
39 B 8469.
40 B 8157, 8159.
41 Ibid.
42 B 8228-29.
43 US 1142.
44 B 8246.
45 B 8249.
46 B 8228, 8248.
47 B 8250.
48 B 8251.
49 B 7813; Stone's statement, 18 April, q.v.
50 B 7814.
51 B 7815.
52 B 7819.
53 B 7816.
54 Stone, 18 April.
55 B 8257.
56 B 8228.
57 B 8197, 8265.
58 B 8179.
59 B 17670-74.
60 B 7823.
61 B 8272; 'The Middle Watch'.
62 P.I.; US 733.
63 *Marconigraph,* January, 1912.
64 US 733.
65 Official Log.
66 B 8275-76; 'The Middle Watch'.
67 B 8279.
68 B 8282; 'The Middle Watch'.
69 B 9038.
70 B 9034, 9045; 'The Middle Watch'.
71 Ibid.
72 B 8286.
73 B 8285-86.
74 B 8289.
75 'The Middle Watch'.
76 P.I.
77 B 8287.
78 B 7824.
79 B 7825.
80 B 7455.
81 B 7429.
82 B 7426.
83 Gibson, statement, April 18.
84 Capt. Lord's Affidavit, Appendix C and *The Boston Evening Transcript,* 19 April 1912.
85 B 6766.
86 B 6783.
87 B 6785.
88 B 6787.
89 B 7438.
90 Gibson, statement, 18 April.
91 B 7832.
92 Stone, statement, 18 April.

Chapter 4

Her stern was swinging, practically dead south

Fourth Officer Boxhall aboard the *Titanic* sent up his first rocket, but the steamer in sight took no notice at all. So Boxhall, helped by the two quartermasters, Rowe and Bright, sent up more at intervals.[1]

Bright was asked by Senator Smith how long the intervals were, but he could not say. "After we would fire one we would go and help clear the boats away, and then we would come back again."[2]

"I would signal with the Morse," Boxhall told Senator Smith, "and then go ahead and send off a rocket, and then go back and have a look at the ship, until I was finally sent away."[3]

Still they brought no response.

"How are the rockets exploded?" asked the senator.

"The rockets are exploded by a firing lanyard."

"They shower?"

"They go right up into the air and they throw stars."

At a later session, Boxhall gave a somewhat different answer to a question from Senator Fletcher: "What was the character of the rockets fired off in the *Titanic,* as to colours?"[4]

"Just white stars, bright. I do not know whether they were stars or bright balls. I think they were balls. They were the regulation distress signals."

He referred to companies' private night signals, and was asked what they were (see Appendix K).[5]

"They are coloured as a rule; stars which you can easily see. These rockets were not throwing stars, they were throwing balls, I remember, and then they burst."

Earlier, Senator Smith had asked Boxhall: "Did they work satisfactorily?"[6]

"Oh, yes," said Boxhall.

"The failure to arouse the attention of this ship was not due to any impaired or partial success of these signals?"

"Not at all, sir."

As for the appearance of these rockets, Boxhall was asked whether or not they "would be regarded as anything but distress signals?"

He answered very sensibly:[7] "I am hardly in a position to state that, because it is the first time I have seen distress rockets sent off, and I could not very well judge what they would be like, standing as I was, underneath them, firing them myself. I do not know what they would look like in the distance."

More than one witness will be able to say what these rockets did look like from a distance; but, first, here are some factual details about the rockets used by the *Titanic*.

The rockets were manufactured by the Cotton Powder Co. Ltd. Known technically as 'socket distress signals', they were then the latest device. The makers proudly advertised them, after they had been approved by the Board of Trade, "as a SUBSTITUTE for both GUNS and ROCKETS in passenger and other vessels . . . The necessity of carrying guns and rockets is entirely obviated and accidents consequently minimized . . ."[8]

"Socket distress signals are fired from a socket, ascend to a height of 600 to 800 feet, and then burst with the report of a gun and the stars of a rocket," Lloyd's Calendar yearly remarked in their section SIGNALS OF DISTRESS. Later Mr Harrison, however, deduced from Lightoller's evidence that the explosion would reach "a height of some 150 to 200 feet", but Lightoller had only mentioned that they burst "at a great height in the air."[9]

Boxhall said that they threw balls, not stars;[10] Lightoller said they threw "a great number of stars";[11] and Lightoller was right. According to another Cotton Powder advertisement, the signals "burst at high altitude showing stars . . . "[12] Like other manufacturers, the Cotton Powder Co. did not specify the range at which their signals could be seen and heard, but they did claim that they could be "seen and heard further than any other means."

Boxhall, Bright, and Rowe continued firing their rockets, but the steamer paid no more heed to the later rockets than she had to the first. She seemed instead to turn away very slowly from the *Titanic,* so that her stern light became visible. At intervals of about five minutes the desperate and frustrated men continued their efforts.

"I assisted the officer to fire them," said Rowe,[13] "and was firing the distress signals until about five and twenty minutes past. At that time they were getting out the starboard collapsible boats. The Chief Officer, Wilde, wanted a sailor. I asked Captain Smith if I should fire any more, and he said· 'No; get into that boat.'"

By that time, according to Boxhall's evidence in London, they had sent up "between half a dozen and a dozen."[14] It would have been easy enough to lose count in more normal circumstances, as at a display of fireworks, unless the number to be fired had been fixed in advance. QM Bright thought, in "probably half an hour", "six were fired in all."[15] Bright could not say if the Morse lamp was used; he did not notice the colour of the rockets, nor, as he was directly asked,[16] look to ascertain it, when they burst. Clearly, he was not a very observant man, and so it was perhaps significant that his number of rockets was so close to Boxhall's. Both also were close to what was certainly the best estimate of all. "About eight" was the number given by Second Officer Lightoller.[17] It was not only the source which inspired confidence in the figure, but, it was to receive exact corroboration quite independently.

Anyhow, the light or lights of the vessel remained in sight, and some of the men in charge of boats were ordered to pull towards her; others did so without specific orders. An important question is, in which direction they had to row. The course of the *Titanic,* at the time of the accident, was S86°W true, a generally westward course. By far the greater number who saw the other ship reported her somewhere on the port bow of the *Titanic.* Hence, if the *Titanic,* after she was stopped, continued heading in the same direction, then that unknown and unanswering ship must have been a little to the south of westward of the *Titanic.* It is beyond question that the *Californian* was somewhere to the north of the *Titanic;* so, it is said, the ship seen by the *Titanic* could not possibly have been the *Californian* (see Diagram 3).

At first sight, in view of so many other things, this is a bold statement, but there is evidence, and very respectable evidence, to support the claim. Boxhall

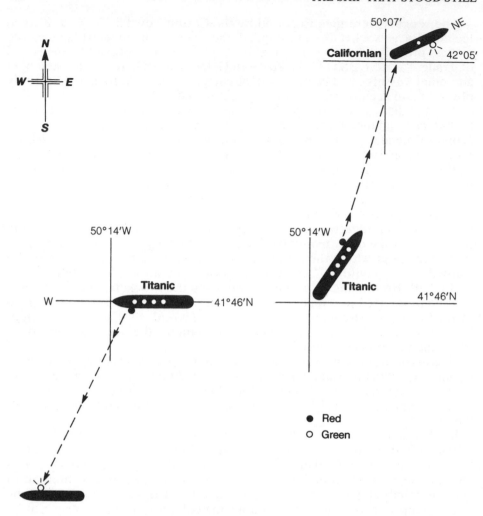

Diagram 3. *Titanic* **heading after collision**
Whether or not the Californian's *overnight position was given correctly, she was certainly north of the ship she saw. Equally certainly, whatever her identity, the ship seen by the* Titanic *was on her port side. Therefore, if the* Titanic *continued heading west after the collision, the ship she saw could not have been the* Californian; *but if the* Titanic *swung north or east of north after the accident, the ship she saw to port could well have been the* Californian.

himself gave evidence at Washington, from which it must be deduced he assumed the *Titanic* was heading west. He said to Senator Smith the steamer was, "almost ahead of us."[18]

"On the same course, apparently?"

"No; oh, no."

"On the same general course?"

"By the way she was heading," said Boxhall, "she seemed to be meeting us."

That is, she would be, as Senator Burton later put it, "on a general course toward the east", which Boxhall did not contradict.[19]

"I saw this steamer's stern light before I went into my boat," he had already said, "which indicated that the ship was turned around."[20]

In my own talk with Commander Boxhall, as he then was, I tried to get a clearer and more direct statement from him. He said he would stick to what he had said at the time; and he also dryly remarked that his recollection, after more than 52 years, was not quite so firm as it had been just two weeks after the accident!

Nor was Boxhall alone in his apparent belief that while she lay sinking the *Titanic* was still on her pre-collision course and heading west.

Third Officer Pitman at Washington testified that at about half past one, while lying on their oars in No. 5 Boat, they saw "one white light."

"In what position was it?" asked Senator Smith.[21]

"It was to the westward. Right ahead —"

"Right on the course of the *Titanic*?"

"Exactly," Pitman agreed.

While Boxhall's opinion must be deduced from his answers, Pitman's was direct and unequivocal.

Another witness of the 'western' school was Alfred Crawford, a First Class bedroom steward, a mature man, with more than 30 years at sea, and an intelligent observer of things he saw. He was in No. 8 Boat, and Captain Smith ordered him to row toward the other steamer. They rowed for hours, all night, but seemed to make no progress.

"Do you know whether you were moving west?" Senator Fletcher asked.[22]

"I do not know the compass, and I could not say."

All the same, the Senator pressed him for a reply.

"Suppose the *Titanic* was going west; then you went northwest?"

"Probably so."

"Toward the light?"

"Yes, sir."

"And then the *Carpathia* appeared in what direction?"

"She came right up around and started to pick up the boats."

"She came from the northeast from you, then?"

"Probably so."

"Assuming you had been going southwest?"

"Yes, sir."

In a counting of heads, therefore, Crawford can be included among those who thought the *Titanic* was heading west, but the value of his evidence on this point is almost nil. In the first place, Senator Fletcher led him with his own assumption that the *Titanic* "was going west"; and, secondly, by another leading question about the direction from which the *Carpathia* approached. In fact, it was not from the 'north-east', but south-east, and is one of the fixed points in this puzzle, which is beyond doubt. At daylight, the lights of the other steamer were no longer visible, and when No. 8 saw the lights of the *Carpathia* coming up astern, they gave up their vain attempt, turned right round and began rowing toward the Cunarder. Having rowed farthest and longest of all the boats towards the other steamer, No. 8 had the longest row back to the *Carpathia,* and was almost the last to be picked up.

An AB, George Moore, was another who evidently believed that the *Titanic* was heading to the west.

"I believe," he said,[23] "the ice we saw in the morning was to the northward of the *Titanic*."

But he, too, was led, in his case by Senator Francis Griffith Newlands of Nevada; and although the report is not quite clear as to whether he was referring to the *Titanic* or the *Carpathia,* he gave an answer that the direction of the ship ". . . in order to go to New York" was "to the westward."[24]

The most interesting, and certainly the most intelligent, supporter of this school of 'westerners', was Mr Beesley.

". . . in the absence of any plan of action," he wrote, "we rowed slowly forward — or what we thought was forward, for it was in the direction the *Titanic's* bows were pointing before she sank. I see now that we must have been pointing North West, for we presently saw the Northern Lights on the starboard, and again, when the *Carpathia* came up from the south, we saw her from behind us on the south-east, and turned our boat around to get to her."[25]

Mr Beesley's boat, No. 13, heavily laden as it was, and obstructed by an iceberg, had a slow row to the *Carpathia,* being, he thought, the eighth or ninth to arrive,[26] he timed the arrival as being no later than about 4.30 a.m.[27] Mr Beesley's timing may well be too early for the arrival of his boat and it is more likely that No. 13 did not reach the *Carpathia* before 5.00 a.m., but this was still early considering that the last boat, No. 8, arrived at about 8.30. As is explained later, the starboard boats had a shorter journey to the *Carpathia* than those on the port side, so it seems probable that, in this case, Mr Beesley was mistaken in his assumption that the *Titanic* was heading west when she sank. In spite of his mentioning the Northern Lights, there is no suggestion that his boat was steering by compass. The bad rowing in No. 13, which Mr Beesley also mentions,[28] makes it highly unlikely that the boat was capable of following a straight course without any fixed mark. In other words, the fact that those in No. 13 "presently saw the Northern Lights on the starboard" seems a very infirm basis for deducing that the *Titanic* was heading north-west when she sank.

The truth of the matter is that after the collision the *Titanic* was not heading west. Probably from the time of the collision, when Murdoch tried 'to port around' the iceberg, he put her head somewhere north of west. She certainly swung towards the north, and her heading may have been north-west, was probably north-east and may even have been due east. There is an abundance of evidence, oral and circumstantial, to prove the point.

Fifth Officer Harold Godfrey Lowe, was very clear in his sworn statement before the British Consulate General in New York where he said 'he had seen a steamer on the port bow', "about 5 miles to the northward of us." Which meant nothing else than that the *Titanic* must have been heading North or somewhat East of North just after 1 o'clock when Lowe made his observation — and "was putting over the starboard emergency boat" No. 1.[29]

In London, QM Rowe was asked whether he had noticed, when he saw the light, if the *Titanic's* head was altering to port or starboard, and he said: "Yes."[30]

"Was your vessel's head swinging at the time you saw the light of this other vessel?"[31] he was asked by Butler Aspinall, one of the five counsel for the Board of Trade.

"I put it down that her stern was swinging."

"Which way was her stern swinging?"[32]

"Practically dead south, I believe, then."

"Do you mean her head was facing South?"

"No, her head was facing North. She was coming round to starboard." (see Diagram 3).

"The stern was swung to the South?"

"Yes."

"And at that time you saw the white light?"

"Yes."

"How was it bearing from you?"

"When I first saw it, it was half a point on the port bow, and roughly about two points when I left the bridge."[33]

Rowe, it will be remembered, had been on the bridge with Boxhall firing rockets for about three-quarters of an hour, until Captain Smith sent him away in charge of Collapsible C, with Bruce Ismay for company.*

Henry Samuel Etches, a First Class bedroom steward, another man with a level head and much assurance, who was in Boat No. 5, was asked in Washington whether he had seen any icebergs.

He had, and also "a very large floe of flat ice".[34] This was the field ice which lay to the west of the *Titanic,* according to all the charts made by various and contradictory hands.

"In what direction?" Senator Fletcher asked.[35]

"I should say it would have been well over on the port side of the *Titanic,* in the position she was going. I should say, by the way we pulled, the direct way we pulled, it must have been on the port side of the *Titanic.*"

Bearing in mind the position of the ice field, the *Titanic,* according to this, must have been heading north to north-east.

Major Arthur Godfrey Peuchen, a chemical manufacturer of Toronto, Ont., and a yachtsman, who, at Lightoller's request, slid down a loose rope to help man No. 6, gave the most convincing evidence of all the witnesses about the direction in which the *Titanic* was heading.

"After you took to the lifeboat, you proceeded to row in the direction in which the ship had been moving, westward?"[36]

The questioner was, once more, Senator Fletcher.

"No; we started right off from the port side of the boat, directly straight off from her about amidship, on the port side, right directly north, I think it would be, because the northern lights appeared where this light we had been looking at in that direction appeared shortly afterwards."

If 'straight off' means, at a right angle from the port side of the *Titanic,* she must have been heading actually due east soon after 1 o'clock in the morning.

It will be noted that while Boxhall and Pitman agreed with their questioners that the *Titanic* was heading west, neither of them seems to have thought about the matter. Presumably, after steaming for four days in a generally westerly direction, the two officers took it as a matter of course that the ship was still headed towards the west. The fact that they knew what her course was at the time of the accident (S86°W) must have confirmed their subconscious belief. But it must be said that with all respect to the opinions of two highly-skilled and experienced seamen, in this instance one can only conclude they were mistaken.

Rowe and Peuchen, who also both knew something about navigation, did take note of the *Titanic's* heading, and bearing in mind that her heading might be changing as time passed, their evidence was similar or complementary.

But if the words of the different witnesses are not decisive, the circumstantial evidence clinches the matter.

As the *Carpathia* came upon the scene from the south-east, if the *Titanic* had still been heading west and the boats on the port side, when they rowed

---

* Like some others, including Bruce Ismay, Rowe had also seen a light on the starboard quarter and he had dutifully reported it to his Captain. The old man then raised his glasses to look and told his quartermaster that the light was not a ship but 'must be a planet' he then lent Rowe his glasses 'to see for himself.' (P.I. from George Rowe [1955].)

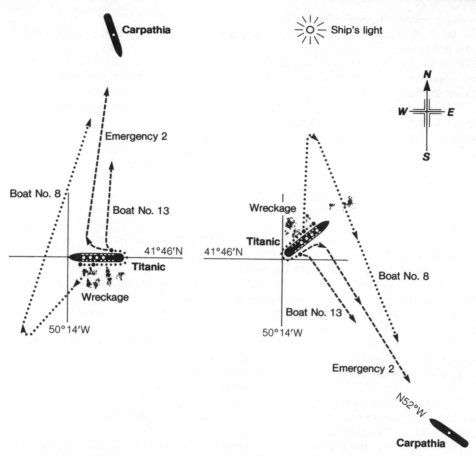

Diagram 4. The *Titanic* headed north of west after the collision

A certainty in a sea of doubt was the direction of the Carpathia's *approach: from the south-east. Hence, if the* Titanic *had continued heading west after the accident, her port boats would have had the shortest row to the rescue ship. In fact, as the diagram on the left, drawn on this hypothesis shows, the exact opposite happened. It was as if the* Carpathia *was coming from the north-west. Emergency Boat No. 2 (Boxhall's boat), nominally a port boat, rowed round the stern of the* Titanic *and became a starboard boat. She was the first to reach the* Carpathia. *No. 13 (Mr Beesley's) arrived eighth or ninth, but as early as about 5.00 a.m. On the other hand, No. 8, which rowed furthest towards the other ship's light, had to run round and did not reach the* Carpathia *until 8.30 a.m. The diagram on the right shows the* Titanic *as she actually headed after the collision, north of west and towards the east, with the same typical port and starboard boat tracks. Major Peuchen indicated the* Titanic *was actually headed east when No. 6 left her.*

away from her generally made for the west or south, while those on the star-board side went west or north — that is, if, in Lawrence Beesley's words, both lots had 'fanned out' — it is clear that the port boats would generally have had the shorter row to the *Carpathia* and the starboard the longer. In fact, the exact opposite is what happened (see Diagram 4).

Remembering that the port boats are the even-numbered, and starboard the odd, we have already seen how Steward Crawford's No. 8 was one of the last to reach the *Carpathia,* which arrived on the scene about 4 a.m. But as No. 8 had made the longest pull towards the other ship, it may be said that experience is not typical. No. 6, which did not waste much effort in trying to reach the light, was also 'almost the last' to board the *Carpathia.*[37]

". . . I imagine we were at least eight hours on the water," said Major Peuchen.[38]

"About what time did you get on the *Carpathia*?" asked Senator Newlands.

"It was after eight o'clock that I looked at my watch; it was something after eight o'clock that we got on."[39]

Andrew Cunningham, steward, in No. 4, said they rowed all night. "Up until about half past seven in the morning, when we went aboard the *Carpathia.*"[40]

Mrs Emily Ryerson, also in No. 4, said in an affidavit: "The *Carpathia* steamed towards us until it was full daylight; then she stopped and began picking up boats, and we got on board about eight o'clock."[41]

AB Joseph Scarrott, in No. 14 said in London it was "daylight" when they got alongside the *Carpathia,* "between 7 and 8."[42]

Last of all to reach the *Carpathia* was No. 12. Lightoller had taken command of this boat, after being transferred with his surviving companions from Collapsible B, overturned and awash. They had stood there for hours, hardly daring to breathe, half-frozen and on the edge of death. With a heroic effort, the indomitable Lightoller finally brought some 75 survivors in the dangerously overloaded No. 12 to safety alongside the *Carpathia* at 8.30.

Mr Beesley wrote that some of the port boats "had to row across the place where the *Titanic* sank to get to the *Carpathia,* through the debris of chairs and wreckage of all kinds."[43]

As for the starboard boats, Mr Beesley's own, No. 13, which although very heavily laden and having to row round a huge iceberg on the way, was alongside "about 4.30".[44] No. 5, according to Quartermaster Alfred Olliver, "was the fourth or fifth" to arrive.[45] William Ward, a saloon steward, attributed the same position to his No. 9.

"I think," he said at Washington, "we were about the fourth or fifth boat to be picked up."[46]

More significant is his evidence that when they started "to pull towards her" it was soon after daybreak.[47]

Mrs Helen W. Bishop, who was in No. 7, said: "[We] arrived at the *Carpathia* five or ten minutes after five o'clock in the morning."[48]

Bruce Ismay in Collapsible C, which was a starboard boat, was also able to give a fairly exact time.

"You boarded the *Carpathia* about sunrise?" asked Senator Smith.[49]

"I think that I boarded the ship *Carpathia* at a quarter to six or a quarter past six."

"Ship's time?"

"Yes, I happened to see a clock somewhere on the ship when I got on her."

C.E. Henry Stengel, in Emergency No. 1, gave this evidence:[50] ". . . I thought we were the first boat aboard; but I found that the boat that had the green lights burning was ahead of us. We were the second boat aboard."

The boat "that had the green lights burning" was Emergency No. 2, and under the command of Fourth Officer Boxhall. Although nominally a port boat, she was in effect a starboard boat. Giving evidence about the steamer he saw, Boxhall was asked how long he saw her stern light.

"I saw it until I pulled around the ship's stern," was his reply.[51] 'I had laid off a little while on the port side, on which side I was lowered, and then I afterwards pulled around the ship's stern, and, of course, then I lost the light, and I never saw it any more."

Boxhall wasted no effort in following the light, in which he had lost whatever faith he had.

He also said: "I think it was a little after 4 o'clock, sometime, when I got aboard the *Carpathia*. It might have been three-quarters of an hour before."[52] But in his first session, he had told Senator Smith: "They told me on board the *Carpathia* afterwards that it was about 10 minutes after 4, approximately."[53]

Emergency No. 2 was certainly the first boat alongside.

All these times of starboard boats should be contrasted with those of the port boats, the next to the last of which, No. 8, before Lightoller's No. 12, did not arrive until about half-past eight. The conclusion must be that, with this evidence added to the direct statements of different witnesses, the *Titanic* was heading somewhere towards the north or slightly east of north. The *Titanic* would then show a red, or port, light to a vessel north of her. Captain Lord, it may be recalled, saw the green, or starboard, light from the unknown steamer as she approached him from the east. Later, after the steamer had stopped, she showed a red light to the watchful mariners aboard the *Californian*. Both green and red lights, in that order, are what the *Titanic* would have shown to a vessel north of her.

The next point to be examined may, therefore, be the direction of the light or lights seen from the *Titanic*. Happily, this can be decided more briefly than the preceding problem.

Fifth Officer Harold Lowe had clearly stated that he ". . . saw a steamer showing her red light about five miles to the northward of us."[54]

Remembering, again, that the *Carpathia* approached from the south-east, the answer once more is to be found in evidence from the boats.

Crawford, again, the steward in No. 8, was asked by Senator Smith what they did from the time they were lowered to the water.

"Kept pulling and trying to make a light . . . We kept pulling and pulling until daybreak. Then we saw the *Carpathia* coming up, and we turned around and came back to her."[55]

In London, Crawford gave similar evidence: "I saw a big ship lit up, and we turned round and went back to her."[56]

Thomas Jones, a seaman, also in No. 8, is worth quoting for the remarkable similarity of his language.

". . . it started to get daybreak, and we lost the light; and then all of a sudden we saw the *Carpathia* coming, and we turned right back and made for the *Carpathia*."[57]

Ernest Archer, an AB, in No. 16, "started to pull toward the light for a time." Then they saw the *Carpathia*.

". . . we turned to go back. I knew that was a steamboat of some kind, so we turned and made back towards the *Carpathia*."[58]

In every instance, the boats which had been rowing towards the light had to make a complete about turn to reach the *Carpathia*. There is no contrary evidence about this from any of the boats!

Before finishing the narrative as seen from the *Titanic*, another matter concerning the ship she saw remains to be examined.

It is regarded as a fundamental argument that the ship seen from the *Titanic* was moving, whereas the *Californian* was stopped from about 10.20 p.m. on Sunday night until about six o'clock next morning. It is not now seriously suggested that the *Titanic* saw more than one ship, for if the abundance of evidence about 'a light', 'lights', ,an imaginary light', 'a codbanker', 'a schooner', 'a fisherman', 'a sailing vessel', 'a steamer' and more, is taken literally, there is no more reason to believe that she saw only two ships than the most heterogeneous fleet ever assembled on the Western or any other ocean. Common sense (an inconstant presence in this mystery, by the way) has accepted it that all the references are to the same single craft, whatever her class or identity.

Boxhall's evidence about her, was by far the most detailed, and he spoke of a steamer 'approaching' the *Titanic*. It is, in fact, only Boxhall, who speaks in detail of a moving ship, but the impression is not permanent. It should also be said that many years after the event, Boxhall still insisted that the steamer he saw so clearly was under way. This statement was made in a public address,[59] and in view of everything he had heard after the disaster, Boxhall was convinced that the ship he saw was the *Californian*. His talk was published in a magazine,[60] which also published an apology in its next issue, though, as we shall see from Chapters 10 and 11, the area of its regret was a good deal larger than truth, at least, appears to have required.

Here, first, is what three other surviving *Titanic* officers said.

In London, Second Officer Lightoller was asked by the Solicitor-General: ". . . throughout the time that you saw this light, so far as you can judge, did it remain stationary, or did it move at all?"

"Perfectly stationary, as far as I can recollect."[61]

Third Officer Pitman, at Washington, said he could not tell whether the light came from a steamer, a sailing vessel, or a lifeboat, "because there was no motion in it, no movement."[62]

Fifth Officer Lowe in his sworn statement before the British Consulate General in New York said: "As I was putting over the starboard emergency boat (about 1 a.m.) somebody mentioned something about a ship on the port bow. I glanced in that direction and saw a steamer . . . When I had got these boats tied together" * — which would have been after 2 a.m. — "I *still* saw these [lights] *in the same position* . . ." [emphasis added].

As for other evidence, Fleet, the lookout, said at Washington, of the "bright light on the port bow," which he saw: "It did not seem to be moving at all."[63] As I have said, when he was an old man, he told me the same thing. "No, it didn't move. It never moved."[64]

Buley, too, has also been mentioned. "She was stationary all night; I am very positive for about three hours she was stationary."[65]

Edith Russell, a First Class passenger, at 87, was still exasperated by it. "There it was, that light, stuck there all night, didn't budge, and we rowed like hell and couldn't get to it."[66]

Rowe, of the rockets, having seen the light from the bridge, saw it later from the starboard collapsible boat, "at about the same sort of distance".[67] "We kept on pulling for it," he told Senator Burton, "because it was the only stationary light."[68]

Steward Alfred Crawford was asked by Senator Smith about the two lights he saw.

"What were they; were they signals?"[69]

"They were stationary masthead lights, one on the fore and one on the main."

And in London, Robertson Dunlop, counsel for the Leyland Line and the officers of the *Californian,* cross-examined Crawford closely.

---

* After leaving the *Titanic* in No. 14, at about 1.30 a.m., Lowe had rounded up boats 4, 10, 12 and D, and had them tied up with his own boat and took command of all five.

"Did they [the masthead lights] appear to remain stationary, or go away, or come nearer to you?"

"They seemed to be stationary."[70]

"Did the other steamer at any time appear to be steaming towards you?"

"No, she seemed to be stationary there."[71]

There is more to the same effect, but it would be tedious to continue. The fact is, the largest number of *Titanic* witnesses, who saw the ship and expressed an opinion, were at least as firm as Boxhall; it was not moving, but stationary. Important as Boxhall's evidence is, the overwhelming probability is that he was mistaken, understandably so, but mistaken all the same.

How, then, might his mistake have arisen?

It is not a common thing even for a professional seaman to meet a ship in mid-ocean that is not moving. In the absence of anything visibly wrong, one expects a ship at sea to be under way. An observer in a ship stopped and in distress, as the *Titanic* was, might easily be misled into thinking the other ship must be moving.

The night was very dark and only her lights were visible.

"You saw nothing of the hull of the boat?" asked Senator Burton.[72]

"Oh, no," Boxhall replied, "it was too dark."

If for any reason her lights changed their relative positions, and over a period of time seemed to grow brighter and then dimmer, as did the lights of the steamer Boxhall saw, it is easy to understand how even an experienced seaman might think the other ship was moving, especially when he had no reason whatever to think the contrary. Clearly, with a couple of thousand fathoms of water under her, she could not be at anchor. Yet, although she must have been stopped, she might very well have created the *illusion* of movement, if she was swinging. Moreover, just because she was not swinging about a fixed point, like a ship swinging at anchor in harbour, any movement she did make would probably be irregular.

What other evidence, if any, is there that bears on this matter?

The lights of a swinging vessel when showing her broadside to the *Titanic* would be very bright — "She had beautiful lights,"[73] said Boxhall — but they would become fewer as she swung around and her stern came into view; "I saw this single light, which I took to be her stern light . . ."[74]

One general comment about Boxhall's 'moving' ship is most necessary. When he speaks[75] about the vessel "as she drew up closer" his seeing first her "green light", then her "red", and finally her "stern light" as she "turned around", the picture he creates is almost unmistakably that of a vessel steaming. But — and it is very big 'but' indeed — an entirely different picture is created when we realize that Boxhall did not see these things, one after another, within the space of a few minutes.

While he was watching the steamer, he was also engaged in another activity altogether. This other activity provides a measurement of time by which we can estimate how long it took the steamer to do what Boxhall saw.

"I would signal with the Morse," he told the Senate inquiry, "and then go ahead and send off a rocket, and then go back and have a look at the ship . . ."[76]

The firing of the rockets took not a few minutes, but about an hour. What Boxhall saw the steamer doing, also therefore took about an hour. Whatever progress she was making must have been minute, and her speed extremely slow, hardly perceptible in fact.

Boxhall himself said: "I do not think she was doing much steaming. I do not think she was steaming very much, because after I first saw the masthead lights she must have been still steaming, but by the time I saw her red light with my naked eye she was not steaming very much. So she had probably got into the ice, and turned around."[77]

This might be described, since no ice was visible from the *Titanic,* as an intelligent *ex post facto* guess.

Bearing in mind this fact that the 'moving' ship, for no apparent reason, took as long as an hour just to 'draw up closer' and finally 'turn around', the first impression created by Boxhall of a vessel steadily proceeding on her course until she turned away is transformed into something very different: a ship hardly moving, if at all. Indeed, the 'moving' ship becomes, even in Boxhall's own description, a drifting ship, making a slow, irregular, rudderless turn; in fact, nothing but a ship that had stopped and was slowly swinging. It is strange that the progress of the ship Boxhall saw seems never previously to have been measured against the time framework of the firing of the rockets; but when the comparison is made, Boxhall's notorious callous steamer that came up to look at the *Titanic's* rockets and then turned her back on them is exposed as an illusion.

After he saw what he took to be the steamer's stern light, Captain Smith sent him away in Emergency Boat No. 2,[78] and soon afterwards he pulled round to the starboard side of the *Titanic* and "lost the light".[79]

Graphic evidence about the mysterious ship comes from Crawford, the steward, who precisely described her masthead lights — ". . . the after light was higher than the foremast."[80] He told of the vain effort of No. 8 to reach the steamer, which he estimated to be ten miles away. There follows an illuminating passage.[81]

"You thought she was coming toward you?" Senator Burton asked.

"We thought she was coming toward us," Crawford answered.

"Why did you think she was coming toward you?"

"Sometimes she seemed to get closer; other times she seemed to be getting away from us."

A suggestive picture: a steamer, which as Crawford also said, "seemed more like she was stationary",[82] but, as he said later in London: "I thought probably she might have been drifting'[83] — a ship not at anchor, but stopped, moved irregularly by wind and current.

Carefully considering all the relevant evidence, and not only part of it, the conclusion must be that Boxhall mistook a stationary, but swinging, steamer for a moving one.

Lastly, let us see if there are any clues to the identity of that swinging vessel.

Telling the Senate Committee about the steamer which the *Californian* saw south of her about 11 o'clock, Captain Lord said: 'When this man was coming along, he was showing his green light on our starboard side, before midnight.'[84]

So the *Californian* would also be showing 'this man' her green light, which is on the starboard side.

"I saw her sidelights through my glasses"' said Boxhall,[85] speaking about the steamer he saw, "and eventually I saw the red light. I had seen the green . . ."

"After midnight," Lord continued,[86] "we slowly blew around and showed him our red light."

"I think I saw the green light before I saw the red light, as a matter of fact," Boxhall emphasized by repeating it.[87]

The steamer he saw "might have been a four-mast ship or might have been a three-mast ship, but she certainly was not a two-mast ship."[88] Later, in

London, perhaps when he had thought more about it, he simply said: "She was, or I judged her to be, a four-masted steamer."[89]

No three-mast ship was known to be in the area that night, but there were several four-masters. They ranged all the way from the *Baltic*, 243 miles away to the south-east, the *Mesaba*, about 200 miles to the eastward, the *Birma*, 70 miles south-west by south, the *Carpathia*, now speeding to the rescue from 58 miles in the south-east, the *Mount Temple*, also turned back to help from 50 miles west-south-west, the *Parisian*, perhaps under 50 miles also west-south-west and Boston-bound, down to the *Californian*, some ten miles north of the *Titanic* and carefully watching.[90]

Sources

1 US 832.
2 Ibid.
3 US 237.
4 US 910.
5 Ibid.
6 US 237.
7 US 910.
8 *Lloyd's Shipping Gazette & Lloyd's List*, 12 April 1912, p. 7.
9 B 14153.
10 US 910.
11 B 14153.
12 *Lloyd's Book of House Flags & Funnels*, 1912 ed.
13 US 519.
14 B 15395.
15 US 832.
16 US 832, 833.
17 B 14160.
18 US 235.
19 US 934.
20 US 933.
21 US 292.
22 US 830.
23 US 564.
24 US 565.
25 Beesley, Dover ed., p. 50.
26 Ibid, p. 54.
27 Ibid, p. 56.
28 Ibid, p. 46.
29 Harold Lowe's signed and sworn statement at the British Consulate General in New York, May 1912.
30 B 17667.
31 B 17669.
32 B 17670-74.
33 B 17674.
34 US 820.
35 Ibid.
36 US 346.
37 US 349.
38 US 350.
39 Ibid.
40 US 797.
41 US 1108.
42 B 460.
43 Beesley, Dover ed., p. 50.
44 Ibid, p. 56.
45 US 529.
46 US 600.
47 Ibid.
48 US 1000.
49 US 951.
50 US 973.
51 US 933.
52 US 911.
53 US 244.
54 Harold Lowe's signed and sworn statement at the British Consulate General in New York, May 1912.
55 US 114.
56 B 18087.
57 US 570.
58 US 648.
59 At the Red House Museum, Christchurch, Hants., England, 1959.
60 *Nautical Magazine*, May 1959 and June 1959.
61 B 14149.
62 US 295.
63 US 358.
64 P.I. Interview with Fleet.
65 US 611.
66 P.I. Interview with Miss Russell.
67 B 17665-66.
68 US 524.
69 US 827.
70 B 17997.
71 B 18010.
72 US 934.
73 Ibid.
74 US 933.
75 US 933-34.
76 US 237.
77 US 934.
78 US 933.
79 US 934.
80 US 829.
81 Ibid.
82 Ibid.
83 B 18054.
84 US 732 & cf. B 6728.
85 US 933.
86 US 732.
87 US 933.
88 US 911.
89 B 15401.
90 For this paragraph, *see* US 1056 & Capt. Knapp's Charts, Nos. 2 & 3, as well as references identifying the ships named as four-masters.

Chapter 5

Rockets

"Anybody knows what rockets at sea mean."[1]

So Lawrence Beesley wrote; 2,201 persons aboard the *Titanic* proclaimed their mortal danger by "calling for help from anyone who was near enough to see,"[2] and a crowd of passengers on the Boat Deck looked up to the sky, to watch the first rocket rise and explode and send out a shower of stars. Mr Beesley was wrong.

Second Officer Stone of the *Californian* saw "one white flash in the sky immediately above this other steamer," and "did not know what it was; I thought it might be a shooting star,"[3] he said later.

"You know distress signals?" Butler Aspinall, one of the counsel for the Board of Trade, asked him.[4]

"I know what they are, yes."

"Was it like a distress signal?"[5]

"It was just a white flash in the sky; it might have been anything."

"I know, but what did it suggest to your mind? What did you say to yourself? What did you think it was?"[6]

"I thought nothing until I brought the ship under observation with the binoculars and saw the others."

Recall here, very early in this vital evidence, Lawrence Beesley's words about the *Titanic's* first rocket: "Up it went, higher and higher, with a sea of faces upturned to watch it, and then an explosion that seemed to split the silent night in two, . . ."[7]

Fifth Officer Lowe had just turned from loading No. 5 Boat to begin on No. 3 when the first 'detonator', as he called it, went off. After that, he said, "they were incessantly going off; they were nearly deafening me."[8]

The black and starry night enveloping Herbert Stone was the same silent night, which had been 'split in two' over the *Titanic* by the explosion of the rocket. But Stone heard not a sound. If the picture he saw was, in more than one sense, a moving one, it was also completely silent. Nor, so far as is known, has there ever been one word from any source to contradict the assertion that none of the watchers aboard the *Californian,* who saw the rockets, heard any sound whatever from them, loud or faint. It has been suggested very tentatively that the slightest shipboard noises, such as emptying an ashcan overboard, would be more than enough to muffle any slight report from the rockets at a distance of ten, seven or even five miles. This may well be true; but as the author of the suggestion himself hastened to add with the remains of his native scepticism, it is impossible to believe that ashcans or other shipboard noises would happen to occur in every case, and certainly no fewer than eight times, simultaneously with the explosion of a rocket. An 'explanation' of such fragility is exactly of the incredible order to 'explain' on the grounds of 'coincidence' the most damning facts against the *Californian*.

To a layman, it certainly is surprising that the rockets which Mr Beesley said 'seemed to split the silent night in two', and which nearly deafened Fifth Officer Lowe, made no sound on a still night, only — according to Stone — about five miles away.[9]

It is a remarkable fact that in the inquiry for an answer, the consultation of experts failed to bring forth any of the layman's astonishment at the silence of the rockets. Neither those, whose experience was mostly practical rather than theoretical, nor the pure scientists, were surprised by the failure of the men of the *Californian* to hear, as well as to see, the rockets at a comparatively short distance.

"Heaven help you," said Mr L.G. Reynolds of Trinity House, "if you have to rely on sound for your safety!"[10]

Coming from Trinity House, his business was, of course, with safety, and particularly with testing rockets, etc. It was surprising to learn that there was a failure of sound — not to produce it, but to propagate it — in no less than a third of the experiments. He spoke also of an 'acoustic shadow zone', the effect of which was that a sound might be inaudible close to the point of origin but perfectly audible much farther away. It is an odd thought that the *Titanic's* rockets might have been heard many miles farther to the North, for instance, than the *Californian,* which undoubtedly did not hear them. One should also bear in mind the time sound needs to travel. At five miles the time of travel would be about half a minute, at ten miles nearly one minute and, to include a favourite distance of the Lordites, at 20 miles almost two minutes. If Stone and Gibson, possibly with the collars of their coats turned up and their scarves round their heads as protection from the cold, would associate the faint muffled report, if audible at all, with the rocket they had seen a minute earlier and not with routine shipboard-sounds seems unlikely. It also seems unreasonable to suggest that the reports of standard socket distress rockets would carry that far.

"Sound," Mr Reynolds summed it up, "as they say, is a last resort."[11]

"Rockets? —," said a master mariner, questioned about the particular problem, "sometimes you hear them, and sometimes you don't."[12]

Sound, it seems, diminishes horizontally according to the law of inverse squares; that is to say, the sound, at a distance of five miles would be only 1/25 of that at one mile from the source, and 1/100 at ten miles. This was the most likely maximum distance between the *Titanic* and the *Californian,* according to the finding of the two inquiries; and even if no other factors were involved, one begins to wonder how much even of Mr Beesley's 'night-splitting' rocket would have been heard at that distance.

Other factors may have been involved, including that of temperature (see Diagram 5).

"Sound waves," wrote Dr V.G. Welsby[13] of the Department of Electronic and Electrical Engineering of the University of Birmingham, "travel faster through cold dense air than through warm light air. Thus, if we happened to have a layer of warmer air over a cold sea, there may have been a significant acoustic velocity gradient with respect to height. The effect of this is to tend to refract sound waves upwards, away from the sea, thus forming what is called an 'acoustic shadow zone'. What I am trying to say is that it is physically possible to have freak conditions for which the sound intensity would

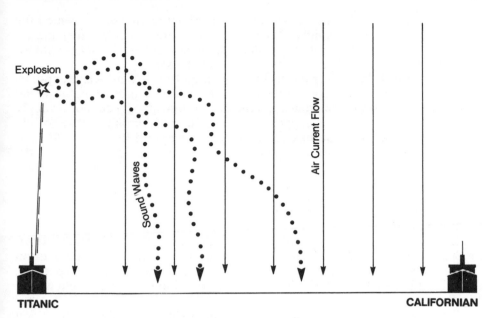

Diagram 5. The *Californian* and the rockets. Diagrammatic representation of sound waves

What every schoolchild knows: warm air rises, cold air falls. The sea was colder than the air. Turbulence was minimal, but the sound waves from the rockets were driven down toward the sea or dissipated by the descending currents of cold air. Data is sparse, but here is a possible reason why the Californian *did not hear the rockets.*

fall off with horizontal distance at a considerably greater rate than is suggested by the simple inverse-square law. I do not know if this possibility has ever been considered but it certainly cannot be ruled out."

Dr Robert Bruce Lindsay, Hazard Professor of Physics at Brown University, Editor of the *Journal of the Acoustical Society of America,* and one of the world's leading authorities on acoustics,[14] quickly and specifically got rid of any notion that the mystery of the silent rockets, if not unique, was certainly rare, by stating that, ". . . problems like the one you mention have been treated in some detail in most books on acoustics for a good many years."[15] He named some of them, and also suggested consulting Dr R.W.B. Stephens of the Department of Physics of the Imperial College of Science and Technology, ". . . a great authority on all aspects of acoustic propagation." The latter agreed with Dr Welsby's tentative opinion,[16] but the difficulty throughout is the lack of sufficient data on which to base a firm scientific judgment. It was pointed out to Dr Stephens that in the region of the *Californian,* at least, the air temperature, from the few figures recorded, was, if anything, lower than that of the sea. Even less is known about the area of the *Titanic,* and nothing, of course, of the intervening area.* From Lightoller's warning to the carpen-

*	*Californian* temperatures:	Air	Water	*Titanic* temperatures:	Air	Water
	14 April. 8 p.m.	30°F	32°F	14 April. 7 p.m.		43°F
	14 April. Midnight	27°F	28°F	14 April. 7.30		39°F
	15 April. 4 a.m.	29°F	29°F	14 April. 8.00 (according to		
				QM Hitchins-US p. 458)		31-31½°F
				14 April. 9.00		33°F

ter about 8 o'clock that the fresh water was about to freeze, it seemed the
temperature was falling rapidly. Possibly, the sea there was colder than the air.
If this was so later, Dr Stephens explained, the sound from a rocket explod-
ing in the air would tend to turn back towards the sea.

The general deduction from all this appeared to be, there was the possibility that because of the conditions which seem to have prevailed, the sound
of the rockets, in simple language, might have diminished much more quickly
than would normally have happened. The apparent 'common sense' of the
layman, as stated and emphasized so often by Captain Lord himself (and
which the writer also found persuasive), that on that calm, still night, the
sound of the explosion of those Cotton Powder rocket signals must have travelled farther than usual is — to put it no higher — not accepted by the scientists or the empirical experts.

Further than that, one cannot go; but it is enough to upset the layman's
'common sense' certainty.

Finally, one must quote the opinion of Mr D.A.S. Little, Technical Director
of Pains-Wessex Ltd., the successors to one of the suppliers of the Cotton
Powder Signals mentioned above. Mr Little, one of the foremost experts on
the subject in the British Isles, has written an opinion which cuts right across
any theory:

"With regard to the lack of sound . . . the only sound would be from socket
distress signals, and these I would consider to have a range of *3-5 miles*."
[emphasis added].[17]

As for young Stone, who in the long run was destined to be one of the most
unfortunate victims of the slowly developing tragedy he unknowingly
observed, after the first 'white flash', he turned his glasses on the ship, when
he saw 'the others'.[18]

"I saw four more then," he said.[19]

"What were they, rockets?"[20]

"They had the appearance of white rockets bursting in the sky."

"Did they come in quick succession?"[21]

"At intervals of about three or four minutes."

So, the five would have been seen from the *Californian* in a period covering perhaps fifteen or twenty minutes.

"I would signal with the Morse," said Boxhall aboard the *Titanic*, "and then
go ahead and send off a rocket, and then go back and have a look at the
ship . . ."[22]

Which makes it clear he did not fire off his eight rockets 'in quick succession', one after the other, or as quickly as he could, but with an interval
between each.

After saying he had seen five rockets, Stone was pressed both by counsel
and Lord Mersey as to what he thought they meant. His replies were remarkably unsatisfactory and unconvincing.

"I thought that perhaps the ship was in communication with some other
ship, or possibly she was signalling to us to tell us she had big icebergs around
her."[23]

How the rising of five rockets could convey any such meaning Stone did
not explain; but for the moment Butler Aspinall did not dispute it. "Possibly,"
he said, "what else?"[24]

"Possibly she was communicating with some other steamer at a greater
distance than ourselves."

"What was she communicating?" Mersey asked him.

"I do not know."

"Is that the way in which steamers communicate with each other?"

"No, not usually."

"Then you cannot have thought that."

He was reminded that he held an officer's certificate,[25] in fact, a first mate's certificate, in steamships,[26] which he had obtained "last December twelve month",[27] that is, December 1910, and that he had been at sea for eight years.

"You applied your mind to the matter, did you not?"[28]

"Yes."

Then, what at the time did he think those rockets meant?

"I knew they were signals of some sort,"[29] the unhappy Stone admitted.

Mersey then again intervened and besought him 'to be frank.'[30]

Stone said he was trying.

"If you try, you will succeed," said Lord Mersey, without, one guesses, much genuine encouragement in his tone. "What did you think these rockets were going up at intervals of three or four minutes for?"

"I just took them as white rockets, and informed the master, and left him to judge."[31]

"Do you mean to say you did not think for yourself? I thought you told us just now that you did think."

"(*No answer*)" is the eloquent entry in the transcript.[32]

"[I] informed the master, and left him to judge."

They are words to mark and ponder. Stone's own succinct summary of this first communication to Lord about the rockets throws a new and unexpected light on its author. In the little we have so far seen of him, he has seemed possibly obtuse, certainly not candid, and most especially stubborn.

Most people in the Scottish Hall that Tuesday afternoon in May 1912, whether they were seamen, lawyers, reporters, or ordinary members of the public, must have shared Mr Beesley's belief that 'anybody knows what rockets at sea mean'.

The questioning of Stone was clearly directed to eliciting from him some awareness of this common knowledge; but with apparent stubbornness he refused to concede an inch. Early on, Stone was asked if he thought the first 'white flash' was 'like a distress signal', and he answered: "It might have been anything."[33]

Stone's evidence in print reads as if he himself did not believe what he was saying; and not without reason.

"You know they were not being sent up for fun, were they?" Butler Aspinall asked him.[34]

"No."

Finally, the direct question was put to him. It was certainly one of the most important in the episode of the *Californian,* and, without exaggeration, a key question in the whole disaster.

"Did you think they were distress signals?"[35]

"No," said Stone.

That, of course, was not the end of it.

Thomas Scanlan, who was representing the National Sailors' and Firemen's Union, went on: "Do you mean to tell his Lordship that you did not know that the throwing up of 'rockets or shells, throwing stars of any colour or description, fired one at a time at short intervals,' is the proper method for signalling distress at night?"[36] Stone agreed he did know it, and he knew it on the night of 14 April.

"And is not that exactly what was happening?" Mersey added.

Stone did not answer, and Scanlan took it up.

"You have heard my Lord put that question. That was what was happening?"[37]

"Yes," said Stone.

"The very thing was happening that you knew indicated distress?"

"If that steamer," Stone began, "had stayed on the same bearing after showing these rockets —"[38]

"No, do not give a long answer of that kind. Is it not the fact that the very thing was happening which you had been taught indicated distress?"[39]

"Yes."

"You knew it meant distress?" Scanlan asked.

"I knew that rockets shown at short intervals, one at a time, meant distress signals, yes."[40]

Scanlan told him not to "speak generally". Didn't he know that very night, "those rockets were signals of distress?"

"No," said Stone.[41]

That was too much for Mersey. Stone was told to think about what he was saying. He had just said it. Wasn't it true?

"It is true that similar lights are distress signals, yes."[42]

"Then you had seen them from this steamer?"

"A steamer that is in distress does not steam away from you, my Lord," Stone answered.[43]

This reply, a key part of Stone's evidence, is, of course, the basis of a main line in the *Californian's* defence. Stone's argument, more explicitly stated than he ever put it himself, seems to have been: "Although these rockets looked like distress signals, they couldn't have been, because the steamer moved as soon as she'd fired the first of them, and it doesn't make sense for a ship in distress to move away from a potential rescuer." There is nothing manifestly absurd in this argument; but what Stone never considered, according to his evidence, is the possibility that he might have been mistaken and that, in fact, the steamer did not move.

After denying that he thought the rockets were distress signals, Stone admitted that some time later he did think they might have been.

"When?" Butler Aspinall asked.

"After I heard about the *Titanic* going down."[44]

Asked if he thought they came from the *Titanic*, he replied, "Not necessarily. They may have come from some other steamer. I did not think that vessel was the *Titanic*."[45]

Stone was also shortly to declare he was "almost certain" the rockets did come from the steamer he was watching, leading to the *reductio ad absurdum* that two ships were in distress and firing rockets. Lord himself admitted that he had never heard of any other ship firing rockets,[46] nor has anybody else, not at the time or ever since.

Gibson was still below, attending to the patent log: Stone was alone on the bridge, just having seen the fifth rocket. It was "Just about 1.10" in the morning.[47] He went to the speaking tube and called up his captain.

"I communicated to him that I had seen white lights in the sky in the direction of this other steamer, which I took to be white rockets."[48]

During the period while the rockets were going up,[49] he had again tried to raise her with the Morse lamp, and once again in vain. It was a little more than half an hour since Lord himself had whistled up to ask Stone if there was any change in the other steamer's bearing.

Stone's evidence about this first, and momentous, report to Lord is almost word for word identical with the statement he had written at the master's request on 18 April, when the *Californian* was still at sea.

"I, at once, whistled down the speaking tube," Stone had written,[50] "and you came from the chartroom into your room and answered. I reported seeing these lights in the sky in the direction of the other steamer, which appeared to me to be white rockets."

Now comes one of the most significant differences between Stone and Lord.

"He [Stone] said he saw a white rocket."[51]

Thus Lord. He said it first in Washington,[52] he said it more than once in London, and he was to go on saying it for many years afterwards; but never once anywhere did he say why Stone, who had just seen no fewer than five white rockets, should "at once" tell Lord he had seen only one. In the story of the later hours of that night there is a wide gap between Lord's memory and the memories of his officers about many other things, large and small; but as Lord said he fell asleep "somewhere after half-past one"[53] and remembered almost nothing until he was called soon after daybreak, this would be at least an apparent reason for the differences, and a real one, if true.

Lord's story of the one rocket is contradicted by his OOW and the apprentice. Both knew and maintained that 'rockets', not 'a rocket', had been seen and reported to him.

Gibson returned to the bridge a few minutes after Stone had talked to Lord.

"What was it he [Stone] told you?" Sir John Simon asked.[54]

"That she had fired five rockets."

"Did he tell you anything else about what he had been doing while you had not been there?"

"He told me he had reported it to the Captain."[55]

Gibson himself saw the last three rockets,[56] and, on Stone's orders, reported to the Captain, "that she has fired altogether eight rockets."[57]

When Chief Officer Stewart relieved Stone at 4 a.m., Stone told him, ". . . at 1 o'clock he had seen some rockets,"[58] and "He told me he had reported to the Captain."[59]

Immediately after Groves had been called with news of the *Titanic*, he rushed to Stone's cabin to know if it was true, . . . and he said: "Yes, old chap, I saw rockets in my watch."[60]

Moreover, Stone, Gibson and Stewart believed the rockets resembled distress signals and came from a ship in some kind of trouble.

There is no dispute that Lord, having heard the news, asked: "Is that a company's signal?"[61] (Stone's version is in the plural: "Are they companies' signals?").[62]

"I had never seen company's signals like them before," Stone answered Lord Mersey in London.[63]

Earlier in his evidence, he said he had answered Lord's question about the companies' signals (and with more characteristic indecision): "I do not know, but they appear to me to be white rockets."[64] It is clear he did not think they were company signals;[65] and no wonder.

If readers will look at the list of 'Private Night Signals', to give them their formal name, of the principal steamship companies trading on the North Atlantic,* they will understand why Stone did not think the white rockets he had seen were company signals.

Boxhall in his evidence in Washington had said about these signals: "They are coloured as a rule,"[66] and Lord himself described them as "signals which

* Appendix K.

resemble rockets; they do not shoot as high and they do not explode."[67] Lord also said in Washington, ". . . you never mistake a distress rocket."[68]

In London, Lightoller, too, gave very clear and succinct evidence on the matter.

"Are there signals of a definite kind and appearance that are known as distress signals?" the Solicitor-General asked him.[69]

"Yes, there is no ship allowed on the high seas to fire a rocket or anything resembling a rocket unless she requires assistance."

That answer was not literally true, as we shall see, but it was very nearly so.

"If you had seen signals like those sent up from another ship would you have known for certain what they were?" the Solicitor continued.

"I have seen them and known immediately."[70]

"We have heard something about companies' signals. Do they resemble these at all?"[71]

"In no way, to my knowledge."

"Would you have any difficulty in distinguishing one from the other?"

"I never had had."[72]

These authoritative words and Lord's own affirmation of the unmistakability of a distress rocket would seem to end the discussion. Nevertheless, three things make it desirable to set out the exact facts about company signals. The first is that it has not been done before, and it is an important factor in the case of the *Californian*. It has been common for one writer to copy another on this subject, without apparently even attempting to get at the facts. The result in recent years has been the conveyance of much misinformation with an air of imperturbable authority.

The second reason for trying to clear up the matter was that Captain Lord, in spite of what he had said about a distress rocket being unmistakable, persisted that night in asking whether the rockets that had been seen from his bridge were company signals. Finally, it has been said from time to time that there might have been some confusion between distress rockets and company signals.

And the third reason is, that although it is now often said, it was not only not true, but was the precise opposite of the truth, that 'rockets were commonplace'. Lightoller's evidence alone, quoted above, which was certainly the voice of a very long and wide experience, might be sufficient by itself to demolish this belief; but the actual conditions prevailing about company signals at the time of the *Titanic* had best be proved by the authentic details.

The legal basis for company signals is to be found in the Merchant Shipping Act 1894 (57 & 58 Vic. c. 60), which incorporated earlier statutes. It was, of course, the law in 1912, and in fact remained so until the passing of the Merchant Shipping Act 1970 (in which, incidentally, there is no longer any reference to company signals). The relevant section in the 1894 statute is the following:

"Private Signals

733 (1) If a shipowner desires to use for the purpose of a private code any rockets, lights, or other similar signals, he may register those signals with the Board of Trade, and that Board shall give public notice of the signals so registered in such manner as they think requisite for preventing those signals from being mistaken for signals of distress or signals for pilots.

(2) *The Board may refuse to register any signals which in their opinion cannot easily*

be distinguished from signals of distress or signals for pilots. [Emphasis added].
(3) (This sub-section authorizes the use of the signals after registration without incurring any penalty)."

About this time, England was at the height of her power and prestige, especially on the sea, where she was unquestionably the leading nation, both in ships of peace, and in maritime affairs generally.

It was in this atmosphere that the Board of Trade was authorized to accept registration of foreign, as well as British, company signals; and the list, issued in pamphlet form from time to time, did in fact contain company signals of many foreign lines.

The Board of Trade register, as will be seen from Appendix K, contains a column, 'Where Used', which precisely defines the area, and whether or not the signal is permitted on the high seas.

In this connection, it becomes of great importance in the case of the *Californian* that the Board of Trade pamphlet reproducing the list of signals registered under the Act is prefaced at the top by the following:

"[Note. — If these signals are used in any other place, for any other purpose than named, they may be signals of distress, and should be answered accordingly by passing ships, and claims sent in for payment of salvage.]"

If Captain Lord, then, had any doubt about the rockets (or rocket) reported to him by Stone, his duty was clear. He should have treated it or them as he would have distress signals.* His failure to do so put him in breach of the instruction of the Board of Trade at the very beginning of the incident, and even on formal grounds, it would seem that he was disentitled to claim that the signals had been a cause of 'confusion'.

The signals, as will be seen from the list in Appendix K. which, although confined to transatlantic lines, is typical of all, were composed of a variety of still and flashing lights, pyrotechnic lights, Roman Candles, coloured balls, etc., and were sometimes combined with blasts on the whistle. The characteristic feature was that the signals were coloured, not white, and that rockets were seldom used in their make-up. The latest available list in 1912 of all the company signals used anywhere in the world — not separately counting many repetitions for different companies of the same group, although listed separately — contains 190 entries. This includes those, mostly foreign, not registered with the Board of Trade (Lloyd's had a record of them). The number seemed remarkably small, compared, for instance, with the number of funnel colours, and although the separate list for private signals of sailing ships was disregarded — even the *Californian* did not claim she mistook a sailing vessel for a steamer — there may have been a decline in the number already since the introduction of wireless; or possibly the number of company signals was never so common as had been suggested by those who claimed to have been tricked by them.

In order to discover what basis, if any, there was for the allegation that the *Californian* might have mistaken the rockets she saw for company signals, this list was examined to find out, (1) if, in spite of Lightoller's absolute statement, any company signals did in fact include rockets in their make-up; and (2) if

---

*   It seems doubtful whether he could have pleaded successfully in the circumstances, typical as it might have been of the *Californian,* that the direction had no application to him, as he was not a 'passing' ship, but a 'stopped' one.

there were any company signals, which, however different in their appearance and make-up from white distress rockets, were uncharacteristically made up of white lights exclusively.

This examination showed, (1) that of the 190 separate company signals in the whole world, the use of rockets in such signals, far from being 'commonplace', was restricted to just five companies:

(i)   *Allan Line,* Glasgow. — The signal was composed of three rockets, blue, white, red, practically simultaneously; *not used on the high seas* (cf. Appendix K).

(ii) *Chargeurs Reunis,* Paris. — A white rocket throwing five red stars.

(iii) *Cunard Line,* Liverpool. — Blue light and two rockets bursting into golden stars and fired in quick succession.

(iv) *American Line.* — Blue, red, blue pyrotechnic lights and two variegated rockets, each throwing blue, red and green balls, the whole practically simultaneously.

(v)   *White Star Line,* Liverpool. — Green pyrotechnic light, followed by a rocket, throwing two green stars, followed by another green pyrotechnic light.

All these five, of which only four were ever used anywhere on the high seas, are thus found to have included colours in their make-up. So, none could be confused with the 'white rockets all throwing white stars' seen from the *Californian,* and company signals containing rockets could be eliminated.

Under (2), of the same world total of 190 company signals, the following four used no colours, but only white, in their signals:

(i)   *City of Dublin Steam Packet Co.* — A lamp showing a bright white light hung over the quarter for a few seconds.

(ii) *Norfolk & North American Steam Shipping Co.,* London. — Two white pyrotechnic lights, fired simultaneously, about 60 feet apart.

(iii) *Siemens Brothers,* London. — A white light produced by burning magnesium wire, followed by a clear light from a good lamp, which shall be darkened five times successively, three times of short duration, one long and one again of short duration, corresponding to telegraph 'Call' signal of the Morse Code.

(iv) *South Eastern & Chatham Railway.* — One bright or white pyrotechnic light.

Again, it seemed next to impossible that any of the above could have been mistaken for the white rockets seen from the *Californian.* Yet the minute possibility must, theoretically at least, always remain, so long as location on the night of 14/15 April 1912, of the ships owned by these four companies was not known.

A careful search was therefore made through Lloyd's various records, kindly placed at my disposal.

The 12 ships of the City of Dublin Steam Packet Co., and the 16 of the South Eastern and Chatham Railway were eliminated immediately, as they did not 'go foreign'.

Siemens Brothers, with their extraordinarily complicated signal, were discovered to own just one ship, the cable-laying *Faraday,* 5,028 tons. This vessel had arrived in London from duty in the North Atlantic on 7 September 1911, and was still in the Thames on 17 April 1912.[73] She could not, therefore, have been some 2,000 miles west, in the *Titanic* area, on 15 April.

There now remained only the Norfolk & North American Steam Shipping

Co.[74] This company traded between the United Kingdom and the United States, and their vessels were certainly to be found in the North Atlantic. There were three of them: *Montauk Point,* 4,822 tons, *Crown Point,* 5,218 tons, and *Eagle Point,* 5,222 tons. It will be noted that all three did at least conform with Captain Lord's opinion that the unknown vessel was of a size 'something like ourselves.'[75] Among all the thousands of vessels in the world's merchant fleets, these are the only three left, whose white company signals might, at least theoretically, have been confused with what the *Californian* saw.

The search of Lloyd's records was resumed.

Eagle Point, it was discovered, sailed from London on 9 March and arrived in Philadelphia on 7 April, where she still was on 15 April.[76]

Crown Point sailed from London on 17 March and arrived in Philadelphia on 5 April, a passage of some 20 days.[77]

The next information about her, after 15 April 1912, is that on 27 April when she was damaged by a coal elevator.

Thus the reasonable inference is that she stayed in Philadelphia after her arrival there on 5 April, and was still there on 15 April.

Finally, *Montauk Point,*[78] the last remaining ship in the world as putative confuser of the *Californian.* Working back from 15 April, there was no word of her that day; nor on 14 or 13 April, . . . I tried the other way. The 16th—! That day she sailed from Liverpool, and so, with her, ends the myth of the *Californian's* being deceived by company signals.

The attempt having been made, and the essential data obtained, any doubt or argument on this aspect of the case is clearly at an end. This remains true even if one takes into account the one remarkable omission from the list of transatlantic passenger lines in Appendix K, that of the Russian American Line. The most exhaustive inquiry has yielded no information whatever about any company signal for that line. The Board of Trade, the Public Record Office, the National Maritime Museum, in England; the Department of Commerce in the United States, and, above all, the Merchant Marine Museum in Odessa, have, one and all, brought the same negative reply. The almost certain inference, therefore, is that the Russian American Line, alone among the transatlantic passenger lines, had no company signal, and need not be considered.

The conclusion is, no known company signals from any known ships anywhere on the high seas that night could have misled the *Californian.* There were no such signals and no such ships, and Lightoller's statement that these signals 'in no way' resembled distress rockets is proved up to the hilt, as, no less, is Captain Lord's own remark, ". . . you never mistake a distress rocket."

"[The rocket] did not worry me," said Lord. "I was still thinking of the company signal."[79]

"The company signal", which Stone had not reported engaged his mind, but the rocket (or rockets), which Stone had reported, did not. It is a strange and hardly convincing statement.

In 1912 company signals were so rarely used on the high seas that it was highly unreasonable for any master to think that a reported rocket (or rockets) would have been a company signal. He would immediately have associated rockets with danger and distress, the thought of company signals would have been very far at the back of his mind, if at all thought of.

Nor does it seem convincing that Lord might have wondered about the number of shipping lines that might have used rockets in their company signals. Lord's sole concern could be summed up in one word: ice, and he did not hesitate to admit it, then or thereafter.[80]

Gibson, having dealt further with the log, rejoined Stone soon after Stone had talked with Lord over the speaking tube, and was told about the five rockets,[81] the report to Lord about them and Lord's instruction to go on using the lamp. Gibson said he got back to the bridge "at five minutes to one",[82] which is a striking example of how varying and approximate were some of the estimates of time that night. If Gibson's time was right, he would have been back about a quarter of an hour before Stone went to report to Lord. To understand the story it is obviously wiser to pay more attention to the events and their sequence than to their timing.

As soon as Stone told Gibson what had happened, the lad at once tried the lamp himself.[83] He got no answer either, but something else happened.

It was for about three minutes that Gibson blinked his lamp at the steamer,[84] and he had just turned his glasses on her to see if perhaps, at last, she was blinking back, when, instead of that, she fired another rocket.[85] He saw it through the glasses. Then came two more, which he saw "through the eye".

"What colour rockets were they?"[86] Sir John Simon asked Gibson.

"White ones."

White rockets — just plain white rockets — those were all they ever saw.

While he had his glasses on the ship when he saw the first rocket, Gibson could see nothing but her lights.

"Still this glare of light?" Mersey asked him, recalling Gibson's earlier description of the ship's after-deck.

("It was all brilliantly lighted at the stern end," Hugh Woolner said, looking at the sinking *Titanic*.)

"Yes," said Gibson.

But he would not agree 'that glare of light' indicated she was a passenger steamer.

"A passenger boat is generally lit up from the water's edge," said young Gibson,[87] who, inarticulate as he was when it came to finding words to define anything that disturbed or puzzled him, was also capable of an occasional vivid phrase.

He said, too, that there was "a pretty considerable distance"[88] from the masthead light of the ship to this 'glare of light' on her after part, which made her out to be at least "a medium size steamer";[89] but for Gibson, a 'tramp' she was born, and a 'tramp' she remained until the end.

"About twenty minutes past one," Gibson went on, "the Second Officer remarked to me that she was slowly steaming away to the south west."[90]

According to Gibson's timing, nearly half an hour must have passed since his return to the bridge, before Stone first mentioned that the steamer was moving.

When Stone himself told Gibson about the five rockets, he said nothing about her moving or 'changing her bearing', as he had reported to Lord.

"When he came, did you give Gibson any information?" Aspinall asked him.

"I told him what I had seen," said Stone.[91]

"What did you say to him?"

"I told him I had seen those white rockets from the ship and that I had told the Captain about it."

"Did you say anything more to Gibson than that?"

"I told him the instructions I had had from the master, and he at once went to the Morse lamp and called up the ship again."

That was all. Had the steamer stopped again, until Stone mentioned this alleged 'slowly steaming away'? Yet, according to Stone's evidence elsewhere, ". . . the ship was altering her bearing from the time she showed her first rocket . . .,"[92] which seems to mean continuous movement.

When Gibson returned to the bridge, he noticed that the ship had changed her position from "right on the starboard beam"[93] to "about two and a half points before the starboard beam".[94] But agreed that as the *Californian* was 'swinging towards the nor'ard,'[95] the lights of a stationary ship "after a bit would bear differently from" him.[96] It should be borne in mind that Gibson never said he saw her moving. In fact when asked directly, he said he had not.[97]

In the twenty minutes that passed, neither of them seems even to have considered calling the Captain again to report the three further mysterious white rockets they had seen. Of such is the kingdom of catastrophe!

Gibson, and with reason, was a good deal more frank than Stone in telling the court what he had seen, and it is a pity that he was not recalled after Stone had given his evidence, to compare some of Stone's statements with his.

"Did you hear any explosions?" Gibson was asked by Mr Laing* for the White Star Line.[98]

"I did not hear any report at all."

"Any stars?"

"Yes."

"You mean stars from the rockets?"

"Yes."

"Were they stars of any colour or were they white stars?"

"White stars."

"Do you know that a distress signal, the regulation distress signal, is a rocket throwing stars?"

"Yes."

"And you knew it then, did you?" Lord Mersey asked.

"Yes."

Laing resumed his questioning.

"And each of these rockets which you saw, which you have described as white rockets, were they throwing stars?"

"All throwing stars," said Gibson.

The hearts of those who did know what rockets at sea meant must have missed a beat.

Fifty years later, what Gibson said he saw was amended by others to "white Roman candle type flares", and in 1965 to "rockets or flares".

But what did Gibson and Stone think the rockets were for?

After Stone had suggested she might be signalling to another ship, or telling the *Californian* "she had big icebergs around her" — which sounded like an improvization and perhaps was — he denied that he or Gibson had said the ship was in trouble and wanted assistance.[99]

Gibson said: "He [Stone] remarked to me that a ship was not going to fire rockets at sea for nothing."[100]

But Stone, giving evidence later, modestly attributed to Gibson the basically similar piece of common sense: "He [Gibson] remarked to me that he did not think they were being sent up for fun, and I quite agreed with him."[101]

But, Stone said: "I made no remark about that at all, about the ship being in distress, the whole time. It did not occur to me after what the Captain said."[102]

---

* Frederick Ninian Robert Laing, K.C. (1856-1931).

Stone was on the bridge and had seen; the Captain was on the settee and had said. So far as Stone was concerned, the Captain's saying was worth more than his own seeing.

"But what had the Captain told you," Aspinall asked Stone, "which would force your mind to the conclusion that this is a vessel which is not in distress?"

"He emphasized the fact about company's signals."[103]

Mersey once more pressed him.

"You did not think they were company's signals?"[104]

"I had never seen company's signals like them before."

"You did not think they were being sent up for fun?"

"No."

"What did you think?"

"I just thought they were white rockets, that is all."

It was an answer to try men's souls. Before Aspinall had done with him, Stone once more leaned on Lord for support.

"I did not think the ship was in distress at the time," he insisted.[105]

"It never occurred to you?"

"It did not occur to me, because if there had been grounds for supposing the ship would have been in distress, the Captain would have expressed it to me."

This was the man Lord had described as "a responsible officer".

Lord, in turn, said: "The Second Officer, the man in charge of the watch, said most emphatically they were not distress rockets,"[106] and, "He said if they had been distress rockets he would most certainly have come down and called me himself . . ."[107]

There is no word in the transcript of either official inquiry that Lord at any time during Sunday night asked Stone directly: "Are they distress signals?" or that Stone volunteered the statement: "They are not distress signals." The above extracts from the London inquiry are said to relate to a talk after the news of the disaster was known. They are inserted here, because they provide an ironical complement to Stone's explanation why he 'made no remark about the ship being in distress', and "the Captain would have expressed it to me", quoted above.

Lord was not worried, because Stone was not worried, and never mentioned distress rockets; Stone was not worried, because Lord was not, and said nothing about 'distress'. It is the kind of explanation, which in the real world, as distinct from that of fantasy where Stone seems to have been living that night, sometimes accounts for tragi-comedies. A and B, two cricketers, see the ball hit into the air. Both run to make the catch. A sees B running and stops; B sees A running and stops; the ball falls between them. On the other hand, it may lead to a *Titanic-Californian* incident, if true. Only, in this case, it happened to be untrue.

Not unnaturally, the Second Officer's almost filial faith in his father-Captain infected the apprentice, young Gibson.

"Did you not think it very curious," Mr W.D. Harbinson, representing the Third Class passengers (who, like the other passengers, were not allowed to give evidence themselves!), asked him, "that so many rockets should be sent up so close to one another?"[108]

"Yes."

"Did you say anything to [Stone] about going to see the Captain and saying this seemed to be a serious matter?"

"No, he told me he had reported it to the Captain, and the Captain had told him to keep calling her up."

But the questions which immediately follow clearly reveal the anxiety which pervaded Gibson's mind, and, if he was accurate, Stone's as well.

"Did Mr Stone say this vessel seemed to be in distress?"[109]

"No; he said there must be something the matter with her."

"Did he make any remarks to you as to the Captain taking no action? Did he say anything to you at the time?"

"No."

"Are you sure?"

"Yes."

"Did you say anything to yourself about it?" Mersey intervened.

"I only thought the same that he thought."

"What was that?"

"That a ship is not going to fire rockets at sea for nothing, and there must be something the matter with her."

"Then you thought it was a case of some kind of distress?"

"Yes."

From the beginning, Stone had demonstrated that he was not a candid or satisfactory witness. His trouble was that he had a secret, and it was a long time before he disclosed it; but it was probably the reason for many of his evasions and exasperating stupidities. Yet, when he was really trying to tell what had been in his mind at the time, rather than to hide it, he said much that perhaps deserved more attention and encouragement than it received.

His account of what happened after Gibson's return to the bridge, for instance revealed something fresh. He maintained that he had thought the rockets might possibly have come "from a greater distance,"[110] from some other ship,[111] and that he had said this to the Captain "the next day,"[112] and "to the Chief Officer and to the Third Officer in conversation."[113]

"Tell me what you said to the Chief Officer?" Mersey asked.[114]

"I have remarked at different times that these rockets did not appear to go very high; they were very low lying; they were about only half the height of the steamer's masthead light and I thought rockets would go higher than that."

"Well, anything else?"

"But that I could not understand why if the rockets came from a steamer beyond this one, when the steamer altered her bearing the rockets would also alter their bearing."

"That pointed to this, that the rockets did come from this steamer?"

"It does, although I saw no actual evidence of their being fired from the deck of the steamer except in one case."

This particular rocket, which Stone said was much brighter than the others, was one of the group of three that Gibson had also seen.

"That, you felt confident," Aspinall continued, "came from the vessel that was showing you these navigation lights?"

"I am sure of it."

He agreed that now he was "almost certain" the rockets did come from the steamer, "Except as I say, that they were very low; they did not appear to go high enough to me."[115]

One may try to guess the time the display ended. If Stone finished with Lord about 1.15, and Gibson returned shortly afterwards; Morsed for three minutes and then saw his three rockets, which Stone said came at the same interval[116] of "three or four minutes" as the earlier five, it would be getting on for half-past one.

("[I] was firing the distress signals until about five and twenty minutes past 1," said QM Rowe of the *Titanic*.)

Of course, Stone and Gibson could not know immediately that there were

going to be no more rockets, none at any rate, from their now familiar neigh-
bour. They continued watching her, and from time to time engaged in useful
maritime activities, Gibson Morseing and Stone from time to time taking
bearings on her under almost continuous observation, calling the Captain in
one way or another altogether three times, and neither of them ever once
thinking that it might be appropriate to waken the Wireless Operator.

"They were not asleep on the *Californian*," writes Mr Peter Padfield![117]

Physically, Stone and Gibson were wide-awake, mechanically busy with
compass, binoculars and lamp, but their minds were full of doubts and anxiety. They knew the rockets were not being "sent up for fun";[118] they felt "there
was something the matter with her", that it "was some kind of distress". But
it was for the master to judge, as Stone had said, and Gibson was under orders
to report to the master as soon as he had any information; but what could he
report? Three more rockets, and the ship apparently changing her bearing?
Clearly that was not new; and if the only reaction of the master to a report of
five rockets and a change of bearing had been an order to go on Morseing, his
response to news of three more would probably be no different, though possibly less civil. That perhaps is what Stone felt. Idly busy, they did nothing
and the sands trickled away.

As it has often been alleged that it was "white Roman candle type flares"
that Stone and Gibson mistook for "white rockets", we must also examine
what precisely Roman Candles are.

Mr D.A.S. Little, already mentioned, has been good enough to supply the
following description:

> In respect of Roman Candles, these are basically cardboard tubes loaded with stars
> which fire in sequence such as the ones seen on November 5th, i.e. you light the
> Roman Candle and after a short delay the first star fires, which in turn lights a
> second, which in turn lights another star, and so on. The average height of a normal
> Roman Candle would be 80-100 feet. If the Roman Candle were used as Company
> Signals, I would think they were coloured with the colour of the stars changing
> during the sequence.[119]

We know that there is no record of any ship using white Roman Candles as
a company signal, and as it has never been seriously suggested that any colour
except white was seen, we may disregard the last sentence in Mr Little's
description. For the rest, the most striking thing is his picture of one star
lighting up the next, one after another . . . How does this compare with the
description of what Stone and Gibson — particularly Gibson — saw?

"And each of these rockets which you saw, which you have described as
white rockets, were they throwing stars?"

"All throwing stars," Gibson said.[120]

Or, in his written report to Captain Lord: "I observed a white flash apparently on her deck, followed by a faint streak towards the sky which then burst
into white stars. . . . She fired another rocket which like the others burst into
white stars."

I leave you, the reader, to judge whether these words more nearly recall
the "Roman Candles", lighting up one star after another, described by Mr
Little, or the *Titanic* rockets with their "shower of stars", that sank down
slowly over Mr Beesley's pages and remain in our memory.

One further point, which so far as I know has never previously been
mentioned, is also worth considering here. Accepting for the moment the
statement that Stone and Gibson did not see rockets, but "white Roman candle

type flares, the stars from which rose only to half masthead height", we know that companies using Roman Candles for signals deliberately restricted the height they could reach (see Appendix K), for the very purpose of avoiding confusion. According to the expert opinion of Mr Little, that height would be about 80-100 feet. The masthead of the vessel concerned, therefore, would be about 160-200 feet above the waterline. The other ship, according to Stone and Gibson, was a "tramp"; or, in Lord's words, "something like ourselves,"[121] "A medium size steamer". The *Californian's* own four masts were about 110 feet above the waterline;* The *Titanic's* only two, about 200 feet. 'Only half masthead height,' if they insist; but certainly masts of exceptional height. Again, let the reader meditate, and let us not for one moment forget that "Roman candle type flares", or any other type of innocuous fireworks, were never once mentioned by Stone, Gibson, or any other of the observers, who in due course will appear, as what they had seen emanating from the other steamer. It was "rockets" or "white rockets" or "white lights which have the appearance of white rockets", or even more ominous and pointed phrases; and never anything else.

Captain Lord himself never claimed to know of any ship except the *Titanic* which fired rockets between 1 and 2 o'clock that night.[122]

It was also suggested in 1912, that what the *Californian* saw may have been flares, which, it was said, were required by law to be carried by Newfoundland Banking schooners to signal to their dories for their safety. An investigation, at my request, kindly undertaken by Canadian Government authorities, brought forth, in January 1965, the following response from Mr E.M. Gosse, the Deputy Minister of Fisheries in St John's, Newfoundland.

". . . I cannot find any laws or regulations stating that signalling equipment should be carried on Newfoundland Banking schooners in 1912. I believe that if such things as rockets and flares were carried, it would have been done on a voluntary basis and I think that the flare would consist of rag saturated with paraffin and set ablaze."

A burning paraffin-saturated rag seems an even less likely source of the white stars seen by Gibson than the Roman Candles.

Lastly, among possible reasons for those fireworks, alleged to have been set off by the "steamer", let us recall Stone's evidence.

"I thought," he said, "that perhaps the ship was in communication with some other ship . . . Possibly she was communicating with some other steamer at a greater distance than ourselves."[123]

Let us lean over backwards once more, and not only grant that Stone in fact did think that, but also that the steamer was actually communicating with "some other steamer". This explanation in the highest degree is improbable, but it is not, on the face of it, as ridiculous as the others we have examined. There is indeed only one objection, but that happens to be conclusive: the *Titanic* never saw any other vessel firing rockets, flares, Roman Candles or even star-loaded, blazing rags. There was, as in due course we shall learn, one other steamer which did fire rockets that night, and for the purpose of informing the *Titanic* that she was speeding to the rescue; but unfortunately nobody aboard the *Titanic* saw them, for she had already foundered.

This exhausts the possibilities suggested from any source; and to this day, the activity of the "steamer" remains shrouded in impenetrable mystery, but

* Calculated from photographs.

much other helpful information was provided about her, from which the
following marine 'Identikit' profile can be built up:

Name:	UNKNOWN
Official Number:	UNKNOWN
International Signal Letters:	UNKNOWN
Builders:	UNKNOWN
Tonnage:	UNKNOWN
Dimensions:	UNKNOWN — 'Apparently a medium-sized tramp'
Speed:	UNKNOWN
Owners:	UNKNOWN
Flag:	UNKNOWN
Port of Registry:	UNKNOWN
Port of Departure:	UNKNOWN
Destination:	UNKNOWN — 'Most probably on passage to the westward.'
Name of Master:	UNKNOWN
No. of Crew:	UNKNOWN
No. of Passengers, if any:	UNKNOWN
Nature of Cargo, if any:	UNKNOWN
Signalling Equipment:	(includes) "Eight white Roman candle type flares."
Engine:	UNKNOWN
First Reported:	Night of 14/15 April 1912.
Last Reported:	Night of 14/15 April 1912.

It was complained that (in spite of this wealth of data), "No properly organized
attempt was ever made in 1912"[124] to find, among others, this vessel, the one
Stone and Gibson said they saw firing rockets. The opening of the files has
revealed that in fact as late as February, 1913, Collectors of Ports in America
and Europe were still reporting non-suspicious vessels with non-disguised
funnels not qualifying for the black spot. As late as 1990, there were still a
number of people who thought she could be identified. Moreover, they fell into
the habit of calling her 'X'. A friend helpfully suggested she be called
Incognita; the American and British enquiries had long ago called her —
Titanic.

Sources

1 Beesley, Dover ed., p. 35.	1966-67, p. 1271.	28 B 7849.
	14 Ibid.	29 B 7850.
2 Ibid.	15 P.I.	30 B 7852.
3 B 7832.	16 Ibid.	31 B 7853.
4 B 7836.	17 Ibid.	32 B 7854.
5 B 7837.	18 B 7838.	33 B 7837.
6 B 7838.	19 B 7840.	34 B 7855.
7 Beesley, Dover ed., p. 35.	20 B 7841.	35 B 7865A.
	21 B 7842.	36 B 8028.
8 US 401.	22 US 237.	37 B 8028-29.
9 B 7819.	23 B 7844.	38 B 8031.
10 P.I.	24 B 7845-47.	39 B 8032.
11 Ibid.	25 B 7848.	40 B 8033.
12 Ibid.	26 B 8022.	41 B 8034.
13 *Who's Who In America,*	27 B 8024.	42 B 8035.

43 B 8037.
44 B 7859.
45 B 7863.
46 B 7000.
47 B 7830.
48 B 7829.
49 B 7875.
50 Stone statement, 18 April.
51 B 6790.
52 US 729.
53 B 7367.
54 B 7464.
55 B 7477.
56 B 7483.
57 B 7552-53.
58 B 8577.
59 B 8594.
60 B 8307.
61 B 6910.
62 B 7870.
63 B 7901.
64 B 7871.
65 B 7903.
66 US 910.
67 B 6937.
68 US 729.
69 B 14169.
70 B 14170.
71 B 14171.
72 B 14172.

73 *Lloyd's Weekly Shipping Index*, 18 April, 1912.
74 *Lloyd's Register of British & Foreign Shipping 1912*, pp. 126, 61.
75 B 6752-3; 6996.
76 *Lloyd's Weekly Shipping Index*, 11 and 18 April 1912.
77 Ibid., April 11.
78 Ibid., 9 May.
79 B 7090.
80 B 7056, 7107, 7111, 7131.
81 B 7883.
82 B 7466.
83 B 7490.
84 B 7495.
85 B 7498-500.
86 B 7501-04.
87 B 7229.
88 B 7331.
89 B 7733.
90 B 7511.
91 B 67883-85.
92 B 8042.
93 B 7439.
94 B 7469.
95 B 7475.

96 B 7472.
97 B 7741.
98 B 7758-66.
99 B 7896.
100 B 7529.
101 B 7895.
102 B 7897-98.
103 B 7899.
104 B 7903-05.
105 B 7993-94.
106 B 7336.
107 B 7374.
108 B 7749-50.
109 B 7751-56.
110 B 7908.
111 B 7909, 7913.
112 Ibid.
113 B 7920.
114 B 7921-26.
115 B 7929.
116 B 7892.
117 Padfield, p. 276.
118 B 7895, 7751, 7756.
119 P.I.
120 B 7766.
121 B 6752, 6754.
122 B 7000.
123 B 7844.
124 M.M.S.A. Petition, 1965, p. 16.

Chapter 6

The "queer light" and more rockets

Being in most ways just an 'ordinary, everyday young man', and certainly without any precognitive gift, Second Officer Herbert Stone could not have foreseen that some 50 years later the rockets he and Gibson had seen would be dismissed as "Roman candle type flares". It might have been a description of some entertaining display of fireworks, unexpectedly produced in mid-Atlantic just for one night and a Sunday night at that! — to while away the dark and freezing hours for Stone and Gibson during their lonely watch. The words might have been the product of ignorance or flippancy; in fact, they were the considered opinion of what had described itself as 'the largest, oldest and most influential Corporation of its kind in existence', the representative body of master mariners, mercantile marine officers and apprentices, called The Mercantile Marine Service Association (in short: the MMSA) and that was disconcerting.

After the eight rockets had gone up, Stone still diligently kept his glasses on the rocket-firing steamer.

"Look at her now, [Gibson]," Stone said suddenly. "She looks very queer out of the water; her lights look queer."[1]

"I looked at her through the glasses after that," Gibson told the British inquiry exactly a month later, "and her lights did not seem to be natural."[2]

He was asked if Stone had told him why he thought "she looked queer."[3] Stone had not; nor had Gibson himself noticed anything wrong with her until Stone drew his attention.[4] But, of course, Stone had earlier "remarked to me that a ship was not going to fire rockets at sea for nothing."[5]

"We were talking about it all the time," he told Mersey, "till five minutes past two, when she disappeared."[6]

Mersey asked him if the Second Officer, because of his remark about the significance of the rockets, had come to the conclusion that this was a ship in distress.[7]

Gibson seemed to hesitate. "No, sir, not exactly," and then he explained Stone meant, "that everything was not all right with her."[8]

"In trouble of some sort?" the Solicitor asked.[9]

"Yes, sir."

Such was the anxious state of mind of the two as a result of the rockets. But ominous as rockets may be, they do not suggest the "queer" or "unnatural".

Lord Mersey had asked Gibson what he meant by "lights which did not seem to be natural."[10]

Gibson's answer was extremely suggestive.

"When a vessel rolls at sea," he said, "her lights do not look the same."

Lord Mersey made an unhelpful contribution to the obvious by remarking that the *Californian* was not rolling, and that there was no sea to make the other ship roll.

"She seemed as if she had a heavy list to starboard," Gibson explained;[11] and, later, "I told him: 'She looks rather to have a big side out of the water.'"[12]

It is a phrase that seemed to throw a sudden light on the dark, mysterious ship. It tormented the imagination of those who first heard it, as it has, ever since, haunted the minds of those who have read it.

Her port light, said Gibson, "seemed to be higher out of the water than what it was before."[13]

To Stone, who gave evidence after Gibson, the lights "looked rather unnatural, as if some were being shut in and others being opened out. The lights appeared to be changing their position — the deck lights."[14] And he lost sight of her red sidelight,[15] but he denied that Gibson had said anything to him about it. When asked what was 'funny' about the changing position of the lights, as it was consistent with the ship's changing her bearing, Stone belittled it, and put forth a fanciful explanation.

"Merely that some lights were being shut in and other exposed and I remarked to Gibson that the lights looked peculiar, unnatural, but when I took the glasses and brought her under close observation, I took it to be due to the fact that very likely she was porting for some iceberg close at hand and was coming back on her course again, showing her other lights, the original lights."[16]

One would like to know if Stone always thought the lights of a ship, which was merely changing her bearing at sea at night, looked "peculiar", "queer" and "unnatural". He was not asked. He did not agree that she was listing, and he professed to distinguish between the "lights", which looked "queer", and the "ship"[17] (which neither he nor Gibson had been able to see at any time, because of the intense darkness).

"The lights are what I call part of the ship," said Butler Aspinall, . . . "You want me to believe, do you, that notwithstanding these rockets, neither you nor Gibson thought there was anything wrong on board that ship; you want me to understand that?"[18]

"Yes," said Stone, astonishingly, having also already said, "a ship was not going to fire rockets at sea for nothing." But, when the truth is known, it is not difficult to feel a certain sympathy for this misguided young seaman.[19]

Gibson, without a burden of responsibility or a secret, had told a significantly different story; and so he continued to the end.

He repeated, "she seemed to be heavily listed to starboard."[20] The white lights, too, seemed higher out of the water, and the after lights "did not seem to be the same as they were before"[21] in relation to the steamer's red sidelight. He said it again and again, but he could not say what the difference was.[22]

As Gibson strained his limited resources to tell the story of the disturbing things he had seen on that still and frightening night in mid-ocean, men leaned forward, hands behind their ears, not wanting to miss a word, and the loads of ostrich feathers on the large hats of the fashionable ladies bobbed impatiently while Gibson hesitated and sometimes stuck.[23]

"Her lights did not seem to look like as they did do before when I first saw them,"[24] he had summed it up almost at the beginning.

Sir John Simon, the Solicitor-General, with the enamel-smooth face and the silky-smooth tones already famous in England, almost pleaded with the youth.

"Could you describe them at all, Gibson?"[25] Simon asked.

"No, sir," said Gibson.

"Just think a minute; do not hurry about it."[26]

But it was no good. Gibson just did not have the words — perhaps nobody had. Yet, a hush slowly fell over Lord Mersey's court; and the feathers ceased to bob.

That the ship seemed to be listing to starboard towards 2 o'clock "conclusively proves", in one of the favourite phrases of the MMSA, that she could not have been the *Titanic,* as the *Titanic* was listing to port. The facts, as distinct from the Association's use of them, are more complex.

Soon after the *Titanic* fatally damaged her starboard side against the iceberg she listed, as might be expected, in that direction.[27] Then, as the water met resistance, it flowed up to a higher deck and rushed, less impeded, to the port side. Thereafter, she certainly listed steadily to port (as she had during the voyage).[*28] As time passed, the list grew worse. Suddenly, the Chief Officer, H.T. Wilde, on the Boat Deck, called out: "Everyone on the starboard side to straighten her up!"[29] Lightoller repeated the cry and the crowd dutifully moved to the starboard side. It may seem remarkable that so large a ship as the *Titanic* could be affected by the movement to one side or the other of the comparatively light weight of even several hundred people. Yet, travellers in undamaged and stable ships may have been surprised to see the apparently disproportionate effect of a movement by a crowd across the deck.

Edward Wilding, one of the designers of the *Titanic* who knew her every rivet and cherished them all, calculated that a movement of 800 people through 50 feet would produce a difference of 2°.[30]

It seems doubtful if the crowd who obeyed the order to move over to starboard numbered as many as 800. Of those still aboard, most of them were either crew or Third Class passengers. The majority of these passengers were still far below the Boat Deck in their quarters. Confused and uninformed, they crowded there, some with their bags containing all they had in the world beside them. Most of them just awaited their end with the negative humbleness of their lowly status. The exact number available to "straighten her up", as Chief Officer Wilde said, is not known, but the theoretical result in degrees did not seem impressive.

"That is to say," said Lord Mersey, "it is negligible?"[31]

But Wilding did not agree. To anybody walking on the deck, he insisted, the effect would be quite perceptible. When this happened, according to Lightoller, it was about "half an hour to three-quarters of an hour before he left the ship",[32] or, as Senator Smith said, before 'the ship left him.'[33]

Sam Hemming, the lamp-trimmer, told the senator of a similar incident. When Hemming last saw Captain Smith he was on the bridge alone, "and he sang out, 'Everyone over to the starboard side to keep the ship up as long as possible.'"[34]

There were some two hundred people there, he thought, all men. Asked how long this was "before the boat went down", Hemming said: "It was some little time." It was about quarter of an hour, he thought, before he "slipped into the water".[35]

Whatever success was obtained in decreasing the port list by either of these manoeuvres would certainly cause some apparent rise of the port light. It seems probable that the movement to starboard directed by Captain Smith came later than Wilde's. It would have been getting on towards 2 o'clock

---

*   And *cf.* the evidence of the mechanical engineer, Norman Campbell Chambers, a First Class passenger: '. . . the ship had had a list to port all afternoon.' (US 1042)

just about when Gibson became aware that "their" ship was listing to starboard.

An onlooker, who literally never moved his eyes from the object he was observing, would not easily notice any continuous change in its condition. For instance, the changing height above the water of the port light of a ship, which only gradually rose (or sank) might escape detection. Any sudden movement would create a new impression. The red light would certainly be, and look, higher than for some time previously, and — possibly — the ship might seem "to have a big side out of the water". Attentive as Stone and Gibson were to the ship they were watching, it is hard to believe that they kept their eyes on her literally without interruption for a period of some two hours. It also seems likely, as Lightoller believed, that as the end approached, the ship would be more tender, and therefore more susceptible to the shifting of weight aboard her.

In other words, it seems not impossible that Wilding may have over-estimated the stability, among the other positive qualities, of the *Titanic,* and that the correction in her port list brought about by Wilde and Lightoller was more than the 2° of his calculation, and considerably more by Captain Smith's command. If so, either rise in the port light would have been more likely to be noticed. It can be said that Stone and Gibson did not "in the least appreciate what was happening". In spite of their intermittent disquiet, they never for a moment seemed to have guessed the full horror of what they were looking at.

"At 2 a.m.," Stone wrote in his report to Lord, "the vessel was steaming away fast and only just her stern light was visible and bearing SW ½W." Her other lights, he must have thought, had gone below the horizon. Her red light, too, list or no list, was out of sight.[36] They had seen her red light, when they came on watch, so she must have been heading somewhere about north-east, as she bore about south-west from them. Now, somehow, she had managed to turn right round and steam away toward the south-west without ever showing the *Californian* her green light. But, said Stone, she "was steaming away fast".

In the same period, about 2 o'clock, somewhere across the intervening sea, the *Titanic* was sinking fast. Her red light was finally under, and most of her other lights forward as well. They got closer to the sea and slowly disappeared under it as she sank. Abaft, she was still well lit; but over the ship, as a whole, there was now much less light than there had been, which could be seen by any observer, either near by in the boats or far away, if anybody happened to be far away watching; and when she finally sank there would be no lights at all.

It seems beyond doubt that however disingenuous — to use no stronger a word — much of Stone's evidence was, he genuinely believed that the other ship was moving.

"Did you really think so?" Lord Mersey asked him.[37]

"I did. The only confirmation I had was the bearings of the compass. Two ships remaining stationary could not possibly alter their bearings."

When Aspinall said: "Altering her bearings did not mean steaming away?" Stone, with his seaman's ordinary knowledge, crisply put learned counsel in his place with the answer: "I do not see how two ships can alter their bearings when stopped."[38]

Whatever was really happening to that steamer with her erratic and unaccountable behaviour, and which, according to Stone, about 2 o'clock in the morning was 'steaming away fast', it needs to be pointed out that this version of the story, that the steamer was recklessly heading straight into the ice field, is told only by Stone.

The *Titanic* did not steam off into the ice field or in any other direction. Hence, Stone's account is one of the chief arguments in favour of Captain Lord. It is repeated over and over again; but it is never mentioned that this, one of the most important matters in Stone's evidence, is not corroborated, as a careful study of the transcript reveals, by the only other witness, the man standing at his side.

Looking at the same ship, Stone and Gibson saw different things. To Gibson, she did not turn around and show him her stern light, which was so significant to Stone. To Stone, all her lights, including her stern light, which did not "suddenly become black", just "gradually faded",[39] "which would be perfectly natural with a ship steaming away from us."[40]

To Gibson, she just remained stationary and slowly disappeared, not steaming, apparently, in any direction. It is true that Robertson Dunlop, when inquiring whether the masthead light was to his left or his right as he looked at it, asked him: "Was that before you saw her apparently steaming to the South-West?", to which question Gibson answered: "Yes."[41] But it is no more significant than Gibson's acceptance of another lead a little before, that the "glare of light" was "aft of the masthead lights",[42] when he had made it clear he saw only one masthead light.[43]

More to the point was Robertson Dunlop's next question after that about "her apparently steaming to the South-West."

"Did you see her turn round?"

"No," said Gibson.[44]

Stone's view, then, is quite distinct from Gibson's, and it may be possible to examine it a little. According to Stone, this remarkable steamer, after showing him her red light and therefore heading about north-east, managed to steam away to the south-west without opening her green light to his view. Although Stone was hampered by the exceptional darkness — but it was as clear as it was dark — it is likely that, although mechanically efficient, he was not a particularly efficient observer. We shall see how he completely missed sighting a steamer, at the end of his watch, when the blackness of night was beginning to be diluted by the oncoming dawn. Be that as it may, the most probable reason Stone did not see the steamer's green light was simple: she never showed it, because she never turned.

Captain Lord, on information from Stone, calculated that the steamer had crossed through some seven points of the compass, "from SSE at 0.50 a.m to SW ½W at 2.10 a.m", and had steamed "at least eight miles." According to Stone's timing, this would have taken from 12.45 a.m. — from the first rocket, when he said, she first changed her bearing — until 2.25 a.m., when she disappeared (see Diagram 14).

Stone's story is, the steamer, having prudently stopped in the ice and remained there quietly for over an hour, suddenly, at 12.45, fires a rocket and begins to move:[45] "steaming into danger", as Lord himself said.[46] The *Californian* affected to believe that the rockets were being fired just as a means of communication, and so the rocket may have been merely a farewell salute to the *Californian,* but, if so, why say 'good-bye' eight times? Having started her hazardous journey, the unknown ship lingers for another hour — a slow goer if ever there was one! — possibly, at first, just trying out the ice, to see if she could crack it, or if it would crack her. However, just before she disappears, she steams away "fast" to the south-west. According to Gibson, she never turned round, so she must have been backing into the ice; according to Stone, crashing into it. Such, at least, is Stone's Own Story.

Mr Padfield describes this as "one more difficult part of his evidence."[47] In

1913, Mr A.M. Foweraker, the inventor of the four ship theory — *Titanic, Californian*, 'X', the non-*Titanic* mystery ship seen by the *Californian* and 'Z', her sister in mystery, the non-*Californian* vessel seen by the *Titanic** — had also been aware of the thin ice over which his theory was moving, and wrote of his hypothetical ship 'X': "It is difficult to account for her moving from a position S.E. true from the *Californian* to disappear in the S.S.W. true without at any time showing her green light, unless she went astern."[48]

Stone did not give evidence in America, but Lord at Washington told how this unknown ship steamed away into the south-west. Both the American and British courts rejected the theory that it was another, and unknown, steamer which fired the rockets, and then steamed away into the ice and after this one-night stand was never heard of again until the supporters of Captain Lord dragged it out of oblivion some 50 years later, at which we shall look later. If Senator Smith and Lord Mersey (not to mention common sense) were right, it would be satisfying to try at least to find out why Stone was wrong.

Stone, taking bearings of the ship and looking at her through his glasses, said, some time after the last of the rockets, 'she is slowly steaming towards the south-west.' This was about the time when, as Lightoller wrote: 'the water was practically level with the main deck,'[49] and she was sinking steadily but slowly.

We recall one of Gibson's memorable phrases, used from his first sight of what he called the "tramp steamer", and repeated more than once, that "there was a glare of white lights on her after deck",[50] once qualifying it as a "faint glare of light."[51] The evidence from the *Titanic* herself about the lights in her after end, already quoted in Chapter 4, is uncontradicted: Steward Crawford — "still burning in the after part";[52] Quartermaster Bright — "The after part of the boat had her lights burning;"[53] First Class Passenger Hugh Woolner — "It was all brilliantly lighted at the stern end."[54]

These were the last lights of the *Titanic,* towards and on the stern, at the south-west end of the ship and shining almost until the last moments, when she was sinking fast.

This, too, was about the time Stone reported seeing his ship "steaming away fast towards the S.W."

The assembly of these passages about the lights and the account of how they went out, not only shows the similarity between what was happening in the *Titanic* and what Stone and Gibson saw, but also contains a hint to solving the puzzle of Stone's moving steamer.

Based on the evidence and personal narrative, this tentative theory that the combined effect of the sinking ship and the pattern of her diminishing lights was the origin of the illusion that the ship herself was in motion at least demands no such suspension of disbelief for its acceptance as its alternative: the fantasy that a steamer, for no apparent reason, on a pitch black night, should suddenly start backing into the ice for a distance (according to Captain Lord) of eight miles, a measure that seemed, and evidently proved to be, suicidal.

Whatever the truth, this was what the watchmen saw, or said they saw, on

---

* The 'four ship' theory may be regarded as opposed to the 'mystery ship' or 'three ship' theory in which only one, unknown, ship lay between the rocket firing *Titanic* and the *Californian.* Each theory has supporters that claim that the rockets seen by the *Californian* were from the *Titanic* and each theory has supporters that maintain that the rockets were fired by the mystery ship 'X' seen by the *Californian.* It is one more example of superb Lordite ingenuity.

this sinister night, distinguished from all others, when Captain Lord received his second call.

It was two o'clock in the morning when Stone finally sent Gibson down with the report Lord had ordered him to make nearly an hour before. The Captain had certainly been most patient, if he was awake.

"I told Gibson," said Stone,[55] "to go down to the master and be sure and wake him up and tell him that altogether we had seen eight of these white lights like white rockets in the direction of this other steamer; that this steamer was disappearing in the S.W., that we had called her up repeatedly on the Morse lamp and received no information whatsoever."

Gibson's version — twice repeated when he came to give evidence — of these orders was somewhat different: "Call the Captain and tell him that that ship has disappeared in the South West; that we are heading West South West, and that she has fired altogether eight rockets."[56]

Mersey naturally asked Stone whether he had said "disappeared" or "disappearing".[57] "Disappeared" was a word, which in the circumstances caught the mind. If Stone had merely said "steamed away" or "gone out of sight" or something similar, the effect would have been less provocative. As it was, Stone did not deny that he had used the verb; the only issue between him and Gibson was about the tense.

"I could not have said that she had disappeared, because I could still see her stern light. I saw this light for 20 minutes after that."

Whether Stone "could" have said it or not that Sunday night, in the report he wrote to Lord on the following Thursday, 18 April, he said he had ordered Gibson "to tell you . . . the steamer had gone out of sight." Gibson, in his report of the same date, actually used the word "disappeared" as coming from Stone. But, of course, Lord had concealed even the existence of these reports from the court. It was a break for Stone, at least.

Gibson said he never saw her stern light.[58] He was "signalling her continuously"[59] and had his glasses on her, when Stone said to him: "She is slowly steaming away towards the S.W."[60]

W.D. Harbinson, counsel for those silent Third Class passengers, asked him: "Could you see whether she was steaming away?"[61]

"No," said Gibson. Then he added: "The Second Officer was taking bearings of her all the time."

The use of the word "could" and not "did" in the question may suggest that his "signalling" prevented his seeing whether or not the ship was moving. But Gibson had also said that he had his glasses on her "at this time",[62] so his "No" must mean that he did not see her "steaming away", which is consistent with his other evidence.

Gibson, who was the first of the two to give evidence, when asked what he understood by "disappeared", answered: "We could not see anything more of her."[63] He then told Lord Mersey that it did not convey to him that the ship "had gone down".[64]

"What did you understand him to mean — that she had steamed away through the ice?"

"That she had gone out of sight."

"Oh, yes," said Mersey. "A ship goes out of sight when she goes down to the bottom. What did you understand by the word 'disappeared'?"

"That is all I could understand about it."

But Mersey was still not satisfied.

"A ship had been sending up rockets; then you are told to go to the Captain and say: 'That ship which has been sending up rockets has disappeared.'

What did you understand the Second Officer to mean? Did not you understand him to mean that she had gone to the bottom?"

"No," said Gibson yet again.

"Then what did you understand, that she had steamed away through the ice?"

"[*No answer*]," says the Transcript,[65] and it is a most significant silence.

When it came to Stone's turn, the question put to him was not exactly the
same. Arising out of his statement that the stern light was gradually "disappearing",[66] he was asked: "Did it have the appearance of being a light on a ship
which had suddenly foundered?"[67]

"Not by any means," he answered emphatically.

On this occasion, he did not ask for clarification, as he might well have
been excused for doing. What does a light "on a ship which had suddenly
foundered" look like?

"When you saw her disappear, did you think something had happened to
her?"

"No, nothing except that she was steaming away."[68]

Whatever was in Gibson's mind, he dutifully proceeded to bring Stone's
report to Lord. This second time, the messenger did not merely blow down the
speaking tube. He went below to the chart-room, found the door closed,[69]
presumably knocked on it, and said he went in. There he found Captain Lord
and faithfully made his report. That report, according to Gibson, let us recall,
was ". . . that ship has disappeared in the South West; that we are heading
West South West; and that she has fired altogether eight rockets."[70]

Lord's only reaction, according to Gibson, was to ask whether the rockets
'were all white', "were there any colours in the rockets at all?"[71]

"What did you tell him?"

"I told him that they were all white."

"Did he give any instructions?"

"No."

"Did he say anything further?"

"He asked me the time."

"What was the time?"

"Five minutes past two by the wheelhouse clock."

Gibson told him that; Lord said nothing more and Gibson returned to the
bridge.[72]

Mersey himself then asked a critical question omitted by the Solicitor-
General.

"Was he awake?"[73]

"Yes, sir," said Gibson.

Stone's account of what Gibson reported to him adds two further details:
Lord had asked "if he were sure there were no colours in them [the rockets],
red or green,"[74] and, "then he told me that as he shut the door he heard the
Captain say something — what, he was not quite certain about."[75] (And, of
course, Gibson did not dare ask him to repeat it!)

There was also one major difference between Stone and Gibson. The latter
had told Lord Mersey that the captain was "awake". According to Stone,
Gibson said on his return to the bridge, "He told me he had woke the Captain
up . . ."[76]

Lord himself said he was asleep during this second call.[77]

It will be observed that Stone's version gives at least some corroboration
to Lord, whereas Gibson's flatly contradicts him. The matter is of great importance in the story.

For the time being, Stone and Gibson just continued their watch; but now as that ship — according to Gibson — was "out of sight", and certainly was 20 minutes later, according to Stone, they had nothing to occupy their time, no more diligent tapping on the Morse lamp for Gibson, no more efficient taking of bearings for Stone.

Being finally satisfied that the ship had now "disappeared", was not just "disappearing", the conscientious Stone once more felt impelled to report to Lord. This was the third and last call to the master about the rocket-firing steamer made by Stone or Gibson during their watch.

This time, Stone did not go below, but just whistled down the speaking tube. Lord himself denied any memory whatever of this third call,[78] as he said he was sound asleep on the settee in the chart room. In order fully to appreciate the features of this final call upon Captain Lord, the reader is referred to Diagram 6, showing the chart-room and Captain Lord's own cabin, the settee being in the former and the speaking tube in the latter. The scale of the diagram unfortunately cannot be guaranteed, but is based on the known beam of the *Californian* as 53.8 feet and the settee as somewhat under six feet.

What happened then in this scene between the two characters, Second Officer Stone and Captain Lord, may perhaps be most clearly set out in nine easy stages, thus:

(1) STONE blows down Speaking Tube.[79]
(2) LORD rises from Settee in Chart-room, walks to Speaking Tube in his Cabin, Distance about 15 feet, but not in Straight Line. LORD BEING FAST ASLEEP.
(3) LORD answers Call: "What is it?"[80] LORD BEING FAST ASLEEP.
(4) STONE: "The Ship from the direction of which we saw the Rockets has disappeared, bearing S.W. to half W., the last I saw of the Light."[81]
(5) LORD: "Are you Sure there were no Colours in the Lights you saw?"[82] LORD BEING FAST ASLEEP.
(6) STONE: "No, sir. They were all White Lights!"[83]
(7) LORD: "All right."[84] LORD BEING FAST ASLEEP.
(8) LORD then walks back from Speaking Tube in Cabin to Settee in Chart-room, Distance about 15 feet, but not in Straight Line. LORD BEING FAST ASLEEP.
(9) LORD RETURNS TO SETTEE, and is STILL/SOON FAST ASLEEP!

All the lines in the above meeting of master and mate are contained in Stone's written statement to Lord of 18 April, his written statement to the Receiver of Wreck on the return of the *Californian* to Liverpool and his evidence in London.

Now, as Captain Lord is not elsewhere credited with somnambulism, this encounter has caused a considerable degree of unease to his supporters. In particular, Stages (2), (5) and (8) are so awkwardly inconsistent with his being as fast asleep as he claimed, that his supporters have been reluctantly driven to drawing the only possible inference. As their reasoning goes, this inference is, of course, not that Lord was not asleep, but that Stone never made the call. Gibson (unfortunately) corroborates Stone, though he times the call, not at 2.40, as Stone said, but an hour later, "about 3.40."[85]

"Did you see him doing it?" the Solicitor-General asked Gibson.[86]
"Yes."
"Did you hear what he said?"
"No."

Apart from the matter of Lord's walking and talking in his sleep, this third report to Lord raised another obvious question concerning Stone, and Aspinall, of course, asked it.

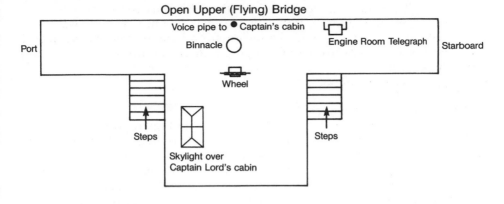

Open Upper (Flying) Bridge

Port

Voice pipe to ● Captain's cabin
Binnacle ○
Engine Room Telegraph
Starboard
Wheel
Steps
Steps
Skylight over
Captain Lord's cabin

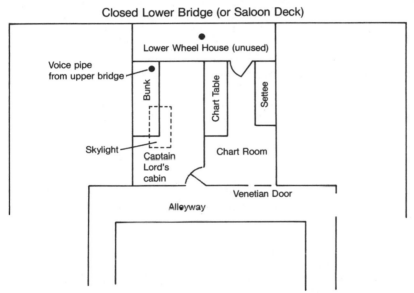

Closed Lower Bridge (or Saloon Deck)

Lower Wheel House (unused)
Voice pipe
from upper bridge
Bunk
Chart Table
Settee
Skylight
Captain
Lord's
cabin
Chart Room
Venetian Door
Alleyway

Diagram 6. Captain Lord's cabin and the bridge of the *Californian*
*Sketch, drawn for clarity rather than to scale. The beam of the ship was actually 53
feet and the settee was under six feet, the two dimensions definitely known. There
was no clock on the upper bridge (B 8141) and no porthole or window in Lord's
cabin. There was a venetian door to the chart-room (B 8171). There are more sketches
made of Captain Lord's cabin and the bridge of the* Californian; *but basically, this
is how Captain Lord seems to have remembered his quarters on the* Californian.

"In view of the fact that when you saw her stern light last you thought
nothing had happened to her, why did you make this report to the
Captain?"[87]

"Simply because I had had the steamer under observation all the watch,
and that I had made reports to the Captain concerning her, and I thought it my
duty when the ship went away from us altogether to tell him."

"But", said Mersey, "why could you not have told him in the morning?
Why wake up the poor man?"[88]

"Because it was my duty to do so, and it was his duty to listen to it."

"It was of no consequence, if the steamer was steaming safely away?"[89]

"He told me to try and get all the information I could from the steamer. I got none and I thought it my duty to give him all the information I could about the steamer."

"Were you anxious about her?"

"No."

"Was he anxious about her?"

"No, as far as I could judge from his answers and instructions."

Herbert Stone was not a man with much curiosity or imagination, but all the same, it is possible that even he may have wondered, as he returned to his vigil, what possible reason there could be for Lord's apparent obsession with "colour" in the rockets. It is a question that deserves examination.

Lord had asked Gibson, ". . . were there any colours in the rockets at all?"[90] or, according to Stone's report of what Gibson told him, "if he were sure there were no colours in them, red or green."[91]

Telling of his own last call to Lord, Stone described the master as being even more pressing. After being informed the steamer had "disappeared",[92] Lord "again asked me if I was certain there were no colours in those lights whatsoever. I again assured him they were all white, just white rockets."[93]

When examining Lord about Gibson's visit (which Lord, of course, said he did not remember), the Attorney-General put a simple question: "Why did you ask if they were white rockets?"[94]

Lord's answer was remarkable. "I suppose this was on account of the first question *they* asked, whether they were Company's signals."

The emphasis has been added to "they", to call attention to Lord's transferring to Stone and Gibson, his own original question (to Stone alone, it will be recalled) about company's signals, when he received Stone's report of the rocket or the five rockets.

"Do just think!" the Attorney pleaded.[95]

"Company signals usually have some colour in them," said Lord.

"So that if they were white it would make it quite plain they were distress signals?"

"No, I understand some companies have white."

We know that answer had a basis in fact, but also how narrow that basis was. Sir Rufus, who presumably did not carry the list of company's signals in his head, and had no more than the common knowledge that white rockets meant distress, sounded exasperated.

"Do really try and do yourself justice!"[96]

"I am trying to do my best."

"Think, you know. Mr Lord, allow me to suggest you are not doing yourself justice. You are explaining, first of all, that you asked if they were white rockets, because companies' signals are coloured. I am asking you whether the point of your asking whether they were all white rockets was not in order to know whether they were distress signals? Was not that the object of your question, if you put it?"

"I really do not know what was the object of my question."

Lord may have wished he had claimed political asylum in Washington; but that was not yet the end. The Attorney next asked him about Stone's call on the tube at twenty minutes to three, and Lord's again asking if Stone "was sure there were no colours in the lights that had been seen."[97]

Lord said he had no recollection of any conversation with the Second Officer between half-past one and half-past four.

What they had seen was strange and mysterious: that ship never answering their lamp; her "queer lights" that "looked unnatural", and, above all, her rockets — and inexplicably silent rockets! — adding their own showers of stars to the star-packed heavens, before she finally steamed senselessly away into the dangerous icefield and disappeared. One thing about it gave Stone no peace and was to torment him until the day he died.

". . . the simplest explanation [is] that at the time these things were happening no one on the *Californian* thought anything of them at all."[98]

Such is the final summary of Mr Padfield; it needs no comment.

We have no hint of what Stone and Gibson talked about as the last of their watch slowly dragged on, and they were left with nothing but the companionship of the dark, ice-clanking sea and the glitter of the crowded sky; but even what had already passed was not the end of the strange things they saw that night.

Still far away, in the south-east, the *Carpathia* was racing on her course of N52°W to the scene of the accident. Her regular speed was 14 knots, but by extraordinary efforts and means, with an extra watch below, and cutting off all heat and hot water throughout the ship, she worked up to 17. She did not yet know that the *Titanic* had gone.

At about 2.40 a.m., Captain Rostron of the *Carpathia* saw very far away a green light a little off his port bow, about where the *Titanic* would be. He took it to be her starboard light, so it must be high out of the water to be seen at such a distance, and he was relieved to see she was still afloat. In fact, what he saw was a green flare, a White Star identification signal, which Boxhall had fired from No. 2 Boat. If Captain Rostron was right in his time, it could only be the phenomenal clarity of the night which enabled the flare to be seen at so great a distance from so low in the water. It seems, however, more probable that Rostron's "2.40" as the time he saw the flare, and thereupon began firing rockets to tell them he was coming, was too early. Mr Howard M. Chapin, an observant First Class *Carpathia* passenger, wrote that "It was after three when we sighted a faint green light off our port bow."[99] That the time must have been later seems to be confirmed by the fact that another half hour passed before any of the *Titanic's* boats heard and saw one of those rockets: just a distant flash and a faint boom; and the time was soon after 3.30.

The *Californian* was then heading about west.[100] It was very soon after Stone's third call to Lord, according to Gibson's timing, that he happened to be looking away to the south from the bridge when he saw something in the sky. It was a rocket; and the time was about 3.40.[101]

He then saw two more.[102]

I once asked Mr Beesley if he had any idea how long it was from the time they heard the *Carpathia's* rocket until she came into sight and then stopped. He thought carefully, and said: "About half an hour to three-quarters." Taking the *Carpathia's* speed at 17 knots and the distance she stopped from No. 13 Boat (Mr Beesley's) as about a mile, it may be the liner was some nine or ten miles away when the "faint boom" of her rocket was heard. If it was no louder than that at that distance, it begins to be less inexplicable that the eight rockets fired by the steamer were not heard by the *Californian*.

Lightoller did not hear them at all.

"Did she (the *Carpathia*) throw up any rockets?" Mr Laing, counsel for the White Star Line asked.

"She did." Lightoller said. He thought he had seen two rockets, "there may have been more" he explained.

"Do you know what sort?"

"The ordinary distress signals, the same as we were using."

"With stars?"

"Yes."

"Were you near enough to hear them?" Lord Mersey wanted to know.

"Oh, no," Lightoller conveyed,[103] making it clear that the sound of the rockets fired by the *Carpathia* were indeed extraordinarily local in their acoustic effect.

Gibson saw the three rockets "right on the horizon".[104] Asked about the first, he said it was a white flash and it went up into the sky.[105]

At the inquiry, when Lord Mersey heard Gibson's account of these rockets, he did not appreciate the terrible significance of the evidence. His mind was not on the *Carpathia* but on the question whether Roman Candles had been fired from the *Titanic's* boats, and at this stage he seemed sceptical about this new series of rockets.[106]

"Are you quite sure," he asked Gibson irritably, "that these three rockets were ever seen by you at all?"[107]

"Yes, Sir. I saw the first one, and I reported it to the Second Officer, and we looked out for more to see if we could see any more — and we saw two more."

When Stone gave evidence later in the afternoon, he told the court:[108] "At about 3.20, just about half-past three, as near as I can approximate, Gibson reported to me he had seen a white light in the sky to the southward of us, just about on the port beam. We were heading about west at that time. I crossed over to the port wing of the bridge and watched its direction with my binoculars. Shortly after, I saw a white light in the sky right dead on the beam." This light was shortly to be followed by two more 'lights'.

He did not think these lights were rockets[109] and Stone's difficulty was, he had not gone and reported this new incident to Lord.

This naturally seemed so incredible to Mersey that it threw doubt on the whole matter. But instead of questioning Stone about the omission, his inquiry was directed to Gibson.

"Were they reported to the Captain?" he asked.[110]

"I reported them to the Second Officer."

"Did he report them to the Captain?"

"No."

"Why not?"

"I do not know."

"If they were really there, why were they not reported to the Captain?"

"I do not know, Sir."

And Stone himself was not asked a word about it by Lord Mersey or any of the counsel.

The eight rockets and the three form an irrefrangible link between the *Californian* and the *Titanic*. This, what the *Californian* saw, it should be repeated, is the decisive factor in the case. If the *Titanic* never saw the *Californian* or any other ship — or, alternatively, saw a dozen ships — cannot alter in the slightest, let alone obliterate, what the *Californian* saw. Even if she had seen no rockets from the other steamer, but only noted the time she stopped, her 'queer lights' and the time of her unaccountable disappearance into the icefield, the incident, in the light of the news of the disaster, must have caused the most painful anxiety to any conscientious shipmaster. But the *Californian* had seen eight white rockets from a steamer in the same position and about the same time as the *Titanic* fired her eight. The supporters of Captain Lord, however, said that Stone and Gibson saw only "eight white

Roman candle type flares" from an unknown steamer; and we searched the records for that steamer at the end of the last chapter. The rockets of the *Titanic* were followed, two hours later, by the rockets of the *Carpathia;* and, sure enough, from about the right direction, that is, the south, at about the right time, the *Californian* saw three more rockets.

The rockets from the *Carpathia* were, of course, less incriminating in themselves: they were not a call for help (though the *Californian's* neglect of them when they were seen could not be excused by that later knowledge). But clearly, it is impossible for Captain Lord's supporters to admit that the *Californian* had seen *Carpathia's* rockets, while denying that they had seen *Titanic's,* which were fired several miles nearer to the *Californian* and from a much higher base.

In 1964, the MMSA privately but authoritatively disclosed to the present writer that the *Carpathia's* rockets were not seen by Stone and Gibson, any more than they had seen *Titanic's* rockets.[111] Of the three "lights" seen by them, one was not a rocket at all, but a shooting star, and the other two rockets were on a wrong bearing for the *Carpathia*. It all was merely one more 'coincidence'.

It may be prudent here to stop a few moments to restate a few elementary facts about the timing of the *Titanic's* rockets.

Lord Mersey found in his report that the rockets began about 12.45 a.m., for which finding there was adequate evidence both at his inquiry and in America. QM Rowe, who helped to fire the rockets, timed their beginning at 12.45. He partly established his finding by reporting he had seen a boat (which we know was No. 7) in the water by 12.25. This, we shall see in a moment, was the earliest of the boats to be launched. If it be asserted that Rowe took 20 minutes to get his "detonators" from near the after-bridge and take them to the bridge, until the time they began from the starboard socket at quarter to one, it is obvious this is a remarkably long time. On the other hand, there may be a simple explanation.

In No. 7 Boat, Dickinson H. Bishop, a First Class passenger, was sent off with his wife, and at Washington,[112] he stated: "I imagine the time the boat was lowered was about a quarter to 1 . . .' It is an article of faith with the Lordites that the rockets must have started much earlier than Rowe said (and Lord Mersey found), because they accepted it that No. 7 was already in the water at 12.25. However, not only does Bishop state (I carefully abstain from saying 'fix'!) the time, but he is supported by Third Officer Pitman, who went next in No. 5, about 12.55.[113] No. 3, one gathers from Fifth Officer Lowe, went about 1 o'clock,[114] and Sir Cosmo Duff Gordon, the notorious passenger in No. 1, told the Attorney-General: "they had just begun [firing rockets] when they were lowering No. 3 Life-boat."[115]

The significance of these three boats is, they include two of the first to leave; they were starboard boats; and could be, and were, observed by Pitman and Lowe on the starboard side where they were working (and where also, from the starboard socket, the rockets were fired). All three boats left, not just about 12.30, but just about 12.45, or quarter to one. This was when the rockets began, Rowe himself said; he had supporting evidence from Bishop, not to mention Stone in the *Californian*. If there is any discrepancy between Rowe's "12.25" in Washington and Rowe's "12.45" in London, it seems as likely as not, that when he had stated his "12.25", he was under the assumption that the ship's clock had been put back. By the time he had reached London he knew that it had not, and so corrected his mistake when he gave evidence at the Mersey inquiry. Alternatively, it may well have taken 20 minutes before the first rocket was fired from the time he first saw and reported No. 7 already afloat.*

Summing it all up, the time of the first rocket, proved by the words of witnesses and the circumstantial evidence of the first three boats on the starboard side, was about 12.45 or a few minutes later. It was at once seen aboard the Californian, and followed by the seven others. After which, the Lordites§ may offer such opinions as they please, without, however, exorcising the basic facts.

If the *Californian* saw none, or only some, of the *Titanic's* rockets, and none of the *Carpathia's,* it must follow that on the North Atlantic that night there were no fewer than four ships firing rockets, or, at any rate, some kind of fireworks:

(1) *Titanic,* which fired about eight.
(2) *Carpathia,* which fired at least three; both these vessels doing so for grave and understandable reasons.
(3) *One unknown and undiscoverable ship,* which fired "eight Roman candle type flares", seen by the *Californian.*
(4) *One other unknown and undiscoverable ship,* which also later admittedly fired two rockets, likewise seen by the Messrs Stone and Gibson; both these unknown and undiscoverable vessels making their signals for unknown and undiscoverable reasons.

It must also be recorded that through the years, Captain Lord's supporters have not followed a consistent line in regard to the rockets.

The earlier statements by Captain Lord's supporters about the rockets should be resurrected here:

(1) "Thus, *Californian,* fast in the ice to the Northward, did not get the appeal for help direct from *Titanic,* but saw the rockets well on the horizon. The Master had been stopped by the ice barriers, and he concluded to wait till daylight . . . The Second Mate Stone and the apprentice Gibson saw the rockets fired by *Titanic,* a strange steamer's hull intervening on the line of bearing . . . This was duly reported to Captain of *Californian,* who, under the circumstances, and probably

* So far as can be ascertained the boats left the ship at the following times, but I think it is necessary to say that these, and indeed, all the times subsequent to the collision which are mentioned by the witnesses, are unreliable:

No.	Starboard Side		No.	Port Side
7	At 12.45 a.m.		6	At 12.55 a.m.
5	At 12.55 a.m.		8	At 1.10 a.m.
3	At 1.00 a.m.		10	At 1.20 a.m.
1	At 1.10 a.m.		12	At 1.25 a.m.
9	At 1.20 a.m.		14	At 1.30 a.m.
11	At 1.25 a.m.		16	At 1.35 a.m.
13	At 1.35 a.m.		2	At 1.45 a.m.
15	At 1.35 a.m.		4	At 1.55 a.m.
C	At 1.40 a.m.		D	At 2.05 a.m.
A	Floated off when the ship sank and was utilized as a raft		B	Floated off when the ship sank and was utilized as a raft

— 'Findings' — Report B.I., page 38. (Beside this table are 28 references to the evidence.)

§ 'Lordites', is the now more commonly used name for the supporters of Captain Lord, and mainly adopted so by themselves. The older name, *'Californians'* is not often used any more.

accepting the judgement of his deck Officer, concluded to wait until daylight."
— MMSA *Reporter,* Vol XXXVIII No. 450, January 1913, article, 'PUSHED
UNDER THE WHEELS OF JUGGERNAUT' by J.D.M.* (Reprinted in "THE
'CALIFORNIAN' INCIDENT", MMSA publication, March 1962.)

(2) "The most likely theory about the rockets is that they *were* the *Titanic's* rockets
. . ." — "The TITANIC and the CALIFORNIAN" by Peter Padfield, February
1965; p. 274.

(3 "The most likely explanation of these later rockets is that they were the *Carpathia's*
rockets as she approached the scene." — Ibid., p. 212.

(4) "It is impossible to escape the conclusion that some, or all, of the rockets they
[Stone and Gibson] saw originated from the *Titanic*." — *Merchant Navy Journal,*
March 1962 (also in MMSA advance press handout), article, "THE 'CALIFOR-
NIAN' INCIDENT . . ." by Leslie Harrison.

Contrast with this last excerpt the following from the 1965 MMSA Petition,
the authorship of the greater part, if not the whole, of which is also commonly
attributed to Mr Harrison:

"As the rockets or flares seen by the *Californian's* second officer and apprentice
did not explode, and as they came from a ship which was steaming away from
them, they could not have been distress signals, and could not have come from
the stationary *Titanic*."
— The Californian Incident Text of a Petition addressed to
The President of the Board of Trade — February 1965, p. 16.

The enormous difference between these statements may remind the reader
of Humpty Dumpty's famous lines when he said, in a rather scornful tone:
"'When I use a word, it means just what I choose it to mean — neither more
nor less.'"

For Gibson and Stone, whose watch was the chief cause of all this controversy, their strange and silent ordeal ended with Gibson going below at a
quarter to four, "to get the Log Gear for the Second Officer,"[116] and Stone
being relieved by Chief Officer Stewart at four o'clock.[117]

Two years and two weeks later, almost to the day, when the dead had been
counted and named, the memorials consecrated and only grief remained, Sir
Alfred Chalmers, Nautical Advisor to the Marine Department of the Board of
Trade until 1911 and himself the survivor of three shipwrecks, wrote his own
exasperated comments on the *Californian's* failure. It had been decided that
there should be "boats for all"; but declaring himself quite "unrepentant"
about the old regulations of the Board, which had been satisfied with even
fewer boats than the *Titanic* had, he went on:[118]

"One other fact which influenced the opinion of the Professional officer is
also borne out in the circumstances in which the casualty occurred and that
is the existence of definite fixed routes which not only tended to lessen the risk
of collisions and to avoid ice and fog but also ensured the reasonable proximity of passing vessels to render timely assistance to one another during the
whole voyage, for when the casualty occurred, one vessel (the 'Californian')
was only about eight miles distance and had it not been for the inexplicable
misapprehension or apathy of the Officers of that vessel an effective rescue
of all would have been possible within an hour or so of the mishap."

It was in this document that Sir Alfred, as quoted earlier, put "the whole

* J.D. McNabb, with an enclosure from A.M. Foweraker.

blame" for the disaster on "the bad lookout" of the *Titanic*, and condemned the court for "a sad lack of logic and consistency, which can only be ascribed to the prevalent grievous [*sic*] decadence of Common Sense and backbone."[119]

But whether it was the bad lookout of the *Titanic*, or the bad regulations of the Board of Trade, or even the "misapprehension" of Gibson and Stone, it made no difference to the one and a half thousand victims of the *Titanic*, for while Gibson and Stone watched, those fifteen hundred perished.

Sources

1	B 7515, 7650.	39	B 7959.	81	Ibid.
2	B 7517.	40	B 7957.	82	B 7307.
3	B 7656.	41	B 7785.	83	B 7312.
4	B 7658.	42	B 7782.	84	Ibid.
5	B 7529.	43	B 7425, 7787, 7791.	85	B 7574.
6	B 7533.	44	B 7786.	86	B 7576-77.
7	B 7535.	45	B 6903.	87	B 7977.
8	B 7538.	46	B 6903, 6904, 6914.	88	B 7978.
9	B 7539.	47	Padfield, p. 276.	89	B 7980-82.
10	B 7518.	48	*Nautical Magazine*,	90	B 7561.
11	B 7522.		Vol. LXXXIX, p. 583	91	B 7952.
12	B 7651.		(June 1913).	92	B 7976.
13	B 7662.	49	Lightoller, p. 232	93	B 7999.
14	B 7943.		(Dover ed., p. 287).	94	B 7289.
15	B 7944.	50	B 7429.	95	B 7290-91.
16	B 7945.	51	B 7719.	96	B 7292-93.
17	B 7996.	52	US 116.	97	B 7307.
18	B 7997.	53	US 840.	98	Padfield, p. 276.
19	See *Daily Mirror*, e.g.	54	US 895.	99	*Paignton Magazine*,
	15 May.	55	B 7949.		August 1912; *Brown*
20	B 7660.	56	B 7552, 7609.		*Alumni Monthly*, April
21	B 7671.	57	B 7972.		1913.
22	B 7680-82.	58	B 7630.	100	B 8008.
23	*Daily Mirror*, 15 May;	59	B 7740.	101	B 7586.
	Manchester Guardian,	60	B 7737.	102	B 7579.
	15 May; *Globe*, 14	61	B 7741.	103	B 14856.
	May; *Daily Sketch*, 15	62	B 7740.	104	B 7596.
	May.	63	B 7611-16.	105	B 7597-98.
24	B 7525.	64	B 7616.	106	B 7594.
25	B 7526.	65	Ibid.	107	B 7591.
26	B 7657.	66	B 7959.	108	B 8008.
27	B (E. Wilding) 20242	67	B 7960.	109	B 8011.
	seq.	68	B 7970.	110	B 7587-90.
28	Beesley, Dover ed., p.	69	B 7554-55.	111	P.I. 29 October 1964.
	20.	70	B 7552.	112	US 1003.
29	US 74.	71	B 7560-65.	113	US 288.
30	B 20934.	72	B 7666-69.	114	US 400.
31	B 20935.	73	B 7570.	115	B 12496.
32	US 74.	74	B 7952.	116	B 7608 & Gibson's
33	US 56.	75	B 7954.		Statement, 18 April.
34	US 671.	76	B 7952.	117	B 8017.
35	US 672.	77	B 7280.	118	[MT 9/920/6] M 12286
36	B 7624.	78	B 7295.		(30 April 1914).
37	B 7968.	79	B 7976.	119	Ibid.
38	B 8050.	80	Ibid.		

Chapter 7

Californian to the rescue

When Chief Officer Stewart took over the watch a few minutes after 4 o'clock that Monday morning, Stone gave him "a full report"[1] of everything he had seen and done during the previous four hours: how he had dutifully reported it all to the master's instructions, when the steamer had disappeared, her bearing — "the whole information regarding the watch". Stewart, on the other hand, says Stone reported the happenings of the watch "very briefly",[2] which is easy to believe, for Stone was probably eager, after that cold middle watch, to return to his warm bunk.

It must all have been a considerable surprise to Chief Officer Stewart. He himself had last been on duty at 8 o'clock the previous night, and when he turned in, about half-past nine, the *Californian* was still pursuing her customary course towards Boston, Massachusetts. And now, this! — Rockets — a blind steamer, and apparently crazy too! — steaming off into the icefield — then, just about half an hour ago, more "lights" or rockets!

Stewart looks over the port beam, in the direction of those three lights ("rockets", said Gibson) and to where the steamer disappeared[3] — south to south-west — but, as she was last seen an hour-and-a-half or two hours ago (Stone and Gibson respectively), Stewart is too late, of course, he can see noth. . . - but . . . hold on there!

Far from seeing nothing, Stewart immediately does see a steamer; it is not hard to make her out — four masts and one funnel. She was stopped, and was an unexpected sight for Stone, who had in fact, missed her completely. It casts some light on the watch-keeping qualities of Second Officer Stone, who, as we know, is not the only ineffective watchman who had been on duty that night. But there are other far more important things arising out of the arrival of that four-masted, one-funnel steamer.

"There she is!" said Stewart, on seeing her. "There is that steamer. She is all right."[4]

"That's not the same steamer!" said Stone instantly. "She has two masthead lights." Thus Stone reported to the court his own reaction to the new steamer.[5]

Stewart's report of Stone was a little different: "Well, he did not know; he said he had never seen that steamer till I pointed it out to him."[6] But the result was the same: Stone disowned her as his own troublesome rocket-firer.

Now exactly why Stewart should have made the comment, "She is all right," when Stone had not expressed any anxiety whatever about his ship, which "disappeared", is but one more instance of the special usage of words and phrases which punctuate the singular vernacular employed by the officers of the *Californian*. The previous night, Captain Lord suddenly says: "The only passenger ship around here is the *Titanic*," when, he alleges, nobody had mentioned a passenger ship; Stone says: "A ship at sea is not going to fire rockets for nothing," which is his highly idiosyncratic way of expressing his opinion that there is nothing much the matter with her; and now Stewart takes a hand at this odd and unreal pastime.

And what about this new arrival on the scene? It was said she was not identified.[7] Lord said, she was reported to have a yellow funnel,[8] and named her as the Canadian Pacific *Mount Temple,* which she might have been, if her funnel was in fact yellow. Other evidence strongly suggests she was the Cunard *Carpathia,* which had the same time as the *Californian,* and stopped just about 4 o'clock in the morning as Stone's watch ended. But whether she was the *Mount Temple* or the *Carpathia,* this is highly probable: the ship was where she was, because she thought she was at the position given by the *Titanic* in her call for help as that where she struck the iceberg, and close to where she sank. That position was approximately where, all night long, Stone and Gibson had watched their "tramp", saw her fire eight rockets, saw her lights gradually getting less, and saw her finally disappear.

It is remarkable that this circumstance has never received the emphasis it deserves.

Let us see what happens next. Stone has now been relieved of his burden of responsibility, and Stewart is the man on watch and in charge. For nearly half an hour, he just waited about on the bridge. He claimed, in spite of what Stone had said, that he thought the four-master might be the rocket-firing steamer.[9]

"I thought she might have drifted back — that she found that she could not get through the ice."

"Now, think about what you are saying," Lord Mersey said. "Do you want me to understand that you thought it was possible that the ship which had steamed away after throwing up the rockets had drifted back and was there before your eyes?"

"At half-past four?" Sir John Simon added.

"In the morning?" Mersey rubbed it in.

"I thought she might have come back, or she might have known something about the other ship."

"Have you ever made that suggestion to a living soul until now?"

"I do not believe so."

"It comes out for the first time in the last minute?"

"I thought all the time," said Chief Officer Stewart, "that that ship had something to do with it or knew something about it."[10]

And, of course, he was right. Whichever ship it was, she knew a good deal about it; but Stewart at the time was so incurious he did not even resort to the well-beloved Morse lamp, let alone use the wireless.

Mersey and Simon pressed him further, so that he finally agreed he did not mean literally the steamer had "drifted back", but had "steamed back".[11]

Each of the *Californian* witnesses was a character, and Stewart, who had been off duty during all the fateful hours and might have been expected to give his evidence with a candour born of his immunity from blame, proved to be extremely devious and unconvincing. An able and intelligent man, with years of experience at sea, what he said, if not the way he said it, must have been intentional. His purpose seems to have been not to tell a plain story of his own minor part in the affair; but, being himself in no danger of criticism - at least so far as the events of the night were concerned — to cover up, as well as he could, for those of his shipmates who were involved and whose careers might be affected.

Arrogant and Olympian though Lord might have been, none of his officers was (in Rufus Isaacs's words) "anxious to make a case against him."[12] On the contrary, the evidence of each was an achievement in loyalty.

In the end, it is probable that the only result of Stewart's efforts was to deepen the suspicion which the undisputed events themselves must have aroused. Stewart, like the others, was a loyal shipmate, but a dubious asset as a witness.

His manner seems to have invited disbelief even when there was no apparent reason for his prevaricating. For instance, when the questioning turned to the rockets, almost automatically, Stewart began to suggest doubt — 'I think . . .,' 'Yes, I believe I asked him if that was the ship that fired them . . .'[13] But when asked if he had asked Stone if the four-master was the ship seen during the night.[14] Stewart, being very positive, said he had asked, and Stone replied he had not seen the ship before. In the statement, given to E.J.M. Bates, the Receiver of Wreck in Liverpool, there was an interesting difference from his evidence in the witness box. Stewart said, when he spotted the four-masted steamer through his glasses: "I saw two white masthead lights and a few lights amidships."[15] In the statement: "On looking through the glass, I saw two masthead lights and a lot of lights amidships."[16] It is not pleasant to impugn the character of a man, who lost his life in a good cause and in the service of his country in 1940, when he had reached the age of 62,* but the first of the matters now mentioned here concerned Stewart's thoughts after the news of the *Titanic* was known; and it is not unfair to say that Stewart did not tell the truth.

"When you heard that," Simon asked, "did it occur to you that the steamer that had been sending up distress rockets might have been the *Titanic*?"[17] It will be observed that Stewart was not asked to concede that the steamer was the *Titanic*. He gave what, after a study of the evidence, can be called a characteristic *Californian* reply: not exactly a lie, completely unresponsive, and decidedly not the truth.

"Not the steamer we saw,"[18] said Chief Officer Stewart.

He was naive if he thought that was the end of it. John Simon was not a man to be unperturbed by so blatant an evasion.

"That is not what I asked you. I will put the question again, if I may," Simon continued politely.[19] He was as smooth as a snake in such encounters, and as deadly. "When you heard that the *Titanic* had sunk that night, did it occur to you that that steamer which you had heard had been sending up rockets, might have been the *Titanic*?"

This time, Stewart did not answer at all. Mersey turned and looked at him sternly.[20]

"Now, come!" he said. "Answer that question!"

And answer it he had to in the end. "'No,' replied Mr. Stewart firmly," according to one newspaper report of the 'scene in court.'[21] "No, I did not think it could have been the *Titanic*,"[22] says the dry official transcript, innocent of all adjectives. But what confidence could one have in the good faith of men who related their story so unwillingly and with so little persuasiveness? It is not surprising that Captain Lord's partisans concentrate on questions of

---

*   Stewart, by then a master, but out of a job, signed on as Third Officer in the Ernels Shipping Co.'s *Barn Hill*, and was killed in the hold, when the vessel was bombed and sunk, 3 miles SSW of Beachy Head on 20 March 1940. (Imperial War Graves Commission: *Lloyd's Supplement*, 1939-40.)

navigation and mostly ignore questions to the navigators.

And so Stewart continued his recollections of what was to be an eventful morning. About 4.30, he went down to the chart-room and woke Lord.[23]

"It's breaking day now," were the words he used, according to Lord.[24]

"When you called the captain," Simon asked, "did you tell him what Stone said he had seen?"[25]

"I told him that the second mate told me he had seen rockets in the middle watch."

"Not a rocket, but rockets?"

"Rockets," Stewart repeated.

Lord's version was that he had been told of only one rocket, but here we shall go on with Stewart's evidence.

"What did the captain say when you said that?"

"He said; 'Oh, yes; I know.'"

Mersey wanted to know if that was all Lord had said, and Stewart enlarged his answer with an important addition.

"He [Lord] said: 'Yes I know, he [Stone] has been telling me.'"

It is not suggested that anybody but Stewart woke Lord. Hence, Lord's "has been telling me" is the equivalent of 'told me'; and it must mean: 'Stone told me about the rockets, not this morning after he came down from the bridge, when his watch was over, but during the watch at 1.05 a.m.'

The result of the passage is that, according to Stewart, Captain Lord admitted Stone had told him of "rockets", not "a rocket".

"Did the captain come on the bridge?" Simon asked.[26]

"At once," Stewart replied, with what the careful reader may be forgiven for calling anticipatory and defensive emphasis.

Once on the bridge, Lord, according to Stewart, discussed his plans, about the possibility of pushing through the ice, and proceeding on the voyage. Stewart, however, asked him if he was not going to the southward to see what the ship was that he, Stewart, "thought had been in distress".

They looked at the ship together;[27] and then comes one more of those incredible failures of communication between the *Californian* officers, which are past understanding.

"Did you tell the Captain," Simon inquired, "that Mr Stone, who had been on watch, thought this was not the ship that had thrown up the signals?"

"No," says Stewart blandly.

"You did not?" Simon repeats.

"No," Stewart says once more.

It is hard to understand why he was not asked to explain or justify his omission in so many words.

"Had you forgotten it?"

"I do not know," said Stewart, "I did not tell him that."[28]

So Lord looked at the ship to the south, and, when asked whether he was going down to look at her, replied, as Simon put it to Stewart: "No, she looks all right; she is not making any signals now."[29]

"Yes," Stewart agrees, "I believe those were his exact words."

We note that Lord, who saw only one masthead light aboard her the previous night, is apparently incurious about finding two aboard her at daybreak.[30]* Lord thinks "she looked all right". "She's not making any signals now."[31]

***

* At Washington, however, when Lord was asked by Senator Fletcher whether the 'yellow-funnel steamer on the south-west of us' was the same as he had seen on Sunday night, he replied: 'I should not like to say. I don't think so, because this one had only one masthead light that we saw at half-past 11.'

"No," Stewart agreed,[32] "but the Second Officer in his watch said he fired several rockets."

"Go and call the wireless operator,"[33] said Lord promptly and just about five hours too late.

One of the smallest mysteries in the *Californian* affair, and an odd one, is why many writers credited Stewart, and not Lord, with the decision, however belated, to call Evans.

In Washington, Lord was not asked about the circumstances under which he finally ordered Evans to be called; but there are several versions of this decisive event. The important and glaring discrepancies occur between the two given by Evans in Washington and London, and Stewart's. The calling of Evans is the second event which seems to cast doubt on Stewart's veracity. Let us see what he says.

Lord has sent him below to call the wireless operator because Stewart has just told him that the vessel to the south is reported to have fired rockets during the Second Officer's watch. The time is 5.40 a.m., ATS.

"Try and remember,"[34] said Simon to Stewart, "what it was that you told him."

"I told him to get out and see what the ship was to the southward."

"I want you to be as accurate as you can. Do you think that was all you said to him?"

"I think so," Stewart answered.

Then followed some further questions about that ship to the southward.

"The ship that Mr Stone had already told you was not the ship that had sent up the rockets?"[35]

"Yes."

"You think that is what you asked him?"

"Yes."

"I must just put it to you. Did you not go to his room and did not you say to him that rockets had been seen during the night?"

"I do not think so, Sir."

"You do not think you did?"

"No."

"And did you not ask him whether he could find out with his Marconi apparatus whether anything was amiss?"

"I told him to call up and see what that ship was to the southward. I remember that distinctly, Sir."

"Did you not ask him whether he could find out whether anything was amiss?"

"I do not think so — No, Sir; I do not remember that."

And here, as an instant contrast, is what Evans said, first in Washington.

"When were you awakened?" Senator Smith asked him.[36]

"About 3.30 a.m., New York time."

"And who awakened you?"

"The Chief Officer."

"What did he say to you?"

"He said: 'There is a ship that has been firing rockets in the night. Please see if there is anything the matter.'"

Two pages later, in the style which was typical of him, the senator had evidently forgotten what Evans had said, and made him repeat it; but as the repetition makes it even more convincing, here it is as well.[37]

"Did you tell me what the mate said," Senator Smith asked, "when he woke you up between 3 and 4 o'clock Monday morning?"

"He came into my room between 3 and 4; opened the door. He knocked at the door, but I was asleep, and he came in. He said he knocked at the door and then came in."

"Was it locked?"

"No; we never lock a door on the ship. He came into my room, and I did not wake up, and he caught hold of me. As soon as he touched me I woke up with a start, and he said: 'Wireless, there is a ship that has been firing rockets in the night. Will you come in and see if you can find out what is wrong — what is the matter?' I slipped on my trousers and called at once. Within five minutes I knew what had happened."

What Evans said in London, when questioned by the Solicitor, is very short.[38]

"You remember Mr. Stewart coming into your room at that time, twenty minutes to six?"

"Yes."

"Just tell us carefully, if you will, what it was he said?"

"He said: 'There's a ship been firing rockets. Will you see if you can find out whether there is anything the matter?'"

One question asked by Clement Edwards, who represented the Dock, Wharf, Riverside and General Workers' Union, should also be quoted.

"Did Stewart say anything to you about a ship being to the southward, would you find out what she was?"[39]

"No, not to my knowledge," Evans answered, making the contrast between his evidence and Stewart's complete.

Which of these two versions rings true? Which of these two witnesses seems to be telling the truth? If it be agreed that Evans is the man to believe, it must be asked why Stewart was giving a severely edited, if not absolutely false, story to the inquiry. The answer must be the rockets. The determination to belittle them is an indication of the consciousness of guilt, which from then on filled the ship.

"Did you," Simon asked Stewart in one of his final questions, "at that time think that anything was amiss?"

"I thought something had happened, yes," says this incredible man.[40] And thinking thus, he says nothing whatever about it to Evans!

Stewart's account of his call on Evans is an insult to the intelligence, and perhaps its chief result was to hint at an atmosphere of conspiracy aboard the *Californian,* at least between the Captain and his Chief Officer. In all charity, the best thing that can be said for Stewart in this matter, as in others, is that he hoped he was helping his skipper.

The effect of Stewart's message[41] was to cause Evans to jump out of his bunk instantly, slip on a pair of trousers and slippers, go to his key at once, start the motor and listen. The speed and urgency of his reaction is a further light, if any were needed, on the alleged routine inquiry Stewart had asked him to make. Hearing nothing, Evans sent out his own CQ call, a general call requesting an answer from anybody listening. In Washington, Evans said: "About a second later, I was answered by the *Frankfurt* . . . He told me the *Titanic* had sunk." Later, in London, Evans said the Canadian Pacific *Mount Temple*, almost at once, was the first to answer him. She said: "Do you know the *Titanic* has struck an iceberg and she is sinking?" She also gave the position, 41.46N:50.14W.

The story of the *Mount Temple's* operator, John Oscar Durrant, has one significant difference. He said he told the *Californian* that the *Titanic* had sunk,[42] and next day admitted he had not been told that himself by anybody, but "came to my own conclusion."[43] In other words, he guessed, and guessed rightly. In the *Mount Temple's* PV, the neutral entry is,[44] "3.25 (5.11 A.T.S.) *Californian* calls CQ. I answer him and advise of *Titanic* and send him *Titanic's* position."

It was then, said Evans in London, that the *Frankfurt* "jumped in" and told him the same thing.[45] Stewart was still waiting in Evans's cabin,[46] and with a hurriedly written message of the *Titanic's* position he went off to fetch Lord. It was then about a quarter to six in the morning.

Exactly what happened after that was described by Lord more than once. In his evidence in London,[47] he said it took 15 or 20 minutes before Stewart returned saying: "There's a ship sunk." "Did he tell you what ship?" asked the Attorney. "No, he went back to the wireless room straight away."

"Did he come back a few minutes after that?"

"Some time after that. He said: 'the *Titanic* has hit a berg and sunk.'"[48]

Curiously, Lord's account given long afterwards was not only more vivid, but also more probable and more like Evans's twice-told story.

But whether the fatal news reached Lord in one piece, or by instalments, before telling what was done about it, there is one other important matter to examine. This, too, might very easily be overlooked, for the evidence of Lord and Stewart tends to gloss over, rather than to reveal, one remarkable fact: even when both of them finally knew at least of the possibility that something was wrong, neither of them made the slightest attempt to find out what had happened.

Let us recall that it was at 4 o'clock when Stewart took over the watch, and he was at once told by Stone about the steamer which had fired rockets. Stewart himself then discovered the four-masted steamer, which, he said, he thought 'knew something about it' or 'had something to do with it'. Being of that opinion, what steps does Stewart take to find out what the four-master knew about the rockets? The answer is none whatever. For half an hour he merely waited about on the bridge, until at 4.30 he called the Captain.

Lord then comes to the bridge, talks with Stewart for about three quarters of an hour about pushing through the ice, or not; turns his engines over at 5.15 for a few minutes; than hears about the rockets, and likewise does nothing for another 15 minutes, or, in all, a whole hour from the time he was called.

"I thought something had happened, yes."[49] Stewart had admitted this; and that was the state of his mind from the very moment Stone had told him the story of the watch.

". . . when the Chief Officer called you," the Attorney-General asked Lord, "do you remember saying to him that the Second Officer had said something to you about a rocket?"

"Yes," Lord agreed, "I said that."[50]

Both men, then, on their own statements, were fully aware no later than 4.30 of something unusual having happened, and so far as they were concerned, they were apparently quite content to remain in a state of ignorance. Between them, these two men allowed more than an hour and a half to pass before they raised a finger to find out what was the matter; or what, if anything, had happened during the night.

Why?

The answer is perhaps suggested in that old article by 'J.D.M.',* already mentioned at the end of the last chapter:

"Thus, *Californian,* fast in the ice to the Northward, did not get the appeal for

---

* J.D. McNabb, a senior Board of Trade examiner.

help direct from *Titanic,* but saw the rockets well on the horizon. The Master had been stopped by the ice barriers, and *he concluded to wait till daylight without courting undue risks by attempting to force a passage in the dark* [emphasis added]. . .'

When Stewart came on watch, and when he called Lord — "It's breaking day now" — it was not yet light; but when he was finally sent off to call Evans, it was light. In those simple words, there is also a possible clue of a much wider kind to the mystery of the *Californian.*

There is little doubt that the talk between Lord and Stewart about that ship to the south finally provided what Freytag called *"das erregende Moment,"* * the instant which sets the whole action alight; but there is considerable doubt as to when that moment occurred.

Lord, it will be remembered, thought "she looks all right". "She's not making any signals now."[51]

Stewart agreed, but told Lord "the Second Officer in his watch said she fired several rockets."[52]

"Go and call the wireless operator!" said Lord.

Those words sound decisive, and were; but when were they spoken? In his evidence, Lord agreed that this conversation took place "just before 5 o'clock".[53] Perhaps it did; but it is quite certain that Evans was not called for another half-hour. Not only his evidence, but the independent wireless logs of other ships provide corroboration of this statement. The alternative is, that Evans was in fact called very soon after five o'clock, received the news of the disaster within a few minutes, and that, somehow, Captain Lord managed to waste almost another whole hour before sending his ship on her mission of rescue. Nobody can believe this. Not only does it fly in the face of the evidence, but it burdens Captain Stanley Lord with such deliberate callousness as would have justified the crudest and most extravagant comments of the ill-informed calumniators, of whom he was later to be the victim. Nothing in the record or the character of the man remotely suggests he was capable of such wilful misconduct, as to ignore the kind of appeal sent out by the *Titanic.*

The overwhelming probability, therefore, is that even if the talk between Lord and Stewart about the ship to the southward did take place "just before 5 o'clock", the facts about the calling of Evans were rather different from the note of urgency suggested by Lord's command: "Go and call the wireless operator!"

It seems probable that even when that, or something similar, had been said by Lord and it had been decided to call Evans, the two remained chatting on the bridge for still another half-hour or thereabouts. It is certainly significant that while Evans says he knew in five minutes what had happened, Lord says "15 to 20 minutes"[54] passed before Stewart returned with the news. Perhaps, in the light of the dreadful knowledge which he was now to receive, his subconscious tried to assuage his conscience by shortening the period of his dilatoriness. Lord certainly, in the words of that old article, did not want to court "undue risks by attempting to force a passage in the dark", and it was safely light when Stewart at last entered Evans's cabin. Nevertheless, it should be repeated yet again, that neither Lord nor Stewart could have had the slightest inkling that the explanation of that "rocket" or "rockets" or of "what was amiss" was the fantastic and overwhelming catastrophe that had actually occurred.

One final statement of Lord's must be included, for it tends to confirm both

---

* The exciting moment.

McNabb's article and the suggestion here made about the deliberate delay in calling Evans. After the publication of the Report of the Mersey inquiry, Lord wrote on 14 August 1912, what he called a "length explanation" in a letter to various papers, including the MMSA's *Reporter*. This letter contained the sentence: "I did not hear of the disaster until daylight, *and that only after it was deemed safe for my steamer to proceed* [emphasis added]."[55] These words are ambiguous, but, as the news of the disaster came through the deliberate act of calling Evans, the implication seems to be that that deliberate act was intentionally postponed until it was light, when Lord considered it was safe for the *Californian* to move, if it should be necessary.

The conclusion of the whole matter seems to be that although the two men, between them, were aware of the possibility of something being wrong from 4 o'clock on, they still preferred to do nothing to confirm or get rid of their anxiety until the darkness had entirely gone. But once they did know, they acted promptly. It is a tiny and withered enough laurel, in all conscience.

The news, when it finally reached Lord, must have been staggering. During the night, when Rostron of the *Carpathia* first heard merely that the *Titanic* was in trouble, he made no attempt to hide his disbelief and astonishment;[56] and, although he wasted no time, as soon as he was convinced of the truth of the news, in turning his ship around and making the most efficient preparations for the work of rescue, there was no doubt about his intense excitement, as well as that of all the other members of his crew. It was the only way ordinary men might be expected to react in the circumstances.

But Lord was far from being an ordinary man. Never dramatic or emotional, whatever feelings the terrible news may have aroused in him, he seems to have given no outward sign. "Great excitement", he himself said, filled the ship;[57] but Lord himself was as cold as the ice which surrounded him. The most appealing and ingratiating of all his supporters, his son, who, of course, denied the entirety of the case against his father, said that if he had ever been "in the awful predicament" in which he was twice officially adjudged to have been, "his reaction would have been quite natural and devoid of any theatricality whatever."[58]

It was a shrewd opinion. Rostron was seen to raise his cap while his lips moved in silent prayer, and ". . . like an electric spark . . . [he] was hurtling around . . ."[59] knowing only that the *Titanic* had struck an iceberg.

Lord, aware of the ultimate catastrophe, though certainly not of its cost, if any, in human life, just concerned himself, coolly and without gestures, in getting the correct position.

He told the Senators in Washington what happened:

"I said: 'Go back again and find the position as quickly as possible.' So he [Stewart] went back, and he came back and said, 'We have a position here, but it seems a bit doubtful.' I said: "You must get me a better position. We do not want to go on a wild goose chase.'"[60]

Very sensible, but also perhaps a shade inhuman.

The *Californian* had stopped at 10.21 the night before,[61] and Lord had arrived at her dead reckoning position of 42.5N; 50.7W.[62] They had stopped till "6 o'clock next morning", Lord said in London, "5.15 we moved the engines for a few minutes and then we stopped on account of the news we received, and waited till 6 o'clock."[63] It was shortly before that, when Evans finally got from the *Virginian* what was called 'an official position' for the *Titanic*, it being the same as that already received 'unofficially' from the *Mount Temple*, 41.46N; 50.14W. It only contradicted the *Mount Temple's* message on the present status of the *Titanic* in stating: "Titanic struck iceberg, wants assistance urgently, ship sinking, passengers in boats. . . ."

Lord worked out the distance. It was no more than 19½ miles. "I immediately got under way . . .," said Lord.[64]

The *Californian* was off to the rescue.

Sources

1 B 8017.
2 B 8576.
3 B 8017.
4 B Ibid.
5 B Ibid.
6 B 8601.
7 B 8613.
8 B 6964.
9 B 8639-43.
10 Ibid.
11 B 8647-49.
12 Mersey, p. 898.
13 B 8602.
14 B 8599-8600.
15 B 8598.
16 B 8612.
17 B 8654.
18 B Ibid.
19 B 8655.
20 *Daily Mirror*, 16 May 1912, p. 5
21 Ibid.
22 B 8656.
23 B 8614-15.
24 B 6876.
25 B 8616-19.
26 B 8621-24.
27 B 8629-31.
28 B 8637.
29 B 8632.
30 US 733.
31 B 8632.
32 B 6966.
33 Ibid.
34 B 8758-59.
35 B 8762-67.
36 US 736.
37 US 738.
38 B 9058-59.
39 B 9164.
40 B 8768.
41 US 736; B 9061, 9065, 9068, 9072.
42 B 9579.
43 B 9591.
44 US 782.
45 B 9082.
46 B 9084-85.
47 B 6970-71.
48 B 6973.
49 B 8768.
50 B 6961.
51 B 8632.
52 B 6966.
53 B 6963.
54 B 6970-71.
55 'The "Californian" Incident', MMSA [1962] p. 17.
56 Rostron, *Home From the Sea*.
57 US 731.
58 P.I.
59 Sir James Bisset, *Tramps and Ladies*, p. 280.
60 US 731.
61 B 6702.
62 B 6704.
63 B 6713.
64 Captain Lord's Affidavit, Appendix C.

Chapter 8

"Half-masted for death, my Lord"

We now come to one of the most apparently controversial aspects of the entire case. The *Californian* reached the *Carpathia,* which was said to be approximately at the position where the *Titanic* had foundered, at the earliest about 7.45 a.m., according to Groves; or, at the latest, about 8.30, according to Lord. If as was found by Lord Mersey's court, the *Californian* was not 19½, but only 10 miles distant from the scene of the disaster, why did it take at the very least nearly two hours to cover the distance?

The short, and comprehensive, answer is that the *Californian* did not — because she could not — steam in a direct line. At any rate, she would not risk doing so.

At the same time, it is well to bear in mind, if the call for help had been received, the *Californian* "Most certainly" 'could have gone to the relief of the *Titanic*'. These plain and unequivocal words are not something lifted from an interim opinion by the allegedly hostile Lord Mersey, and perhaps out of context; but they express the emphatic and reiterated opinion of none other than Captain Lord himself.[1]

They were spoken in Washington in a passage of Lord's evidence, which is not often mentioned but is of great significance, and were uttered on the afternoon of 26 April in the latter part of his testimony.

"You were asked by Senator Smith a moment ago," Senator Fletcher addressed Lord,[2] "whether, if the wireless operator on the *Californian* had been on duty, would have picked up this message from the *Titanic* giving the alarm?"

"Yes," said Lord.

"Could you have gone to the relief of the *Titanic* at that time?"

"Most certainly," Lord answered.

"You could have gone?" the Senator repeated.

"We could have gone; yes."

"The engines were not running then," Senator Fletcher went on, almost as if he were offering a way of escape to Lord, but the latter, as will be seen, would have none of it.

"The engines were stopped; perfectly stopped," Lord agreed.

"But you could have gone to the *Titanic*?"

"The engines were ready," Lord explained. "I gave instructions to the Chief Engineer, and told him I had decided to stay there all night. I did not think it safe to go ahead. I said, 'We will keep handy in case some of these big fellows come crunching along and get into it.'"

Unless these words are an idle boast — and Lord does not seem the kind of man to engage in idle boasts — what can they mean, except that "in case some of these big fellows" get into trouble in the ice, the *Californian* will be there ready — able — and willing to help them out?

Lord's words were spoken to a friendly and largely uninformed audience. It was only later, in London, when it was clear to Lord that the enormity of what had happened was not likely to be so easily overlooked by the sceptical and probing experts of the British inquiry that the tone of his defence underwent an abrupt change. Contrast the foregoing passage with these questions asked by Robertson Dunlop on 14 May, less than three weeks later.[3]

"Assuming that she sank somewhere between two and three, could you, in fact, if you had known at 1.15 a.m. in the morning that the *Titanic* was in distress to the southward and westward of you, have reached her before, say, 3 a.m.?"

"No, most certainly not," said Lord.

"Could you have navigated with any degree of safety to your vessel at night through the ice that you, in fact, encountered?"

"It would have been most dangerous."

At this answer, Mersey himself intervened to save Lord from the pit which his eager acceptance of Robertson Dunlop's leading questions had so efficiently dug for himself.

"Am I to understand," the Commissioner asked Dunlop, "that this is what you mean to say, that if he had known that the vessel was the *Titanic* he would have made no attempt whatever to reach it?"

"No, my Lord. I do not suggest that," Dunlop answered; and then pirouetting 180 degrees in the air, he continued with another question to Lord. "What would you have done? No doubt you would have made an attempt?"

"Most certainly I would have made every effort to go down to her," Lord agreed with the same emphasis as he had just infused into his answers with an almost exactly opposite meaning.

"Would the attempt from what you now know in fact have succeeded?" This was in fact Dunlop's final question to his sorely pressed client.

"I do not think we would have got there before the *Carpathia* did," Lord answered, as desired, "if we would have got there as soon."

It is not a performance which irradiates truth. It is important to emphasize the contrast between Lord's earlier evidence in Washington and the statement he made in London. What had changed so radically as to bring about this difference? The answer is, precisely nothing. The difference is merely the result of Lord's having decided to alter the basis of his defence.

Apart from not having received the distress call, he now said he could not have got there in time, because of the distance separating him from the *Titanic*.

The speed of the *Californian* is, of course, the first factor to identify.

On a full consumption of coal, Lord said in London, her full speed was 12½ to 13 knots.[4] In Washington, he had told the Senators, they averaged "on our present consumption 11 in fine weather."

"In case of distress," Senator Smith asked, "I suppose it would be possible for you to exceed that considerably?"

"Oh," said Lord, "we made 13 and 13½ the day we were going down to the *Titanic*."[5] They were at full speed then, "driving all we could."

But the start of the trip, according to the log, which Lord brought with him from Boston and read in part, was very different.

"Six o'clock proceeded slow," Lord read, "pushing through the thick ice."[6]

"6.20 clear of thickest of ice; proceeded full speed, pushing the ice" (see Diagram 7).

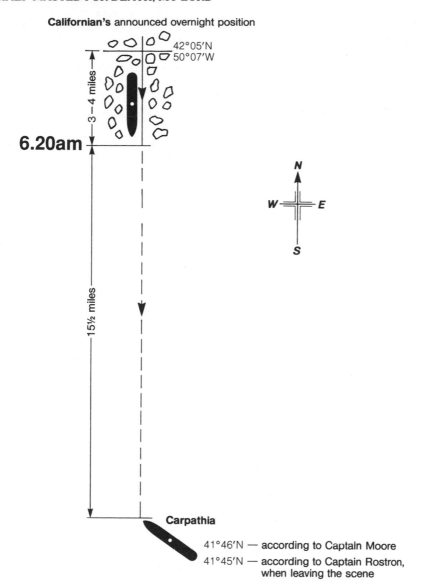

Californian's announced overnight position

42°05'N
50°07'W

3 – 4 miles

6.20am

15½ miles

N
W — E
S

Carpathia

41°46'N — according to Captain Moore
41°45'N — according to Captain Rostron,
when leaving the scene

Diagram 7. The *Californian's* distance from the *Carpathia*: according to Captain Lord
Through the thickest ice after 3-4 miles; if his overnight position was correct, at 6.20 a.m. he still had 15½ miles to go.

Exactly how slowly the ship moved when she first set out was indicated by Stewart (who was responsible for writing up the log).

"What pace were you making for the first three or four miles?" he was asked by Clement Edwards.[7]

"We were going very, very slow," said Stewart. He could not give any idea "how slow", because he said he had not been on the bridge very much at that time.

"Just crawling through?" Edwards suggested.

"Just crawling through the ice," Stewart agreed.[8]

The interesting and important thing about this is, that if the estimate is correct and the *Californian* steamed even as much as four miles through the ice in the first 20 minutes, she must then have had still another 15½ to go before she reached the given position of the *Titanic,* that is, if the overnight position of the *Californian* as 19½ miles from where the *Titanic* sank was correct.

Let us go back to see something more of what happened aboard the *Californian,* when the news about the Titanic was received, and afterwards, during Captain Lord's effort to join in the rescue.

Whether or not Captain Lord himself was excited is not certain, but he could not escape knowledge of the feeling all around him.

Groves was aroused by Stewart with the words, or "words to that effect": "The Titanic has sunk, and the passengers are all in the water ahead of us."[9]

In fact, Groves had already been disturbed by the sound of ropes being thrown on the deck above his head, and he realized that the boats were being got ready to swing out.[10] Before he had time to wonder why, Stewart was in his cabin and telling him to get up onto the bridge. When Groves heard the reason, he jumped straight out of his bunk and dashed the two or three yards diagonally across the alleyway to Stone's cabin.[11]

Stewart had already disappeared about his duties. That very morning, this very mate, and in the approving company of his dawdling skipper, had idled away a whole hour and a half, rather than rush intemperately to the wireless cabin and discover the specific cause of eight recently observed distress rockets. Captain Lord was an efficient and cautious seaman, who metaphorically kept his feet preferably on the ground, but certainly never in the ice, and his Chief Officer was, it appeared, of the same stamp. When it eventually became light, and, as Lord himself later wrote: "was deemed safe for my steamer to proceed," this dashing pair — their minds now possibly not unaware of opportunities for salvage* — finally stripped the veil from the secret, with the appalling result we know.

Thus, Stewart could not now spare another second to give Groves any details, not even to convince his young shipmate that the fantastic news was true, In fact, nobody aboard the *Californian* now had a second to waste. If the captain's heart had throbbed partly at the prospect of material reward, the others were stirred only by eagerness to help the new giant in distress. All hands were up and on the job.

At 6.30, Lord had hauled a coal basket to the main truck,[12] put a man in it, equipped him with binoculars and ordered him to keep a good lookout for the Titanic§ — he probably needed no urging. He had told Chief Engineer Mahan, a Greenock man two years older than himself,[13] to get out all the speed he could and never mind the coal. Lord did not have the resources enjoyed by Rostron aboard his *Carpathia,* but whatever a man could do with the *Californian* by way of preparations, he did. He only wanted to help. So far, all he knew — all anybody aboard knew — was the *Titanic* had gone down, though in view of the contradictory wireless messages received, not even that was yet absolutely certain. It was bad enough. Lord only wanted to help, that was all everybody wanted, no doubt. Meanwhile, the ice was being bumped aside vigorously, the engines banged and pounded out their 13 knots

---

* "That any seaman would wilfully neglect signals of distress is preposterous and unthinkable – there was everything to gain and nothing to lose." Thus Lord who was acutely aware of the possibilities and value of salvage, as he said specifically. He also emphasized the bad wages which were paid in those days. (Letter from Lord to MMSA *Reporter*, 14 August 1912.)

§   See Appendix G.

and more, and in his wireless cabin young Evans was now tapping away at his key almost without stopping to listen. Still over a hundred miles from the disaster,[14] Gilbert William Balfour, a Marconi travelling inspector in the *Baltic*, had the "first signals with the *Carpathia*, but were unable to work him, owing to persistent jamming by the *Californian*, who was talking all the while."[15] Balfour, in the *Baltic's Procès Verbal*, refers to "persistent jamming by *Californian*", "impossible for us to work", "long, irrelevant conversations", "*Californian* still monopolizing the air with his remarks. Carrying on conversations with every station". He was chatting to the German *Prinz Adalbert*, the Russian *Birma* — especially the *Birma* — and his neighbours at sea were to find that he was to go on talking nearly all the morning, till past midday.[16] Not a word of what he said has been preserved, unfortunately. Having been asleep so long, Evans at his wireless was now almost like a child mad with excitement over a new toy.

Thoughtless it may have been, but understandable; and young Evans actually was not only an efficient and responsible operator, but a youth of high principle, unyielding to the temptations which in those days were often dangled before the underpaid telegraphists for interesting, but private, stories.

At some time during the run south, and still before anybody, not even Evans himself, knew the true and appalling nature of the disaster, Evans did manage to find time to talk to Gibson, or, more probably, to listen to Gibson. He told the story in Washington.

Senator Smith asked him: "What did the first mate or any other officer of the ship or member of the crew tell you about Captain Lord being notified three times that a vessel was sending up rockets?"[17]

"Well," Evans began, "we have talked among ourselves, but —"

At which, surprisingly, the Senator sharply interrupted

"One minute. I do not want any idle gossip. If you can recall anything that was said by any officer of your ship about that matter, I would like to have you state it; and if you cannot, say so."

Evans said the mate had not told him anything about it, nor any other officer, but "I think the apprentice did."

"Give it as near as you can," Senator Smith insisted.[18]

"Well," said Evans, "I think he said that the skipper was being called; called three times. I think that is all he said."

"Who was meant by the skipper?" Senator Smith (characteristically) asked.

"The captain, sir."

"Was being called, or had been called?" The curiosities of *Californian* locutions not unreasonably required translation.

"Had been called, sir."

The Senator then asked Evans, twice of course, in successive questions, whether he had heard any officer speak about it.

"Well, I do not remember any other special individual, but I know it was being talked about a lot."

"Collectively?"

"Yes, sir."

"There was a lot of talk about it, but you cannot recall any individual who spoke to you about it?"

"No, sir; except the apprentice. I think he told me that he had called the captain."

"Did this talk occur on board the *Californian*?"

"Yes, sir."

"Immediately after the accident to the *Titanic*?"

The answer which Evans was now to give about when Gibson told him how he had called the captain three times, induced Smith to repeat himself in what at first seems his usual fashion. But, from his insistence and the precise care of his questioning, it seems clear that on this occasion his examination was not only justified but shrewd. Smith must have realized the enormous significance of what Evans had said, and probably he could hardly believe what he had heard.

Had Gibson, then, told Evans about calling Lord, in Smith's words, "Immediately after the accident to the *Titanic*?"

"*Before we got to the* TITANIC; *yes, sir,*" said Evans[19] (Emphasis added).

"Before you reached the *Titanic*?" Smith repeated.

"Before we reached the scene of the disaster," said Evans, lest the words he had used create any ambiguity.

"Monday morning?"

"Yes, sir."

"Before you reached the scene of the disaster?" Smith asked yet again.

"Yes, sir."

And the questioning continues as follows:

"The men on the ship talked about it, did they?"

"Yes, sir."

"Generally?"

"Yes, sir."

"What did they say? What was said?"

"From people taking up the conversation I knew it was said that rockets had been seen — had been fired. They did not know what rockets they were. I know they said that rockets had been fired off, and the captain had been roused."

"How many times?"

"Three times, I think it was, sir."

"Is that all you heard said?"

"That is all I can recollect; yes, sir."

He had more to tell of what was said aboard later, but we must pause here.

Evans makes it clear beyond any reasonable doubt that when the sinking of the *Titanic* first became known aboard the *Californian,* but before there was any word about loss of life, and therefore before the enormity of the possible consequences of the negligence aboard the *Californian* was realized, Gibson instantly and unhesitatingly linked the rockets he had seen with the *Titanic,* and only with the *Titanic*. None of the questions and objections about the rockets — about their not making any sound; reaching only half-mast high; being signals to another (never identified) ship in distress; coming from the wrong direction, indeed some of them not even being rockets at all but shooting stars, and the others, at worst, company signals or Roman Candles, and certainly impossible for any of them to have come from the *Titanic*! — not a single one of these arguments, which later were to become so familiar in the armoury of Captain Lord's supporters, was even thought of by Gibson, at least, early that morning. Nor did his evidence stand alone.

When Groves was called by Stewart, he jumped straight from his bunk, rushed across the alleyway to Stone's cabin and saw him there almost immediately after the Chief Officer had left him.[20]

"I went only to his door,"[21] Groves told Lord Mersey. "He was just getting dressed himself then, and I said, 'Is this right, Mr Stone, about the *Titanic*?' I told him what the Chief Officer had said. He said: 'Yes, old chap, I saw rockets in my watch,' and I went straight back to my cabin."[22]

Groves had not stopped to dress before calling on Stone.[23]

"Did he say where the rockets were, or what sort of rockets, or anything of that sort?" Groves was asked.[24]

"As far as my recollection goes all he said was he had seen rockets in his watch, but at that time I did not pay particular attention to what he said, except that he had mentioned rockets."

"You do not remember more than that he mentioned rockets?"

"No, nothing more."

Mersey, of course, understood and remarked on the importance of the conversation,[25] and urged Groves to try to recollect it. Groves then enlarged it:[26] "Yes, that is right." Stone, he said, confirmed the news about the *Titanic*. "Hurry up and get dressed; we shall be wanted in the boats. I saw rockets in my watch."

"That conveys to me the notion," said Lord Mersey, "that when he said he saw rockets in his watch he was referring to the rockets which he believed had come from the *Titanic*. Did he give you that impression?"

Whatever "impression" Stone gave, it should be pointed out that he had never, in his evidence, told the court he believed the rockets had come from the *Titanic*.

"Well," Groves replied, "it is rather difficult for me to say what impression I got then because I was rather excited, but I have told you what he said to me and what I said to him."

In his memoir of 1957, Groves wrote that Stone's reply on being asked if it was true that the *Titanic* had sunk was: "Yes, I saw her firing rockets in my watch."

The importance of the incident lies not in the exact words used by Stone, but in the undoubted fact that he, exactly like Gibson, instantly mentioned the rockets he had seen when the sinking of the *Titanic* first became known.

Having dressed quickly and got to the bridge by about 6.50, Groves was told by Lord to turn his glass on the ship, some five miles to the east on the port beam, which was soon to be identified as the *Carpathia*. Then, for the first time, came an unequivocal indication of the terrible news.

"After I had been looking at her," said Groves, "I made out she had her house flag half-mast."[27]

At this, Lord Mersey asked what seems a strange question even for an ordinary informed layman, let alone a former President of the Admiralty Court.

"What is that?"

"Her company's flag," Groves explained.

"Is there any significance in its being half-mast?" Lord Mersey continued in a manner worthy of Senator Smith himself.

"It is half-masted for death, my Lord."

"That is how you understood it at the time?" Mr Rowlatt resumed the questioning.[28]

"That is what I understood it to mean."

"It was because of the disaster to the *Titanic* that this vessel was flying her house-flag half-mast?"

"Yes."

As the *Californian* had rushed on, the news of the rockets quickly spread through the ship. Nobody, of course, spoke to Captain Lord about the matter, but it seems that by the time the half-masted Cunard house flag brought its plain announcement of death an excited discussion was already under way.

The *Californian* continued steaming south along the edge of the ice "for a little time," said Groves, "after I had told the Captain she had a red funnel with a black top and the house-flag half-masted, and the next thing that was done we starboarded."

In fact, they seem to have overshot the mark. Lord said the *Carpathia* bore north-east from him, which agrees with Rostron's very important statement contained in an affidavit sworn in New York on 4 June:

> "The first time that I saw the *Californian* was at about eight o'clock on the morning of 15 April. She was then about five to six miles distant, bearing W.S.W. true, and steaming towards the *Carpathia*."[29]

This estimate of the time he first saw the *Californian* is a repetition of Rostron's official report to the Cunard at Liverpool of his experiences, which had first been published on 20 April, about six weeks earlier:

"At 8 a.m. the Leyland steamship *Californian* came up. I gave him the principal news and asked him to search and I would proceed to New York."[30]

The first comment, and much the less important, to be made on the passages from Rostron's affidavit of 4 June, quoted above, is this: whatever the distance between the *Californian's* starting point and the *Carpathia,* it is clear from both Lord and Rostron that the final leg of the *Californian's* approach was from somewhere in the south-west, not on the west to east course as shown on the charts issued, through many years, by the supporters of Captain Lord.

But the last scene as the *Californian* finally reached the *Carpathia* has yet to be described. Whatever the exact time — Lord put it at 8.30 — the Cunarder was busy taking the survivors aboard from the *Titanic's* boats, absorbed in the climax of the operation, which was to make her the most famous rescue ship in maritime history.

The *Californian* came to within half a mile of the *Carpathia* and stopped.[31] The *Carpathia,* having put a signal on her jumper stay that she wanted to semaphore,[32] asked as her first question if the *Californian* had any survivors aboard. It must have tasted bitter. But the *Californian* did not, of course, yet know any details, and according to Bisset, an officer on the wing of her bridge signalled with hand flags: "What's the matter?" At Rostron's order, Bisset replied:

"*Titanic* hit berg and sank here with loss of fifteen hundred lives. Have picked up all her boats with seven hundred survivors. Please stay in vicinity to search for bodies."[33]

Groves's version — and he is the other principal source — was that Lord himself, immediately after saying he had no survivors aboard, asked if he could be of any assistance and got the answer, "No."[34] Who was signalling from the *Californian* is not stated, but it was not Groves, although he was reading the messages. Groves told his story a month to the day after it happened; Bisset wrote his 47 years later; but there is no important difference between them.

The two ships got into wireless communication, and, Bisset said, Rostron sent a message: "I am taking the survivors to New York. Please stay in the vicinity and pick up any bodies." According to Groves, it was "Captain Lord [who] suggested that we should search down to leeward."[35]

At 9 o'clock, the *Carpathia,* in bright sunshine, was steaming away to the south-west.[36] Groves said it was "almost exactly 9 a.m., because I heard her bell strike."[37]

With two sharp strokes on the bell of the departing *Carpathia* clanging over the ice-scarred sea — and in that hour some must have recalled the tolling of a funeral bell — the *Californian* began her search.[38] Lord described what he saw. The *Carpathia* had taken aboard 13, which was most of the *Titanic's* boats, and was carrying them to New York;[39] but Lord found "several".[40]

One of the boats contained four or five suitcases abandoned by the passengers.[41]

There were also "deck-chairs, cushions, planks."[42]

"Collapsible boats?"

"I saw two collapsible boats."

"Any wreckage?"

"Yes."

"Much?"

"Not a great deal."

It was generally agreed that compared with the magnitude of the catastrophe, there was little wreckage.

He found no lifebelts floating, or bodies. And, of course, nobody living.[43] Lord was an unemotional man, cold in manner, and certainly not "theatrical". Yet, icily rational though he was, he may have hoped to find somebody living. He searched carefully and diligently, of course; but he failed to join in the rescue, and fate denied him the smallest comfort.

Sources

1 US 728.
2 Ibid.
3 B 7406-9.
4 B 6675.
5 US 716.
6 US 718.
7 B 8780-81.
8 B 8783.
9 B 8297.
10 Groves, 'The Middle Watch'.
11 B 8301-02.
12 US 721.
13 Official Log.
14 US 1057, 1056.
15 Ibid.
16 US 1058, 1063.
17 US 744.
18 US 745.
19 Ibid.
20 B 8299.
21 B 8310.
22 B 8307.
23 B 8302.
24 B 8305-06.
25 B 8308.
26 B 8310-11.
27 B 8331.
28 B 8335.
29 B 25551.
30 *Boston Post*, 20 April 1912.
31 *Tramps and Ladies*, p. 291.
32 B 8354.
33 *Tramps ans Ladies*, p. 292.
34 B 8359-60.
35 B 8362.
36 *Tramps and Ladies*, p. 295.
37 B 8367.
38 US Senate Report, p. 13.
39 Ibid.
40 B 7031.
41 B 7031-38.
42 B 7031.
43 B 7031-38.

Chapter 9

Where was the *Californian*?

"Until now, the two great unknowns in the tale were the actual position of the *Titanic* and the actual position of the *Californian*." So wrote Dr Robert Ballard, one of the three expedition leaders who had found the wreck of *Titanic* in 1985. "The stern section sits on the ocean bottom at 49° 56' 54" W, 41° 43' 35" N . . . (The centre of the bow section is located at 49° 56' 49"W, 41° 43' 57" N.) This means the *Titanic* sank roughly 13.5 miles east-south-east [sic] of her CQD position."[1]

The stern section is here considered, as this part of the wreck is judged the closest to the position where the *Titanic* sank.[2]* The exact distance from the CQD position, in a straight line and in modern terms, is then 13.0 miles at a bearing of 101° true from North (or 13.0 miles east by south in 1912 terms). In practical terms it puts the *Titanic* 12.75 miles east and 2.4 miles south of her CQD position. These figures would not have surprised a number of reliable witnesses who had sped to the rescue of the *Titanic* in the early hours of 15 April 1912.

By accepting Dr Ballard's figures, we know now the most probable final position of the *Titanic*. However, this still leaves any impartial reader with the important question: 'Where was the *Californian*?'

Before we consider that important question, let us first look at the navigational evidence concerning the *Titanic* and what the friends of Captain Lord have said about it.

"One man's guess against scientific navigation! That's what they had to accept to condemn Captain Lord!"

So said supporters of the scientific navigator, Captain Lord, concerning the *Titanic's* position, the guesser being Fourth Officer Boxhall, who had worked it out, and, it was alleged, guessed wrong. In fact, said the Lordites, the *Titanic* was miles farther South than her CQD latitude of 41.46N, and therefore really out of sight from the *Californian*. All this was part of the plot, it was said, to saddle Lord with the blame.

"They wanted a bloody goat", Lord, as an old man reported his friend Frank Strachan§ saying, "and they got you!"[3]

---

* To the layman this may be also the position where the *Titanic* sank. Expert opinion, however, will differ. Dr. G. Langelaar, former head of the Technical Department of Smit International, the renowned Dutch salvage company, stressed that a number of factors (sinking time, drift, underwater current, the amount of air trapped in the ship) may cause the wreck to "plane a couple of miles (2-3 miles) away from its surface position". (P.I.)

§ Frank Strachan, Leyland agent in the US (Brunswick, Ga.) He later got Lord a job with Latta.

He laughed too, though bitterly, and there is no doubt he believed it.

The truth, however, has little to do with guesswork, and nothing at all to do with a plot against Lord.

We turn first to the *Titanic* herself. The starting point is at 7.30 on the Sunday night, when Lightoller, on the 6-10 watch, took stellar observations,[4] "and they were beautiful observations," said Boxhall.[5]

Boxhall, as we have already said, at 28, had been at sea for 13 years,[6] had an Extra Master's certificate, and had had twelve months' training in navigation and nautical astronomy in a navigation school in Hull. It was he who worked out the position of the *Titanic* after the accident from Lightoller's observations, and so if he did guess on that immensely important occasion, he was, at least, well equipped. Let us see what happened.

"Would there not be some danger of your mistaking a figure," Senator Burton asked him in Washington, "or something of that kind, that is, written down by another person?"[7]

"When you take stars," Boxhall explained, "you always endeavour, as they did that night, to take a set of stars. One position checks another. You take two stars for latitude, and two stars for longitude, one star north and one star south, one star east and one star west. If you find a big difference between eastern and western stars, you know there is a mistake somewhere. But, as it happened, I think I worked out three stars for latitude and I think I worked out three stars for longitude."[8]

"And they all agreed?"[9]

"They all agreed," said Boxhall.

Lightoller, it seems, had carefully got not one star, not two, but three each for latitude and longitude. It would have been an exceptional *gaffe*, it is said, if Boxhall had, starting with those sights, got the ship's position wrong. But, of course, it was the 7.30, not the disaster, position he was working out "after 8 o'clock". The figuring took some time. "Yes," he said, "I finished before 10 o'clock, because I gave Mr Lightoller the results when I finished."[10]

The probability is that he had at least a correct starting point for the later calculation, in the form of a correct ascertained position. Unfortunately, with the loss of the *Titanic's* log, we do not know the 7.30 position.

We turn next to Boxhall's London evidence, where he gave a detailed account of the means by which he arrived at his famous "41.46 N.; 50.14 W.".

The Solicitor-General asked Boxhall: "So that what you had to do after the disaster had occurred would be to take the position on the chart at 7.30, take your course, take your speed and calculate where you would be?"[11]

"Yes, from the 7.30 position I allowed a course and distance which gave the position. I worked it out for 11.46 as a matter of fact."

This is a point to note. Most other observers put the time of the collision at 11.40. Boxhall, however, having put it six minutes later, in effect allowed the ship six minutes more steaming, and, at full speed; or, at any rate, the fastest speed she had yet achieved.

"Can you tell me," Simon went on, "what speed you assumed as between the 7.30 position and the time you struck?"

"Twenty-two knots."[12]

Lord Mersey intervened: "Is that right?," and Simon then asked Boxhall why he took 22 knots?

"I thought the ship was doing 22 knots," was the obvious, but not very illuminating, answer. But the questions that followed did elicit the information, given without prevarication or hesitation, that precisely explained the factors in Boxhall's reckoning.

"Was it an estimate," Simon continued, "you formed on any materials as to revolutions or as to the patent log?"

"No," said Boxhall, "I never depend on the patent log* at all. It was an estimate I had arrived at from the revolutions, although I had had no revolutions that watch; but taking into consideration that it was smooth water and that there ought to have been a minimum of slip, I allowed 22 knots."

"As far as you remember, was there any discussion as to whether 22 knots would be right, or did you do it on your own?"

"I did it on my own; there was no discussion at all."

Simon was asking Boxhall if he thought "now" that he had "formed a proper estimate", when Lord Mersey interrupted with another, and also very pertinent, question: "Did you ask the Captain as to the speed?"

"No, I did not," Boxhall answered.[13]

In the talk given by Commander Boxhall in 1959 about the *Titanic,* he explained that Captain Smith told him the first position sent out was "the 8 p.m. dead reckoning one, and asked how it compared with the 7.30 p.m. star position, and was told that this showed the ship to be ahead of the DR position. Thereupon he [Captain Smith] gave orders that this should be given to the wireless operator for transmission. And that, explained Commander Boxhall, was why the *Carpathia* received two positions."[14]

The dispute, of course, was about the final position, and this was the one which Sir John Simon was investigating.

"As far as you know now, as far as you see now from the information you have, and had, is 22 knots about right?"

"Yes," said Boxhall, "I feel pretty easy on that."

Fifty-two years later, when I asked him much the same question, I received much the same answer.

But Captain Lord's supporters were far from easy about it all. On the contrary, when they applied their minds to the passage quoted, it seemed not only the veritable anatomy of a guess, but one of the grosser outrages of the outrageous twentieth century. And, it had been perpetrated at the expense of Captain Lord.

It is also worth observing, that, when all is said, Boxhall undoubtedly wanted his ship to be found and himself, at least, to be saved!

A master mariner asked for an expert opinion, has said: "Boxhall was asked to do just a simple job and he did it adequately." Nor is that the last word about Boxhall's guesswork.

In Washington, Senator Burton had another, separate hearing with Boxhall. Remembering what Boxhall was to disclose later in London about the methods he had used to obtain the position of which he was so sure, he gave a piece of information to Senator Burton that has the authentic and unexpected ring: "One of the first things that Captain Rostron said after I met him was: 'What a splendid position that was you gave us.'"

Boxhall was than asked what position he had given, and he answered, of course, "41.46 and 50.14."[15]

"And you are satisfied that was correct?"

"Perfectly."

The senator finished the matter with another question about Rostron.

"You are sure it was right, and Captain Rostron said it was?"

"Captain Rostron said it was a very, very good position," he insisted.[16]

---

* It read 260 miles at the time of the collision, Q.M. Rowe told Senator Burton, i.e. for about 11 hours and 40 minutes of steaming. Not allowing for slip or drift, we obtain a speed of about 22.3 knots.

"I may state this," Captain Rostron informed Senator Smith and his colleagues, "that the position given me by the *Titanic* was absolutely correct and she was absolutely on her track, bound for New York."[17] Seventy four years later Dr Ballard confirmed Rostron's conclusion about the *Titanic's* track by stating that "the *Titanic* was exactly on course".[18]

Captain Lord's own proceedings when fixing his overnight position were not subjected to anything like the minute scrutiny to which Boxhall had to submit — the complaint of Lord indeed was that his figures were rejected almost without examination — but he described what he did, in his affidavit of 25 June 1959:

"Allowing S.89.W (true) 120 miles from my noon position, and also taking into account the latitude by Pole Star at 7.30 p.m., I calculated my position as being 42°5' N., 50°7'W."[19]

It will be noted that Lord did pretty much what Boxhall did. Lord had the advantage of Stewart's Pole Star sight at 7.30; but Boxhall had Lightoller's cast-iron (one would have thought) three stars, also at 7.30. The *Californian* sent out her position by wireless, and so, as we well know, did the *Titanic*. In fact, the big difference between them, we are told, is that Lord got his figures right and Boxhall (and presumably Lightoller as well) got his wrong.

Now let us look at the *Californian* herself, and see how her case is put by Captain Lord. His noon position on the Sunday, 14 April, was 42.5N; 47.25W, by observation, and at 5 o'clock Stone took two observations of the sun to check the longitude. These details are reported in the affidavit sworn by Captain Lord. Of more interest is the fact, which has already been described soon after the beginning of the story, that about half-past six (Groves put it an hour earlier), the *Californian* passed three icebergs five miles to the South. The interest of the occurrence lies in the action Lord took at 7.30, which was to send a report of these bergs to the *Antillian,* giving his position as 42.5N; 49.9W. This, of course, was hours before the disaster, and, as Lord said, there could be no question of preparing an alibi. At 7.30, Stewart reported a latitude by Pole Star of 42.5°N, and finally, when the ship stopped in the ice at 10.21 that night, Lord worked out his position as 42.5N; 50.7W.[20] His course had been S89W (true).

Up to this point, there can be no question whatever, whether Lord's reckoning and that of his officers was right or wrong, of any attempt at deception or falsification. How and when and why Captain Lord came to insist that the *Titanic* was really 30 or 32 miles south of him when she hit the berg — 11 or 13 miles farther than she reported — is another matter; but once he made it a keystone in his defence, he never yielded an inch in his reliance on that argument. Both the American and British inquiries refused to accept his figures.

After the verdicts had been given, on 17 October, Lord wrote to A.H. Gill, his Member of Parliament:

"As I mentioned to you in Bolton some time ago, I admit there was a certain amount of 'slackness' aboard the 'Californian' the night in question, but I strongly maintain that the position I gave at the enquiry was correct, and there hasn't been any evidence produced to prove the contrary, and until such evidence is produced or proof of my log-book being 'cooked' I am entitled to the benefit of that document."[21]

This letter, found in the Board of Trade files, raises more than one point. One wishes in vain to know what "slackness" Captain Lord spoke about to Mr

Gill. His supporters admit none. But it is no more than his opinion that there had been no evidence to prove his position wrong.

Looking now at the *Carpathia,* it is evident that, for the supporters of Captain Lord, no ship is more awkward to criticize than this celebrated rescue vessel that had sped to the *Titanic's* rescue and ultimately took all survivors to New York. Yet, an essential part of the argument that the *Titanic* was far south of her given position depended on showing that the *Carpathia* did not know where she was going, or where she was when she got there. It is a situation which might seem to call for a certain degree of tact. But to the defenders of the *Californian,* one, Boxhall, was a careless guesser; the other, Bisset, in the *Carpathia,* was the author of "a tissue of nonsense" and a "twister of facts". How then does Captain Rostron of the *Carpathia,* whom Bisset described as "my old friend, superior and shipmate", "my old friend and mentor",[22] fare with these stern, if hardly modest, judges, the Lordites?

The *Carpathia's* own story of her voyage is to be found in two main sources: the evidence of her captain at the US inquiry in New York, and later in London, and from two books. The first of these is Rostron's volume of memoirs, *Home From the Sea,* published in 1931, and the other, Bisset's second volume of his trilogy, *Tramps and Ladies,* which did not appear until 1960.

Whatever support there was from the *Carpathia* herself that she did not actually have to steam 58 miles to reach the scene of the disaster derives from Bisset's book, and it is understandably given much weight by Captain Lord's defenders. It is only as a witness against the *Californian* that they regard Sir James Bisset as "so wide of the mark" that what he writes is presumably not even worth mentioning.

Bisset's evidence "against" his own ship, the *Carpathia,* is a different matter. (It should be made clear that the word 'against' certainly did not express Bisset's intention, but is chosen here to express the use made of his narrative by those who claim to deduce a contradiction between it and what was arithmetically possible).

Bisset informs his readers that at 2.40 a.m., when the *Carpathia* still had 25 miles to go,[23] they sighted a green light, which at first was thought to be the *Titanic's* starboard light, but later was known to have been only a flare from Boxhall's boat. It is said it would have been impossible to see such a flare from that distance. Five minutes later, at 2.45, Bisset spotted an iceberg and reported it to Rostron, who "reacted promptly in a seamanlike manner, altering course to starboard and reducing to half speed." When he was sure the ship was clear and no other obstruction in sight, he put her back on her course, and resumed full speed. This was certainly some diminution of the run at full speed.

At 3.15, Bisset writes, the *Carpathia* was "within twelve miles of the *Titanic's* wirelessed position." It is pointed out that in spite of the slackening of speed to avoid the 2.45 iceberg, which, however brief, according to Bisset himself, certainly took place, the *Carpathia* must have steamed 13 miles in the 35 minutes between 2.40, when she sighted the green flare, and 3.15. As Bisset says she was making 16 knots, this was clearly impossible. The probable explanation is that the time of "2.40" for sighting the green flare was too early and more likely, after 2.50 but before 3.30, the *Carpathia* was then already much closer to the CQD position.

At 3.30, half an hour before the arrival, "there were numerous bergs surrounding us, and small growlers of ice grinding along our hull plates." At this time, therefore, Captain Rostron is reported by Bisset, so it is said, to have reduced speed to "Half" for the last 30 minutes of the run and then to

"Slow". This, however, is a clear misreading of Bisset's story. He writes:

> "Captain Rostron reduced speed to half, and then to slow, as the *Carpathia* was steered cautiously towards a green flare sighted low in the water, at a distance difficult to judge in the continuing peculiar conditions of visibility. It appeared likely but at first was not certain, that this flare was from a lifeboat."

The reduction of speed to Half — if it took place — began not at 3.30, when the icebergs surrounded the *Carpathia,* but only from the time, which is not stated, when she began steering towards the green flare. The engines were stopped at 4 a.m., and they arrived in three and a half hours.

It is clear that apart from the question of the *Carpathia's* speed during the last half-hour, her distance to the scene of the wreck, as Bisset describes the run, could not have been 58 miles.

Bisset's account of the *Carpathia's* famous dash to the rescue in any event is not unique, for Rostron also told the story, and there is a difference between them about the speed of their ship:

> "The *Carpathia* was a fourteen-knot ship, but that night for three and a half hours she worked up to seventeen knots. One of the first things I did, naturally, was to get up the Chief Engineer, explaining the urgency of matters and, calling out an extra watch in the engine-room, every ounce of power was got from the boilers and every particle of steam used for the engines, turning it from all other uses, such as heating."

Those lines appeared in 1931, 19 years after the *Titanic;* but within days — almost within hours — of the wreck, Rostron had been examined in detail about the speed he had maintained. This was the evidence he gave in New York on 19 April 1912, the opening day of the Senate investigation.

"I knew the *Titanic* had struck ice," Rostron said.[24] "Therefore, I was prepared to be in the vicinity of ice when I was getting near him . . . I went full speed, all we could —"

"You went full speed?" asked Senator Smith. It was his first morning, indeed his first hour, and he lost no time in starting to prove that the twentieth century had discovered one of its most exasperating characters. Still, William Alden Smith was a good man and better equipped than most, for he had a built-in repeater.

"I did," said Rostron, "and doubled my lookouts, and took extra precautions and exerted extra vigilance. Every possible care was taken. We were all on the *qui vive*."

It was in London, almost exactly two months later, on 21 June, that Rostron told the same story and testified that he had got up to 17½ knots out of the *Carpathia*.[25] One further quotation from the London evidence is worth giving, for it provides a convincing detail about the speed the ship was making. The Attorney-General was asking about the iceberg which caused Rostron to put the ship's "helm hard-a-starboard and put her head around quick and pick up"[26] the first boat (Boxhall's) on the starboard side, instead of the port, as he had at first intended.

". . . At what speed were you going when you saw this iceberg about a quarter of a mile from you?"[27]

"I should think we were making something about 15; the engines had been stopped for about three minutes — probably between 13 and 15 knots at the time."

The question was later repeated.

"Then you say, although your engines had stopped and had been stopped for something like three minutes, you were still making somewhere about 13 to 15 knots?"[28]

"Yes."

Now, these questions and answers taken from the New York and London hearings all seem so clear that they would need no comment, were it not for a passage in Mr Harrison's article, "The 'Californian' Incident", of March 1962. There he says of the *Carpathia* that "only slightly over two hours of her dash to the rescue" were made "at a steady course and speed". The remainder of the time she was zig-zagging through many icebergs ("a feat of seamanship for which there can be nothing but the highest praise"), and the last 25 minutes she was going "cautiously" "at slow speed".

The version of Rostron's story is in places substantially different from Bisset's (though not nearly so much as asserted by the Lordites); but is unquestionably a flat contradiction of Mr Harrison.

As a footnote to the statement that the *Carpathia* was "zig-zagging through many icebergs", Rostron was asked in London, by the Attorney-General about them —

"As I understand, from what you tell us, you saw six bergs from a quarter to 3 to 4 o'clock?"[29]

"Yes, we passed these to get up to the position," he replied.

In fact, he gave a similar reply to four similar questions in all.[30] Rostron was not a man given to exaggeration, and when it came to stating their number he said they had seen six icebergs, but no more; and dangerous enough though they were, they were probably not so hampering to speed or course as is implied by Mr Harrison's phrase, "zig-zagging through many icebergs". Rostron himself makes no such suggestion.

Mr Padfield says Rostron "was never specifically asked whether he had *slackened* [emphasis in original] speed at all during this time, while he was dodging the bergs."[31]

He may not have been asked, but nevertheless he supplied the information, and indeed summed up the whole question of the speed of his ship. This appeared in a passage in his book,[32] additional to what he had said at the two inquiries, and it also differed from Bisset's statement that they slowed down when the first iceberg was encountered.

"Almost at once" Rostron wrote "the second officer [i.e. Bisset] reported the first iceberg. It lay two points on the port bow and it was the one whose presence was betrayed by the star beam. More and more now were we all keyed up. Icebergs loomed up and fell stern; *we never slackened, though sometimes we altered course suddenly to avoid them* [emphasis added]. It was an anxious time with the *Titanic's* fateful experience very close to our minds. There were seven hundred souls on the *Carpathia;*[*] these lives, as well as all the survivors of the *Titanic* herself, depended on a sudden turn of the wheel."

But clear as Rostron is that the *Carpathia* not only did not slow down, but kept going all out until she arrived within a few hundred yards of Emergency Boat No. 2 about 4 a.m. one of Rostron's officers has said to me, "he always insisted that he found the *Titanic* exactly where he figured he would."

Mr Harrison, in the article already quoted, has said, on the other hand, ". . . there can be no doubt that the *Carpathia* actually encountered the lifeboats at least ten, and more probably 18 miles to the south-eastward of the DR position given by the *Titanic*."

---

* Bisset says 1,035 – *Tramps and Ladies*, p. 283.

We note here, for instance, that Captain Lord himself put the *Titanic* no more than some 13 miles from her Dead Reckoning position (i.e. about 32 miles south-south-east from the *Californian's* overnight position). Mr Harrison concluded "there can be no doubt" that it was "more probably 18 miles", five miles farther than even Lord himself estimated and no less than 37 miles from the *Californian*.

Before concluding with what Rostron said, there is one circumstance already mentioned, but most apposite here: the *Carpathia's* rockets. The *Californian*, according to Mr Padfield, saw those rockets,[33] either at 3.20, as Gibson and Stone said originally,[34] or possibly about 3.30, when Mr Beesley saw them, or even as late as 3.40.[35] Whenever it was, the *Carpathia* was still about eight miles to the far, or south, side of the *Titanic's* position from the *Californian*. If the latter was 37 miles from there, the rockets must have been 45 miles from the *Californian*.

At Washington, Captain Lord, when asked if he could have seen the *Titanic* rockets 'from the position she was supposed to have been in' (i.e. 19½ miles from the *Californian*) answered: "I do not think so. It would have been way down on the horizon. It might have been mistaken for a shooting star or anything at all."[36]

Gibson saw those three *Carpathia* rockets "right on the horizon",[37] and Stone saw the second "at such a very great distance that if it had been much further, he wouldn't have seen it at all".[38] It is an interesting thought that if the *Carpathia's* rockets were some eight miles beyond the *Titanic's* position, and if the *Californian* was not 19½ miles, as Lord said, from it, but only 10 miles, as both inquiries found, the *Carpathia's* rockets would have been about 18 miles away and not so very different from what Lord described as "way down on the horizon". What is absolutely certain is that the *Californian* could not have seen the *Carpathia's* rockets from 40 miles away, according to Lord's figures, nor *a fortiori* from 45, according to Mr Harrison. Yet the *Californian* did see the *Carpathia's* rockets.

Mr Harrison is also of the opinion that another, subsequent unidentified steamer, saw the "passing" *Carpathia*, while she fired her rockets and sent up her blue Cunard flares.

"What must the watchkeepers in that vessel have thought, and . . . what were they supposed to do? . . Evidently they applied common sense to the problem, shrugged their shoulders, and made no attempt to do anything about it . . . Lord Mersey found no reason for criticism of this technically improper use of distress signals or of its possible consequence of creating confusion in another ship: he did condemn the *Californian*, however, for *her* inactivity when faced with a comparable situation."[39]

One could stop and reflect here if this is Mr Harrison's opinion of a seaman's common sense, but it is of more interest to see if this 'unidentified steamer' cannot be identified.

Captain Rostron told Sir Rufus Isaacs on the 28th day of the inquiry: "We saw mast head lights quite distinctly of another steamer between us and the 'Titanic'. That was about (a) quarter-past three."[40]

"The mast-head lights?"

"Yes, of another steamer, and one of the officers swore he also saw one of the side lights."

"Which one?"

"The port side light," said Rostron who did not see any sidelights himself. (Gibson had seen the rockets two points before the port beam,[41] the *Californian* must thus have been showing the ship firing those rockets her red port light.)

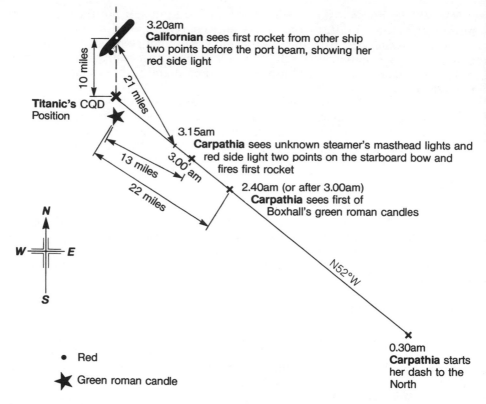

3.20am
Californian sees first rocket from other ship
two points before the port beam, showing her
red side light

10 miles

21 miles

Titanic's CQD
Position

3.15am
Carpathia sees unknown steamer's masthead lights and
red side light two points on the starboard bow and
fires first rocket

3.00 am

13 miles

2.40am (or after 3.00am)
Carpathia sees first of
Boxhall's green roman candles

22 miles

N

W —— E

S

N52°W

×
0.30am
Carpathia starts
her dash to the
North

• Red

⭐ Green roman candle

Diagram 8. *Carpathia's* **dash to the north and sighting of an unknown steamer**
At 12.30 a.m. 15 April, the Carpathia *heads full speed toward the sinking* Titanic, *her course is N52W.*
At 2.40 a.m. the Carpathia *sees Boxhall fire a green Roman Candle — the White Star company signal — half a point on the port bow. If the timing is correct this should be over a distance of some 22 miles.*
At 3.15 a.m. the Carpathia *sees the two masthead lights of a steamer, two point on her starboard bow. One officer says he also sees her red sidelight. Captain Rostron thinks the ship is between him and the* Titanic.
At about the same time, 3.15 a.m., the Carpathia *fires the first of her three rockets. At 3.20 a.m. Gibson in the* Californian *sees the first of the three rockets, two points before the port beam, from the new stranger coming up from the south-east.*
The line of direction, in which the Carpathia *saw the stranger, crosses some ten miles north of the position Captain Rostron in the* Carpathia *was heading for. The only ship seen at dawn on the line in which the* Carpathia *saw the masthead lights and a red port light was none other than Captain Lord's command — the* Californian. *(Or, as Mr A.M.Foweraker in 1913 called her: 'The mystery ship X'.)*

"And how was the light bearing?" Lord Mersey wanted to know.
"About two points on the starboard bow."[42]
"On your starboard bow?"
"On my starboard bow; that would be about N. 30, W. true," explained Rostron.
When this information is projected on a chart the unidentified steamer is no longer a complete stranger.
The line, on which Rostron and his officers saw the steamer, crosses about ten

miles, or less, north of where the *Carpathia* found the lifeboats. In that position the *Californian* was seen at dawn, before she got underway (see Diagram 8).

Rostron may have thought that the stranger was *between* him and the *Titanic;* but it is more likely that she was not and that she was in fact North of where the *Titanic* had sunk.

If we now apply Mr Harrison's questions and answer to this more familiar ship, we see that she never was that much of a stranger anyway: particularly the questions 'What must the watchkeepers in that vessel have thought, what were they supposed to do?' and the answer: 'they made no attempt to do anything about it,' seem to apply to only one known ship that night, and she was none other than the *Californian.*

In January 1913 J.D. McNabb had, like Mr Harrison, struggled with the unidentified steamer too.[43] A map supplied by his anonymous friend the "Sea Lawyer" showed the bearing of the steamer seen by the *Carpathia,* projected over the track of McNabb's mysterious steamer X as seen by the *Californian.*

Turning back to the *Titanic;* it was admittedly more due to Rostron than to anybody else that her reported position was generally unquestioned.

"The great thing about Rostron was, he was a great navigator." So wrote a former shipmate, who served under him in several of his commands.[44]

"There was nothing slapdash about Rostron & of the navigators around that night I would certainly place Rostron & his team at the top of the list. *I have no doubt at all that had Rostron been Master of the* Californian *that night all the lives would have been saved* [emphasis in original]."[45]

Rostron was certainly not infallible; no man is (Captain Lord, of course, according to his supporters, alone excepted), and he says, for instance, of the *Californian* , "she carried no wireless . . ." though that mistake is understandable and pardonable. But he continues, ". . . and all the night had been lying not many miles away, hove to because of the ice."[46]

Next, and of capital importance in the whole story, is Captain Rostron's statement that neither of the ships he saw when daylight came was the *Californian.* "It was daylight about 4.20 a.m. At 5 o'clock it was light enough to see all round the horizon. We then saw two steamships to the northwards, perhaps seven or eight miles distant. Neither of them was the *Californian.* One of them was a four-masted steamer with one funnel, and the other a two-masted steamer with one funnel."

Now, if the *Californian* was in fact only ten miles north of the *Titanic's* position, why did Captain Rostron not see her, why did he actually deny that she was there? It is hardly surprising that Rostron's words should invariably be cited as strong evidence in Lord's favour. There is also a surprising answer to this question.

Let us thus look at what another observer from the *Carpathia* says about the first sighting of the *Californian.*

"While we had been picking up the survivors," Sir James writes in his second volume, *Tramps and Ladies*: "in the slowly increasing daylight after 4.30 a.m., we had sighted the smoke of a steamer on the fringe of the pack ice, ten miles away from us to the northwards. She was making no signals, and we paid little attention to her, for we were preoccupied with more urgent matters; but at 6 a.m. we had noticed that she was under way and slowly coming towards us.

"When I took over the watch on the bridge of the *Carpathia* at 8 a.m., the stranger was little more than a mile from us, and flying her signals of identification. She was the Leyland Line cargo-steamer *Californian,* which had been stopped overnight."[47]

There was, it should be noted, only five minutes' difference between *Californian* and *Carpathia* times. Now, the *Carpathia* was stopped soon after four o'clock in what Captain Rostron reckoned was the given position of the *Titanic*.

If the findings of two official inquiries about the distance between the *Californian* and the *Titanic* were correct, Bisset's account of what he saw, and when he saw it, is exactly what might be expected.

But, it may, and should, be asked, why was Bisset alone in bringing this deadly evidence against the *Californian* and Captain Lord? The short answer is, Bisset is not the only witness from the *Carpathia*. When he wrote: ". . . we had sighted the smoke of a steamer . . ." he was not using a formal expression, but making a literal statement. Nor, finally, were he and Captain Rostron at odds.

For convenience, all this hitherto unpublished and decisive material from the *Carpathia,* and the account of its discovery, will be collected and set out in detail in Chapter 19, in the story to be told of the search for the solution to the *Californian* mystery. Nor do the new witnesses come only from the *Carpathia*.

As the *Carpathia* left the scene, Captain Rostron sent a message to the Cunard Line in New York. A copy of it was made at "7.55 a.m." next morning, according to a memorandum on it by somebody in the White Star office, where a Cunard man brought it. There was no hour stated on the Marconigram itself. It read thus:

"Carpathia to Cunard, New York. Latitude 41.45; longitude 50.20 west. — Am proceeding New York unless otherwise ordered, with about 800, after having consulted with Mr Ismay and considering the circumstances. With so much ice about, consider New York best. Large number icebergs, and 20 miles field ice with bergs amongst. ROSTRON."[48]

The *Titanic* had given her latitude as 41.46N. Rostron in the above message said his was 41.45N, a difference of only one minute, or a mile to the south.[49] It is difficult to believe that already early on that Monday morning, 15 April, Captain Rostron had begun fabricating evidence against a man, for whose misfortune he actually felt and expressed the greatest sympathy. Nevertheless Rostron's latitude was much more north than that found by the *Californian*.

The evidence presented by the *Californian* as purported corroboration of her own correct navigation and the fallibility of that of the *Titanic,* was the noonday position of the *Californian* on Monday, 15 April, which was 41.33N; 50.9W[50]

This was afterwards treated as the crucially important observation, but we discover one surprising and most significant thing about it: Lord himself took no part in it. "I did not personally take an observation this day," he swore in his same affidavit of 25 June 1959.

Is it reasonable to suppose that Lord would not even have bothered to take an observation himself that noon, if, at the time, he had regarded his own position of the previous night and that of the *Titanic* of the immense importance he later attributed to both? It may be said in reply, that Lord could not have realized how far south the *Titanic* had been, until after the position at noon was taken; but that is a cock that will not fight, as we shall realize, when we discover just how long afterwards it was, and under what circumstances, Lord first raised the matter of the *Titanic's* position, and why he felt it necessary to push her as far south as he could.

Anyhow, they had good sights, said Stewart; all the officers (except Captain

Lord himself of course) took part in the observation and all agreed.[51] They had travelled about four or five miles from the wreckage, when the observation was made. Basing his calculation on this noon position, Lord reckoned the position of the wreckage, when he left it after abandoning his search, was 41.33N; 50.1W.[52] This would be about 32 miles south of the *Californian's* overnight position of 42.5N; 50.7W,[53] and Lord afterwards maintained that the position of the wreckage was also the real position where the *Titanic* collided with the berg. A mere three hours earlier the *Carpathia* sent out her position on starting back to New York, she had placed this same wreckage at 41.45N, only one mile south of the *Titanic's* reported position, but no less than 12 miles north of Lord's calculation. It is clear that both these ships could not be right; but before any further comment about the startling difference between the two calculations, as one possible test of its correctness, we must try to find out how long after the *Californian* gave up the search, her observation was made.

The *Carpathia,* leaving Captain Lord to search, set off for New York at 9 a.m., with, in Commodore Bisset's words, "our load of sorrow."[54]

"11.20 proceeded on course N. 59 W. by compass." So Captain Lord read his log entry to the tribunals at Washington and London,[55] when he told of the abandonment of his fruitless search. Groves, in his evidence, said the *Californian* searched till "Ten-forty exactly. That is when we resumed our course."[56] How he came to be so precise about the time he did not say; nor was he asked; but, according to him, the search was given up and the course resumed forty minutes earlier than the time stated in the log. Bisset goes even further in truncating the *Californian's* search, for he writes that Captain Rostron received a wireless signal from Lord that he had found no bodies and was resuming his voyage, "An hour later . . .",[57] that is, after the *Carpathia's* own departure, which would be 10 o'clock.

Now, after the MMSA took up Captain Lord's case for the second time many years after the event, in 1959, the General Secretary, Mr Harrison, in his article 'The "Californian" Incident', adduced that the *Californian's* noon position of 41.33N; 50.9W was strong support for Lord's estimate that the true position in which the *Titanic* sank was 41.33N; 50.1W. The reason, wrote Mr Harrison, was that this noon position was taken "barely twenty minutes after they had left the scene on resuming their voyage to Boston." The *Californian's* own log, quoted above, put the time at which she resumed her voyage at "11.20". Hence, the noon position was taken not "barely twenty minutes" later, but at least forty minutes later, and if Groves was right, an hour and twenty minutes later. Bisset would make the lapse of time no less than two hours.

Mr Harrison's mistatement of "barely twenty minutes" for the minimum of forty minutes derived from the *Californian's* own log is typical of the many errors which disfigure, and dilute the effectiveness of the propaganda for Captain Lord.

The next link in the chain of evidence about the overnight position of the *Californian* is Captain James Henry Moore, master of the Canadian Pacific *Mount Temple*. Moore was a veteran with 32 years at sea, 27 of them having been on the North Atlantic.[58]

His ship, the *Mount Temple,*[59] 8,790 tons gross, was bound West for St John, New Brunswick,[60] from London and Antwerp, with 1,461 steerage passengers aboard.[61] At 12.11 a.m.,[62] ATS, which was 1 hour and 46 minutes ahead of New York,[63] 15 April, John Durrant,* the sole wireless operator,

---

*   John Oscar Durrant, 1891-1951.

heard the *Titanic's* distress call. The night steward took the message to the captain,[64] who turned the ship round,[65] worked out the position, and by about 12.30 was going back on a course of N65° true at his full speed of 11½ knots. His own position when he turned back was 41.25N; 51.14W *.[66]

Captain Moore went and saw his Chief Engineer and said: "Go down and try to shake up the fireman, and, if necessary, even give him a tot of rum if you think he can do any more."[67]

He believed the man got his rum. Anyhow, the *Mount Temple* did pretty well. When she turned back, she was about 49[68] § miles from the *Titanic's* position, and at 3.25, when Moore figured he was still 14 miles away, he stopped "on account of the ice getting so thick". After that, he went on again, but slowly.

"We are not to enter field ice under any conditions,"[69] was how Moore described the instructions of the Canadian Pacific to their captains. In these circumstances, and with his custom and practice of exceptional caution, it was an earnest of Captain Moore's courage and efficiency as a master mariner, as well as of his devotion to the humane traditions of his calling, that he set off so promptly and unhesitatingly on his mission of rescue. With his crew, he altogether had aboard about 1,609 persons. It was a considerable responsibility.[70]

Soon after 3 o'clock, Moore had seen a schooner coming from the opposite direction.[71] When the *Mount Temple* started back towards the *Titanic*, there was also a tramp steamer of about 4-5,000 tons on Moore's port bow, going "Almost in the same direction. As he went ahead, he gradually crossed our bow until he got on our starboard bow . . ."

Then, in answer to Senator Smith's question as to "whether her funnel was of any special colour," Captain Moore said: "If I can remember rightly it was black, with some device in a band near the top."[72]

It was about half-past four when the *Mount Temple* finally arrived at what Captain Moore reckoned was the position of the *Titanic*.[73] The tramp which had crossed his bows was a little to the southward and ahead of him,[74] but otherwise she found nothing whatever.[75] There was no sign of the *Titanic* nor of any wreckage, boats or bodies. Confronted by thick ice, the Canadian ship slowed down and stopped, trying in vain to find a way through.

Captain Moore came to the conclusion that the *Titanic* had given the wrong position,[76] and when morning came, he got a prime vertical sight, that is, a sight with the sun bearing due East. He got two observations in fact, one giving him 50°9½'W and the other 50°9¾'W,[77] within a quarter of a mile. He was already some three miles to the eastward of the position the *Titanic* had given, 50°14'W, and so he concluded that as she could not have got through the "great pack of ice", her real longitude must have been still farther east. He figured it as "at least eight miles."[78] On the other hand, he twice made it clear that he found nothing wrong with the latitude given by the *Titanic*.

". . . I think, after all, the *Titanic* was further east than she gave her position, sir," he told Senator Smith. "In fact, I am certain she was."[79]

"East or south?" Smith asked.

---

* A misprint in the hearings on page 759 gives the position as "41° 25' north and 51° 41' west". (Some 68.4 miles, 253° true, from the CQD position.) This is corrected four questions later where Captain Moore states: "The longitude was 51° 14' west." (With the given latitude 41° 25' north this is 49.5 miles, 245° true, from the CQD position.)

§ In fact this was 68.4 miles, bearing 72°, from the CQD position and 80.2 miles, bearing 76°, from where the wreck was found.

"East, sir," said Captain Moore.[80]

And, again, even more emphatically —

"Does the fact that you found no evidence of the wreck," the Senator interrupted him, "when you got to the *Titanic's* reported position tend to confirm you in the idea that her position was eight miles further to the southward?"

"No; to the eastward."[81]

"To the eastward?" Senator Smith repeated.

"Yes," said Captain Moore.[82]

What, then, is the significance of all this, so far as the *Californian* is concerned? Merely this: Captain Lord's supporters made much of the allegation that the *Titanic* got her reckoning wrong, and sent out a wrong position, relying heavily on the evidence of Captain Moore of the *Mount Temple*. The *Titanic,* it is asserted, was actually much farther from the *Californian,* specifically much farther south from the *Californian,* than her given position; but no attention is called to the fact that Captain Moore gave no support whatever to this proposition, for he did not question the given latitude. In fact, he supported it. His first sight of the *Carpathia* was from the reported position of the *Titanic,* when the Cunarder was picking up the boats. She was not, certainly, in the given longitude, but she was in the given latitude, that is, due east and would indeed have been just about where that rocket-firing steamer had been, just about where, next morning, that four-masted discovery of Stewart was lying and no more than a few miles from where 73 years later the French-American expedition found the wreck of the *Titanic.*

But one other matter, and more important by far than Captain Moore's circumstantial and navigational evidence, is a piece of direct evidence in his story. This describes his first sighting of the *Californian.*

Captain Moore said, when he had failed to find a passage through the "ice pack" to the south, he had turned round again and was once more in the reported position of the *Titanic,*[83] "thinking I might pick up some soft place to the North." It was then "about 6 o'clock in the morning". At that time, he sighted the *Carpathia* on the east side of the ice pack. She was about five or six miles away. At the same time, he sighted the *Californian.*[84]

"As I was going to the north," said Captain Moore, "the *Californian* was passing from east to west.[85] . . . He was then north of the *Carpathia,* and he must have been, I suppose, about the same distance to the north of the *Carpathia,* as I was to the westward of her."[86] (See Diagram 9).

In other words, as early as "about six o'clock in the morning" the *Californian* is already no more than five or six miles away from, north of, the *Carpathia.*

The *Californian* at 6.20, according to her log, when having gone "very, very slow" and having "just crawled through" some four miles of ice, according to Stewart's evidence, she began to proceed "at full speed, pushing the ice" — once more in the words of the log.

Lord's evidence was that between six and half-past, he was "making anything between S. and SW."[87] "I was pushing through field ice,"[88] "two or three miles of it"[89] and the *Mount Temple* was in sight.

If Moore is right, and we shall find that his evidence is corroborated and supplemented in most convincing fashion, the value of the time factor as proof in itself of the alleged great distance of the *Californian's* overnight position from the *Titanic's* CQD position is at an end. The fact that from the time, about 6 o'clock, when the *Mount Temple* sighted the *Californian,* then only five or six miles north of the *Carpathia,* the *Californian* still required considerable time to reach the *Carpathia* was due almost entirely to the great

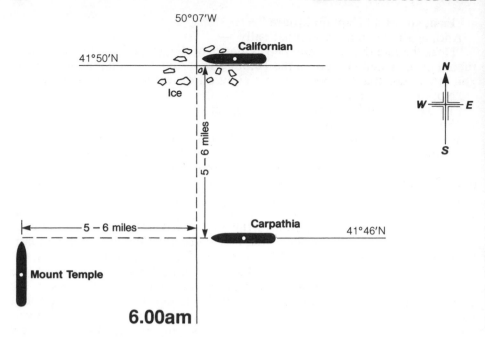

Diagram 9. The *Californian's* distance from the *Carpathia:* according to Captain Moore in *Mount Temple*
Captain Moore in the Mount Temple, *five-six miles west of the* Carpathia, *sights the* Californian, *which he estimated was five-six miles north of the* Carpathia.

difficulty of the approach through the ice, both at the beginning and when she had to turn to reach the *Carpathia.*

If there be any question about the effect of the difference of time on the sighting by Captain Moore, it should be noted that the difference according to the evidence of the respective Marconi operators, Evans and Durrant, between the *Californian* and the *Mount Temple* was only nine minutes.* [90]

It is also a remarkable fact that the very first independent evidence which serves as a test of the *Californian's* overnight position at once shakes its credibility. Needless to say that, so far as I know, this is nowhere mentioned in any of their numerous writings on behalf of Captain Lord.

A piece of circumstantial evidence must now be taken into the story, for it strongly suggests that when the *Californian* started from her overnight position she must have been farther south than Lord believed, even taking into account some 7½ hours of drift. Lord estimated that he was not clear of the ice until half-past six and covered only "two or three miles" while he was in it. If he was right, he would still have to cover at least 16½ miles before he reached the *Titanic* position, marked, as he agreed, by the *Mount Temple.* [91] The highest estimate of his speed he gave at Washington, was 13-13½ knots. In London, he attributed the latter figure to his Chief Engineer. "I estimate it at 13," he said. [92] He had passed the *Mount Temple* at half-past seven, Lord also said. Granting all the maximum figures in his own favour, and disregarding the probability that even when the *Californian* broke out of the thickest ice, she still could not steam by the shortest route, we are still faced by the arithmetical difficulty of getting this hypothetical 13½ knot steamship over 16½

* *Evans:* 1 hr 55' ahead of New York; *Durrant:* 1 hr 46' ahead.

miles in 60 minutes at the outside, though again we know it is very probable she passed the *Mount Temple* a good while before 7.30. Even if drift of a whole knot is added, the *Californian* is still light by two miles. So much for Captain Lord's own figures.

Let us, however, try another available set of figures. Characteristically, these derive from his loyal Chief Officer, being more in favour of his master than Lord's own. Moreover, they are conveniently, if not perhaps quite convincingly, supported by the log.

In his evidence, Stewart's description of the "very, very slow pace"[93] of the *Californian* through the ice, when she was "just crawling",[94] applied not to Lord's "two or three miles", but to "three or four".[95] According to the log, however, which was kept by Stewart, it was not half-past six, as Lord said, when they were clear of the ice, but "6.20".[96] Both Lord and Stewart were almost certainly guessing; but let us now accept Stewart's guesses. If the *Californian* completed her 'crawl' by 6.20, during which she covered four miles, she would still have to steam another 15½ by 7.30. At 13½ knots. It is by arithmetic theoretically possible. Practically, it seems improbable.

There is only one clear and realistic alternative, and that is, that the distance between the starting point of the *Californian's* dash to the south and the *Titanic-Mount Temple* position was substantially less than the 19½ miles calculated by Lord. This means that her overnight position must have been farther south than reckoned.

The Mersey findings were that the assessors had advised that the distance of the *Californian* from the *Titanic* was "not more than eight to ten miles."[97]

There is other cogent evidence, and from the *Californian* herself, which tends to confirm Captain Moore's estimate that the *Californian* was only five or six miles north of the *Carpathia* "about six o'clock in the morning". This comes from Third Officer Groves, who gave much graphic and convincing detail.

Groves was woken by Stewart about 6.40, told that the *Titanic* had sunk and that he was wanted on the bridge.[98] He dressed and went up, by which time the ship "had got a good speed on" and the lifeboats were being swung out.[99]

"Now it is getting on for 7?" he was asked.

"I suppose by the time I got on the bridge it would be about 6.50; but you understand the time is only approximate."[100]

Asked if there were any other vessels in sight, Groves said: "There was a four-masted steamer abeam on our port side."[101]

"What steamer was that?"

"I did not know at the time, but I knew afterwards she was the *Carpathia*." (See Diagram 11).

He did not know which direction the *Californian* was going, but he thought the *Carpathia* was about five miles off — "possibly more, possibly less, but about five."[102]

"Did you look at her with the glass?"[103]

"I did."

"Who asked you to do that, anybody?"

"The captain."

He made out her red funnel with a black top and her house flag. He also saw two other vessels, one being the *Mount Temple*, which was on their starboard side, when he first saw her.[104]

"How far off was she, do you think?"[105]

"Well, when I noticed her first — I had been paying particular attention to this other steamer [*Carpathia*] — I should think she would be perhaps a mile and a half away from us."

"Nearer than the *Carpathia?*"

"Much nearer than the *Carpathia.*"

When Groves saw the *Mount Temple,* she was stopped again in the ice. When Captain Moore first saw the *Californian* about six o'clock in the morning some five or six miles north of the *Carpathia,* he said: "She [the *Californian*] was there shortly after me . . ."[106]

Comparing this with Groves's story, it will be seen how closely they fit. When Groves came on the bridge somewhat later, the *Californian* must have been heading in a southerly direction, and although still bumping the ice, she was going at a good speed — probably all out. The *Mount Temple* was only about a mile and a half ahead. It seems probable that as this was the position about 6.50 a.m., the *Californian* was up to the *Mount Temple* earlier than 7.30. Moreover, also at 6.50, Groves said,[107] the *Carpathia* was already abeam on the port side, which would be to the east, about five miles away.

From an unexpected source, there is one more piece of independent corroboration that the distance between the overnight position of the *Californian* and that of the *Titanic* was much shorter than Captain Lord and his supporters tardily preferred it to be. When the Allan liner *Virginian* arrived in Liverpool from Halifax, N.S., on the morning of 21 April, her master, Captain G.J. Gambell, told of the wireless messages concerned with the disaster, which he had received or sent, and including his first communication with the *Californian* on Monday, the 15th, at 5.45 a.m. ATS.* [108]

This very important story, which received wide international coverage, was reported most fully and accurately in *The Times* (London) of 22 April, from which the quotations here are taken.

"She [the *Californian*] was 17 miles north of the *Titanic*," said Gambell, "and had not heard anything official of the disaster. I sent a Marconigram to her as follows: '*Titanic* struck iceberg, wants assistance urgently, ship sinking, passengers in boats . . .'"

Presumably Gambell's "17 miles" as the *Californian's* distance from the *Titanic* was his equivalent of Lord's 19½ and also derived from the estimated overnight position of the *Californian.*

At Washington, Lord reported getting the message from the *Virginian* "at 6 o'clock", which may fairly be regarded as agreeing with Gambell.

Senator Smith then asked: "You heard nothing further from that source?"[109]

"From the *Virginian*? I had a message about an hour and a half after. He said: 'When you get to the scene of the disaster, will you please give me particulars of what is happening?'"

According to Lord, therefore, it must have been about 7.30 when he received Gambell's request in his second message.

Lord does not say when or what he replied, but Gambell, who seems to have had an unusually exact mind, does: "She at once replied: — 'Can now see *Carpathia* taking passengers on board from small boats. *Titanic* foundered about 2 a.m.'"

The *Californian's* bridge, according to Lord, was 40 feet above the water.[110] Applying the usual formula (1.144 $\sqrt{Ht}$, where Ht = the height of the observer above the water in feet), the *Carpathia* could not have been much more than

* This is variously reported as "5.45 a.m." in *The Boston Herald* of 22 April and "4.45 a.m." in *The New York Times* of 23 April; but we know from Evans's evidence in London that he was first in touch with the *Virginian* "about a quarter to six ship's time," so clearly ATS in both ships was the same. The P.V. of the *Virginian,* however incomplete it was, shows that, like the *Californian's,* her wireless messages were being logged by New York time.

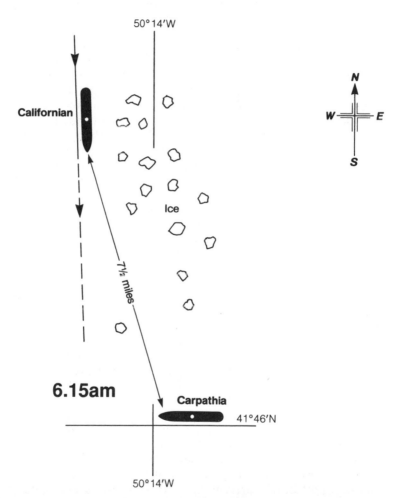

Diagram 10. The *Californian's* distance from the *Carpathia:* according to Captain Gambell in the *Virginian*

Captain Gambell of the Virginian, *Halifax-Liverpool, received the* Titanic *distress call at 12.40 a.m. ATS, 15 April, and relayed the same position to the* Californian *about 5.45 a.m. The* Virginian *was not yet in sight when she received a Marconigram from the* Californian *that she could see, and was apparently 71/2 miles from, the* Carpathia *about 6.15 a.m.*

seven miles away, and probably less, when Lord replied to Gambell. At first sight, Gambell seems to provide remarkable circumstantial confirmation of Lord's "19½ miles": it had taken him an hour and a half of hard steaming to get to within seven miles of the *Titanic's* position, as marked by the *Carpathia*.

Unfortunately for Lord, however, Captain Gambell's story is actually a flat contradiction of Lord's evidence at Washington that an hour and half passed before the second message from the *Virginian* was received. Evidently, as soon as he had finished with the *Carpathia, Frankfurt* and *Baltic*, Gambell instantly turned again, as we would expect, to the *Californian:*

> "At *6.10 a.m.* [emphasis added] I sent a Marconigram to the *Californian:* [his request to be told about conditions at the *Titanic* when the *Californian* got there] *She at once replied:* [emphasis added] 'Can now see *Carpathia . . .*" etc.

It mattered little that *The New York Times* reported the *Californian's* reply as "6.14", or that Evans must have used a few minutes for his transmission, so that possibly — though not probably — Gambell might not actually have received Lord's message before 6.20-6.25; nor did the bearing of the *Carpathia* from the *Californian* matter, when the latter "at once replied". Neither does it make the slightest difference, that at about that time, or perhaps a few minutes later,* the *Californian* informed the Russian liner *Birma;* that "she [was] only 15 miles away from [the] position given by the *Titanic*."[111] The friends of Captain Lord may regard this recently found message 'as important new evidence',[112] its true significance is reduced to zero when at the same time the *Carpathia* was already in sight and less than seven miles away. At that moment, it was the distance alone between the two ships, *Carpathia* and *Californian*, and not the distance between the reported position of the *Titanic* and that of the *Californian*, that weighed in the scales of judgement, and that distance was less than seven miles.

The unique importance of Captain Gambell's narrative is that by pure chance it contains circumstantial corroboration of the fact that it was not "an hour and a half", or 90 minutes, after 6 a.m. or thereabouts, before it could be shown that Captain Lord was only some seven miles from the *Carpathia*, but only half an hour, or, most probably, a mere 25 minutes.

On any showing, it still took the *Californian* about an hour and 25 minutes, according to Groves, to reach the *Carpathia* at eight o'clock. Whoever was right, there is one final piece of apparent support for Captain Gambell's time, and it comes from Captain Lord himself.

On Friday morning, 19 April, in Boston, when Lord had not yet decided to add to his defence the alleged wrong reckoning of the *Titanic* and his own distance of more than 30 miles from the scene, he told the reporter of the newspaper, *The Traveller:* "Long before we got to the scene, we saw the *Carpathia* picking up the life boats from [the] *Titanic . . .*" "Long before" is a vague phrase, but it is perhaps not far-fetched to guess that if Gambell's message had in fact arrived at 7.30, as Lord asserted, he might have said: "An hour before we got to the scene . . ." The words Lord actually used to the reporter somehow suggest a much longer interval before she finally arrived.

Captain Moore, Groves, Lord himself, and the circumstantial evidence unexpectedly provided by Captain Gambell, together all point in one direction. It is probable, as Lord said, he had to steam much more than 19½ miles to reach the scene of the wreck; but it is almost beyond doubt that the distance in a straight line, 'north and south, between the *Californian's* overnight position and the *Carpathia* must have been much less than 19½ miles.

The name of another sea captain in the story, and not yet mentioned, is

---

* 6.00 o'clock *Birma's* time or 6.25 (or 6.20 according to *The Daily Telegraph*) *Californian's* time.

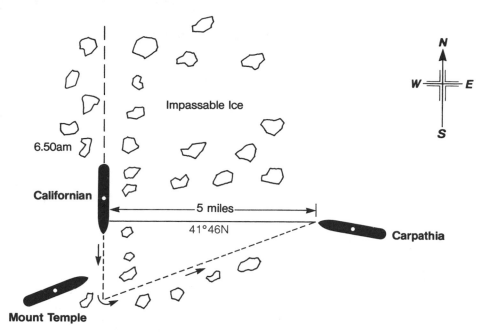

Diagram 11. The *Californian's* distance from the *Carpathia:* according to Groves in the *Californian*

Third Officer Groves sights the Carpathia *from the bridge of the* Californian, *abeam, five miles to the east, and* Mount Temple *to starboard, about 1¹/₂ miles to the south. This diagram also shows the later track of the* Californian *through the ice to the* Carpathia, *as described by Captain Rostron.*

Ludwig Stulping, who was in command of the Russian-American Line SS *Birma,* 4,588 tons, bound east to Rotterdam and Libau. The *Birma,* which until 1905 had been better known as the *Arundel Castle* in the Cape trade, on the morning of 25 April was suddenly publicized by *The Daily Telegraph* with a heavy black headline on p.16: 'THE TITANIC DISASTER; STORY OF THE BIRMA', a story occupying most of the page, a chart[*] and three illustrations.[113]

The story, which was written by a passenger, an English-born journalist of San Francisco, Charles Edward Walters, was certified as accurate by Captain Stulping, First Officer Alfr. Nielsen, Purser C. Hesselberg, and the two English wireless operators, Joseph L. Cannon and Thomas George Ward. It was dated 22 April, and sent to the *Telegraph* from "off Dover". A considerable part of the narrative was a complaint — quite justified, it would seem — of the rude and ungrateful response to the Russian vessel's offer of stores and other help, by the *Carpathia* and all the other Marconi-equipped ships (the *Birma* having the De Forest system of wireless), which for the remainder of the crossing flatly refused even to give her any information about the disaster. But Mr Walters also reported that when the *Birma* reached the given position "After daylight", they "found at once that it must be wrong." There was no sign of the wreck. They passed "enormous icebergs" . . . "yet it was obvious that none of these could have damaged the *Titanic,* for to the north-east of us lay enormous ice floes, extending for miles. The *Titanic,* coming westward, would have been warned by these floes that large bergs were about."

---

[*]   See Appendix E, page 362.

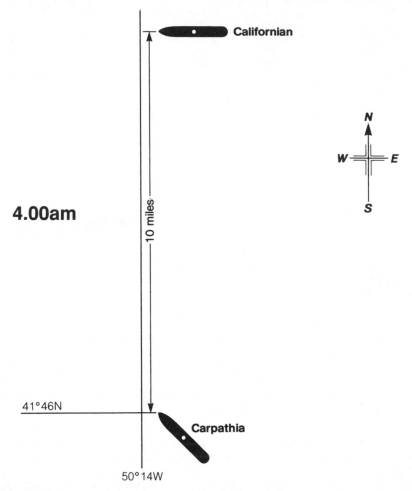

Diagram 12. The *Californian's* distance from the *Carpathia:* according to four *Carpathia* officers
When they had arrived and stopped at the position of the Titanic, *at least* four *of the* Carpathia's *officers said they saw the* Californian *stopped ten miles to the north.*

"We soon heard by wireless," Mr Walters continued, "that the *Carpathia* was picking the boats up north of the ice floe."

What was described as a "a rude chart" accompanied the story (see Appendix E, Diagram II). This chart was a copy of the chart prepared by Captain Stupling of the *Birma.* On his original chart an X marks the place reached by the *Birma,* which she estimated to be the given position of the *Titanic,* though earlier in his story Walters had stated the latitude as received by the *Birma* to be '41.44N (instead of 41.46N), the position of the X reads as 41.49½N, 50.12W. The *Birma's* story gave no figures, but a double XX, east of the ice floe (at about 41.34N, 49.35W), on the chart, which is said to mark the *Carpathia's* position, was appreciably south and east of the X, the *Titanic's* reported position, according to the *Birma.*

There is, however, a significant contradiction between this XX on the chart and the narrative.

"The ice floe was approached by us from the south-west," Walters writes, "until we reached the point marked X, when it was obvious that the location given must be wrong. We then saw the *Carpathia* on the *north-easterly* [emphasis added] side of the floe . . ."

It is interesting that the first intimation the *Birma* had of the presence of the *Carpathia* was in the message received that she was picking up the boats "north of the icefloe". The origin of that message is not stated; but there is something of more importance to be noted. It is clear that if the location of the XX on the chart is correct, Walters must have written that the *Carpathia* was on the south-easterly side of the floe from X. Whether "north-easterly" was a mistake or a typographical error for 'south-easterly', or whether the XX was placed too far south cannot be decided. Bearing in mind the testimony of other witnesses (including, of course, Captain Moore), and considering the vivid and apparently accurate quality of Mr Walters's story as a whole, my own guess is that when he first sighted the *Carpathia* that morning, she was to the north-east of him, as he wrote, not south-east, where she would have been if the XX on the chart is correct.

How the *Carpathia* found the boats in spite of the alleged "wrong position" is also considered by Mr Walters.

"The *Carpathia* got there in time and saved the survivors, whether by chance in striking the position or warned in time by being on a different course; . . ." or, possibly, by luckily bad navigation!

Having seen the *Carpathia* on the north-easterly side of the floe, the narrative continues, "and, being asked merely to stand by, and seeing the vessel engaged in picking up the boats with the survivors, we circled around the floe, first to the south, in order to avoid being crushed by the ice; then, after turning the lower corner, we turned north-eastward, up to the point marked XX, which is the spot on which the *Carpathia* 'stood' while picking up the boats."

One thing clearly emerges from the story of the *Birma*. Exactly as in the evidence of Captain Moore of the *Mount Temple*, the substantial discrepancy — assuming it existed — between the *Titanic's* given position and the alleged real position was not in the latitude, but in the longitude. Captain Moore confirmed the correctness of her given latitude as 41.46N; Captain Stulping, although giving no figures, seemed from his chart to place the *Titanic* south of that latitude. The narrative, if correct, would seem to place the *Titanic*, if anything, even north of the given latitude; and, of that narrative, Captain Stulping and his officers certified, ". . . the facts in the foregoing report . . . are correct, to our knowledge and belief."

It is necessary, therefore, also to point out that in any event, a careful reading of the whole of the *Birma's* story shows that it is not, as always stated by Captain Lord's legion, full and unequivocal corroboration of his statement that the *Titanic* was actually considerably south of her reported position. The *Birma* provides consistent support for that assertion, as do Lord's supporters, only if attention is paid exclusively to the chart and the Captain's certificate without mentioning the possibly even more significant statement in Mr Walters's report that he first saw "the *Carpathia* on that north-easterly side of the floe, . . ."

The real value of the *Birma's* story, however, must be enhanced by the fact that its chief purpose was evidently to be found in the desire of a fair-minded and indignant Englishman to vindicate the conduct of a brave and chivalrous foreign sea captain and his crew, who had tried hard to help an English ship in distress, and had been insulted for their pains. The question of the *Titanic's* position was merely incidental to the main object of trying to right that wrong. But that was not the end of it.

On Stulping's rude chart XXX marks the spot "where S/S B passed S/S/ C proceeding SW." Presumably this meant: where the *Birma* passed the *Californian* proceeding south-west. The position of the triple X is at about 41.21N, 49.37W or well south and east of the noon observation of the *Californian,* and only shows how rude the chart indeed is. Still, in October 1990 Mr Padfield told the viewers of the BBC's *Newsnight* that "the *Birma* found the wreckage roughly where Dr Ballard found the wreck of the *Titanic*" and deduced from that "that Captain Lord was one of the better navigators that night." The narrative from the *Birma* had not mentioned the finding of any wreckage, in fact it was stated that "no wreckage of any kind was seen", the story only told where the *Birma* observed the *Carpathia* picking up the survivors. Presumably Mr Padfield meant this position as the place of the wreckage. What "roughly" then means in Mr Padfield's conception can be determined when plotting the wreck position against the double-X on the map of the *Birma,* rude as that map is said to be. The surprising result from such a plot is that the *Carpathia* was engaged in the rescue some 16 miles east of the position where the wreck of the *Titanic* was found and — if the Lordites' favourite latitude of the double-X on the map is accepted, as undoubtedly Mr Padfield does — some nine miles south of that location. To consider these distances as "roughly where Dr Ballard found the wreck of the *Titanic*", is precisely as accurate as is Mr Padfield's conclusion "that Captain Lord was one of the better navigators that night."

The truth is far more complicated than rough estimates and unsupported conclusions will reveal, and a good deal more confusing if not all the available evidence is taken into consideration.

As we know now, the wreck of the *Titanic* was located 12.75 miles east and 2.4 miles south of the position Boxhall calculated. Of all the navigators, that night and later; Boxhall, Captain Rostron, Lord, Moore, Stulping and Dr Ballard (though he may not be regarded as a navigator, he had the best and most modern equipment to have navigational problems solved for him), only Captain Lord eventually pushed the position of the *Titanic* 10-12 miles south, and his friends later as far as 18 miles. Captain Rostron, Captain Moore and Dr Ballard all agreed independently that the latitude, as given by the *Titanic,* was correct within one to two-and-a-half miles. Even Captain Lord regarded the latitude correct before he decided to place the *Titanic* much further south, and we shall look at that story in more detail in Chapter 11.

The longitude of the *Titanic* has not had that aura of fierce dispute, but it was the only possible significant error in Boxhall's dead reckoning, being nearly 13 miles west of the wreck position. The *Titanic* was nonetheless on her course when she collided with the iceberg, just not as far along it as her stated position put her. We now know that Boxhall stood corrected by Captain Moore of *Mount Temple* who said the *Titanic* was "at least eight miles" east of her given position. The *Birma* put that position on her rude chart some 26 miles east of that position, which is clearly too far east. Captain Moore is surprisingly closer to the truth; Dr Ballard agrees with him within less than five miles.

At the Senate inquiry Boxhall had to answer to Captain Moore's finding. "The Captain of the *Mount Temple* maintains," Senator Burton, in his separate hearing with Boxhall, said, "that the course as conveyed by the distress signal was wrong; that the *Titanic* was actually eight miles distance from the place indicated. What do you say as to that?"[114]

"I do not know what to say," said Boxhall. "I know our position, because I worked the position out, and I know that it is correct." He then told the

Senator about Rostron's compliments on the position he had worked out, already quoted.

Beside Moore and Stulping there are no other sources that can clarify the longitude of the *Carpathia's* rescue work. Both Lord and Rostron had steamed away before they made their observations. How far they had steamed is not known.

The Lordites have never made much of an argument over the longitude of the *Titanic*; they considered the alleged southern position of the *Titanic* of much greater importance. Their persistent and continuous claims that the *Titanic* was much more south of her given position were, of course, instantly demolished by the finding of the wreck and the publication of its position; but not a word of recognition for being at fault so grievously and for so long was ever heard. Instead, the new evidence was proclaimed to be in recognition of Captain Lord's navigational evidence which had always been right and that he "was one of the better navigators that night."

Mr Harrison observed that "Captain Lord's navigation was accurate to within five or six miles."[115] He arrived at this conclusion by including the "nine hours [sic] after the TITANIC sank" and "checking back to 2.20 a.m." from what is also known as the noon observation of the *Californian,* "41° 33' North, 50° 01' West." To claim that a noon observation reveals the accuracy, within five or six miles, of the dead reckoning overnight position of more then ten hours earlier, would be far from correct.

A more prudent observation is that of all navigators in the area only Captain Lord's navigational figures for his ship's overnight and early morning latitude were inaccurate and considerably north of where he actually was, incredible as this may seem for such an experienced captain and his equally experienced and devoted officers.

This is not the last word that can be said on this subject, and in Chapter 19 the examination of the *Californian's* relation to the *Carpathia* will be conclusively cleared and concluded.

Whatever the real reason for the *Californian's* error was, it did not bother Captain Lord much then or later, nor did it his friends.

In the bright sunlight of the morning of 15 April, with his house flag and the ensign at half mast, Lord turned his ship away from the wreckage and steamed off for Boston.

Sources

1 *The Discovery of the Titanic,* p. 199.
2 Ibid. p. 205.
3 *A Titanic Myth,* p. 188.
4 B 15638.
5 US 931.
6 US 209.
7 US 931.
8 US 932.
9 US 932.
10 Ibid.
11 B 15639.
12 B 15643-47.
13 B 15648-49.
14 *Nautical Magazine,* May 1959, p. 263.
15 Ibid.
16 US 932.
17 US 25.
18 Dr Ballard's address to the annual Associates Dinner of the Wood's Hole Oceanographic Institute, 15 April 1986.
19 'The "Californian" Incident', p. 4.
20 B 8706 - Pole Star at 10.30; B 8798 - Pole Star at 7.30.
21 [MT 9/920/6] M 31921.
22 'Commodore', pp. 204, 212.
23 *Tramps and Ladies,* pp. 282-285.
24 US 27.
25 B 25390.
26 B 25401.
27 B 25467.
28 B 25472.
29 B 25507.
30 B 25423, 25515, 25516.
31 Padfield, p. 270.
32 *Home From the Sea,* p. 64.
33 Padfield, p. 212.
34 B 8008.
35 B 7586.
36 US 729.
37 Ibid.
38 B 8009-10.
39 *A Titanic Myth,* p. 173.

40 B 25552.
41 Statement Gibson.
42 B 25559.
43 'Under the Wheels of
    the Juggernaut',
    January 1913, map 2.
44 P.I.
45 Ibid.
46 *Home From the Sea*, p.
    68.
47 *Tramps and Ladies*, p.
    291.
48 US 183, 184, 1139.
49 *Home From the Sea*, p.
    65; Affidavit, 4 June
    1912; US 26; B 25405,
    25499.
50 B 8821; Lord's
    affidavit, 25 June 1959.
51 B 8819, 8818, 8820.
52 B 7039.
53 B 6704, 6823.
54 Bisset, *Tramps and
    Ladies*, p. 295.
55 US 723, B 7267.
56 B 8369.
57 "Tramps and Ladies",
    p. 295.
58 US 757 & P.I from Capt.
    Hatty A. Moore.
59 George Musk, A.M.
    Inst. T., *Canadian
    Pacific Afloat 1883-
    1968.*

60 B 9413.
61 US 769.
62 B 9451.
63 B 9436.
64 B 9456.
65 US 760.
66 US 759.
67 US 760-63.
68 US 760.
69 B 9261.
70 B 9282.
71 US 763-64.
72 US 763-64.
73 US 766.
74 US 765.
75 US 767.
76 US 777.
77 Ibid.
78 Ibid.
79 Ibid.
80 Ibid.
81 Ibid.
82 Ibid.
83 US 778-779.
84 US 779-780.
85 Ibid.
86 Ibid.
87 B 7005.
88 Ibid.
89 B 7388.
90 (Evans), B 8935;
    (Durrant), B 9436.
91 B 7257.
92 B 7261.

93 B 8780.
94 B 8783.
95 B 8780.
96 US 718.
97 Mersey Report, p. 46.
98 B 8293-97.
99 B 8313, 8315, 8319.
100 B 8321.
101 B 8323-24.
102 B 8326.
103 B 8329-31.
104 B 8342.
105 B 8345-46.
106 US 778.
107 B 8323.
108 *New York Times*, 23
    April, p. 2.; *Times*
    (London) 22 April,
    p. 22.
109 US 732.
110 B 6997.
111 Radio scrap log of
    Joseph Cannon radio
    operator of the SS
    Birma, first published in
    The Daily Telegraph,
    p. 32, 16 July 1990.
112 *The Daily Telegraph,*
    p. 32, 16 July 1990.
113 *The Daily Telegraph,*
    25 April 1912.
114 US 931.
115 *The Case for Captain
    Lord*, Harrison [1989]

Chapter 10

On her way to Boston

"11.20 proceeded on course N. 59 W. by compass."[1]

So Lord read from his log to the tribunals at Washington and London, when he told of the abandonment of his fruitless search. Before she gave up, the *Californian* steamed near the seven remaining empty boats. In bright sunshine, and steaming away fast to the south-west, the rescue ship was hidden from the *Californian* among the icebergs in less than 20 minutes. The *Californian* made a turn to starboard, followed by one to port.[2] On an ice floe about a mile or so distant, Groves, peering through his glasses, saw figures moving and drew Lord's attention in the hope that they might be human, but Lord said they were seals. He was almost certainly right, but all the same Groves, who was extraordinarily cautious in matters relating to the value of human life, never entirely got rid of a doubt about Lord's decision.[*]

We have mentioned two other times at which the *Californian* is said to have abandoned their search, first, Bisset's,[3] an hour after the *Carpathia* set off for New York, when Rostron received a message from Lord that he had found no bodies and was resuming his voyage. This would be about 10 o'clock. Groves in evidence gave the time at "Ten-forty exactly".[4]

So, the *Californian* went on her way again, seeing a great deal of ice, and having, in the words of Groves, "to absolutely force" their way "through a particularly long field about half a mile wide."[5]

About this time probably, far away, the first step was taken which was to introduce the *Californian* to the world, the first public stage in the story which was soon to turn this obscure British cargo boat into a vessel of international notoriety. It came in the form of a wireless message sent via Cape Race at 4.35 p.m. New York time by Captain Herbert James Haddock of the *Olympic* to "ISMAY, New York and Liverpool," and read as follows:

"*Carpathia* reached *Titanic* position at daybreak; found boats and wreckage only. *Titanic* had foundered about 2.20 a.m. in 41.16 north [*sic*] 50.14 west; all her boats

---

* It has been asserted more than once that the failure of the *Californian* to find anything, when even after the mission of the *Mackay-Bennett* and the *Minia* bodies were found, is further proof of the ineptitude of the *Californian*. My own effort to investigate the matter on both sides of the Atlantic was certainly frustrated by the lack of relevant documents. ITT World Communications Inc. regretfully announced to me the mysterious loss of the *Mackay-Bennett's* log at New York, following its survival for more than 50 years at Halifax, N.S. In England, the ship's report to the charterers, the White Star Line, likewise mysteriously vanished from the possession of the Cunard Company, the residuary legatees. I, at least, can form no conclusion on the matter, for or against the *Californian*.

accounted for; about 675 souls saved, crew and passengers; latter nearly all women and children; Leyland Line SS *California* [*sic*] remaining and searching position of disaster; *Carpathia* returning to New York with survivors. Please inform Cunard. HADDOCK."* [6]

By that time the *Californian* was on her way to Boston, frustrated and quite unaware that although she had no survivors aboard, and could not contribute a merest mite of information toward relieving the anxiety of two continents, she had become a focus of interest, albeit a minor one, and was to remain so for some days until she made her landfall. Apart from the big and obvious question which dominated the ship, and generated intense interest among her crew, there was another unexpected, if lesser, emotion very much alive in the heart of at least one member of her company.

About half-past nine that morning, the approximate time of many ships in the disaster area, Durrant, the *Mount Temple* operator, overheard Balfour, the Marconi inspector in the *Baltic*, reprimanding Evans, of the *Californian* for his excessive activity over the air: "Stand by immediately. You have been instructed to do so frequently. Balfour, Inspector."[7] It was but the latest of several such messages, and they had given rise to much resentment in young Evans at what he considered the unfair treatment he had received. At 4.52 p.m. on the Monday afternoon, Ernest James Moore, the senior operator in the *Olympic*, received this message from the *Californian:*

"We were the second boat on the scene of disaster. All we could see there were some boxes and coats and a few empty boats and what looked like oil on the water. When we were near the *Carpathia* he would not answer me, though I kept on calling him, as I wanted the position. He kept on talking to the *Baltic*. The latter says he is going to report me for jamming. We were the nearer boat to the *Carpathia*. A boat called the *Birma* was still looking."[8] Evans himself, it appeared, was unconscious of having done anything wrong. Moore discreetly replied: "that would take note of fact that in cases of distress nearer ships should have precedence."[9] In the light of what happened afterwards, there is a certain irony in Evans's insistence on their having been the "second boat on the scene" and on their nearness to the *Carpathia;* but so far as the *Olympic* was concerned, his message by chance served to provide the first authentic report of the disaster after Rostron's.

There is not much other information of what happened aboard the *Californian* the remainder of that momentous day. Nearly the whole of her 900-mile passage to Boston was through fog; in a sense, it was symbolic. Because of the fog Lord and his officers were "tired out".[10] The ship was seething with talk of the rockets seen in the middle watch, and it is tempting to speculate about the conversation in the mess that night. Captain Lord, characteristically remote, had nothing to say about the rockets to anybody; that, at least, is what he was to tell Lord Mersey,[11] though there was some talk between him and Stone. A more normal man might have made it his business to try to find out if anybody besides Stone and Gibson had seen anything (and if he had,

---

* "... Immediately that telegram was received by me," Mr Phillip A.S. Franklin, the US Vice-President of the International Mercantile Marine Company told Senator Smith, "it was such a terrible shock that it took us a few minutes to get ourselves together. Then at once I telephoned, myself, to two of our directors, Mr Steele and Mr Morgan, jun., and at the same time sent downstairs for the reporters. I started to read the message, holding it in my hands, to the reporters. I got off the first line and a half, where it said, 'The *Titanic* sank at 2 o'clock a.m.,' and there was not a reporter left in the room – they were so anxious to get out to telephone the news.' (US 179)

Lord might have received some remarkable and unexpected answers); but Lord controlled his curiosity.

The ship's log, which would be the usual source for at least the formal account of the previous night's extraordinary events, has either disappeared or is no longer available for scrutiny. Nevertheless, we do know the official story the *Californian* was to preserve for posterity of the strange and mystifying experience that had gone on so long while Stone and Gibson stood their watch. We know the exact words and the precise number. In the accounts of adventures by sea, it is unique and unparalleled. It is complete silence.

Lest the uninformed reader believe that this statement is an exaggeration or a joke, we may fittingly turn now to the story about that log as told briefly by Captain Lord, and more fully by Chief Officer Stewart, in whose evidence it is a revealing and fascinating passage.

Rather oddly, it was only toward the end of Lord's evidence that the log was mentioned, when Lord Mersey said that Lord had produced it, and asked if the Attorney-General had examined it. When he replied that he had not, Mersey turned to Lord.

"Is there any reference in your log to your steamer having seen these rockets?"[12]

"No, Sir."

"Or this mysterious ship which was not the *Titanic*?"

"No, Sir."

"It is not usual to record these things in the log?"

"We never realized what these rockets were, my Lord. If they had been distress rockets, they would have been mentioned in the log."

"But the next morning you knew the *Titanic* had gone down?"

"Yes."

"Did you make no record then in your log of the signals you had seen?"

"No."

And he would not budge. The Second Officer had "said most emphatically they were not distress rockets,"[13] and no entry was made. Lord was, of course, consistent. If only unanimity of recognition as distress rockets was the qualification for entry in the log, then Stone's reported blackballing of them was enough for exclusion.

"Is there anybody on board your boat," Mersey persisted, "who thinks they were [distress rockets]?"

"Not to my knowledge, my Lord," was the reply; and charity must attribute it to some lapse of memory. When Lord stood at the witness table that morning, it was already public (and sensational) knowledge in America and Britain that at least one member of the crew did think they were distress rockets — though perhaps Lord would have justified his reply by saying he had posted that particular seaman as a deserter,[14] and he was no longer 'aboard his boat'!

Lord finished his answer: "I have not spoken to any of the crew about it." And on that we have already commented.

But the fundamental dishonesty of excluding any mention of the rockets from the log arises not from any single sophistry, but from the total impression created. Look at the log and nothing had happened: an ordinary quiet Sunday night at sea; question the watch, and in fact something extraordinary and sensational had happened. Moreover, whether or not those signals were regarded as distress rockets, we have seen how, immediately the news of the *Titanic* was received, Gibson and Stone instantly connected them with the disaster. Probably Lord, Mersey and perhaps the Attorney-General, had not read the transcript of Evans's most deadly evidence in Washington; certainly, no attempt was made to use it against Lord. One wonders what more brutal, though no more effective, cross-examiners than Rufus Isaacs, such as Edward Carson or Richard Muir, who were also in practice at that time, would have done with such material. It is improbable that Lord's statement that he had not spoken to any of the crew about the rockets would have been allowed to lie undisturbed.

At the next day's hearing, Groves was asked by Sir John Simon a number of questions about the scrap log.[15] It was kept in a thin blank book, "a cargo book",[16] of which they kept a number on board, and it was Groves's job to rule them up,[17] the first heading being "Hours".[18] The scrap log was destroyed from time to time,[19] the permanent entries being made in the Chief Officer's log. The book which covered the period of the middle watch for the night of 15 April — Stone's and Gibson's watch — he assumed had been thrown away.[20] "I expect it went over the side," he said, though he did not know definitely. He had come on duty "about 6.50"[21] again, and as officer of the watch again at 8 a.m. that Monday,[22] but he had not looked back in the scrap log to see what entries,[23] if any, had been made by Stone.

It must be said this is a surprising admission. When first asked if he knew whether there was any reference to the rockets, he answered: "I saw none myself."[24] Mersey at once intervened and asked him if he had looked, and Groves admitted he had not,[25] and was then rebuked and told to be careful how he answered.

"If you had been on the bridge instead of from 8 to half-past 12, from 12 to 4," Lord Mersey asked him,[26] "and had been keeping the scrap log book, and had seen a succession of white rockets with stars going up from this vessel, which you speak of, or from the direction of this vessel, would you in the ordinary course of things have made a record of the fact in your scrap log?"

"Most decidedly," Groves said, "that is what the log book is for."

"So I should have thought. Then it would have been the business of the man who had charge of this book to record these facts?"

"I think so, my Lord."[27]

The answer was obviously less positive than the preceding one, and not probably because Groves was any less certain about it, but because it did not require as much intelligence as he undoubtedly possessed to see where the line of questioning was going to take him.

"Who was he?" Mersey went on. He had been listening to Stone for some hours the preceding day giving evidence about his watch.

"Mr Stone was on watch."

"And, therefore, if Mr Stone did what you think was his duty, this scrap log book which was thrown away, or which at all events cannot be found, would contain a record of these rockets having been seen?"

"Yes, my Lord" — and this was it! — "but it is not my duty to criticize a senior officer, though."

"I am asking what is the ordinary practice." And with that, Mersey finished the examination of Groves. In sharp contrast with most of the other witnesses, Groves made admissions, when truth or common sense required. The impression created on all who heard him was most favourable, Captain Lord (and supporters of after years) alone excepted.

Chief Officer Stewart, who made his first substantial contribution to the story when he took over the watch at four o'clock, was perhaps the finest specimen of a *Californian* witness. We have seen his début: when Captain Lord apparently believed the steamer to the south was the one of the night before, Stewart did not correct his mistake; when he first heard the *Titanic* had sunk, he did not think the steamer that threw up rockets might have been she; when he called Evans, he did not ask him to find out if anything was wrong because a steamer had been firing rockets, although that was why Lord had sent him to call Evans. We shall now see that his evidence about the log, for which he was responsible, casts no blemish on this record.

It is when Stewart comes on duty at 4 a.m. next day, for the Morning Watch, after the adventures of the night, that his log becomes something other than a true record, and his attitude to it a fitting subject for criticism.

He said he had entered into the log book everything he found "on the scrap log sheet."[28]

"You observe there is nothing at all in your log book about seeing distress signals?"

Even Stewart could not deny that. Here, it should be noted that the questioning proceeded on the assumption that the rockets seen had been distress rockets; but I have been told that it would not have been customary to have omitted any reference to 'company signals", if any such had been sighted at sea, and especially from a vessel apparently stopped in the ice.

The questioning proceeded.

"Is there anything?"

"No, nothing," said Stewart.

"Nothing at all?"

"No."

"No reference to any of these events of night at all?" It seemed that Simon had not yet examined the log, and he apparently found it a little hard to believe.

"No," said Stewart for the third time.

"Does that convey to you," Lord Mersey asked, "that there was no reference to these events in the scrap log?"

"Yes, my Lord."

Simon resumed the examination, and his question provided a test for Stewart.

"Give us your views. Supposing you were keeping the scrap log on a watch when you were in ice, and supposing you saw a few miles to the southward a ship sending up what appeared to you to be distress signals, would not you enter that in the log?"

Lord Mersey had asked Groves the same question, and had promptly received the answer: "Most decidedly, that is what the log book is for."[29]

And Stewart? — His answer is printed thus: "Yes — I do not know."[30]

Mersey thereupon jumped at him with the understandable exclamation: "Oh, yes, you do?"[31] The fact that, as a quirk of style of these British transcripts,* a question mark appears rather than an exclamation mark, cannot conceal even on the cold page the obvious anger aroused by yet one more attempted evasion by this most disingenuous witness. Stewart then gave a further and better answer: "Yes, I daresay I should have entered it, but it was not in our scrap log book."

"That is not what I asked you," said Simon.[32] "What I asked you was — apply your mind to it — supposing you had been keeping the scrap log in those circumstances and you saw distress signals being sent up by a ship a few miles from you, is that, or is not that, a thing you would enter in the log?"

---

*   Another, for instance, is the invariable alteration of such conversationalisms as 'wouldn't' into 'would not'.

"Yes," Stewart finally conceded the point. He seemed almost to want to make it clear that he was fighting a rearguard action, rather than trying to help discover the truth. Nor was this the end of it.

"How do you account for it not being there?" Mersey asked him.

"I do not know, my Lord."

"It was careless not to put it in, was it not?"

"Or forgetful," blandly replied Chief Officer Stewart.

"Forgetful?" Mersey repeated. "Do you think that a careful man is likely to forget the fact that distress signals have been going off from a neighbouring steamer?"

"No, my Lord."

"Then do not talk to me about forgetfulness."

Stewart's answer seems either impudent or frivolous, but was perhaps merely thoughtless; thoughtless in the sense that he was thinking only of covering up for his shipmates. It was certainly stupid. Lord had, at least, a possible, if not convincing, reason for the silence of his log in that Stone was said not to have regarded the rockets as distress signals.

"The scrap log book," Simon went on, "is intended to be kept at the time, is it not, as the things happen?"

"Yes, sir, but they generally write them up at the end of the watch."

At four o'clock, when he went on watch, Stone told him about the "signals", how they had sent messages about them to the Captain three times; and he, Stewart, was going to "take charge of this same sheet of paper".

"Did not it occur to you that it was odd that there was nothing entered on the scrap log book?"[33]

But Stewart said he had not noticed it then. Nor had he himself made entries "on the same sheet of paper" between four and eight o'clock; but he had done so at eight.[34]

"Did not you notice it then?"[35]

"I noticed there was nothing on it then."

"But by that time you had had the message that the *Titanic* had sunk?"[36]

"Yes."

"Did not you notice it then?"

"I noticed there was nothing there."

And twice more, Simon, for once with almost Smith-like insistence, got Stewart to admit that he had noticed the scrap log was blank about the period "between midnight and four".

"And you have told us, in your view, it would be right to make such entries?"[37]

"Yes."

"Did you ever speak to the Second Officer about it?"[38]

"No."

"Or the Captain?" Mersey asked him.

"No."

"Or to anybody?"

"No, my Lord."

The piece of paper would be used until midnight on 15 April, and Stewart would then write the entries into the log book from the scrap log.

"And do you say you then destroyed the record for 15 April?"

"Yes."

"When you destroyed it, did you notice then there was no record on it about these distress signals, did not you notice that?"

"No, I just copied it off as it was."

This was the final question put to Stewart about the log, and it seems as superfluous as the answer was unresponsive. But the substance of Stewart's evidence needs little comment. That he did not speak to Stone about the blank scrap log, when he first noticed it, at eight o'clock on the Monday morning, when they were approaching the *Carpathia,* with all the excitement prevailing, is easy to understand; but that at no time afterwards did he ask Stone for any explanation, or even mention the matter to Lord, seems to indicate that Stewart, whose job it was to write up the log, regarded it with indifference. After his evidence, Lord's own presentation of his log as an authentic and reliable record, in his letter to his MP, cannot be taken at face value.

The silence of the log about the rockets and all the events of the Sunday middle watch causes the sobering thought that there was not a written word, not even a hint in the official papers aboard the *Californian,* that a single person in the ship had ever seen anything at all which might have been connected even remotely, with the disaster. There was not a link or trace between the *Californian* and the *Titanic* in her last hours. Unless somebody 'split', if Captain Lord's misdemeanour was ever to become known, chance would have to take a hand.

Next day, 16 April, Rostron sent Lord a message of thanks and said the surviving *Titanic* officers had reported all her boats had been accounted for.[39] Early that same morning, Captain Haddock of the *Olympic* also received from Philip A.S. Franklin, the joint US chief of the White Star and Leyland Lines, this frantic message:

> ". . . Instruct *Californian* to stand by scene of wreck until she hears from us or is relieved or her coal supply runs short. Ascertain *Californian* coal and how long she can standby by . . .[40]

At 2.55 a.m., when that message arrived,[41] the *Californian* was perhaps already some 120 miles from the "scene of wreck", and its irrelevance to the real circumstances is one instance of the results of the bad communications that prevailed.

Now, already within these few hours, the chance that was to take a turn in Captain Lord's fate and expose his entanglement with the *Titanic* came onto the scene. Among the *Olympic's* passengers was Roy W. Howard,* then only 29 years old, but already News Manager of the United Press. With that, almost but not quite, infallible flair for news, he now sent out a Marconigram that the *Californian* had recovered some bodies of the *Titanic* victims, which would be taken to Boston.[42]

The story instantly got headlines on both sides of the Atlantic. Lord's secrecy, log or no log, was over. Inevitably, inquiries were rushed at him from Boston and other papers.[43] The *New York American* was interested specifically in "Astor's body"; the *Boston American* asked: "How many bodies" and "survivors"; J. Fitzpatrick, of *The Boston Post,* urged him: "Send collect any news even if slight and survivors aboard relieve world's anxiety."

From the *Olympic* came an inquiry whether George Wick, the Youngstown, Ohio, millionaire, was aboard. Having had her name first made known to the world by Captain Haddock of the *Olympic,* the *Californian* had now definitely become "news", because of Roy Howard's scoop, and apocryphal though it was, Lord's replies to all the inquiries must have been a repetition of nega-

---

* Roy Wilson Howard: Jan. 1, 1883-Nov. 20, 1964.

tives, and none of them would have contained even a hint of the only story he could have told, that concerning the events of Sunday night.

Far more important to him than any of these communications from strangers was a message which now arrived from the Boston agent of his owners, the Leyland Line: "Press reports you were near *Titanic* and have remains on board. Have you anything to report."[44]

It was now Thursday, 18 April, and Lord was on the spot.

The P.V. of the *Californian* has disappeared from the archives of the Marconi Marine Company. A search of the Boston press brought to light, in an early edition of *The Boston Post* of the next day, 19 April, a rewritten but obviously accurate, account of Lord's answer:

> "Captain Lord, upon receiving the distress signal, forced the slow-going freighter to the limit of her speed and reached the scene six hours after the Titanic had gone to the bottom.
>
> "According to his message, he cruised about, but saw no signs of bodies of the passengers who went down in the whirlpool caused by the suction as the Titanic's massive hulk sank."[45]

It will be observed that there is not a word in this message either about Sunday night.

The same day, 18 April, Lord received a second message from the Boston office of Leyland's. This may have been the first step in the sequence of events that now followed; it certainly had an important place in them. It read:

> "18th April, 1912.
> *From*: Leyland   *To*: Commander, *Californian*
> Understand press representative on board *Winnissmeret*. You may permit them aboard steamer unless in your judgement this is undesirable."[46]

From the first Leyland wireless message of 18 April, we get the remarkable information that Lord had sent no report at all to his owners of the Sunday night's incidents, and the company were no doubt surprised to learn from the newspapers that their *Californian* had been near the *Titanic*. It has already been pointed out above that on the Monday night there was not one official word aboard the *Californian* in writing to connect her with the *Titanic* after the collision with the iceberg. We find the same thing was still true on Thursday. Save for the creative imagination of Roy Howard, Lord's failure to report to Leyland, coupled with the total silence of his log, had made it theoretically possible that the owners would have been kept permanently and completely in the dark about the proximity of the *Californian* to the *Titanic* during the hours of the tragedy. This omission of Lord to send even a short preliminary report by wireless, with perhaps a promise of details to follow after arrival in Boston, has been cited as strong evidence of his bad faith and guilty conscience. The admitted incontrovertible facts are undoubtedly extremely suspicious, but still not yet, at least in my opinion, conclusive beyond reasonable doubt.

It was only at Boston, as we shall have to describe, that Captain Lord first descended from an area of conduct, which was certainly marked by bad judgement or bad luck, or even by negligence, or possibly something morally different and worse, into another territory, where, a seemingly Faust-like, 'Evil, be Thou my Good!' might have composed his precept. Then, indeed, something positively false and amoral without question determined his course.

It is possible that the demand from Leyland's for a report from him, received on 18 April, was what prompted his request to Stone and Gibson for their statements.* From his 1959 affidavit and the statements themselves, however, it seems more likely that Lord had asked for them before receiving Leyland's Marconigram. The news of the imminent meeting with the press was probably only the catalyst which brought about the prompt completion and delivery of the narratives. Clearly, Lord wanted to fortify himself with them before facing the reporters.

Yet, one cannot help asking why, if he was really so unworried about the events of the night, he asked for these statements at all? Let us recall the main features of his case: the ship they saw was certainly not the *Titanic;* she was about the same size as themselves; she had no wireless; the rockets she fired — if she fired them — were not distress signals; she was not in distress, and she steamed away. Why, then, give the entire episode a second thought? The sum of it all, according to Lord, was as devoid of significance as if it had never happened; certainly, it had not the slightest connection with the *Titanic.* In other words, by this line of reasoning, the *Californian* was in the same relationship to the disaster as any other ship on the North Atlantic that night, which had not seen a strange steamer stop at 11.40 p.m.; which had not seen that steamer fire — or apparently fire — eight rockets; which had not seen that steamer's lights "look queer"; which had not seen her listing; and which had not seen her "disappear" at 2.20 in the morning. Again one wonders how many masters of any such steamers, which had seen none of these things had asked their officers of the watch, after hearing of the sinking of the *Titanic,* to turn in an account of their watch during which the disaster took place.

Whenever it was that he had asked for the reports, something unexpected and surprising must now be mentioned about the request or order. It was made secretly. Whether Lord actually forbade Stone and Gibson to disclose to their shipmates what he had asked them to do is not known. He had, of course, no right to give any such order, and common sense suggests that it would have been no more than a request. In any event, the fact is that amid all the talk of the rockets, which had filled the ship since early Monday morning, nobody aboard — except perhaps Stewart, who was in Lord's confidence — seems ever to have heard of the assignment given to Stone and Gibson. Nearly 50 years afterwards, Groves was astonished to receive copies of the two statements,[47] and Groves was probably the most alert man in the whole crew. Certainly, there was no hint of the existence of these documents at either the Washington or London inquiries. Possibly, the first public reference to the two narratives, with quotations from them, was in a letter supporting Lord, headed "Under the Wheels of the Juggernaut", in the MMSA's magazine, *Reporter,* for February, 1913.[48] This was more than six months after the Mersey Report, and Lord himself had sent the author of the letter, A.M. Foweraker, copies of the statements. They had a limited circulation among professional readers; and it is no exaggeration to say that until they were published by the MMSA in March 1962, the original stories of Stone and Gibson were generally unknown.

"At about 12.45," Stone wrote in his statement, "I observed a flash of light in the sky just above that steamer."

Although Stone "thought nothing of it," "Shortly after" he saw another light, "which I made out to be a white rocket". By 1.15, he wrote he "observed three more the same as before, and all white in colour." It was then he reported to Lord, and said he had seen "five". Hence, he himself included the first "flash of light" in his count of the number of rockets he had seen, and there can be no doubt that it was in fact a rocket and the first rocket fired by the *Titanic*.

So far as I know, there has never been any direct comment on this point; but the fact here is that Stone, who did not even know of the existence of Q.M. Rowe of the *Titanic,* when he was writing his statement, timed the first rocket he saw from the bridge of the *Californian* at exactly the time, "about 12.45", that Rowe said the first rocket was fired from the *Titanic*. What must an ordinary reader or investigator, with no axe to grind, conclude from this identity?

The second point to be mentioned here occurs in Gibson's statement. Like that in Stone's Report, it has also not hitherto been the subject of comment, but it is even more important as it identifies the ship Gibson and Stone were watching.

"Arriving on the bridge again at that time ['about five minutes to one']," Gibson wrote, "the Second Officer told me that the other ship, which was then about 3½ points on the Starboard bow, had fired five rockets . . . I then watched her for some time and then went over to the keyboard and called her up continuously for about three minutes. I then got the binoculars and had just got them focussed on the vessel when I observed a white flash apparently on her deck, followed by a faint streak towards the sky which then burst into white stars. Nothing then happened until the other ship was about two points on the Starboard bow when she fired another rocket. Shortly after that I observed that her sidelight had disappeared but her masthead light was just visible, and the Second Officer remarked after taking another bearing of her, that she was slowly steering away toward the S.W. Between one point on the Starboard bow and one point on the Port bow I called her up on the Morse lamp but received no answer. When about one point on the Port bow she fired another rocket which like the others burst into white stars."

Quite unknowingly, Gibson was writing circumstantial and detailed corroboration of the key part in the story of a man he did not know, and which was not yet told. Closely examined, the two stories unexpectedly identify the ship which fired the rockets and prove beyond any reasonable doubt that she was the *Titanic*.

Gibson's and Stone's words on the one side, and Boxhall's on the other were delivered quite independently, in fact, the two young men in the *Californian* did not even know of the existence of the third in the *Titanic,* nor he of theirs. The two parts were told at different times and at different places, but they meshed as completely as if they had been planned together around a single table (see Diagram 13).

Boxhall said twice he saw first the green, i.e. the starboard, light of the three- or four-masted steamer. At this ship, which was showing him her starboard side, he must have fired seven rockets. He did not mention the figure,

Diagram 13. The rockets-beyond doubt
(To understand this diagram — the most important of all, for it shows how the events in the Californian *and the* Titanic *fit together like the pieces of a jigsaw puzzle — the reader should follow the numbers in sequence, revolving the page as required. Beginning at 1, one will see from aboard the* Titanic, *as Boxhall saw her, the other ship — the* Californian, *although he did not know her name then. Turning the page to 2, the reader's viewpoint will next be that of Stone aboard the* Californian, *looking towards the* Titanic, *her name likewise unknown to him at the time. So on to 8, when Gibson supplied that final element of proof.)*

1. 12.45am

2. 12.45am

4. 12.45am

5.

6.

7. 1.30am

8.

● Red
○ Green

N W E S (compass)

1. From about 12.45 a.m., Boxhall in the Titanic began firing rockets at the other ship, which was on her port side and would therefore have seen the Titanic's red light. Boxhall first saw the ship's green light, and was certain she 'was not a two-mast ship'.

2. At about 12.45 a.m., Stone in the Californian saw the other ship fire a rocket. He could see her red light, while at intervals she fired five rockets. The Californian was heading east-north-east, but swinging slowly to the south, and was showing her green light to the vessel firing the rockets. Gibson was below while the five rockets were being fired.

3. Boxhall fired altogether seven rockets while he could see the green light of the other ship.

3. Later, Boxhall in the Titanic saw the other ship's red sidelight, as well as her green. She had two masthead lights, and 'she had beautiful lights'. He 'judged her to be a four-masted steamer', and he thought she was moving.

4. Gibson returned to the bridge of the Californian and heard about the rockets. Stone said the other ship began to move towards the west when she fired her first rocket, but he never saw her green light, so she could not have turned. Either she backed away toward the west, or he was mistaken. Gibson never saw the other ship move at all. He did see her fire two more rockets. He noticed the Californian's own heading, which was still easterly, and the other ship must have seen her green light.

5. Gibson also noticed the Californian's head was falling away toward the south, and when she pointed there the other ship would be able to see her red light as well as her green.

5. Gibson also noticed the Californian's head was falling away toward the south, and when she pointed there the other ship would be able to see her red light as well as her green.

7. Boxhall later saw the other ship's red side-light alone. He fired one more rocket, his last. Eight in all, Lightoller said were fired. The last went off about 1.30 a.m.

8. Stone and Gibson saw the other ship fire an eighth rocket, which proved to be the last. Gibson noticed the Californian was then heading toward the west, when she must have been showing her red light alone to the other ship. It was then about 1.30 a.m.

but Stone and Gibson, between them, provide it. Then, says Boxhall, he saw her red, i.e. port, light, and he fired his final, eighth rocket at this ship now showing him her port side. Again, Boxhall does not give the figure, but Stone and Gibson, once more, do.

After Stone had seen the first five rockets, Gibson comes back to the bridge. During his absence, the *Californian* has swung "towards the nor'ard",[49] and her head is "falling away to northward and eastward".[50] The result is, the rocket-firing steamer is nearer the *Californian's* bows. Time goes on, and Gibson sees the ship fire two rockets. She has now fired seven in all, while the *Californian* had her green light showing to him.

More minutes pass, and the *Californian* continues her slow swing, and finally she shows her red, or port, light to the stranger.

"After midnight," said Captain Lord, "we slowly blew around and showed him our red light."[51]

Gibson, too, notes this, and then says the steamer fired another rocket, her eighth. He could not know it at the time, but it was also her last.

Summing it up: from Boxhall, we learn that he must have fired seven rockets while the other steamer was showing him her starboard side.

From Stone and Gibson, we learn that the *Californian* was showing the unknown steamer her starboard side while she fired seven rockets.

From Boxhall, we learn that he must have fired his last, or eighth, rocket while the other steamer was showing him her port side.

From Gibson alone, we learn that the *Californian* was showing the unknown steamer her port side, while she fired her eighth rocket. It is the last, and clinching, detail.

Sources

1 B 7267.
2 'The Middle Watch'.
3 *Tramps and Ladies*, p. 295.
4 B 8369.
5 B 8371.
6 US 179.
7 US 782.
8 US 1139.
9 Ibid.
10 *The Boston Evening Transcript*, 19 April 1912, p. 8.
11 B 7337.
12 B 7329-33.
13 B 7336-37.
14 B 7061.
15 B 8503 *seq*.
16 B 8518.
17 B 8515.
18 B 8529.
19 B 8508.
20 B 8532-33.
21 B 8554.
22 B 8555.
23 B 8553.
24 B 8552.
25 B 8529.
26 B 8561.
27 B 8562-64.
28 B 8721-27.
29 B 8561.
30 B 8727.
31 B 8728.
32 B 8729-33.
33 B 8739.
34 B 8740-42.
35 B 8743.
36 B 8744-47.
37 B 8748.
38 B 8749-56.
39 'The "Californian" Incident', p. 15.
40 US 181.
41 US 1140.
42 *Daily Herald*, 18 April 1912.
43 'The "Californian" Incident', p. 15.
44 Ibid., p. 16.
45 *The Boston Post*, 19 April 1912, p. 11.
46 'The "Californian" Incident', p. 16.
47 P.I.
48 'The "Californian" Incident', p. 31.
49 B 7475.
50 B 7774.
51 US 732.

Chapter 11

Boston: Captain Lord crosses his Rubicon

I

It was Captain Lord's first trip to Boston,[1] and also the first visit of the *Californian*.[2] As it turned out, this was also the only time master and ship appeared together in Boston harbour, and never before or later did this unknown captain and undistinguished vessel, both normal subjects for routine back-page shipping announcements, arouse so much expectation.

At 8.17 p.m., the night before, when the *Californian* came abeam the South Wellfleet wireless station, a further message was despatched to Leyland's in Boston:

> "Arrived scene of *Titanic* disaster 8.30 a.m. 15th. All survivors taken aboard *Carpathia*. Have not any and did not see any bodies. Lord."[3]

It was 1 o'clock Friday morning, 19 April, when the *Californian* arrived at Boston Light,[4] and there she waited the rest of the night. Lord's message had been plain and emphatic; sufficient to put an end to any lingering hope that this ship might have aboard any *Titanic* survivors or the remains of any victims. Neither sorrow nor hope is entirely rational, however, and it is hardly surprising that at 7 o'clock the Clyde Street pier of the Boston and Albany docks in East Boston was lined with scores of anxious relatives and friends of *Titanic* passengers.[5] The original plan to have the reporters meet the ship before she docked had been changed, and so many of them were also on the pier, impatiently awaiting her.[6] The *Californian* was in any event the first ship that had been near the *Titanic* to arrive in Boston since the disaster.[7] John H. Thomas, the local agent of the International Mercantile Marine, owners of both the White Star and the Leyland Lines, who had sent the two wireless messages to Lord, had told Edwin T. Curtis, the Collector of the port, that he was willing to allow reporters with customs passes to board the ship. Thereby he incidentally won a nod of approval for treating the press with more consideration than had the Cunard Company the night before in New York when the *Carpathia* arrived.

As soon as the gangplank was lowered there was a rush onto the deck,[8] but a representative of Leyland's first had a few minutes of private conversation alone with Lord in his cabin. When he appeared, there were many anxious inquiries. Lord's first words proved more effective than his South Wellfleet message of the previous evening. Quietly, he told the crowd that his ship had no bodies aboard.[9] Although the *Californian* had cruised about the area where the *Titanic* had gone down "for more than six hours", according to one report, though others put it as "three", they had found nothing. The bereaved listeners were disheartened, but finally convinced. Most of them then left the ship, with many in tears. A large touring car with four young men in it drove up to the dock soon after the *Californian* tied up, and one of them named Endicott at once jumped out and asked if perhaps the bodies of Mr and Mrs Straus had been recovered. Being told they had not, he gave the news to his companions, who were relatives of the deceased, and the car drove off.

Captain Lord now had to face the reporters. One can safely assume this was the first encounter with the press he had ever had in his life, and although he seemed quite at ease it must have been an ordeal. He refused to be photographed, but otherwise was "agreeable" and "talked readily",[10] and this, too, in spite of the fact that he was said to be tired out after the strain of being in almost constant fog[11] from the time the voyage to Boston had been resumed.

The story he told was simple and easy to understand.

"Leyland Liner Rushed to Scene of Titanic Disaster but Found Only Wreckage"

Such was a typical headline in *The Boston Traveller.*[12]

"My wireless operator, C.F. Evans, received the SOS message at 5.30 Monday morning," Lord told that newspaper, "when we were 30 miles north of the scene of the frightful disaster. This message was sent from the steamship *Virginian.* I do not know where the *Virginian* was at the time."

All the papers that day or the next, in what may be described as the first phase of the Boston episode, had much the same report of Lord's description of his trip to the scene of the wreck, but the *Globe* was perhaps a little more vivid. They were separated from "the scene of the catastrophe", Lord was here reported as saying,[13] "by great masses of ice, including a number of large bergs and field ice, which in places was two miles wide." After Evans told them the news, "we set about reaching the scene of the accident as quickly as possible."

"At best, however, it was slow going. At times, nervous and anxious as we were, we hardly seemed to be moving. We had to dodge the big bergs, skirt the massed field ice and plow through the line of the least resistance. For three full hours, we turned, twisted, doubled on our course — in short, manoeuvered one way or another — through the winding channels of the ice."

"Long before we got to the scene," the *Traveller's*[14] report continued, "we saw the Carpathia picking up the life boats from Titanic, and were close in when the last of the boats were hauled on board the Cunarder. We steamed as close to the spot as we could, but there was no sign of life about. For three hours I remained steaming about the spot, hoping to be able to pick up something, or recover some body, but we saw nothing."

The *Traveller* also had a detail reported nowhere else: "Running close to the Carpathia, the cries and wailings of the women and children could be heard in spite of the fact that they had been taken to the cabins and staterooms, where they were attended by those on board the rescue ship.* The ocean was smooth and calm and the weather was fine, but there was a desolate aspect about the place that impressed us all on board the Californian. No

---

* A possible, though questionable, detail, especially to those familiar with Mr Beesley's story of the silence of the survivors. John R. Joyce, Boston banker, a passenger in the *Carpathia,* corroborates Mr Beesley. He said: "But there was no demonstration. No sobs – scarcely a word spoken. They seemed to be stunned." (*Boston Herald,* 19, p. 3)

other ship was in sight but the Carpathia. I do not know where the Virginian was then."

Lord also described the wreckage:[15] "Of course the waters were pretty well littered with wreckage, but we were really a bit surprised, considering the size of the wreck, that there wasn't more. We seamen would describe the amount of floating material as 'scant wreckage', but I suppose a landsman would have thought that the waters teemed with floating stuff. The wreckage consisted of cushions, chairs and similar things."

"At the end of three hours, our search having been without result, we put on steam and headed for Boston."[16] The distance was approximately nine hundred miles.[17]

It seems that nobody asked Lord directly why the SOS from the *Titanic* had not been received until the early morning, and nowhere was the reason stated that Evans was off duty. Lord was reported as saying that the *Californian* was 30 miles north of the wreck[18] and also as "20 miles" from the scene; but he made no point of that (let alone asserting that the *Titanic* had given the wrong position). All the emphasis was on the difficulty presented by the impassable ice.

"I never in all my marine career saw so much ice," he told the *Boston Daily Advertiser,* which was literally true, as he was to testify later that he had never before been in field ice at all.

"S.S. CALIFORNIAN NOT
ABLE TO AID IN RESCUES"

" 'S.O.S.' SIGNALS RECEIVED
WHEN IN BIG ICE FIELD"

These, accordingly, were the headlines to the *Advertiser's* report, and all the papers, after getting the master's story, gave similar importance to the ice. It was the ice and the ice alone, Lord implied, which had prevented him from giving any effective help.

Such was Captain Lord's story, a tragic tale of human goodwill and efficiency, frustrated by chance and the power of nature. It was modestly told and accepted not only without question, but with respectful compliments.

"It took some mighty good seamanship," commented *The Boston Globe,* "to pilot the freighter through the narrow winding channels of the ice, and although her officer used every effort to keep her going as fast as possible, there were times when circumstances made it necessary for her to proceed at a snail's pace. Some faint idea of what conditions were in the North Atlantic at that time may be gained from the fact that it took this 13-knot steamer, going at her best under the circumstances three full hours to cover the 30 miles which separated her from the scene of the disaster."[19]

Amid the unanimous acceptance of Captain Lord's straightforward story, there was only one curious and rather puzzling detail.

"Captain Lord was asked," reported *The Boston Traveller*, "in what latitude and longitude he was when he first received the S.O.S. message from the Virginian, and his reply was that he could not give out 'state secret', and that the question would have to be answered by those in the office."[20]

The newspaper made no comment, but *The Boston Evening Transcript* did.[21] The language of its report of the same matter at once suggested a certain scepticism. According to the *Transcript,* Lord "said that the reporters were requesting what he termed 'state secrets', and that the information would have to come from the company's office. Ordinarily when a steamer reaches port and has anything to report, figures giving exact positions reckoned in latitude and longitude have always been obtainable from the ship's officers. Later at the White Star office and in the presence of Manager John. H. Thomas, Captain Lord said that when he received the message the Californian's position was 42.05 north latitude and 50.00 west longitude. The message gave the Titanic's position as 41 degrees 46 minutes north latitude and 50 degrees 14 minutes west longitude."

The *Transcript's* reporter was evidently sufficiently interested to follow up the question of the *Californian's* position by taking Lord at his word and going to the office. We do not know where aboard the ship Lord's interview with the reporters took place, nor whether it was in the presence of any of the crew; but we do know that, once again, the *Transcript* man tried to dig a little deeper than any of his colleagues. It seems he wanted to question Evans, but "Wireless operator C.F. Evans had nothing to say." A barbed remark then follows: "So far as was apparent his vocal organs were not impaired."[22]

It may be putting it too high to say that this reporter did not believe Lord's story, but he clearly indicated that he had some doubts and was conscious of something more to the story than had been told. His report continues: "An agent of the line boarded the steamer immediately after she docked and was closeted with Captain Lord in his cabin for a few minutes before the reporters saw him. Possibly nothing transpired beyond regular routine business as it is customary for an agent to communicate with the commander of a vessel as soon as possible."

The implication is plain, but as the writer was clearly an accurate and fair-minded journalist, he adds his opinion about Lord, which has already been partly quoted: "However, Captain Lord was agreeable and talked readily except in the instance of latitude and longitude." The information is then given that the night before John H. Thomas "sent a wireless message to Captain Lord telling him to give to reporters any information that he might have regarding the disaster." This seems a clear hint that if anything was being kept back, the person responsible was probably Captain Lord himself and not the officials of the Leyland Line.

With this single exception the Boston newspapermen accepted Lord's story at its face value, without question or reservation. And why not? They had no reason to suspect that this particular British merchant skipper, in spite of his remarkably distinguished appearance, was any different from, and less to be trusted than, the average member of a much respected calling. The reader who knows what really happened is in a better position to judge the nature and value of Captain Lord's narrative.

One may give Lord the benefit of the doubt when assaying his motive for not communicating with his Boston office; but it is not reasonable to acquit him for his conduct at his first press meeting. His subsequent statements at Boston, soon to follow, provide overwhelming corroboration that his glaring lack of candour at his first interview with newspapers was no snap decision, but a deliberate policy. His log was blank; nobody knew of the statements by Stone and Gibson. Not a document aboard the ship, so far as any stranger knew, could contradict him, and, he must have believed or hoped, not a voice would dare. There was cause for him to be disturbed, if he was; for he, a truthful man hitherto, had decided to plunge into falsehood. His story was intended to, and did, deceive. At Boston, Captain Lord had crossed his Rubicon.

Whether or not any of Lord's officers and crew were within earshot while he was being interviewed, all soon were able, that day or the next, to read in the local newspapers what he had said. The *Titanic,* of course, occupied the greater part of the front pages, but the *Californian* was not by any means smothered.

We cannot be sure whether the publication of Lord's interview was actually the provocation for the events which resulted in breaking the true story of the *Californian,* as distinct from Lord's version of it, but it certainly had an early place in the revelation. The opening of the files of the *Titanic* by the British Board of Trade has unexpectedly disclosed the real story of how and by whom the sighting of the rockets was first made known to the world. The material is quite different from the story always accepted and ante-dates it by several days.

Some time after the *Californian's* meeting with the *Carpathia* on the Monday, and certainly before 11 p.m. on Friday, 19 April, a letter was written, perhaps aboard the *Californian,* which contained a largely correct account of the sighting of the rockets, and the repeated calling of Captain Lord. It was addressed to England.

That letter must have been written before 11 p.m. on Friday night, 19 April, because it was surely in a mailbag aboard the *Lapland,* when that vessel sailed from New York on Saturday with the next despatch of mails for Northern Europe, including England. Among more important things, it served to expose the vanity of Captain Lord's hope that his crew would remain silent, for it was written by none other than the ship's carpenter, W.F. McGregor. With his appearance in the story, the second phase of the *Californian's* Boston episode opens.

II

Having obtained 24 hour's leave from Saturday night, McGregor set out for Clinton, Massachusetts,[23] a small town of some 13,000 inhabitants, about 34 miles north-east of Boston. His letter, whether written at sea or only after Captain Lord's meeting with the press in Boston, had been composed in a spirit of great indignation. It was intended as a protest and possibly with the object of getting some action taken. The letter was already on its way to England, but the carpenter had not cooled off by the time he came to the end of his journey.

Although he took it upon himself to interfere in Captain Lord's plan for concealing the truth about the *Californian,* and to that extent was an agent of history, very little is known about W.F. McGregor. As the ship's carpenter he was of senior rating in the *Californian* and only surpassed in pay by the Officers, Engineers and Chief Steward. His position and craft was highly respected and one would not expect a man of his trade to be given to unverifiable gossip.

Still he remains as shadowy a figure as any of the lower deck, but with hints of acquaintances superior in the British social hierarchy to those of average seamen. Born in Liverpool,[24] he was a mature man of 41. This was not his first voyage in the *Californian,* although it was to be his last. He was paid £7 per month, he lived in Liverpool, and he had a relative in Clinton. When the *Californian* arrived back in Liverpool on 10 May, he took the balance of the pay due to him and left the ship and the sea for good. The rest is silence.

That McGregor's trip to Clinton was more than a mere family visit became clear on Tuesday evening, when the local newspaper, the *Clinton Daily Item,* appeared with a sensational front-page story. Although its circulation was only 3,000 and limited to the readers of a small town, it is an historic document, for it broke the *Californian* story, and first publicly disclosed anywhere in the world that rockets had been seen by her on the night of the disaster. Never previously republished in its entirety, the story read as follows:[25]

"CALIFORNIA [*sic*] REFUSED AID
Foreman Carpenter on Board this Boat Says Hundreds
Might Have Been Saved FROM THE TITANIC

According to a story told by the foreman carpenter on board the steamship California, that boat was within ten miles of the Titanic when that steamship met its fate, and but for the orders of the captain could have aided the Titanic and probably saved hundreds of passengers. This story was told to John H.G. Frazer of this town by the foreman carpenter who is a cousin of Mr. Frazer, but because of a possible outcome of these facts the name of the man is withheld.

Mr. Frazer's cousin was in Clinton Sunday on a leave of absence from Saturday night until Sunday night while the California was docked at Boston. It is said the ship will probably never sail again under the same captain as a result of his action on the night of the disaster. The story as told to Mr. Frazer is to the effect that the California, which belongs to the Leyland line, which is under the same control as the White Star Line, was within 10 miles of the Titanic when she struck the iceberg. At this time the California was sailing just ahead of the Titanic but had seen a big field of ice and in order to avoid it turned south and went round the big mass. It is also said that the wireless operator on board the California notified the Titanic and all other vessels in that vicinity of the presence of the big ice field.

It was shortly after the California had gone by the ice field that the watch saw the rockets which were sent up by the Titanic as signals of distress. The officer on watch, it is said, reported this to the boat, but he failed to pay any attention to the signals excepting to tell the watch to keep his eye on the boat. At this time the two boats were about 10 miles apart. It being in the night the wireless operator on board the California was asleep at the time.

It is said that those on board the California could see the lights of the Titanic very plainly, and it is also reported that those on the Titanic saw the California. Finally the first mate on the California, who, with several of the officers had been watching the Titanic, decided he would take a hand in the situation and so roused the wireless operator and an attempt was made to communicate with the Titanic. It was then too late, as the apparatus on the Titanic was out of commission. The operator did, however, catch the word 'Titanic' which was probably being sent from the Carpathia or some other boat, and this information was given to the captain. He immediately ordered the boat to stop and was very much concerned as to the fate of the Titanic after that, but it was far too late. The California had during this time continued ahead under full steam and by the time the name of the boat was ascertained it is believed to have been about 20 miles away.

The California turned back and started for the scene but it is a very slow boat as compared with the Carrpathia [*sic*] and several others, and although the Carpathia was about 50 miles away when it first learned of the accident it was able to get there much sooner than the California. The next morning the California learned from the Carpathia that it had reached the scene and that the Titanic had gone down and that all the survivors had been picked up. According to Mr. Frazer's cousin the captain of the California had the appearance of being 20 years older after the news reached him. The California proceeded to Boston.

It is the belief of Mr. Frazer's cousin that the captain will never be in command of the California again and he told Mr. Frazer that he would positively refuse to sail under him again and that all of the officers had the same feeling. Mr. Frazer says according to the story as told him that had the captain of the California turned back when the rockets were first seen hundreds of the Titanic passengers could have been taken off on that boat."

It will be noticed that McGregor did not claim that he himself had seen anything; nor did he talk directly to the newspaper. One can deduce that he was asleep during the critical middle watch and probably did not wake up until the *Californian* was hurrying to the scene; hence, the erroneous statement that the vessel continued on her course during the night. There are other mistakes as well, some of which perhaps were due to inaccurate repetition by Frazer of what McGregor had told him. Nevertheless, this was the first even roughly true account of the *Californian's* Sunday night. Hitherto, her sighting rockets had not even been suspected. It is also a red-hot, first impression of the indignation prevailing aboard the ship, which could not have been guessed from any of the arrival stories, with their picture of a crew united (if silent) behind their eloquent skipper, all disappointed but all conscious of having done their best. It seems certain that if McGregor's story had appeared in a Boston or New York newspaper, it would have exploded across the nation.

It was only Boxhall's evidence on Monday which carried the incident of the 'mystery ship' seen from the *Titanic* to the front pages of America. Next morning, 23 April, *The New York Times* headed its report of Boxhall's evidence:[26]

"SHIP FIVE MILES OFF AS BIG LINER SANK
No Clue to the Identity of the Craft, but Others Saw Her Light"

By then, some enterprising Boston reporter must have seen the Clinton story and rushed off that very Tuesday night to interview Lord again, for his new story appeared next morning, 24 April, in *The Boston Post*. Lord "stoutly denied" that his was the ship which was said by *Titanic* survivors to have "passed within five miles of the sinking steamer and ignored distress signals."

It was on this occasion, and for the first time, that Lord said his vessel "had sighted no rockets or other signals of distress."[27] He repeated that the *Californian* was stopped all night in the ice field, with her engines and dynamos shut down. The impression conveyed, if not intended, was that for this reason the wireless was not working, and so the *Californian* did not hear the distress signal until next morning, when it was received from the *Virginian*.

This story bore the headlines:[28]

"LEYLAND LINER GOT NO SIGNALS
Wireless Not Working, Though But 20 Miles Away"

but Lord's own words should be quoted: "The wireless operator retired about 11 o'clock, and up to the moment of shutting down no message of distress or any signal of distress was received or sighted." These careful words are literally true, as no doubt Lord intended them to be.

In England *The Liverpool Echo* on 24 April and under the headings:[29]

"ALL MIGHT HAVE BEEN SAVED
LEYLAND LINER CAPTAIN'S ADMISSION"

had got word of the story too and stated: "It is now suggested that the steamer whose lights were seen from the deck of the Titanic by the doomed passengers must have been the Californian." But, on the other hand, there was also an opinion that the *Hellig Olav*,[30] westbound from Copenhagen, may have been the "so-called mystery ship". As that vessel docked in New York as early as 17 April,[31] and it was calculated that the spot where the *Titanic* struck was some 1,080 miles from New York,[32] the 9,939-ton Danish vessel, with a top speed of 15½ knots,[33] soon necessarily ceased to be a suspect. Her owners, the Scandinavian-American Line, issued a statement on 24 April that the *Hellig Olav* was, in fact, at least 350 miles west of the *Titanic* at the time of the accident.[34]

To a *New York Herald*[35] man in Boston on Tuesday night, when asked about those rumours which had been coming out of Clinton, Massachusetts, that the *Californian* "was within sight of the *Titanic* and failed to respond to her calls for assistance," Lord loftily dismissed the charge with the words: "Sailors will tell anything when they are ashore." It was a comprehensive and Olympian judgement and was intended primarily to dispose of the Clinton reports; but there must have been a few among the crew who might have applied the words to Lord himself. The *Herald* published the story in New York next day, 24 April, and included in it a direct quotation from Lord about his wireless:

"With the engines stopped, the wireless was, of course, not working, so we heard nothing of the Titanic's plight until the next morning."

". . . if he had known of the *Titanic's* plight, all of her passengers might have been saved." So tamely commented *The New York Herald,* and there seems to have been no instant reaction elsewhere in America to this disingenuous explanation. *The Liverpool Echo* diligently followed up the matter, and declared on the 25th: "Inquiries in the highest shipping quarters in the city to-day point to a different conclusion . . ."[36]

"'It is unthinkable,' said a leading shipowner, 'that the dynamos were cut off . . .'" and informed opinion was that the *Californian* was no exception to the general practice that the wireless and the ship's engines were not linked, and it was no excuse for the inactivity of the wireless that the engines were stopped. As the wireless was not working, the real reason must have been that the operator "had gone to rest, expecting that no more messages would reach his vessel that night. There was no blame attached to the operator in this, but the whole deplorable story shows that the operators were not numerous enough to staff the apparatus in a prolonged crisis . . . The feeling experienced next morning when the terrible catastrophe was revealed must have been heart-rending."

This true and quite blameless explanation for the silence of his wireless Lord himself certainly published later; but he never denied that he had, at least, originally, attributed it to the stopping of the ship's engines. It was a stupid thing to have done, as it could so easily be disproved, unlike other false statements he undoubtedly made, which were speciously convincing. In any event, it will be observed that to his sole explanation of his inactivity, when he arrived at Boston, which was the ice, he had now added the factor of his wireless. On Thursday morning, 25 April, *The Boston Globe* at last specifically mentioned McGregor's Clinton visit, although, of course, without naming him. Under the heading:

"DENIAL ON THE CALIFORNIAN"

it reported: "One who said he was in the crew of the Leyland steamer

Californian and who was visiting relatives in Clinton last Sunday night is alleged in a statement printed in the Daily Item of that city, to have said that the signals of distress sent up by the Titanic were seen by the Californian and ignored. The name of the man is not given. According to this unnamed authority, the Californian was within 10 miles of the Titanic when the accident occurred . . ."[37]

John H. Thomas, the loyal and diligent agent, at once came to the defence. "The story is perfectly absurd," he declared. "Captain Lord is a brave man and an able officer and to say that he would not have responded to signals of distress and gone at once to the rescue of any ship in peril is simply ridiculous."

"He was specifically equipped for such work, too, having six big lifeboats aboard his ship."

Every word of which, about man and ship, was true. Thomas went on to say that on his arrival Lord had "reported to me the relative positions of the Titanic and the Californian, he having gotten the position of the Titanic from the Virginian. The vessels were 20 miles apart."

He said that "no signals could possibly be seen at this distance" and "the story should not be dignified by a denial."

Captain Lord, the Globe continued, "simply ignored the story yesterday. 'Here are some facts,' he said, 'and you can see for yourself.'" He then gave the position of the Californian, when she stopped in the icefield, 42.05N; 50.07W, and the position of the Titanic, as given by the Virginian, 41.46N; 50.14W. "'This shows that the Titanic was 18 miles due south of us and seven miles west, which would make her 20 miles away . . . We started as soon as we learned where the Titanic was, at 6 o'clock. The ship was driven for all she was worth. We stopped alongside the Carpathia at 8.30. We remained there four hours, thinking we might find someone floating on wreckage.'"

All this Lord had said before. On the day of his arrival, when his latitude and longitude were alleged to be "state secrets", he had casually said that at the time the Virginian's message was received, "we were 30 miles north of the scene."[38] But now, being clearly anxious to prove, with the aid of latitude and longitude, his exact distance from the wreck, he offered an additional and gratuitous piece of information. Although never mentioned by his partisans, it is something not to be forgotten by others.

"We also checked up in regard to the [Titanic's] position,'" said Captain Lord, "and found it to be what it had been reported by the Virginian [i.e. 41.46N; 50.14W]."[39]

Leaving aside for the moment the fact that the Californian's overnight DR position must have been wrong we find Lord here, when relying on it to show he was not ten miles from the Titanic, as McGregor has alleged, but 20, using as a prop in support of his own reckoning nothing other than the accuracy of the reported position of the Titanic. This was the man who was later to make it a key part of his defence that the Titanic had made a mistake and given out the wrong position. Here, Lord gives it unexpected, but specific, confirmation. Nor was this the end of it. In his final Boston interview, with the Journal, he again implicitly confirmed the correctness of the Titanic's position.

Ten days had now gone by since the disaster, and the Globe printed Lord's statement without comment. It then continued with the statement that the wireless operator had gone to bed about 11 o'clock the night before, and was not called until 5 a.m. on Monday.

Stewart now gets into print for the first time.

"The first thing picked up by the operator, says First Officer Stewart, was a confused message from the Frankfurt in which it was made out finally that the Titanic was sinking . . ."

During the night, it was said, Lord did not see any vessel which might have been that reported within five miles of the *Titanic*.

"Between noon of 14 April and noon of 15 April the Californian steamed 129 miles, which would indicate that she was tied up somewhere. She steamed 275 miles in the following 24 hours. All this, it is said, appears in the ship's log and is easy of verification."

"The Californian is due to sail on Saturday, and as she was nearest to the Titanic apparently when the accident occurred Captain Lord will probably be a witness before the British Board of Inquiry.

"None of the crew yesterday would say they had seen any signals of distress or any lights on the night of Sunday, 14 April. One of them said he did not believe that any one else did. The chances, he added, were that any one on deck that night was not looking for signals of distress but was more likely looking for some warm place in the lee, as it was very cold."

One must speculate whether the *Globe* reporter, while garnering this meaty story, happened to encounter carpenter McGregor! The newspaper, in any event, could add itself to the roster of those which Lord had received and deceived. But, as it happened, this was the last day on which Captain Lord's house of cards was still standing. The anonymous McGregor, angry but disinterested, had first asserted that Captain Lord had built a house of cards. On this same 25 April, another character, by no means anonymous, but with a desire and gift for personal publicity, and, again unlike the carpenter, not entirely disinterested, took action. This new champion of truth — and other less respectable causes — at once had a devastating effect and blew over the whole of Captain Lord's fragile structure. This new entrant on the scene was an assistant donkeyman and his name was Ernest Gill.

III

His entrance marked the opening of the third and final phase of the *Californian's* Boston episode.

We do not know the complete story of how Gill came to tell — actually, to sell — his story to *The Boston American*, but by Wednesday evening, 24 April, he had already made the deal.[40] That evening, he met Evans, who had gone ashore, "outside the North Station or the South Station" — Evans could not remember which — and said "he had been up and told the newspaper about the accident."[41] It is possible that Gill's original motive was only, as he said, to prevent Lord's "hushing up the men", without thought of self-gain. Whatever may be thought of Gill, he at least was not afraid to sign his name. The disclosure that Harold Bride, the *Titanic's* surviving wireless operator, had been paid a thousand dollars by *The New York Times*[42] for his story, was not made in Washington until the following Monday, 29 April; but Gill throughout gives the impression of having an eye to his own interests, not necessarily always unfairly, and quite probably he needed no example from Bride or anyone else to get the idea that he might make a good thing out of his own contribution to history. At any rate, the newspaper, which printed his story, whether on their own, or Gill's initiative, was no small, up-State newspaper, but a large city member of the Hearst chain. *The Boston American*, like the rest of the Hearst press, was a sensational, yellow newspaper; but sometimes it did also campaign for respectable causes.

The Californian *in Dominion Line colours, 1902.*

The cast in pictures

Same picture of the Californian *retouched to Leyland Line colours.*

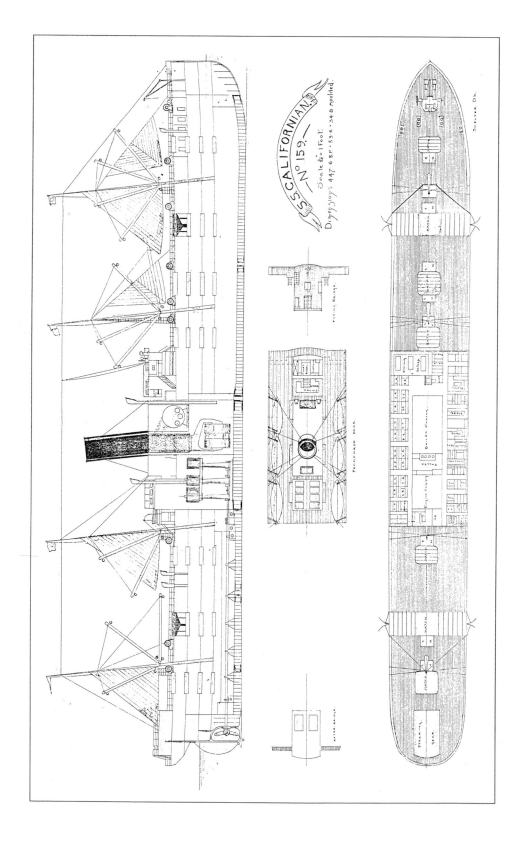

S.S. CALIFORNIAN
Nº 159.
Scale 1/32 = 1 Foot.
Dimensions 447.6 B.P. 536.34.8 moulded.

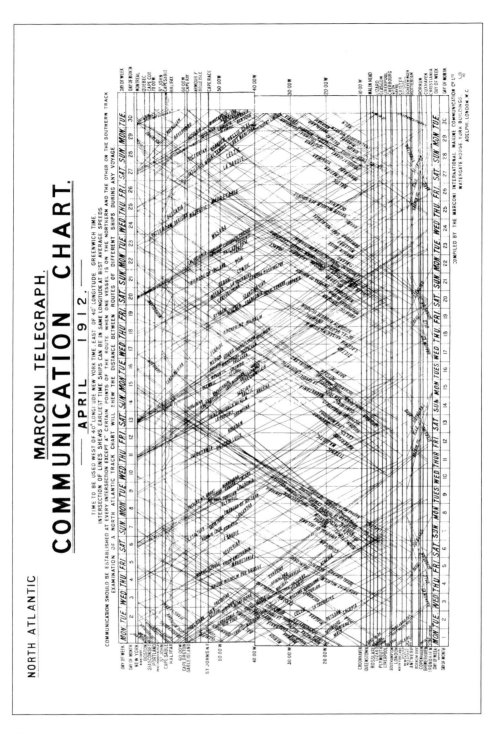

Opposite *Plan of the* Californian. (Courtesy: Rob Caledon Ltd, Scottish Record Office)

Above *The Marconi Communication Chart for the North Atlantic for April 1912 that young Evans, the* Californian's *Marconi operator, needed, but 'in the hurry of getting off again' did not get.* (Courtesy: Marconi Co.)

Above Titanic *ready to leave her fitting out berth, Johnson's Wharf, at Harland & Wolff for her half a day sort trials in Belfast Lough.* (Photo: courtesy Stanley B. Jackson)

Left *Fitting the* Titanic *out continued in Southampton over the Easter holiday, when the ship was dressed for the day but her decks were still cluttered with ship's stores.*

Right *Captain Edward John Smith of the* Titanic, *photographed at Southampton, on the bridge of his last command.*

Below Titanic's *near collision at Southampton, with the SS* New York, *(middle) photographed from the deck of the* Titanic. *On the left is the SS* Oceanic *who nearly broke her mooring lines.*

Above *Last look at the* Titanic *from Southampton as she steamed to open water on her way to Cherbourg. Note her slight list to port.*

Below *The* Titanic *at night. This washed drawing is often said to be a photograph. It is however, an artist's impression — made in England — of the ship at anchor at Cherbourg. It nevertheless gives a good impression of how the* Titanic *appeared at night to anybody watching her broadside lavish illumination. The two masthead lights on her main or after mast are fiction as the* Titanic *did not carry masthead lights on her main mast at all. The smoke issuing from the fourth, dummy, funnel is also fiction.*

The next six photographs show wireless operators involved in the drama:

Above left *John George Phillips,* Titanic. (Courtesy Marconi Co.)

Above *Harold Sydney Bride,* Titanic. (Courtesy Marconi Co.)

Left *Harold Thomas Cottam*, Carpathia.

Below *Cyril Furmston Evans*, Californian.

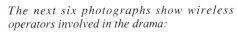

Above left *Gilbert William Balfour, Marconi Travelling Inspector, happened to be on the* Baltic. (Courtesy Marconi Co.)

Above right *John Oscar Durrant*, Mount Temple. (Courtesy Marconi Co.)

Below *Captain Lord and his officers in 1912. Photograph taken on the voyage before the* Californian *became notorious. Seated: left to right: Captain Lord and Chief Officer George Frederick Stewart. Standing: left to right: Second Officer Herbert Stone and Third Officer Charles Victor Groves. The two little girls pictured were children of passengers on that voyage.*

Above *Captain Lord in 1920. These pictures are very much preferred by the supporters of Captain Lord and used in almost all their publications. Lord at this time was employed by Lawther Latta.*

Below left *Captain Lord in 1926.*

Below right *Captain Lord's son, Stanley Tutton Lord (left) and Mr Leslie Harrison.*

Above *The only eyewitness drawing of the* Titanic *firing one of her eight rockets. The sketch was made by steward Leo James Hayland.* (Courtesy Mr W. Lord)

Below Titanic *lifeboat No. 6, only half filled, bobbing gently on the empty ocean. The boat could have held some 68 persons, but she carried only 28 survivors. Like most port side boats she was among the last to arrive at the* Carpathia.

Above *Lookout Fred Fleet in 1912.*

Above right *Lookout Fred Fleet in 1964.* (Photo: Leslie Reade)

Below left *Second Class passenger Mr Lawrence Beesley in 1912.*

Below right *Mr Lawrence Beesley in 1958.* (Photo: Leslie Reade)

Above *SS* Carpathia.

Left *Captain Arthur Henry Rostron of the* Carpathia. (Courtesy: Mrs Margaret E. Howman)

Above right *SS* Mount Temple. (National Maritime Museum, Greenwich)

Right *Captain James Henry Moore of the* Mount Temple. (Photo: courtesy Captain Harry A. Moore)

Above *Shelter deck of the* Californian.

Above right *The* Californian *at the time of her arrival, photographed from the* Carpathia *by one of her first-class passengers, Mr Louis M. Ogden.* (National Archives, New York City)

Middle right *The two signal flags on the* Californian's *main mast. The hoist, first pendant — or code flag — over the 'J' flag, conveys the signal 'I have a headway'. The half-masted house flag, seen here also on the main mast, which supporters of Captain Lord choose to identify as the coal basket in which AB Ben Kirk was hoisted to spy for the sunken* Titanic *(see Appendix G).*

Below right *The icefield, photographed by Mr Louis M. Ogden from the* Carpathia *as she steamed from the scene of the disaster.* (National Archives, New York City)

Below *The* Californian *photographed from the* Carpathia *by first-class passenger Mrs Mabel Fenwick.*

Above *The four surviving officers of the* Titanic. *Left to right: Second Officer Charles Herbert Lightoller, Third Officer Herbert John Pitman, Fourth Officer Joseph Grove Boxhall. In front: Fifth Officer Harold Godfrey Lowe.* (Courtesy: the late Mrs Sylvia Lightoller)

Below *Crowd outside pier 54 in New York awaiting the arrival of the* Carpathia.

Above right *Senator William Alden Smith, Chairman of the Senate Sub-committee of Inquiry.* (Library of Congress)

Above far right *First session and first witness of the US Senate investigation, held at the Waldorf-Astoria Hotel in New York. Bruce Ismay (hand at moustache) being questioned by Senator Smith (opposite him and with arm resting on table).*

Right *The US Senators and the man who initially had their utmost interest. Top, left to right: Senator Theodore Elijah Burton (Ohio), Joseph Bruce Ismay, Chairman and Managing Director of the White Star Line, Senator Jonathan Bourne (Oregon). Bottom, left to right: Senator Francis Griffith Newlands (Nevada), Senator Duncan Upshaw Fletcher (Florida), Senator George Clermont Perkins (California).*

CLINTON DAILY ITEM.

VOL. XIX. NO. 306. (Established 1895) CLINTON, MASS., TUESDAY EVENING, APRIL 23, 1912. PRICE ONE CENT

FIEFIELD TROUBLES

Husband and Wife Tell their Troubles to Judge Smith in District Court

CASE CONTINUED AGAIN

DEMURER SUSTAINED

Judge Hardy Hands Down Finding in Case of Robinson vs. Coulter

SAYS "NO LIBEL"

STRIKE IS THREATENED

Weavers at the Lancaster Mills go to Office and Make Demands

TO HOLD MEETING

CALIFORNIA REFUSED AID

Foreman Carpenter on Board this Boat Says Hundreds Might Have Been Saved

FROM THE TITANIC

STATE BOARD IS AGREED

Favorable Action Taken on Plans for the Abolition of the Grade Crossings

SUPERIOR COURT NEXT

As a result Capt. Lord and Wireless Operator Evans of the Californian have been subpoenaed to appear before it, although the steamer is to sail Saturday morning.

The summons came after, but apparently had no connection with the story told yesterday by Ernest Gill, second donkeyman aboard the Californian.

CAPT. LORD DENIES STORY

"I saw a white rocket about ten miles away on the starboard side," he swore, in an affidavit. "It was not my business to notify the lookout, but they could not have helped but see them."

This story Captain Lord branded as a lie, in talking to a Journal reporter last night. He declared he believed Gill had been paid to tell the story.

"If I go to Washington it will not be because of this story in the paper, but to tell the committee why my ship was drifting without power, while the Titanic was rushing under full speed.

"It will take me about ten minutes to do this," Captain Lord declared.

"FALSE," ASSERTS SHIP'S CAPTAIN

Notwithstanding the fact that he with his wireless operator had been summoned to appear before the Senate committee that is investigating the sinking of the Titanic, Capt. Lord said last night the charges which had been printed in an evening paper were all "bosh."

"Everything that was printed in the story is a falsehood and any person who reads the affidavit of this man 'Gill' and knows anything about the sea will know that the stories that are being circulated among the crew that Gill

received $500 for the affidavit have some foundation."

"In the first place, do you think that any man who had been at work in the engine room or a ship for four hours would come out on the deck and stand there with the thermometer registered 27 degrees, smoking cigarettes?

"In the second place, don't you think that if any signals were sent by this man (if he was on deck) they could not have been seen by the officers and men on the bridge?

"Every officer and man of this crew is an Englishman and a white man, and no Englishman will stand by and see anybody or anything in distress without trying to lend assistance.

"Mr. Stewart, the first officer, was on the bridge during the times that the signals were supposed to have been seen, and he can tell you himself that nothing of the kind was seen by him or any of the men who were on watch with him.

"We got in among the ice about 10.30 P.M. and immediately shut off steam and drifted from that time until we received a message from the Virginia saying that the Titanic had struck an iceberg, was sinking and wished for assistance, and that time was about 2.30 A.M.

"Everything had been quiet during the night and no signals of distress or (Continued on Page 2—Column 1.)

---

nly Roosevelt Paper In B
evelt And His Campaign

Left *Captain John Joseph Knapp, US Navy Hydrographer.* (US Navy)

Below left *Second Officer James Bissett, Carpathia 1912.* (Courtesy: Angus and Robertson)

Below *Commodore Sir Ivan Thompson.* (Courtesy: Cunard Line)

Right *Front page of the* Clinton Daily Item, *23 April 1912. "CALIFORNIA* (sic) *REFUSED AID". Carpenter W.F. McGregor (not mentioned by name) broke the news of the* Californian's *dubious role in the drama.*

Opposite bottom left *Ernest Gill in Boston, after making his affidavit.*

Opposite bottom right From the Boston Journal, *front page, 26 April 1912. Captain Lord's denial that any signals were seen and his claim that Chief Officer Stewart was on the bridge and would support his denial*

HON. THEODORE E. BURTON

J. BRUCE ISMAY

SENATOR BOURNE

FRANCIS G. NEWLANDS

SEN. FLETCHER

SEN. GEO. C. PERKINS

Above and below *Port and starboard views of the* Titanic, *by chance taken by two photographers at the same time, at Johnson's Wharf, Belfast, just before the ship started her trials. The starboard view was taken by Stanley B. Jackson, the port view by Harland & Wolff's official photographer.*

Above right *The* Californian *in 1915.*

Below right *Scottish Hall, of the London Scottish Regiment in Buckingham Gate, being prepared for the* Titanic *Inquiry. The court had for each group its own right place; counsels up front and ladies up in the gallery. A large map of the North Atlantic Ocean (partly seen at the far left) and a half model of the* Titanic *were installed; as were, a few days later, curtains behind the Commissioner and his Assessors to improve the poor acoustics of the military drill hall.*

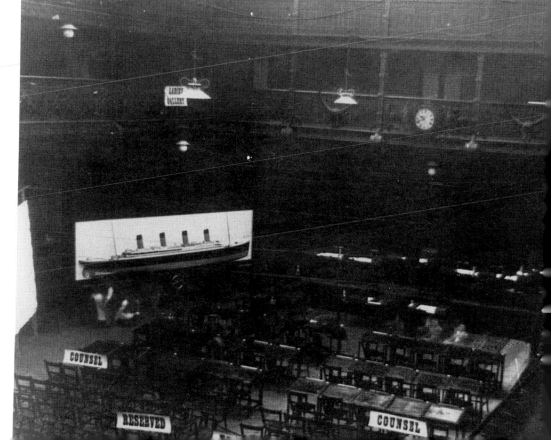

Above *The Californian witnesses. Left to right: Fireman George Glenn, Greaser William Thomas, Wireless Operator Cyril F. Evans, Apprentice James Gibson, Second Officer Herbert Stone, Seaman William Ross, Third Officer V. Groves and Chief Officer George F. Stewart.* (Courtesy: The Illustrated London News)

Left *Captain Lord on his way to the Inquiry a month after the disaster, 14 May 1912.*

Above *The Wreck Commissioners' Court in Scottish Hall in session. Behind the raised tables the Commissioner (second from the left) and his assessors; in front and on the floor, two of the stenographers who recorded the proceedings.*

Right *Mrs Sylvia Lightoller who attended all sittings of the Mersey Inquiry.* (Courtesy: Mrs Claire Rowe)

Above left *Wreck Commissioner Lord Mersey.*

Above right *The Attorney-General, Sir Rufus Isaacs.* (Courtesy: Lord Reading)

Left *C. Robertson Dunlop, Counsel for the Leyland Line, Captain Lord, and officers of the Californian.* (Courtesy: Mrs C. Robertson Dunlop)

Below *Senior Engineer E.C. Chaston, RNR.* (Courtesy: The Daily Mirror)

Above left *Rear Admiral Somerset A. Gough-Clatrope, RN.* (Courtesy: The Daily Mirror)

Above right *Captain Arthur W. Clarke.* (Courtesy: The Daily Mirror)

Below left *Professor J.H. (later Sir John) Biles.* (Courtesy: The Daily Mirror)

Below right *Commander F.C.A. Lyon, RNR.* (Courtesy: The Daily Mirror)

Left *Mr Leslie Harrison; until 1975 the General Secretary of the Mercantile Marine Service Association.*

Below *The* Samson.

Samson
Ex Belsund
Tromsö
506 Tons
Juni 1926

Above *Captain Henrik Bergethon Naess near the end of his life.* (Fotograf Schröder, Trondheim, Norway) **(Inset)** *Henrik Bergethon Naess at the time of the incident.* (Courtesy Norsk Polarinstitutt, Oslo, Norway.)

Below *Magic memories: extract of letter from Captain Naess: the* Samson *meets the* Titanic *'south of Cape Hatteras'. ('As it might be of some interest, I allow myself, since there is room left, to inform you, that when we were on the sealer 'Samson' in the southern part of the ice — south of Cape Hatteras, we saw the* Titanic, *just at the moment when she sent up her rockets . . .' Letter from Captain Naess in Norsk Polarinstitutt. (Courtesy: Norsk Polarinstitutt)*

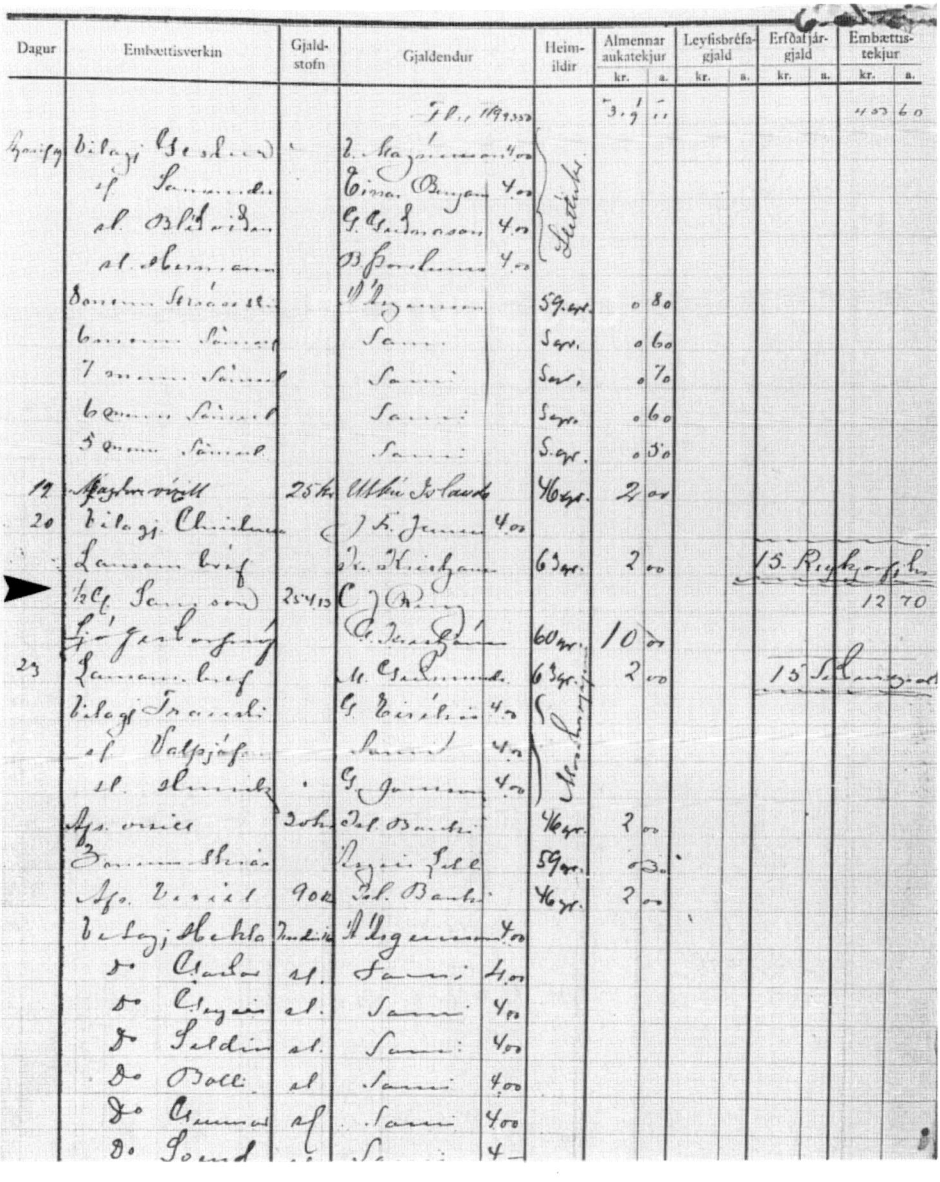
Dagur
Embættisverkin
Gjald-stofn
Gjaldendur
Heim-ildir
Almennar aukatekjur
Leyfisbréfa-gjald
Erfðafjár-gjald
Embættis-tekjur
kr. a.

The entry for April 6 **left** reads "1/4 C1 Samson", or fourth class, for which a duty of 1/20 of her tonnage in Icelandic crowns — 25.40 kr — was charged. Half that duty (1/2 G or 1/2 Gjald) — 12.70 kr — was charged on subsequent arrivals. Lighthouse duty was payable only at her first arrival in harbour and all charges were payable on arrival.

Date	**Official Business**	**Subject or Charge**	**Charge or Payer**	**Lighthouse Duty**	**Para of Law**	**General Extra Duty**	**Licence Duty kr. a.**	**Legacy Duty kr. a.**	**Office Charge kr. a.**
1912									
April 6	1/4 C1 Samson	254.13	C.J. Ring	63.50				25.40	
April 20	1/2 G Samson	254.13	C.J. Ring					12.70	
9/5	1/2 G Samson	254.13	C. Ring					12.70	

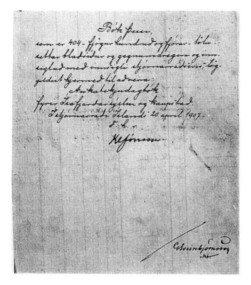

This book,
which contains 404 — four hundred and four — numbered pages and sealed with the ministries seal is herewith legalized to be:
An extra revenue day book. (or journal)
For the sheriff in Isafjordarsyla and the township of
Isafjordur.
The Ministry for Iceland 20 April 1907.

F.h.r.
(In the name of the Government Counsel)
K. Jonson

G. Sveinbjörnsson

(The book was in use up to 1914.)

Below Carpathia *Officers, 1912. Back row: Italian Doctor; Second Officer James Bissett; Mr Roth, Hungarian supernumerary officer; Chief Engineer; First Officer Horace Dean; Assistant Purser; Purser E.F.G. Brown; Arpad Lengye, Hungarian Doctor. Centre row: Chief Officer Hankinson; Captain Arthur H. Rostron; Dr Frank McGhee. Front row: Third Officer Eric Rees; Fourth Officer Geoffrey Barnish. The picture was signed by Captain Rostron and his five officers for surviving Fifth Officer Harold Lowe of the* Titanic.

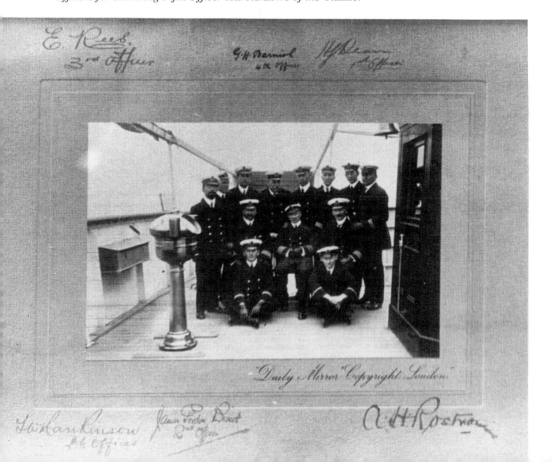

31st. August 1965

Dear Mr. Reade,

Thank you for your letter of
August 26th, and my apologies for the
delay in replying to your previous letters.
My father never, at any time,
discussed with me or with my brother
and sister his part in the "Titanic"
story. But my mother tells me (and
this is all that she will tell) that, as
you say, he was sure that distress
rockets were being fired. As you say,
he was in a very difficult position, as
a very young Second Officer, on the

First and last pages of a letter from John A. Stone to the author.

This is all the information I can
give you, and hope that your book
will be a success & and that my
father's part in the Titanic affair
will be treated fairly, as he deserved,
and sympathetically.

Yours sincerely,

John A Stone

Leslie Reade.

On Thursday morning, 25 April, it had the headlines:

"SAYS HE SAW THE TITANIC'S ROCKETS"[43]
Ernest Gill, Donkeyman on the Californian, Says His Captain Ignored the Signals"

Gill's story, in the form of an affidavit, was then printed, and read as follows:

"I, the undersigned, Ernest Gill, being employed as second donkeyman on the steamer *Californian,* Capt. Lord, give the following statement of the incidents of the night of Sunday, April 14:

I am 29 years of age; native of Yorkshire; single. I was making my third voyage on the Californian.

On the night of April 14, I was on duty from 8 p.m. until 12 midnight in the engine room. At 11.56 I came on deck. The stars were shining brightly. It was very clear and I could see for a long distance. The ship's engines had been stopped since 10.30 and she was drifting amid floe ice. I looked over the rail on the starboard side and saw the lights of a very large steamer about 10 miles away. I could see her broadside lights. I watched her for fully a minute. They could not have helped but see her from the bridge and lookout.

It was now 12 o'clock and I went to my cabin. I woke my mate, William Thomas. He heard the ice crunching alongside the ship and asked: 'Are we in the ice?' I replied, 'Yes; but it must be clear off to the starboard, for I saw a big vessel going full speed. She looked as if she might be a big German.'

I turned in, but could not sleep. In half an hour I turned out, thinking to smoke a cigarette. Because of the cargo I could not smoke 'tween decks, so I went on deck again.

I had been on deck about 10 minutes when I saw a white rocket about 10 miles away on the starboard side. I thought it must be a shooting star. In seven or eight minutes I saw distinctly a second rocket in the same place, and I said to myself, 'That must be a vessel in distress.'

It was not my business to notify the bridge or lookouts; but they could not have helped but see them.

I turned in immediately after, supposing that the ship would pay attention to the rockets. I knew no more until I was awakened at 6.40 by the Chief Engineer, calling, 'Turn out to render assistance!'

'The Titanic has gone down,' he explained. I exclaimed and leaped from my bunk. I went on deck and found the vessel under way and proceeding full speed. She was clear of the field ice, but there were plenty of bergs about.

I went down into the engine room on watch and heard the Second and Fourth Engineers in conversation. Mr. J.C. Evans is the Second and Mr. Wooton[*] is the Fourth. The Second was telling the Fourth that the Third Officer had reported rockets going up in his watch. I knew then it must have been the *Titanic* I had seen.

The Second Engineer added that the captain had been notified by the apprentice officer, whose name, I think, is Gibson, of the rockets. The skipper had told him to Morse with a light to the vessel in distress. Mr Stone, the second navigating officer, was on the bridge at the time, said Mr Evans.

I overheard Mr. Evans say that Morse lights had been shown, and more rockets sent up. Then, according to Mr. Evans, Mr. Gibson went to the captain again and reported more rockets. The skipper told him to continue to Morse until he got a reply, but no reply was received.

---

*   His name was actually 'Hooton'; *see* Appendix J.

The next remark I heard the Second pass was, 'Why the devil didn't they wake the wireless man up?'

The entire crew of the steamer have been talking among themselves about the disregard of the rockets. I personally urged several to join me in protesting against the conduct of the captain, but they refused, because they feared to lose their jobs.

A day or two before the ship reached port, the skipper called the quartermaster, who was on duty at the time the rockets were discharged, into his cabin. They were in conversation* about three-quarters of an hour. The quartermaster declares he did not see the rockets.

I am quite sure that the *Californian* was less than 20 miles from the *Titanic,* which the officers report to have been our position. I could not have seen her if she had been more than 10 miles distant, and I saw her very plainly.

I have no ill will toward the captain or any officer of the ship, and I am losing a profitable berth by making this statement. I am actuated by the desire that no captain who refuses or neglects to give aid to a vessel in distress should be able to hush up the men.§

ERNEST GILL.
Sworn and subscribed to before me this 24th day of April, 1912.
SAMUEL PUTNAM, Notary Public.

With Gill's affidavit, the *American* also published, of course, an explanatory story, with another set of arresting headlines:[44]

"ADMITS HE SAW ROCKET SIGNALS
Captain Lord of 'Californian' Saw Ship Within Five Miles of Him
Sending Up Rockets —
Made No Attempt To Go To Her —
Seaman Gill Tells Damaging Story —
Says Crew Wanted To Protest Captain's Act in Not Answering . . ."

"The Californian of the Leyland Line," the piece began, "was the ship which was sighted by the Titanic, but which refused to respond to her signals of distress. Captain Lord of the Californian thought it was some small vessel and refused to risk his ship by sending her through the ice at night to the rescue.

"These charges are made in affidavits by Ernest Gill, second donkeyman on board, who is on his way to testify before the Senate Investigating Committee. They were repeated in the presence of four members of the crew and a notary public, and by an officer of the ship, who affirmed them in a confidential communication to the BOSTON AMERICAN."

The story proceeds to tell of the vain attempt to call Captain Lord and of the tardy wakening of Evans:

"The chief officer rushed into the wireless man's room, tore him from his bunk and exclaimed:

'For God's sake, get to your key. Some ship has been sending rockets all night and we have done nothing.'

"Then the message from the 'Virginia' [*sic*] was 'caught', and 'As soon as Captain Lord knew that it was the Titanic of his own line which had sunk he rushed the Californian full speed to the rescue . . . Captain Lord's ship was in the ice and

---

* Boston American: 'consultation'.

§ Boston American: 'hush up the matter'.

he stopped his engines. He feared to proceed through the ice, even on such a night, because of the ever present danger that a berg might strike his ship.

"When once he learned of the Titanic trouble, however, according to Gill, he forced his vessel to do her best."

The *American* published Gill's affidavit and story only in its morning edition of that day, 25 April. Apparently the editor felt that McGregor's story — though the carpenter was not named — in the *Globe* of the same morning, had taken much from the value of his scoop. But the fat, of course, was now finally and irredeemably in the fire; and yet again the patient Boston newspapermen journeyed over to the Clyde Street pier. This unprepossessing vessel had become front page news; and one of the papers even took a picture of her, lying in her dock.[45]

A *Boston Post* reporter boarded the ship Thursday night with a copy of Gill's affidavit in his hand. As soon as Lord saw him he let fly. The calm he had preserved after McGregor's attempt had disappeared, for the time being anyhow.

"I will have absolutely nothing to say"[46] were his opening words to the *Post* man. "I'll answer no questions. I told you fellows my story the other day, and now you are taking stock in what that fellow has to say."

The reporter asked the captain if he would deny Gill's charges. Lord refused to deny them, but taking the copy of the affidavit in his hand, he said: "You don't have to ask me to deny what this man has to say, but just look at these statements and judge for yourself."

He pointed out that the *Titanic* had struck the berg "at 20 minutes to midnight, and here this man says he saw the vessel proceeding at full speed about midnight, some 20 minutes after the accident. That's all I will have to say."

It was an effective, if not absolutely final, blow at Gill, and more will be said about his picturesque "big German" vessel in the next chapter. He did not hesitate to call his assistant donkeyman, quite bluntly, a liar. He also said that Gill had been paid $500 for his affidavit, and he, Lord, anticipated no difficulty in convincing the Senate Committee "of his entire innocence of any ignoring of signals from the Titanic."

At 6 o'clock, Thursday evening, Guy Murchie, the US Marshal at Boston, received a wire from Senator Smith[47] to subpoena Lord and Evans and have the ship's log brought to Washington. An hour later, Murchie personally served the two men aboard their ship at her pier. What one might have expected to be a routine incident turned out to be somewhat more complicated and much more protracted. Lord at once got into touch with John H. Thomas by telephone.

"I am perfectly willing to go to Washington and appear before your American investigating committee," he told the *Boston Herald* reporter.[48] "I would, of course, like to sail as originally planned, but anything that I can do I am willing to do."

Thomas, too, next day, when the town was full of reports that the White Star or the Leyland Line or the International Mercantile Marine, or perhaps all together, had tried to prevent Lord and Evans from going to the inquiry, told how willing he was. After he had received the call about the subpoena being served on Captain Lord, "I thought the matter over a few moments and then told them to go to Washington."[49]

Lord was willing, Thomas was willing, perhaps even Evans (whom nobody asked) was also willing. Yet, four hours after he had served the subpoenas,

Murchie telegraphed his report to Colonel D.M. Ransdell, the Senate Sergeant at Arms, that the two were to testify, "but are now* 10 p.m. prevented from going by White Star officials."[50] Whether this was a misunderstanding, or whether perhaps the officials were not quite so co-operative with the government as Mr Thomas later maintained, cannot be decided; but there is no doubt about Murchie's own opinion, for his telegram continued: "Believe they have important information. Please advise me further, and will bring them to Washington if necessary."

But Murchie's readiness for arrests and handcuffs proved unnecessary. After Thomas had heard about the service of the subpoenas, he did not, as he later told the *Boston American,* "think it over for a few minutes" and then tell Lord and Evans to go to Washington. What he actually did was to telephone Philip Franklin, the IMM chief in New York, asking that their depositions might be taken in Boston, "rather than compel them to go to Washington, with the risk of not getting back in time to have the steamer sail."[51] The departure of the *Californian* from Boston had been planned for Saturday morning, 26 April, and Franklin at once tried to reach Senator Smith in Washington on the long-distance telephone. Smith was too busy investigating the *Titanic* disaster against the clock to take time off, and just sent out word through his secretary that the two potential witnesses must come to Washington. Franklin then called Thomas back and said he "hoped they could without doubt catch the midnight train."

Whatever Captain Lord may have been thinking while these talks were going on, he was not surprised at what had happened. Some time that day, after Gill's story had been published in the local *American,* Lord had gone and sat down in his cabin and drawn a rough sketch of the position of the ice and the course he said his ship had sailed to the *Carpathia.*[52] On the back of the drawing he had written a number of notes.

"What did you do it for?" Lord Mersey asked him in London.

Lord was perfectly frank: "After the statement that this man Gill made in the papers that we were supposed to have ignored the *Titanic* signals, I knew at once there would be an enquiry over it."[53]

After supper the previous night, Chief Engineer Mahan had come along and told him that a fireman, William Kennerdale, was ill in the forecastle and spitting blood.[54] Lord ordered Mahan to get a doctor at once, and went to see the man, who said he was feeling better. That was 9.30. Then Kennerdale had another attack, and by the time the doctor came aboard just before ten o'clock, the fireman was dead. That meant there would have to be a report to the Consul, possibly an inquest, arranging the funeral and other unforeseen jobs.

Thomas was packing Lord and Evans off to Washington, but first there were still more reporters to see. Gill had not been aboard since Wednesday night and his 'dunnage' had gone. The *American* had said he was on his way to Washington — in fact he was already there — to tell his story, but Lord angrily said to the *Herald* man he could see no reason why such "a story should be told, especially since such obvious unsailorlike deeds were admitted in the affidavit."[55]

"Do you suppose that any man of any race whatsoever would see signals of distress and fail to report them either to the bridge or the lookout?" he asked. "Can you imagine a man realizing that fellow-sailors were in dire

* There is a misprint of substance in the US 'Hearings', page 688, where "not" is printed for 'now', and has been the source of much misunderstanding and confusion.

straits failing to notify someone that he had seen such signals?"

Lord then questioned whether Gill could see any masthead lights at ten miles with the naked eye, and continued: "Gill received six pounds a month wages. . . . He was a good man according to the report of his superior officers and I can conceive of no reason, other than financial, that would cause him to talk such poppycock."

This *Herald* story was notable from several points of view, and not least because of the *Californian* united front presented to the outside, hostile world.

"Captain Lord's story," the *Herald* continued, "of the Californian's position and the other occurrences on that night was corroborated by First Officer Stewart, Second Officer Stone, and the quartermaster on duty at the time. Stone emphatically denied that he had notified Capt. Lord of any rockets, as he had seen none, nor had any been reported to him. He also denies that he signed any statement, under compulsion by the captain, stating that he had seen any signal of distress."

The conscientious reporter, not yet satisfied, interviewed also several members of the crew, not named, who 'declared they had heard nothing of any ship in distress and that they considered it remarkably queer that Gill had said nothing about it to them and that he had not reported it to the watch on duty . . .'"

It will be noted that two names, Groves and Gibson, are glaringly absent from the united front of self-approval which Lord and his officers pronounced upon themselves. In view of the oft-repeated statement that the contemporary press were shrieking for the condemnation of Captain Lord, it is worth dwelling in detail on such a story as this. Knowing as we do what had been said by McGregor, Groves and Gill himself, it is difficult to escape the conclusion that in reporting what would appear to the stranger to be unanimous support of their captain by his crew, the *Herald* reporter must either have been deliberately or fortuitously selective in his sampling of lower deck opinion.

Captain Lord, however, before catching his train to Washington, had his last interview with a Boston newspaper, and it was the most ingenious and inventive of all. It was given to *The Boston Journal*. Lord spoke freely and with vehemence to what had proved a friendly paper, and the story appeared next morning on the front page under a two-column heading:

"CALIFORNIAN'S CAPTAIN WARNED TITANIC OF ICEBERG BEFORE WRECK"

This story, which was published on Friday, 26 April,[56] when Lord was already on his way to Washington, gives so remarkable an impression of the gap now separating at least the undisputed facts from his version of them that it should be set out very fully.

It begins with an introductory statement:

"The Leyland liner Californian, which is now berthed at East Boston, warned the Titanic of the iceberg danger in time to enable the liner to protect herself, according to information which came to the Senate committee which is investigating the disaster at Washington yesterday.

"As a result Capt. Lord and Wireless Operator Evans of the Californian have been subpoenaed to appear before it, although the steamer is to sail Saturday morning.

"The summons came after, but apparently had no connection with the story told yesterday by Ernest Gill, second donkeyman aboard the Californian."

Then follows a short quotation from Gill, of his having seen a white rocket ten miles away on the starboard side, but that it was not his business to report it.

"This story Captain Lord branded as a lie, in talking to a Journal reporter last night. He declared he believed Gill had been paid to tell the story.

"'If I go to Washington it will not be because of this story in the paper, but to tell the committee why my ship was drifting without power, while the Titanic was rushing under full speed.

"'It will take me about ten minutes to do this,' Captain Lord declared."

Notwithstanding that he and the wireless operator had been subpoenaed:

"Captain Lord said last night the charges which had been printed in an evening paper were all 'bosh'.

"'Everything that was printed in the story is a falsehood and any person who reads the affidavit of this man Gill and knows anything about the sea will know that the stories that are being circulated among the crew that Gill received $500 for the affidavit have some foundation.

"'In the first place, don't you think that if any signals were seen by this man (if he was on deck) they would not have been seen by the officers and men on the bridge.

"'Every officer and man of this crew is an Englishman and a white man, and no Englishman will stand by and see anybody or anything in distress without trying to lend assistance.

"'*Mr. Stewart, the first officer, was on the bridge during the times that the signals were supposed to have been seen, and he can tell you himself that nothing of the kind was seen by him or any of the men who were on watch with him.*'"
(Emphasis added.)

Lord then told how they had got into the ice about 10.30 p.m. shut off steam and drifted until they got a message from the 'Virginia' [*sic*] 'about 3.30 A.M.' that the *Titanic* had struck an iceberg, was sinking and needed assistance.

"'Everything had been quiet during the night and *no signals of distress or anything else had been seen,* and about 5 o'clock in the morning, which is my regular time for getting up, *I told Mr. Stewart to wake up 'Wireless' and have him get in touch with some ship and get an idea of what kind of an ice field we had gotten into.* (Emphasis added.)

"'Wireless' got to his instruments within a few minutes and started to call up any ships that were near by. *He tried for a number of minutes to get an answer and was about to give up* when he heard an answer of some kind. (Emphasis added.)

"'He could not make out what the message was and told Mr. Stewart so, when suddenly he said: 'A ship is sinking.' Mr. Stewart told him to find out where the ship was and what it was.

"'The Ship with which we were talking was the Frankfurt, a German ship, and the operator was so excited with the news that he was trying to give us that he was trying to send it both in German and English, with the result that we could get nothing and were calling him and trying to get him to send the message slowly when we heard another ship calling.

"'The Frankfurt was told to close up and stop, and then we got a message from the Virginia [*sic*] in which we were told that the Titanic was sinking and the passengers were being taken off in the lifeboats and that more assistance was needed.

"'We got the location of the Titanic, and after figuring out our location we found that we were between 19½ and 20 miles from where the Titanic *was supposed to be*. (Emphasis added.)

"'We put on full speed and *raced* through the field of ice *to the place, but when we arrived there* we found that the *Carpathia* had arrived before us and they told us that they had picked up twenty boat loads of people and that there was nothing else for us to do. (Emphasis added.)

"'We looked around the vicinity for some time, but being unable to find anything at which we could lend assistance, we started on our trip. Any of the officers or crew of my ship can tell you the same story.

"'It is all foolishness for anybody to say that I, at the point of a revolver, took any man into this room and made him swear to tell any kind of a story.

"'No member of the crew has ever been in this room, and none of them come near the place except to clean up.

"'If any of you gentlemen is a notary you are at liberty to take my sworn statement, for what I have told you, and any other man on the ship will tell you the same story, which is the truth.

"'The position of my ship was given to you gentlemen when you first came aboard, after I arrived on this passage, and you will find that the positions that I gave then will be the same as I am giving you now.

"'This man Gill was making his second trip on this ship and he has now left the ship and has overstayed his leave.'"

So ends Captain Lord's last statement to a Boston newspaper.

This statement, it will be seen, is, in parts, true: that is to say, the parts which are mostly of minor importance.

The *Californian's* log showed that at midnight the temperature of the air was 27°F (-3°C),[51] and it seems a valid point to question whether Gill would stand smoking on deck in such cold. More will be said about this in the next chapter.

Captain Lord's boast that "every officer and man of this crew is an Englishman and a white man" may also be allowed to pass, although not literally true. The entire crew may have been "white", but at least five of them, and perhaps six, were foreigners, Austrian, Germans or Dutchmen.*

Worth more attention is Lord's reference to the *Californian's* position, for it coolly omits any hint of his original refusal to disclose latitudes and longitudes on the ground that they were "state secrets"! It is some indication of the serene impudence of this remarkable man's dominating personality that evidently not one person present dared remind him of this awkward fact.

Most of Lord's fanciful description of Evans's CQ call after being wakened by Stewart, although very far from the facts, is not of much significance.

The important and significant part of this section of Lord's story is the reason alleged by him for having called Evans at all. We already know that Evans himself said he was woken up by Stewart and told: "Wireless, there is a ship that has been firing rockets in the night. Will you come in and see if you can find out what is wrong — what is the matter?"[58] Stewart's version, on the other hand, was that he woke Evans and said to him: "I told him to get out and see what the ship was to the southward."[59]

The reason Lord now actually did give for waking Evans — to "get an idea of what kind of an ice field we had gotten into" — was quite new, quite insignificant, and wholly false.

---

* *See* Appendix J.

Let us pay some attention now to Lord's estimate of the distance of about 20 miles between his position and "where the *Titanic* was supposed to be". Here he was, almost on the point of departing for Washington. Lord unquestionably did realize he was going to Washington not just as an ordinary witness, but to state his defence to the investigators — and to the world. That being so, one must ask why he did not take advantage of the opportunity provided by this interview of hammering home what was later to become one of his main arguments in support of his complete innocence. Already he had neglected similar opportunities at earlier interviews of making the same point; now, he had one final chance of flattening Gill with a single blow, before he even faced the Senators. Why didn't he say plainly and bluntly: "Gentlemen, the whole charge is absurd! The fact is the *Titanic* gave the wrong position. Actually, we were so far apart, it was physically impossible for us, the *Californian* and the *Titanic,* to have seen each other. Perhaps my ex-Assistant Donkeyman would explain that!"

Instead, having remarked that they figured out that their "location" was some 20 miles "from where the *Titanic* was supposed to be", he goes straight on with his story of putting on full speed and racing through the ice to "the place", where they found the *Carpathia*. In other words, so far from making an issue of the *Titanic's* position, Lord here tacitly accepts its correctness, and goes on about something else.

Finally, the most calculated and flagrant of all Captain Lord's excursions on the wrong side of his personal Rubicon: his calling on Stewart as a witness, or rather, a non-witness, to the rockets.

Let his words be repeated and weighed:

"Mr. Stewart, the first officer, was on the bridge during the times that the signals were supposed to have been seen . . .'

The reader certainly has not forgotten that Stewart, far from being on the bridge when the "signals" were seen, that is between about 12.45 and about 1.30, was in his bunk and asleep. It is hard to believe, too, that Captain Lord had forgotten it. But the reporters had not seen the *Californian's* watch list.

". . . and he can tell you himself," said Captain Lord, "that nothing of the kind was seen by him or any of the men who were on the watch with him . . ."

What, then, is to be said of Captain Lord's story, as a whole, on this occasion? It differs actually in degree, rather than in kind, from his earlier interviews with the Boston papers. Not one of them, to anybody knowing the facts, bears the impress of honesty, and one is driven to ask whether any of them can be reconciled with the words of a man, "comfortable in his mind"[60] and with nothing to hide. The impression left by his final story in *The Boston Journal,* above all, is so damning that it is hard to think of any convincing answer Lord could have given to an accusation of plain falsehood, short of being able to claim that he had been grossly and most damagingly misquoted. Yet, never from first to last, is he known to have made the slightest complaint of that kind.

Lord's situation might be compared with that of a doctor who decides at 1 o'clock on a bitter winter night that a patient, who has called him, can safely wait for his attention until daylight; and wakes to hear the fantastic news that not only the patient but 1,500 have died in the night as the result of his refusal to answer the call. Adding to his inadequate moral fortitude his customary arrogance when challenged, Lord was driven to intentional falsification. The episode cannot be forgotten. It was a permanent and unanswerable exposure of his own consciousness of guilt.

Having finally disposed of the press, and Thomas having made the necessary travel arrangement, Captain Lord, accompanied by Evans, caught the 1 a.m. train for Washington and evidence on oath.[61] It was to be a day of triumph.

Sources

1 *Boston Traveller*, 19 April 1912, p. 7. NB: All dates are April, 1912, unless otherwise stated.

2 *B Evening Post*, 19, p. 8.

3 B Post, 19, p. 11.

4 Ibid.

5 *B Advertiser*, 20, p. 7.

6 *B Globe*, 19, p. 4.

7 *B Herald*, 19, p. 2.

8 *B Advertiser*, 20, p. 7.

9 Ibid.

10 *B Evening Transcript*, 19, p. 8.

11 *B Globe*, 19, p. 4.

12 *B Traveller*, 19, p. 8.

13 *B Globe*, 19, p. 4.

14 *B Traveller*, 19, p. 7.

15 *B Globe*, 19, p. 4.

16 *B Traveller*, 19, p. 7.

17 *B Evening Post*, 19, p. 8.

18 *B Advertiser*, 20, p. 7.

19 *B Globe*, 19, p. 4.

20 *B Traveller*, 19, p. 7.

21 *B Evening Post*, 19, p. 8.

22 Ibid.

23 Clinton, Mass., 42.36N., 71.44W.; 13,075 pop., 1910 Census.

24 Official Log.

25 *Clinton Daily Item*, 23, p. 1; Rowell (and Ayer) 'American Newspaper Directory', 1913, p. 390.

26 *New York Times*, 23, p. 1.

27 *B Post*, 24, p. 5.

28 Ibid.

29 *Liverpool Echo*, 24, p. 8.

30 US 1114.

31 *Liverpool Echo*, 24, p. 8.

32 US 175.

33 'Lloyd's Register'; 1912.

34 *B Globe*, 25, p. 5.

35 *New York Herald*, 24, p. 4.

36 *Liverpool Echo*, 25, p. 8.

37 *B Globe*, 25, p. 5.

38 *B Traveller*, 19, p. 7.

39 *B Globe*, 25, p. 5.

40 US 746.

41 US 747.

42 US 896.

43 *B American*, 25 and affidavit also printed at US 710, 711.

44 *B American*, 25.

45 *B Herald*, 26, p. 9, heading: "Liner Charged with Deserting Titanic".

46 *B Post*, 26, p. 6.

47 US 688.

48 *B Herald*, 26, p. 1.

49 *B American*, 26, p. 1.

50 *B American*, 26, '10 o'clock Baseball Extra' ed., p. 2, col. 2; US 688.

51 *B Journal*, 26, p. 1, cols. 3, 4; US 689.

52 B 7395, 7385, 7410-11.

53 B 7396.

54 Official log, p. 14.

55 *B Herald*, 26, p. 1.

56 *B Journal*, 26, p. 2.

57 US 1142.

58 US 738.

59 B 8758.

60 B 6983.

61 *B American*, 26, p. 2.

Chapter 12

Fact and fantasy from a donkeyman

The Sub-Committee of the Committee of Commerce was appointed by the US Senate to inquire into the *Titanic* disaster on 17 April, and by 4 o'clock the following afternoon, its Chairman, Senator William Alden Smith of Michigan, and Senator Francis Griffith Newlands of Nevada were on the express for New York.[1] Senator Jonathan Bourne of Oregon was to join them the next day, and they would ultimately be further reinforced by Senators Theodore Elijah Burton of Ohio, Duncan Upshaw Fletcher of Florida, George Clermont Perkins of California and Furnifold McLendel Simmons of North Carolina.[*]

Under much attention from the Press and the general public, Senator Smith and his colleagues started their investigation in the Waldorf-Astoria Hotel in New York on Friday, 19 April. In the week that passed before Captain Lord attracted Smith's attention, the enterprise had moved from New York to Washington. There, in the large Majority Caucus Room of the Senate Office Building,[2] Smith and his six colleagues began their first session at half-past ten on Monday morning, 22 April. In contrast with the opening of the London inquiry ten days later, there was enormous public interest. A shoving, yelling crowd of five hundred people, mostly fashionably-dressed women, rushed to get in, and large as the room was, the number of would-be spectators far exceeded its capacity. In the confusion and uproar, witnesses and others having business with the inquiry had to fight their way through.

Next day, 23 April, the hearing had moved again and from then on took place in the much smaller room of the Territories Committee.[3] It was there that on the morning of 26 April, Senator Smith, at the end of the second questioning of Philip A.S. Franklin, Vice-President of the IMM, asked: "Is the Captain of the *Californian* here, or the Captain of the *Mount Temple*?"

Neither had yet been seen, and Smith decided to excuse Franklin and called Ernest Gill.[4] In 24 hours the name of this assistant donkeyman may have become known to some hundreds of thousands of newspaper readers.

Gill was 29 years old, and one of the London correspondents who listened to him that morning, cabled that he was an "honest working fellow with a Yorkshire accent and reddish hair." A sketch of him drawn during his comparatively brief appearance before the committee shows this rather mysterious young man as having a moustache and sharp features (the caption, incidentally, credits him to the *Carpathia*).

---

[*] For biographical details of this illustrious company the reader should turn to Wyn Craig Wade's *The TITANIC: End of a Dream*, Rawson, Wade Publishers, New York, 1979.

Smith began by reading Gill's sworn statement to him and then putting the question: "I will ask you, witness, whether this statement is true?"[5]

"Yes, sir," said Gill, "that is correct."

The almost inevitable mistake made in the examination of Gill, which was conducted chiefly by Senator Fletcher, was in asking him certain questions demanding some knowledge of navigation, which Gill was no more capable of answering sensibly than, say, Senator Smith himself.

"I am not a sailor," Gill declared frankly, when he appeared later in London.[6] "I do not know anything about the latitude or longitude."

Gill knew the *Californian* was "headed for Boston"[7] and that the rockets, when he first saw them, were "on the starboard side, forward". These replies to Senator Fletcher were unexceptionable (assuming Gill had seen anything at all); but he was next asked: "Was the *Californian* passed by the *Titanic,* her course being the same as the *Titanic's* course was originally?"

"I think she must have passed the *Titanic.* The *Titanic* must have passed us first, because we were floating, and that would take a lot out of our way. We were a slower boat."

"After the *Titanic* struck the iceberg," Senator Fletcher went on, "did the *Californian* pass by the *Titanic?*"

"The only way I can account for this, we were stopped in the ocean, and it is not natural for a ship to keep her head one way all the time. She must have been drifting."

It is no more easy to discover what Gill meant than it often is to understand the meaning of an ordinary witness on a matter of direction or speed in an accident case with a motor car, when he does not drive. The form of the Senator's question also opened an objection to Gill's doubters and opponents, because whatever he may have seen he certainly never saw the two ships on the same course 'originally' or at all. He probably meant that he knew that both must have been headed generally west, one to New York and the other to Boston. The *Californian,* Gill knew, had stopped before the *Titanic,* which he claimed to have seen with her 'couple of rows of lights' and still steaming west; but his own ship, now drifting to the will of the wind and the sea, had turned round and was heading back to the direction from which she had come.

The examination then established[8] that the *Californian* had got under way about 5 o'clock in the morning and proceeded to deal with the rockets Gill claimed to have seen.[9] They looked to be "pale blue or white," said Gill, but when an attempt was made to pin him down to colour, he said: "It would be apt to be a very clear blue; I would catch it when it was dying. I did not catch the exact tint, but I reckon it was white."

"Did it look as if the rocket had been sent up and the explosion had taken place in the air and the stars spangled out?"

So far Gill had said ". . . when I saw it it was not very plain" and had not mentioned "stars" at all; but he was quick to seize on the Senator's suggestion.

"Yes, sir; the stars spangled out. I could not say about the stars. I say, I caught the tail end of the rocket."

He saw no "lights on the steamer", "signs of it", "Morseing", "noise", "escaping steam", nor indeed, and absolutely mysterious, "sign of the steamer at the time" of the rockets. It was "a very clear night" and "it could not be 20 miles away", and the witness seemed to have been as conscious of the mysterious disappearance of the steamer in half an hour as the reader is to this day, and probably more so than was Senator Fletcher at the time.

According to Gill's sworn statement, he saw the steamer about midnight, and he told his mate William Thomas she was "going along full speed". About half an hour later he went up on deck to have a smoke and the ship, somehow, had completely disappeared.

When asked:[10] "You estimate that the rockets went up not over 20 miles away from the *Californian*?" he himself told Senator Fletcher, ". . . she had not had time to get 20 miles away by the time I got on deck again." Yet she had undoubtedly gone, and if not over the edge of the earth presumably into some other region of the imagination.

"As I understand," the Senator summed it up, "you never did see the ship, did you?"

"No, sir; not without the one I seen, [? 'unless she was'] the big ship, that I told my mate was a German boat — not without that was the ship in question, the *Titanic*."[11]

"You think it may have been the *Titanic*?"

"Yes, sir.[12] I am of the general opinion that the crew is, that she was the *Titanic*."

In his evidence[13] he also said he first saw her "At four minutes after* 12 exactly," and attempted to explain by the time he "was working with the fourth engineer at a pump that kicked" how he was able to time the event so precisely. If he was convincing about that his version of the sighting itself was extremely unconvincing, as will be discussed later in this chapter.

It is also to be noted that when Gill came to give his evidence in Washington about "a big German" "going along at full speed", as described in his statement, he had a different story.

"Was this ship moving at that time?" [i.e. at "four minutes after 12"] Senator Fletcher asked.[14]

"*I did not take particular notice of it, sir* [emphasis added], with the rushing to call my mate" was Gill's surprising reply. This was probably the truth, accepting his statement that he had seen a ship at all.

He goes on: "I went along the deck. Suppose I am going forward, now; I could see her over there [indicating], a big ship, and a couple of rows of lights; so that I knew it was not any small craft. It was no tramp. I did not suppose it would be a 'Star' boat. I reckoned she must be a German boat. So I dived down the hatch, and as I turned around in the hatch I could not see her, so you can guess the latitude she was in. As I stood on the hatch, with my back turned, I could not see the ship. Then I went and called my mate, and that is the last I saw of it."[15]

"Did you observe the rockets go up in the direction this ship was as you first saw her, from where the *Californian* was?" Senator Fletcher asked.

"It was more abeam, sir; more broadside of the ship."

Senator Smith asked him why he thought the ship he saw, or thought he saw, was a German.[16]

"Because the German ship would be heading to New York at about that time."[17] [Which ship?]

"Heading for New York?"

"*Or from New York* [emphasis added]. It is in that vicinity we meet those boats."

It is not a cogent explanation.

Gill also was asked[18] when it was he had heard the engineer officers

* He probably said 'afore' (i.e. 'before'), which the American reporter understood as "after", but the point made here is unaffected.

discussing the failure to call Evans, the wireless operator.

"Twenty minutes past 8 on Monday morning." As a man concerned with engines, he was given to precise timings.

A further passage in his evidence made it clear he did not admit he had deserted from the *Californian* or been dismissed.

"I belong to the ship now," he insisted.

Smith was finished with him shortly before 1.20,[19] when the adjournment was taken, and it would seem that in spite of the one correspondent already quoted, and even before Captain Lord gave evidence Gill had not made a very favourable impression.

The small but significant differences in the two versions of Gill's evidence can best be appreciated, if read consecutively. So, on the whole, it seems convenient to anticipate the course of events and examine here the evidence he was to give later in London on 4 June. A thorough study concerned only with the *Californian* requires a comparison between Gill's evidence in London with his earlier stories in Boston and Washington, and a note of the remarkable discrepancies among the three. To the Attorney-General, however, the *Californian* was only a minor, if important, part of the inquiry. When the truth was established in America that the *Californian* had seen rockets, which was later confirmed in elaborate detail in London, the Attorney was naturally little concerned with differences in Gill's three sworn statements. Nevertheless, they remain important in an attempt to unravel the puzzle.

Gill's Boston statement was not read or put to him in London.

He told Mr Rowlatt how he was going along the deck "and looked over the starboard rail and saw a large steamer. It could not have been anything but a passenger boat — she was too large. I could see two rows of lights which I took to be porthole lights, . . ." To these, for the first time, he now added "several groups of lights which I took to be saloon and deck lights. . . ." He also said: "I knew it was a passenger boat. That is all I saw of the ship."[20]

He thought: "She was a good distance off; I should say not more than 10 miles, and probably less."[21]

There seems to be a fluency and assurance and literacy about these answers, as indeed about most of his London evidence, which is entirely fresh.

"Did you notice whether she appeared to be moving?"[22]

"I did not stand to look at the ship . . ."

(In Boston: "I watched her for fully a minute . . ." in the extreme cold and in his thin clothes, as he himself later also pointed out in London;[23] and all this in a ship in which he "had no interest".)[24]

". . . but I supposed she would be moving. I did not expect a ship to be lit up like she was and stationary, and nothing to stop her, because I could see the edge of the ice flow, the edge of the field of ice; it appeared to be 4 or 5 miles away."[25]

In answer to Lord Mersey's intervention,[26] he explained: "Well what appeared to be the edge, sir. It was darker."

His statement that he had seen the edge, or what he took to be the edge, of the ice, also now made a first appearance. In his Boston affidavit he had only deduced it: ". . . it must be clear off to the starboard, for I saw a big vessel going along full speed. She looked as if she might be a big German."[27]

His timings were about the same. He saw the ship "before" he went off watch at midnight[28] — and if one is not going to hold exact timings against other witnesses, Gill too may be forgiven his Washington "at four minutes after [or, 'afore] 12 exactly" — and he was up on deck again for his cigarette "after one bell"[29] — "Between half-past 12 and 1," Rowlatt explained.

"Did you see the steamer then?" he asked Gill.[30]

"No, I could not see anything of the steamer at all. She had disappeared. She had either steamed away, or I do not know what she had done. She was not there."

"I do not understand that," Lord Mersey remarked,[31] but unfortunately did not pursue the matter. Nobody else was sufficiently interested to ask a single question about what surely is — to paraphrase a famous phrase — a puzzle within a mystery. Instead, accepting Gill's statement, Rowlatt went on to ask him: "Did you see anything in the direction where the steamer had been?"[32]

His answer is substantially a repetition of his American evidence, but again it seems to me to have a new air of literacy. Moreover, while in America he gives the impression of being a humble, almost Uriah-Heep-like fellow (quick and ready to agree with the suggestions of his superiors) in London, he spoke like a man of some force and independence, standing on his own feet. Before he left the witness box, we shall see him even reproving the Attorney-General himself for vagueness!

"I had pretty nearly finished my smoke,"[33] this extraordinary character began his account of what he had seen, "and was looking around, and I saw what I took to be a falling star. It descended and then disappeared. That is how a star does fall. I did not pay any attention to that. A few minutes after, probably five minutes, I threw my cigarette away and looked over, and I could see from the water's edge — what appeared to be the water's edge — a great distance away, well, it was unmistakably a rocket; you could make no mistake about it. Whether it was a distress signal or a signal rocket I could not say, but it was a rocket."

(In his Boston statement, remember: "I said to myself: 'That must be a vessel in distress.'")[34]

The answer is also reminiscent of Stone's evidence about the rockets he saw seeming to come from "a greater distance past the ship",[35] the difference — and a decisive one, of course — being that he also saw the ship.

Gill was next asked if what he had seen "was in the same direction from you as the steamer had been . . ."[36] His answer was a singular miscellany of misused and contradictory nautical terms, which perhaps better emphasized the accuracy of his remark: "I do not know anything about the latitude or longitude", than served as a reply.

"It was slightly astern of where I had seen the steamer. The steamer was more than ahead of us, just on our quarter, as we say, and the light was more astern. It was more abeam of our ship."[37]

Probably he means the rockets seemed to be more amidships.

Robertson Dunlop's cross-examination, on behalf of the Leyland Line and the *Californian's* officers, brought out that Gill thought he "had no business to report" what he had seen to the officer in charge of the ship.[38]

"You did not attach much importance at the time apparently to what you say you had seen?"[39]

"No, not any importance," this singular young man agrees; he, let us still remember, being the observer who decided he was looking at a ship in distress. "It was a signal, and other people on the ship, the proper people would attend to that. It was nothing to do with me."[40]

After he had heard about the *Titanic,* it occurred to Gill that this signal might have been of some importance.[41]

"I do not quite follow," the Attorney-General interrupted. "Is it suggested that signals were not sent up?"[42]

"No, I am not suggesting that," Dunlop replied.[43] Then he put this question to Gill: "What I am suggesting is that neither you nor anyone who saw those signals attached at the time any importance to them?"

"I do not know whether anybody else did who saw them, but I did not."[44]

So did Gill repeat his indifference to what he had regarded as "a vessel in distress".

The Attorney-General and Lord Mersey at once stepped in protectively to remind Mr Dunlop respectively: "What he said was, 'It was nothing to do with me,'" and "He is a donkeyman, working in the engine-room."[45]

Dunlop also supposed Gill would have his interest in salvage? and was promptly put in his place: "Yes, Sir; but that is not the question; we are not talking about salvage."[46]

(Lord, during his life, also pointedly drew attention to that item, to suggest the gross improbability of his own alleged inactivity).

Sir Robert Finlay, for the White Star Line, then briefly cross-examined the very self-confident donkeyman, and he too elicited some remarkable answers.

The *Californian* had two masthead lights, said Gill.[47]

"Not a side-light."

"Not steaming lights, not red or green lights, but plenty of side-lights, if you call them side-lights; I mean for illumination."

"Was the vessel that carried these lights moving?"

"Well, I did not stay long enough to see whether she was moving or in what direction she was going. She was there; she was a ship passing; and I had no interest in her, merely that she was a ship. She was a big ship, I could see that at a glance; in fact, I did not think she was a British ship . . ."

Dunlop came back to ask him whether the ship was heading in the same direction as the *Californian*.[48] In Washington, questions of this kind by Senator Fletcher had made the man look a fool if nothing worse. In London, somehow Gill's answers read like a brush-off to Robertson Dunlop, and he actually winds up capitalizing on his own particular skill with a neat epigram.

". . . I did not stay long enough," said Gill to Dunlop, "to observe which way she was going. No doubt if I had stayed another minute, I could have been sure of the direction."

"But you have, have you not, stated what the heading of this vessel was when you first saw her?"

"Yes, but, of course, they said, was she moving? I did not think the ship would be standing still with nothing to stop her."

He admitted having made the "remark" that the vessel was heading in the same direction as the *Californian*.

"Is that right or wrong? Do you want to correct it?"

"Well, I do not know."

"Do you think she was heading towards Europe or towards New York?"

"I do not know about that. I am not a sailor. I do not know anything about the latitude or longitude. *My compass is the steam gauge.*"

And Robertson Dunlop, a future Admiralty silk, of some fame, sat down.

But it was when the Attorney-General began his short re-examination with the question: "Have you been seen by the solicitors of the *Californian* since you have been home?", that the precise-minded assistant donkeyman rose to his summit with an implied rebuke on the leader of the bar of England.

"How do you mean?" Gill asked *him*. "Will you be more explicit?"[49]

Sir Rufus obliged: "I am anxious to understand from you whether since you returned to this country you have made a statement to anybody?"[50]

Gill said he had, to "a Board of Trade official" "at the Wrecks' Office."[51]

"That, of course, we know; that is the deposition. Do you mean you have made no other statement?"[52]

"None whatever."

"And you have not been seen by anybody?"

"No."

"I am not suggesting there is any harm in it; I only want to know the fact."

"No, I am telling you the truth; you asked me and I am telling you."

"You are perfectly right," the Attorney conceded. "You are justified in what you have said in America by what has transpired since."[53] He went on to say he was not going to ask questions in detail, because the *Californian* evidence was before the court, but he wanted to make it clear to Dunlop, ". . . that I disagree entirely with his observation that, according to the evidence, nobody paid any attention to these rockets. I have the evidence." Lord Mersey agreed that it was not in accordance with his recollection. Nor, of course, was it in accordance with the facts, and no attempt years afterwards by any apologist for Captain Lord can alter these facts.[54]

That was the end of Ernest Gill's evidence and his hour of glory. One is left with the problem of first trying to explain the astonishing change (as it seems to me) that was displayed by one who, through an accident of circumstances, was treated at the time, and in fact became, a key witness, and has ever since been so regarded.

On the afternoon of Gill's evidence at Washington, Evans, the Marconi man, first put into the official record of the case[55] the idea that Gill's disclosure was born of a desire to earn $500. In point of time, the notion, as we shall learn, had already been published in greater detail and with considerably more force. Evans expressed no opinion about the value of the suggestion; but Lord himself, having promptly denounced Gill to the reporters as a liar, ever after regarded the explanation of Gill's whole story as simple, and he assumed the £5 10s donkeyman was tempted by the $500.

In the contest of Gill v. Lord at Washington, it was almost certainly only a minority who preferred Gill. Apart from the beginning of his experience in the sighting of that "German" steamer and its sequel, which are as striking and convincing as 25 carat gold, no less and certainly no more, his story, as pointed out during its course, is punctuated with equally explicit, though less obvious, and much less important, improbabilities.

In London, on the other hand, though this evidence was still burdened with the steamer, as a whole he seemed to have created a quite different, and more favourable, impression. Some of the minor demands, at least, on our credulity, have been removed. Although he even added "saloon and deck lights" to his steamer, he evidently gave her only a hurried glance, instead of loitering along the freezing deck in his thin flannel suit[56] to ponder over details of this vessel in which he "had no interest". In his London version, Gill rushes below to the warmth of his cabin, nor, when he goes up again for his cigarette, does he stay on deck incredibly long. The so significant and graphic (but *ex post facto*) words: "That must be a vessel in distress!" also discreetly disappear, to the general gain of credibility. As already said, his character, as a whole, also seems to have taken on some dignity and self-respect, and his views are forcefully expressed. In spite of Gill's assurance that he had not seen anybody, it is almost as if somebody of skill and finesse, who wanted to exploit Gill's evidence against Captain Lord to the utmost, had taken this ignorant and uningratiating man in hand and carefully coached him about the things to say and those to suppress, and also how to say them.

All these characteristics seem to recall one witness who had preceded Gill, and whose intelligence and candour, above all, had created a universally favourable impression, and not least because candour was not universal among the *Californian* witnesses. This evidence gravely damaged the credibility of Lord's defence, and in the end was preferred to it and the evidence of the senior officers. The witness was, of course, Third Officer C.V. Groves. Now, if the apparent similarity in some of the qualities of the evidence of two such very different characters as Groves and Gill rested on personal opinion alone, it would hardly be worth mentioning; but it does not.

Fairness to Captain Lord requires that a curious fact, not hitherto considered in this context, be described. When, on 25 April, *The Boston American* first published Gill's affidavit, it announced that the charges were not made by Gill alone. It said his charges "were repeated in the presence of four members of the crew and a notary public, and by an officer of the ship, who affirmed them in a confidential communication . . ." The paper said it was withholding the officer's name; but, if made at all, it seems most likely that the "confidential communication" came from Groves, the only alternative being an engineer. The "confidential communication" did not apparently affirm all Gill said — for one thing, Groves knew nothing of the statements made by Stone and Gibson.

"According to the officer," the newspaper reported, "Captain Lord was called from his bunk three times by the officers of the watch, Mr. Stone or the apprentice officer, Mr. Gibson, and notified that some vessel in distress was discharging rockets ten miles away."

On learning the facts of the disaster, Groves had not the slightest doubt that the ship he had seen, and which later fired the rockets, was the *Titanic*.[57] The more he heard, as time passed, the firmer his belief became, and in fact it never changed for the remainder of his life.

Groves sailed in the *Californian* from Boston on the afternoon of Saturday, 27 April, reaching the Huskisson Dock in Liverpool on the following Friday week, 10 May,[58] and so far as is known he never saw Gill again. It is true that after the *Californian* returned to Liverpool, Lord and three of his officers reported to the Wreck Commissioner and to the Marine Superintendent of the Leyland Line; and Lord incorrectly reported seeing Gill.[59]

But this was clearly a mistake of memory.

"I think you came back by the *Cestrian,* the next boat of the same company?" Rowlatt asked[60] Gill in London.

"Yes," Gill confirmed.

Lloyd's records show the *Cestrian* did not leave Boston until Sunday, 5 May,* and arrived in Liverpool on 15 May. This was actually the day on which Groves gave the main part of his evidence, and he sailed again in the *Californian* on Saturday, the 18th. Gill's second performance as a witness, did not occur until 4 June.

The reference in *The Boston American* to the "confidential communication" from the unnamed ship's officer, with the possibility of some association between Gill and Groves, and the suspicion, however faint, that the latter might have influenced Gill, proves to be completely negative, and does nothing to explain the transformation of Gill in London, let alone the major mysteries in his story; and at the end, as at the beginning, we are left facing the puzzle of Ernest Gill.

From the point of view of history, as we already know, Gill had been anticipated, and although hitherto universally regarded as the man who broke the *Californian* story to the world, it is now definitely established that the secret was actually disclosed first by the anonymous ship's carpenter whose name

* Though she was advertised to sail on 4 May.

was not discovered until 52 years later, and then only through somewhat bizarre circumstances. It was Gill, however, who had both the taste and the urge for personal publicity, and Gill who achieved the detonating result. This is why it is still important to try to discover the truth about him.

At opposite poles in relation to Gill stand the Attorney-General and Captain Lord, and there would be little difficulty if either was completely right in his estimate of the man. To the Attorney, Gill was a witness of truth, "and he was fully justified in what he said in America"; to Captain Lord, he was merely a case of an unscrupulous £5 10s per month donkeyman seeing and grabbing an opportunity of making a pleasing sum of money — $500 being the generally accepted figure aboard the *Californian* — by selling a completely false and fraudulent tale.

Now, there are two main points in Gill's story, one which on the face of it is impossible to incredible, the other which, likewise at first sight, is very probably true. The first, of course, is that "very large steamer"; the second, the rockets.

It is at this stage we shall introduce a document never widely known in the story of the *Californian,* and long since forgotten. Fortunately rediscovered, it throws some light on the darker recesses of Gill's astonishing, and too readily accepted, tale. Paradoxically, the obscurest parts became the most brightly lit.

On 26 April, the day after *The Boston American* had launched Gill's sensational affidavit, a rival newspaper, *The Boston Herald,* without deigning to name its competitor, published its own *Californian* number. The *Herald* ran as its final item an interview with one of the chief characters in the affidavit, none other than Gill's own cabin mate.

"William Thomas, a donkeyman," the story began, "was Gill's 'bunkie' and was highly indignant yesterday [25 April] that his name had been brought into the affidavit. 'I knew nothing about this affidavit,' he said, '. . . Gill woke me up soon after 12 o'clock that night, and I asked him why he was so late.''It's all right, the engines aren't running,' he answered. 'Then I heard a bumping against the side of the ship, and I asked if it was ice. He said it was. . . .

"'I think that Gill would have told me if he had seen rockets. I don't believe that he could see a ship ten miles off if there was one, because the change from the engine room to the deck partly blinds a man, and besides that night it would have been easy to take fixed stars for vessels' lights and shooting stars for rockets."[61]

The first thing to note about this statement is that it indicates Gill made his affidavit without the co-operation or knowledge of his friend William Thomas; but there is no reason to draw any adverse inference from Gill's failure to observe such a refinement as obtaining Thomas's permission to use his name. Thomas was 46, no less than 20 years older than Gill, and it is possible he regarded the younger man as in some way under his authority. Thomas confirmed Gill's important evidence that he was late, apparently very late, but reassures him with the information that the engines are not running and the ship is in the ice.

What did Gill say at the time? According to Gill, a great deal; according to Thomas, his sole hearer, nothing but that the ship was stopped because of ice.

Thomas also says: "I think that Gill would have told me if he had seen rockets," but here, it would appear, Gill's story is far less vulnerable. According to him, and to Thomas himself, he saw the rockets, if he saw them at all, when Thomas was already in the engine room attending to oiling the steering gear, his routine job.

In fact, the most impressive thing by far in Gill's whole story is his timing of the rockets. "I had been on deck about ten minutes," he says in his affidavit, "when I saw a white rocket about ten miles away on the starboard side."

That would make it about 12.40. Rowe in the *Titanic* and Stone in the *Californian* independently timed that first rocket at about 12.45. It is a striking similarity.

At first glance, it seemed his story of the rockets was very probably true. A closer examination leaves that opinion unaltered. His failure to see the steamer at the same time is not perhaps absolutely incomprehensible. It may be that from the deck, which was some feet below the bridge, where he stood, or perhaps sat, as he smoked, he could not see, or he overlooked, the lights of the steamer firing the rockets.

Of the rockets themselves, as he truthfully said in London, he gave them no importance at the time, and, of course, did not tell anybody. Later, after he realized the significance of what he had seen, and decided to try to offer his experience for sale, the rockets alone, without a ship, could not have seemed impressive enough to bring in a rich enough reward — they had, after all, failed to impress Gill himself when he saw them. It was then he probably decided to add those unfortunate words, "That must be a vessel in distress". Although they prudently disappeared from his London evidence, their effect was still present.

But Gill's apocryphal caption to the rockets was not the end of his creative activity. After trying to make some money and while brooding over the whole enterprise, even the words about "a vessel in distress" must have seemed inadequate. Gill was evidently shrewd enough to understand his story had to be not only convincing, but also sufficiently sensational. He was a little man aiming at probably the richest prize he had ever imagined he might win, and he did not want "to make a muck of it."

It has been frequently emphasized that it is unrealistic to place too much trust on exact times of various incidents stated by participants in the story. In this instance, however, we are faced with an exceptional issue. At four minutes to twelve "exactly" — giving Gill's "four minutes *after* twelve", as reported, the meaning he really intended — we have him seeing the brightly-lit steamer going along at full speed. But at only a few minutes after 11.40, we also have Groves and Lord seeing a steamer not only not brightly-lit, but also stopped.[62] With such a discrepancy, not only of time, but also with the difference between "full speed" and stopped, it is unavoidable that the testimony of Gill — the odd man — should instantly sound exceedingly doubtful, if not positively suspicious. Gill was forced to time his steamer that late, because he was caught by the fact that the time he left the engine room could easily be checked with the Fourth Engineer, Mr Hooton. Yet these are only the less formidable of the difficulties built-in to Gill's steamer.

Soon after 12, Stone has seen the steamer stopped; at 20 minutes past midnight, Gibson has also spotted her[63] — four in all now. But, when Gill comes back on deck about 12.30 for his smoke, something inexplicable in material terms seems to have happened: his brightly-lit passenger ship has completely vanished. The truth in his experience trapped him again.

His whole case was, not that the watch and the captain had failed to see the rockets, but that, having seen or heard of them, they failed to answer them. If they had seen the rockets, they must inevitably have also seen that brightly lit steamer, which was sending them up. But if he had seen no such steamer, the watch presumably had seen none either. What should or could he do? He had been bold enough to add a steamer when he felt his story needed bolstering with one, so he would be bold enough to remove her when he feared she might prove too heavy a burden for his fragile narrative and sink it, and him, with her. So remove her he did. Her disappearance made an even more unlikely story, and he knew it. He had appeared almost proud of not being a seaman. He might be ignorant of latitude and longitude, but he must have known a good deal about knots and revolutions, and how many would have to be made to take that "big vessel" completely out of sight — not just hull down — from his height of about 30 feet above sea level in half an hour.

Gill, therefore, hoped to protest at least the appearance of honesty by finessing the problem, so to speak, and calling attention to the phenomenon himself — "She had either steamed away, or I do not know what she had done. She was not there."[64]

In Washington, after Gill had made his exit from the witness stand, the inquiry adjourned before calling the next witness, who was Captain Lord himself.

Sources

1 *Evening Telegram,* New York, 18 April.
2 Ibid., April 23, p. 1.
3 *New York Globe,* April 23, Night Ed., p. 2.
4 US 710.
5 US 711.
6 B 18215.
7 US 711.
8 Ibid.
9 US 712.
10 Ibid.
11 Ibid.
12 US 713.
13 Ibid.
14 Ibid.
15 Ibid.
16 Ibid.
17 US 714.
18 US 713.
19 US 714.
20 B 18136.
21 B 18137-38.
22 Ibid.

23 B 18162.
24 B 18208.
25 B 18137-38.
26 B 18144.
27 US 710.
28 B 18134-35.
29 B 18156.
30 B 18155.
31 Mersey, p. 408.
32 B 18157.
33 B 18157.
34 US 710.
35 B 7908.
36 B 18158.
37 B 18158.
38 B 18193.
39 B 18195.
40 Ibid.
41 B 18196.
42 Mersey, p. 409.
43 B 18198.
44 Ibid.
45 Mersey, p. 409.
46 B 18199.

47 B 18206-08.
48 B 18210-15.
49 B 18216.
50 B 18217.
51 B 18218-19.
52 B 18220-23.
53 Ibid.
54 *See,* e.g., Padfield, p. 276.
55 US 746.
56 B 18162.
57 P.I., 1955, and see Chapter 20.
58 *Liverpool Express,* 11 May.
59 Captain Lord's Affidavit, Appendix C.
60 B 18172-73.
61 *Boston Herald,* 26 April, p. 9.
62 B 8211.
63 B 7424.
64 B 18155.

Chapter 13

Captain Lord's 'At Home' in Washington

When Captain Lord and Evans finally arrived in Washington, the committee was still at its luncheon recess. Lord himself had not enjoyed the journey. It was his first trip in a pullman and he found the experience unpleasant. He could not sleep and it made him feel sick.[1]

When he arrived at the Senate, in accordance with the practice of the Committee, he was soon shown into the chamber where the hearing was to be continued, and sat next to P.A.S. Franklin. Nearly 50 years afterwards, Lord tried very hard, but in vain, to recall Franklin's name. He had no trouble in remembering that next to Franklin sat Bruce Ismay.

If anybody, having read the account of the suspicious and rather unfriendly negotiations which preceded the summoning of the *Californian* witnesses to Washington, had expected a somewhat anxious meeting between Lord and his employers, and especially in view of Gill's evidence just completed, he would have been surprised at what actually happened.

Franklin identified himself to Lord as the Manager of the White Star in New York. Then Lord gave a strange and unexpected glimpse of these two professional men in different sides of the shipping business, alone and confidentially close together on what may have seemed like unfriendly territory, but unobserved for the moment by laymen's eyes and unheard by hostile ears.

According to Lord there was a spirit of conviviality over the meeting. It is a line that jars. Thinking of the grim purpose of the whole elaborate activity, with its senators and secretaries, its clerks and reporters and various functionaries, all basically concerned with an inquest into the deaths of 1,500 persons; and remembering, too, the extremely serious reason for Lord's own visit, it is hard not to wonder what Franklin and Lord found to be convivial about. Perhaps it was the already notorious ignorance of Smith about maritime matters.[2] At any rate, Lord got on famously with Franklin.

Lord sat talking to Franklin for about ten minutes or longer before Smith returned to resume the inquiry at about three o'clock; and the cheerful little prologue was over. But Lord's examination which followed could hardly have been more friendly.

The agreeable picture of his afternoon in Washington while the senators listened and a lady sketched him, lingered in his memory for the rest of his life. Nobody doubted anything he said, or questioned his judgement. Lord always insisted on his friendly reception. At times it almost seemed as if Captain Lord was 'at home' and Senator Smith and his five colleagues were Lord's bemused guests. He was to suffer a more alarming experience in his native land.

It is an interesting fact that Lord's evidence in the American 'Hearings' occupies 18 pages of the transcript,[3] but it is not until the 14th page is reached that a question was asked about "distress rockets". Until this point, Lord had quoted from his log, giving his Sunday night position, when he stopped, 42.5N; 50.7W; earlier, at 6.30, when he passed two large icebergs at 42.5N; 49.10W; and later warned the *Titanic* that he was stopped in the ice, and the *Titanic* told him "to shut up, or stand by, or something, that he was busy".[4] Then, Lord told how it had taken him about 2½ hours to get to the *Carpathia* on the Monday morning, and that he estimated the reported position of the *Titanic* some 19½-19¾ miles from his own position, where he had stopped; how he had doubled the lookout on the Sunday night;[5] the ice warnings he had had, from the *Nieuw Amsterdam* as early as 9 April (when the *Titanic* was still safely tied up to the New Dock in Southampton), from Captain Barr of the *Caronia* on the 13th, and a report from the *Parisian* on the 14th of the same icebergs he presumably later saw himself. Lord explained he himself had had little experience of ice, only small bergs in the North Atlantic, but "I have seen any amount of it around Cape Horn, but that was when I was in a sailing ship." He told them, reading again from his log, of his weather that Sunday, from "Four a.m., fresh wind, rough and westerly; sky overcast and heavy shore showers," all the way to "Midnight, calm and smooth sea; clear weather; ship surrounded by ice."

It is noteworthy that from first to last the senators were never curious enough to look at the log themselves.

"Would you like to see the log?"[6] Lord asked blandly, when they were questioning him about the ice reports he had received.

"No," said Smith, "I want you to read that into the record, if you please."

"'From *Caronian* [sic] to Captain *Californian* . . .'", Lord droned on.

Here was a man who had nothing to hide, for he knew very well that anything that would have been safer hidden had just been left out. As we know, there was not a word about the rockets or the strange behaviour of the strange ship to raise any question that might ruffle the routine tranquillity of those pages. It is a question whether the senators would have had wit enough, even if they had examined the log for themselves, to realize that that egregious document was no less fraudulent for what it did not contain than it would have been if it had been stuffed with matter that was positively false. As it was, the senators trusted the log without even glancing at it themselves.

Captain Lord went on to say that it would have taken him "At the very least, two hours"[7] to reach the *Titanic* on Sunday night, if he had received her CQD. Like other master mariners, he seemed to think very little of the idea of giving his man in the crow's nest glasses, and the only time he had done it was when he was looking for the *Titanic,* with a man up the foremast in a coal bucket. He told them where he had seen the largest icebergs — to the south-east — but he had no idea how much larger than the *Olympic* or *Titanic* that largest berg would have been.

There followed next an amiable discussion about the colour of the icebergs by day and by night.[8]

Lord conceded as much as he could. After all, he had begun by telling them he had not had much experience of ice, but if the senator wanted him to bestow on them the benefit of this small experience, why should he refuse? Everything was going so smoothly, it would have been foolish to strike a dissenting note. Clearly, these senators were a far more agreeable group than that rough and sceptical crowd of Boston newspapermen!

It was when the questioning turned to the rules governing the duties of wireless operators aboard ship that Lord's answers seemed to reveal a little more of what was beneath the surface of the man,[9] and of his inability, typical of the average captain of the time, to appreciate the potentialities of wireless. Even to Bisset, it hadn't been much more than a toy up to the time of the *Titanic*.[10] Lord knew Evans had been off duty that night, and he agreed, "most certainly" he would have caught the CQD if he had been at his post.

"If you were to have the service of a wireless operator at a time when he might be of most service," Smith asked, "when would it be, ordinarily, day or night?"

They considered the little problem.

"As it happens," Lord pointed out, "there are so many one-operator ships around that at night time most of these fellows are asleep; and he would be more useful in the daytime. We would get a great deal more information in the daytime, as it happens now.

"Would it not be well to have your wireless operator at his post on duty at night, when other eyes are closed, in order that any possible signal of distress might not escape your attention?"[11]

Lord might very well have observed that a distress signal is not bound by time, and is possibly as common during daylight as at night. But he did nothing of the kind. Instead, he gave an answer, which was not only inept in itself, but coming so shortly after his own tragic failure to use his wireless at the one moment in all his life when he needed it most, gave a hint of why he had failed. It was almost as if Captain Lord was deliberately pitting the limited human vision of an officer on watch against the range of wireless — even the wireless of 1912.

"We have the officer on the bridge," said Lord, "who can see as far at night as in the daytime."[12]

Lord's failure to use his wireless at the crucial time on the night of Sunday, 14/15 April 1912, has passed into the cautionary tales of the sea and of many radio men the world over ever since. In spite of the unequivocal decision of this very Senate Committee on this issue, the investigation of why Captain Lord permitted Evans to sleep through those hours was not begun until Lord faced the much more severe tribunal in London nearly three weeks later, but already this egregious answer cast a strange light on the sort of mind which bred such a failure. Senator Smith was too polite that afternoon to make an appropriate comment, but he did not allow the answer to pass completely.

"But the officer on the bridge could not see the *Titanic* even with glasses, you said, that night."[13]

"No," Lord admitted.

"The wireless operator," Smith went on, "could have heard the call from the *Titanic* if he had been at his post of duty?"

"Yes; he would have heard that." That may be thought of as an admission that might have shattered a man of ordinary self-confidence; it seems to have left Captain Lord utterly unperturbed.

"Do you know whether the wireless service works more satisfactorily at night than it does in the daytime, and with greater accuracy?"

"I believe it gets a longer range,"[14] Lord answered correctly. "I do not know that there is any more accuracy, but you can reach farther."

At this point in the proceedings, astonishing to relate, it seems that the examination of Captain Lord was complete, at least so far as Senator Smith was concerned.

"Do any of the other Senators," he asked, "desire to ask any questions?"[15]

Quietly, the spring afternoon had droned on, never for a single moment suffering the sharp prick of reality. Here, in this same room, that very morning, Ernest Gill had made a definite accusation, true or false, that this man, now present on the witness stand and giving sworn evidence, this sea captain and holder of an extra master's certificate, the highest qualification of all, had wilfully neglected to render assistance to a vessel in distress; and not one of the senators present had so far seemed sufficiently interested to ask a single question on that subject.

Senator Bourne accepted the invitation of his Chairman, and said: "I simply want to ask, Captain, whether the wireless operator had any regular hours or not? If so, what were they?"[16]

Lord replied that he did not think there were "any regular hours. I understand they are usually around from seven in the morning to half-past two, and then I think they lie down, because I never, as a rule, receive any messages between half-past two and four. I presume they are asleep."

"You think it is better to have two operators on every ship, do you, so as to have continuous service."[17] In fact, of course, Lord had said nothing whatever of the kind; but he accepted the idea rather daintily.

"It would be much nicer. You would never miss a message, then."

Finally, Senator Fletcher asked him about the lookouts he kept on after the engines were stopped; and Lord said, in what might be described as the answer at a climacteric, although the answer itself was not of much importance: "We discontinued the one on the forecastle head. We just kept the one on the crow's nest."

I have used the word 'climacteric', though one might, with equal accuracy, have said it was Lord's final answer in his period of near irrelevance. If Lord, as the fact was, had been summoned to Washington primarily because of Gill's revelations, and to a much lesser extent because of his own ice warning to the *Titanic* (which actually provoked only 20 of 227 questions asked of him to this point), it must fairly be said that until now the Committee had done little but beat round and round the bush until it could beat no more.

The transcript gives no clue as to whether the decisive question then asked was the result of a sudden memory of Gill, or whether in fact it had long been ready.

"Captain," said the Senator, "did you see any distress signals on Sunday night, either rockets or the Morse signals?"[18]

It is clear from the manner of his third answer following, that Lord could not have hesitated an instant before he flung back his answer. The reader should remember that this was the first occasion ever that Lord departed from what till that moment had been his defence to the charge, and repeated again and again: ". . . no signals of distress or anything else had been seen." And he had called on Stewart, who he falsely said had been on watch at the relevant time, to "tell you himself that nothing of the kind was seen by him or any of the men who were on the watch with him."

His defence now assumed its second form, and Lord answered Smith's question thus: "No, sir; I did not. *The officer on watch saw some signals, but he said they were not distress signals*' [emphasis added].

"They were not distress signals?"[19]

"Not distress signals," Lord repeated.

"But he reported them?"

"To me." Then, evidently deciding that these senators should receive no more deference from him than he had paid to the reporters in Boston, he said: "I think you had better let me tell you that story."

"I wish you would," Smith promptly agreed; and forthwith gave up any further notion of questioning this imperious seaman until he was ready to

answer. The dominance that Captain Lord had established over his inter-
rogators that afternoon, and not underestimated by him, is suggested by
Smith's reply, which displayed an unwonted diffidence.

This is the story Lord told, which is given here in full.[20]

"When I came off the bridge, at half past ten, I pointed out to the officer that
I thought I saw a light coming along, and it was a most peculiar night,* and
we had been making mistakes all along with the stars, thinking they were
signals. We could not distinguish where the sky ended and where the water
commenced. You understand, it was a flat calm. He said he thought it was a
star, and I did not say anything more. I went down below. I was talking with
the engineer about keeping the steam ready, and we saw these signals coming
along, and I said: 'There is a steamer coming. Let us go to the wireless and
see what the news is.' But on our way down I met the operator coming, and
I said: 'Do you know anything?' He said: 'The *Titanic.*' So, then, I gave him
instructions to let the *Titanic* know. I said: 'This is not the *Titanic*; there is no
doubt about it.' She came and lay, at half past 11, alongside of us until, I
suppose, a quarter past 1, within 4 miles of us. We could see everything on
her quite distinctly; see her lights. We signalled her, at half past 11, with the
Morse lamp. She did not take the slightest notice of it. That was between half
past 11 and 20 minutes to 12. We signalled her again at ten minutes past 12,
half past 12, a quarter to one, and one o'clock. We have a very powerful
Morse lamp. I suppose you can see that about ten miles, and she was about
four miles off, and she did not take the slightest notice of it. When the second
officer came on the bridge, at 12 o'clock, or ten minutes past 12, I told him
to watch that steamer, which was stopped, and I pointed out the ice to him;
told him we were surrounded by ice; to watch the steamer that she did not
get any closer to her. At 20 minutes to one I whistled up the speaking tube and
asked him if she was getting nearer. He said: 'No; she is not taking any notice
of us.' So, I said: 'I will go and lie down a bit.' At a quarter past 1 he said:
'I think she has fired a rocket.' He said: 'She did not answer the Morse lamp
and she has commenced to go away from us.' I said: 'Call her up and let me
know at once what her name is.' So, he put the whistle back, and, apparently,
he was calling. I could hear him ticking over my head. Then I went to sleep."[21]

It was the natural end of the story. One wonders if Franklin sighed to
himself: 'So much for Gill!' Certainly, nobody listening to Lord could have
suspected that whether or not Gill's report of the alleged intimidation of the
quartermaster was true, Lord had in fact quietly obtained from both Second
Officer Stone and Apprentice Gibson confidential reports of the rockets they
had seen and of the disappearance of the strange, unresponsive ship. Senator
Fletcher did not know that, though he knew about stock exchanges; nor
Senator Burton, who knew about taxation; nor Senator Bourne, who thought
up the parcel post in America; nor Senator Simmons, who knew how to disen-
franchise Negroes; not even Senator Perkins, who knew a little about ships;
and certainly not Senator Smith.

None of them could have guessed, according to the report of Second Officer
Stone, he had told Lord at a quarter past one the ship had fired not one rocket,
but five, which news at once brought Lord's own order to "Call her up and let
me know at once what her name is!" Having given that imperative order, it
was clear from the master's own words he had then placidly gone to sleep, this,
too, being the first time Lord himself had chosen to file "Sleep" as his own
preferred and official defence. None of them apparently resented that, and

* Through a mistake, this is printed "light" in the 'hearings'.

all their Chairman, Senator Smith, asked was: "You heard nothing more about it?"[22]

"Nothing more," said Lord, "until about something between then and half past four, I have a faint recollection of the apprentice opening my room door; opening it and shutting it. I said: 'What is it?' He did not answer and I went to sleep again. I believe the boy came down to deliver the message that this steamer had steamed away from us to the south-west, showing several of these flashes or white rockets; steamed away to the south-west."

Could anybody have guessed from this that Captain Lord had in his possession a report from this very "boy" describing these "flashes or white rockets" thus: "I then got the binoculars and had just got them focussed on the vessel when I observed a white flash apparently on her deck, followed by a faint streak towards the sky which then burst into stars?"

If Senator Smith had really known his job and been efficient, he would have issued further subpoenas there and then, or at latest, at the end of the day's hearing, ordering the attendance of Stone and Gibson in Washington; but Lord had clearly overwhelmed the Committee. Smith just asked him[23] to suppose that the *Titanic* had used her Morse lamp and fired rockets "for a half to three-quarters of an hour after she struck ice, would you, from the position of your ship on a night like Sunday night, have been able to see those signals?"

Her Morse lamp was "an utter impossibility", Lord said and he did not think they could see her rockets. "It would have been way down on the horizon. It might have been mistaken for a shooting star or anything at all." The apprentice Gibson had made no such mistake, but the Committee hardly knew his name.

Smith then asked if Lord had seen anything of the *Amerika* during his voyage, and then went on to a number of unimportant and irrelevant questions about the *Frankfurt,* which vessel reappeared from time to time in their questioning. He next obtained the story of how the news of the disaster finally reached the *Californian* through the waking of Evans, which has already been closely analyzed in a previous chapter.

Senator Fletcher, towards the end of Lord's examination, asked for some further particulars of the ship. "Let me ask you a question with reference to that steamer you saw four miles away. What was her position in reference to your ship —"[24]

Lord quickly interrupted him: "Pretty near south of us, 4 miles to the south."

And Fletcher continued his question: " — as to being on the starboard or port side?"

"Well, on our ordinary course, our ordinary course was about west, true; but on seeing the ice, we were so close we had to reverse the engine and put her full speed astern, and the action of reversing turned the ship to starboard, and we were heading about north-east true."

It was then Lord continued with information which was of the most deadly significance for his case.

"When this man was coming along he was showing his green light on our starboard side, before midnight. After midnight we slowly blew around and showed him our red light."

"And he passed south-west?"

"He was stopped until one o'clock, and then he started going ahead again; and the second officer he reported he changed from south-southeast to west-southwest, 6½ points; and if he was 4 miles off, the distance he travelled I estimated to be seven or 7½ miles in that hour."

"Was he ever any closer to you?"

"No, sir."

"Were you able to tell what kind of ship it was?"

"The officer on watch, and the apprentice there, and myself — I saw it before one o'clock, before I went to the watch [*sic* — chart?] room — were of the opinion that it was an ordinary cargo steamer."

"Did you see the funnels?"

"No, sir. It had one masthead light and a green light, which I saw first."

It will be remembered that Groves had seen her red light, as had Stone and Gibson.

"You could not hear any escaping steam, or the siren, or the whistle?"

"No, sir."

Finally, Smith asked him: "Have you any idea what that steamer was?"[25]

"Not the faintest," said Lord. "At daylight we saw a yellow funnel steamer on the southwest of us, beyond where this man had left, about 8 miles away."

"Do you suppose that was the same one?"

"I should not like to say. I don't think so, because this one had only one masthead light that we saw at half past 11."

It will be remembered that when Stewart and Lord looked at that ship together at dawn, Stewart did not tell his skipper that Stone had reported she was not the ship that had fired the rockets. Nor did Lord make any remark about her showing two masthead lights.

Lord's evidence was now almost at its end. Apart from his story of the "ordinary cargo steamer" and Gill's of the "big German", the Committee, up to that day, had already heard 18 witnesses from the *Titanic,* who had testified about a light or lights they had seen, which they thought came from another ship.

Yet, once again it must be said, the decisive evidence of this vital issue comes not from the *Titanic,* but from the *Californian.* That afternoon, Captain Lord had made his own contribution to it, and it was his opinion — honest though it may have been — that the ship which approached him and showed first her green light and then her red, was an "ordinary cargo steamer". And, although it was still a profound secret, Lord also had the statements of Stone and Gibson, the latter of which destroyed him.

Lord now faced Senator Smith's final questions. His two replies to Gill's charges, different though they were, showed that the enamelled front of his pride had not even been scratched. He had first disposed of the Boston newspapermen with a complete and brazenly false denial; now, he must have felt satisfied that his quiet self-confidence, which at times was indistinguishable from quiet arrogance, had more subtly, but with equal finality, misled these amiable, and admittedly ignorant, American politicians.

"From the log which you hold in your hand, and from your own knowledge," Smith asked him finally, "is there anything you can say further which will assist the Committee in its inquiry as to the causes of this catastrophe?"

"No, sir; there is nothing; only that it was a very deceiving night. That is all that I can say about that. I only saw that ice a mile and a half off."

It was finished. Later, when he got back to Liverpool he was to write Smith a letter [26] formally correcting "a wrong answer" he had given, when he had been asked if he could give the temperature of the water from his log book; but now, there was not another thing he need say. He was complimented on his evidence and Evans took the stand.[27] Lord did not stay to listen. He himself was certainly absolved.

Lord, of course, was anxious to return to his ship in Boston, but his going before Evans's evidence was surely as typical as it was strange. It recalls his "convivial" preliminary chat with Franklin and is a further indication of his detachment, his exceptional removal from common feelings. Curiosity at least, if not a spirit of comradeship, might have impelled another skipper to delay his departure for an hour or so and to lend the moral support of his presence while the 20-year-old Evans faced the ordeal of being examined; but not Stanley Lord. Perhaps he thought Evans could take care of himself; more likely he never thought about it at all.

Evans, described next day in London[28] as "a rosy-faced lad of twenty", but whose glasses give him in the rare photographs a clerkly appearance, began his evidence with a short account of his career. This was his third trip in the *Californian*.[29]

"Where were you Sunday, 14 April?" Senator Smith wanted to know.[30]

Evans then gave an hour-by-hour report of how he had passed the day:

"From 7 o'clock in the morning until half past 8 I was on duty. From half past 8 to 9 I was having my breakfast. From 9 o'clock to half past 12 I was on watch. From 1 o'clock to 3 o'clock I was on watch. From 3 o'clock to half past 5. At half past 5 had my dinner. From 6 o'clock I was on watch. I was on watch until 5 and 20 minutes past 11. I heard the *Titanic* working. I put down the phones and I turned in."

The seaman's Sunday: a mere 15 hours' labour and two full hours for his meals, a siesta perhaps and — possibly — his orisons.

Just before turning in he had heard the *Titanic*.

"What time did you receive the CQD call from the *Titanic* Sunday night?" Smith asked.

"I did not receive it, sir."

"You did not receive it at all?" The Senator was plainly shocked, but presumably only by the young fellow's desertion of duty, because Lord had already told him the *Californian* had not heard the CQD.[31]

"No, sir," said Evans, and next told how he had earlier sent, at 6.30 p.m. ATS,[32] the ice report to the *Antillian* of the three large icebergs, which the *Titanic* overheard,[33] and then of his call to the *Titanic* about 11 o'clock.

". . . The Captain told me[34] he was going to stop because of the ice, and the captain asked me if I had any boats, and I said the *Titanic*. He said: 'Better advise him we are surrounded by ice and stopped.' So I went to my cabin, and at 9.05 New York time I called him up. I said: 'Say, old man, we are stopped and surrounded by ice.' He turned around and said: 'Shut up, shut up, I am busy; I am working Cape Race,' and at that I jammed him."

He explained what 'jamming' meant and said he had listened to the *Titanic* sending private messages to Cape Race, "and at 11.35 I put the phones down and took off my clothes and turned in."[35]

Before Evans came to his story of the rockets, he readily gave the senators much other information. He told how he had jumped out of bed, "slipped on a pair of trousers and a pair of slippers" and rushed to his key. In "almost a second" the *Frankfurt* answered his CQ, and then came the matchless dialogue — but typical of its time — between the two young men:

". . . The DFT answered me. He said: 'Do you know the *Titanic* has sunk during the night, collided with an iceberg?' I said: 'No; please give me the latest position.' He gave me the position. I put the position down on a slip of paper, and then I said: 'Thanks, old man,' to the German operator, . . .'[36]

The *Virginian* then broke in[37] with the same news and the same position. Stewart was standing by and no doubt desperately impatient to return to Lord on the bridge, but Evans said: "Wait a moment; I will get an official message."

He got that, as distinct from what was regarded as "just conversation", and Stewart dashed off to Lord.

The mention of the *Frankfurt* invariably stirred the Committee, and so Smith at once asked: "Did you have any difficulty whatever working with the *Frankfurt* operator?" and followed with many more questions about that vessel and her operator. The Committee knew by this time that Phillips of the *Titanic* had been exasperated by the *Frankfurt's* delay in any positive response to his distress call, and had said: "You are a fool, keep out!"[38]

Having dealt for the time being with that ship, Smith asked whether Evans had been in communication with the *Parisian* and the *Amerika,* and then what his wages were per month.[39]

"£4."

"And board?"

"Yes."

"You have your board on the ship, and room?" Four pounds per month and all this for a 105-hour week!

"Yes," Evans admitted.

Evans's manner seems to have become more cautious, when he was asked by Senator Fletcher, as he shortly was, about Gill.

"Do you know Gill, who was a member of the crew of the *Californian* — Ernest Gill?"[40]

"I think I have seen him; yes, sir."

"Did you ever have any conversation with him about that ship that was seen that night throwing up rockets?"

"I think so. Practically everybody on the ship — it has been common talk on the ship."

He did not know when the rockets were seen, nor from what direction as he had turned in. Gill had not made "any special statement" to him about his published statement; and he did not "think" Gill had said anything about how he came to make it. Questions about the *Californian's* wireless and his calling by Stewart then followed.

Fletcher went back to Gill. His question was to bring forth from the reluctant witness the first detailed evidence the world had heard of the rockets the *Californian* had seen, Captain Lord's denial of the very sight of which was still on sale on the Boston newsstands.

"Did Gill, the donkeyman, ever talk to you about a story he was telling about the sending up of the rockets by a ship that night?"

"I think he may have mentioned it to me."

"When?"

"Everybody on board has been speaking about it amongst themselves."

"The captain too?" Fletcher asked — whether innocently or slyly one is left to guess.

"No, sir. I have never spoken to the captain about the matter of rockets, at all."

"None of this talk you have heard on the ship was in the presence of the captain?"

"No, sir."

"In a general way, what was the talk with reference to that, that you heard on the ship?"

"Well, I could not say. It was just simply the usual talk about the rockets." This is a strange answer. Its two parts are, of course, contradictory.

"Were the rockets described?" was Fletcher's next question.

"Not to my knowledge, no, sir. I never heard them described." He could not know that Captain Lord had Gibson's description in his possession.

"Do you know whether they were distress rockets, or some other kind of rockets?"

"No, sir; I do not. I did not see them, myself."

Senator Burton took up the examination, and referred to Evans's statement that "everybody was talking on board about these rockets."

"Do you mean by that that they were saying that they themselves had seen the rockets, or that there was merely talk about it on the ship?"

"There was talk about it, and some of them said they had seen it, and some said they had not."

The following three questions from Senator Burton have gloomy importance, as they unexpectedly brought forth even from this conscientious young man what the experienced student of the case comes to recognize as a peculiar *Californian* answer.

"With how many did you talk who said they saw rockets that night?"[41]

"Nobody."

"Did you talk with anybody?"

"No one in particular."

"Can you tell any one you talked with who said he had seen rockets that night?"

"No, sir."

Each of these answers was untrue, and stupidly untrue. In an attempt to discover the approximate lapse of time before Evans reverted to his practice of telling the truth, a spoken and timed reading of the intervening matter indicates that no more than about five minutes afterwards[42] he admitted that Gibson himself had told him he had seen rockets, which statement Evans shortly repeated twice more.

That "intervening matter" comprised firstly questions about the *Californian's* wireless,[43] which he answered freely and apparently with enthusiasm. Senator Smith, who had taken up the questioning again, also asked whether "your mate" said "how he knew that there had been rockets fired?"[44]

"No, sir," Evans replied.

And he did not know why he had not been called when the rockets were first seen.

There now comes the immensely important and significant passage in Evans's testimony already set out at the time in the narrative when the event he described occurred. This was Gibson's telling him "before we got to the *Titanic* . . . before we reached the scene of the disaster,"[45] on Monday morning, how rockets had been seen during the night, and how they had tried three times in vain to call Lord. Immediately the news was known that the *Titanic* had sunk, those rockets were identified as hers, or, at the very least, were associated with the disaster. Fifty years later, the Lordites complained that the alleged enemies of Captain Lord "jumped to conclusions", but on the morrow of catastrophe, the first to "jump to conclusions" were the crew of the *Californian* themselves. Others would say that the instant connecting of the rockets with the *Titanic* by Gibson and many others was no more than obvious common sense. Common sense may not have been on the watch that Sunday night, nor in command either, but what happened in those very early hours after the news was received proves that it had not entirely fled the vessel.

"Was there any talk of this kind after you left the scene of the sinking of the *Titanic*?" Smith asked Evans.[46]

"Yes; it has been talked about all the time since then."

"They have talked about it all the time since then?"

"Yes, sir."

"As an unusual and extraordinary occurrence?"

"Yes, sir."

The questioning turned to the Morse signals,[47] and Evans said he remembered Gibson telling him he had called up on the Morse lamp.

"He started to call up the *Titanic*?" Smith asked. Dull as the man was generally said to be, and lulled just recently by Lord's tranquillizing evidence, the apparent effect of young Evans's unwilling but devastating evidence was to alarm the senator also into associating the *Titanic* with the rockets the *Californian* saw.

"I do not know whether it was the *Titanic* —" Evans began.

Senator Burton asked: "Was there anything said about the direction in which these rockets were seen? Did they say that they were off where the *Titanic* was sunk?"

"Nobody specified any special direction where they came from. From the south they were."

"The direction in which the *Titanic* was?"

"I would not be sure about that." He was still doing the best a truthful man could for his shipmates, but that answer was certainly true.

"In all this conversation, did they say these rockets came from that boat which the captain has mentioned or that they came from the *Titanic*?"

"They did not know which."

But Burton pressed him:[48] "Was it said that the rockets were those which had been sent up by the *Titanic*? Was that the talk on board ship?"

"Some of them seemed to think so, and some not, sir."

Evans was now asked whether anyone had told him Gill "was to receive $500 for a story in regard to these rockets — anyone on your boat?"

"I think the donkeyman mentioned it."

"What did he say?"

"He said: 'I think I will make about $500 on this.'"

Gill had told him that on Wednesday night, when they had met outside the station.[49] Significantly, Gill also "asked if I was not going back any more. He said he had been up and told the newspaper about the accident."[50] What Evans was doing ashore, he did not say, but Gill seems at once to have thought it possible he too was leaving Captain Lord and his *Californian* for good.

Smith asked further questions about Gibson.

"And that apprentice told you he saw these rockets?"[51]

"Yes, sir; he said he saw rockets."

"He said he saw rockets?"

"Yes, sir."

Smith asked him if he knew whether Gibson, too, had got anything for his story or given out any story.

"I do not think for a moment he told anybody other than the people on the boat." His indignation sounds through the cold print.

"But you got your information directly from the apprentice who was on the bridge with the officer?"

"Yes, sir."

"That he himself had seen rockets the night the *Titanic* went down?"

"Yes, sir."

"Did you hear the captain say that he saw rockets?"

"I heard so the next day. I did not hear anything about it the same day."

"You heard him swear to it here a few moments ago?"*

"Yes, sir."

"White rockets, he said, did he not?"

---

* Lord, of course, had not sworn to that.

"I think so."

Smith then asked Evans if he himself had been offered or received any money for any information about the *Titanic* and the *Californian,* and Evans said he had not.[52]

Evans refused to admit to Fletcher that Stewart "evidently considered these rockets were distress rockets."[53]

"But he would not ask you to inquire —" Fletcher began again.

"He said to find out," Evans interrupted him.

Stewart's story, which had not yet been given to the world, was, as we know, that he had never mentioned rockets or trouble or anything but the need to find out the name of a ship to the south. One must regret that Stewart was not summoned to Washington.

"Stewart would not ask you to inquire unless he apprehended there was some trouble?" Fletcher pressed on.[54]

"I do not know." Evans, still doing what he could for this unworthy colleague, then, it seems, tried to throw a little dust in their eyes. "Two or three days before that I got word from another operator that there was a boat wanting to be towed, an oil tank.* She was short of coal, and wanted to be towed, and I believe he thought it was her: I would not say. He did not happen to mention it to me; he has not mentioned it to me."[55]

It is not worth taking the space to demolish this attempted excuse for Stewart, though one may mention in passing that it was this 'oil tank' which was a factor in the reassuring early story that the *Titanic* was safe.

The final questions to Evans came from Senator Smith and were about money received for information about the *Titanic*.[56] Evans repeated that he had received none and would accept none.

"Why?"

"I do not think it is right to receive money for anything like that."

"That is all; you may be excused."

"Thank you," said Evans, and began his journey back to the *Californian* at the Clyde Street Pier in Boston.

The withdrawal of Evans was the close of the *Californian* case in Washington, except for parts of the evidence of the navy's hydrographer. Although some of the questions towards the end of Evans's examination contain a hint that erosion of the immense effect of Lord's evidence had perhaps already begun, there is no doubt he had been the star witness of the day.

The master of the *Californian* had never been in trouble for a moment. In any terms, it had been a triumph, as the British and American papers were to declare next day.

As between Gill and Captain Lord, *The New York Tribune*[57] said Gill "made far from a favourable impression," whereas "Stanley Lord, captain of the Californian, told on the witness stand a direct and straightforward story, which won the respect and confidence of the nautical men present," an opinion shared by *The Daily Telegraph* of London, which said: "Captain Lord's evidence was the most impressive recorded to-day . . ."[58]

"We can hardly hesitate," asserted *The Globe*[59] in London on Saturday evening, "as to the version we must accept. The statement of the Californian's master is so circumstantial and is so perfectly supported by her log, that we ought to assume it to be correct . . ."

* This was the German oil tanker *Deutschland* of the Deutsche-Amerikanische Petroleum Gessellschaft (DAGP). Her call for assistance on 14 April had brought the *Asian* of the Leyland Line to her side the next morning and a tow into Halifax.

To anybody knowing more about the facts than did the writers of those opinions, Captain Lord's statement on the witness stand is undeserving of the praise it received. At the time, it was clearly, even if unconsciously, a tribute to the forceful character of the man rather than his matter, a truth which would emerge only after the ordeal of the cross-examination he was to endure in London.

Evans's story, which although necessarily largely hearsay, and told with reluctance, at the very least tended to raise questions about Lord and to strengthen Gill's evidence, if not his character. It seems to have aroused no comment whatever and in many of the English papers it was not even reported. This omission may have been due partly to the time difference between Washington and England. Assuming Evans finished his evidence and left the stand at about five o'clock, as seems probable, it would already be 10 p.m. in England, and deadlines might be involved.

But that Saturday, after Gill, Lord, and Evans had all been seen and heard in public, except for the one reporter, already mentioned, who described Gill as "an honest working fellow. . . .", not a word of criticism could even be inferred against the "bronze-faced, middle-aged Englishman", who had made such a "Strong Impression".

What Gill had said, it is true, was the basis for such headlines as "AMAZING EVIDENCE FROM THE CALIFORNIAN" and "LIVERPOOL MAN'S AMAZING EVIDENCE", — only that "amazing evidence" was not accepted. The "mystery" also, it was agreed on both sides of the ocean, was far from solved, and *The Evening News*[60] of London said: "whether this amazing tangle will ever be unravelled is doubtful."

So, with an easy mind, at 5.20 p.m. on Saturday afternoon, 27 April, Captain Lord sailed from Boston and headed for home.[61]

The shadowy McGregor was a true prophet, for it was his last voyage in command of the *Californian*.

Sources

1 *Daily Telegraph*, 27 April, p. 13.
2 Ibid.
3 US 714, *seq.*
4 US 715.
5 US 718.
6 US 719.
7 US 722.
8 US 724-25.
9 US 726.
10 *See* e.g. Bisset. *Tramps and Ladies*, pp. 149, 275.
11 US 726.
12 Ibid.
13 Ibid.
14 US 727.
15 Ibid.
16 Ibid.
17 US 727.
18 US 728.
19 Ibid.
20 Ibid.
21 Ibid.
22 US 729.
23 Ibid.
24 US 732.
25 US 733.
26 US 1142.
27 Ibid.
28 *Daily Telegraph*, 27 April, p. 13.
29 US 733.
30 US 734.
31 US 716.
32 US 735.
33 US 734.
34 US 735.
35 Ibid.
36 US 737.
37 Ibid.
38 US 738.
39 US 738, 739.
40 US 741.
41 US 743.
42 US 747.
43 US 743.
44 US 744.
45 US 745.
46 US 746.
47 Ibid.
48 Ibid.
49 Ibid.
50 US 747.
51 Ibid.
52 US 746.
53 US 748.
54 Ibid.
55 Ibid.
56 US 749.
57 *New York Tribune*, 27 April, p. 1.
58 *Daily Telegraph*, 27 April, p. 13.
59 *The Globe*, 27 April, p. 1, 'Notes of the Day'.
60 *Evening News*, 27 April, p. 1.
61 Official Log.

Chapter 14

The Mersey inquiry and the lavatory maker of Victoria Street

Senate Resolution 283, which directed its Committee of Commerce to investigate the causes of the wreck of the *Titanic,* was dated 17 April,[1] and as we know Senator Smith was at work not later than the following evening. What seems to be the first official mention in public of a British inquiry was made in the House of Commons on that same Thursday, 18 April, when Sydney Buxton, the President of the Board of Trade, in reply to questioning about lifeboats, said there would be an inquiry.[2] A minute dated 19 April in a Board of Trade file, which deals with ice reports from incoming ships, reads: "Perhaps it would be well to order a formal investigation in respect of the loss of the 'Titanic' at once."[3]

On 22 April, Buxton told the Commons: ". . . I am in communication with the Lord Chancellor with a view, if possible, to the special appointment of a person recognized as of high judicial authority as a Wreck Commissioner, under Section 477 of the Merchant Shipping Act, 1894."[4] Later the same day, he explained that under the Act there were four courses which might be taken with regard to a wreck, the last being "to request the Lord Chancellor to appoint a Wreck Commissioner. The last course has not been taken for many years . . ."[5] In view of the unprecedented size and nature of the disaster, however, this was the course he proposed to take. That evening, 22 April, Buxton said: "I am glad now to be able to announce that Lord Mersey . . . has been good enough to undertake the responsible and arduous duty."[6]

It should be made clear — because of the innuendo that here was a venal public functionary, the "Wreck Commissioner", lurking in the wings, dagger in hand, waiting to come forward on cue to destroy an innocent British sea captain — that there was no such permanent officer of state as a "Wreck Commissioner". The appointment was *ad hoc*, and the Wreck Commissioner would be expected to resign after he had fulfilled his function, which in due course Lord Mersey did.

The interests of the general public, Mr Buxton told the House in answer to many questions on the subject, would be represented by the Law Officers of the Crown,[7] although — somewhat awkwardly, it may be thought — they, the Attorney-General and the Solicitor-General, were also the counsel for the Board of Trade.

On 29 April, the announcement was made of the appointment of five assessors who were to assist Lord Mersey.[8] They were appointed not by the Lord Chancellor, who had chosen Lord Mersey, nor by the President of the Board of Trade, but by the Home Secretary, so, if there was a conspiracy to "rig" the inquiry against Captain Lord, presumably the name of Reginald McKenna must be added to the growing number of malefactors.

The names of the assessors had already been given to the Press, but in line with the interest shown by the Commons, after McKenna's statement, there were several questions concerning Professor Biles. Members were assured that he had not designed either the *Titanic* or any other Harland & Wolff ship.[9]

The Labour leader, Will Crooks, had already asked "the right hon. Gentleman how it is, after the approval of the House, there is no assessor representing purely the Labour side and no assessor representing the travelling public?"

McKenna replied that the function of assessors was to act as expert advisers to the judge, not to sit in any representative capacity.

Crooks persisted; whereupon McKenna said his "hon. friend" was "mixing up the proper subject for evidence with the proper subjects to be advised upon by expert advisers, who are called assessors. No doubt passengers and persons representative from the Labour point of view will be called as witnesses."[10]

Mr McKenna's "hon. Friend" was undoubtedly "mixed", but no more wrong in fact than was the certainty of his Rt. Hon. friend Reginald McKenna that "passengers and persons representative" for Labour would give evidence, for neither of which categories was a representative spokesman allowed to open his mouth.

It was in this vigilant atmosphere that the inquiry was initiated. For his three months of work, Lord Mersey received a thousand guineas*[11] for his expenses, but no other emolument.

John Charles Bigham,[12] later Lord Mersey, in some ways was not a typical English judge. A Liverpool man, he was born on 3 August 1840[§] and was the son of a prosperous merchant. He was educated not at one of the ancient British public schools, followed by Oxford or Cambridge, but at the Liverpool Institute and the University of London. After this, he took the even more unusual course of studying at the Sorbonne and in Berlin. He was not called to the Bar until he was 30, but his comparative seniority, backed by a much wider experience than that of the average junior barrister, became an asset he confidently exploited to the full. Without any physical advantage, and indeed handicapped both by a lack of inches and an indifferent voice, he practised on the Northern Circuit, where the shrewd businessmen of the booming cotton and shipping trades were more impressed by a good brain than a handsome face and an imposing presence. Bigham's mind was keen, and his slow speech and plain and direct advocacy were distinguished in an age of florid (and time-consuming) rhetoric. His style appealed to business clients and juries of businessmen, and within a few years he had achieved success.

In 1885, he took silk, and thereafter he built up an enormous practice. When the Commercial Court, the aim of which was to administer the law with a minimum of procedural formality, was established in 1895, Bigham, as his friend and biographer Theo Mathew wrote, was "ever ready to accept an invitation to confine his arguments to the essential points." His methods as a judge in the same court, after he had been raised to the bench in 1897 by Lord Halsbury, were similar. The disadvantage of this practice was that the unsuccessful party was sometimes more aware of what seemed the judge's impatience, and even rudeness, than of the justice of his decision.

---

*   Then, $5,103 – the highest sum paid at the inquiry was the Attorney-General's fee, £2,458 ($11,926). Captain Lord received for his attendance and expenses £7-0-6 ($34.31).

§   d. 3 September 1929.

Bigham was not much interested in politics, but nevertheless he made several attempts to enter Parliament, which he finally succeeded in doing in 1895.

Bigham was a useful judge, with a wide experience in the law, but he was criticized more than once when presiding over criminal trials, both for bias against the accused and for undeserved leniency. Between 1909 and 1910, he served as President of the Probate, Divorce and Admiralty Division, and on his retirement because of ill health, he was raised to the peerage as Baron Mersey of Toxteth and became a member of the Privy Council.

Today, Lord Mersey's name is linked with the subject of maritime disaster, for, after the *Titanic* inquiry, he presided in 1913 over the International Convention on Safety of Life at Sea, and then inquired successively into the wrecks of the *Empress of Ireland* in 1914 and the *Falaba* and *Lusitania* in 1915.

The five assessors appointed by the Home Secretary to assist him with the technical aspects of the inquiry were, Professor John Harvard Biles, LL.D., D.Sc., Rear Admiral the Hon. Somerset A. Gough-Calthorpe, CVO, RN, Commander F.C.A. Lyon, RNR, Captain Arthur Wellesley Clarke, and Mr Edward Catmore Chaston, RNR. The names of this quintet were probably little known to the general public, but in shipping circles it was felt that no better qualified group could have been selected. Moreover, their skills and experience were sufficiently diversified as to fit them to deal with all questions likely to arise.

John Harvard Biles (1854-1933), whose middle name perhaps had more significance in America than in England, was the only one of the five who had never followed the sea as a profession. Instead, he had occupied the chair of Naval Architecture at the University of Glasgow since 1891, longer than any other professor holding a similar position in the country. Biles had served his apprenticeship at Portsmouth Dockyard and later entered the Naval Construction Department of the Admiralty. After a short time, he joined the private firm of J. & G. Thomson of Clydebank as their naval architect. It was in that capacity that Biles took part in the design of the famous ships, *City of New York* and *City of Paris,* finally named *New York* and *Philadelphia,* respectively. Among his works was a book entitled *Modern Steam Turbines,* but Biles was perhaps best known as an expert on bulkheads and the sub-division of ships. Under one name or another, his *Philadelphia* was in more than one accident, including breaking her starboard propeller shaft and wrecking the engine, running on the Manacles and, finally, in 1920 colliding with a whale; but the bulkheads of Professor Biles survived everything. He served on many government committees and wrote and lectured much on technical subjects. An article of his entitled 'The Loss of the Titanic' had appeared in *The Engineer* of 19 April, because of which it was suggested that Biles had already made up his mind;[13] but the criticism was rejected. Biles was a man of considerable independence as well as of immense knowledge. His reputation was unimpaired, and he continued to be esteemed both as a practitioner and a theoretician, as he had been in the moulding loft on Clydebank and as he was in his professorial chair at Glasgow. He was honoured with a knighthood a year after the *Titanic* inquiry.

In later years a knighthood was also awarded to Captain Arthur Wellesley Clarke,[14] an Elder Brother of Trinity House, and whose nominee as assessor he was. Trinity House, of course, has charge of the lighthouses, lightships, buoys and beacons around the English coast and most pilots are, or were, licensed by the Elder Brethren. It fulfils some of the functions performed in the United States by the Coast Guard. Captain Clarke had been retired from the sea for several years, but had kept, it was said, "closely in touch with everything in connection with the mercantile marine of the present day,"[15] and it was because of his exceptional knowledge of the merchant service that Trinity House had nominated him.

Rear Admiral the Hon. Somerset A. Gough-Calthorpe was only 42 years old, and must have been one of the youngest officers ever to reach flag rank, Nelson and Beatty being perhaps the two most notable to have surpassed his achievement,[16] as both were promoted to Rear Admiral when under 39. Gough-Calthorpe, during 1902-5, had served as Naval Attaché to Russia, Norway and Sweden, and in October, 1918, he was to make another notch in history by signing the Armistice with Turkey on behalf of the Allied powers at war with her.

The fourth assessor, Commander F.C.A. Lyon, had commanded P. & O. liners, which although very different from what in those days was often called "the Atlantic ferry", had provided him with much experience of passenger ships. Since coming ashore he had become a well-known assessor and had himself conducted inquiries into maritime cases.

Edward Catmore Chaston,[17] a Newcastle man, who for 13 years had held a senior engineer's commission in the Royal Naval Reserve and was the senior engineer assessor to the Board of Trade, completed the team. He was a man of wide theoretical and practical experience. A prominent member of the North East Coast Institution of Engineers and Shipbuilders, Chaston had read a number of technical papers to this body. He was the surviving partner in the firm of Havelock and Chaston, consulting engineers, of Newcastle-on-Tyne, and had been a member of many inquiries into marine casualties, including the *Parisiana,* burnt and abandoned at sea, the *Empress of Britain,* sister ship of the unfortunate *Empress of Ireland,* and the *Ashanti,* in which an explosion had killed an engineer and three other seamen. He had gone to sea at the age of 21, and had served for more than 22 years in the Atlantic trade between Glasgow and New York and the Canadian ports. Afterwards, Chaston was in the Prince Line in the South Atlantic, trading to the River Plate. Chaston, in short, was at the top of his profession, although unable, in terms of a then current British joke, to answer to the call of "Mac!" * at the engine room door.

The secretary of the inquiry was a man of unusual experience and exceptional ability.[18] Starting as a soldier in the Grenadier Guards, he had also been an attaché in the British embassies in St Petersburg, Constantinople and Peking; also, a war correspondent for *The Times,* an explorer and the author of books about little-known parts of Asia, the China Incident of 1900 and other topics. Retired from the army, he entered the Board of Trade as a civil servant, and there had already served as secretary to Royal Commissions on such divers subjects as motor cars, lighthouses and vivisection. The British Government had decorated him with a CMG (Companion of the Order of St Michael and St George) and the Imperial Ottoman Government of Turkey with the Order of Medjidie (Third Class). He had fought (unsuccessfully) two parliamentary elections and had married a daughter of an Admiral of the Fleet. This exceptional man in 1912 was 40 years of age and was the Hon. Charles Clive Bigham (1872-1956). By one of those charming coincidences which occur in fairy stories, rich families and the upper echelons of British politics, this paragon of secretaries happened to be none other than the son and

---

* The engine room staff in those days was traditionally manned by Scottish labour.

heir of the Wreck Commissioner himself.

Such then were the personnel of the court of inquiry. None had ever been in prison; but if some of Captain Lord's supporters in after years were right, and these men, among others, were now preparing to "rig" the forthcoming investigation so as to ruin Captain Lord, then Wreck Commissioner, assessors, the Honourable Clive Bigham and all, must so far have been very lucky or very cunning to have deceived the country into regarding them as men of honour.

The country in fact was on the alert about being deceived, as may be inferred from the Commons attitude to the inquiry, reported above. There was, of course, widespread grief and shock because of the disaster, but neither panic nor hysteria. The notion fostered by the Lordites that Britain was smarting under a national humiliation caused by the loss of her greatest liner on her maiden voyage was a distortion of the real feeling that prevailed. There seems to have been none of the infatuation attaching to the *Titanic,* which may transform a person or a thing into a symbol of national perfection. The British people, moreover, were still calm enough not to exaggerate the *Titanic* into a national disaster. There was precious little sentimentality among ordinary people about the mercantile marine as a national service. Cargo boats were about as 'romantic' as coal mines; the luxury liners as remote from the average man as the Ritz Hotel; and the seamen who manned both, if ever thought about at all by the non-seagoing tens of millions, were regarded as potential trouble-makers and as yet one more source of the bitter industrial disputes which were tearing England apart and even threatened revolution.

This was the England into which, without the public's knowledge, the *Californian* was now unexpectedly introduced. It is a curious story and was unknown until the files were examined.

In the last weekend of April, the Senate inquiry was still going on, and several weeks were to pass before its Report, accompanied by Senator Smith's speech, was published. Report and speech, of course, both dealt with Captain Lord and the *Californian;* but on 29 April, Lord and Gill had already given their evidence, and, as far as public opinion can be gathered from the Press — there were no complicated opinion polls in those days — the issue was decided. The Press of both countries had accepted Lord and rejected Gill. The incident of the *Californian* was finished, and up to that time — a fortnight after the disaster — there is not a word in any document in the files showing any intention of summoning Lord or anybody else from the *Californian* to the inquiry, which was soon to begin. Captain Lord, as we have seen, returned to Boston from Washington, convinced that he had dealt with the senators even more satisfactorily than he had with the Boston Press. Nor, as the *Californian* made her way home, now two days out from Boston, could he have had any reason to anticipate trouble ahead. But he reckoned without Mr Gerard J.G. Jensen. This mysterious gentleman was somebody Captain Lord did not know and had never heard of, but he was to have an important, and indirectly decisive, effect on Captain Lord's future career.

From various sources, we know that Mr Jensen was a civil engineer practising in and before, the year 1912, at 14 Victoria Street, London SW. He was either a partner in, or had some other association with, a long-established firm, dating back to the 80s of the last century, called 'The Sanitation Company'. He had a telephone number, the classical-sounding telegraphic address, 'Cloacalis, London', and he lived his life remote from matters maritime, occupied with drainage, water supply and sewage disposal. One A.S. Everett was secretary of the firm, and a Mr Sidney Herbert Marshall was its manager. None of these details has even the remotest apparent connection with the steamship *Californian,* and after a diligent search in likely, and even unlikely, directions, they are the sum of what is known about Mr Gerard J.G. Jensen. The Institute of Civil Engineers have no record of him, the Electoral Register knew him not and even the Roll of Ratepayers overlooked him. A man whose very occupation must have caused him to scatter a hundred clues about himself and his interests has left no more than a name with a hint of Danish descent.

The explanation of why this obscure maker of lavatories, with no known interest or activity in public affairs, should have been so much exercised by the *Californian* as to take the trouble suddenly to intervene in the *Titanic* inquiry is surprising. In the England of 1912, with a class stratification even more rigid than that of today, this professional man is found to have a friend, who was a friend of W.F. McGregor, the socially humble, if temperamentally rebellious, carpenter of the *Californian.* The unexpected result of this indirect connection was to make Mr Jensen responsible for bringing the *Californian* directly to the notice of Sydney Buxton, the President of the Board of Trade.

The *Lapland,* with the American mail aboard, as well as most of the survivors of the *Titanic* crew, arrived at Plymouth on Sunday, 28 April. In one of her mailbags was the letter posted by McGregor in Boston on 19 April and addressed to his unknown friend somewhere in England. By next day, the friend, wherever he was, had received the letter and at once got into touch with Jensen. The latter probably read it, but if not he was certainly given a full knowledge of its contents and he acted without delay.

That Monday evening, Jensen posted a letter of his own, the envelope being postmarked, "London SW 6.30 p.m.", and addressed to "The President, Board of Trade, Whitehall, S.W."

Within was a single sheet of a grey-white notepaper of British quarto size, handwritten throughout on both sides, with the word "Confidential" prominent and underlined near the top of the first page.

It read:

" April 29th, 1912

The President
Board of Trade

<u>Sir</u>
'Titanic' Enquiry

I think I am discharging a public duty in bringing the following matter to your notice & to suggest that at the forthcoming enquiry witnesses should be called & closely examined from the Leyland Co's S.S. 'Californian'. My information is from a letter written by the carpenter of the 'Californian' to a friend of his but I should be obliged if you would consider the source of your information as confidential.
Briefly stated the facts are:-
1 That while the Californian was lying in the ice with engines stopped, the Titanic's signals of distress were seen by various members of the crew.
2 That the matter was reported to the Capt of the Californian on at least three occasions.
3 That the Californian's Captain took no notice of the matter.
4 That the signals were reported to the First Officer when he relieved the Captain in the ordinary course.

5 That the First Officer then set his Marconi operator to work & got in touch with the 'Titanic' — but that it was then too late to be of service.

6 That the Californian was within 10 miles of the Titanic & could have saved every soul, had her Captain responded to the call for help.

7 That Newfoundland fishing boats are occasionally run down by the Californian & other liners & no attempt is made to save the lives of the fishermen in the endeavour to keep time in crossing the Atlantic.

Yours faithfully,
Gerard Jensen" [19]

If this letter is compared with the story published in the *Clinton Daily Item* six days previously, 23 April, it will be noted how much closer it is to the known facts. The error in the newspaper story, which did not come direct from McGregor, but through his cousin, John H.G. Frazer, that the *Californian* was moving when the rockets were seen, is corrected; and Jensen also states that Lord was called "on at least three occasions". Whether the charge about the *Californian* contained in paragraph seven was true seems very doubtful, but a similar charge was made more than once at the time of the disaster in respect of the fast mail boats.[20]

A formal acknowledgment, without comment, was sent to Jensen on 1 May[21] and the letter was sent to, and read by, a number of officials, including Sir Walter J. Howell, the Assistant Secretary and Chief of the Marine Department of the Board of Trade, and their Solicitor, Sir R. Ellis Cunliffe. Whether Buxton himself saw the letter is not known, but the Receiver of Wreck in Liverpool, E.J.M. Bates, appears to have been informed of the charge made against the *Californian,* for he was shortly to take statements from members of her crew. The documents in the Receiver's office were destroyed by bombing during the Second World War, so one cannot be sure of the instructions issued to Bates, as there is no copy in the files. The importance of Jensen's letter is not the probability that it initiated the examination of the crew of the *Californian* on her return to Liverpool, but the certainty that it was the earliest document, being exactly two weeks after the disaster, in which an accusation against Captain Lord was made to the Board of Trade.

The inquiry began on Thursday, 2 May, in the drill hall of the London Scottish Regiment in Buckingham Gate. Some confusion occurred before the proceedings began, as the band of the Scots Guards usually rehearsed in the hall on Thursdays, and they duly appeared with their instruments. They were turned away, as were a number of ladies who had come to listen to the rehearsal.[22]

The hall was large and had accommodation for 300 members of the public, but in contrast with America, there seemed to be little public interest in the inquiry. Some 50 counsel and 60 pressmen had taken their places shortly before 11 o'clock, when the inquiry was due to start, but the chairs reserved for the public behind a crimson cord drawn across the center of the hall from wall to wall were two-thirds unoccupied. The gallery reserved for ladies had but three occupants. One of these was Mrs Sylvia Lightoller, wife of the *Titanic's* Second Officer, who was present at all 36 sessions and heard the reading of his Report by Lord Mersey on 30 July.

On the wall was a sectional plan of the *Titanic,* and to the right of the dais a 20-foot model of the ship and a chart of the North Atlantic.

Before the opening, the Law Officers and other counsel gathered in the billiard room for a consultation, but were almost immediately driven out by a violent escape of gas. This incident very soon seemed to typify the unsuitability of the hall for its present purpose. At ten minutes past eleven, Lord Mersey, followed by the five assessors, entered and, after bows were exchanged with counsel, took their seats.

Lord Mersey quietly said: "The inquiry is now open into the loss of the Titanic." It was at once discovered that the acoustics were so bad that not a word could be heard at more than a few feet.

Very soon there were protests and a suggestion that the inquiry be moved to more suitable premises. Next day, *The Pall Mall Gazette* commented: "Why a place about as suitable as Charing Cross Station should have been selected is one of those secrets of the official mind which is past finding out. Lord Mersey is surely not expected to emulate the vocal feats of a drill-sergeant . . ."

Lord Mersey, of course, spoke in nothing but his usual tones, but what he said soon after the proceedings began was enough to cause a bigger row than any drill sergeant in full cry had ever created. The Commissioner refused to hear the counsel for various unions, including the Shipwrights' Association, the Dockers' Union, and the Imperial Service Guild, which represented the officers. In addition, he had excluded the counsel for the more radical Seafarers' Union in favour of the conservative Sailors' and Firemen's Union, whose Secretary, Havelock Wilson, had sent a cable of warm sympathy to Bruce Ismay.

"The Titanic inquiry has not begun well," said the *Daily News*,[23] which could not understand why "If a person is interested at all, . . . he [has] not a right to be represented throughout . . .?"

Much could be written about the Mersey inquiry as a reflection of the society in which it functioned, just as the Senate inquiry was an instrument of the American democracy. Here, comment must be limited, and no more than an attempt can be made to convey the atmosphere and manner of this British investigation, before which Captain Lord and other *Californian* witnesses were to appear. Its informal appearance, with Commissioner and counsel in ordinary morning dress instead of legal wigs and gowns, was the deceptive front for an inquisitory instrument almost as rigidly bound by unwritten rules as British society itself. In sharp contrast with the American inquiry,* [24] of the many surviving passengers in Britain alone, who could have given evidence, no more than two First Class passengers — three, if Bruce Ismay was regarded as a passenger — were allowed to enter the witness box. (The Mersey inquiry heard 97 witnesses). The exclusion of all in the First Class, except Sir Cosmo and Lady Duff Gordon, although probably surprising to the uninitiated, was not an obvious defiance of any specific object of the inquiry, as no specific issue was raised about the First Class passengers. The total absence of any testimony from the Third Class survivors is different, as two of the 26 questions addressed to the inquiry for answers (Nos. 21 and 24)[25] did in fact raise the issue whether the Third Class passengers had been discriminated against in their access to the boats.

On 21 June, one of the last days of the inquiry, Clement Edwards, who represented the Dockers' Union, remarked that no passengers had been called and said: "I think in the public interest it might be well if the learned Attorney-General indicated why that course had been taken."[26]

Sir Rufus replied: "I am quite ready to do so. I thought I had already done

---

* Of the 87 witnesses who gave evidence to the Senate inquiry – orally, by affidavit, or by other documents – 21 (including Ismay) were passengers. The number comprised: *First Class:* ten oral, eight affidavits; *Second Class:* one affidavit; *Third Class:* three oral.

so, but I will state it in two sentences. We found it useless to call passengers
who could only state what had already been stated by the officers and crew
who have been called. If I had found in any proof or document submitted to
me that any passenger could prove anything which was in conflict with what
had been said on any material point, of course, I should have called them.
As your Lordship knows, at an early stage, and since, as intimated to my
learned friend, Mr Harbinson,* who naturally had some statements before
him, I would call any passenger whose proof or statement was put before me,
if it added anything to the testimony which we already have. My own view,
after consideration of a great many statements was that it was useless repetition, and that therefore it was unnecessary to put it before the Court."

"That will probably be satisfactory to Mr Edwards," said Lord Mersey.

According to the instincts and traditions of the British ruling class, who
were conducting the inquiry, it seems that the Third Class passengers,
although not expressed, were precisely what they were; Third Class passengers. Their place in British society was well understood and had a long
history. They were of those who in their little spare time formed the crowded
and dingy background at all ceremonial rejoicings, past and present, from
Royal progresses to public hangings; but their lifelong occupation was to
till the land and mine the coal, to toil in the factories and man the ships,
without whose labour in fact there never could have been a First Class
Britain, and who were, in short, both the base of Britain's greatness and
society's bottom. As such, ideally they should not be seen and certainly
never heard.

Nobody understood this better than Lord Mersey, the Attorney-General
and the other high and important personages, who had arranged and constituted the *Titanic* inquiry. Lord Mersey was quite satisfied by the Attorney-
General's explanation of the exclusion of the Third Class passengers.[27]

Meanwhile, after the first day's meeting and the complaints that nobody,
whatever his rank in society, could be heard, an attempt was made to find a
more suitable place for the inquiry. A former roller-skating rink in Aldwych
was inspected, but in the end the inquiry was continued at the Scottish Hall.
A sounding board was fitted above the platform on which the court sat and the
chairs were brought closer to it, so that the acoustics which had been impossible at the beginning were improved until they merely "left much to be
desired",[28] and so they remained to the end.§

In spite of what an objective observer might consider to be the extremely
unsatisfactory opening of the inquiry, British self-satisfaction about it, except
in radical circles, remained undented. The popular *Daily Graphic* on 3 May
ran a headline over portraits of Mersey and others: "NO 'PREPOSTEROUS
SMITHS' HERE", and the explanatory caption beneath read, ". . . The names
of the Commissioners [*sic*] . . . are guarantees that the English inquiry will be
marred by no incidents such as have made the Senate inquiry in Washington
ridiculous . . ."[29]

On the other hand, to put the picture in perspective, a few days later, Horatio
Bottomley, in his frequently scurrilous weekly *John Bull*, had the heading:

* Counsel for the Third Class passengers, who were allowed representation without articulation.

§ The irregularity of the acoustics was apparent, for instance, during the evidence of George Elliott
Turnbull, Deputy Manager of Marconi Marine. Counsel heard him discussing the amount of traffic between
the *Titanic* and Cape Race, when Lord Mersey suddenly complained: 'You do not speak loud enough for
me to hear you at all well' (Mersey, p. 361). Elsewhere, some of the repetitive questions and inconsequential comments may have resulted from the bad acoustics.

"'TITANIC' TRICKERY ANOTHER WHITEWASHING ENQUIRY? — THE FARCE OF THE PROCEEDINGS — BOARD OF TRADE AS BOTH DEFENDANT AND PLAINTIFF!"[30]

The *Californian* arrived in Liverpool on the completion of her only notable voyage on Friday evening, 10 May. She had made the passage in a day less than two weeks, and in contrast with the excitement and publicity that had marked her arrival in Boston, her return to her home port aroused only the smallest general interest. Apart from the routine notice in the shipping papers of her arrival and berthing in the Huskisson Dock, a careful search of the British Press yields only one story of more than a line or two in which the ship is even mentioned. This appeared next day, 11 May, in the *Liverpool Express,* and is headed:

"ARRIVAL OF THE CALIFORNIAN NO FURTHER INFORMATION"

The *Californian,* it was said, was "really the nearest vessel to the *Titanic*," but because of the ice she had stopped her engines and "lay to, with the result the Marconi was not working." Otherwise, she would have received the distress signal and hastened to the *Titanic's* assistance, "with the probability of hundreds of lives being saved."

"No additional information was obtainable last evening," the report continued, "it being pointed out that the story of the Californian's participation in the disaster had already been fully told at the American inquiry."

On her homeward passage she was said to have followed a course 160 miles farther south than when outward bound, and an unnamed member of the crew said he had never seen such fields of ice.

And that was all. Neither here nor elsewhere did it even occur to anybody to interview Captain Lord.

"After the return of the Californian to Liverpool," said Lord, "I reported to the Wreck Commissioner and to the Marine Superintendent of the Leyland Line, Captain Fry. While in the latter's office, Mr Groves, the Third Officer, volunteered the opinion that the ship seen from the *Californian* on the night of 14 April was the *Titanic*.[31] This was the first occasion I had heard him make such a statement[32] and I duly commented to this effect to the Marine Superintendent."

Groves said: 'There was absolutely no doubt her being a passenger steamer, at least in my mind.'[33] But Lord disagreed.

If Lord was accurate in this passage, he could not have been as surprised as he claimed to be, when Groves repeated his opinion to Captain Fry. In his evidence at the British inquiry, Lord, as we know, said the other ship was "something like ourselves."[34]

Moreover, in his affidavit of 25 June 1959, he swore that the remark Groves made to Captain Fry, which provoked his comment: "That's the first time I've heard him say that," was not that the unknown ship was "a passenger steamer", but that she was the *Titanic*.

Following the meeting with Captain Fry, certain members of the crew then gave statements to the Receiver of Wreck, E.J.M. Bates. Who, and how many, they were, is only partly known. The list published more than once is incorrect, at least in that it mentions "two apprentices", for Gibson was the only apprentice.

At any rate, Lord said[35] he was summoned by telegram to appear before the inquiry on 14 May, and he travelled up to London the previous evening.

Presumably, Stewart, Stone, Groves, Gibson and other members of the crew also received telegrams and went at the same time. Now, although as he insisted ever afterwards, he was again to appear before an inquiry only as a witness and not as a defendant, he may not have been entirely free of anxiety.

The ambivalent procedure of the inquiry enabled the Law Officers, Sir Rufus Isaacs and Sir John Simon, who were the leading counsel for the Board of Trade, not only to call witnesses, but also to have the exceptional privilege of cross-examining them. In Washington, if Senator Smith and his colleagues showed any bias at all, it was not against the poorer passengers or ordinary seamen. In London, there was a notable difference. Throughout, one is conscious of a lack of sympathy with those who had only recently been through a fearful ordeal, and there was no democratic nonsense, as in Washington, of dignifying any humble and dim-witted ordinary seaman by addressing him as 'Mr' For his part, the ordinary seaman of England, with his inadequate education and vague view of society, knew only that 'they' were running the inquiry, just as 'they' ran everything else in England.

Lord himself, unlike his crew, could not have enjoyed the peace of mind that is said to come from resignation, for he was an educated man and he must have known something at least of the reputation of Rufus Isaacs, the Attorney-General, and its possible consequences for himself.

In his manner, Rufus Isaacs was normally a friendly man. Years afterwards, Lord declared he wasn't friendly from the beginning.[36] Neither the transcript of the evidence, nor the memory of two witnesses I consulted, corroborates this opinion,*[37] and a few years before the inquiry, A.G. Gardiner, a famous Liberal editor, had written: "Mr Isaacs wins by wooing . . . He is so pleasant and amiable that it is a pain to disagree with him; . . . He does not browbeat a witness, or hector the judge, or dictate to the jury. He pervades the court with a sense of polite comedy."[38]

Lady Lloyd George, too, writes of him about this time as being "full of raillery and charm, handsome and debonair . . ."[39]

But, of course, there was much more to Rufus Isaacs than charm and friendliness, manifest and abundant as they were, for these qualities were still remembered at the Bar more than a decade after he had become Lord Chief Justice. Immensely ambitious and immensely hard-working, his pre-legal career had included a variety of experience. As a boy, this son of a Jewish fruit merchant had run away to sea, where his courage and ability as a boxer had saved him from the worst of the bullying; later, he spent a couple of years in Germany as his father's agent; then came a short period on the Stock Exchange, ending in disaster and a burden of debts, which he ultimately paid to the last penny. He finally came to the Bar 'rich in worldly wisdom' and achieved success almost immediately. In those days, and for many years afterwards, outstanding members of the English Bar enjoyed a popular fame comparable with that of stars of the theatre, or, later, of football or television. This was especially true of a small number, whose practice led them to appearing in sensational criminal trials. Rufus Isaacs disliked criminal work and did very little of it. Nevertheless, his great skill as a cross-examiner had enabled him to expose some of the most devious and obdurate villains of the century. Always polite, always persistent, sometimes in that quiet, beautiful voice, he would ask a totally unexpected question that brought its victim down in sudden and total catastrophe.

Boldness and courage may or may not have been the qualities he most

---

* Lord's opinion of Mersey expressed at the same time was: 'Hostile! At once.'

admired, but, without doubt, timidity and cowardice were those which he most despised and considered shameful. It was a characteristic not without consequences to Captain Lord.

Rufus Isaacs was usually friendly and approachable, and merciful too, but he could also on occasion be forbiddingly different. Of his first encounter with him during the 1914 war, Chaim Weizmann wrote: "It was as if I had run into an iceberg."[40]

This was the famous antagonist, so much more formidable than Senator Smith, whom fate had now brought into action against the obscure sea captain from the North of England. In the long and glittering career of Rufus Daniel Isaacs, 1st Marquess of Reading, Lord Chief Justice, High Commissioner and Special Ambassador to the United States, Viceroy of India and Foreign Secretary, his encounter with Stanley Lord was no more than a minor, and soon forgotten, incident. None of Reading's biographies describes it; *"Californian"* and "Stanley Lord" are names which are absent from all the indexes, nor do the family papers show any substantial connection with the cases of both the *Californian* or the *Titanic;* but for Captain Stanley Lord, Tuesday, 14 May 1912, was a day which was to change his life. In Boston, his bold falsehoods had made clear his realization that he had something to hide; in London, on that day, Rufus Isaacs, with a single, short question in cross-examination, showed what it was. By penetrating into the most secret recesses of Lord's mind, he exposed the fact that Lord had no answer to the accusation against him.

Washington had been a day of triumph; London was to see a catastrophe.

Sources

1 US 1.
2 [Hansard] Official Report, Fifth Series, Parliamentary Debates, Commons 1912 Vol. XXXVII 515. 18 April.
3 [MT 9/920/1] M 10307. [1912].
4 [Hansard] op. cit., 774.
5 Ibid., 852.
6 Ibid.
7 Ibid., 1 May 1869.
8 Ibid., 1510, 29 April.
9 Ibid., 1 May 1870.
10 Ibid.
11 Cd. 6738, 1913.
12 *Times,* 4 Sep 1929; *Law Journal,* 7 Sep 1929; *Dictionary of National Biography 1922-30,* p. 81, P.I.
13 Cf. [MT 9/920/2] M 11927 [30 April].
14 P.I., July 1964.
15 *Journal of Commerce Report,* p. xvi.
16 A.T. Mahan, *The Life of Nelson,* 2nd ed., p. 244;

Rear-Admiral W.S. Chalmers, *The Life and Letters of David, Earl Beatty,* p. 104.
17 *Journal of Commerce* Report, p. xvi; P.I.
18 Ibid., p. xvi.
19 [MT 9/920/1] M 12148.
20 *See,* for instance, Beesley.
21 [MT 9/920/1] M 12148.
22 This account of the opening of the inquiry is based mostly on the Press of 2 and 3 May, including the *Standard, Pall Mall Gazette, Morning Post, Daily Graphic, Daily Mirror.*
23 *Daily News,* 3 May, editorial, p. 4.
24 US "Hearings".
25 Mersey "Report".
26 Mersey, p. 706.
27 *See,* for instance the 21st Day's Hearing, 11 June, Harbinson for the Third Class v. The

Commissioner & The Attorney-General.
28 *Morning Post,* 3 May, p. 9.
29 *Daily Graphic,* 3 May, p. 1.
30 *John Bull,* 11 May, p. 586.
31 Capt. Lord's Affidavit, Appendix C.
32 Ibid.
33 Ibid.
34 B 6752, 6996, 6997.
35 Capt. Lord's Affidavit, Appendix C.
36 'The Other Ship', p. 14, 26 March 1965.
37 *Daily Mirror,* 14 April 1962.
38 A.G. Gardiner, *Prophets, Priests and Kings,* p. 158.
39 Frances Lloyd George, *The Years That are Past,* p. 43.
40 Chaim Weizmann, *Trial and Error,* p. 203, East and West ed.

Chapter 15

Question 6944

It was the seventh day of the inquiry and the first time public interest was really aroused.[1] Long before 10.30 when the hearing was due to begin, the public seats were filled and the Ladies' Gallery was also well occupied before Lord Mersey and the assessors took their seats. The character of the audience, too, had changed. Hitherto, the public had been represented by casual observers, 'the man in the street'; but on that Tuesday morning, it was said, "Ninety per cent. of those who sat in the body of the hall were fashionably-dressed ladies, while others looked down from the Ladies' Gallery." All this excited anticipation, however, had been caused not by the prospect of hearing the *Californian* witnesses — whose coming was in fact not generally known — but by the expectation of seeing Sir Cosmo and Lady Duff Gordon cross-examined.[2] As this suddenly notorious couple* were still at sea in the *Lusitania,* their evidence was postponed, no doubt to the disappointment of the Society audience, which were now confronted with getting what entertainment they could from yet one more group of undistinguished and unpromising seamen. That afternoon, there was a widely-publicized matinée at Covent Garden in aid of the *Titanic* Fund.[3] The King and Queen were present, having driven to the opera house in an open landau; Sarah Bernhardt had come over specially from Paris; Mischa Elman played; Pavlova danced and other famous artists contributed their services. Yet, that evening, the *Titanic* event of the day was not the brilliant occasion at Covent Garden, lit though it was with world-famous names, but the story told at Scottish Hall by three hitherto unknown British seamen in plain clothes, whose evidence had unexpectedly disclosed a new and strange sensation which instantly gripped the imagination of the metropolis.

It had begun in the morning when the Attorney-General announced that he proposed to call some witnesses from the *Californian.*[4] There was an issue between the master and the officers and, certainly, "an assistant donkeyman", who said that the *Californian* had seen distress rockets from a vessel and had taken no notice of them. Whether or not that vessel was the *Titanic,* as the donkeyman said, could be determined only after hearing the evidence. Sir Rufus said that it was "a little difficult" to say that this had a direct bearing on the questions submitted "so far" for Lord Mersey's consideration, but as some of the evidence was material to those questions, and statements had been made and evidence "given elsewhere", he thought it "desirable" that

---

* It was said that Sir Cosmo had bribed the crew of their almost empty boat not to go back to attempt any rescue of those in the sea.

the court "should hear what there is to be said." He did "not propose to go into it at any length". In fact, the *Californian* witnesses took the best part of two days. Lord was followed by Gibson and Stone, and the next day, Groves, Stewart, Groves (recalled) and Evans were heard.

Mr Robertson Dunlop asked to be allowed to appear for the Leyland Line — "the owners, master and officers" — but Lord Mersey said he should watch, "and, if you find any attack is made upon your clients, then you can ask me to allow them to go into the box."[5] Captain Lord afterwards complained that, having met Mr Roberts, the manager of the line, in the court, he was just introduced to Robertson Dunlop, but had no opportunity of any useful discussion with him before or after his evidence.[6]

Wearing a blue suit that would have merged with any crowd, Lord himself was so distinguished in appearance that most of the reporters attempted some description of him.[7] He was "bronzed and deep-voiced", "sea-reddened", "tall", "lean" and "clean-shaven"; had "a wrinkled brow", "spare features and high forehead", and he was "bald to the crown of his head". Most of them also commented on his "self-possessed manner" or said he was "at his ease"; but the time came when neither his curt denials nor his evasions and inconsistencies shielded him from the armoury of questions shot at him, and his "self-possessed manner" hardened into defiance, while he rapped the table, behind which the witnesses stood, his face more arrogant even than usual. Afterwards, when judgement had been given and he stood condemned, he wrote to the Board of Trade, with surprising and touching humbleness: "I am told that at the inquiry I was a very poor witness, this I don't dispute . . ."[8]

Most of the evidence given by Lord and the other *Californian* witnesses has already been reported and discussed in the sequence of the events to which it relates. It is significant that of the six *Californian* witnesses, apart from Gill, it was Lord and Groves, according to contemporary reports and recollection of a few who heard them, who most impressed their listeners. "Opera glasses and lorgnettes were raised by ladies," said a newspaper about Groves, "as, smart and alert, he stepped to the witness-table."[9] He answered Mr Rowlatt "quietly and confidently", as he did all the other counsel who questioned him, and, above all, in contrast with most of his shipmates, he was clear and frank. Evans was uncontroversial and told the truth; Gibson, the most damaging witness from Lord's point of view, who involuntarily blew his captain's case to pieces, did his best to tell his strange story and was honest; Stewart was not; and Stone was trapped by his conscience and a number of contradictory emotions.

Lord began his evidence with particulars of his ship and the voyage to Boston, to the time he stopped on Sunday night because of the ice. The Attorney-General then asked the question which led to one of the crucial subjects, whether the unknown ship was a passenger steamer.

"Now close upon 11 o'clock did you see a steamer's light?"[10]

"I did," said Lord.

Lord's account of the sighting of the ship has never received the close examination it requires. It is not easy, as altogether he gave no fewer than four versions of the matter. He and Groves were the only two who saw the steamer when she first came into sight as a single light and there is sharp contradiction between Lord and Groves about many, if not most, of the important details concerning the ship. The course of the steamer's approach and the apparent extinction of many of her lights when she stopped, especially.

The story — more precisely, stories — told by Lord, lacked the minor, but obvious, puzzles of Groves, but foundered because its basis was that he saw a ship, not the *Titanic,* which also fired eight rockets.

Of Lord's four versions of the sighting of the steamer, three differed in significant details from one another. The passing of the years and the decline of memory might account for some of the differences, but the first two versions were so close together in time, and so soon after the event that failure of recollection cannot explain their contradictions.

Version 1.

This was given at the U.S. Senate inquiry described in Chapter 13. It was the earliest in point of time, being told only 12 days after the disaster. (In Boston, just five days after it, Lord, we recall, had seen nothing at all, no steamer, rockets, or signals of any kind, nothing whatever, except, of course, ice.)

"When I came off the bridge, at half-past ten," Lord told Senator Smith, "I pointed out to the officer [i.e. Groves] that I thought I saw a light coming along . . . I went down below. I was talking with the engineer . . . and said, 'There is a steamer coming . . .'"

Version 2.

This was Lord's evidence in London on 14 May, exactly a month after the events he was describing, and no more than three weeks after *Version 1.* It was now "close upon 11 o'clock" when he first saw the steamer's light.[11]

"I must put this to you," said the Attorney-General. "Do you remember about a quarter-past 11 on that night, that is the night of the 14th, his telling you that he had noticed a steamer — that is, the third officer, Mr. Groves?"[12]

"No, I do not."

"Did you ask about her lights?"[13]

"Not then."

"At any time?"

"No. A quarter to 12 was the first time I ever mentioned anything to him about the steamer, that I recollect."

These are astonishing answers. They contradict, of course, not only Groves's evidence of his report to Lord about the approaching steamer, but, more surprisingly, Lord's own evidence at Washington. The poor quality of his memory, which might be the only honest explanation of these replies, is hard to accept, as its failure appears to be coincidental and coterminous with his interests.

The next question was: "Did he say to you that she was evidently a passenger steamer?"

"No."

"And did you say to him: 'The only passenger steamer near us is the *Titanic*?'"

"I might have said that," Lord replied, "with regard to the steamer, but he did not say the steamer was a passenger steamer."

This is another strange answer. Let us try to imagine the scene and the lines. Lord having just arrived on the bridge, Groves points out the steamer.

'There she is, sir.'

'The only passenger steamer near us is the *Titanic*,' Captain Lord retorts with the prize *non sequitur* of a singularly inconsequential evening. If Groves had said nothing about 'a passenger steamer', why Lord should have introduced the term in referring to the other steamer is inexplicable. Groves, we know, said plainly and throughout he was convinced the other steamer was a passenger steamer, and had so reported to Lord. Lord's reply, in that context, makes sense, even though he himself might have made it for the very reason that he did not believe the other ship was the *Titanic*.

Lord Mersey then took up the questioning. Referring to Lord's statement to the Receiver of Wreck in Liverpool, he asked, "You said, according to your statement: 'The *Titanic* is the only passenger steamer near us.' You said that to him [Groves]?"[14]

"She was."

"But you said it to him?"

Lord now gave a new answer, and substantially different from his earlier one: from "I might have said that . . ." to "I do not recollect saying it."

From Lord's point of view, this may be more credible, but it is also suspect, as it once again craves in aid his conveniently infirm memory.

"Did you know of any other passenger steamer near you except the *Titanic*?" Sir Rufus asked.[15]

"I did not."

"But you knew the *Titanic* was not far from you?"

"I had no idea where the *Titanic* was."

"But you had been in communication with it?"

"Yes; but I never had its position."

This would have been a fair answer to the preceding question alone, but it did not stand alone. Lord had already agreed that the *Titanic* was "near" — he even emphasized it, "She was" — but for some reason he will not admit she was "not far", and he justifies his answer by saying that he "never had" her position.

Let us bear in mind that this is the man, who, according to one of his supporters, gave "such straightforward, sailor-like answers to his tormentors."[16]

It was also in this part of his evidence that Lord said that the steamer approached from the eastward after the *Californian* had stopped;[17] that he went and asked Evans what ships he had, and Evans replied: "Nothing, only the *Titanic*."[18] Lord told the Attorney: "You can never mistake those ships — by the blaze of light."[19] He told Evans to let the *Titanic* know "that we are stopped, surrounded by ice,"[20] which was the message that was to raise a storm, as Phillips, who was working Cape Race, told Evans to "keep out"[21] or "shut up".* Answering the Attorney's question about sidelights on the approaching steamer, Lord said: "I saw a green light,"[22] and he believed "She was something like ourselves," "A medium size steamer."[23] He had seen only one masthead light,[24] but he told the court that Groves informed him next day, or the day after, that he had seen two.

Lord's supporters point to this answer especially as evidence of his good faith. Perhaps it is. It has never, however, been my belief that Lord resorted to falsehood consistently or from choice. He was neither a practised nor an habitual liar, but a hitherto normally truthful man, whose one act of misconduct had placed him in a quite unforeseeably terrible situation. Trapped in it, he was in the position of a man of hitherto blameless character, who has yielded to a sudden criminal impulse, and terrified by the possibility of exposure, tells any lies that may seem necessary to protect himself. This was the reason for Lord's blatant falsehoods at Boston and for the shifty incredible passages in his London evidence. It remained for the Attorney-General, as we shall see, to identify and hold up for the general inspection the exact nature of the things which Stanley Lord had done and knew he had done, and which had driven him to such desperate courses.

---

* 'Shut up' actually does not appear in the transcript, but "keep out" was taken to mean the same. However, as Evans said: "And you do not take it as an insult or anything like that." (B 8998-9).

Version 3.
Captain Lord's next version of the sighting of the steamer is contained, very concisely, in the affidavit he swore on 25 June 1959, after he had decided to try to reopen his case.

"At 10.30 p.m.," he said, "as I was leaving the bridge, I pointed out to the Third Officer what I thought was a light to the eastward, which he said he thought was a star."

This, it will be seen, is a return to Washington and *Version 1*.

Version 4.
What, so far as I know, is the final version, was given in February 1961, in the recorded conversation and, as a result of Mr Harrison's veto, may not be quoted here, but once more (as in *Version 3*), it was soon after the *Californian* stopped, that is a little after 10.20, that a light was first seen by Lord.

Allowing for the fact that the affidavit (*Version 3*) and *Version 4* date from nearly half a century after the event, it is interesting that they depart radically from Lord's London evidence (*Version 2*), and repeat the general substance of the first public version at the American inquiry.

"If you say it three times, it's true," according to 'The Hunting of the Snark'. It may be; but one is inclined to look for corroboration. Whether Lord first saw the steamer from the bridge, as he said several times, or while standing below on the deck, according to his London evidence, does not matter greatly, except possibly for the time factor, as we shall see.

Groves's story never varied. In his version, he did not see the ship about 10.30, in Lord's company, but alone and not until considerably later. Then, he always asserted, it was he who came down from the bridge and reported the ship — "a passenger steamer" — to Lord, while the latter was in his cabin. This was exactly where one might expect him to be. With his own ship safe and stopped, and a temperature of 30°F/-1°C. on deck, there was no particular reason why he should have lingered outside in the freezing cold longer than necessary. His question to Groves: "Can you make anything out of her lights?" was not inconsistent with his having already seen the ship some time previously from the saloon deck, when she was farther away.

Anybody but Lord might have said to Groves: "Yes, I saw her myself some time ago. What do you make of her lights now?" But the taciturn, rank-conscious Lord of 1912 preferred to keep his conversation with his junior officer to the minimum.

The time of the first sighting is of more importance than the place from which the steamer was seen. In London, Lord accepted Attorney-General's suggestion that the time was "close upon 11 o'clock"; but if it was in fact soon after 10.30, according to Lord's twice public-repeated assertion, the ship would have been steaming for about an hour before she stopped. If Groves was right in saying he first saw the light about 11.10, she would have been moving for only half that time before she stopped. As there is no dispute that it was the same steamer that Groves and Lord saw, and that she stopped in the same place, it follows that she must have been steaming twice as fast if Groves was right.

It was only in the aftermath of the tragedy that the initial identification of the ship in sight acquired enormous importance. Groves gave through the years three versions of Lord's words and when they were spoken.

Version 1. In 1912 Groves told Lord Mersey that Lord had said to him on the bridge: "The only passenger steamer near us is the *Titanic*."[25]

Version 2. In a 1955 letter Groves, recalling the incident in detail, wrote: "When he [Lord] came on the bridge he remarked 'That will be the 'Titanic' on her maiden voyage.'"[26]

Version 3. Two years later, in 1957, when Groves wrote his recollections in 'The Middle Watch', he attributed the same words to Lord: "That will be the 'Titanic' on her maiden voyage", but here Lord had spoken them in his quarters below, where Groves had gone down to report the stranger.

Looking at these three versions, it is obvious that the difference between version 1 and 2 is the exact words Lord may have spoken, not their substance. Nor is there a difference in timing; it was during Lord's three minute visit to the bridge, which Groves said was at about 11.45,[27] that Lord had made his remark about the *Titanic*.

Between version 2 and 3 the difference is the timing. Version 3 would have been somewhat earlier in time than version 2, or at about 11.30,[28] before Lord came to the bridge.

Without doubt version 2 would clinch the matter as to the identity of the ship observed by Lord and his Third Officer: it was the *Titanic* and the *Titanic* alone Lord thought he was watching.

Version 1, corroborated by Lord's own evidence,[29] and version 3, both show Lord's awareness that if Groves was right and it was a passenger steamer approaching, it must have been the *Titanic*, nor did Lord ever deny that.

Looking at the character of Lord and Groves, their stake in the case and their evidence as a whole, it seems that Groves's versions of the exact words spoken by Lord are true in their substance. It seems possible that the remark might have been made by Lord without even thinking, as the automatic sequel to his information from Evans, and without checking it against the evidence of his eyes. Nor does this possibility exclude another, that, very soon, on thinking of what he was looking at, he concluded that the ship he saw was not the *Titanic*, even though he did not bother to express his change of opinion at the time. Finally, neither of these possibilities excludes yet one more, that this — to Lord — unlikely-looking vessel was nevertheless the *Titanic*.

Altogether, whatever test is applied, it seems more probable that Groves is closer to the truth than Lord. Which means, that Groves did report the ship to Lord; and, far more important, that whatever were the precise words spoken at that time, Groves did say the vessel in sight was a passenger steamer. Groves very probably knew that the *Titanic* was on her maiden voyage, but the evidence is that it was midnight before he was informed that she was close to the *Californian*.

We now turn to the story of Lord's unused wireless. It seems, at least to one observer, to have an almost nightmare-like quality. There was the unknown steamer firing one rocket after another; there was the sleeping Evans alongside his instrument in perfect working order; and there was the skipper, whether physically asleep or not, certainly mentally comatose about the obvious needs of the situation. Across the years, as we read the evidence of Lord sending Stone back to yet another exercise on the Morse lamp, we feel the urge to cry out: "The Marconi, man! Use your wireless!"

In London, astonishing as it seems, the Attorney-General examined Lord for several hours without putting a single question to him about his failure to call Evans. It remained for Thomas Scanlan, counsel for the National Sailors' and Firemen's Union, to raise the issue.

Having established that Evans went off duty, "So far as I was concerned," according to Lord,[30] ". . . at 11 o'clock, after he had sent the last message,"* Scanlan asked the crucial question, which had been omitted in Washington and so far in London.

"When you were in doubt as to the name of the ship and as to the meaning of her sending up a rocket, could you not have ascertained definitely by calling in the assistance of your Marconi operator?"

Lord's reply was as astonishing as it was revealing.

"When?" he exclaimed, "At 1 o'clock in the morning?"[31]

Scanlan did not think the suggestion so outrageous as Lord's shocked tone indicated. "Yes," he said; and Lord then gave his explanation.

"This steamer had been in sight, the one that fired the rocket, when we sent the last message to the *Titanic,* and I was certain that the steamer was not the *Titanic;* and the operator said he had not any other steamers, so I drew my conclusion that she had not got any wireless."[32]

Now, even if this statement is a truthful report of what was in Lord's mind at the time — which is not beyond all doubt — it is a fallible piece of reasoning. Granting his premise that the steamer was not the *Titanic,* it by no means follows that she did not have wireless, even though Evans "had" only the *Titanic.* If, as Lord had said previously, "she was something like ourselves . . . a medium size steamer",[33] she too would almost certainly have had only one operator. He might have been off duty already, or temporarily away from his set, while Evans was calling the *Titanic;* or he might not have answered at all, even if he was sitting with the phones on his head, as the *Californian's* ice message was addressed specially to MGY (the *Titanic's* call sign). Anybody determined to find out why that ship had fired even one rocket would not have failed to try his wireless, without regard to his previous 'conclusion' that she had none.

Clement Edwards, counsel for the Dockers' Union, later asked: "I think you said that you did not give any instruction to the Marconi operator to try and ascertain the name of this vessel?"

"No," Lord agreed, and then added: "I did at 11 o'clock."[34]

This is a surprising piece of information, for more than one reason. If, as he had told Scanlan, he was so entirely uninterested in that steamer, he should have been asked to explain why he had told Evans to get her name. It is the only time Lord made this statement, either in his evidence or in his reminiscences. If it had actually happened, it is remarkable that he did not refer to it, when he was asked why he had not brought Evans into action after hearing about the rocket. Instead of the unconvincing explanation he did give, it would have been more believable if he had plainly answered: "I'd already told my operator to call her at 11 o'clock to get her name, and he could get no reply, so I assumed she had no wireless." But he said nothing of the kind. Nor did Evans. There is not a word in his evidence either in Washington or in London about any such request from Lord. It is hard to believe it was ever made.

Scanlan asked him if it would not "have been quite a simple thing" to have called up Evans when he was in doubt about the ship's name and the reason for her sending up "rockets".

"It would if it had worried me a great deal, but it did not worry me. I was still thinking of the company's signal."[35]

"At all events, now in the light of your experience, would it not have been a prudent thing to do?"

* In fact, Evans did not go off duty until 11.35.

"Well," said Lord, as if it were the merest trifle, "we would have got the *Titanic's* signal if we had done."

He persisted in his refusal to believe that the other ship had wireless.

"But as a mere matter of precaution," Scanlan persisted,[36] "when you were in doubt and left word that someone was to come down to your cabin and give you a message, would not it have been a proper thing to have tried the experiment?"

"Well, I was waiting for further information. I had a responsible officer on the bridge, who was finding this out for me."

Judging from Lord's unwillingness to agree even with that innocuous suggestion, one begins to glimpse the strength of his bizarre and muddled thinking — or prejudices — about wireless. If he was sincere, this answer, taken with his statement in Washington that his officer on the bridge could see as far at night as by day and his astonishment at the notion of calling Evans at one in the morning, indicates the comparative value, in Lord's opinion, between "a responsible officer on the bridge" and a 'precautionary experiment' with the wireless.

In his very next answer, Lord finally conceded that it would have been no trouble "whatever" to have called Evans,[37] and that if the steamer had wireless, "he could have spoken to this vessel."

"If she had had wireless,"[38] he repeated yet once more, as inch by inch he fought his stubborn rearguard action.

"If you had done this, you would have found out whether she had wireless?"

"Very likely. If she had had it, we would have got her."[39]

"If she had had it, you could have ascertained directly in what trouble she was when she sent up the rockets?"

"Yes."

It was Scanlan's last question about the wireless in a most destructive cross-examination.

Four other counsel, representing various interests, next questioned Lord. They included T.B. Roche for the Marine Engineers, who asked very pertinently about Lord's "respect for the ice" and his unwillingness to move his engines until "5 o'clock" because of it.[40]

"Was that the reason, perhaps, why you were not so inquisitive as to these signals as you might otherwise have been?"

"No," said Lord, "that had not anything to do with it."[41]

Perhaps it had not, but there is much to suggest that it had nearly everything to do with it.*

The Attorney-General then, very tardily, also asked about the wireless.

Lord agreed that, when he was not satisfied that "the rocket" was "a company's signal", he might have called the Marconi operator without any difficulty whatever. He understood the idea of Marconi telegraphy, but could not use it; he also knew about CQD and SOS signals, but could not receive them because they went too quickly for him.[42]

"They would have been able to distinguish the signal as long as she [the *Titanic*] was giving it?" Mersey asked Lord.[43]

"The operator would. I do not think anyone else on the ship would."

"The operator would, if you had called him?"

"Yes."

And that was Lord's last word on his failure to call Evans.

---

* cf. Lord's letter of 14 August, when it was "deemed safe for my steamer to proceed".

"That silly man, who wouldn't use his wireless!"[44]

In those few words, Captain Rostron of the *Carpathia,* more than once in a spirit of dismay and impatience, but mercifully not questioning Lord's honesty, summarized the whole episode.

It goes without saying that Lord's apologists do not blame him for not using his wireless; but neither they nor anybody else questions the crucial importance of the matter. It was indeed the most important of the mechanical, as distinct from the human, factors entirely under Lord's control. In spite of his own almost contemptuous dismissal of the wireless, it was the make-or-break of the material factors in the whole story. Without it, to use more appositely the words already mentioned as applied to Boxhall's evidence, "there would have been no *Californian* incident."

Of course, Lord did not know about the *Titanic's* fate; but we shall shortly see what he did know. If he had called Evans at once, he might have been faced with the risk of also having to move his ship at once in the darkness. In McNabb's words: "he concluded to wait till daylight without courting undue risks by attempting to force a passage in the dark . . ."

When the appalling news finally reached Lord, he must soon have realized that his legal and moral position would be hopeless, if he admitted that he knew, when it still mattered, that rockets had been seen and he had not called his wireless operator. When he did admit he first knew of "several rockets", from Stewart next morning, his instant response, he said, had been: "Go and call the wireless operator!"[45] Any alert and humane skipper would, of course, have given that order; and Lord knew it.

However, the admission of knowing about one rocket and the true statement, which must be corroborated by Stone, that he had asked whether it was "a company signal", provided him with a positive defence. To say that he had thought five rockets were nothing but the belated acknowledgement of his lamp would be too much to believe; but he might convince with one. At most, he could be criticized for having made a mistake; but nothing worse.

At any rate, between Boston and Washington, Lord contrived his new "one rocket" story, and in Washington he appeared to have got away with it — he could hardly foresee that in London he would be hoist with his own one-rocket petard; and be ruined by it.

It remains thus to report the decisive passage in Lord's evidence in London, which is also the end of his defence.

The series of questions by the Attorney-General, which led to the single most important one in the whole case, follows Lord's evidence about the sighting of the steamer, already discussed. It comes before the inquiry into the wireless and other topics examined in this chapter and earlier, but it has been fittingly reserved for the closing pages of this report of Lord's evidence in London, as it was the climax of his story.

We begin with Question 6902.[46]

"Did you remain in the chart room," Sir Rufus asked Captain Lord, "when you were told that a vessel was firing a rocket?"

"I remained in the chart room, when he told me that this vessel had fired a rocket."

"I do not understand you. You knew, of course, there was danger in this field of ice to steamers?"

"To a steamer steaming yes."

"That is why you stopped?"

"Yes."

"And you knew also that it was desirable, at any rate, to communicate with the *Titanic* to tell that there was ice?"

"Yes."

"You had done that?"

"I had done that."

"And you knew that this vessel, whatever it was, that you say had stopped —"

"Had stopped, yes."

"I do not understand — it may be my fault —"

"Shall I explain it to you?"

"What do you think this vessel is firing a rocket for?"

"I asked the Second Officer. I said, 'Is that a company's signal' and he said he did not know."

"That did not satisfy you?"

"No, it did not."

"I mean whatever it was, it did not satisfy you that it was a company's signal?"

"It did not, but I had no reason to think it was anything else."

Here, Lord Mersey intervened: "That seems odd. You knew that the vessel that was sending up this rocket was in a position of danger?" And Lord repeated his agreement: "If she moved, yes."

"What do you think the rocket was sent up for?"

"Well, we had been trying to communicate with this steamer by Morse lamp from half-past 11, and he would not reply."

"This was a quarter past one?"

"Yes, we had tried at intervals from half-past eleven."

"What do you think he was sending up a rocket for?"

"I thought it was acknowledging our signals, our Morse lamp. A good many steamers do not use the Morse lamp."

"Have you ever said that before?"

"That has been my story right through — my impression right along."

The reader, who has followed Lord at Boston and Washington can judge the accuracy of that answer. The Attorney then resumed the examination.

"Just let me put this to you. When you asked him whether it was a company's signal he said he did not know. That would not satisfy you?"

"No."

"Was it then you told him to Morse her and find out what ship it was?"

"Yes."

"After the white rocket had been sent up?"

"After the white rocket had been sent up."

"And did you tell him to send Gibson, the apprentice, down to let you know this reply?"

"Yes."

"What was the message that Gibson brought down to you then?"

"That morning? I did not get it, not to my knowledge, I never got it."

"You had seen the rocket or you had heard of the rocket?"

"Yes."

"You want to know what the rocket is?"

"Yes."

"You have been trying to find out by Morsing (sic) him?"

"Yes."

"And you have failed?"

"Yes."

"Then you say to him that Gibson was to come down and tell you what the result of the Morse signalling was?"

'Yes."

"And then, I suppose, you remained in the chart room?"

"I remained in the chart room."

"And you did nothing further?"

"I did nothing further myself."

"If it was not a company's signal, must it not have been a distress signal?"

"If it had been a distress signal, the officer on watch would have told me."

"I say, if it was not a company's signal, must it not have been a distress signal?"

"Well, I do not know of any other signal but distress signals that are used at sea." This is Answer 6936.

"You do not expect at sea, where you were, to see a rocket unless it is a distress signal, do you?"

"We sometimes get these company's signals which resemble rockets; they do not shoot as high and they do not explode."

Lord in 6936 has now conceded that he knew of only company's signals or distress signals at sea, and also that one *white* rocket has been reported to him. As for his answer about "company's signals which resemble rockets", the reader who has heard there were but five rocket company's signals in the world, four of them coloured, and the fifth, which was white, throwing red stars, can judge whether this was a candid or a disingenuous answer. It is also worth recalling that the Board of Trade prefaced its list of company's signals with the note that if "they are used in any other place, or for any other purpose than name,* they may be signals of distress, and should be answered accordingly by passing ships . . ."

"You have already told us that you were not satisfied that was a company's signal," Sir Rufus persisted.[47] "You have told us that?"

"I asked the officer, was it a company's signal."

Then Mersey interrupted again.

"And he did not know?"

"He did not know," Lord agreed.

"You have told me already some few minutes ago —" the Attorney began again.

"Very well, sir."

"— that you were not satisfied it was a company's signal. You did not think it was a company's signal?"

"I inquired, was it a company's signal."

"But you had been told that he did not know?"

"He said he did not know."

"Very well, that did not satisfy you?"

"It did not satisfy me."

Then at last, came the climactic Question 6944.

"Then, if it was not that, it might have been a distress signal?"

"*It might have been.*"[48] [emphasis added].

The Attorney-General followed this answer with a question he had already asked three times, and the number of its repetitions probably is the mark of his astonishment.

"And you remained in the chart room?"[49]

"I remained in the chart room."

Thousands of words about the *Californian* were to follow before the end of the Mersey inquiry, and even more thousands, not excluding this book, in the three-quarters and more of the century that had passed; but Lord's four short words, "It might have been", spoken in a second of time and gone forever, save

---

*   Such as "answering our Morse lamp?"

on the printed page, are really the end of the case. It requires a minimum of reflection to realize those words constitute a confession.

Whether those who heard them understood their enormity one may doubt, or whether Lord himself realized that the simple and deadly question to which they were the answer had finally exposed and dragged into the light the veritable nerve of the dark and hitherto profoundly secret knowledge, which, as in a classic tragedy, had been the cause of his moral downfall, by the reduction of an honest man to deception and from deception to unadulterated falsehood.

Exactly a month after Lord had given his evidence, 14 June, on which day the 24th hearing of the inquiry took place, Sir Rufus mentioned the questions which had been put to the Court at the beginning.[50] At the end of the evidence, further questions might be added.

"According to my view at present," he continued, ". . . the only question which should be added is one relating to what I may call compendiously the 'Californian' incident. There is no question in the twenty-six before you which would cover that . . ."

On 19 June, the 27th day of the hearing, the Attorney-General mentioned Question 24:[51] "What was the cause of the loss of the 'Titanic,' and of the loss of life which thereby ensued or occurred?"

"To that," he said, "I propose to add this question: 'What vessel had the opportunity of rendering assistance to the 'Titanic,' and, if any, how was it that assistance did not reach the 'Titanic' before the 'Carpathia' arrived?'"

Dunlop was not in court and it would seem that he was not notified that the question was to be submitted. Captain Lord himself certainly had no knowledge of it.

His case was argued by Robertson Dunlop on 28 June, the 33rd day of the inquiry.

Charles Robertson Dunlop, with an excellent legal degree from Oxford and destined for a leading place at the Admiralty Bar, was 36 years old. He was the last of the many counsel for various parties to address the court before the Attorney-General's final speech, and he was greeted by Lord Mersey with the inquiry: ". . . how long do you think you will take to convince us that the *Californian* did not see the *Titanic's* lights?"[52] He answered: ". . . about two hours." He opened with an expression of "the profound regret" of the owners and the master that they had been unable to render any assistance to the *Titanic;* but, as Lord said he had had no communication with Dunlop whatever after giving his evidence,[53] the expression of this "profound regret", at least, must have been assumed rather than personally authorized.

Dunlop admitted that he had been present very rarely during the inquiry.[54] He attempted to show, with the aid of the log, that the *Californian* was on a course, S89W true,[55] from which she could not have seen the *Titanic,*[56] and had stopped in a position over 20 miles from the wreck.[57] When Mersey put him on the spot by asking him whether they saw the signals or not, Dunlop admitted that they saw "certain signals"[58] which were not distress signals but "private night signals". On the other hand, if they were distress signals, they did not come from the *Titanic.*[59]

". . . If they were distress signals," said Lord Mersey, "whether they came from the *Titanic* or not, you ought to have made for them."[60]

Dunlop insisted that he was interested only in signals from the *Titanic.*[61] Lord had said she was not the *Titanic;* Stone and Gibson thought she was a tramp, and Gill, who claimed to see a passenger ship after 12 brightly lit, was contradicted by Groves, who saw the other ship's light go out at 11.40. One or the other must be wrong;[62] and as for Groves's view that it was the *Titanic* — "his evidence was largely the result of imagination stimulated by vanity."[63]

About the navigating lights, Dunlop made a point of saying that the *Titanic* would have shown her green light to the *Californian,* whereas, said Groves, Stone and Gibson, the other ship had shown her red.[64] Mersey then called attention to Lord's having seen the green,[65] but Dunlop claimed that the reds had it by three to one.[66] Mersey thought this might have been explained by the *Titanic's* swinging, but Dunlop said it could not be. He, of course, overlooked the time lapse, and although Mersey knew the evidence better than Dunlop — for instance, Mersey had a vague memory of Rowe's evidence, which the Attorney identified,[67] about the *Titanic's* swinging — Mersey could not collate the apparent discrepancies about the sidelights with the evidence from the *Titanic* about porting round the iceberg. Even less could he refer to the relevant evidence, when Dunlop sought to demolish the alleged identification of Gill's steamer with the *Titanic.* Gill was said to have had his steamer heading north-east. But, said Dunlop, there was no evidence of the *Titanic's* having turned round and headed towards Europe.[68] Nobody in court, it seems, knew of the evidence of Major Peuchen, the yachtsman, at Washington, who had unmistakably indicated that was precisely where the *Titanic* was heading when he left her.[69] Dunlop no doubt could have objected to the reading of Peuchen's evidence from the US 'Hearings', but hardly to a statement that such evidence had been given.

Citing the evidence, Dunlop maintained that the *Titanic* and the *Californian* were never in sight of each other,[70] and the ship seen by the *Titanic* was not the *Californian,* because the latter "unfortunately was stopped until 6 o'clock in the morning."[71] He then mentioned Rostron's denial of seeing the *Californian* before 8 o'clock, and the miscellany of fishing boats and other vessels reported by various witnesses. The rockets seen by the *Californian* "could not possibly have been the rockets of the *Titanic,*" and he thought it probable that the steamer seen by the *Californian* and that seen by Boxhall were different. Then followed his remarkable assertion that it was no part of "the loyalty owed by one shipowner to another" to try to implicate another's ship.[72] He said Groves was mistaken in his identification of the *Carpathia,* when he reached the bridge,[73] but omitted the significant bit of evidence that the ship Groves saw had her flag at half-mast.

Dunlop then mentioned the Hansa Line's *Trautenfels* as a vessel being near the scene on 14 April, and "having done . . . what the witnesses from the *Californian* say the steamer which they saw did."[74] The German tanker *Paula* and other named vessels were also possible; but the *Trautenfels* was "the best, because she steams to the S.W."[75]

Mersey listened patiently, and abstained from remarking that although they were "all very good", they all had the notable difference of not having reported on arrival that they had had to fire eight, or any, rockets at all. Dunlop, however, asserted that the rockets seen by the *Californian* were "answering rockets"[76] or requests to stand by, not distress signals, and they were white, the same colour as the *Titanic's,* because "most rockets are white rockets."[77]

The reader knows this was true, but the inference was very different from that suggested by Dunlop, for white rockets were only distress rockets.

It was here the Commissioner summed it all up by saying that at all events the *Titanic* had sent out white rockets and the *Californian* had seen white rockets; the *Titanic* sent up about eight rockets, and the *Californian* had seen about eight.

"Yes, it is a coincidence," said Mr Dunlop, no doubt with a straight face.

"Yes," Lord Mersey echoed, "it is a coincidence."[78]

The last point on this part of Dunlop's argument was that Stone and Gibson were misled, because when the steamer began firing her rockets she also began steaming away to the south-west (Gibson himself said he did not see her moving). She was not herself in distress, but was perhaps going off in answer to some other vessel.[79]

Rather surprisingly perhaps, Dunlop then put his case on the opposite assumption that the unknown ship was the *Titanic* and the rockets were hers.[80] Even if that were true, Lord was not to blame, because "he was lulled into a state of security and unsuspicion by the reports that he got."[81] Yet, even if he had made the attempt, he could not have reached the *Titanic* in time, and no lives would have been saved. The effort indeed "might possibly have only added the *Californian* to the *Titanic* tragedy."[82]

But even if Mersey took an unfavourable view of Lord's conduct, and thought his conduct merited rebuke, there were three grounds why the report should refrain from rebuking him. The first was "public policy". It would be "a grave mistake" to censure Captain Lord, for it would put "into the hands of foreign critics a weapon of attack on the reputation of the British Mercantile Marine, of which we are very justly proud and jealous."[83]

In this final portion of Dunlop's address, which occupied some 27 minutes, Mersey listened in complete silence, without a single word of interruption. It is difficult, however, for the reader to refrain from a gasp of astonishment at the sheer wrong-headedness, not to say cynicism, of this first 'ground' for not censuring Lord.

The second reason for keeping silent was very different. Dunlop submitted a substantial question of law, and one deserving most serious consideration.[84] He maintained that the court had no jurisdiction to censure Lord, whose conduct was not one of the subjects to be considered by the inquiry. Lord had attended as a witness only, and if the Board of Trade had intended to make him a party to the inquiry he should have been served with a notice in the form prescribed by the law.[85] It was not until a month after Lord had given evidence, on 14 June, that a question was added covering the *Californian,* which would enable the court to censure him. The stated object of this new question had been to obtain a finding on the facts from the Commissioner, which would enable the Law Officers of the Crown to decide whether Lord should be prosecuted under the Maritime Conventions Act, 1911, Section 6. If that was so, Lord should have known before giving evidence, been informed what the charge was, and heard the evidence of the other witnesses, before giving his own. Dunlop might, of course, have added that Lord would also have had the right to refuse to give evidence at all, as it might incriminate him. Dunlop did complain that "Captain Lord has been treated here in a way which is absolutely contrary to the principles on which justice is usually administered, or on which these inquiries are generally conducted."[86]

Dunlop's last plea was that Lord had already been "sorely and severely punished".[87] Whatever the reason for his inactivity, it was not due "to any wilful disregard of duty", and his "ordeal of public criticism and public censure" would be warning enough, without censure from the court, to him and other masters of the "strict duty" that lay upon those who go to sea of rendering assistance to ships in distress.

"I venture to think," he ended, "that if your Lordship does not censure him then truth and justice and mercy will meet together in your Lordship's report."[88]

It was, on the whole, a brave effort; but a careful reader of the complete text of the speech will notice that, from beginning to end, this discreet advocate had omitted any reference whatever to Question 6944.

That omission was, of course, repaired by the Attorney-General in his comments on the *Californian,* which came at the end of his final address on the whole *Titanic* case, on 3 July, the 36th day of the hearing.

"First of all," he said in opening his speech,[89] "the view which I take of it is that so far from being desirous of bringing home to the Captain of the *Californian,* or to any of the officers of the *Californian,* that they saw distress signals and that they took no step after they had seen them, I am most anxious, and have been throughout, to find some possible excuse, for the inaction on the part of the *Californian.* It is not a case of desiring to bring home to them that they did not do their duty; our anxiety and your Lordship's anxiety would be, if possible, to find some reason to explain the failure by them to take any steps when they had seen distress signals. I can only say that to me it is a matter of extreme regret that I have come to the conclusion that the submission I must make to you, is that there is no excuse. Whether I am right or wrong in that is, of course, for your Lordship's consideration."

". . . the Captain," he continued, "does not admit that they were distress signals, but he admits that they might have been . . . having seen the distress signals, the *Californian* took no steps, except to attempt to do Morse signalling with a light . . . The comment I make upon it is that for the master of a British vessel to see distress signals, whether they come from a passenger steamer or not, and whether they come from a passenger steamer of the size of the *Titanic* or not, is a very serious matter . . ."[90]

He made it clear that Captain Lord had not been summoned "to answer some attack upon his certificate", and was not on trial, and that Lord Mersey was not being asked to do more than express his opinion on the facts.[91]

Now, on this 36th day of the inquiry, when the Attorney-General was finally dealing with the *Californian,* Lord Mersey showed that he was still uneasy about his position with regard to the case, and with Captain Lord's rights.

"Let me put it quite plainly,"[92] he insisted. "If Captain Lord saw these distress signals and neglected a reasonable opportunity which he had, of going to the relief of the vessel in distress, it may very well be that he is guilty of misdemeanour. That is so, is it not?"

"Yes, under the Merchant Shipping Act, 1906."

"Am I to try that question?"

"Certainly not."[93]

"I think not."

"Certainly not, my Lord. I never asked and could not ask your Lordship to try that question, but, nevertheless, the facts, which you are asked to find, whether they reflect upon him or not, are material to the inquiry."

"The facts I can find, but I do not want, unless I am obliged to do it, to find a man guilty of a crime."

"No, my Lord."

"I do not think I have tried him for any such purpose."

"I agree."

"And, moreover, as you know perfectly well, he might, if he had had any idea that he was going to be tried for a crime, have said when he was in the witness-box: 'I refuse to answer these questions because they may incriminate me.'"

"Yes."

"But he did not do that, you know."[94]

That concluded the colloquy. It is given here in full, because it is important for two reasons: first, the discussion illuminates the attitude towards Captain Lord of two of the chief participants in the proceedings, who, if his champions are right, must also have been the two leading conspirators in what was alleged to be a "rigged" inquiry — "rigged", of course, against Captain Lord;

second, it contains a forecast of the correct ending to the case.

Sir Rufus than pointed out the different considerations which would apply, if it were to be decided whether Captain Lord had committed a crime. "... I should be very sorry to do an injustice to Captain Lord," he said, "and I am very anxious that in any event nothing should be said as a conclusion by your Lordship which would suggest that he had committed a misdemeanour . . . The material points are first of all whether the *Californian* saw distress signals. One answer of the Captain seems to me quite disposes of that."[95]

One may assume he was about to cite Question 6944, but before he could do so, Lord Mersey stopped him.

"I don't know," he said, "whether it will relieve you at all in the trouble you are taking, but I think we all are of opinion that the distress rockets that were seen from the *Californian* were the distress signals from the *Titanic*."[96]

It will be noted there was no question as to whether the signals seen were distress rockets and that Lord Mersey had not impatiently jumped to conclusions alone in his alleged prejudice against Lord, as criticized by the Lordites, but that he made his views known only after consultation with his assessors. *The Shipping World* of 10 July alone seems to have considered this worth mentioning.

Having read much of the evidence, the Attorney quoted Questions 6944 and 6945, ending with Lord's statement, "I remained in the chart room", and commented: "Now, my Lord, that establishes quite clearly this, that he thought it might have been, and the moment a man thinks it might have been a distress signal and does not know what else it could be, I should have thought it really means that he knew — I will not say he was quite certain — but he knew at any rate this, that there was a serious possibility of some vessel being in urgent need of assistance close by. It is very difficult to understand. I find it very difficult to understand in reading through all this evidence why it was that in those circumstances he remained in the chart-room and took no step."

"... I am unable to find any possible explanation of what happened," Sir Rufus said, "except it may be that the Captain of the vessel was in ice for the first time, and would not take the risk of going to the rescue of another vessel which might have got into trouble, as he thought, from proceeding through the ice when he himself had stopped. But even that does not explain why they did not call up the wireless operator to ascertain what the condition of things was. We have heard no explanation of it. I think your Lordship is left absolutely in the dark with reference to it."[98]

He seems to have been so impressed by the impenetrable mystery of Lord's silence that he thought it right to caution against any attempt at speculating about the causes for it, which were not supported by facts. In expressing this opinion, he used words which later attained some notoriety because of the quite baseless innuendo they were said to contain.

"One can only conjecture," he said, "and I do not know that it is perhaps quite safe to speculate upon the reasons that made Captain Lord neither come out of his chart room to see what was happening, nor to take any step to communicate with the vessel in distress, even such a very slight effort as to have the wireless operator called up."[99]

It was said that these words amounted to a charge of drunkenness against Lord. Had the statement stood alone, without a reference also to the wireless, there might have been firmer ground for the belief that the Attorney was hinting that Lord was drunk. There was, of course, not a scintilla of evidence which gave the slightest hint of Lord's being in that condition. On the contrary. Stone had recounted in detail his two conversations with Lord, and Gibson had said flatly that when he entered the chart-room, the master was "awake". One may close this topic with an extract from a letter by Groves, written near the end of his life, and published here, by permission, for the first time:

> ". . . there are two points concerning which I hold strong views. The first is the question of the sobriety of Captain Lord. Although I was with him for only some three months, it is quite long enough to know whether or not a man is of temperate habits. I never saw him take a drink or heard of him desiring one and he was thoroughly abstemious, always."[100]

Rufus Isaacs was one of the most popular men of his day at the Bar, and was remembered with affection long after he had passed from the scene; but even his admirers were aware of the few limitations in his generally formidable equipment. "Poverty of language and occasional ambiguity" were the words once used to me by one of his friends in speaking of the man who ultimately rose so high,[101] and it seems probable that an instance of this weakness is to be found in his phrasing of the caution which was sometimes understood as a hint of Lord's insobriety.

The Attorney-General concentrated on the decisive effect of Question 6944. He could not foresee all the details of the various defences put forward in later years by Lord's supporters, but we can see that Lord's fatal and unadorned admission that he knew it was possible that a distress rocket had been fired, and dragged from him at that, put paid to his many defences and the glut of technical inconsistencies and impossibilities alleged on his behalf. Compared with the moral (and legal) consequences of that admission, what difference could it make whether Lord saw one masthead light or two, or whether the ship seen by the *Titanic* was stopped or moving? Grant that Lord was justified in trusting his "responsible" officer on the bridge, he was, at best, guilty of incompetence in failing to support that responsible officer by not summoning the wireless operator to his aid. If the *Carpathia* had reached the *Titanic* in time and saved everybody still alive, so that there was not a single casualty after Lord first knew of the one rocket he admitted, he would have been favoured by phenomenal indulgence from the President of the Immortals; but it would not in the slightest degree have altered or mitigated his own failure in the supreme moment of his life to respond to the kind of demand that was an inherent part of his calling. He was, therefore, exposed as unworthy of the responsibility he accepted when he took command of a ship. That Lord knew in his own mind the true quality of his act, long before his admission, we have seen from his later behaviour. Put it comprehensively: grant the whole of the case advanced by, and for, him, down to its ultimate absurdity that the eight white rockets seen from his bridge were not rockets at all, but a duplicate set of eight "white Roman candle type flares", and it does not lighten by a minim the burden of his guilt from the knowledge that the rocket might be a signal that human beings in the black night were calling for help, whether from the *Titanic* or the most ancient and rustiest tramp, matters not at all. And Stanley Lord had chosen and preferred to do nothing. That his punishment may have been as disproportionate as that of Oedipus may be true; but to say that he was the victim of the greatest miscarriage of justice in the history of British marine inquiries is in itself a travesty of justice. Pity has a place in judgement, but its indulgence should not be a perversion of truth or a contempt on valour.

At the end of Lord's cross-examination by the Attorney-General, Lord Mersey had asked when he was going to sea and Lord answered: "On Saturday."[102] Evans, the last witness, having finished his evidence the day after Lord, Wednesday, and the 'three or four other witnesses' from the *Californian* being told they were not wanted, the Solicitor-General asked what the *Californian* witnesses should do.[103]

"As far as I am concerned," said Mersey, "they may go . . . They are going to sea, I understand."[104]

"Yes," Robertson Dunlop repeated, "they are sailing on Saturday."[105]

They did; but Lord was not among them. After his return home, he was told by Captain Fry, the Leyland Marine Superintendent, that he was to be relieved of his command. So, Lord went and removed his 'gear' from the ship.[106] He was never aboard her again, but, for the remainder of his life, to those who knew, his four words and their consequences had branded him, "Lord of the *Californian*."

Sources

1 This account of the scene is based chiefly on the *Globe*, 14 May, p. 7 and *Daily Mirror*, 15 May, p. 3.
2 Mersey, p. 144.
3 Evening papers, 14 May and daily 15 May.
4 Mersey, p. 145.
5 Ibid.
6 Capt. Lord's Affidavit, Appendix C.
7 *Globe*, 14 May, p. 7; *Daily Sketch*, 15 May, p. 6; *Daily Mirror*, 15 May, p. 3; *Standard*, 15 May, p. 9; and some P.I. from a few eye witnesses.
8 10 August, quoted in MMSA Petition, Feb 1965, p. 50. The original covering four foolscap sheets is in [MT 9/920/6] M 23448.
9 *Globe*, 15 May, p. 6.
10 B 6715.
11 Ibid.
12 B 6826.
13 B 6828-31.
14 B 6835-36.
15 B 6838-40.
16 Padfield, p. 277.
17 B 6716-17.
18 B 6721, 6723.
19 B 6725.
20 B 6737.
21 B 6744, 8993.
22 B 6728.
23 B 6752, 6754.
24 B 6809.
25 B 8215.
26 P.I.
27 B 8481.

28 B 8169.
29 B 6831.
30 B 7080.
31 B 7082.
32 B 7083.
33 B 6752, 6754.
34 B 7173.
35 B 7090-91.
36 B 7094.
37 B 7095.
38 B 7097.
39 B 7098-99.
40 B 7134-35.
41 B 7136.
42 B 7318-25.
43 B 7327-28.
44 P.I.
45 B 6966.
46 B 6902-37.
47 B 6938-43.
48 B 6944.
49 B 6945.
50 Mersey, p. 611.
51 Mersey, p. 688.
52 Mersey, p. 831.
53 Capt. Lord's Affidavit, Appendix C.
54 Mersey, p. 831.
55 Mersey, p. 832.
56 Mersey, p. 836, 834.
57 Mersey, p. 832.
58 Ibid.
59 Ibid.
60 Mersey, p. 836, 834.
61 Mersey, p. 833.
62 Mersey, p. 834.
63 Mersey, p. 835.
64 Ibid.
65 B 6759.
66 Mersey, p. 835.
67 Ibid.
68 Mersey, p. 836.
69 US 346.
70 Mersey, p. 834.

71 Mersey, p. 837.
72 Ibid.
73 Mersey, p. 838.
74 Ibid.
75 Mersey, p. 840.
76 Ibid.
77 Mersey, p. 841.
78 Mersey, p. 842.
79 Mersey, p. 843.
80 Mersey, p. 844.
81 Ibid.
82 Ibid.
83 Ibid.
84 Ibid.
85 Rule 3, Merchant Shipping Act, 1894, form of statement of questions to be raised. Rules set out at p. 723 of statute.
86 Mersey, p. 845.
87 Ibid.
88 Ibid.
89 Mersey, p. 895.
90 Mersey, pp. 895-96.
91 Mersey, p. 896.
92 Ibid.
93 Ibid.
94 Ibid.
95 Ibid.
96 Mersey, p. 897.
97 Ibid.
98 Mersey, p. 900.
99 P.I. *ca*, 1926, at the bar.
100 P.I. Captain C.V. Groves's papers, 1959.
101 Ibid.
102 B 7342.
103 Mersey, p. 194.
104 Ibid.
105 Ibid.
106 Capt. Lord's Affidavit, Appendix C.

Chapter 16

Judgement days

On Tuesday, 28 May, Senator Smith presented to the Senate the unanimous Report of the Committee of Commerce on their inquiry into the "causes leading up to the destruction of the steamship *Titanic,* with its attendant and unparalleled loss of life, so shocking to the people of the world."[1] The Report by itself covered 19 printed pages, and it was accompanied by a number of exhibits, consisting of analytical lists of crew and passengers, bringing the total to 66 pages.

Before this final stage of the inquiry was reached, on 18 May, just one day more than three weeks after the *Californian* witnesses had been heard, Captain John J. Knapp, USN, Hydrographer of the Bureau of Navigation, Navy Department, had given evidence.[2] After describing more than 25 years of activity of the Bureau in publishing monthly charts of the North Atlantic and other bulletins at shorter intervals, including a daily memorandum containing news of perils to navigation, all based on, and collated from, numerous reports from ships, Captain Knapp went on to analyse the navigational evidence concerning the *Californian.* One of the charts he presented, No.2, and his memorandum and comment on it, are reproduced.* As will be seen from Senator Smith's speech below, the Committee were convinced by his evidence. Captain Knapp concluded that if the *Californian* was in the position given by Lord, she could have reached the scene in two hours, but if she had been in the "hypothetical position" shown in the chart, she "certainly could have reached the *Titanic* in a little over an hour after she struck."[3]

It is hardly surprising that Captain Knapp is far from being the Lordites' favourite American. Complaint is made that he did not realize and say that the evidence was "inadequate to prove that *any* [emphasis in original] specific ship was the mystery ship."[4] In other words, all Knapp should have done was to dismiss from his mind the most important evidence of all from the *Californian,* that she had seen the rockets. In the absence of his doing so, it follows, according to this argument, that because (as it was ironically emphasized) "Knapp was a nautical man",[5] "Is it possible to believe that [he] was uninfluenced by pressure from outside or by the general hysteria?"[6] That is, Captain Knapp was at the very least unprincipled and certainly professionally incompetent. Perhaps because the question is rhetorical, we are not told the precise reward in dollars and cents, or in other material benefit, Captain Knapp derived from his dishonorable conduct.[§] His evidence is also called ". . . the turning-point in the *Californian* incident", because, without it, "Mersey . . . would have

* *See* Appendix E.

paused in his headlong attempt to prove Lord guilty."[7] This, it seems, is a deduction, entirely unsupported by evidence or any other known circumstance.

At the same time, it is necessary to point out that Captain Knapp obviously accepted Gill's story about what Knapp called "the large steamer". The hydrographer had the advantage of seeing and hearing Gill, and Knapp was undoubtedly a man of great skill and — in the circumstances it seems not impertinent to add — of unquestioned integrity. Nevertheless, it seems to me that he may well have looked on Gill as merely one more human unit in supplying oral data about a technical problem, and that he did not compare its credibility with that of the evidence concerning the other ship, which was given by other members of the *Californian* crew, whom he mentioned, but, with the exception of Lord, did not name. In spite of this, as said in Chapter 12, where the reasons are set out, I am convinced that Gill did not see "the large steamer". If Gill is disregarded in Captain Knapp's memorandum, its validity still remains unaffected, as its conclusions follow with no less logic from the evidence about the other ship, given by Groves, Stone and Gibson.

The Committee made various recommendations, including the following: boats for all, and passengers and crew assigned to them before sailing; every "ocean" steamer carrying 100 passengers or more should be equipped with two electric searchlights; "radiotelegraphy" should be regulated, and there should be an operator on duty day and night; "the firing of rockets or candles on the high seas for any other purpose than as a signal of distress be made a misdemeanour"; certain structural alterations for increasing safety should be introduced in all seagoing steamships carrying 100 or more passengers, the construction of which began after the date of the Report.[8]

Some of these recommendations were clearly prompted by the incident of the *Californian,* but other passages in the document directly concerned that vessel:

"VESSELS IN VICINITY OF STEAMSHIP 'TITANIC'"
At this time the Committee thinks it advisable to invite attention to the reported positions of the vessels in the vicinity of the *Titanic* when her calls of distress were being sent out.

The *Californian,* of the Leyland Line, west-bound, was in latitude 42° 05' north, longitude 50° 07' west, and was distant in a northerly direction 19½ miles according to the captain's figures (p. 717)." [†]

The Report then mentioned, with their positions and distances from the *Titanic,* the *Mount Temple, Carpathia, Birma, Frankfurt, Virginian, Baltic* and *Olympic,* the last being about 512 miles to the westward. It continued, later:

"STEAMSHIP LIGHT SEEN FROM THE STEAMSHIP 'TITANIC'"[9]
Sixteen witnesses from the *Titanic,* including officers and experienced seamen, and passengers of sound judgement, testified to seeing the light of a ship in the distance, and some of the lifeboats were directed to pull for that light, to leave the passengers and to return to the side of the *Titanic.* The *Titanic* fired distress

§ *(on opposite page)* Mr Padfield was considerably more informative about the "rigged" British inquiry than about the "framed" American one, and named the specific rewards given to the malefactors. Baron Mersey was granted a Viscountcy, although very tardily; and Rufus Isaacs, the string of honours and offices, of which the reader has already been informed.

† i.e. US 717.

rockets and attempted to signal by electric lamp and Morse code to this vessel. At about the same time the officers of the *Californian* admit seeing rockets in the general direction of the *Titanic* and say that they immediately displayed a power-ful Morse lamp, which could be easily seen a distance of 10 miles, while several of the crew of the *Californian* testify that the side lights of a large vessel going at full speed were plainly visible from the lower deck of the *Californian* at 11.30 p.m., ship's time, just before the accident. There is no evidence that any rockets were fired by any vessel between the *Titanic* and the *Californian,* although every eye on the *Titanic* was searching the horizon for possible assistance.

THE STEAMSHIP 'CALIFORNIAN'S' RESPONSIBILITY[10]

The committee is forced to the inevitable conclusion that the *Californian,* controlled by the same company, was nearer the *Titanic* than the 19 miles reported by her captain, and that her officers and crew saw the distress signals of the *Titanic* and failed to respond to them in accordance with the dictates of humanity, interna-tional usage, and the requirements of law. The only reply to the distress signals was a counter signal from a large white light which was flashed for nearly two hours from the mast of the *Californian.* In our opinion such conduct, whether arising from indifference or gross carelessness, is most reprehensible, and places upon the commander of the *Californian* a grave responsibility. The wireless operator of the *Californian* was not aroused until 3.30 a.m., New York time, on the morning of the 15th, after considerable conversation between officers and members of the crew had taken place aboard that ship regarding these distress signals or rockets, and was directed by the chief officer to see if there was anything the matter, as a ship had been firing rockets during the night [p. 736].* The inquiry thus set on foot immediately disclosed the fact that the *Titanic* had sunk. Had assistance been promptly proffered, or had the wireless operator of the *Californian* remained a few minutes longer at his post on Sunday evening, that ship might have had the proud distinction of rescuing the lives of the passengers and crew of the *Titanic.*"

After all the verbosity and repetition of the hearing itself, the Report was an unexpectedly brief and businesslike document, and its recommendations seemed necessary and sensible. With the exception of the recommendation about searchlights in merchant ships, they were also generally similar to what was to follow from the Mersey inquiry.

The Senate Committee's findings on the *Californian,* insofar as they were based on the evidence from that ship were, it is true, not completely accu-rate. The Committee, let us recall, heard only Gill, Captain Lord himself and Evans. It was Gill alone, and not "several of the crew" who testified about the "large vessel going at full speed"; and even he said nothing about her "side lights". Moreover, Gill timed his apparition not at "11.30 p.m. ship's time", but just before midnight. Of no importance, but also imprecise, was the state-ment that "a large white light" had been "flashed" from the "mast" of the *Californian.*

Senator Smith presented the Report with a speech, which, on the whole, even after more than three quarters of a century of dire competition, retains its outstanding place in any anthology of embarrassing Senatorial oratory. It is the overblown style, and not the content, which embarrasses the reader; but it is a fact that the packed chamber, which Smith addressed, were consider-ably moved and listened attentively to the end, with many of the women, who crowded the gallery, in tears.[11]

---

* i.e. US 736.

The speech was disfigured by a number of irrelevant mistakes; but nevertheless, this landbound legislator had got hold of the most essential point of all, that the *Californian* had seen rockets, and her captain had not even bothered to call the wireless operator.

In the United States, his findings on the *Californian* were frequently mentioned in the newspapers, but, perhaps surprisingly, comment was scant. An exception was *The New York Tribune,* which, after criticizing Captain Smith, continued: "Nor is it easy to disagree with him [Senator Smith] in thinking that a tremendous responsibility rests upon the Captain of the Californian for his failure to ascertain the facts concerning the ship which only a gunshot away was making signals of distress."[12]

In fact, from an examination of scores of British, American, continental, and what were then called 'colonial', newspapers and periodicals, one gets the firm impression that the Report, as a whole, was approved by the majority. Outside the United States, where Smith's speech received comparatively little notice — perhaps because its emotionalism and hyperbole were not so unusual — it was often held to have damaged the effect of his Report. Typical of this view was the London *Daily Express,* which under the heading "Bombastos", said: "the grotesque oration of Senator Smith" deprived the Report "of much value".[13] *The Evening News* spoke of "Smithery and Georgery", comparing the senator's speech with the alleged extravagance of Lloyd George's language.[14] *The Evening Standard* under the heading "The Amazing Smith", strongly condemned his oratory, but went on: "But in the midst of this mass of wild verbiage there are embedded some important suggestions. The attack on our Board of Trade is virulent enough, but it calls for attention in the House of Commons when our own inquiry is concluded. So is the indictment of Capt. Lord of the Californian, which is a serious matter that cannot well be allowed to rest."[15]

Generally, after the contempt and hostility that had been Smith's usual portion since Britain had first heard of him, his final performance received more respect than might have been expected. The more radical the paper, the warmer was the approval of Smith. *The Star* said: "The report blames the Board of Trade, Capt. Smith, and the Californian; and in no case will the apportionment of blame cause the least surprise in this country . . . We may depend upon it that in some light or other, heroic or otherwise, the Californian will figure conspicuously in its report."[16] *John Bull* was, after its fashion, enthusiastic about Smith, as it had been from the first:

"The report of Smith of Grand Rapids, on the *Titanic,* is precisely what everybody reading the evidence with unbiased mind must have expected it would be. Stripped of its Grand Rapids rhetoric, it beats the British Board of Trade into a pulp," and so on. It includes a summary of the finding on Lord, and ends, "After these smashing conclusions, the Mersey Court may, if it chooses, whitewash the Board of Trade and recommend medals for the directors of the White Star Line."[17]

The Manchester Guardian, although of the opinion that the Report "does not seem to be a first-rate piece of work," also said: "As it turns out, several of the Committee's conclusions — those, for instance respecting . . . the inaction of the Californian — are very much what it is generally expected that we shall have from Lord Mersey."[18] *The Spectator* included the verdict on the *Californian* among "the more important conclusions" arrived at;[19] and both *The Daily Chronicle* and *The Globe* thought judgement on Captain Lord should be suspended until the British court of inquiry published its report.[20]

It is worth recalling here that, although the Mersey inquiry had heard the

Californian witnesses some two weeks before these comments, no formal request had yet been made to Lord Mersey for any finding on the incident. It was apparently taken as a matter of course, by the public, at least, that part of Lord Mersey's job was to give some kind of judgement on the *Californian*. This is far from saying, as do the supporters of Captain Lord, that there was a scream from the mob for a scapegoat, which was reinforced by the American report. The Press, as will be gathered from the above extracts, was very temperate.

More than a month of the Mersey inquiry remained after the Senate Report was published. Having heard 97 witnesses and nine speeches from counsel, the court adjourned on the 36th day of the hearing, which occurred on Wednesday, 3 July.

At the end of his address, the Attorney-General said to Lord Mersey: ". . . the latitude which you have seen fit to allow . . . so that all questions might be asked which would be of the slightest use, has . . . very much narrowed the range of controversy, when we get to the end of the Inquiry . . . on many of the points it has been shown quite clearly there can be no dispute . . . The result of it has been that, in any event, everything has been put before this Court, and I hope that your Lordship will be satisfied of that, that all the evidence that can have been of use to you has been presented to you . . . I leave the matter to your Lordship for your Report."[21]

"Very well," said Lord Mersey. "Thank you, Mr Attorney. I will try to get this Report out in reasonable time."

And, with that, the Court adjourned *sine die*, in other words, without a stated day for its resumption.

It was just under four weeks after the adjournment, on Tuesday, 30 July, that Lord Mersey brought his inquiry to its end at Scottish Hall, where it began, and read his Report. On p. 43, the passage which concerns the *Californian* begins:[22]

"5.-THE CIRCUMSTANCES IN CONNECTION
WITH THE S.S. 'CALIFORNIAN'.
"It is here necessary to consider the circumstances relating to the S.S. 'Californian'.

Lord Mersey then went through the evidence as given by the various witness and finally concluded:

"There are contradictions and inconsistencies in the story as told by the different witnesses. But the truth of the matter is plain. The 'Titanic' collided with the berg at 11.40. The vessel seen by the 'Californian' stopped at this time. The rockets sent up from the 'Titanic' were distress signals. The 'Californian' saw distress signals. The number sent up by the 'Titanic' was about eight. The 'Californian' saw eight. The time over which the rockets from the 'Titanic' were sent up was from about 12.45 to 1.45 o'clock. It was about this time that the 'Californian' saw the rockets. At 2.40 Mr. Stone called to the Master that the ship from which he had seen the rockets had disappeared. At 2.20 a.m. the 'Titanic' had foundered. It was suggested that the rockets seen by the 'Californian' were from some other ship, not the 'Titanic'. But no other ship to fit this theory has ever been heard of.

"These circumstances convince me that the ship seen by the 'Californian' was the 'Titanic', and if so, according to Captain Lord, the two vessels were about five miles apart at the time of the disaster. The evidence from the 'Titanic' corroborates this estimate, but I am advised that the distance was probably greater, though not more than eight or ten miles. The ice by which the 'Californian' was surrounded was loose ice extending for a distance of not more than two or three miles in the direction of the 'Titanic'. The night was clear and the sea was smooth. When she first saw the rockets the 'Californian' could have pushed through the ice to the open water without any serious risk and so have come to the assistance of the 'Titanic'. Had she done so she might have saved many if not all of the lives that were lost."[23]

The Court also specifically answered the 26 questions submitted by the Board of Trade.[24] Question 24, already mentioned, was in three parts. Part (b) had been added, and read:

"What vessels had the opportunity of rendering assistance to the 'Titanic' and, if any, how was it that assistance did not reach the 'Titanic' before the SS. 'Carpathia' arrived?"[25]

The Answer given by the Court was:

"(b) The 'Californian.' She could have reached the 'Titanic' if she had made the attempt when she saw the first rocket. She made no attempt."

The terse, direct style of Mersey's address, devoid of adjective or emotion, is deadly. Its effect was far greater than Senator Smith's no doubt sincere, but heart-broken, phrases. His magniloquent sentences, awash with tears, had dimmed few English eyes, but Lord Mersey's unperturbed prose momentarily stunned even the Lordites. In later years, when they had recovered sufficiently, they gripped their pins and needles, and Lilliputian-like, hammered away at the granite surface of the findings, not, it is true, at their base, which was the pronouncement on the rockets, but at such subsidiary details as the apparent unconsidered acceptance of Gill's obviously incorrect timings. Yet, this clearly was among the "contradictions and inconsistencies", which Lord Mersey himself had mentioned in the final passages of his findings. Those two last paragraphs, summarizing the essential facts about the *Californian,* stand indeed, after more than three quarters of a century, unshaken and unanswerable, and in the canon of *Titanic* literature are deservedly renowned.

As the Attorney-General had asked, Mersey did no more than announce his findings of facts. Among the recommendations at the end of the Report was No. 22: "That the attention of masters of vessels should be drawn by the Board of Trade to the effect that under the Maritime Conventions Act, 1911, it is a misdemeanour not to go to the relief of a vessel in distress when possible to do so."[26] This was clearly the result of the inactivity of the *Californian,* and, very soon, the Board of Trade had printed a special leaflet embodying this recommendation, which was widely distributed,[27] but in the finding itself, no recommendation was made, no opinion was expressed, no word of condemnation uttered. In all this, likewise, there was a contrast between Smith and Mersey. Smith had said that if Lord had been vigilant as "the dictates of humanity" prompted, there was "a very strong probability that every human life . . . could have been saved," and "The conduct of the captain of the *Californian* calls for drastic action by the Government of England . . ." Mersey, basing his findings on 70 citations of evidence, all, incidentally, from *Californian* witnesses, found as a fact that as the ice surrounding the *Californian* "was loose ice", she could have pushed through it, "without any serious risk", to reach the *Titanic.* Or, as the Maritime Conventions Act, 1911, stated, 'it was possible to have gone to the relief of the vessel in distress.'

Mersey also found it was a fact, that if she had pushed through this loose ice when she saw the first rocket, she could have reached the *Titanic* in time to save perhaps every life; but, "She made no attempt"; or, again in the conclusion of the same statute, her master having failed to go to the relief of a vessel in distress, had been guilty of a misdemeanour. Mersey stopped short of stating the legal consequences of Captain Lord's failure, or of telling "the Government of England", as the senator had, what they should do. The next move, if any, was up to that government.

One comment it is necessary to make on the last of Lord Mersey's findings of fact. This, although oddly enough never mentioned by Captain Lord's friends, is of far greater weight than the various "contradictions and inconsistencies" on which reliance was based, and so partly contributed to the findings, thereby provoking a spate of sarcasm and complaints.

The *Californian,* declared Lord Mersey, was surrounded "by loose ice". He then adds that she "could have pushed through the ice to the open water without any serious risk and so have come to the assistance of the 'Titanic.'" The careful reader will observe that, while, as already said, no fewer than 70 citations of evidence from the *Californian* formed the basis of the findings, not one of them supports these concluding findings, which are indeed the most decisive of all.

What evidence there was from the *Californian* to some extent actually contradicts Lord Mersey's statement.

"Could you," Dunlop asked Lord, "have navigated with any degree of safety to your vessel at night through the ice that you, in fact, encountered?"[28]

"It would have been most dangerous," said Captain Lord, instantly taking the hint.

But Lord, we know, was a devious witness, and with an obvious interest in making the passage to the *Titanic* sound as dangerous as he could. More significant is what Groves said. He had no doubt that the other ship was the *Titanic,* and that the *Californian* should at once have gone to her assistance when the first rocket was seen.

"At the time you left the bridge was it a clear night?" Scanlan asked him.[29]

"Quite clear."

"Was it so clear that your captain could have picked his way, even through that icefield, to the ship which you saw?"

"He could have picked his way through there, but it certainly would not have been a particularly safe proceeding. There is no doubt he could have done it."

This is a judicious answer and probably a correct one, but a good way from Mersey's announcement that the passage could have been made "without any serious risk". There is no uncertainty whatever about the ice conditions when the trip was finally undertaken in daylight. At the scene of the disaster, the water may have been clear, with comparatively distant bergs as the only ice in sight; but from north and west, there was a unanimity of evidence from the *Californian,* amply corroborated by the independent *Mount Temple,* about the thickness, and indeed frequent impassibility, of the icefield some five hours after the first rocket. It still remains, therefore, to ask whether Lord Mersey was right or wrong in making his decisive finding that the *Californian* was surrounded only by loose ice; and, if he was right, what was the basis for his finding. If the ice was in fact as described, it seems that the *Californian* could have safely reached the *Titanic,* even though, in Groves's words, it "would not have been a particularly safe proceeding."

The evidence, and what was probably in Mersey's mind, came not from the *Californian,* but from Lightoller. He said that the light he saw was "not over 5 miles away."[30]

"Was there any field ice or pack ice about the *Titanic* about this time," Mersey asked him, "anything that could be seen anywhere?"

"No, my Lord."

"Then there was nothing to prevent a vessel as far as you could see, coming to the *Titanic*?"

"Not as far as I could see. You are speaking of the night-time?"

That evidence was as good as any, but it is not the end of the matter. In describing what happened after the ship had stopped, Lord said she was surrounded by "loose ice" and was one-quarter to half-a-mile from the edge of a low icefield. He could not see any clear place to get through and so decided to remain stopped until daylight. When he sent for the Chief Engineer they examined the density of the ice. Like Mersey, as said above, they decided she was surrounded "by loose ice". Obviously, the distance between his own "findings" and Mersey's was inconsiderable and very different from his, Lord's evidence.[31]

It is true that Sir Ernest Shackleton, the Antarctic explorer, in his expert evidence, said: "I think field ice for a ship of the class of any ocean liner is almost as bad as an iceberg, because at a speed like that, the kinetic energy is so enormous and field ice is very often 20 feet deep; it is like running on a rock almost."[32] Clearly, this opinion did not apply to 'loose ice', and to a ship, not of 46,000 tons, running at 22 knots, but to a 6,000-tonner, making 13 at the outside.

The time when Captain Lord and Chief Engineer Mahan "examined the density of the ice" must have been about 10.30, or more than two hours before the first of the rockets was seen. The conversation in which Lord disclosed this talk with Mahan did not take place until 47 years after he had given his evidence.

Already in existence at the time, although withheld from the Court and everybody else, was Stone's statement of 18 April, quoted in full in Appendix D. Near its beginning, is a passage, which may serve as the final item in support of Lord Mersey's judgement that the *Californian* was surrounded "by loose ice", through which she "could have pushed without any serious risk . . .", even though it is not formal evidence and was unknown to him. The time of which Stone wrote, moreover, was just before he went on the bridge, that is, not earlier than midnight, and so only about 45 minutes before the first rocket.

"You showed me a steamer," Stone writes to Lord, "A little abaft of our Star-beam and informed me she was stopped. You also showed me the *loose field ice* [emphasis added] all around the ship and a dense icefield to the southward."

Mersey's singular carelessness in failing to name the source for his last, and decisive, finding, catches the eye, just because it is unique, at least in the *Californian* case; but when the query is answered, it confirms his own generally high standard of care and accuracy.

Mersey's duty, of course, was to discover the causes of the disaster, and not to be affected by sentiment. Yet, one feels that a word of praise for bravery or of sympathy with suffering, where appropriate, would have been no breach of that duty, and perhaps more fitting than his two solitary and indignant interventions on behalf of Bruce Ismay and Sir Cosmo Duff Gordon, who were otherwise already massively (and expensively) defended. In short, as was to be anticipated, Lord Mersey inevitably ran his inquiry as a member and agent of the ruling class in a class-ridden country. It is necessary to make these comments, but it is equally necessary to insist that, within his limitations, he was still an honest judge, and one must dissent from the application of the word "travesty" used by the defenders of the *Californian* to describe his conduct of the inquiry and his Report. There were complaints of "whitewash", and with some reason, but, on the whole, the Report achieved its purpose, and its consequences prevail among the trading ships of all nations to this very day.

On both sides of the Atlantic, the Press generally approved of the Report. The keynote of the editorial in *The New York Tribune* was, "Experts say 'Ditto' to laymen".[33] It pointed out that Mersey's findings were "mere echoes of Senator Smith's report . . .," which truth was a frequent theme in the American Press; and thus was the once much-derided nautical ignoramus implicitly vindicated.

The finding on the *Californian* also was approved by a very large majority in all grades and shades of the Press. *The Times* said: "The severest blame is implied rather than expressed, and it concerns the Californian. The proofs that the Californian saw the distress signals of the Titanic and could have come to her . . . are set out with a deadly conciseness and merciless logic."[34] *The Evening Standard* thought that the Report "takes an indulgent view of the conduct of everybody concerned, with the exception of the Captain of the Californian . . . This is the most tragic feature of the whole affair . . ."[35]

The Daily Express believed the *Californian* "remains a mystery of the sea, which deserves further elucidation. It was contrary to every tradition of the sea services; it is a blot upon the honour of the mercantile marine; it exacted fearful penalty."[36] Several papers passed similar severe comments on Lord, the strongest perhaps being *The Daily Telegraph:* ". . . The Commissioner has reached other conclusions which must occasion the deepest regret and humiliation . . . there were sins of omission, which, if they did not directly contribute to the disaster, greatly exaggerated its effects. After patiently sifting all the evidence, the Commissioner has reported that 'The lights seen by the steamer Californian were those of the Titanic'; . . . This is the indictment which is held to have been proved against a British shipmaster. It stands on record for all time; it calls for no comment, for the condemnation is as unmitigated in its simple severity as it is unmerciful in its stern recital of the probable consequences of this fatal lapse from the high standard of conduct on the sea, accepted by sailors everywhere as a commonplace duty which none would dare to escape even at personal peril. This portion of the report stands out as a thing apart — a horror which in the days to come will wound the human instinct of the race wherever the story of the Titanic is recounted . . ."[37]

Yet, in some papers there was no opinion at all on the *Californian,* even though they had much to say about the Report as a whole. Others merely reported the finding. Of these, *Le Temps* of Paris was typical: "Il est établit que c'est bien le *Titanic* qu'a aperèu le *Californian.*"* [38]

There was also, creditably enough, an occasional expression of sympathy with Lord. So, *The Manchester Guardian* thought there was "no need to do more than indicate the contrast between the parts played in this tragedy by the Carpathia and the Californian; it would be inhuman as well as supererogatory to try in any way to add to the penalty that the event has laid upon one who failed under the test of an almost incredibly splendid opportunity . . ."[39]

---

* It has been firmly established that it was the *Titanic* that was observed by the *Californian.*

The Daily News, which, after the Smith Report had recommended suspending judgement on Lord, now pleaded for Captain Smith and continued, "nor should Captain Lord of the Californian — deplorable as his conduct was — be made the scapegoat because the disaster, having been precipitated he did not break the force of the tragedy . . ."[40]

A surprise of the Press reaction was the number of blanks on the *Californian* in the shipping and engineering press. *The Shipping World, Syren and Shipping, Fairplay* and *Engineering*[41] had not a word between them, and *The Engineer*[42] contented itself with the observation, ". . . of the circumstances regarding the S.S. Californian we need say nothing."

Shipping Gazette & Lloyd's List Weekly Summary found it "An agreeable feature" that the Report had paid a tribute "to the conduct of nearly everybody whose name is associated with this Atlantic tragedy. Unhappily this is not said of Captain Lord of the *Californian*. He is told that if his vessel had gone to the assistance of the *Titanic,* as she could have done, 'she might have saved many, if not all, of the lives that were lost.' This is by far the most terrible sentence in this report."[43]

In view of its unreasoning support given to Captain Lord years later, there is a certain irony in the candid, but compassionate, opinion expressed by *The Journal of Commerce* at the time: ". . . The praise to Captain Rostron, of the Carpathia, stands out in strong contrast to the simple narrative of the facts in regard to the action of the Californian, but we think that Lord Mersey has wisely confined himself to the statement of the circumstances, the suffering which Captain Lord must necessarily already have experienced being quite enough punishment for the unfortunate error of judgment which he undoubtedly committed."[44]

The Maritime Review of Cardiff, already mentioned in connection with the Smith Report, was again exuberantly on Lord's side: ". . . nothing succeeds like success, while nothing fails like failure! The world is asked to believe that the skipper of the Californian knowingly lost the chance of his life. The world will please itself as to what it believes. Personally, Captain Lord need not bother unduly because of our opinion."[45]

Later,[46] when Lord himself had written to the Press, Captain Ward, editor of *The Maritime Review,* remarked: "Personally, we are of the opinion that Captain Lord need not have explained. It was altogether unnecessary — to his professional brethren, who hold him blameless," and when Horatio Bottomley of *John Bull,* who dismissed Mersey's Report as "£30,000 Worth of Whitewash,"[47] wired *The Maritime Review,*[48] "Please tell me what that white rocket would mean," the editor contemptuously replied in print, ". . . the rocket was, really, the Man in the Moon lighting his pipe . . ."

It would seem that Captain Lord's own characteristic arrogance was reflected at least in part of the nautical Press, as previously mentioned, and nowhere is there apparently much embarrassment that hundreds of travellers had paid their fares and lost their lives as a result. In addition to the egregious, if also eccentric, *Maritime Review,* an article in *The Nautical Magazine* for August, 1912, headed, "The *Titanic* Inquiry", and signed "Editor", contains this sentence, "The speeches of counsel have nothing of value for us, they can be ignored";[49] and earlier in the same issue, in an extensive and colourful paragraph on Lord himself, it is said: "The Court *thought* [emphasis in original] that the rockets seen by the *Californian* were the distant rockets of the *Titanic,* and in view of this *thought* [emphasis in original] did their best to ruin the career of Captain Lord. We can only trust that his owners will take no notice of this dry, legal, wretched stuff . . ."[50] Besides its support for Lord, the whole piece is infused with hostility towards the Board of Trade and contempt for the general public.

There were many more comments on the *Californian,* but those already quoted are a fair sample, and representative not only of the British, but also the foreign press, where comment was made on the incident.

All this time, Lord himself was at home in Wallasey. He had been suspended, as already said, and Captain William Masters, the son of the former captain of Leyland's *Columbian* in the Boston-London service, took over command of the *Californian.*[51] Masters was to remain the captain of the now notorious vessel until 9 November 1915, when a German submarine ended her career, off Cape Matapan, while she was on a voyage as a troopship between Saloniki and Marseilles.*[52]

In his 1959 affidavit,[§] Lord described his own reaction to Lord Mersey's Report in these measured terms: "I first read the findings of the Court of Inquiry in the Press and while naturally not at all pleased at the references to myself, I was not unduly concerned as I was confident that matters would soon be put right."

He had been kept on full sea pay and bonus and told that he would be reappointed to the *Californian,* but after the publication of the Report, he was informed on 13 August that he could not be given another ship. The Liverpool management of the Leyland Line supported him; but, according to Lord, "one of the London directors, a Mr Matheson [*sic*], K.C., had threatened to resign if I were permitted to remain in the company . . ."

Captain Lord was undoubtedly an outstanding man, but professionally, through his own choice, by provincial measurement. Whether he knew it or not, and presumably he did not, since he did not even get the man's name right, he now had the bad luck to run into not just "one of the London directors", but one of the top men of his time in his field. This was the redoubtable Miles Walker Mattinson, K.C., later Sir Miles Mattinson. This truly unique personality, having had a dazzlingly brilliant academic career in the law, unexpectedly followed it by no more than routine success at the Bar, and combined that with consistent and unequivocal failure in politics and parliament. He finally decided his destiny lay in the City. There, his financial genius exploded and rapidly established him not only as a source of legends, but, more important, as a man of power in several industries, including shipping, with his Leyland directorship numbered among the lesser of his distinctions.[†] It was Lord who resigned.[53]

He then approached the MMSA, and at once wrote a letter to the Press setting out his case as he then chose to frame it. This letter as published in *Syren and Shipping* of 21 August, was dated 14 August.[54] It is substantially the same as that he had already addressed to the Board of Trade on 10 August, and appears in the next chapter.

Meanwhile, on publication of the Report, *The Daily Graphic* had said: "We submit that the matter cannot be allowed to end there. Under the Maritime Conventions Act of 1911 it is a misdemeanour not to go to the relief of a vessel in distress when possible to do so, and it is most desirable that the

---

* She sustained one casualty, R.J. Harding, a member of her crew, whose name is duly commemorated among the many thousands of merchant seamen in the memorial on Tower Hill.

§ *See* Appendix C.

† Mattinson was born three months after the charge of the Light Brigade in the Crimean War (1854) and died three months before D Day in the Second World War (1944).

master of the Californian should be prosecuted, not in any vindictive spirit, but as the best means of bringing the evidence of this Act to the knowledge of captains who are oblivious of their moral obligations."[55]

Sources

1 US Senate Resolution 283, 62nd Congress, 2nd Session, Report No. 806, p 69.
2 US 1111 *seq.*
3 US 1118-19.
4 Padfield 160.
5 Ibid., 164. 165.
6 Ibid., 165.
7 Ibid., 160.
8 US Senate Report, pp. 18, 19.
9 Ibid., p. 11.
10 Ibid.
11 American and British press reports, e.g., *Daily News,* 29 May, p. 1.
12 *New York Tribune,* 29 May, p. 6.
13 *Daily Express,* 29 May, p. 4.
14 *Evening News,* 29 May, p. 4.
15 *Evening Standard,* 29 May, p. 7.
16 *The Star,* 29 May, p. 2.
17 *John Bull,* 8 June, p. 718.
18 *Manchester Guardian,* 29 May, p. 6.
19 *The Spectator,* 1 June, p. 858.
20 *Daily Chronicle,* 29 May, p. 4; *The Globe,* 29 May, p. 1.

21 Mersey, p. 901.
22 Mersey Report, p. 43, *seq.*
23 Ibid, p. 46.
24 Ibid, p. 62.
25 Ibid, p. 71.
26 Ibid, p. 73.
27 [MT 9/920/6] M 25042.
28 B 7407.
29 B 8382-83.
30 B 14140-42.
31 Capt. Lord's Affidavit, Appendix C; Mersey Report, p. 46.
32 B 25116.
33 *New York Tribune,* 31 July, p. 6.
34 *The Times,* 31 July, p. 7.
35 *Evening Standard,* 31 July, p. 9.
36 *Daily Express,* 31 July, p. 4.
37 *Daily Telegraph,* 31 July, p. 10.
38 *Le Temps,* 1 August, p. 2.
39 *Manchester Guardian,* 31 July, p. 8.
40 *Daily News,* 31 July, p. 6.
41 *Fairplay,* 1 August, p. 42; *Engineering,* 2 August, p. 161; *The Shipping World,* 7 August, p. 189; *Syren and Shipping,* 21 August, p. 264.
42 *The Engineer,* 2 August, p. 125.
43 *Shipping Gazette & Lloyd's List Weekly Summary,* 2 August, p. 488.
44 *The Journal of Commerce,* 31 July, p. 6.
45 *Maritime Review,* 3 August, p. 339.
46 Ibid., 24 August, p. 79.
47 *John Bull,* 17 August, p. 204.
48 *Maritime Review,* 31 August, p. 111.
49 *Nautical Magazine,* August 1912, p. 128.
50 Ibid., p. 123.
51 *New York Tribune,* 29 May, p. 1.
52 Ministry of Defence (Master's Report, H.S. 1138, Ref. ADM 137/1138).
53 Some of the facts here are also in Lord's affidavit.
54 *Syren and Shipping,* 21 August, p. 269.
55 *Daily Graphic,* 31 July, p. 4.

Chapter 17

Why Captain Lord wasn't prosecuted

"IMMEDIATE"
Not later than 1 August that word was written in Sydney Buxton's hand-writing on a note asking for the question to be considered whether "it is desir-able, or practicable, to institute proceedings against Captain Lord."[1]

Now, since the opening in 1964 of the *Titanic* files to 1914, for the first time can one know what really happened. Before, at best, only an intelligent guess could be made about the argument which was said to have taken place within the fastness of the Marine Department of the Board of Trade on the subject of prosecuting Captain Lord.

Lord Mersey's Report, with its Findings of Fact, was published only on Tuesday, 30 July, but here, no later than Thursday, 1 August, was the President of the Board, the minister responsible for formally starting a prosecution should there be one, already beginning his inquiry. The hitherto sluggard Board, it seemed, was swift to action. On that same first day of August, Sir R. Ellis Cunliffe, the solicitor to the Board, was also responsible for the first of several memoranda on the topic, to be composed by various officials.

"Captain Lord," he wrote, "gave his version of what happened in the Witness box here and in America, he might have taken the objection that he declined to reply lest he should incriminate himself; he did not do so & though the Wreck Commissioner did not accept his views explanations or excuses I would not advise a prosecution of Captn. Lord under Sec 6 of the above Act [i.e., the Maritime Conventions Act, 1911] under the circumstance. I need hardly add that his punishment is already very great. Moreover he was in Ice & stopped by the Ice to a certain extent for I believe the 1st time."[2]

That being the instant verdict of the highest legal professional authority at the Board of Trade, it might have been thought the enterprise would be nipped in the bud, but in fact more than six weeks were to pass before the last word was written on the possible prosecution.

Independently of any proceedings, and presumably first in point of time, was the decision about the reply to be sent to Lord, who had written:

"10 Ormonde Street, Liscard, Cheshire.
August 10th, '12

The Assistant Secretary, [Sir Walter J. Howell]
Marine Department, Board of Trade, London.

Dear Sir,
With reference to Lord Mersey's report on the *Titanic* disaster, he states the

Californian was 8 to 10 miles from the scene of the disaster.

I respectfully request you will allow me as Master of the *Californian* to give you a few facts which proves she was the distance away that I gave of 17 to 19 miles. April 14th 6.30 p.m. I sent my position to the *Antillian* and *Titanic,* this gives me 17 miles away, and you will see it was sent some hours before the disaster. April 15th about 6.30 a.m. gave my position to S.S. *Virginian* before I heard where the *Titanic* sunk, that also gave me 17 away. I understand the original Marconigrams were in Court.

The evidence of Mr. Boxhall of the *Titanic* who was watching the steamer they had in view, states she *approached* them between one and two a.m., the *Californian* was stopped from 10.30 p.m. to 5.15 a.m. next day.

The steamer seen from the *Californian* was plainly in view from 11.30 p.m. the one seen by the *Titanic* was not, according to her lookout men seen until 0.30 a.m.

Capt. Rostron of the *Carpathia* states when at the scene of the disaster: "*It was daylight at 4.30 a.m. I could see all around the horizon, about 8 miles North of me* (this was the directions the Californian was) *there were two steamers, neither of these was the 'Californian'*". Had the *Californian* been within 10 miles from the *Titanic* she would have been in sight at this time from the *Carpathia,* as she was in the same position as when stopped at 10.30 p.m. the previous evening.

With regard to my own conduct on the night in question I should like to add a little more. I had taken every precaution for the safety of my own ship, and left her in charge of a responsible officer at 0.40 a.m. with instructions to call me if he *wanted* anything, and I lay down fully dressed. At 1.15 a.m. (25 minutes after he had seen the first signal) the officer on watch reported the steamer we had in sight was altering her bearing, in other words was steaming away, and had fired a rocket. I did not anticipate any disaster to a vessel that had been stopped nearly for an hour, and had ignored my Morse signals, and was then steaming away. I asked him was it a Company's signal, and to signal her and let me know the result. It is a matter of great regret to me that I did not go on deck myself at this time, but I didn't think it possible for any seaman to mistake a Company's signal for a distress signal, so I relied on the officer on watch. Although further signals were seen between 1.15 a.m. and 2.0 a.m. I was not notified until 2.0 a.m., and then I had fallen into a sound sleep, and whatever message was sent to me then, I was not sufficiently awake to understand, and it was sufficient indication to anyone that I had not realised the message, by the fact that I still remained below, curiosity to see a vessel pushing through the ice would have taken me on deck. The message sent to me at 2.0 a.m., was, I heard later, to the effect that the steamer we had in sight at 11.30 p.m., had altered her bearing from S.S.E. to S.W.½W. (to do this she must have steamed at least 8 miles, the *Titanic* did not move after midnight) and had fired eight rockets, and was then out of sight.

The question of "drink" has been raised as the reason I could not be roused. I don't drink, and never have done.

Further signals were seen after 2.0 a.m. but the officer was so little concerned about them, that he did not think it necessary to notify me. I was called by the Chief Officer at 4.20 a.m., and in conversation he referred to the rockets seen by the Second Officer. I immediately had the wireless operator called, heard of the disaster, and proceeded at once, pushing through field ice to the scene, and I would have done the same earlier had I understood, as I had everything to gain and nothing to lose.

There is the conversation between the Second Officer and the Apprentice while watching the vessel, that they thought she was a tramp steamer, this is their opinion at the time, which is most likely the correct one.

My employers, the Leyland Line, although their nautical advisers are convinced we did not see the *Titanic,* or the *Titanic* see the *Californian,* say they have the utmost confidence in me, and do not blame me in any way, but owing to Lord Mersey's decision and public opinion caused by this report, they are reluctantly compelled to ask for my resignation, after 14½ years' service without a hitch of any description, and if I could clear myself of this charge, would willingly reconsider their decision.

If you consider there was any laxity aboard the *Californian* the night in question, I respectfully draw your attention to the information given here, which was given in evidence, which also proves was not on my part.

I am told that at the inquiry I was a very poor witness, this I don't dispute, but I fail to see why I should have to put up with all the public odium, through no fault or neglect on my part, and I respectfully request you will be able to do something to put my conduct on the night in question, in a more favourable light, to my employers and the general public.

> I am, Sir,
> Your obedient Servant,
> (Signed) Stanley Lord.[3]

Like everything Lord wrote or said, apart from merely formal or routine matter, this letter deserves study for any light it may cast on his extraordinary and fascinating character. The general tone of the letter gives not the smallest indication that Lord was aware that the primary concern of the Board of Trade about himself at the very time he was asking for something unusual, if not unprecedented, was not what they could or would do for him, but whether or not they should there and then try to put him in prison. With his own knowledge, more complete naturally than that of anybody else on earth, of what had really filled his mind during and since the critical night, Lord writes not one word, of course, to recall that less than four months had passed since he had told an almost completely untrue story in Boston, and under three, since Rufus Isaacs in London had wrung from him his answer to Question 6944 that he knew a distress rocket might have been fired. These two basic and incriminating events might never have occurred. Nor, it should be noted, not during all his 84 years — he was 35 at this time — did those two facts apparently ever again enter his consciousness, let alone trouble it. These are the two gravest, albeit silent and absent, matters in this letter; but they are far from being all that must provoke questions about Lord's good faith.

After Stone's misguided, but stubborn, fight to protect his captain as well as himself, one cannot avoid a feeling of contempt at the captain's attempt to shift his responsibility to his subordinate: "I didn't think it possible for any seaman to mistake a Company's signal for a distress signal, so I relied on the officer on watch."

Stone had reported "a" white rocket, and it was Lord himself who had at once initiated the fiction of the company's signal (or signals) by asking: "Is it a company's signal?" to which Stone replied: "I've never seen a company's signal like that." One notes as attempted proof that he had not understood the meaning of the second call the almost jaunty statement: ". . . curiosity to see a vessel pushing through the ice would have taken me on deck." Lest any mitigation of his frivolity be attempted on the ground that he was asleep, we recall Gibson's flat statement that he, Lord, was not asleep — of which statement there is, of course, no mention in this letter. One notes finally Lord's admission that he "was a very poor witness," about which a little will be said shortly.

For the recipients of the letter, the immediate question was whether a copy should be sent to Mersey to read; but Sir Walter Howell wrote to Buxton, who was on holiday, that he was "certainly of opinion that it would be better not. Lord Mersey and his Court have delivered their judgement, and there is an end of the matter as far as they are concerned. I think if you communicated anything now, whether from Capt. Lord or anyone else concerned, it might be misunderstood, and would create a bad precedent . . ."

"I agree. S.B."[4]

That was to be the last word about Lord's first effort to obtain further consideration for his case, and on 29 August Howell signed a letter to Lord, the substantive part of which read: "In reply I fear all I can say is that all the circumstances attending the casualty have formed the subject of a searching investigation by a Court of Inquiry, the Board of Trade would not feel justified in taking any steps with regard to our present statement."[5]

It may be worth observing it had apparently originally been intended by the Board of Trade to send their letter addressed to "Stanley Lord Esq.," and it was only later thoughts which permitted them to accord to Captain Lord the rank to which he was still in law entitled.[6] It has often been said by Lord's supporters that there was "a lawyer's, not a seamen's case" against him, but the fact of the matter is, there was a much stronger feeling of disbelief and hostility toward him among some at least of the seamen who were familiar with the *Californian*. There can be no doubt about the opinions of the assessors at the inquiry, nor about that of Captain A.H.F. Young, the Professional Member of the Marine Department. On 17 August, the latter wrote this memorandum following Lord's letter:

> "in view of the fact that signals of distress were reported to Capt. Lord and no action was taken by him with a view to rendering assistance at the time those signals were made it appears that as the President has decided that he is not to be proceeded against for misdemeanour he has been treated with very great consideration and, I think, any further action is unnecessary."[7]

But Captain Young returned to the subject again in a further note on 2 September:

> "I was not aware until the 13th ultimo that it had been decided not to proceed against Capt. Lord, but I have had the opinion from the first that a special Inquiry shd. have been ordered not only as to his neglect to answer to Distress signals, but also as a consequence of such almost inexplicable neglect, into his competency to continue to act as a master of a British ship. It appears to me also on reading the observations of the Attorney General at the Titanic Inquiry that he was clearly of this opinion. From the point of view of 'gross misdemeanour' — I think an Inquiry should have been held, but as I gather from this paper, that it has been decided by the President no to do so — I cannot well offer any further observations."[8]

Captain Young, Sir Walter Howell (the Assistant Secretary of the Marine Department) and Sir Hubert Llewellyn Smith, who was the Permanent Secretary, all did actually 'offer further observations', and while inclined to lean to the view that there should be no prosecution — "his punishment is already real and very heavy" (Howell);[9] "Capt. Lord's fault carries its own punishment" (Young)[10] — consideration was given to the possibility of proceedings under Section 470 of the Merchant Shipping Act, 1894, because of "any gross act of misconduct" or, by Section 471, for the forfeiture of his certificate through "incompetence or misconduct unfit to discharge his duties." They were afraid* of a public protest if Lord was allowed to go scot free, and it was decided that yet one more opinion should be asked of the Assistant Solicitor, Mr E. Potter.

Potter's views follow:

> "Captain Lord was summoned to appear at the inquiry as a witness but was not made a Party to the proceedings. On the 7th day of the hearing Mr. Robertson Dunlop asked the Commissioner for leave to appear under Rule 5 of the Shipping Casualties &c. Rules on behalf of the Owners, Master and Officers of the 'CALIFORNIAN' but the Commissioner declined to deal with the application at that time and said that if anything required explanation he would let Mr. Dunlop know.
>
> "In fact, however, thereafter Mr. Dunlop cross examined the witnesses and at the close of the Inquiry addressed the Commissioner on behalf of his Clients so that for practical purposes though possibly not technically, it may be said that Captain Lord became a Party to the proceedings under Rule 5. But the most that the Court could find was that lives might have been saved if the 'CALIFORNIAN' had gone to the rescue earlier. They could not find as a certainty that lives would have been saved. The Inquiry was into the loss of the 'TITANIC' and loss of life from her. The Court could not find that the loss of the 'TITANIC' and the loss of life from her was caused by 'the wrongful act or default' of Captain Lord (Section 470-(1)(a) and there was therefore in my opinion no power to deal with his certificate.
>
> "It seems to me to be very doubtful whether the conduct of Captain Lord comes within the contemplated meaning of the words 'misconduct rendering him unfit to discharge his duties' in Section 471 (1) which is the Section giving the Board power to order a L.M.B. [Local Marine Board] Inquiry. But apart from that to prove that Captain Lord had been guilty of 'a gross act of misconduct' it would be necessary to show that he had knowledge of the events, was a free agent, and notwithstanding this, acted or refrained from acting deliberately, and I do not think this could be done on the evidence given at the Inquiry before the Wreck Commissioner."[11]

This opinion, dated September 17th, was neither very valorous nor very clear. If a successful defence to a prosecution under Section 470 has to depend on proof that lives were actually saved, then it would seem to follow that a failure to save life, however expert and brave the attempt, must ensure an unfavourable verdict; which is clearly absurd. On the other hand, under Section 6 of the 1911 Act, there was an obligation on a master of attempt "so far as he can do so without serious danger to his own vessel, her crew and passengers (if any) [to] render assistance to every person . . . who is found at sea in danger of being lost . . ." The words used by Mr. Potter to indicate the impossibility of proving against Captain Lord under Section 470 'knowledge of events,' 'being a free agent' and 'notwithstanding this, acted or refrained from acting deliberately' are all contradicted by the events themselves that occurred, and it is difficult to see what defence there would have been to an indictment based on Section 6 of the 1911 Act. Captain Lord admittedly knew of *a* rocket — *res ipsa loquitur* — "the thing speaks for itself" — and he did nothing whatever about it, although there was nothing on earth to have stopped his finding out why it was being fired, if he had cared to use his wireless; but

---

* "In any case we shall be attacked for acting in far less clear cases than this, and in letting Capt. Lord hold his Certif . . . WJH, Aug. 30, 12" – M 23448/12 (in MT9/920/6).

even that was not the end of it. A jury might very well have believed the evidence of Stone and Gibson that Lord had been told of eight rockets, not one rocket. Moreover, a prosecution determined to get all the facts would have obtained statements from some of the reporters in Boston, who had been metaphorically buried under Lord's avalanche of falsehood, with a view to their giving evidence at the Old Bailey in London. There is no reason to doubt that the American Government would have given any necessary help, and whether or not Captain Lord had chosen again to give evidence, it is exceedingly difficult to imagine any convincing explanation he, or anybody on his behalf, could have devised in answer to the unequivocal and deadly testimony that could have been offered to an Old Bailey jury by those Boston reporters.

In his letter to the Assistant Secretary, above, Lord wrote: "I am told that at the inquiry I was a very poor witness," . . . which was true; and, in his letter to the Press: ". . . a nautical man rarely makes a good witness," which was untrue. If Captain Lord had been a more practised offender, he might have refused to give evidence at all. On the other hand, if he had been innocent, he would probably also have given evidence but told the truth, in which case he might well have been a much better witness, "nautical man" though he was. Captain Lord made "a very poor witness" because he gave the strong impression of frequently not telling the truth, even though the inquiry never heard a report of the most direct and impudent falsehoods he had uttered. Had the Boston witnesses been heard and Stone's and Gibson's secret statements been known, his situation would have been immeasurably more difficult, as he would have had to find a credible answer to the simple and comprehensive question: "Why did you say that no signals of any kind were seen and that your Chief Officer was on watch at the time and could corroborate you?"

Within the Board of Trade itself, however, the general opinion leaned toward mercy. Nor, with its own questionable record on safety regulations, was this tendency at all inappropriate. It was widely felt that Lord's act had brought its own punishment, and although it may be that the future was to show that common opinion had exaggerated both the extent and endurance of Captain Lord's own sensitivity or sense of responsibility, the issue of prosecuting him finally faded away when the last Second Divisions Clerk, A.D. Donald, added his initials to the file on 2 October 1912.

Long before this date arrived, Buxton had insisted that the Board issue to masters and others a notice implementing Mersey's Recommendation No. 22, that is a reminder of their obligations to render assistance to vessels in distress. In August, accordingly, Handbill No. 310 was published by the Board of Trade and widely distributed. It read as follows:

"HANDBILL NO. 310
NOTICE TO
MASTERS OF VESSELS

The report by Lord Mersey on the loss of the S.S. 'Titanic' contains the following recommendation:-

'That the attention of Masters of vessels should be drawn by the Board of Trade to the effect that under the Maritime Conventions Act, 1911, it is a misdemeanour not to go to the relief of a vessel in distress when possible to do so.'

In calling the attention of Masters of vessels to the above recommendation the

Board of Trade desire to lay stress on the fact that it has always been the duty of masters to proceed to the assistance of a vessel in distress, and this duty exists apart from the statutory obligation placed upon masters by the Maritime Conventions Act passed last year. The Board do not doubt that apart from the Statute Law, such services will be rendered in the future as in the past in accordance with the best traditions of the Merchant Service.

At the same time the Board wish, in accordance with the recommendation, to draw the attention of masters and other persons in charge of vessels to the effect of the recent enactment; and to point out that, should they fail in carrying out their duty in this respect, they render themselves liable (as the offence is punishable as a misdemeanour) to punishment under Section 680 of the Merchant Shipping Act, 1894, by fine or imprisonment for two years with or without hard labour.

WALTER J. HOWELL,
Assistant Secretary,
Marine Department.
Board of Trade,
August, 1912.
M.22,457/1912
Handbill No. 310"

Meanwhile, for the next several months, Lord was corresponding with Rostron, Lightoller, and others in an attempt to obtain information from them to show that the *Californian* was not the guilty ship. It says much for the candour and compassion of Rostron and Lightoller particularly that they received his approach with the greatest sympathy and with any scrap of fact or with any suggestion that seemed likely to be helpful to him.

"Dear Lord," Rostron wrote[12] to him from the *Carpathia* in New York on 5 September 1912, "I was very glad to hear from you and hope things are looking brighter for you."

Unfortunately, the Rostron family have no knowledge of Lord's letter to their father. A good deal of its contents, however, can be inferred from the remainder of Rostron's reply:

"I'm sorry," it continues, "I cannot give you any detailed description of the two steamers seen by me.* All I know — one, a four-masted one-funnel steamer dodging about. I suppose amongst the ice to Nd.; the other, two masts and one funnel coming from W. to E. straight on his course. I did not see colour of funnels or notice anything which might distinguish either. You can imagine I was quite busy enough.

"Can't you get your position when stopped and get approx. courses you steered with speed, to where we met?

"I'll do what I can, but you know I can only say what I know and what I saw, and 'pon my word it isn't much and I'm sorry too.

"If you can suggest anything I should be happy to help you, but you see I know so little and have said all I really do know too.

"Anyway, Lord, you have my sympathies. I understand more than I can say especially about the calling business.§

---

*   *c.f.* Rostron's affidavit.

§   Rostron had told his younger shipmate Ivan Thompson, later Sir Ivan Thompson, that the reference to "the calling business" related to Lord's letter to him in which Lord had said "It would not have happened if I had been called properly." (P.I. from Sir Ivan Thompson; 22 November 1963.)

"I may state *for your private information* [emphasis in original] I have had quite long talks with Captain Bartlett* about you.

"With best regards,
Yours sincerely,
(Signed) A.H. Rostron"

It is poignant and significant that in these early months, when the tragedy was still fresh, all the seamen concerned trust Lord and took him on his own terms; none gave even a hint of any doubts of his innocence. What was going on in Lord's own mind at this period must remain guesswork; but it can be only shocking and illuminating to ask what would have been the reaction of Rostron and Lightoller, if Lord at this time had repaid their own frankness by saying to them (if he still remembered!):
"I lied at Boston, when I proclaimed to the world that we saw no signals of any kind, and invoked the corroboration of my Chief Officer to confirm my lie"; and "I confessed to the Attorney-General in London I knew that at least one distress rocket might have been fired."

A new factor appeared in his problem with the dispatch on 6 August of a letter [13] to him, quite unexpectedly, from Quebec by W.H. Baker, an officer in the Canadian Pacific *Empress of Britain*. Baker wrote that he had been moved into the *Mount Temple* at the last minute on her homeward voyage after the *Titanic,* and had heard aboard the Canadian ship an account of many startling things that were said to have occurred on the fatal night:

> "The officers and others told me what they had seen on that eventful night when the *Titanic* went down, and from what they said, they were from ten to fourteen miles from her when they saw her signals. I gather from what was told me that the Captain seemed afraid to go through the ice, although it was not so very thick. They told me they not only saw her deck lights, but several green lights between them and what they thought was the *Titanic*. There were two loud reports heard, which they said must have been the "finale" of the *Titanic;* this was some time after sighting her, I gathered. The Captain said at the inquiry in Washington, that he was 49 miles away, but the officers state that he was not more than 14 miles off. I must tell you the men were fearfully indignant that they were not then called upon to give evidence at the time . . . These fellows must feel sorry for you knowing that you could not, in the face of this have been the mystery ship . . ."

As a result of this letter, Baker put Lord into touch with Notley, the Third (or Fourth, according to Lord) Officer of the *Mount Temple*.[14] Notley had lunch with Lord, confirmed Baker's story, and offered to give evidence if called upon, but would not volunteer to do so. Lord promptly animated his MMSA, and by 27 August, the Secretary, C.P. Grylls, was writing Sir Walter Howell a letter "in strict confidence" giving the names of various *Mount Temple* officers (but not, incidentally, Notley's), from whom it was suggested that statements should be taken when the vessel next arrived in London.

Lord's supporters in later years themselves publicly admitted this attempt to shift the blame from the *Californian* and Captain Lord to the *Mount Temple* and Captain Moore was "unfortunate". Moore and the Marconi operator Durrant both published denials when the ship arrived in St John, N.B., that she had seen any signals from the *Titanic*.[15] Moore, too, later gave extremely

* Charles Alfred Bartlett, Marine Superintendant, White Star Line, Liverpool.

long and detailed evidence in Washington, supported by a very complete wireless PV,[16] and received a warm compliment from Senator Smith for his "care and solicitude" for his 1,461 passengers and the property in his care.[17] He also gave evidence in London, supported there by Durrant as well.

The results of an attempt by *The New York Tribune* at St John as early as 25 April to secure confirmation of the reports about the *Mount Temple's* having seen rockets or other signals were curious: it was said that Second Officer Heald "could tell a lot, but it was not his business to talk"; Dr Bailey said he "was not a navigating officer, and he was in no position to say anything"; and, once more, Third Officer Notley, "who was said to have been on watch, could not be found."[18] Moreover, at no time while the *Mount Temple* evidence was being given in Washington or London was a single word of protest or contradiction raised by any passenger or member of the crew. Unless the evidence of Captain Moore and Durrant in Washington and London was, in Sir R. Ellis Cunliffe's phrase of 6 November, "a tissue of lies",* Lord's contention that the *Mount Temple* was between the *Californian* and the vessel sending up rockets was "utterly impossible". Likewise, the story alleged to have been attributed to the passengers and certain members of the *Mount Temple's* crew must also have been without foundation.[19] It must be remembered that, unlike the various editions and impressions of Lord's story, Captain Moore's evidence, although more detailed in Washington, was the same in London, and the very complete PV first presented by him before the Senate committee, if it was a forgery, had already been smoothly and expertly concocted by Durrant as early as 26 April, when Moore left for Washington.

In addition to the MMSA,[20] the Leyland solicitors, Hill, Dickinson & Co.,[21] and Lord's M.P., A.H. Gill,[22] attempted to implicate the *Mount Temple;* but when potential witnesses from that ship were asked to stand up and be heard, there was a complete and sudden silence. It is not surprising that in one of the *Mount Temple* files opened in 1964, Cunliffe was also found to have written as early as 2 September: "If there be anything in these allegations it is a matter for grave comment that those who make them have not hitherto communicated with the Board of Trade."[23] Nor did any one of them, passenger or seaman, do so, in 1912 or ever thereafter.

Nevertheless, was the *Mount Temple* story true or false?

Its origin is obscure; but so far as it concerned the passengers, at least, it seems to have had some connection with a dispute in which a certain Dr Quitzrau or Quitzman became involved.[24] Holder of a steerage ticket, he was given a Second Class cabin because of the crowded steerage, but when found on the Saloon deck and asked what class ticket he held and replying, "Steerage", he was ordered from that deck. Later, on the night of the disaster, the doctor, whose confidence in Captain Moore's seamanship clearly disappeared simultaneously with his own exit from the Saloon, "was awakened by a sudden stopping of the machinery . . . was told that the *Titanic* had struck an iceberg and was sinking, and that the light of her distress signals had been seen." The doctor, likewise, was also for some reason unavailable to give evidence.

It seems possible that observers in the *Mount Temple*, when she had arrived on the scene of the *Titanic's* given position, and was stopped there by ice, may have seen the green flares that Boxhall was sending up, and perhaps even the lights of the approaching *Carpathia* as well. Such may have been whatever material basis there might have been for the entire episode.

As a matter of logic, the last word on the *Mount Temple* must be the deci-

---

* *See* Appendix F.

sive fact, that even if the case against her were put at its highest, that she was the steamer seen by the *Titanic,* of which there is in fact not a shred of evidence, even adding her to the scene cannot subtract the *Californian.*

Going back to 1912 and 1913, Lord made a further effort to persuade the Board of Trade to reopen his case on 8 August 1913. He then sent them the four anonymous articles entitled "A Miscarriage of Justice", by A.M. Foweraker, the solicitor of Carbis Bay, Cornwall, and subsequent correspondence in the April, May, June and July 1913 issues of *The Nautical Magazine.* Lord pointed out that he had no acquaintance with Foweraker; yet this file is found to contain an ineffable memorandum by Second Class Clerk A. Donald, which includes these words: "It is claimed that there was no acquaintance between Capt. Lord and the writer of these articles, but it is plain that the writer deliberately set out to clear Capt. Lord."[25] One wonders why Mr Donald believed Lord had sent them to the Board.

Earlier references to this series have already credited Albert Moulton Foweraker with the origin of the "4 Ship Theory", but he had contrived it without any new evidence whatever. The heart of his defence of Lord was that the inquiry had come to the wrong conclusion on the evidence. At the same time, profoundly enmeshed in the technical thickets of navigation composing this argument lay the implication that no blame attached to Lord, if it had been proved that the rockets seen by the *Californian* were not those of the *Titanic.* It remained for a contributor, who signed himself, "MASTER MARINER (RETIRED)", to bring to the surface and fittingly deal with this bold and irresponsible notion:

> "Sir: I have read the articles which have appeared in your last three numbers *re* the *Californian* and the *Titanic.* It has always appeared to me, and to many others with whom I have discussed the subject, to be a mere matter of detail whether those on board the *Californian* saw the *Titanic* or they did not? They evidently saw a vessel of some sort firing rockets, a signal of distress. It was the duty of the *Californian* to have gone to her assistance. They did nothing! Whose fault it was is only known to Captain Lord and his officers. They might not have been able to get near her on account of the ice, but they might have *tried.* There is no dispute, I think, about their having seen a vessel firing distress signals."[26]

It is to Foweraker's credit that having been thus directly challenged, he showed himself at least on one occasion in a more humane category than Lord's customary supporters by admitting in a letter [27] in the following issue of the magazine, that if the *Californian* had seen a ship firing distress signals, she should have tried to get to her.

With that admission, whatever moral basis the articles may have had collapsed. But in addition, as mentioned already, other weaknesses honeycombed this series, which were of a specious, but actually hollow, complexity. An admission was made, without any attempt at explanation, that "something unusual was taking place in regard to the lights of this vessel" seen by Stone and Gibson — the lights they said "looked queer".[29] Mr Foweraker also found "it difficult to account for her moving from a position S.E. true from the *Californian* to disappear in the S.S.W. true without at any time showing her green light, unless she went astern."

In the result, after a series of official-to-official memoranda of no very profound kind, the Board of Trade, in the person of Ernest J. Moggridge, wrote to Lord once more on 4 September 1913: ". . . I am directed by the Board of Trade to state that they have carefully considered the statement to which you refer, but, as you were informed in August last year, they are unable to re-open the matter."

By this time, Lord had started on a new career. As the result of the intervention of Frank Strachan, of Brunswick, Georgia, the United States agent for the Leyland Line, in February, 1913, Lord entered the employment of Nitrate Producers' Steam Ship Co. Ltd., owned by Lawther Latta & Co. Ltd., at a salary of £20 per month, with a monthly bonus of £5, and received the command of their steamship *Anglo-Saxon*, 4,263 gross tons.[30]

Strachan, said Lord, had not believed the charge against him, and Lawther Latta & Co., in contrast with Captain Young's question as to whether Lord was fit to hold his certificate as a British sea captain, wrote this on 21 January 1913, in reply to Lord's application:

"Dear Sir,
We have to acknowledge receipt of your straightforward and frank letter of yesterday, the tone of which we appreciate, and naturally, we observe it is possible you may not have had a proper opportunity of setting out your case. So far as our recollection of the examination goes, the chief point against you was not so much as to whether it was your command that was nearest the *Titanic,* but the alleged fact that rockets were seen by your officers, that you were called, but remained callous to the call. Be that so or not, the circumstances were altogether exceptional, and not such as it appears to us sufficiently serious to condemn the reputation of any man . . ."[31]

This letter is worth a moment's reflection. What, one wonders, would the Messrs Lawther Latta & Co. consider "sufficiently serious to condemn the reputation of any man". Barratry, perhaps, the misappropriation of a cargo of nitrate? Lawther Latta were generally known as a very hard firm, as may be guessed from their reaction to Lord's own letter to them and their verdict on his conduct.[32]

Lord invariably maintained that whatever their reputation may have been, he himself had never been treated so well. Certainly, Stanley Lord and John Latta, two men who knew their jobs, got on admirably.

The war came in 1914 and Lord served at sea throughout. He transported horses, took part in a practice for an early form of combined operations, and in the many dangers of the war at sea. Although one of the junior masters, in 1916 Latta had Lord supervise the fitting out of his largest ship, the *Anglo Chilian*, 9,079 gross tons, and gave him the command. Lord was chased by submarines, but never caught.[33]

And the war faded the *Titanic*.

". . . the aftermath of the *Titanic* Inquiry in those days was not such as to affect me personally or professionally in any way, I decided to let the matter drop," he declared in his 1959 affidavit.

So time passed. The memorials to the *Titanic* engineers could be seen in Southampton and on Pierhead in Liverpool and in London and to others in New York; but the only thing most people vaguely remembered now about the *Titanic* was her name and the iceberg, and how she was trying to break the record, and went down with all hands, and a second cousin of a friend of Shirley's niece was a baby who was saved in the last lifeboat, and Captain Jones (or, Smith??) put his megaphone to his white beard and shouted, "Ladies and children first! Be British!" and then shot himself, and everybody joined hands and sang "Nearer, My God, To Thee".

Lord's indifference inevitably increased. He was happy and prosperous and, of course, innocent. For the comparatively few, with a real interest, when everything less had faded from the memory, the plain, incontrovertible and essential facts about him and his *Californian* remained: eight distress rockets had been seen and eight distress rockets had been ignored. As Lord settled down and reconciled himself to unquestioned innocence and obscurity, so, gradually perhaps but certainly, did those plain facts of the rockets tell everything about the *Californian* for all, his early sympathizers and his critics alike. Lightoller and Rostron both in terms repudiated their initial support of Captain Lord.[34]

In March 1927, after 14 years of service with Lawther Latta, Lord was compelled to retire because of trouble with his eyesight.[35] He was then only 49 years old. On 17 July 1928, Sir John Latta wrote him a testimonial, in which he said: ". . . he had our entire confidence, and we regard him as one of the most capable Commanders we have ever had."[36]

The sailor was home from the sea.

Sources

1   [MT 9/920/6] M 22457.
2   Ibid.
3   [MT 9/920/M6] M 23448; or published in 'The "Californian" Incident'.
4   [Ibid.] M 22457/12.
5   [MT 9/920/M6] M 23448; or published in 'The "Californian" Incident'.
6   Ibid.
7   Ibid.
8   Ibid.
9   Ibid.; M 22457/12.
10 [MT 9/920/M6] M 23448; or published in 'The "Californian" Incident'.
11 Ibid.
12 'The "Californian" Incident', MMSA, [March 1962], Exhibit W, p. 40.
13 Ibid., Exhibit R, p. 35.
14 Capt Lord's Affidavit, Appendix C.
15 *Boston Post*, 26 April, p. 6.
16 US 769, *seq.*

17 *New York Tribune*, 25 April, p. 1.
18 Ibid.
19 [MT 9/920/6] M 31921/12.
20 [Ibid.] M 25699.
21 [Ibid.] M 26040.
22 'The "Californian" Incident', p. 43; contains the B.O.T. letter, returning letters left by Gill, rejecting exculpation of *Californian*, but undertaking to examine any *Mount Temple* statements obtained by Lord.
23 [MT 9/920/6] M 25699.
24 *New York Tribune*, 26 April, p. 1.
25 [MT 9/920/6] M 24407/13.
26 *Nautical Magazine*, August 1913, p. 198.
27 Ibid., September 1913, p. 304, "Correspondence", letter from "The Writer".
28 Ibid., June 1913, Vol.

LXXXIX, No. 6, p. 583.
29 [MT 9/920/6] M 244407/1913.
30 Capt. Lord's Affidavit, Appendix C; letter, Lawther Latta: Lord, 30 January 1913 ('The "Californian" Incident', p. 46); 'Lloyd's Register', 1913.
31 "The "Californian" Incident', Exhibit EE. 2., p. 46.
32 'The "Californian" Incident', 1962, pp. 46-48 inclusive.
33 P.I.; *Commutator* of 'Titanic Enthusiasts of America', September 1964.
34 P.I., confirmed by some published sources, e.g. C.H. Lightoller, '"Titanic" and Other Ships'.
35 Capt. Lord's Affidavit, Appendix C.
36 'The "Californian" Incident', Exhibit FF. 3, p. 48.

Chapter 18

"The Norwegian Fairy Story"

"I am Lord of the *Californian*!"

The authoritatively[1] and, no doubt, also characteristically expressed words of introduction, fell flat.

The tall, spare old man stood in the General Secretary's office in the Mercantile Marine Service Association at Nautilus House in Liverpool. He was now 81 years old, and behind his glasses there was an expression of half-amusement at the astonishment he evidently believed his mere appearance in these surroundings was creating. For many years, he had been living across the river in happy retirement with his wife and son, and, since she had died, at least contentedly with him alone. He had shown no interest for a long time in the Association (though his membership had never lapsed), nor indeed with anything to do with that old story. In fact, he had not even told his son what he intended doing; nor had he made an appointment, so it was clear what a sensation his bare pronunciation of the two names, "Lord" and "*Californian*" must inevitably cause in this well-informed place. In view of the sequel, it was ironical, it did not; but the simple fact, although an odd one, is that Leslie Harrison, then the General Secretary, had never heard a word about Captain Lord or the *Californian*. As Mr Harrison, like any holder of a master's certificate, even of his generation, born only in 1912, knew at least a little about the *Titanic,* that made it extraordinary too. The gap in his knowledge was swiftly repaired.

Captain Lord had been provoked into this surprising and unprecedented expedition by the film made from Walter Lord's book of the same name, *A Night to Remember.* Whether the old seaman had made an exception to his rule and read the book is not clear. He claimed to have thought very little of it, but he was not the most objective critic of *Titanic* literature. He certainly did not see the film which, in dealing with the *Californian* episode, departed from the book by embroidering the incident with various inaccuracies;[*] but the reports that must have come to him either personally or through the newspapers, of which he was a vast reader, were enough to decide him, after some 45 years, to try once again to have the Finding of Fact by Lord Mersey against him reversed.[2]

Mr Harrison was at first sceptical, although it seems to have been the last time he ever did have any doubts. At the outset, even before he had ascertained whether the MMSA still had any of the *Californian* papers in its morgue,

---

* e.g. by referring to the non-existent passengers aboard the *Californian,* and showing Captain Lord under bedclothes.

he felt bound to tell Lord that his society was constantly receiving similar requests for their help to try to reverse ancient grievances, and almost as often being compelled through the conviction that there was really no case, to turn the applicant away. He would as usual, he said, have to be convinced beyond doubt that Lord had a genuine and serious complaint. In spite of the blitz and the long interval of inactivity, it was soon found that the Association had in a file of its magazine, *The Reporter,* the long letter from A.M. Foweraker, 'Under the Wheels of the Juggernaut'. Very soon after that, Mr Harrison was profoundly convinced that Captain Lord was indeed the victim of injustice.

The legal authority for Captain Lord's claim was thought to be found within the Merchant Shipping Act, 1894, which was, and until the passing of the succeeding act of 1970, remained the basic code of law governing the working lives of British merchant seamen. The relevant portion of the statute read as follows:

"Rehearing of inquiries and investigations.

Section 475. The Board of Trade may, in any case where under this part of this Act a formal investigation as aforesaid into a shipping casualty . . . has been held, order the case to be-heard either generally or as to any part thereof, and shall do so —
(a) if new and important evidence which could not be produced at the investigation or inquiry has been discovered; or
(b) if for any reason there has in their opinion been ground for suspecting that a miscarriage of justice has occurred.

It perhaps should be said here that, unlike Mr Harrison, I first heard of Captain Lord and the *Californian* at the time of the *Titanic* tragedy, and since becoming generally familiar with the story at the age of maturity, I have had no doubt of the justice of the findings of the American and British inquiries about Captain Lord. Nevertheless, since beginning the research for this book, if the results had justified it, I should not have hesitated publicly to change my opinion. A fair claim may therefore be made to scrutinize the campaign for Captain Lord undertaken by the MMSA, which has become part of the *Californian* story; but the subject is far more important than, and goes much beyond, personal considerations.

As in similar democratic attempts by an organization at openly trying to change public opinion about a particular political issue or on an alleged case of injustice, the actual work is necessarily delegated by the mass of the members to a few executives. This must be more necessary than usual with such a body as the MMSA, comprising some thousands of master mariners in command, who spend most of their lives at sea. It is very probable in fact that only a minute number can even have read the complete evidence and other relevant material relating to the *Californian* alone, let alone to the whole *Titanic* disaster. In such circumstances, the membership, while giving the honour and the prestige of their professional reputation to the support of the campaign, had the right to rely on the good faith and the sense of responsibility of those acting in their name in what they considered a good cause.

If actual knowledge of the case among professional seagoing officers was so minute, it is easy to believe that ignorance of Captain Lord and the *Californian* among the general public was virtually complete. Starting with that condition and constantly recurring public forgetfulness, there was from the beginning the opportunity of taking advantage of both, but of course a responsibility not to do so. Part of the difficulty of the case was that Lord himself, for decades, had forgotten and buried the fatal fact at the base of his whole case that he had once long ago betrayed his own guilt. In the fight for Captain Lord, during the last 30 years from its inception, its progress was substantially unopposed, and so far as the public were aware, uncontradicted, because uncontradictable.

The lack of knowledge in average readers, however, must surely have prevented them in practice from testing and exposing mistatements repeatedly started and staged by the supporters of Captain Lord.

More important was Mr Harrison's statement, in 'The "Californian" Incident' of March 1962, that it was "impossible" not to believe that Stone and Gibson had seen the *Titanic's* rockets. Thereafter, he never again referred to it, but only — although with a hint of inconsistency — denied they had seen rockets — or the *Titanic's* rockets — or anything but "Roman candle type flares" — or it would seem, anything else the Lordites chose.

The Board of Trade dismissed both the 1965 and 1968 MMSA Petitions, on 8 September 1965 and 26 July 1968 respectively, with a minimum of explanation. Nor did the Board respond to the repeated demands to give specific reasons for their decisions. Possibly they sought to avoid being entangled in a long and irrelevant argument; and the short answer to any issue of "injustice" in Petitions I and II was Captain Lord's own answer to Question 6944. Yet, with the exception of the dismissal of the two petitions, the campaign continued unchecked and almost unquestioned.

To recount, therefore, in some detail one episode of importance largely organized by the Lordites has a threefold purpose. It is an intrinsic part of the narrative; it is further illustrative of their method and technique; and it is an affirmation of principle in protesting at, and thereby publicizing, an act its perpetrators might prefer erased from memory. The word "would" originally stood in place of that "might"; but the resurrection and exploitation of the story in 1968 raised a question about the Lordites' opinion of their handiwork. In any event, here is released this tardy tortoise of truth in the general direction of a flying, repeatedly triumphant, dismissed, but lately reanimated and not entirely forgotten fantasy.

On the night of 19/20 April 1962, soon after the 50th anniversary of the *Titanic,* the BBC reported in their 'Merchant Navy Programme' a Norwegian television feature of the previous Monday, 16 April. The BBC told of a Norwegian ship, which having been poaching seals, came within ten miles of the *Titanic,* saw her rockets, but fearing that these meant that her poaching had been discovered, steamed away without taking action.

Although the BBC for some reason had not mentioned the vessel's name, the original programme had, and this broadcast effected the introduction to England, or perhaps the whole of Britain, of the notorious story of the *Samson.*

The campaign for Captain Lord had got well started with his affidavit in June 1959,* but though Lord himself died early in 1962 in tranquil circumstances, which we shall look at in the final chapter, nothing stayed the struggle to vindicate him. Its whole basis, it was said privately a few days before the annual meeting of the MMSA, might be changed because of the *Samson.* Meanwhile it was still being checked; how much and at what pace, cannot be ascertained, but on 30 April Mr Harrison said: ". . . while, at the moment, I have an open mind on this question, it hardly seems that the Norwegian authorities would broadcast this report unless it had some reliable basis."

---

* *See* Appendix C.

The checking of the *Samson* must have been proceeding quite rapidly, because at the meeting four days later, 4 May 1962, there was a preliminary introduction by way of a press release from the MMSA. Neither the Norwegian broadcast nor the BBC had got the *Samson* into the world Press, but this handout did. Dated 3 May, it opened:

> "In April, 1912, Mr. Henrik Naess (now deceased), First Officer of the Norwegian sealing vessel 'Samson', submitted a confidential report to the Norwegian Consul in Iceland in which he stated that during the night of 14th/15th April [1912], the 'Samson' was operating in the Newfoundland area. During his watch, he sighted 'two big stars' to the south which he thought had a 'peculiar position'. he instructed the masthead lookout to study them through binoculars, and received a report that they were not stars, but 'lanterns and a lot of lights'. A few moments later several rockets were seen and shortly afterwards all the lights suddenly disappeared. Mr. Naess' report continues:-
>
> "'The Samson's position was such that it was feared that we might be taken for violating territorial borders, and the lights out there meant that there were Americans in the neighborhood. When the lights went out this probably meant that we had been observed, the rockets being, maybe, signals to other ships. We therefore changed course and hurried northwards. When dawn came, there was no sign of ships anywhere.'
>
> "After the ship's arrival in Iceland, Mr. Naess learned from a newspaper of the *'Titanic'* disaster. From the 'Samson's' log, he checked that both time, date and position of the disaster coincided with their own observations. His report concludes: 'We now understand the meaning of the lights and rockets we had seen. We had been ten nautical miles away when the 'Titanic' went down. There we were, with our big excellent ship and eight boats in calm, excellent weather. What might we not have done, if we had known? Alas, we had no radio on board.'"

Particulars of the *Samson,* obtained from 'Lloyd's Register' for 1912 and other sources give the following information: the sealer was a wooden bark of 506 tons gross, with auxiliary steam engines. Built in 1885 by Larsen of Arendal, her approximate dimensions were 148' in length, 31' beam, 17' depth. She was registered at Trondhjeim, owned by Acties Salfanger Dpsk. Samson (managers Aug. Fosse), and her master since 1909 had been Captain Carl Johann Ring.* To complete details obtained later: she had three masts, with a single funnel abaft of the mainmast, and a large bowsprit, In 1930, after alteration, she was owned by the Byrd expedition to the Antarctic and she was named City of New York. She stranded off Yarmouth, N.S., on 30 December 1952, and was later burnt out.

The information was derived from the Norwegian Television Authority and was the foundation of the speech made by Mr Harrison at the meeting of the MMSA, where he declared that Naess's report seemed "absolutely authentic", and went on, "If the ship seen from the *Titanic* was in fact the *Samson,* then it is conclusive proof that Captain Lord was indeed the victim of the grossest miscarriage of justice in the history of British marine inquiries." This was 4 May. A little earlier, 16 March, in his article, 'The "Californian" Incident' in *The Merchant Navy Journal,* Mr Harrison said: "... it may well be considered he was the victim ....," etc. This was before the discovery of the *Samson,* and it began to seem that, if that little craft could be proved to have been an "absolutely authentic" caller and walker-out on the *Titanic,* Captain Lord's

* Died 22 June 1918, after his ship, the *Eglantine* was torpedoed in the North Sea.

claim to be the victim of the greatest miscarriage of justice by sea would be strengthened in proportion to the difference between ". . . it may well be considered he was the victim . . . " and ". . . he was indeed the victim . . .".

To an open minded student of the case, it was more difficult to follow how the *Samson* clinched with "conclusive proof the enormity of the alleged injustice done to Captain Lord. No more than the abortive attempt at entangling the *Mount Temple* 50 years earlier, did the *Samson,* even if the story were true, seem to advance Lord's cause by one inch (see Appendix F). Even if the *Samson* saw the rockets, how did that make the *Californian* not see them, or un-see them, whichever be the correct term? And, if that could not be done, how did the *Samson* make Lord a victim of injustice in any degree? The matter has been succinctly put more than once by saying. "Adding the *Mount Temple* (or the *Samson*); or any and every ship from A-Z, for that matter, not excluding the *Flying Dutchman* and the *Mary Celeste*, cannot subtract the *Californian.*"

The pleasure of joining the chorus of congratulations from the men of goodwill to the men of the MMSA on her arrival* was regrettably denied to the rest of us by a built-in, and very obvious puzzle, which had escaped only the press and the BBC. This was the reason for the *Samson's* flight from the *Titanic*. One did not have to be a seaman or a specialist to know that in 1912 territorial waters extended, with rare exceptions, to no more than three miles from the coast.§ Even if the *Samson* had been seal-catching illegally, why should she have been afraid of Americans on the high seas? Americans didn't rule the seas, not in 1912 anyhow (that, "at heaven's command", was still Britain's function, and even the Royal Navy arrogated no police powers to itself in mid-Atlantic). If the *Samson* was within ten miles of the *Titanic,* she must have been hundreds of miles from the nearest land, American or any other. There had been no comment whatever on this elementary point, but the story just didn't make sense.

Who was First Officer Henrik Bergethon Naess, and why had he, and not his skipper, Captain Ring, made the statement? Why had 50 years passed before publication? When had this statement been made, and under what circumstances?

But, above everything, the chief riddle, first assumed to be a newspaper mistake in the first obscure report, had become apparently unanswerable in the specific words of Naess himself in the MMSA release: ". . . it was feared that we might be taken for violating territorial borders." Here was a professional body starting a radical new argument for its cause on the foundation of a document suspect on its face, and endorsing it as apparently "absolutely authentic".

An attempt to obtain some light on the puzzle by examining a copy of the original script of the Norwegian programme was not even acknowledged by the broadcasting authorities in Oslo (Norsk Rikskringkasting); nor was a second; and in the late summer of 1962 a personal inquiry by a friend in Oslo brought the reply that "there was no script".

Time passed. Then, in a notable press release dated 12 March 1963, the MMSA made some memorable announcements. The paper was an extract from

* "At least, it's *new!*" said an un-Californian *Californian* buff happily; but, as Horace wrote, *Fronti nulla fides,* or, "Appearances are deceptive".

§ The territorial waters of Newfoundland, Canada, which were closest to the scene, were, by the Canadian "Customs and Fisheries Protection' Act of 1906, officially set for "three marine miles". For the territorial waters of the United States of America the same rule applied.

the Spring issue of the *Merchant Navy Journal,* dated the next day, 13 March.

First, in his "Command Notes", Mr Harrison declared, ". . . subsequent developments have justified the statement . . ." that Captain Lord "was the victim of the grossest miscarriage of justice", etc. This was now common form, and through the pages of the November 1962 issue of the United States Naval Institute *Proceedings,* Mr Harrison had already introduced it on the Western side of the Atlantic.

In March 1962 Mr Harrison had laid it down that "if the ship seen from the *Titanic* was in fact the *Samson"*, that would be "conclusive proof" Captain Lord was the victim, etc. Now, almost exactly a year later, Captain Lord clinched the title. In their press release, the MMSA announced the decision:

> "We now believe that the ship seen from the sinking *Titanic* was the Norwegian sealer *Samson,* the *Californian* herself being over twenty miles away."

Gone were the "If" and the "Maybe". Within the minor world of the whole *Californian* controversy, here was a momentous announcement. The MMSA had taken its stand. Obviously, their inquiry in Norway had been more fruitful than mine, and as their case was now riveted to the *Samson,* they had obtained the facts to make the story credible by getting rid of its basis, which was First Officer Naess's fantasy about those mid-Atlantic "territorial waters"* But there were other points to be noted in this press release. It was based, of course, on the MMSA's "4-ship theory", and for the time being, let us look at it accordingly.

If it was the *Samson* the *Titanic* saw, we know from Naess, she was ten miles away, and turned northwards. At that time, according to Captain Lord, the *Californian* was under 20 miles from the *Titanic.* How did it happen that the vigilant *Californian* failed to see the *Samson,* after her northward turn, and as she necessarily got closer to the Leyland ship?

Even without that examination, there is one piece of evidence from the *Titanic* herself, which has a decisive bearing on the acceptance by the MMSA of the Norwegian sealer as "The Other Ship". We already know Boxhall described that ship, the steamer, probably with four masts, possibly three, but certainly not two. At another session, he fixed her distance at "about 5 miles, and I arrived at it in this way. The masthead lights of a steamer are required by the Board of Trade regulations to show for 5 miles, and the signals are required to show for 2 miles."[3]

"You could see that distance on such a night as this?" Senator Burton asked.

"I could see quite clearly."

But still the senator was not satisfied, and pressed him.

"You are very sure you are not deceived about seeing these lights?"

"Not at all."

"You saw not only the mast light but the side lights?"

"I saw the side lights," Boxhall answered. "Whatever the ship she was, she had beautiful lights. I think we could see her lights more than the regulation distance, but I do not think we could see them 14 miles."

Anyhow, it is clear the ship the *Titanic* saw must have had better than average lights.

The *Samson* when it comes to her lights, does not match up to Boxhall's picture of his brilliant stranger: the *Samson had oil lamps.* 'Lloyd's Register'

---

* "We worked out the position then [*Titanic,* Lat. 41.46 N.; Long. 50.14 W.] to the best of our ability, and the *Titanic* we found 1,080 miles from New York, about 600 miles from Halifax; . . ." P.A.S. Franklin. (US 175.)

for 1912, and for every issue until 1919-20, which contains her last entry under that name, discloses that even then she did not have electric lights.

Expert nautical opinion is that it would have been impossible for the *Titanic* to have seen the *Samson* at ten miles. At five miles, on a clear night (as it was), it is said, it might have been possible to see white lights from her, or several white lights seeming to be one, but neither of her sidelights, green or red, could have been seen.

"The *Titanic* did not see the *Samson!*" So say the seamen.

Without going further, this might seem to put paid to the pretensions of the *Samson;* but we shall look further.

As for the hypothetical ship — not, of course, the *Titanic* — seen by the *Californian,* she was, according to this press release, "most probably on passage to the westward. On encountering a belt of ice, some four or five miles wide, which lay in a north/south direction in the vicinity of 50 degrees W "she turned to the northward. Proceeding up the edge of the icefield, she sighted the *Californian,* lying stopped slightly on her port bow. After approaching to within four or five miles the stranger also stopped, heading ENE'ly, at approximately 11.40 p.m. apparent time ship."

Now this short passage is an attempt to defuse, so to speak, the explosive quality of the *Californian's* own evidence about the approach of the ship she saw.

That ship was surely on passage to the westward, just as the *Titanic* was, because Captain Lord himself saw her green light, as she came up closer in the southward. Groves, Stone, Gibson and Lord himself later all saw her red light — and never again her green — after she stopped. This meant she had then turned to starboard, or to the north, or even anywhere east of north. There was no evidence whatever that she had turned to the northward, as asserted here, before she stopped. Why, then, was it said? The answer is, the *Titanic* also turned north, or even headed east, after she stopped as well, and this might distract the reader's mind from the *Samson.*

It is also stated that after this oncoming ship turned to the northward, "she sighted the *Californian*". One asks, what is the basis for this statement. If the ship was the *Titanic,* the complaint of Mr Harrison is that she didn't see the *Californian;** if the ship was the one-eyed tramp put forward for the defence, one is tempted to ask for the source of this information.

"At about 1 a.m.," it is said, "the stranger got under way, *turning to star-board* [emphasis added], and on a SSW'ly course, steamed slowly into the icefield . . ."

We already know that neither Stone nor Gibson, the only witnesses, saw her turn to starboard; and also, that as far back as 1913, that very failure of hers to turn to starboard or to port, had shaken even A.M. Foweraker, "unless she went astern" (for eight miles, according to Captain Lord). (See Diagram 14). Mr Padfield, two years after their press release, in 1965, was also to find this "difficult".

So far, that little matter of the rockets had somehow not yet been mentioned. It was to provide the occasion for a notorious début in print, if not in reality.

"Between approximately 12.45 and 1.45 she ['the stranger'] *may have fired* [emphasis added] eight white Roman candle type flares, the stars from which rose [not, e.g.'may have risen'] only to half masthead height."

Stone and Gibson, together, certainly saw eight "objects" — let us call them — fired; but yet there seems to be a feeling of doubt in the above state-

---

* Perhaps a distinction is made between "sighting" and "seeing" a ship; an indulgence, that is, in the *Californian* casuistry introduced by Captain Lord, who agreed that the *Titanic* was "near us", but would not admit she was "not far".

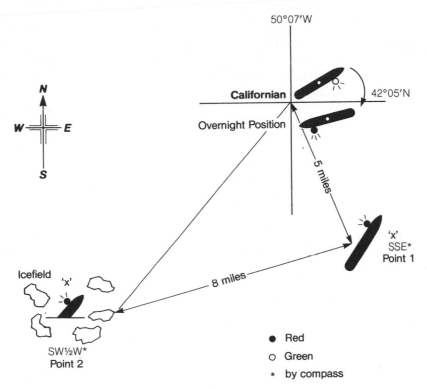

Diagram 14. Captain Lord's story of a mystery steamer

Using only Captain Lord's data, this is the ship seen from the Californian, *bearing SSE, five miles away (Point 1). Here, as Stone and Gibson watched, she fired eight rockets, and from here, Stone reported and Lord repeated, she steamed, for no discernible reason, into the icefield and out of sight, bearing SW¹/₂W (Point 2). It will be noticed, to have got there, she must have turned, but we know from Stone and Gibson, who only saw her red, and never her green light, she did not turn. Hence she must have steamed stern first, again for no discernible reason, and, by Captain Lord's calculation, she steamed no less than eight miles to get to Point 2. Alternatively, after firing her eight rockets, she never moved at all, before she "disappeared" — which, however, is to adopt the story of Gibson, the only other eyewitness who testified. Gibson's story of the steamer which didn't move or turn, of course, fits the facts — or the* Titanic.

ment. On the other hand, only Stone remarked, and not before one month after the event, that they had gone "only to half masthead height"; but even though Mr Harrison evidently believed they may not have been fired at all, he had no doubt whatever they didn't get up very high.

So, this "little book" was ready to go out into the world and make its case. How it would fare would soon be known. Some months earlier it had been announced that the BBC were to broadcast on a national programme a radio documentary on Captain Lord's case. It was during the preparation of this programme eventually called 'The Other Ship', that Mr Beesley was visited by Mr Harrison and a Mr Stanley Williamson of the BBC,[4] and strongly urged by the former to alter certain passages in his book, written 50 years previously. Incidentally, this also proved to be a preliminary stage in the Petition of 1968, and no doubt also constituted part of what was described in 'The

Other Ship' as "four or five years of exhaustive enquiries".

'The Other Ship' was broadcast on 26 March 1963, by the BBC Home Service in a 45-minute series called 'Trial By Inquiry'. The authors were Arthur Swinson and Stanley Williamson, the latter being also the Producer. "Research" was credited to Leslie Harrison. The series had little regard for public inquiries as a means of discovering truth.

Although other points about the *Californian,* discussed elsewhere in this book, were mentioned, the origin of the piece was, of course, the discovery of the *Samson.* All the characters were given their real names.

The programme opened with a speech taken from the Association's *Samson* handout: "In April, 1912, Mr. Henrick [*sic*] Naess . . . made a confidential report," etc. Immediately there followed the now notorious words of Naess, "The *Samson's* position was such that it was feared we might be taken for violating territorial waters, . . ."* Two more speeches, and Naess was abeam of what probably was the M.M.S.A.'s favourite line in all literature: "We had been 10 nautical miles away when the *Titanic* went down."[5]

At this very early stage in the programme, listeners must have sat up with a jerk, their brows puckered, their scepticism aroused, every one of those hundreds or thousands or millions in 1963 recalling how the *Titanic* in 1912 had foundered hundreds of miles from land.

There is no need to follow 'The Other Ship', point by point, along her 45-minute passage on the air waves. Gibson, whose evidence had destroyed Captain Lord and sunk the *Californian,* and would have sunk the *Samson* too, naturally made no appearance, and his name was scarcely mentioned. A good deal of space was given to the rockets, but of some thousands of questions asked of the *Californian* witnesses at both inquiries, undoubtedly the single most important of them all, the shattering Question 6944, was just left out.[6] Even Lightoller — of all men! — was used to argue Lord's case by describing the nature and method of using modern distress rocket signals, commonly still called "rockets";[7] but omitted was Lightoller's other swift-following answer, ". . . there is no ship allowed on the high seas to fire a rocket or anything resembling a rocket unless she requires assistance." Instead:[8] "In a recent interview, recorded at his home in Northern Ireland, Captain Alec Kane, an acquaintance of Captain Lord, discussed the question:

> *KANE*: Oh yes, yes, during the night there were a whole lot of rockets fired but everybody knows that in those days firing of rockets was a practice among merchant seamen. All the Atlantic shipping lines had rockets of their own to identify themselves by sea. They used to say two liners passing in the Atlantic could only recognise each other if these rockets were fired.
> *NARRATOR*: So the rockets which Stone saw could well have been 'company's signals'. . . ."[9]

Even without saying, "Flags-? Wireless, Captain-?" the reader who has read the detailed analysis of company signals in Chapter 5, will realize it is no exaggeration to say there is scarcely a word of truth in the verbatim extract quoted above.

Much was made of the *Titanic's* alleged wrong position. Rostron's affidavit that he did not see the *Californian* at five o'clock was quoted,[10] but not his four-times repeated statement that the *Titanic's* position was "correct"; nor Captain Lord's own repeated statement to the same effect. Not a hint either that almost

---

* The press release had had, ". . . *territorial* borders".

exactly a year before, Mr Harrison himself had written — and no apology is made for quoting it again — "It is impossible to escape the conclusion that some, or all, of the rockets [Stone and Gibson] saw originated from the *Titanic.*" To have resurrected that buried admission would have required less than ten minutes of "exhaustive enquiries", but it might have confused even this most marine-minded of radio audiences, as, most certainly, they would have been puzzled and made uneasy, by the strange sight of the "queer lights". So the audience were spared that knowledge too; but, as has been said, one can't include everything.

'The Other Ship' was a resounding success, and was repeated on 8 April and 27 September in that same year, 1963.

"The B.B.C. broadcast," wrote Mr Harrison early in 1964, "marked the turning of the tide, so far as the legend of the *Californian* is concerned."

Still more aware of the "territorial waters" than of the turning of any tide, my own inquiries continued, first to Iceland, and later to Norway, for any information about the visit of the *Samson* in 1912; and for confirmation of the existence of the "Confidential report to the Norwegian Consul in Iceland" by First Officer Naess.

"... about the sealer *Samson* ... So far I have heard nothing and as to Reykjavik, I have closely examined the Harbour list for April 1912 but there is no mention of *Samson* ..."

So wrote Hr Lárus Sigurbjörnsson, Librarian and Archivist of the City Council of Reykjavik, to me on 12 May 1964.

An inquiry to the Norwegian Embassy in Iceland was passed to Oslo, and on 25 June 1964, the Norwegian Embassy in London wrote,

"... The material in the Foreign Office archives was some time ago, in co-operation with the Norwegian State Broadcasting Corporation, thoroughly investigated, but no information relating to the movements of the Norwegian ship 'Samson' at the time of the Titanic disaster was found."

A later letter from Oslo included the following:

"... The sources of information upon which the programme was actually based remain entirely unknown to this Ministry." — Hr. Erik-Wilhelm Norman, Head of Archives, Kgle. Ultenriksdepartment (Norwegian Royal Foreign Office), August 20th, 1964."

The "Confidential report to the Norwegian Consul in Iceland" by Hr Henrik Naess, which two years previously had so impressively opened the MMSA's press release on the *Samson,* was now somehow beginning to look too confidential for the authorities in Iceland or Norway ever to have heard of it. That saucy, poaching little *Samson,* so unlike other candidates of the MMSA for the part of "The Ship Seen From the Sinking *Titanic"* , possessing as she did a known name, tonnage and other things that go with real ships, was herself looking a little hazy in the mists of the far north.

"The real mystery," Mr Harrison insisted, "... is how two Courts of Inquiry could come to such a fantastic decision."

Then, through the intervention of Hr Harald Brinchmann, the well-known Norwegian publisher, news at last came from Hr Kjell Arnljot Wig, Norwegian television producer of the *Samson* show of 16 April 1962. It seemed that the

Samson section had lasted only "two or three minutes" and recorded "the main points of some new material made available to us about the supposed presence" of the *Samson* "in the waters where the 'Titanic' went down that very night."

Hr Wig went on to say he had never been able "to get hold of Mr Naess's original diary, although there is reason to believe that it exists, deposited in some safe." He said he had kept an authorized copy of an extract relating the happenings in the *Samson* on the night of the disaster, and would have it translated and sent to me.

Some time later, in sending me a translation of his own copy, Hr Wig described how he had acquired it, and said he had been informed "that Mr Naess, during all these years [i.e. between 1912 and some 40 years on] had lived in a certain state of fear due to the responsibility he felt for having withheld information which ought to have been submitted to the authorities at an early stage . . ."

The inference from this letter is unexpected. Assuming, as one can, that Hr Wig was justified in taking "this new information" (as he called it) "at face value", it now appears that First Officer Naess lived in fear for years, not because of the possible consequences of his "confidential report to the consul", but because of his failure to make a confidential, or any, report to the consul or any other authority. The inability of the Norwegian Foreign Ministry to find this ever more mysterious document becomes less surprising; and increasingly so by the source of its date, "April 1912", assigned to it first by the MMSA, and later repeated. Whether it was born in the Norwegian Consul's houses in Isafordur or Reykjavik* in 1912, or at Nautilus House, Liverpool,§ in 1962 seems to be not free from doubt. Certainly, there is no date either in the original Norwegian text or in the English translation, which Hr Wig was good enough to have made for me by Lt. Cdr. Hans Stoerman Naess (no relation of Henrik Naess) of the Royal Norwegian Navy.

The ease with which this extract from the diary progresses from inaccuracy to improbability and arrives, via a hitherto unreported impossibility, at its memorable and notorious climax, gives it a rare, possibly unique, distinction.

"*Over jul 1912* . . .", or in English, "After Christmas, 1912", First Officer Henrik Naess begins, after mentioning that an ear ailment had compelled him to go ashore, and that for a time he had been "stone deaf", "I had two good offers of work . . ."[11]

One of those offers was that of a mate's job in the *Samson*.

This is the third line of the extract, and one is stopped immediately. Here is one of the only three dates in the document, and it must be wrong, unless Naess was offered the mate's job about eight months *after* the *Titanic* was sunk. The date is the same in the Norwegian original — "*Over jul 1912*". Presumably, "1912" is a mistake for "1911", and we proceed.

Now, in search for an explanation, however far-fetched, for the "territorial borders" (or "waters"), one wondered if the *Samson* had really been hunting seals in American waters or even on the American shore. The only trouble is that the diary gives it no help whatever. On the contrary, the *Samson* seems neither to have hunted nor caught seal, shark, or any other living creature, not even sea serpents.

* Norway had two Consulates in Iceland; an Honorary Consul at Reykjavik; Mr Tjodolf Klingenberg, who, just as the Honorary Vice Consul at Isafordur, Mr Gudmundur Hanneffon, was not of Norwegian, but Icelandic origin.

§ The MMSA headquarters at that time.

She left Tönsberg on 8 February, with 45 men aboard under Captain Ring ("a sailor to his fingertips", but evidently no diarist), and Naess later writes of ice off Newfoundland.

"We . . . kept on a south-westerly course until noon the next day."

From the later context, that must be noon, Sunday, 14 April.

"According to our calculations and the noon observations we should then be level with Cape *Hatteras* and we found quite rightly that we were" (see Diagram 15).

I pause for cape identification.

Cape *Hatteras,* North Carolina: 35°15'N; 73°32'W, some 1200 miles from the position of the *Titanic,* encountered (if at all) by the *Samson* almost exactly twelve hours later.

Apart from the fact that Hatteras is *south* of the scene of the disaster, the *Samson,* according to Naess, ". . . continued to the south-west the whole afternoon until darkness set in;" in other words, getting farther and farther in the wrong direction.

The name "Hatteras" is underlined in the translation, as it is in the Norwegian text, and perhaps it is an indication that the typist was also stopped by this name, for it is the only one so marked.

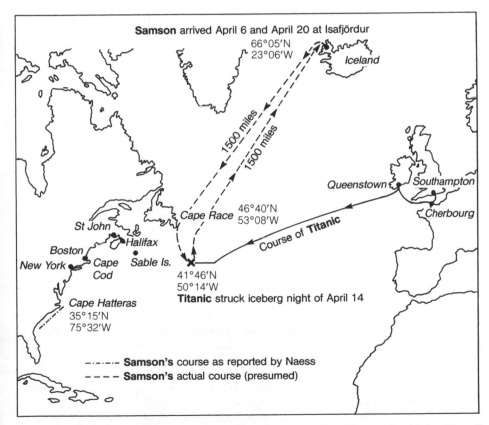

Diagram 15. Courses of the *Titanic* and the *Samson.* "The Norwegian Fairy Story"
Besides showing the track of the Titanic, *this map depicts two wonders: (1) the* Samson *seeing the* Titanic *firing rockets in the ice south of Cape Hatteras, and (2) as described in the text, how, to see the* Titanic *anywhere, the* Samson *had to cover some 3,000 miles in 13 or 14 days at seven knots.*

Possibly "Hatteras" is another mistake, this one for Cape Race, and, at least, if the *Samson* was in the latitude of Cape Race at noon, and continued steaming south-west, she would not be going away from the *Titanic*. But the location of Cape Race is (regrettably) 46.40 N; 53.08 W, that is, over 300 miles north of the *Titanic* at midnight. So, the *Samson* would have had to steam almost that distance in twelve hours, and the speed needed would have been about the same as the *Mauretania's,* then the fastest ship in the world.

I soldiered on.

The description of the meeting between the *Samson* and the putative *Titanic* was substantially the same as that already quoted:

"Just before twelve o'clock I strolled out on deck to wait for my relief . . . I noticed two large stars on the horizon far down to the south. 'Those stars are hanging very low', I said to the bridge hand. 'Nip up to the crow's nest and see what you can make of it.' I thought it possible that it could be American seal-catchers lying on the edge of the ice barrier. The bridge hand climbed up and pointed his telescope towards the stars.
'That is no star!' he shouted from above, 'they are lanterns, and I can see lots of lights.'
A moment passed and then suddenly some rockets rose against the sky."

But the remarkable capacity of this short extract from Naess's diary to provide one surprise after another is not yet exhausted, and now follows one more unexpected and inexplicable happening:

"Thereafter [i.e. after the rockets] all the lights were suddenly extinguished and it was dark. We saw no more."

Why Naess's *Titanic* put her lights out, we can only guess. Then follows the passage in the diary where the *Samson* got a chill down the spine, realized they were in territorial waters; there were Americans about; they had spotted the *Samson* and signalled the fact (somehow!) by rockets to other ships. So, without wasting a moment, the *Samson* got her 25- or 125-knot engine going, and, "We therefore started manoeuvering northwards to get out of sight."

Whether the *Samson* started northwards from south of Cape Hatteras, as she claimed, she did not see the *Californian,* then admittedly only ten miles away, nor did the *Californian* see her. Naess goes on to describe how the *Samson* got damaged in the ice and took refuge in Iceland, where, it is said, repairs were made. There, the Consul has Skipper Ring and Naess to dinner.

"Have you heard the latest ghastly news?" asks the Consul.

No, they had not; so he tells them.

"'When did this happen?'" asks the diarist. "There was something inside me which made me think." The Consul tells them that too, and gets a newspaper. Then follows the passage, almost identical with the stunning finale of the MMSA's press release, already quoted.

Ring and Naess go back on board, newspaper in hand.

"I looked at the log" — only Naess, by the way — and the paper shows, "both the time, date and position were exactly according to our notes." All becomes clear. There they had been "ten nautical miles away when the 'TITANIC' sank," with their "large vessel", "eight wonderful boats" and "lovely, calm weather". What could they "not have done in the way of rescue work, if we had only a notion of what was going on right in front of our noses. Had we only had a radio for instance . . .," and, one adds, not been plagued with territorial waters, for instance.

Thus, with that unfinished sentence, and the suggestion of a sigh, the extract from the diary ends.

After the success of 'The Other Ship', the *Samson* received further serious consideration as a candidate for being the non-*Californian* by Roy Anderson in his book, *White Star,* which contained a picture of the ship and a chapter in support of the MMSA's campaign.

Anticipation accordingly was keen about the use the MMSA would make of the *Samson* in its forthcoming Petition to the Board of Trade on behalf of Captain Lord. How would the Association follow up its own public announcement that it was its belief that the *Samson* was the ship seen by the *Titanic*? Would it solicit congratulations on its good fortune and acumen? But also, as the Board of Trade might be expected to show more curiosity than the general press, and more nautical knowledge than the general public, how would it explain those "territorial waters"?

The answer came on 5 February 1965, which saw the publication of what proved to be the first Petition by the MMSA for Captain Lord. There was neither jubilation nor justification. There was not a single word of any kind about the *Samson*. Abandoned at the altar! It seemed incredible. Surely the Association could not just coolly and quietly have abandoned its whole "solution"?

If that was in fact the reason, at the press conference aboard HQS *Wellington* on the day of publication, it seemed justified. The conference was more than half over before, suddenly, a reporter raised his hand about the subject. The writer, who was present, found him hard to hear, but the substance of his question was understandable.

'Mr Harrison,' he asked, 'wasn't there a boat — was it last year? You said — a Swedish whaler or something?'

"Oh," said Mr Harrison quickly, "you mean the *Samson*. She was a Norwegian — a sealer; we couldn't do anything with that — much too speculative! Next, please?"

The *Samson* disappeared, and was heard of no more. Years passed; new wars began; man busied himself also getting ready to take off from his old planet for the moon; but the Lordites were not distracted and now quietly prepared a nest for their nautical phoenix. On 19 February 1968, the BBC presented the public in their Northern and Northern Ireland services with a television version of 'The Other Ship'. It was called 'Captain Lord and the Titanic', and was in the same 'Trial By Inquiry' series. 'The Other Ship' had been so big a success, without, so far as I know, any protest or adverse criticism, that presumably the BBC felt safe in repeating the programme.

Question 6944, "the queer lights" and Gibson were again all omitted; Lightoller's evidence was again mistreated to help Lord's case; and, in a statement the value of which we have the material to judge, the narrator declared: ". . . the rockets, which Stone saw could well have been company signals."

The "territorial waters" again washed away any credibility from the story; but it was the sudden revival and use made of the *Samson,* which demonstrated the superiority of television over radio. Three years earlier, that vessel had been sunk in silence and without trace, one had thought, by her own sponsors, the MMSA. Now, she made an unexpected reappearance.

"A few years ago," the narrator began the episode, "a startling document came to light — the reminiscences of a Norwegian seaman called Henrik Naess . . . One passage of his book [*sic*] tells of an incident . . .," and so on.

The narrator held up a book for all to see, and delivered his account of the notorious incident, as if reading from it. However, on 6 April 1970, it was learned that Naess's son, Hr Harald Naess, had confirmed in Bergen that his father's journal had never been published.

"... the trial was very cleverly put over," wrote Thompson Hamilton, former secretary to Tom Andrews and his successor Edward Wilding. "... The narrator ... also brought forward some new evidence which he read from a book which was an autobiography by a Norwegian shipmaster of a seal fishing vessel . . ."[12]

Not all viewers were misled. *The Radio Times* of the BBC refused to publish a letter of protest from Sir Ivan Thompson about "Captain Lord and the Titanic", filled though the letter was with damaging facts, some from the Commodore's personal experience. It was only after attempted censorship and some delay that the letter was published in a Southampton newspaper, and later in Liverpool.

The letter, published here by kind permission of Lady Thompson, reads as follows:

"Dear Editor,
The B.B.C. I Programme 'Trial by Inquiry' last Monday night was of course pure Propaganda for Captain Lord's supporters. It just consisted of carefully selected snippets of the evidence. The main witness 'Gibson' who blew Lord's story sky high, was carefully omitted from the cast. Mr. Dunlop, Lord's counsel, was introduced, but his plea on Lord's behalf: 'The Captain admits he made no effort but if he had gone at speed there might have been another Titanic.' Second Officer Stone's statement 'They don't fire rockets for nothing, and there's something funny about that ship' were also omitted and most important of all the direct question 'Why didn't you call your Wireless Operator' and the answer 'when, at one o'clock in the morning'. If Lord had called his Operator, of course he would have been committed, and would have had to make an effort.

Let's review the whole sorry story. On August 27th, 1912 the Secretary of the M.M.S.A. wrote to the Board of Trade 'From information given to us, there appears to be strong grounds that the lights seen from the Titanic were those of the MOUNT TEMPLE and not the Californian.' This letter was marked Private and Confidential. In reply the Board of Trade wrote: 'In so grave a matter we can scarcely take action on information given in strict confidence contained in a letter marked "Private and Confidential". As nobody came forward to substantiate the accusations made by the M.M.S.A. the Mount Temple affair gradually faded out until 50 years later, when in 1962 a Pamphlet widely distributed by the M.M.S.A. in which the letters — Re the Mount Temple were repeated. Though in a foreword by Mr Harrison, the Secretary of the M.M.S.A. it was stated: 'Navigationally this appears to be an impossibility.' At this time Captain Burns was the manager of the Canadian Pacific Line at Liverpool, and I was the President of the M.M.S.A. Captain Burns thought this attempt to shift the blame from Lord, to another British Shipmaster Captain Moore of the Mount Temple, was very wrong, and I agreed with him. Captain Moore was dead, but his son who was also a Captain in the Canadian Pacific Line was still alive. I promptly resigned as President of the M.M.S.A.

Since then they have never mentioned the Mount Temple, but in 1963 the B.B.C. put out a Radio Programme on the Home Service based this time on the Norwegian Fairy Tale about the 'Samson'. The Mate of the 'Samson' had read about the Titanic in a newspaper, and said he checked with his log and it showed that the Samson was ten Nautical miles away from the Titanic that night. I suppose the Samson log like that of the Californian has disappeared. There is no mention of the Captain of the Samson, nor if he even had heard the Fairy Tale. The Samson was a sealer (though she was shown on the T.V. Programme as a full rigged ship.) The Mate's statement was: 'Our position was such, that it was feared we might be taken for violating Territorial Waters.' When it was pointed out that the Titanic sank about 1000 miles outside Territorial Waters, this story like that of the Mount Temple died a natural death. If Commander Lightoller had thought the B.B.C. would use him in a propaganda programme on Lord's behalf he would have turned in his grave."

This incident, whether connected or not, was similar to many attempts to prevent expressions of opinion considered unfavourable to the interests of Captain Lord, an aspect of the campaign not yet mentioned. Because of its possibly wider consequences, it was possibly even more serious.

The loudly proclaimed sensational discovery of the *Samson* in 1962, had not gained universal acceptance. Marine author Peter Padfield wisely did not mention the *Samson* in his 1965 published crusade for Captain Lord; *The TITANIC and the CALIFORNIAN*. He apparently agreed with Mr Harrison that the *Samson* was "much too speculative" and could not be used for his book. It seemed, however, different 25 years later, when public opinion had to be mobilized and influenced. So on 29 October 1990 Mr Padfield informed the audience of BBC's *Newsnight* about his views on the *Samson:* "Now that ship [the *Samson*] appears to be about the size the *Titanic* witnesses described and she did the same sort of thing the *Titanic* witnesses described. In fact she came towards the *Titanic,* stopped and then went away again, which can't be said of the *Californian* of course."

In fact and of course Mr Padfield, who had examined both the British and American enquiries for his book, had forgotten the overwhelming evidence from *Titanic* witnesses, already mentioned, that indicated a stationary steamer, and not a small sealer moving toward and from the *Titanic* or moving at all.

Mr Padfield was not the only supporter of Captain Lord who had made a 180 degree turn on the "much too speculative" *Samson* story. None other than the best of all Lord's friends had, as we know now, turned around too. In 1986 Mr Harrison rejoined the believers in the *Samson* story and opened a chapter in his book with the old details and explained that the *Samson's* alleged involvement could not "be obtained in a legally admissible form" and for the time being, — that is for nearly thirty years now — has "to be regarded as a tantalising glimpse of the possible solution of the riddle of the identity of the ship seen from the *Titanic*."[13]

To turn back to the search for less prepossessed and more reliable sources. Word had come from Norway: "The story of Samson and Titanic was certainly known before 1962". Perhaps because Naess's account of his meeting with the *Titanic* seems never to have been critically examined in his own country, as it had been in America on its first appearance in 1912 the incident remained, over the years, an accepted part of the Titanic story. Without any excitement, therefore, the statement from Norway that it certainly was not new in 1962 was coolly reinforced with precise collaboration. On at least three occasions, two of them printed and published, which can be exactly dated and identified, the incident was mentioned.

First, in the *Norsk Geografisk Aarbok 1916-1919* ('Norwegian Geographical Yearbook') published in 1921 at what was then Christiana, at p.238, is a short account, which could have emanated only from Naess himself. We learn: ". . . on this voyage they passed the 'Titanic' about an hour before she ran into the iceberg. With its 12 big long-boats 'Samson' could have had the opportunity of rescuing many, if the people on board had known what a drama was taking place nearby."

The discrepancy between this story and the "Journal" as to the number of boats and, more important, the alleged time of the encounter, will be noted.

Second, on 9 June 1928, the Trondheim newspaper *Arbeider-Avisen*, on page 2, published an interview with the celebrated seal-hunter, who by that time had become "Captain" Naess. Having told how in 1912 he had joined the *Samson* the newspaper continued: "It was during this expedition that he experienced an event that in strangeness and horror far surpassed the many days and nights in the Arctic Ocean."

Naess then gives a shorter version of his original story, but complete with the essential elements of "hunting on illegal territory", fear of the Americans, the lights and rockets, and eventual news in Iceland about the wreck of the "gigantic steamer" *Titanic*.

Finally, in a long letter dated 18 November 1939, from Naess to Adolf Hoel, the former head of the Polarinstitutt, now in the library there, the remorseful adventurer indulges once more in what seems to have been his favourite confession.

". . . when we were on the sealer 'Samson' in the southern part of the ice-south off Cape Hatteras, we saw 'Titanic' just at the moment when it sent up its rockets . . ."

Between 1928 and 1939, he had reduced the number of their boats from 12 to 8. On the other hand, since 1921, instead of choosing to "pass the *Titanic* an hour before she ran into the iceberg," he now selects a more promising time for the meeting. But, they had caught no seals; they had rescued not a soul from the *Titanic*.

". . . we could have performed a great deed," Captain Naess laments, perhaps with a rum toddy in reach.
"Instead the tour had been a complete miss."

Still, he had seen the *Titanic* back once more in the ice south of Cape Hatteras.

Apparently, part of the same document was made available to the MMSA through Henrik Naess's son and described as Naess's unpublished memoirs by Mr Harrison, who briefly mentioned them in his book,* but the contents of the memoirs are not revealed, nor commented upon. Cape Hatteras is not mentioned and the readers where thus spared that piece of valuable information too.

Commodore Sir Ivan Thompson remembered first hearing of the *Samson* in May or June 1912 while his ship was loading timber in a Texas port. A newspaper first called it "The Norwegian Fairy Tale" in 1913, which became a common saying on the North Atlantic.[14]

It was also as far back as 1964 that a "new" story reached me of a Norwegian sealer, which had told a story exactly similar to the *Samson's*. For a stunned moment, it looked like a real coincidence; but the name of this second sealer was nothing other than *Samson*. And the date of the original disclosure of her adventure; again, 1912.

A world sensation had been about to get off the ground when a would-be corroborative detail in this story was incautiously disclosed: the reason the *Samson* fled was her fear that she was in territorial waters. The hard-headed men of 1912, and understandably more knowledgeable about the facts than the public of 1962, at once asked how the *Samson* could have seen the *Titanic's* rockets from anybody's territorial waters. Certain it was, if she was ten miles from the *Titanic*, she was hundreds of miles from the nearest shore. Somebody else said, the *Samson*, if not a red herring, was certainly a Norwegian *gafol-*

* p. 196.

bita; but it seems the preferred and popular name for the alleged adventure among the public and North Atlantic seamen was that said to have been conferred by an American newspaper, "The Norwegian Fairy Story". The still-born sensation was washed away in floods of tears, not of sorrow, but of mirth.

Probably, the original claim made by the MMSA in 1962, to have found in the *Samson* something hitherto unknown, and of sensational importance, was made in good faith. It would have been unreasonable to have asked for more knowledge from this British guild than from the Norwegian Broadcasting Corporation, which might have provided a partial excuse for the *Samson* episode. On the other hand, the exclusion of the *Samson* from the 1965-Petition might charitably be interpreted as caution, however belated, in using so questionable an instrument of propaganda. Perhaps also, as proud and ancient a body as the MMSA might have felt humiliated (wrongly, in my opinion) to have publicly admitted a mistake about the *Samson,* and decided to let her be quietly forgotten, as indeed she was.

One last, and important, gap in the story was filled in 1970. Acting on information from Norway, passed by me to him, more than six years after my first inquiry, Hr Lárus Sigurbjörnsson in Iceland, with the help of a retired sheriff in Isafjörthur, Hr Jóhann Gunnar Olafsson, had an examination made of an old "Supplementary Revenue Book", as it was described, for 1912. There, dated 6 April and 20 April, two entries were found about the *Samson.* They appeared to be, respectively, date of arrival and of departure, but I soon learned that they were not. In fact the dates recorded were the dates that Captain Carl Ring came into the Goverment's Counsel Office of Isafjordur, which was no more than a simple small building, and paid the taxes that the *Samson* owed by her presence in that town. The date of departure was unrecorded, but it was guessed at 7 April.

For the first time, also, there was information about her speed, with her 75 horse power auxiliary engine, the *Samson* could do about 6 knots, and some-what more if her sails were also in use. Now, the distance to the position of the *Titanic* and back was over 3000 miles, or about 500 hours of steaming, say 21 days, or 19 possibly, if under sail as well. On this reckoning, which is deliberately made generous on the side of the *Samson,* it is apparent that the vessel could not have got within ten miles of the *Titanic,* as Naess claimed, on the night of 14/15 April, and still checked in at Isafjord, which the book shows she did, on 20 April. In other words, these two routine entries in this "Supplementary Revenue Book" of Isafjörthur, whichever way they are used, finish the *Samson.*

In February 1973, the National Archivist of Iceland, Hr Bjarni Vílhjálmsson, had the relevant pages of this "Supplementary Revenue Book" microfilmed and personally certified their authenticity.

It should be emphasized, nonetheless, that Naess's journal, with its absur-dities about those "territorial waters" and encountering the *Titanic* "south of Cape Hatteras" — repeated also in his interview with the *Arbeider-Avisen* and his letter to Professor Hoel — may be said to destroy themselves.

Some final thoughts about the puzzle of Henrik Bergethon Naess and his *Samson:* to those who remembered the laughter and scorn in 1912, which greeted his "territorial waters", and instantly created "The Norwegian Fairy Story", he was naturally regarded as a clumsy liar and nothing more. In the eyes of those veterans of 1912, the ready acceptance of Naess by the Lordites of the 1960s, added nothing to their respectability or intelligence, let alone the credibility of their cause. Apart from this *Titanic* incident, however, Naess seems to have had a certain standing in Norway among Arctic explorers and

others in similar spheres. The great name of Nansen himself was once linked
with his. But a possible rational explanation of the incident seems beyond
discovery. His fantasy, moreover, was persisted until as late as 1939. A photo-
copy of his 1939 letter to Dr Hoel, holograph in Naess's careful and obviously educated handwriting, shows that in his "account" of the incident, he
had first left out mention of Cape Hatteras, but it appears, carefully inserted
even if above the line.

It is, however, just possible that one further passage in his "Journal" may
provide the right end to the story of the *Samson,* and so bring this chapter on
"The Norwegian Fairy Story" also to an end. It immediately precedes his
report of strolling out on deck just before midnight and noticing "two large
stars on the horizon . . ." which proved to be the . . ., one hesitates what to call
her. Anyhow, First Officer Naess writes:

> "We were on six hour watches . . . *I was on watch in the evening but sat down
> below drinking a rum toddy with the skipper . . .*"

The italics in the above are my own. This picture created by these few words
is surely rare, and possibly unique in its impudent candour. Bearing in mind
that the *Samson* was only a seal-hunter, and not a well-run ship like, say the
Californian, the conduct of Naess yet seems a little below par: the conscientious officer of the watch, not out on deck in the cold where his duty was,
but below in Skipper Carl Ring's cheery warm cabin, and vigilantly scan-
ning not the line of the horizon through his glasses, but the level of spirits in
his glass . . . that's south of Cape Hatteras . . . in territorial waters . . . with
the Americans on their tails . . .

Can it be that a partial explanation and an excuse for "The Norwegian
Fairy Story" are just a widow's cruse of rum toddy on a freezing cold night?
But clearly more than rum is needed to excuse or explain the fantasy of the
MMSA. Possibly, their whole campaign might charitably be dismissed as
"The Liverpool Fairy Story".

The so-called "Mystery Ship", conceived as early as 1912 by A.M. Foweraker,
had, in the 1960s, mainly and foremost through the energies of the MMSA,
started a whole new life and although dismissed as "much too speculative"
after a few years, it still endures to this day and is not to die that easily.

In 1976 a brand new candidate for the position came forward, virtually out
of the blue. It did not do well at its launch and was quickly forgotten, but in
1989 it reappeared and was lovingly embraced by the growing band of well-
meaning, but mostly ignorant, amateur *Titanic* searchers; which largely, and
growingly, make up the blaring rearguard for the defence of Captain Lord.

The suitor this time was the German oil-tanker *Niagara,* owned by the
"Deutsch-Amerikanische Petroleum Gesellschaft" * (DAGP) of Hamburg
and its story is as incredible as its solution is simple.

According to her First Officer, Mr Hofmann, the *Niagara,* on her way from
New York to Hamburg, was near the sinking *Titanic.*

On the night of 14/15 April 1912 he and others saw, to the north-west of
them, two masthead lights, two sidelights and a lot of other lights of what
seem to be a passenger liner. Somewhat later, when they had passed, they
saw the lights in a strange and tilted perspective, the front light being low
and the rear light high out of the water. After that they saw no more lights, but
did see rockets, fired from the same direction and they concluded that the
rockets were part of "a celebration on board" the passenger liner, which

* The "German American Petrol Company".

Hofmann regarded as "nothing unusual" and they did not investigate. Not until Hamburg did they learn of the *Titanic,* and their mistake.

The story dates back to 1938 when a Mr J. Hunck finished his "Chronicle of the Waried Oil-Tanker Shipowners Ltd 1862-1922."* The chronicle was never published, but some copies did survive.

The German marine writer Mr Jochen Brennecke found and used the chronicle for his book *Tanker,* and the *Niagara* story he featured for his magazine, *Schiff und Zeit,* published by him for the German ship-lover-market. It appeared in the third edition of the magazine for 1976. Brennecke did not publish the story in support of Captain Lord, but simply out of general interest for the *Titanic.* And so the *Niagara* appeared as the so-called "Mystery Ship" in public for what was probably the first time.

A quick look at the available sources for the *Niagara; Lloyd's Weekly Shipping Index* and the prominent Hamburgian shipping papers for April 1912, dismissed the story instantly, and branded it as another *Titanic*-yarn. According to these sources the German *Niagara* had left San Francisco on 4 April for a voyage to Chingkiang near Nanking, China.[15] On 1 May she passed Whampoa, near Canton.[16] In short, she was not on the North Atlantic, but on the North Pacific, or on the other side of our globe.

Confusing in the *Niagara* story is the existence of the *Niagara* of the "Compagnie Générale Transatlantique" better known as the French Line. There are no reports from the French *Niagara* that connects her with the *Titanic,* other than that she reported on her arrival in New York, on 15 April, that she had run into ice which pierced two holes in her hull below the waterline. (The SS *Kura* and the SS *Lord Cromer* also reported damage by ice on their way to New York.)

A close examination of all the so-called "Mystery Ships", be they the illegally sealing *Samson* in American territorial waters, the courageous *Mount Temple* or the Pacific trading *Niagara,* reveals only that none of the claims made on their behalf stand scrutiny.

As yarns they make a great contribution to the *Titanic* legend, but as historical contributions to the mystery of the *Californian,* their value is nil, nor do they excuse the *Californian* or the conduct of her captain, but rather disfigure, and dilute the effectiveness of the campaign on behalf of Captain Lord.

Sources

1 *A Titanic Myth,* p. 163.
2 P.I., from Mr Harrison, several showings of the film and Foreword by Stanley Tutton Lord to *The* Titanic *and the* Californian by Peter Padfield.
3 US 934.
4 P.I., almost contemporary with event.
5 "The Other Ship", reprint from Annual Report, MMSA, 1963.
6 Ibid., p. 11.
7 B 14155.
8 "The Other Ship", p. 11.
9 Ibid., p. 12.
10 Ibid., p. 7.
11 Opening of special translation of Naess journal.
12 P.I., letter from Thompson Hamilton, 18 March 1968.
13 *A Titanic Myth* pp. 195-197.
14 P.I. from Sir Ivan Thompson; letter of 5 October 1963 and a
meeting on 3 September 1965.
15 Lloyd's Weekly Shipping Index, Steamers, 11 April 1912.
16 Telegraphische Schiffsmeldungen, Neue Hamburgische Börsen = Halle, Hamburgischer Cörrespondent, 2 May 1912. (Universitait und Staats Bibliotheek [D602], Hamburg.)

* Chronik der Waried Tankschiff Rhederei GmbH 1862-1922.

Chapter 19

The confession of Herbert Stone

No utterance or document in the whole case of the *Californian,* without exception, would be so important as a confession by Herbert Stone that he knew distress rockets were being fired.

The protagonist or leading character in the tragedy being Captain Lord himself, the cautious reader may be stopped by that unqualified statement and impelled to ask whether a confession by the captain would not be far more important. It would, had not Captain Lord already confessed, by his answer to the Attorney-General's climactic Question 6944: if that rocket was not a company's signal, then "it might have been a distress signal?"

The clash of wills between the two men was then at last decided, and four fatal words were wrung from Lord's guilty conscience: "It might have been."

In their context, the meaning of these four words was this, and nothing else:

"I knew a distress rocket might just have been fired; *I knew, therefore, that human beings might be in danger of death – and I remained in the chart room.*"

As the charge against him — morally, if not legally — of which he stood accused, was that he had ignored distress signals, his words were nothing but a confession.

Though no heading, embodying that event, can be found in any of the growing literature in support of Captain Lord, the confession has existed for well over three quarters of a century. It is not even denied by the Lordites, because it is not really admitted to exist, and, of course, is not specifically publicized or explicitly commented upon. It is at best suppressed or belittled. Mr Padfield made no mention of it ever and Mr Harrison's only comment has been. "Not knowing why the signals reported by Stone had been sent up, Lord could only agree. 'It *might* have been'".[1] Yet it is a fact, since 1912; on record; in print, and available to any objective inquirer, or even to a "frank partisan". Undenied, undeniable and unequivocal. So much then for Captain Lord's confession.

The most important immediate goal remaining, therefore, to an independent investigator was the question of Second Officer Herbert Stone. One knew, of course, generally, that Stone, too, had told a pack of lies in Boston, but no more than that. In an interview with *The Boston Herald* of 26 April 1912, almost all names familiar to us, with the notable exceptions of Groves and Gibson, made their contribution, large or small, to the mosaic of falsity.

One knew also that Stone had repeated in London that he did not think they were distress signals,[2] but the whole agonizing tribulation which the young man suffered at the witness table in Scottish Hall made it clear that he was very different in his attitude to the case from, say, either Lord or Stewart; and this impression was confirmed by such recollections as were still available from the few survivors who had actually been present and heard him.

Shortly before the writing of this work was actually decided, a circumstantial story was received[3] that Stone had once told a friend, an officer in the mercantile marine, as it used to be called, that he always thought the rockets "were distress signals and I tried my best to get Lord up but he wouldn't leave the chartroom." After long delays, communication with this officer, by this time a retired master, established that Stone's friend or acquaintance, had indeed reported a conversation with Stone, how he had attempted to call the Captain, and other matters already recorded; but not a word of Stone's own views on the rockets.

". . . With regard to my conversation with Stone, I cannot actually recall him saying, 'he always thought they were distress signals.'. . ."

Stone, moreover, was very far from being the only puzzle, human or material, to be investigated.

One of the obvious items that provoked inquiry was the fact that certain witnesses from the *Californian* were not called. It will perhaps be remembered that after Evans, who was the last *Californian* witness (apart from Gill, who did not appear until more than two weeks later), had given his evidence, the Solicitor-General said: "From the 'Californian' there is this donkeyman, Gill, who is not here at present, and who gave evidence in America. I have three or four other 'Californian' witnesses, but it does not appear to me they would add anything."[4]

A short conversation followed between him and Lord Mersey. Dunlop was asked if he wanted them, and he agreed they did not "add anything"; and so, these unnamed witnesses, together with the six, who had testified, were all dismissed.

With the proofs* in front of them, it seemed very probable that Simon and Dunlop were right when they agreed that these three or four possible further witnesses from the *Californian* would not "add anything". On the other hand, it would be interesting to find out, whatever they had intended to say, for there must have been some reason, in the first place, why they had been summoned to London with the other six.

Clearly, it would be an advantage to know, who these uncalled witnesses were, but the whole thousand pages of the *Titanic* "Proceedings" contained next to no help on the subject. However, very soon after the return of the *Californian* to Liverpool, statements were in fact taken by the Receiver of Wreck, certainly from all six who gave evidence and no doubt at least from the other "three or four" as well. It seemed logical to apply to the Receiver of Wreck in Liverpool in the hope of finding, long undisturbed in his cellar, the whole lot of the wanted papers, and perhaps more, thus ending the search almost before it had begun. That hope was extinguished without delay, when back came the answer that the old Receiver had been long gone, his old office long bombed and the old papers long burnt, the last two achievements, of course, being among the many of the Luftwaffe over the City of Liverpool. Fortunately, the Official Log of the *Californian* had escaped the blitz.

Thinking a bit, it seemed possible that, even as in many matters of life and

---

* Statements of what the potential witnesses would say, in possession of counsel, but not the judge.

death in our society, it might be money which could prove the clue to a more intelligent or logical means of finding the names of these men. Possibly a state paper which set out the costs of the *Titanic* inquiry.

A document, long buried in one of the hundreds of volumes in the State Paper Room of the British Museum, of typical government folio size and as fresh as if it had never been opened, as it probably hadn't been, since it returned from the binders in 1913, had the answer. The title page read:

RETURN OF THE EXPENSES INCURRED BY THE BOARD OF TRADE AND OTHER GOVERNMENT DEPARTMENTS IN CONNECTION WITH THE INQUIRY INTO THE LOSS OF THE S.S. "TITANIC"

The price, one halfpenny, in those days was the equivalent of one cent.

The officers, including Marconi Operator Evans, (listed as 3rd Officer and Stone as 1st Officer) are separately listed under the heading: "Officers of other vessels — on the opening page, which also starts the list for; "The crew of *"Titanic"* —

On page 3 the lower ranks of the *Titanic* are continued and listed in the second column together with the "Crew of other vessels — and here the first four names reveal the identity of all the uncalled *Californian* men.

	£	s.	d.
E. Gill, Donkeyman, 'Californian'	9	18	0
W. Ross, A.B., 'Californian'	3	2	6
G. Glenn, Fireman, 'Californian'	3	7	6
W. Thomas, Greaser, 'Californian'	6	14	0

That is all. Three of them. The names and occupations were certainly a surprise, but perhaps the reason for these three being sent to London was to be found in their stories, which meant, after checking their names in the Official Log, trying to find the trio to get their stories. The search would have to begin with the forbidding application to the Record Office for Seamen and Shipping in Cardiff; but, at least, I should now know I was looking for the right men. Probably all three were dead, but even so, it seemed not improbable that they had told their stories to their families, who might still be living, and willing and able to repeat what they knew. That would not be legal evidence, but it was the truth, not its form, that interested me. The log confirmed the occupations given in the "Return" to the three retrieved from anonymity, and also that there was only one "Thomas" in the crew. I had discovered that Thomas had already told his story.

W. Thomas was the bunkmate of Gill, and, it will be remembered, he was interviewed in Boston, when he did a good deal to undermine an important part of his mate's story. It is clear that anything of interest he could have said in London, he must already have told *The Boston Herald* in 1912.

The attempt to find George Glenn began through Cardiff, and after various unsuccessful approaches to different organizations and individuals, false trails and bad clues, followed and perforce abandoned, authentic information from a somewhat unexpected source brought the search to as successful an end as was possible. As all the "wanted" persons were (unfortunately in the circumstances!) respectable citizens unknown to the police, it was only through a lucky chance of friendly relations happening to exist between a local police force and some of their civilian neighbours that any help might be obtained from that quarter. Yet, it was through this means that George

Glenn was traced. The Chief Constable of the town in which he had lived was able to say that Glenn himself had died in 1952, but his son was alive and residing at an address disclosed.

As soon as could be conveniently arranged, a meeting took place[5] with Mr George Herbert Glenn (the eldest son of the late George Glenn) who was not born until after 1912. It seemed that Glenn had actually written an account of his experiences on the Sunday night, but most regrettably, once again, this, and many more of his father's, and other family, papers were destroyed in a German air raid. There was probably more detail in the written account than survived in the son's memory, even though he had heard the story more than once from his father. In any event, Mr George Herbert Glenn, on 10 September 1965, made a statutory declaration, of which the following is the substance:

"(1) . . . I am the eldest son of the late GEORGE GLENN, of . . ., who died in 1952.
(2) My father was at one period of his life a merchant seaman, and he served as a stoker or fireman in the Leyland Line steamship *Californian*. He was aboard the ship in that capacity on her voyage from London to Boston, Mass., beginning April 5th, 1912.
(3) During the night of April 14th-15th, at sea, my father was on deck of the *Californian* with another fireman, whose name I do not know, when he saw rockets being fired from another ship. *My father drew the attention of the Officer of the Watch to the rockets.* [Emphasis added].
(4) The information contained in the foregoing Paragraph (3) was obtained from my father. I was a boy at the time, but I remember his telling me of the incident.
(5) (This Paragraph is a detailed identification of his father in various newspaper photographs by Mr. George Herbert Glenn, which were shown to him, and his recollection of another he remembered, but which probably was among the papers destroyed. As there can now be no dispute that Glenn was one of the uncalled witnesses, these details are omitted).
(6) My father's and other family papers were destroyed during the last war in a German air raid.
(7) I make this statement voluntarily and without any monetary or other inducement, and solely in the interest of truth, and because I am informed that the information it contains is of historical importance in connexion with the questions of the part played by the S.S. *Californian* in the loss of the *Titanic*.

DECLARED at, etc. (*Signature*) G.H. GLENN

before me, etc. (A Commissioner for Oaths)"

By the time six *Californian* witnesses had given their evidence there could not be the slightest doubt that the *Californian* had seen rockets; so assuming the above declarations reproduced the substance of what Glenn's evidence would have been — and there is no reason to question it — a quick run through his proof might have justified the opinion that it would not "add anything". A closer look though at Paragraph (3) shows that Glenn — and possibly his unnamed companion as well — could certainly have added at least one new detail. Unlike Gill, Glenn apparently had a conscience responsive to more than one stimulus, and the sight of those rockets was among them. Instead of deciding, as Gill had, that they were none of his business, (Mr Glenn could not say whether his father had been on watch at the time), Glenn promptly went and pointed out the rockets to Stone. If Glenn had been called, he might have made even more trouble for Stone, and it is easy to understand why Robertson Dunlop readily agreed to Glenn's dismissal unheard.

Whatever else may be said, it is apparent that Glenn's untold story, at least, is a flat contradiction of the allegation by the MMSA that the "Attorney-General" had these three witnesses dismissed because their evidence would have supported Captain Lord.

There now remained only the story of William Ross, AB, for whom a search had begun at the same time. It proved to be much longer and more difficult, even before it was given up. Every means used in the hunt for Glenn was tried with Ross and failed.

Then, in a sense, literally out of the blue, came unexpected and authentic information about William Ross.

A letter from the Acting Chief Constable of Liverpool, Mr H.H. Balmer, announced: ". . . information has been received that William Ross died two years ago in Canada, where his wife and three children are still living. A copy of your letter has been forwarded to Mrs Ross in order that she may write to you if she so desires."

Many more weeks followed before it seemed clear that Mrs Ross, for doubtless good reasons, had no such desire. But eventually, she did write, and later, a longer letter followed from her eldest son, Mr Kenneth William Ross.[6]

As described by him, William Ross, the AB, must have been an exceptional character.

". . . The fact that my father passed away almost three years ago," wrote Mr Kenneth William Ross, "has rather dulled our memory of the events which took place as he described them to us.

The sea, of course, was in my father's blood until the day he died, although he had been a 'landlubber', as the saying goes, for many years. In fact, we, his children, do not really remember him as a seaman, but nevertheless we were very much aware that the sea was close to his heart. To give you an example, who ever heard of the ceiling at home being called the 'deckhead' — we did; and bed was always a place to 'bunk' for the night.

However, to bring the conversation back to the Titanic is to recall how he was walking on deck that evening back in 1912. The stars were out and *he could see flares on the horizon which were interpreted as some kind of distress signal*." [Emphasis added].

It seems only right to draw the attention of the inventors of the "Eight Roman candle type flares" to the fact that William Ross, as a voice from the past and the dead, through the memory of his son, offers this confirmation of their original creation. They may make what use they please of this fresh information, provided they invariably observe the condition that it be used, contrary to their practice, unseparated from the interpretation given to those "flares" by William Ross, "as some kind of distress signal".

Mr Ross also wrote: "We have no idea why he was not called to give evidence," and he expressed his regret that his father himself could not answer, as presumably he would have done "in more detail".

Although only the substance of the stories of Glenn, the fireman, and Ross, the Able Seaman, have been recovered, and can be given only as hearsay; and that of William Thomas, the greaser, only through a newspaper interview, they are all, it seems to me, deserving of belief. Their names, and these reports of their frustrated evidence, may, without exaggeration, be regarded together as the answer to the puzzle of the uncalled witnesses. In its light, it is interesting to read the reference to the matter, in the February, 1965, Petition of the MMSA over the signatures of Captain W.W.P. Lucas, President, and W.L.S. Harrison, General Secretary:

"At the British inquiry there were available some additional witnesses from the *Californian* who were not actually called upon to give their evidence. These must have included at least one engineer officer, who could have testified if necessary to the fact that the *Californian's* engines were stopped all night. Of even greater value to Captain Lord would have been evidence confirming the distance steamed on the morning of April 15 from getting under way at 6 a.m. ship's time and arriving at the scene of the disaster at 8.30. This was crucial if his evidence as to the distance which separated the two positions was to be accepted.

"In addition, there can be little doubt that the witnesses included the quartermasters and lookouts who were on duty during the night, and whose evidence might have served to confirm the second officer's conviction that he did not see any distress signals from the nearby ship.

"Neither Mr. Dunlop nor the Attorney General thought it necessary to call any further witnesses from the *Californian,* however [Appendix 10].* Mr. Dunlop undoubtedly considered that he had brought before the Court the full story of the events of the night as they appeared to the *Californian's* witnesses. If any other members of the crew had made statements which conflicted with the story told by Captain Lord, then it is certain that the Attorney General would have called them. The fact he did not confirms any evidence which they could have given would have merely been in support of Captain Lord's story — a story which quite evidently the Court had already decided to reject."[7]

One is impressed by the typical assurance of the affirmation that the uncalled witnesses "must have included at least one engineer officer, . . .", and "In addition, there can be little doubt [they] included the quartermasters and lookouts who were on duty during that night . . ." As the reader now knows, these were all guesses, all intelligent and all wrong. The attribution to the Attorney-General of the fresh piece of villainy of suppressing these witnesses, because they would have helped Captain Lord is a gross mistatement. Actually, the fact that it was Lord's "very nice gentleman", Sir John Simon, the Solicitor-General, and not the Attorney-General, who initiated the dismissal of Thomas and the two others, may charitably be regarded merely as a manifestation of the characteristic inaccuracy of these documents.

A more important question than the uncalled trio of witnesses, and a decisive one, was the question of what the *Carpathia* saw. Commodore Bisset, in his second volume of autobiography, *Tramps and Ladies*, wrote: ". . . in the slowly increasing daylight after 4.30 a.m., we had sighted the smoke of a steamer on the fringe of the pack ice, ten miles away from us to the northwards, She was making no signals, and we paid little attention to her, for we were preoccupied with more urgent matters; but at 6 a.m. we noticed that she was under way and slowly coming towards us.

"When I took over the watch on the bridge of the *Carpathia* at 8 a.m., the stranger was little more than a mile from us, and flying her signals of identification. She was the Leyland Line cargo-steamer *Californian*, which had been stopped overnight, blocked by ice."[8]

Taking into account the time, bearing and distance from the *Carpathia* of the *Californian* according to Bisset, this was terrible evidence for the support-

* Appendix 10 to the Petition reprints the discussion before the witnesses were dismissed.

ers of Captain Lord. It meant, that wherever the *Titanic* had been, the *Carpathia* was on the spot, and only some ten miles north of it, as early as soon after 4.30 a.m., there too was the *Californian,* just where she had been all night. To others, with an unbiased view of all the evidence, it was exactly what one might have expected, and confirmed Groves, Captain Moore and what was to be inferred from Captain Gambell of the *Virginian.*

Bisset was a particularly awkward customer for the Lordites. In addition to his high reputation, he was known to have had the inconvenient habit of making contemporary notes. Their method of dealing with him was similar to that used towards other adverse evidence. Mr Harrison derided Bisset's book as a "tissue of nonsense".[9]

Although Bisset was corroborated by Captain Moore and others outside the *Carpathia,* as said before, why had one never heard of others in the ship herself, who could speak about the propinquity of the *Californian* as had the man who was her Second Officer at the time? After all, Bisset had not written, for instance: "*I* had sighted . . .," but had used the plural throughout — ". . . *we* had sighted the smoke of a steamer . . . *we* paid little attention . . . but at 6 a.m. *we* had noticed . . ." Whom if anybody, did he have in mind?

On the other side, indeed, and often and legitimately cited by the Lordites, was the affidavit of Captain Rostron of 4 June, that, "At 5 o'clock it was light enough to see all around the horizon. We then saw two steamships to the northwards, perhaps seven or eight miles distant. Neither of them was the *Californian.* One of them was a four-masted steamer with one funnel, and the other a two-masted steamer with one funnel. The first time that I saw the *Californian* was at about eight o'clock on the morning of April 15th. She was then about five or six miles distant, bearing W.S.W. true, and steaming towards the *Carpathia.*"[10]

It was a matter which invited at least an attempt at solution.

The officers of the *Carpathia,* on the historic voyage of the rescue were, in addition to Rostron as master and Bisset as Second Officer, Chief Officer Thomas William Hankinson, First Officer Horace Dean, Third Officer Eric Rees and Fourth Officer Geoffry Barnish. All of them, except Bisset, it will be seen from the note below, died before the end of the war in 1945.[*] Communication was made with the Rev. John Geoffrey Barnish, the son of Fourth Officer Barnish; but a search of his father's papers revealed only his copy of the famous *Carpathia-Titanic* gold medallion presented to those who took part in the rescue, "to the amusement of the latter," as Mr Barnish wrote, "and the disappointment of those who would rather have had the cash value."

From Mrs Sylvia Lightoller, the widow of the *Titanic's* Second Officer, came some valuable information. Lightoller, in October and December 1912, while at sea in the *Majestic,* had written two very sympathetic replies to Captain Lord; and yet, certainly not later than 1935, when his book, *Titanic and Other Ships* was published, he had written about the rockets: "'Why were we firing these signals, if there was no danger?' was the question, to which I replied that we were trying to call the attention of the ship nearby, as we could not get her with wireless. *That ship was the 'Californian'* [emphasis in original]."[11]

In a celebrated radio broadcast in the following year, Lightoller repeated and enlarged upon the subject, and in fact never afterwards changed his

* Hankinson, 21 April 1936; Rostron, 4 November 1940; Barnish, 21 November 1941; Dean, 6 February 1943; Rees, serving as Commodore, R.N.R., on Russian convoy, missing, presumed lost, 16 April 1942, and Bisset died, 28 March 1967. (Cunard Pension Fund, Press and other private sources.)

conviction, that the *Californian* was the nearby ship. This view is the more striking, as it is very probable he had formed no opinion about her identity until some time afterwards.

As Lightoller won his desperate battle with the sea, and brought No. 12 Boat, the last of them, and overloaded with no fewer than 75 people, alongside the *Carpathia,* a voice came down to him: "Hullo, Lights, what are you doing down there?"[12]

It was First Officer Horace Dean, who had been his best man. Whether it was Dean, or some other officer of the *Carpathia,* who first mentioned the position of the *Californian,* cannot be said. The fact of the matter is, as reported by Lightoller to his wife, he learned aboard the ship during the return passage to New York, that at least three of the ship's officers, besides Bisset, saw the *Californian* "early on the morning of the 15th, the Monday," about eight or ten miles to the north of the *Carpathia* (see Diagram 11). These officers were Horace Dean himself, Third Officer Rees and Fourth Officer Barnish. When asked if it was not possible to give any estimate of the time, the word "early" was repeated, but it was said that Lightoller's information was that when the *Californian* was first sighted from the *Carpathia* by these three officers, "she was not moving". An inquiry of Mrs Lightoller as to whether or not Chief Officer Hankinson also saw the *Californian* brought the answer that, as far as her recollection went, Lightoller never told her. Finally, it was also reported by Lightoller that he had been told that "some of the passengers" of the *Carpathia* had also seen the four-masted ship stopped to the North.*

A comparison of this report with Bisset's account of his first sighting of the *Californian* in his book shows how close is Lightoller's information, as repeated by his wife. The fact that, in legal terms, it is strictly hearsay and would be inadmissible as evidence, does not affect its probative force. Nor can there be much doubt that the story, coming as it did direct to Lightoller from the three officers, who had actually seen the *Californian* when and where and under the circumstances they described, was the chief reason why he ceased to have any question about the identity of the ship whose "single light", as he described it, he himself had seen from the *Titanic.*

Mrs Lightoller, who was then a young woman of about 25, "went everywhere with him; we did everything together." Lightoller, who was 13 years older then she was, had fallen in love with her at first sight, when as a girl of 16, she had stepped up the gangway of his ship, the *Suevic.* Mrs Lightoller had some vivid memories of the *Californian* witnesses, but, having just had her husband restored to her after a greater danger than even that adventurous man had ever surmounted, she was, like others in the hall, burning with indignation at the *Californian's* original neglect of the rockets; and by the evident cool reaction produced by them on at least two of the witnesses from that ship. It was in fact only Lightoller's own discreet reminder: "You can't kick a man when he's down, my dear," that induced her to shake hands with Captain Lord.

Far more important, and indeed of the greatest importance, because the account came from somebody associated with the persons actually concerned, were the recollections of a shipmate of Rostron and other *Carpathia* officers. The seaman was Ivan Thompson,[§] who began his sea career with the Joseph

---

* In what proved to be the last meeting with Mrs Lightoller, a few weeks before her death on 3 October 1969, she repeated before some half-dozen people, that her husband, shortly before he died in December 1952, had discussed the *Californian* with her, and had no doubt of Captain Lord's culpability.

§   Died 22 July 1970.

Chadwicks-Drum Line, then went to the Harrison Line and finally to the Cunard. There he ultimately rose to command of the "Queens", to the post of Commodore and was knighted.

"I was the first Cunard officer," he says, "to go to a White Star ship — I joined the *Majestic* when the old MAURI finished and afterwards for many years I was master of the *Britannic* and the *Georgic,* so I spent well over 20 years sailing with White Star personnel and during this time every detail of the fatal night was discussed over and over. I sailed with Bisset on many ships. Dean, Barnish and Rees were all Officers on the *Carpathia* at the time, and they were all shipmates and friends. *They were all adamant that they saw the Californian stopped ten miles away when they arrived at the 'Titanic's' position. All three watched her approach, while they were busy with the 'Titanic's' boats. They told me this* [emphasis added]. Bisset certainly wasn't the only one who saw her approaching. Rees was an emotional Welshman, and when we were shipmates on the *Laconia,* there were several occasions when he walked out of the wardroom because Lord's name was mentioned. Lightoller (the real hero of the 'Titanic') was a friend and to his dying day he was *sure* [emphasis in original] the other ship was the *Californian* — Boxhall was next to me on the seniority list, and of course I was on the Atlantic that night, so I feel I have had chance to learn all the facts."

It is not surprising that with this knowledge and this background, Sir Ivan Thompson at once resigned the presidency of the MMSA, when an attempt was made in 1962 to revive the old discredited story about the *Mount Temple* being "the other ship", and not the *Californian.*

It will be noticed that, as in Mrs Lightoller's report of Commander Lightoller's statement, Chief Officer Hankinson of the *Carpathia* is again absent from Commodore Thompson's account of the incident.

As for Sir Arthur Rostron, Thompson says: "I sailed under Rostron's command in several ships, including the first *Mauretania,* and we often talked 'Titanic'. He was sorry for Lord (weren't we all?), but he used to refer to him as, 'That silly man who wouldn't use his wireless.'"

Rees, Barnish and Dean told Thompson that they had questioned Rostron about his affidavit, in which he said he did not see the *Californian* at dawn, when the other officers did so, and *Thompson himself* did the same, when the opportunity came.

This was Rostron's answer:

"I know. Dean and others, and some passengers, said they saw the *Californian* and watched her approaching. *Well, I was mistaken. I had so much to do, I wasn't thinking of the Californian and didn't recognise her.*" [Emphasis added].

Trailing more than three quarters of a century behind the unrecorded after-incidents of the great disaster, one often has the frustrated feeling of a sluggard camp-follower. Somebody with persistent curiosity and exact mind would have to write it down, there and then, as nearly verbatim as possible. As it was, the admission of his mistake meant probably nothing to Rostron, who, as his daughter said, had much sympathy for Captain Lord. For his four officers, who had themselves seen the *Californian* in her tell-tale position early that April morning, their skipper's correction of his affidavit, unofficial as it was, removed something untrue from the record, as it did for Ivan Thompson, who had only heard the facts from the four officers. Yet this is the first occasion on which Rostron's withdrawal of his affidavit has been published. Nor can it henceforth be questioned, save at the price of questioning also the honesty of the men who heard Rostron's admission.

Rostron's correction of his affidavit is of prime importance in the case of the *Californian*. It not only knocks probably the most impressive and respectable prop from the defence of Captain Lord, but this withdrawal of what, from the *Californian* point of view, was assuredly the key point in Rostron's affidavit, served to rationalize his evidence.

It seems clear that Rostron made his mistake because he did not realize that the four-master he first saw to the north was the same steamer he finally identified as the *Californian,* when she was coming towards him from the west-south-west. Even without Rostron's explicit alteration of his affidavit, there would be strong grounds for suspecting he had made a mistake, and why. With his correction disappears whatever exiguous support for Captain Lord still remained in the *Carpathia* evidence, even after Rees, Dean and Barnish had corroborated Bisset.

The times mentioned by these four witnesses and Rostron fit no more with the exactitude of a timetable than any other series in this tragedy, and no more surprisingly or vulnerably. If anything, they are remarkably consistent. Further, as it certainly gets later, so different witnesses independently estimate the distance between the *Californian* and the *Carpathia* to be diminishing (which even the Lordites would probably not dispute); but the most significant thing is that the two ships are much nearer to each other much earlier than they could have been, if Captain Lord's estimate of his position, although honestly reckoned, had been correct.

Another piece of evidence came from First Class passenger Spencer V. Silverthorne, a buyer for Nugent's department store in St Louis. While he trembled from the bitter cold, in No.5 Boat, he watched "the lights of two steamers, one much closer than the other. They rowed toward the closest one, and she proved to be the *Carpathia*. The other ship," Mr Silverthorne remembered, "was the *Californian* and she came up much later."[13]

Wherever the *Carpathia* was, when she arrived on what the survivors in the lifeboats, at any rate, regarded as the scene of the *Titanic* disaster, even if Captain Lord (and later the MMSA) knew they were wrong, there too was the *Californian;* stopped ten miles away, as she had been since 10.21 the previous night, blind, deaf, and, if not deliberately indifferent, certainly completely inactive and useless. The *Carpathia's* relation to the *Californian* is now conclusively clear and its examination concluded (see Diagram 16).

While information was being sought about the *Carpathia,* an attempt was also being made to find Herbert Stone. After a long effort to make communication, in June 1965, a letter arrived from his son, Mr John A. Stone, who said that his father had died suddenly of a cerebral haemorrhage in September 1959. In the reply, the oft-repeated, but never confirmed, rumour was set out in detail with a request for comment. Stone was reported to have said: "he was sure from the beginning that what he saw was distress rockets." A month passed, and there was no reply, so another letter followed. Six weeks went by, and still there was silence. Another letter followed, trying to set out the case for getting Stone's own views as accurately as possible, whatever they might have been, apart from his evidence, so as to be able to repeat him fairly. The historical importance of the issue, it was asserted, should be given preference to any personal considerations. Yet one more week went by, and then came a reply.

We met the following night[14] in the cafeteria of a crowded and noisy railway station. Inevitably, no doubt, one searched the son's face for resemblances to his father, but they were not obvious, at least, not to the young man of 24 of 1912, whose likeness was the only one known. A large, baldish man, clean-shaven, with glasses, in the early 40s, obviously with an academic turn of mind, very musical, far removed from the sea . . .

Questions were put to him about his father, as he sipped his coffee, glancing surreptitiously now and again at his watch. This was the climax of the case. The son told everything he knew, which was considerable; but it was difficult for one's mind not to slip back to that May day in 1912, as the young officer battled desperately for a peculiar cause not his own. A strange character Herbert Stone must have been, he and Stanley Lord, both of them in their different ways.

Herbert Stone must have had an unhappy journey home after his grinding ordeal at Scottish Hall . . . 1500 lives had been lost, *1500*. He had recently been married, and presumably he was still living, where the log placed him, at 72 Wadham Road, Bootle. There doubtless his young wife was waiting for him. The Liverpool papers, too, were full of it, perhaps even more than London's — she was a Liverpool ship. The rockets not answered, the 1500 lives lost. What sort of marriage, what sort of life would it be, starting like that? The shadow of it must have been over her, as it had been over him.

All of which might have been fanciful, though not very. But there was not a word of fancy or imagination in what the son had written about his father; "he was sure that distress rockets were being fired."

Sources

1 *A Titanic Myth,* p. 74.
2 B 7856A.
3 P.I. from a retired master mariner, 1963.
4 Mersey, p. 193.
5 P.I. The meeting took place in 1965.
6 P.I., obtained mostly in 1966.
7 1965 Petition, p. 24.
8 Bisset, *Tramps and Ladies,* p. 291.
9 P.I. from L. Harrison, October 1964.
10 B 25551.
11 Lightoller, Dover ed., p. 289.
12 P.I. from Mrs Lightoller, 1964 and following years.
13 P.I. from Mr Silverthorne, 14 July 1955.
14 June 1965.

Chapter 20

Why it happened

"What was the matter? Was the captain drunk?"

That question has sometimes been asked by persons coming fresh upon the basic and incredible facts of the *Californian:* eight distress rockets seen, and eight distress rockets unanswered.

The captain, of course, was not drunk. If he had been, there would have been a cruder scandal, but no mystery.

The governing principle of Captain Lord's supporters was to avoid what was incomparably the first and greatest task confronting them, to explain convincingly why the rockets were practically ignored. Instead, they concentrated on a myriad of contradictions, real or factitious, every one of which, compared with the rockets, was a trifle. In Chapter 18, a report of the *Californian* campaign was supplied and in this final chapter these minor items will be disposed of, and an attempt made to supply what is probably the real and unexpected explanation of the fundamental mystery.

The reader scarcely needs to be reminded of the frequent and distinctive practice of the Lordites of relying on evidence which is said to support their man and blandly ignoring the rest. Apart from this distillation of evidence, great stress is also laid on certain propositions, which are claimed to have the demonstrable truth of a theorem of Euclid, but which in fact defy common sense and ignore common experience.

In the first Petition of the MMSA,[1] for example, it is said, if only two ships had been concerned, "they must first have sighted each other at about the same time. No technical knowledge is needed to understand this point." No technical knowledge, in fact, is needed to understand this is a bad point. Here, on the one hand was the largest ship in the world, brilliantly lit, rising some 70 feet above the sea and moving at more than 21 knots. The other ship, the *Californian,* of some 6000 tons, with a freeboard of only 11 feet,[2] was lying stopped, her flying bridge only 40 feet above the waterline. The *Californian* had her two masthead lights, port and starboard red and green lights, stern light and probably a few lights from portholes and elsewhere. She carried no passengers, and although her lights were described by Boxhall as "beautiful",[3] she was lit that night no more than would have been usual with any medium-sized freighter.

The physical conditions were altogether exceptional. Mr Beesley quoted one of the captains[4] who gave evidence in Washington — he was probably paraphrasing Captain Lord himself — as saying: "he did not remember seeing such a night before." In an inky black night, behind the *Californian* was a sky filled with so many stars of unusual brilliance that even experienced travellers and professional seamen commented on the extraordinary spectacle. It does indeed require no technical knowledge to understand that such a phenomenally brilliant sky on such a dark night and on such a flat black sea, with an absolutely unprecedented lack of swell, on which Lightoller had commented,[5] so far from making mutual and almost simultaneous sighting between these two ships almost certain, would have made it most improbable. The argument has in fact been put to several naval officers and experienced merchant seamen, and all have expressed the obvious opinion that in these exceptional conditions, they would expect the *stopped, comparatively small, comparatively sparsely lit Californian* to see the *huge, fast-moving, brilliantly-lit Titanic* before the latter saw the *Californian,* and in fact long before the *Titanic* did so. One retired master mariner and active admiralty assessor told me he would not have been surprised if the *Titanic* had never spotted the *Californian,* even at five miles away, in the particular conditions. Such was the professional opinion on what the first MMSA Petition described as: "This single vital point, that is, the vast time difference between the sightings not only completely and finally disposes of the case against Captain Lord but should have been clearly evident as such to both courts of inquiry."[6] Neither Court was as stupid as this Petition betrays itself.

Simultaneous sighting between the two vessels must have been unlikely, even if the lookouts of the *Titanic* had been as perfect as machines, which was far from being the case.

It must be emphasized in any event that although the Lordites say "nearly two hours", or, when they switch to Captain Lord's 10.30 version, "two and a half hours", passed between the time Groves first saw his passenger ship, and the *Titanic* her "three or four-masted ship", the facts are different. The *Titanic* first saw her ship, no more than ten minutes after she struck, or even perhaps at the very time; but, at most, no more than half an hour after hitting the iceberg, that is, when the boats began to be cleared.

The *Titanic* lookouts certainly did not see the *Californian* at the time of the collision. Apart from any possible deficiency in their quality — and it was criticized at the time and since — expert opinion, or even the exercise of any visual imagination, can understand why the *Titanic* failed to see the *Californian,* which was in sight. Groves and Lord, particularly, spoke about that "very deceiving night", when stars were mistaken for ships' lights and ships' lights for stars. Any stationary ship with only a few lights — however bright — was likely not to be seen as quickly as she would have been normally on a night with fewer, and a normal number of, stars. Paradoxical as it may seem at first, the final and satisfying explanation of an apparent contradiction, and the subject of one of the favourite 'challengers' of the Lordites, is really simple and obvious: the *Titanic* did not see the *Californian,* not because she was not there, but merely because *the multitudinous stars acted as effective, although temporary, camouflage.*

A much more impressive argument for Captain Lord, and in my view, at first encounter, the least vulnerable of all, is the other concerned with lights, that is, the alleged small number of them on the other ship.

When Captain Lord said: "You can never mistake those ships — by the blaze of light . . . a ship like the *Titanic* at sea, it is an utter impossibility for anyone to mistake," unlike the effect of so much of his evidence, he raised not disbelief or doubt, but carried instant conviction. We know he was wrong nevertheless on this occasion, but he raised a problem, which demands an attempt at solution.

Unfortunately, we do not know what Glenn and Ross, the uncalled witnesses, who saw the rockets, thought about the lights of the other ship, or even whether they saw them. Our knowledge, therefore, must come exclusively from characters on one side or the other of the controversy, that is, Lord, Stone, Gibson and Groves (I exclude Gill, who on this point seems plainly untruthful). While much of what Lord and Stone said was evasive, and some of it in Lord's case, at least, also false, there is no doubt that both believed the stranger had too few lights for a passenger steamer. Gibson also said more than once he thought the ship was a "tramp", but this opinion was decisively undermined for any impartial reader by his vivid reference, also repeated, to the "glare of light on her after deck".[7]

Groves, then, is the only witness who said unequivocally that the other ship "had a lot of light" at any time, which was when he first saw her. He also said, of course, she was "undoubtedly a passenger vessel". In spite of this, if the ship had just gone quietly on her course until she was out of sight of the *Californian,* it would have been easy to believe that Groves had somehow been mistaken, and all that had happened was, a medium-sized steamer, at largest, had steamed past some miles to the south. Or, as Mr Harrison wrote after more than a decade of labouring in vain to explain away what happened with the *Californian* after the *Titanic* hit the iceberg and fired her rockets: "If, however, you take from the *Californian* and the *Titanic* such uncontradicted and consistent evidence as is available before any confusing rockets were fired and seen, the following perfectly simple situation is revealed . . ."[8] Or, as any believer in happy endings and a far, far simpler and better world than we know, might write: "If we look at the situation prevailing in Elsinore, Denmark, before any confusing murder of the King occurred, and his son Prince Hamlet was ordered to avenge him, the following perfectly simple situation is revealed . . ."

Unfortunately, it is the confusing murder of Hamlet *père* and the confusing rockets which complicate any preceding "simple situation" and make it irrelevant. It is the complexities which make the drama that concerns us.

The strange ship did not just steam past the *Californian,* as we well know; but let us for the last time review what she really did, but picturing her in our imagination now, as having very little light. Groves now agrees with Stone and Lord about this. I omit Gibson, because his evidence seems a significant addition to the opposite view.

First of all, the ship stopped. Stone testified Groves told him this had happened at 11.40 (when the *Titanic* stopped). Then she lay still for over an hour, the only thing she did being apparently to ignore the *Californian's* Morse lamp. Beginning at 12.45, said Stone and Gibson, she fired eight white rockets bursting into white stars (about the same time the *Titanic* fired eight such rockets). Those rockets make no sound, which, to a layman, seems puzzling. Expert opinion, on the other hand, is (surprisingly) not at all puzzled.

Stone says to Gibson: "there must be something the matter with her" . . . Gibson agrees, "that a ship is not going to fire rockets at sea for nothing" . . . and "there must be something the matter with her" . . . Gibson thinks "it was a case of some kind of distress."[9]

Stone said, Gibson "remarked to me once that he did not think they were being sent up for fun, and I quite agreed with him."[10]

Then, suddenly, the two anxious young men realize that something new and strange is happening to this vessel.

Stone remarks to Gibson: "Look at her now; she looks very queer out of the water; her lights look queer,"[11] and: "Have a look at her now, Gibson, she seems to look queer now."[12]

Gibson says: ". . . her lights did not seem to be natural."[13]

Stone "merely thought it was a funny change of her lights,"[14] and "I remarked that the light looked queer."[15]

Gibson says: "She looks rather to have a big side out of the water,"[16] and "she seemed to be heavily listed to starboard."[17]

Stone notices there is something "funny" or "odd" about her lights: "I noticed the lights looked rather unnatural."[18]

Finally, soon after two o'clock, the vessel "disappears" (about when the *Titanic* foundered).

An unprejudiced investigator can hardly fail to be chilled by this deadly likeness to the last hours of the *Titanic* drawn exclusively by *Californian* witnesses. Against the truly overwhelming identification of the unknown ship with the *Titanic*, there is only one factor, her lack of light. Let us ignore Groves's evidence on the other side completely, and accept it that the *Californian* saw her display little light.

We know from Gibson's statement of 18 April that the other ship was beyond any doubt the *Titanic;* and numerous writers have described that her lights were blazing; but here we are trying, without Gibson's help, to find out why the *Titanic* gave the impression at an apparent distance of no more than four to seven miles of being lit as scantily as a tramp.

Part of the answer is found in the heading of the *Titanic,* for when she ported round the iceberg and turned her bow north and towards the *Californian,* she showed, to any observer on the *Californian,* her darkest side; the bridge and her fore ship. It was in this part of the ship that Lamp Trimmer Sam Hemming had closed the fore scuttle hatch, from which there was a last "glow". He had done so on First Officer Murdoch's order at about 7.15 p.m.[19]

The answer must also be found in the extraordinary physical conditions of that night. The Principal Technical Officer of the Ministry of Transport once suggested that abnormal refraction might have been the cause of lights being seen much farther away than would ordinarily have been possible.[20] Nor was he the only authority who formed that opinion.[21] The assessors, who knew their job, estimated the real distance between the two ships as considerably more than it seemed to the experienced observers in either vessel, and as much as ten miles.

In other words, it was only because of the unusual conditions that the ship's lights were seen as clearly as they were at that distance.

Bearing in mind the abnormal sights from that ship and the decisive things she did, the firing of her eight rockets, the strange appearance of her lights, her list and her disappearance, the conclusion must be that at ten miles, from the position of the *Californian,* on this night this was how the *Titanic* looked.

At that distance, the puzzle of the failure of each ship to see the Morse lamp of the other ceases also to be a puzzle; and, at ten miles, the silence of the rockets would also be quite normal — Mr Little, we remember, put their range of sound at three to five miles. On the other hand, abnormal refraction might also explain the remarkable distance at which the *Carpathia* saw the green flares from Boxhall's boat.

As said above, the scarcity of light is Captain Lord's most impressive argument. As such, it has been treated in this book in isolation, and with everything deliberately loaded in favour of it: disregarding Groves's contradicting evidence and, necessarily ignoring Gibson's statement which by itself destroys it.

Next, we glance at the strange argument about the "limited" damage to the *Titanic,* which is said to "prove" the *Californian* was not near her. This "limited" damage has already been compared with the "limited" extent of the wound of somebody shot through the heart; and expert opinion has been quoted on the unlimited absurdity of the theory.

A far more arresting claim is that Boxhall saw a moving ship, when the *Californian* was undoubtedly stopped, and so the ship at which Boxhall fired his rockets could not have been Lord's command. Near the end of his life, Lord himself was in the habit of voicing his indignation about this matter.

"Well, there are two things I've always stressed. The *Californian* stopped in the ice at 10.20 and her engines never moved. The *Titanic* came up, stopped. There was nothing in sight when she hit the berg. Nothing, by two lookout men and two expert officers on the bridge. They saw nothing. Now how could it possibly have been the *Californian* that they saw? *Californian* never moved. This steamer approached them. You don't want any technical adviser to point it out — it's all bunk, isn't it? Those two things would prove to me — and prove to any nautical examiner — that the *Californian* couldn't have been the ship. They proved that she never moved after 10.20, and they proved that the *Titanic* never saw anything after she hit the berg until the steamer they saw steamed towards them. Dammit, that clears everything, doesn't it? Clears everything."[22]

If this *reductio ad absurdum* had been an accurate statement of the facts, the argument would have been as formidable as that relating to the fewness of the lights. Actually, by far the greater part of the *Titanic* evidence never contradicted *Lord's* claim. It was agreed that the light or lights of the ship seen never moved. Among those who said so were Second Officer Lightoller, Third Officer Pitman and Fifth Officer Lowe. The Lordites, of course, ignored all those, and others, and depend on Boxhall, who gave a circumstantial account of how the steamer he saw approached the *Titanic* and finally steamed away. It has been suggested, and not for the first time, that Boxhall was mistaken, and saw a drifting and swinging ship as a steaming one.

What I believe has not previously been pointed out is that whatever Boxhall saw this three- or four-masted vessel doing, was not compressed into a few minutes, but was spread over about an hour. This is measured and checked by the time Boxhall took firing the rockets, from about 12.45 a.m., until Captain Smith sent him away in Emergency Boat 2. If the other ship was really steaming, she was undoubtedly only crawling — Boxhall himself said she was doing 'very little', — and the probability from the circumstances, and certainly from the weight of the evidence, is that she was not steaming at all.

As to the distance of the *Californian* from the *Titanic*, one of Lord's very important, though very tardily proclaimed, points of defence, after so much already said, let us merely sum up:

(1) The *Californian* was much closer to the *Titanic* than any other known vessel.
(2) Lord claimed that the *Titanic* gave the wrong position, and she was really some 13 miles farther to the south, or more than 30 miles from the *Californian*.
(3) The crude chart of the *Birma* gave some equivocal support to the belief that the *Titanic* was south of her given position, but the accompanying narrative did not. On the other hand, Captain Lord was contradicted by:
(4) Captain Lord of the *Californian* (no other!), who twice said in Boston, before he had decided to rely on the *Titanic's* alleged wrong position, that the *Titanic's* position, as given him by the *Virginian,* was correct.
(5) Captain Moore of the *Mount Temple,* who twice said that although the *Titanic* was some eight miles east of her given position, she was not south of where she had said.
(6) Captain Rostron of the *Carpathia,* who said four times the *Titanic's* position was correct. Moreover, when he left the scene of the wreck, he gave his own posi-

tion as only one mile south of the *Titanic's* latitude.

(7) Dr Ballard who found the wreck only two miles south of the *Titanic's* stated latitude.

But whether the *Titanic* was right or wrong, the vital thing was how far was the *Californian's* overnight position from the *Carpathia,* which reached, and became a marker for, the scene of the wreck soon after 4 a.m. Remembering the *Californian* started from her overnight position about 6 a.m., and began by crawling through the ice:

(1) In the *Mount Temple,* Captain Moore saw the *Californian* about six o'clock, heading west, and already as early as that, only five or six miles north of the *Carpathia.*

(2) In the *Californian,* then steaming south, Groves saw the *Carpathia,* about seven o'clock, abeam on the port side, about five miles away.

(3) In the *Virginian,* which kept about the same time as the *Californian,* Captain Gambell received a message from the *Californian* about 6.20 that she could see the *Carpathia* picking up the boats, and she must thus have been less then seven miles away.

(4) In the *Carpathia,* Second Officer Bisset, soon after daybreak, about 4.30, saw the *Californian* stopped, ten miles to the north. She was also seen by First Officer Horace Dean, Third Officer Eric Rees and Fourth Officer Geoffrey Barnish. About six o'clock, she was to be seen under way, coming slowly towards the *Carpathia.* Steward J.W. Barker also saw her at this time.[23] Captain Rostron saw a four-masted ship with one funnel seven or eight miles away to the north about five o'clock. He said she was not the *Californian;* but later admitted he had been mistaken and agreed that she was.

Only the *Birma* gives the slightest help to Captain Lord's case if the narrative of her Captain and Officers as printed in *The Daily Telegraph* of 25 April 1912 is ignored. For the rest, the *Mount Temple,* the *Virginian,* the *Carpathia* and the information form the *Californian* herself place the *Californian* at the latest, before seven o'clock, and at the earliest, 'after 4.30,' ten miles or less north from the scene of the wreck. The evidence is crushing.

And so to the heart of the matter and the most important subject of all, the rockets.

"Rockets" were no favourite topic in Lordian literature; it enjoyed no special prominence on the summit of the mountain of rhetoric raised to the cause. On the contrary, it was the comparatively minor contradictions and confusions which engaged the indignant and muddled devotion of the faith, and if every one of these had been justly decided in Captain Lord's favour, the fact that he ignored the rockets would still justify the finding against him.

Captain Lord himself first tried to suggest the rockets were "company signals", and his followers ever after claimed they could have "confused" Stone.

"I had never seen company signals like them before," said Stone himself of them.[24] Nor had anybody else.

Let it be recalled, if Captain Lord was in doubt about any "company signals" reported to him, his duty according to a direction from the Board of Trade was clear: *he should have answered them as distress signals.*

Let it be further recalled, no ship in the world had as a company signal a white rocket or white rocket throwing white stars, such as Stone and Gibson saw. It has been shown here for the first time, only three ships in the world had any kind of company signal composed exclusively of white lights. Although the signals were unmistakably different from white rockets (two white pyrotechnic lights, fired simultaneously 60 feet apart), as the three ships might have been on the North Atlantic on the night of 14/15 April 1912, an attempt was made to locate them. Two of them were found to be in the port of Philadelphia. The third, it has not been possible to locate beyond theoretical doubt; but it has been possible to ascertain that on 16 April, the *Montauk Point,* this last ship left on earth that theoretically might have confused the skilled mariners of the *Californian,* sailed from Liverpool,[25] some two thousand miles north-east of the position where the *Titanic* sank. It is maintained that confusion by company signals is at an end.

As for the real rockets, as distinct from the fireworks entertainment promoted in after years by the second and subsequent notions of the Lordites, from as early as 1913 until as late as 1965, it was admitted that the rockets seen by the *Californian* did come from the *Titanic.* It was nevertheless asserted that Captain Lord's inactivity should not have been penalized. The 1913 opinion of the retired "Master Mariner" that it was "a mere matter of detail" whether the rockets came from the *Titanic* or some other vessel has been quoted. Here, let us quote words not hitherto published, those of Sir James Bisset, while living in Australia, during an unsuccessful attempt to compel him to withdraw what he had written about the *Californian* in his book; these words, let us remember from the man, who, in public, sought compassionately to excuse Captain Lord:

"The Titanic fired distress signals — the Californian saw the Distress Signals — the Californian did nothing & 1500 lives were lost."[26]

Of the four-ship theory, that is, that not only the *Titanic* and the *Carpathia,* but two other unknown and undiscoverable ships also had fired rockets, in more than three quarters of a century never a single voice was raised to say: "I saw those rockets!" let alone to claim: "I, a habitant of the globe of the earth, was one who fired them!" Questions about these factitious recurrences were sunk in a sea of times and technicalities, where the Lordites painstakingly likewise drowned common sense for good measure.

The last words on the second Petition of the MMSA in 1968 must record it was based on a statutory declaration made by Mr Beesley on 21 February 1963, in which he said the last of the eight rockets from the *Titanic* had been fired before his lifeboat, No. 13, cleared the vessel's side. According to the Mersey Report, while cautioning that all times subsequent to the collision were unreliable, this boat left at 1.35 a.m.[27] Mr Beesley, in his book, implied that No. 13 was lowered much earlier, at 12.45 a.m.[28] As stated above, the MMSA were eager to get the *Titanic's* rockets fired and finished before 12.45 a.m., when Stone saw the first of them. Hence, the Petition maintained that, in the words of the Merchant Shipping Act, 1894, Section (1) (a), "new and important evidence, which could not be produced at the investigation or inquiry has been discovered," and that, under the Section, the Board of Trade were bound to re-hear that part of the case which concerned Captain Lord.

There is no reason to doubt that Mr Beesley would have returned to England in 1912 to give evidence, had he been asked to do so;*[29] but all his "new and important evidence" was already available to the MMSA in February 1965, when the first Petition was presented. The reason for not using it then, according to the Association, was their confidence that the Petition would succeed "on its technical merits", and to spare Mr Beesley, then 85 years of age, "unwelcome publicity".[30] At the time he was being pressed to make a statutory declaration, his family tried to caution him against the possibility of

* He actually returned in the *Laconia* in July 1912.

such publicity. It also was the only statutory declaration Mr Beesley made in relation to the *Titanic,* in those later years of his life.[31]

When the first Petition was dismissed in September 1965, Mr Roy Mason, then Minister of State (Shipping), wrote to the MMSA that the President of the Board of Trade had rejected it, because, among other reasons: "Your petition does not suggest that there is any new and important evidence which could not have been produced at the formal investigation into the loss of the Titanic . . ."[32] Mr Beesley having died in February 1967, the MMSA apparently dusted off Mr Beesley's 1963 four-year old declaration and suddenly saw in it "new and important evidence". The result was Mr Beesley's tardy and posthumous fathering of the 1968 Petition. Like most of the Lordites' propaganda, it was marred by errors of substance, and its misleading statements have already been mentioned.

Although Lord Mersey rightly gave his caution about the times of the launching of the boats, there is much less doubt about the order in which they left the ship. There is none, for instance, that No. 13, Mr Beesley's boat, left before Emergency No. 2, to which Boxhall, who was firing the rockets, was ordered away by Captain Smith. One would expect the firing of the rockets to have continued until Boxhall left, and there is no doubt that it did. The evidence comes from himself and other sources, including No. 13 itself.

Reginald Robinson Lee, the lookout with Fleet at the time of the collision, was also in No. 13.

"Did you see any rockets sent up from the *Titanic*? the Attorney-General asked him.[33]

"Yes, sir."

"Before you left the vessel?"

"Before *and after.*" [Emphasis added].

John Edward Hart, the Third Class Steward, was in No. 15, which came down immediately after, nearly on top of, No. 13, and gave similar evidence.[34]

"At the time you were leaving in No. 15 boat, were there rockets being sent up?" Mr Scanlan asked.

"Yes; rockets had been fired sometime previous to that."

"You saw that yourself?"

"I saw the rockets fired; yes."

It seems almost superfluous to add that neither Lee nor Hart was mentioned in the second Petition. The Board of Trade very properly dismissed it on 26 July 1968.[35]

It is not hard to understand how Mr Beesley in his old age came to make a mistake about the time of the last rocket. It was a matter, as was said, of ". . . wearing down an old man with talk, undue persuasion, and long past his bedtime;" it is less easy to discover why almost certainly he made a mistake of no less than about 50 minutes too early in the time he apparently stated in his book for the departure of No. 13 Boat.* But one final thing about this Petition should be said. With nothing but pity for Captain Lord, and an amiable desire to help his supporters, Mr Beesley's scientifically trained mind nevertheless would not allow him to lend the support of his name to plain nonsense. It is, therefore, not only relevant, but due to his memory, to state here that only a few months before his death, and more than three years after

---

* One might guess that he had retarded his watch by 47 minutes – the total amount of the ship's clocks were due to be put back – and took the time from it; but since his death it has been impossible even to discover for certain whether the watch he had the greater part of his life was with him aboard the *Titanic*. His family, it must be said, had no high regard for his respect for time.

signing his only statutory declaration dealing with the *Titanic,* Mr Beesley sent for the present writer. While discussing the evidence of Stone and Gibson about "the queer lights", Captain Lord's statements in Boston, and Herbert Stone's confession, all of which greatly impressed the old man, and the two last of which he had not previously known, he firmly declared that he had no doubt that the *Californian* had seen the *Titanic* and her rockets.[36] That, and not this posthumous petition, of such dubious origin, was Lawrence Beesley's last word on the subject.

At the end of the last chapter, we quoted the climactic words in the letter from Stone's son which plainly and frankly admitted that his father had confessed to the charge that he knew distress rockets were being fired.

It is the most important single new fact discovered in this inquiry.

Something more about it must be said; but in the setting of his experience as it actually happened, the unfortunate Stone was not alone with the rockets. Besides Gibson and Gill, there were the firemen George Glenn and his mate, who watched them, Glenn, at least, so concerned that he went and called Stone's attention to what was happening. Then, from Canada, as a voice from the dead, through the memory of his son, came the story of AB William Ross, who saw what he called "flares" "on the horizon, which were interpreted as some kind of distress signal." And, most vivid of all, the simple and unforgettable words of Gibson that what he had seen were "white rockets", throwing "white stars", "all throwing stars".

Here, for the first time, two further, and most significant, details can be added.[37] In private, Gibson said many times that "he did not know it was the Titanic." This is a clear indication that while he held to the view he expressed in his evidence that the other ship looked like a tramp, he later agreed she must have been the *Titanic*. This interpretation is corroborated by the other detail, likewise never previously disclosed. According to a most reliable close relative, Gibson also claimed "on several occasions" that "he was the very first to see *the distress signals* [emphasis added]." That his claim contradicts the accepted evidence is true, but in this context does not matter. The description he gave in his evidence of what he saw could only be distress rockets. The important thing is that, for the first time, Gibson himself used the specific words, "distress signals".

Against the words of these eyewitnesses, Glenn, Ross and Gibson, we remember Herbert Stone in London, standing rock-like and alone, unyielding through a long and almost unbearable ordeal, defiantly at bay, admitting that the other ship's lights looked "queer" admitting she must be in some kind of trouble, admitting that "rockets wouldn't be sent up for fun"; but shifting his ground and stubbornly evading the issue, until he finally lied and said flatly that he did not think that what he saw were distress rockets.

For years afterwards, elusive and uncorroborated rumours drifted about Liverpool and Merseyside that Herbert Stone of the *Californian* had confessed that he really had known what he had seen were distress rockets. This was mentioned in the letter to Stone's son, which finally evoked a reply.

In the case of the *Californian,* this letter is a document of finality and of unequalled importance:

"........

31st August 1965,

Dear Mr. Reade,
Thank you for your letter of August 26th, and my apologies for the delay in replying to your previous letters.

My father never, at any time discussed with me or with my brother and sister his part in the 'Titanic' story. But my mother tells me (and this is all that she will tell) that, as you say, *he was sure that distress rockets were being fired* [emphasis added]. As you say, he was in a very difficult position, as a very young Second Officer, on the threshold of his sea career. But there is no doubt that he felt very deeply about it and was extremely troubled at the time of the enquiry. Knowing my father, and here I speak of my knowledge of him as a man, not as his son, I am quite sure that he would never do anything dishonourable and he would always do his duty.

There is no doubt that this unfortunate episode had a great effect upon his career, as he never had command of his own ship, although colleagues have praised his seamanship . . ."

Details of Stone's subsequent career follow, and the letter concludes as follows:

"This is all the information I can give you, and hope that your book will be a success and that my father's part in the Titanic affair will be treated fairly, as he deserved, and sympathetically.

Yours sincerely,
John A. Stone"

This frank and simple letter rings true in every word. It must have been a painful one to write, and it may be permissible to pay tribute to its moral courage. In a lesser man, the filial devotion, which shines through it from beginning to end, might have subordinated the demands of historical truth to a prudent silence. The impression of candour and directness was confirmed at the meeting which immediately followed, and at which some further information was obtained.

Lloyd's records and some Board of Trade documents, discovered only after considerable effort and search, finished forever the invention of the 'confusing company signals': the evidence itself disposed of the *ex post facto* "Roman candles" and "non-exploding flares"; and now, here published for the first time, Stone's own well-authenticated confession pins down the fact that what the middle watch of the *Californian* saw on that tragic night were distress rockets and nothing else; and Herbert Stone, at least, knew it at the time. The reason he fenced so desperately with the question, and eventually took refuge in a lie is more subtle than obvious self-interest. It is one of the decisive issues in the case, and an attempt to explain it is a final task outstanding.

One ship, and one ship only, was in distress that night, and fired rockets, and that was the vessel seen by the *Californian*. Her identification as the *Titanic* was, we recall, unwittingly but conclusively proved by Gibson. It is ironical that it was Captain Lord himself who was responsible for obtaining this final piece of evidence against himself. He it was, who ordered Gibson and Stone to make reports on what had happened in the early hours of 15 April, and it was in Gibson's paper that the clinching details were contained.

Gibson's apparently innocuous statement about the *Californian* showing her red light to the other ship when she fired her eighth rocket is, therefore, actually a built-in bomb which finishes any defence for Captain Lord to the specific charge concerning the *Titanic,* just as he had already destroyed himself morally by his own answer to Question 6944. There may be various reasons why the devastating significance of Gibson's words has never previously been pointed out. Once it is, there can be no further doubt that it was the *Titanic,* and nothing but the *Titanic,* which the *Californian* saw firing her eight rockets. Those rockets, unanswered in 1912, remained unanswerable ever after.

It could fairly be said, without adding another word, the case for Captain Lord is dismissed, and that is the end of the story. Yet, nobody who has delved into the mystery, would be content to end his labours there and so abruptly. What really happened that night has now been told, but not why. The why is inextricably bound up with the most important character in the drama, Captain Lord himself, and his relationship with his Second Officer. Something more, therefore, still needs to be said about this remarkable man, and hitherto blameless master mariner.

At the time, and shortly afterwards, it was almost unanimously agreed that the verdict was just.

Seamen generally, even more than those who scarcely knew one end of a ship from the other, believed most emphatically so about the adverse decision against Lord in both countries. This did not, of course, prevent some, among them Rostron and Lightoller, from an expression of human sympathy with a fellow seaman in trouble.

More typical was Captain Young, the Professional Member of the Marine Department of the Board of Trade, who, we recall, was the most persistent of all for pressing the law against Captain Lord, for having a special inquiry "into his competency to continue as master of a British ship". Another was a retired master, who had been only a young officer in 1912 (and he was typical of many). Not for a moment would he entertain any excuse for Captain Lord.[38]

"When you hear a man may be drowning," he said, "you don't stop to reckon the odds; you go at once and try to pull him out, even if you've got a wooden leg — or a dud engine. Lord's duty was clear. He should have gone out on deck — seen for himself — called up on his wireless and gone to help, ice or no ice! He did none of these things."

He himself had once been similarly tested and answered an SOS immediately. "And so would any seaman," the old man growled.

Nature itself had handicapped Captain Lord for his ordeal with a handsome but sculptured countenance of stone, that seemed neither to invoke, nor to welcome, sympathy in 1912. In all his long hours at the witness table he had uttered not a single word of regret — he was surely not a figure to awaken public compassion.

Although a fascinating study certainly, he seems the very reverse of the jolly and companionable skipper he depicted himself in his recollections. In Chapter 10, the resumed passage to Boston has been described. "Comfortable" in his mind as he later claimed to be,[39] he yet quietly ordered Stone and Gibson to give him reports of their eventful middle watch. There can be little doubt that they were wanted in the desperate hope of allaying his unspoken fear that those rockets were the *Titanic's*. When they did not, they were equally quietly buried.

Not a document, not a written word, linked the *Californian* with the last hours of the doomed liner, during which Lord played a leading, if entirely inactive, part. Only the chance intervention of Roy Howard, who had mistakenly reported that the *Californian* had bodies onboard, ultimately led to the exposure of the story even to Lord's owners, and the outside world. So far from being "comfortable" in his mind he was a deeply troubled man.

If he had thought for a moment that the ship calling for help was the *Titanic,* one can hardly doubt that Lord would have gone for those rockets at once — or tried to. The weakness, and the evil, in Lord was that believing the trouble came from a ship like his own, in the words of McNabb, he "concluded to wait until daylight".

The reason, of course, was his fear of the field ice, of which he had no experience, and which at the time he probably exaggerated. More than anything else, that fear explains, although it cannot excuse, Lord's misconduct. It was the decision of a cautious and calculating, rather than an impulsive, man; and it was a fatal one.

It happened because Lord was the man he was, an individual, and like nobody else; because of the decisions he took, and, because of one fortuitous circumstance — his relationship with Herbert Stone.

Boston was nearest in time to the event itself, and in Boston this troubled man decided upon his course. There, in the Boston Public Library, the record of what he said at the time still lies, in more than one sense, columns of it, hundreds and thousands of words of it, a web of omissions and positive falsehoods; open to anybody with a persistence for the truth (including his supporters!), never before told in the story of the case; as good as new.[*]

One cannot know whether this spate of untruth was carefully prepared in furtherance of Lord's apparent policy of deceiving anybody deceivable, or whether it consisted of exceptional improvisations in the general pattern, a kind of marine *Commedia dell'Arte*. That he was more restrained and intelligent in his conflict with the facts later in Washington and London cannot undo what happened in Boston. One may pity a proud and hitherto upright man in such straits; but there, under the shadow of the Boston Customs Tower, where Lord betrayed himself as a panic-stricken and unrestrained deceiver, he himself killed the legend of his innocence, then and forever.

It is ironical that Lord, unlike Stone, suffered very little for his part in the *Californian*. His reputation with Sir John Latta was so high that, as his trouble with his sight had proved to be only temporary, he would have been welcomed back at any time. Lord, however, had had enough of the sea, and although he was under 50 on his retirement in 1927, and lived to be 84, he never again left England. Unlike many seamen, he had always been prudent financially, and this useful trait, supplemented by a number of inheritances, not only enabled him to retire when he did, but also accounted for the material comfort of his life. Spent with his wife and son at his home in Wallasey, it was one of exceptional happiness.

For an active and able man of 49, in effect deliberately to have turned his back on the world seems extraordinary. His service with Latta's, which he often said had been his happiest days at sea, cannot explain it. The unique place Captain Smith had once held with the White Star Line was similar to that Captain Lord soon won with Latta's Nitrate Company (incidentally, a much more prosperous, if less glamorous, enterprise). When there was a new ship, Lord got the command; and his career with Latta terminated not in a catastrophe, but with his reputation at its summit.

As the memory of the *Titanic* itself faded, Lord was forgotten, and only rarely did reports, usually of a hostile kind, in which his name figured, reach him from different parts of the world. It was said, for instance, with his world in ruins after the *Titanic*, "he crept away and drank himself to death in a slum"; about the time of his retirement, in Boston it was said he had left the sea because no officers would serve with him. Lord seems to have met all such stories with only passing resentment or even indifference. These attacks did not hurt much, because the truth was vastly different. One who knew him as well as anybody, has written: "the *Titanic* catastrophe, after the initial

* *The Boston Journal* for 26 April 1912, containing the most lurid of Lord's inventions, is available only at the Library of Congress, Washington, D.C.

impact, did not worry him in the least."[40] Groves and Stone might brood secretly over their very different responsibility in the affair, but Lord was made of tougher fibre. He seems very soon to have reached the comforting conclusion that he had nothing to reproach himself with. The dreadful exposure of his inner state of mind at Boston was apparently gone and forgotten, never to be thought of again. It certainly had never been known in England; and Question 6944 was but the largest gap in the unread official record.

More than once Lord asserted that he had never read a transcript of his evidence, or Evans's; nor a composite report of the inquiry. If this was literally true, it meant he did not read a newspaper in Boston either on that Saturday.[41]

And later, after London, when all the evidence was in, and judgement given, and the books began to be written and continued to be published over the years, he did not read them either.

Not a single book, not even the evidence did he ever read.[42]

And if at any time he came upon a book about the *Titanic,* he stopped reading it, Lord claimed. Nobody could tell him anything about the *Californian.* How could they? He was there and his critics were not. He knew all that had gone on, better than anybody. He'd not seen the *Titanic,* no matter what they said.[43]

He was an old man when he said that, known to all who met him for his good humour and unfailing charm; but when he suddenly ripped out his contempt for evidence and authors and anybody who dared express an opinion contrary to his own, the old arrogance and scorn of contradiction possessed him, and there, for a few moments, was a startling resurrection of "Lord of the *Californian*", the man who dominated and despised; and was condemned.

One asks nevertheless whether the real reason he read nothing about the *Titanic* — if it was true — was as he said, or that he could not bear to do so. It does not affect his innocence; nor could it undo Boston.

His was a long retirement, stretching out to 34 years.[44] Lord had no one dominating interest. He joined the Wallasey Golf Club, but only for the game, not its social side; he read biography and good fiction, and newspapers voraciously. The cinema did not interest him, nor modern music, but in a household of musical knowledge and catholic taste, his own preference was for the tuneful operettas and musical comedies of the period. He took no part in politics, but, of course, was an ardent Tory, which in such circles in England does not count, as it is part of nature.

Lord's life was centered almost entirely in the present, and the *Titanic* and *Californian* apparently had receded far back in his mind. The 35-year old Captain Lord, who had disciplined his ship almost by the very appearance of his face alone; who said little to anybody, and nothing at all to most; who had no sense of humour and ruled by the rules, without exception and without forgiveness, had disappeared. In his place was a very approachable, gentle old man. Time had mellowed the grim countenance of the master of the *Californian.*

His charm was inescapable, and he had the rare quality of turning even a casual acquaintance into an enthusiastic and permanent supporter. The impression of integrity and technical efficiency created by him remained in the memory even after his death. He had become not a mellower version of, but seemingly a different man from, that stern and unyielding figure who had stood at the witness table in Scottish Hall, suffering a slow and inescapable psychological stripping. The result was an emotional refusal to accept even the theoretical possibility that Lord could have been wrong. The climax of the blind belief in him was the charge that the only explanation of the two adverse verdicts was plain dishonesty: "frame-up" in Washington and a "rigged" inquiry in London.

The real Captain Lord in his 80s, usually accompanied by his pekingese, Chin, seemed neither a "victim" nor a villain, but merely a universal charmer. He joked frequently, and did not exclude the irritating results of his own occasional lapses of memory, which was in fact usually exceptionally clear.

One cannot escape the suspicion that it was the character of Lord himself, rather than any merit in his case, which persuaded Mr Harrison to give the support of his organization to a difficult and hopeless campaign. Many who made Lord's acquaintance, but who had hitherto not read the hundreds of pages of evidence and other documents bearing on the *Californian* — those on the *Titanic,* generally, extend to thousands — fell under the spell of the old sea captain. It seems that Mr. Harrison too believed in the skill and integrity of this outstandingly fascinating old man of the sea.

Thereafter, in his few remaining years, Lord took an active and enthusiastic part in the preparation of his case; and here Groves comes back briefly into the story.

It was near the end of his life, when living in retirement in Suffolk, that, much against his will, Groves was persuaded to turn his mind back to the *Californian*. Since that traumatic experience he had made for himself by far the most successful career of any member of the *Californian's* crew (see Appendix J), beginning with the early attainment of his extra master's certificate. He was an enthusiastic Mason and a keen yachtsman, and on the Suffolk coast the stocky, retired sea captain, with the white hair, thrust-out jaw and deep blue eyes was a well-known and very popular figure.

A quiet and sensitive man, but an entertaining talker, there was at least one topic on which he never started a discussion. *Titanic* and *Californian* were names he never uttered, and even men who had known him well for years never suspected that he had been concerned in the great disaster. His acute, even exaggerated, sense of responsibility, it seems, caused him to blame himself, at least in part, for the great loss of life. As he wrote, if he had only realized that the magnetic detector of Evans's wireless needed winding, the whole story would have had a less tragic ending.[45] Lord, as we have seen, who was so much more at fault, could live for many years with his mind untroubled by the *Titanic;* but not Groves.

The two met only once, 13 years later in 1925, and then very briefly and by chance in Sydney N.S.W. Neither recognized the other, and it was only after some time that Lord realized who he was talking to.

"Are you Lord of the *Californian*?" the companion of Groves enquired a day or so later as the two met Lord walking along the quay: "What of it?" Lord snapped,[46] as if overwhelmed by sudden, unpleasant, memories.

In the serenity of his old age Lord believed Groves was a publicity-seeker, and bitterly resented the fact that the Mersey inquiry had preferred this junior officer's evidence to Stewart's, Stone's and his own.[47]

In contrast, Groves had no hostile feelings towards his former skipper, and so, in 1959, during the early stages of the renewed campaign for Captain Lord, he ultimately was persuaded, out of fairness to Lord, to a discussion about the case in his Ipswich home. Having "strong views" about the matter, he afterwards spontaneously wrote his testimony to Lord's sobriety. Truth was Groves's only criterion, and on another matter he refused his support. His firmly expressed opinion at the inquiry in 1912 that the ship he had seen was the *Titanic* was naturally no help to Lord's friends, and a determined attempt was made to get an admission from him that Lord Mersey "brought pressure to bear upon you to express an *opinion* [*sic*] which was preferred to Captain Lord's navigational *evidence*" [emphasis in original].[48]

But Groves could take care of himself. He would not apply that type of reasoning to the *Titanic*.

"There is absolutely no question whatsoever," he wrote, "that [Lord Mersey] did not influence me at the inquiry in any way and I cannot see any grounds for anyone asserting that he did so. Young as I was at the time, I am perfectly sure nobody would have attempted to do so."[49]

He felt so strongly about it, in fact, that he repeated his denial:

". . . I must again repeat that from Lord Mersey downwards nobody influenced me in what I thought and what I said. I see no reason to contradict anything which I said at the Scottish Hall . . ."[50]

Because of the doubts which from time to time the MMSA professed to have about Groves's final opinion of the identity of the ship he saw, it should perhaps be repeated that until his death, which occurred in 1961, he never changed his opinion about this either.

"I have never had the slightest doubt whatsoever," he wrote in a letter in 1955, which expressed his views to the end, "that the ship which I saw on that evening in April, 1912, whilst we were stopped in the ice was indeed the 'Titanic'."[51]

In the crisis of the *Californian,* Second Officer Herbert Stone had a more important part than Groves, and, with Captain Lord, the most vital of all. When all the questions and problems concerned with technical or material matters have been answered or solved, there still remains the intangible factor of personality, which, as already said, in my view was decisive. The core of this matter is the relationship between Stone and Lord.

In his old age, Lord reported Stone saying to him: "I would have pulled you out, if there'd been any trouble!"[52]

Perhaps Stone even said it, though it seems in the highest degree unlikely. Whether or not Lord was as fast asleep on his settee at the crucial times as he claimed, there was the direct evidence of Gibson, who said flatly that Lord was awake — it is hard to believe that Stone would have been morally capable of the determination and familiarity of actually laying his hands on Lord under any circumstances.

Before now, nothing, as far as I know, has ever been published about Stone's background, but it is of importance in trying to understand his actions, or lack of them, on the night of the disaster, and the story he told later.

Stone came of a North Devon family, and the reason he went to sea was significant. He left home and took up a maritime career because of what was described as a "difficult" father.

If it stood alone, it would be incautious to deduce too much from the cause which drove Stone to sea — it was not an uncommon thing for boys to run away to sea, then or later — but the circumstances in which Stone found himself in the *Californian* served to strengthen the effect of his troubled past.

It is not difficult to understand the disturbing elements in Stone's situation. Stone could not, and did not, find his fellow officers very congenial. He had left his home as a boy of 16 to escape from his father; now, he found himself in a ship commanded by an exceptionally dominating and remote skipper. Lord was clearly a much better man than himself, and aboard ship there was no place to escape from him.

Lord's mere presence was enough to arouse in the already insecure Stone a feeling of such inferiority as amounted to actual fear. He could not escape, but he avoided Lord as much as he could by taking to his bunk whenever he was off duty. Aboard ship, this was well known; and afterwards, the fear that Stone had for Lord, if not common knowledge, was at least known to persons astonishingly remote from the *Californian*. Charles Burlingham, for instance, counsel in New York for the White Star Line in some of the litigation after the wreck, was aware of the unusual situation.[53]

That Stone's attitude towards Lord was neurotic is apparent from the nature of some of his evidence. During the firing of the rockets, Stone betrayed an almost infantile faith in the infallibility of Lord. Here was a grown-up, weather-beaten, moustached ship's officer answering questions by quoting his captain, much as an obedient child might justify his conduct by repeating, "Papa told me." It becomes less incomprehensible (and less humiliating) if we bear in mind the boyhood of the man, who was watching the stars of the white rockets hanging in the sky.

Stone was no fool; at least, he knew distress rockets when he saw them, and he was sure distress rockets were being fired, even though the master seemed obsessed with "company signals". Three more had gone up since the five he had reported, when the master had ordered him to send Gibson down to report again, when he had news. Stone had no doubt there was something wrong with the ship; and following the rockets came the disturbing "unnatural" change in the lights. At this point, a normal man of average force of character would have disregarded Lord's order to send Gibson below, and instantly have gone himself. He would indeed have "pulled" Lord out.

To Stone, however, there lay below, whether asleep or awake, another father figure, who was even more "difficult" than his own. From the time that passed after the last rocket was fired, before any communication was made to Lord, Stone hesitated, almost incredibly, for about half an hour, no doubt weighing the known against the unknown. In the end, unable to summon enough moral courage to go and confront the captain himself, it was Apprentice Gibson he sent below to deal with Captain Lord. The man in the key position was mentally handicapped in dealing with the special situation.

It is an interesting fact, and perhaps a hint of the limit of his own indulgence with weakness, that although Groves had witnessed and knew a great deal about Stone's neurotic fear of Lord, he always believed nevertheless that the blame for the failure of the *Californian* rested much more heavily on Stone than on Lord.

There is no reason to doubt Herbert Stone's physical courage under ordinary circumstances, but equally no reason to have any faith whatever in his moral ability to contradict, oppose and, worst of all(!), even correct an order from this dominating father figure. Groves laboured under no such crippling psychological burden. He himself has written that he would have had Evans called at once, and if the suggestion has been rejected, he would have gone immediately to the Chief Officer. Groves was positive that Stewart would have acted promptly; which inevitably would have led to a more honourable ending to the *Californian* incident.

When the day came for Stone to tell his story on oath, he was in a dilemma. The decisive factor, however, was his subconscious feeling that if he did speak out, he would not only be disloyal to his captain, but he would be betraying and incriminating his own father. We know what Stone actually said.

He paid heavily for his loyalty and his fears.[54] He was deeply troubled at what he had done, and, as we know, confessed the truth to his wife, and to her alone; but that was not the end of it. He never forgot that terrible night; but he never said a word against Lord or anyone else. Nor would he ever discuss the matter, even with his children; but his whole career was greatly affected by it. He had the reputation of being a competent seaman, and he himself was pathetically certain that if it had not been for the *Californian,* he would have risen to command.

In 1933, bad health drove him from the sea, and thereafter he worked in the Liverpool docks for the rest of his life. He was on his way to work there one morning in September 1959, when he had a cerebral haemorrhage and died a few hours later. He was 72, and died penniless.

Anybody who reads the evidence without bias will probably agree with Groves, that Stone was more directly responsible for the delinquency of the *Californian* than Lord himself; but, morally, it is a different matter. Lord, in a moment of weakness, made a deliberate decision to disregard a call for help at sea, and so his act was in a different category from negligence or a mere error of judgement on a technical matter.

After Captain Lord had decided to fight again his cause of the *Californian,* the subject became a favourite conversation piece at home; but it was not darkened by such memories as the unhappy fate of Herbert Stone.

Captain Lord had reduced the whole case to a simple, cast-iron argument, "*Californian* never moved", and there is no doubt that unlike the things he had said at Boston long ago, he believed in it implicitly. Chin, the pekingese, would bark indignantly, the grandfather clock would chime loudly; Vermeer's "Woman With A Water Jug" glowed from the print on the wall, and everybody else believed it too.

In this home of comfortable and unswerving respectability such monstrosities as any guilt attaching to the *Californian* clearly had no place.

But one who met Lord in those last years of his life, and who did know all the facts of his ordeal, must have asked: "Is this the cold-blooded inventor of Boston, the man who deliberately fabricated a story, which deceived most of the shrewd ship reporters of a great maritime city?"

This provides the basis of the last reason why it happened: the Lord of 1912 was not the Lord of 1962. On that April night certainly, character was indeed fate.

Stanley Lord died in Wallasey of a renal infection on 24 January 1962, at the age of 84. The struggle to reverse the decision against him was then well under way. He left an estate of £21,234, and made certain bequests to religious bodies and charities.[55]

It remains to make a few final remarks about the vigorous effort of 'officially restoring his reputation as a shipmaster'.

It was frequently said by the Lordites (and possibly others), that in condemning Captain Lord, a grave slur was cast on the reputation of the British mercantile marine itself. The finding against Lord implied that the other officers of the mercantile marine, who in one way or another had contradicted him, were vindicated. The complement to this situation has naturally not been mentioned by Lord's supporters, but it should be made clear. The reversal of the condemnation of Lord would imply a rejection of those loosely described, and for convenience, as his "opponents". These included not only all his own officers — except perhaps Stewart, judging by part of his story — but also Captain Moore of the *Mount Temple,* Captain Gambell of the *Virginian,* Captain Rostron of the *Carpathia,* Second Officer — afterwards Commodore Sir James — Bisset, First Officer Dean, Third Officer Rees and Fourth Officer Barnish of the same ship; Second Officer Lightoller and Fourth Officer Boxhall of the *Titanic.* All these officers were no less men of honour and skill than Lord

THE SHIP THAT STOOD STILL

himself, and it is hard to see why their posthumous condemnation would not
cast an even larger shadow over the reputation of the British merchant navy.
Nor is that the end of it.

In addition to the opposition of his fellow officers, Lord was opposed also
by the US Senate Committee, who, it may be argued, are no concern of the
British Board of Trade. The condemnation by the British inquiry is, of course,
the point in issue, and the reversal of the finding would condemn Lord Mersey
and his five assessors. If Captain Lord was right, all these men, Americans as
well as British, every single one of them, was wrong.

All the varied persons above are dead, but among those still living are close
relatives of the deceased. The reversal of the verdict against Lord would necessarily inflict on these innocent persons the painful knowledge that it had now
been officially held that their deceased relatives were either incompetent or actually corrupt. It must be further pointed out, that any new inquiry, would necessarily have to depend exclusively on documents and legal arguments.

The evidence against Lord was overwhelming. That concerning the most
important issue, the rockets, was so damning that his supporters were plainly
intimidated and preferred to make loud noises on little puzzles of relative
unimportance. Moreover, the evidence in Lord Mersey's Report, which formed
the basis of the finding against Captain Lord, was drawn, with one possible
exception (Sir Ernest Shackleton, the Antarctic explorer), out of their own
mouths, exclusively from the *Californian* witnesses themselves. Even if it
took no account of the considerable amount of new material, including Lord's
statements in Boston and Stone's confession, presented in this book, any
competent and unprejudiced tribunal would inevitably be compelled to confirm
the 1912 decision.

In the circumstances, it is right to ask whether there would be any
justification for spending public money on a new inquiry in such a clear case.

Although a valiant fighter against the despotism of bureaucracy, a Lord
Chief Justice, who was ironically perhaps the worst in modern times, once,
in a minor case,* coined a phrase which won enduring fame. He said: "It is not
merely of some importance, but is of fundamental importance that justice
should not only be done, but should manifestly and undoubtedly be seen to
be done."

Lawyers, as a class, are far from being the last group in the country to
claim that justice and the law are identical. It has been said that as Captain
Lord's certificate had been neither cancelled nor suspended, the law was that
he could not appeal against the censure implied in Lord Mersey's finding.
The point was argued in the case of *The Royal Star,*§ with the master in exactly
the same situation as Captain Lord. The court there held that the master was
entitled nevertheless to appeal against the censure; but whether that judgement
would be followed seems doubtful for more than one reason. The status of
Captain Lord at the inquiry, whether only a witness or a party, it was said,
"contains a forecast of the correct ending to the case".

The friends of Captain Lord, with much emphasis, not to mention an equal
amount of inaccuracy and a disregard for an abundance of inconvenient
evidence, have asserted that justice was assuredly never done in his case.
The answer to this charge is clear and unequivocal: justice most decidedly was

---

* *Rex V. Sussex Justices, Ex parte McCarthy* [1924] *1 K.B.* 256 *at p.* 259.

§ (1928 p. 48). Incidentally, with Charles Dunlop, then a K.C., appearing as counsel for the unnamed
master.

done. If it be further claimed on Captain Lord's behalf, in accordance with the principle set out above, that justice was not anyhow seen to be done, it again seems to me there can be only one answer: it was not.

The basis for this opinion is the extremely dubious argument of the Attorney-General about Lord's status when he gave his evidence, and what appears to be the still undecided question of any right of appeal to the courts in his particular situation, which, in any event, he did not even attempt to exercise.

Nevertheless, even after Lord's death, he was entitled to some "relief", in that before he gave his evidence he was not cautioned that, if he preferred, he could remain silent. The relief Lord might have claimed must have been limited to an official acknowledgment of an infringement of a legal right, a breach of natural justice, and the damages would probably have been no more than nominal. A judicial inquiry in Lord's case would be useless, even in the unlikely event of one being granted. It might be that the only means of putting the matter right would be to take the appropriate steps to secure the intervention of the Parliamentary Commissioner, the popularly named 'Ombudsman'.*

Any declaration granted posthumously to Lord would be materially and practically quite valueless, and its sole purpose would be publicly to restore the integrity of the principle that justice should be "seen to be done". To many, the whole proceeding might seem completely academic, if not positively objectionable as a piece of effete and time-wasting legal ceremonial.

In our society, however, whether British or American, where in recent times the power of the executive (particularly in Britain) has enormously increased, but where, in contrast with totalitarian practice, the principle of protecting the rights of the individual against the state is still theoretically admitted, a public acknowledgment of a wrong done in this case would have a rare and peculiar value. The wrong was committed many years ago (and would be barred by any statue of limitations) to a man now dead, who himself certainly did not have "clean hands". In this age especially, where the individual has been despised and mocked and murdered by a hundred dictators of all sizes and colours, it is better to be over careful about a wrong to any individual, rather than blatantly contemptuous of it, particularly when, as here, we are confronted with what is as much a moral as a legal issue.

Fiat justitia, ruat coelum, which in the case of Captain Stanley Lord alone, may be translated:

"Let justice be seen to be done, though heavens fall
From the weight of white stars as distress rockets call."

Sources

1 MMSA Petition 1965, p. 6.	6 MMSA Petition 1965, p. 6.	11 B 7515.
2 Official log.	7 B 7429.	12 B 7650.
3 US 934.	8 USNI *Proceedings*, August 1969.	13 B 7517.
4 Beesley, Dover ed., p. 42.	9 B 7756.	14 B 7991.
5 B 14199.	10 B 7895.	15 B 7996.
		16 B 7651.
		17 B 7660.

* This official, whose institution was inspired by Scandinavian precedent, has the function of putting right certain wrongs to the citizen for which the courts have no remedy; but the Ombudsman's powers were determinedly restricted and limited by the Government when the office was established. In modern Britain the executive is an exceedingly jealous god.

18 B 7943.
19 B 17707-9.
20 P.I.
21 P.I. Professor Stephens *et al.*
22 *A Titanic Myth,* p. 188.
23 *New York Times,* April 19.
24 B 7901.
25 *Lloyd's Weekly Shipping Index,* 9 May 1912, and cf. Chapter 5.
26 P.I. 18 July 1969.
27 Mersey Report, p. 38.
28 Beesley, Dover ed., pp. 38-39, 30.
29 P.I.; L.B.; L.R.
30 MMSA Petition, February 1968, pp. 6, 7.
31 P.I.
32 *Liverpool Echo,* 8 Sep 1965.

33 B 2582-83.
34 B 10103-10104.
35 Commons Hansard, 26 July 1968-280.
36 P.I. Final meeting with L.B., Northwood, Middlesex.
37 P.I. 22 Sep 1969. Letter from Gibson's widow.
38 P.I., July 1968, personal interview.
39 B 6983.
40 P.I.
41 *Cf.* US newspapers, 27 April 1912.
42 Ibid.
43 P.I. from L. Harrison, October 1964.
44 P.I. The writer has sought, and been favoured with, the best possible information

about Captain Lord.
45 'The Middle Watch'.
46 *A Titanic Myth,* p. 158, and P.I. Groves and L. Harrison.
47 P.I. from Groves and L. Harrison.
48 P.I. Capt. C.V. Groves's papers.
49 Ibid.
50 Ibid.
51 Ibid.
52 *A Titanic Myth,* p. 189.
53 P.I., obtained in New York.
54 P.I., September 1965 - letter and interview.
55 Chief Probate Registry, Somerset House, Calendar of Grants Vol. 1 JKL 1912, Vol. 8, 1962.

Addendum

The 1990–1992 Reappraisal

Between 1975 when Leslie Reade finished the last chapter of his book and 1993, when it was finally published, a whole new way presented itself to the friends of Captain Lord to have the case for the *Californian* reopened and to reappraise Captain Lord's role in what had generally become known as the 'Californian Incident'.

In 1989 the British Ministry of Transport established an investigative branch that was to look into maritime accidents that needed to be investigated officially, more often than not because of public demand. This branch was given the name 'Marine Accident Investigation Branch' (MAIB). Its powers are to investigate marine accidents on their own account, or by order of the Secretary of State, and — if so chosen, usually for preventive purposes — to make their reports public.

The continuing lobby by Captain Lord's supporters directed their attentions to the MAIB from its very early days, and eventually, on 29 May 1990, the Investigation Branch formally sent the Secretary of State for Transport, Cecil Parkinson, their papers and information suggesting the opening of a reappraisal of the Californian Incident.[1]

One may wonder what the information was that the Branch had submitted to the Secretary of State for Transport. Mr Leslie Harrison apparently knew what it was: "The Department of Transport have already concluded that the Titanic and Californian were probably 20 miles apart," he wrote on 21 June that year (1990). Earlier, he had said that: "In a letter dated 3 August 1988, it was stated on behalf of the British Department of Transport that they had carefully considered the evidence, including that provided by the finding of the TITANIC's wreckage, and concluded that in all probability the CALIFORNIAN was 'substantially further' from the TITANIC than Lord Mersey had found." Mr Harrison found that: "This is an official tacit admission that Captain Lord was completely innocent of the charge that he could have saved 'many if not all' the lives that were lost."[2]

On 6 June,[3] a week after the MAIB had submitted their proposal to the Department of Transport, Cecil Parkinson had indeed decided in favour of the reappraisal, and the Investigation Branch could therefore get to work. It set its goals and terms of reference; in short these were:

(a) To establish as far as possible the positions of the *Titanic* and the *Californian*.
(b) To consider whether *Titanic* was seen by *Californian*.
(c) To consider whether distress signals from *Titanic* were seen by *Californian* and, if so, whether proper action was taken.

(d) To assess the action by Captain Stanley Lord of the *Californian*.

The references seemed short, but certainly adequate.

Captain Thomas W. Barnett, a then recently retired Merchant Navy officer of wide experience, and formerly a surveyor for the Investigation Branch, was commissioned to look into the matter. He was to present his findings to the Chief Inspector of Marine Accidents, Captain Peter Marriott, and prepare a report.

All this had happened in complete and official silence and not a word had leaked to the outside world. For more than a month the silence prevailed. Then, *The Daily Telegraph* (London) broke the news on 9 July 1990. A day later it already seemed to know the result of the whole exercise.

Shipwreck inquiry 'will clear Titanic scapegoat at last'

it announced on 10 July 1990.

"There is no doubt about it," said Mr Harrison equally confident the same day, "they must know they are leading up to a vindication of Captain Lord," he enthusiastically anticipated, and he had every reason to be so confident.

The friends of Captain Lord had been informed of the reappraisal no less than some two and a half weeks before[4] the Press heard of it[5] and seized upon the story instantly and massively. Only a week before that was the Press Office of the British Government first and officially informed of the reappraisal.[6]

Captain James de Coverly, Deputy Chief Inspector of MAIB, had informed Mr Leslie Harrison, Mr Peter Padfield, Mr Stanley T. Lord (Captain Lord's son) and some others, apparently all supporters of Captain Lord, on 20 June 1990 "that the Secretary of State, Cecil Parkinson, [had] decided that [the] Branch should commission a reappraisal of the evidence concerning Captain Lord." It was intended that a report would be published when Captain Barnett had completed his task, but no publishing date was given.[7]

No wonder that expectations were high in the ranks of Captain Lord's supporters. "If the investigation turns out as we hope," Mr Padfield said, "it will be a personal triumph for Leslie Harrison." [8]

Captain Barnett was soon to find an avalanche of information descending on his desk. Leslie Harrison "is making available to the new inquiry between 40 and 50 documents from 1912 attached to an affidavit sworn by Captain Lord in 1960 [sic: 1959],"[9] wrote Barry O'Brien, the *Titanic*-man of *The Daily Telegraph*, who had broken the news of the reappraisal.

It was not the only information given to Captain Barnett. He naturally had information from both sides of the argument and both sides of the ocean. Mr Harrison was but one among many others who had submitted documents for or against the argument.[10]

An odd aspect of the whole exercise was its name. In the Press it had been called "a re-examination", "an investigation", "a re-evaluation", "a 'low key' enquiry", "the reopening of the 1912 inquiry". It all meant the same, of course, but not once was the official name "Reappraisal" mentioned. However, there is some significance in this phrase that should not be overlooked. "It is not a Formal Investigation nor a rehearing of the Formal Investigation of 1912: . . . to conduct such proceedings would be entirely outside the powers of the Marine Accident Investigation Branch or of any individual. What is taking place is a reappraisal of the particular matter of the involvement of the *Californian*, taking account of evidence which was not available in 1912

— particularly, of course, the discovery of *Titanic's* wreckage."[11] explained Cecil Parkinson.

The Merchant Shipping Act of 1970 rules that the Board of Trade (since 1983, Department of Trade and Industry) may order the whole or part of a case to be reheard, if new and important evidence has come to light or if there is reason to suspect that a miscarriage of justice had occurred.

The new and important evidence, in the eyes of the supporters of Captain Lord, was this time, of course, the discovery of the wreck. This evidence, interesting in itself as it may be, but which by its sheer nature, says nothing about the overnight position of the *Californian,* was not to be used for a formal investigation, but for a reappraisal. This meant that whatever the outcome, the 1912 verdict would legally, and historically, remain untouched.

"On the particular matter of the CALIFORNIAN's distance from the TITANIC," wrote Mr Parkinson, "it is correct that Mr Harrison (and others) are aware of earlier work done within the Department which suggested that the distance was in the order of 20 miles; it is partly because of this work that I considered a more thorough reappraisal necessary."[12]

What this earlier work had been was not revealed. Surely the publication of the exact position of the wreck in 1987 has been part of it, but it also seems that work done much earlier had great influence on the decisions made in 1990 and later. In the early 1960s Captain J.H. Quick, a General Surveyor for The Board of Trade, had filed a report in which he found that the two ships had been some 20 miles apart.[13] Apparently Captain de Coverly found Captain Quick's report, for whatever reason, more convincing than Captain Barnett did. Beside that, over the years the file with letters in support of Captain Lord, complaining about the treatment he had been given, had grown to two feet.[14] ". . . there have been, over many years, numerous approaches to the Department on the subject of CALIFORNIAN's involvement in the tragedy. All have to be dealt with, and our files show that they occupied a quite significant amount of staff time."[15] wrote Cecil Parkinson, making it clear that his Department was more than tired of the endless argument.

Lacking this and other detailed information, the Press tried to keep the story going throughout July 1990, and they found willing support in the friends of Captain Lord. *The Sunday Telegraph,* under the heading:

Titanic scapegoat 'victim of clubmen's conspiracy'

quoted Mr Padfield who had again voiced his old belief that Captain Lord was "made the scapegoat" and that "it was not the sort of conspiracy where you have documentary evidence, more a case of talks in club chairs. It has every sign of a gentleman's agreement, if you like, that Lord would be got."[16] Mr Harrison was quoted in practically all the papers airing the beliefs he had held for over 30 years and with which the reader is now familiar.

But other, and most professional, opinions were heard too, though the space given to them was sparse to say the least. Captain A.B. Yarker of Croydon, Surrey, felt that the rockets were overlooked: "Rockets fired at sea must always be treated as distress rockets," he prudently and accurately observed. "Thus, when he [Lord] learnt that rockets had been sighted, the Master of the Californian, instead of turning over and going back to sleep, should have gone to the assistance of the vessel firing them. Whether or not this vessel was the Titanic would have become instantly apparent had he woken up his radio operator and ordered him to activate his set."[17]

Dr Robert Ballard, who had the wrath of the 'Californians' brought upon him by saying in his book that the position of the *Titanic* "does not decisively weight the scales for or against Captain Lord" and observed the "strong possibility" that the *Californian* was south and "well east of her calculated position",[18] remained "sceptical of Lord's innocence" and thought "the new investigation [was] sort of silly."[19]

While Captain Barnett was reappraising the old and the new evidence, the Press Office said that his final report was to be made public shortly before Christmas 1990. It was not, neither was it by the end of January, or early February 1991, as the Press Office said later. Nor was it half way through April as was expected next. "Any day now" the Press Office said at the end of April. "Oh no, not before the end of the year [1991]" the Investigation Branch said at almost the same time.

Captain Barnett had asked those who could give him valuable information to submit that information before the end of the first week of November 1990 so he could close his investigation and write his report.

Within a few months he was ready, and in mid-March 1991 he submitted his report to the Investigation Branch. However, Barnett's report was not to be published then, nor has it been to this day.

On 2 July 1991, the Department of Transport wrote in a letter to the impatient hordes of Captain Lord's legion, who had fired off restless letters to the Department inquiring when their hero would finally be officially exonerated, that Captain Barnett "had submitted his findings and report to the Chief Inspector of Marine Accidents in March 1991" and because of the thoroughness of his report, the Chief Inspector needed to be equally thorough, and that a review was then being undertaken. After he was finished with the review the Chief Inspector would advise the Secretary of State — then Malcolm Rifkind, who had taken over from Cecil Parkinson in November 1990. When the advice had been considered by the Secretary of State an announcement would be made.

This letter revealed something entirely new. So far it had been made clear that Captain Barnett's report would be published when he was finished with it. Now it became apparent that his report would first be reappraised — so to speak — by the Chief Inspector of Marine Accidents, Captain Peter B. Marriott. In fact Captain Marriott delegated Barnett's report to Captain James de Coverly, the Deputy Chief Inspector of Marine Accidents.

Captain de Coverly's position in the exercise was unfortunately somewhat subverted by himself at the start of the reappraisal in July 1990, when he stated that: "Preliminary studies of the evidence suggest the Californian was substantially further from the Titanic than Lord Mersey found — possibly 20 miles, as Captain Lord said."[20] He may well have regretted this statement as it may have indicated prejudice, but whatever it was, he kept to his statement till the end.

After the Department's letter of 2 July 1991 there was a long silence which lasted for months. Then on 23 February 1992 Cecil Parkinson asked his successor, Mr Malcolm Rifkind, about the outcome of the reappraisal[21] and criticized the year-long delay in publishing the report.[22] "The Branch [MAIB]," he later explained, ". . . has been under tremendous pressure from current investigations and must attend to priorities. But the captain's son is not getting any younger,* and this was a tremendous slur on his father: he was vilified. If a wrong was done it should be put right, or at least the case should be authoritatively summed up. I do not know what is in the report, but it will be

---

* Mr S.T. Lord was in his 80s.

nice to have it before the anniversary, when old allegations will be dragged up. Certainly the new evidence looks quite promising from Mr Lord's point of view."[23]

Again the supporters of Captain Lord had every reason to be optimistic, even 'jubilant'; "they scented victory", *The Sunday Times* noticed. "Having come so close to clearing his name," Mr Harrison said to *The Daily Telegraph,* "these inexplicable delays are extraordinarily disappointing."

A month later, 25 March, Cecil Parkinson's question to his successor had proved to have done its work, and it was announced that on 2 April, 12 days before the 80th anniversary of the tragedy, the report of the reappraisal would be issued; it was, and under the heading:

RMS "TITANIC"
Reappraisal of evidence
Relating to
SS "CALIFORNIAN"

It was not Captain Barnett's report, but a report made by the Deputy Chief Inspector Captain James de Coverly. The reader is referred to this remarkable work of modern marine investigation for details. However, the most important conclusions reached, are given here in brief:

"TITANIC was in approximate position 41 47N 49 55W when she struck the iceberg at 2345 hours 14 April, and in position 41 43.6N 49 56.9W when she foundered.

The position of the CALIFORNIAN cannot be deduced so accurately and opinions are divided. However, it is concluded that CALIFORNIAN was probably between 17 and 20 miles from TITANIC.

It is possible that TITANIC was seen by CALIFORNIAN due to abnormal refraction permitting sight beyond the ordinary visible horizon; but more likely that she was not seen.

TITANIC's distress signals were seen, and that proper action was not taken; however, any reasonable action by Captain Lord would not have led to a different outcome to the tragedy, as CALIFORNIAN would have arrived well after TITANIC had sunk."

The report was disappointing, to say the least, for Captain Lord's legion. It had found that the *Californian* had seen the distress rockets of the *Titanic* and should have taken action, but it had done nothing.

The two ships were also closer than the supporters of Captain Lord ever wanted to admit. But the report had found two main different distances between the two ships: Captain Barnett, concluded the ships were "between 5 and 10 miles apart"[24] or "between 5 and 7 miles".[25] (A distance of 8 to 10 miles is used throughout the report, too.) Captain de Coverly, who had further examined Captain Barnett's report, found they were 17 to 20 miles apart, "probably 18 miles", just as he had stated two years earlier before the reappraisal had started. The Deputy Chief Inspector's distance, with all its implications, was accepted for the final conclusions and fully endorsed by the Chief Inspector of Marine Accidents, Captain Marriott. It should, however, be realized, as it does not seem to be in all circles, that a Chief Inspector always stands by his Deputy Chief Inspector and will almost automatically endorse his findings, as much as the Secretary of State will accept the Chief Inspector's Report without question.

The supporters of Captain Lord claimed to know why Captain Barnett's findings were rejected; his report was "completely unacceptable" to the Chief Inspector so that it was "referred downwards" to the Deputy Chief Inspector "who rewrote it completely".[26]

Not only do the different findings of the distances between the two ships make it a remarkable report;* the shifting of blame to Herbert Stone, with whom they sympathize, but who they feel "was seriously at fault" and "should have gone down himself to the Master when there was no proper response from him",[27] is remarkable for it distracts from the real responsibilities of Captain Lord. Perhaps in the 1990s more self-initiative is expected from young officers, but in the autocratic era prior to World War I, this was quite different and not accepted as normal, and certainly not by Captain Lord.

As for the nautical assessment of the positions of the two ships, the *Californian's* proved to be the most difficult of all for the MAIB. Whatever position was reached by either Captain Barnett or Captain de Coverly it was based on what the possible currents could have been that night and even the days before the incident. It is here that the report finds its nautical weakness; there is no clear evidence as to the prevailing ocean currents in the area for that night, and the fact that the ice had drifted so far south is no proof that it had drifted south over longitude 50 W. The map of the New York District Court of 1915 (see Appendix E) and the fact that all the bodies of the victims were found considerably east of the wreck position, completely shatters this hypothesis. Nor was the icefield "in a roughly north/south direction" as the report states,[28] but in a roughly SW/NE direction as all independent maps show (see Appendix E).

Captain Barnett assessed that a southern current had influenced the *Californian* since noon 14 April. No doubt he based this on Stewart's testimony that between noon 13 April and noon 14 April, the *Californian* found herself 39 minutes of latitude (equal to 39 miles) more south of where she expected to be.[29] Captain Barnett believes that the *Californian* did not correct adequately for this set. This, if true, would indicate a southern set of about 1.6 knots.

Captain de Coverly did not support these findings and considered "the full strength of the (southern) current was only felt when close to the ice field."[30] He argued that:

(a)§ ". . . a southerly current in the region of the accident was unusual" and "even more unusual . . . further east."

This overlooks the possibility that such currents could have existed as shown in Stewart's evidence mentioned above.

---

* A number of strange mistakes have also crept into the report. It may have taken some 21 months to produce this document, but in the end there seems to have been some undue haste: The name of the Captain of the *Titanic*, Edward John Smith, is mistakenly given as E.C. Smith (page 4, 2nd paragraph) and in one place 'north' was used by the nautical men of the MAIB for south (paragraph 3(d), page 10, 4th paragraph). This mistake is also found back in Annex 3, the area map of the incident, where the position of the sighting of Boxhall's green Roman Candle is drawn in north or on the starboard side of the *Carpathia's* course line, while the text of paragraph 3(d) correctly states that it was seen on the port bow, thus to the south.

§ The points, (a) to (e), can be found in full on pages 10 and 11 of the report.

(b) "The Pole Star sight taken by the Chief Officer (Stewart) at 1930 hrs (which) gave . . . latitude — 42°05'N . . . (the same) "as that observed at noon".

Captain de Coverly feels that this indicates that the set of the current "was nil, at least until 1930 hrs, unless either the observations were in error or false evidence was given" and one is left to speculate which it really was; no current, error or falsehood.

(c) Since the *Californian* had steered a course slightly south of west, and had radioed to the *Antillian* the sighting of three icebergs at 42°03'N, which was essentially the latitude of the Pole Star observation Stewart had made an hour later, the current must have been north, not south.

Again Captain de Coverly overlooks the possibility of error in the *Californian's* navigation, which here could be attributed to the 180 degree turn of current from south to north.

(d) The fact that the *Carpathia* saw Boxhall's green Roman Candle half a point on her port bow, suggests to Captain de Coverly that "the boat which it came from must have been to the north [sic: what is meant, of course, is south] of CARPATHIA's course line and" he added "it follows that during the two hours the ship [*Carpathia*] must have been set to the north".

It is hard to understand why Captain de Coverly chose this possibility out of so many. With equal authority he could have given the following reasons: Both the boat and the *Carpathia* were set south, but the boat drifted in a locally stronger current. Or: Both the boat and the *Carpathia* were set north, but the *Carpathia* was set in a locally stronger current.

How difficult it must have been for Captain de Coverly to come to a definite decision on what the currents were is shown in his selected belief that the *Carpathia* was set to the north by the net effect of the current she encountered.

His final argument (e), already discussed, concerned the position of the icefield.

Still, Captain de Coverly felt he could conclude authoritatively "that *Californian* was between 17 and 20 miles from the *Titanic* at the time of the collision, bearing about NW by N from her" and that the *Californian* could possibly see the *Titanic* because of abnormal ("super–") refraction, permitting sight beyond the ordinary visible horizon; unless there was another ship between the *Titanic* and the *Californian,* possibly this ship was indeed the *Samson.*

The area where the incident occurred is not specifically known for the super-refraction phenomena and it is remarkable if it existed that night and through dawn the next morning when the *Californian* was seen by so many witnesses hove to ten miles to the north of the *Carpathia*. Captain de Coverly certainly realized this and stated that he did "not consider that a definite answer to the question 'was TITANIC seen?' [by the *Californian*] can be given."

There seems to be no doubt that Captain de Coverly tried his best and performed his work as accurately as he could, but when one reflects on his findings, one cannot escape the feeling that behind the officially published goal there lies a practical, and possibly more modern, reason for the whole exercise. Cecil Parkinson wrote: "If Captain Barnett's reappraisal ends the matter it will, in the long run, have saved time and staff resources." For *The Times* he explained that he "felt it would be less expensive and more just to try to settle the matter."[31] From this it seems that the authorities were more concerned with laying the matter to rest than anything else. As Mr Parkinson predicted, Captain Barnett's report did this; but Captain de Coverly's report missed that goal entirely, however good his intentions were. Mr Harrison, however, feels that the two differences in distance found between the ships, "make the Report valueless". Nevertheless, the Ministry of Transport "considers the matter closed."[32]

For the supporters of Captain Lord it was far from a victory, and the jubilant mood quickly subsided. The report was first called "a shambles of contradictions",[33] but after the first anger had died down, the mood changed to grouching murmur. "It is politics," one *Titanic*-club in America grumbled. Mr Leslie Harrison initially made only one comment: "the report was ambiguous, although it cleared Lord of the main charge of blame," he remarked.[34] Captain Lord's son, Stanley T. Lord, said "he was disappointed that his father had been only partly exonerated, but pleased that the report cleared him of blame for the loss of life."[35] After these statements, the two main supporters of Captain Lord declined to comment; Stanley Lord only adding that "anything to do with the Californian and the Titanic has the shadow of Lord Mersey hanging over it."[36]

But this was not the end of it. Wanting to give Mr S.T. Lord a fair chance to comment upon the findings of the reappraisal, I telephoned him and asked him for his reaction. Reluctantly, he replied: "They were too far away, there is nothing they could have done. That is all there is to it!"[37] He then hung up, breaking off the telephone connection as if the *Titanic–Californian* incident had come to an end there and then. It is not, of course, "all there is to it".

An American *Titanic*-enthusiast and, near Washington-based private eye, who refers to himself as 'The Commissioner of TQ III' (*Titanic* Enquiry III), has not only criticized that part of the report of the reappraisal that he and his friends do not like, but also announced that the "other known facts and implausibilies [sic] [of the case] will appear in a forthcoming book".[38]

The first of Captain Lord's supporters who gave, though privately, a substantial comment on the report of the Reappraisal was none other than Mr Leslie Harrison. In the second ('vanity'*) edition of his book *A Titanic Myth*, published in the summer of 1992, Mr Harrison added a Preface and an Epilogue.

In the "Preface to the Second Edition" of his book, Mr Harrison states that the wreck of *Titanic* was found in "1986", "fourteen miles away" from her position accepted in 1912. Both figures are of course wrong; the wreck was found in 1985 and its position was made public by Dr Ballard in the last half of

Diagram 16. *Titanic* and *Californian* positions
Titanic *as in her CQD calls, the wreck position as found by Dr Robert Ballard, et al. Plus the* Californian *according to Captain Lord, Captain Barnett, Captain de Coverly, the* Californian *as seen from the* Carpathia; *and the position in which the* Titanic *sank, according to Captain Lord and his most devoted supporters, until the position of the wreck was made public by Dr. Ballard in 1987. After that, the friends of Captain Lord never mentioned that position again, but maintained that "he [Lord] was the better navigator that night".*

---

* i.e. privately published; in this case through the *Self-Publishing Association* in England.

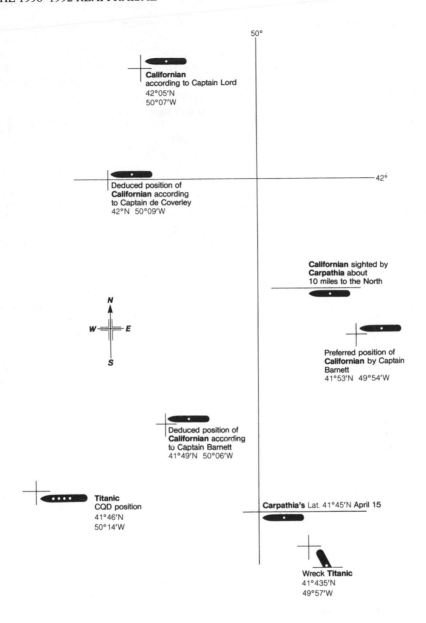

50°

Californian
according to Captain Lord
42°05′N
50°07′W

42°

Deduced position of
Californian according
to Captain de Coverley
42°N 50°09′W

N
W — E
S

Californian sighted by
Carpathia about
10 miles to the North

Preferred position of
Californian by Captain
Barnett
41°53′N 49°54′W

Deduced position of
Californian according
to Captain Barnett
41°49′N 50°06′W

Titanic
CQD position
41°46′N
50°14′W

Carpathia's Lat. 41°45′N April 15

Wreck **Titanic**
41°435′N
49°57′W

Position in which **Titanic** sank, 30–32 miles south of
Californian according to Captain Lord and his most devoted
supporters, until the wreck position was made public in 1987.

1987, which proved less then 13 miles away from the *Titanic's* CQD position.

The Epilogue is even more remarkable; it attacks Captain de Coverly, and quite undeserved at that, for not accepting all the views that Mr Harrison has held for so long about the *Californian* and Captain Lord, but then: "Though it be honest, it is never good to bring bad news", Shakespeare wrote.

Captain de Coverly may have concluded a most favourable distance of about 18 miles between the *Titanic* and the *Californian* for Mr Harrison's campaign, but he is given precious little gratitude for it. "An admission of failure", Mr Harrison scorns when he reflects on Captain de Coverly's hope that those who wish to speculate further will do so rationally and with regard to human characteristics.

It is Mr Harrison who cannot agree with Captain de Coverly's conclusion that the ship seen from the *Californian* came from the east. "All the evidence is," writes Mr Harrison, "that she came from the westward", and he regards it "a fundamental error" that "technically invalidates the Report."[39]

It seems that this is Mr Harrison's last stand. Gone are the rockets (or the Roman Candle type flares of some sort or description) from the arguments in support of Captain Lord. They are mentioned no more; neither in the Epilogue, nor in his address at the launch of his privately published book, and the other friends of Captain Lord adopt the same attitude. It is as if no rockets were ever fired from the sinking *Titanic*.

For the last time then: the overwhelming evidence about the ship seen from the *Californian* is that she came up from the east. Both Captain Lord and his Third Officer Groves (the only two men known to have given evidence or an account of some sort of the sighting of the ship) agreed that she did; Captain Lord saw her to the south showing a green light, and thus the ship was on a westerly course. Groves said, and always maintained and insisted, that the ship he had seen was "coming up on the starboard quarter" of the *Californian* and that she must be going "westward". He was always sure she was indeed the *Titanic*. (See Chapters 3 and 15 for details.)

Another difference of opinion between Mr Harrison and Captain de Coverly concerns the alleged difference of time between the two ships. Captain de Coverly does not accept a difference of time between the two ships, and Mr Harrison finds this "another important omission", ignoring all evidence (presented in full in Chapter 2), that there was very little, if any, time difference at all.

In short, Mr Harrison's disagreement with Captain de Coverly, goes on for several pages of familiar Lordite literature, all of which has been dealt with and dismissed in this book.

In the two closing paragraphs of his book Mr Harrison hints, as do other supporters of Captain Lord, to the ongoing battle of the Lordites when he asks: ". . . is the report open to amendment in the light of reasoned criticism?" and answers: "It would be an unforgivable act for it [the Department of Transport's opportunity to close the controversy] to be cast aside."

It was one inarticulate and insignificant Lordite who, after reading the Report, and with growing dismay, obstinately announced: "I shall appeal this!" I have no doubt that here Leslie Reade would have instantly quoted from Laurence Sterne's *Tristram Shandy*, "'Tis known by the name of perseverance in a good cause, — and of obstinacy in a bad one."[40] And so sum up the whole sorry case for the *Californian* and her Captain.

Sources

1 P.I. Press-Office.
2 'The Case For Captain Lord', L. Harrison (1989).
3 P.I.
4 Letter from Captain J. de Coverly to Mr L. Harrison, 29 June 1990.
5 *The Sunday Telegraph*, 7 July 1990.
6 Press Office, London.
7 Letter from Captain J. de Coverly to Mr L. Harrison, 29 June 1990.
8 *London Observer Service*, July 1990.
9 *The Daily Telegraph*, 10 July 1990.
10 P.I. from The Rt. Hon. C. Parkinson, November 1990.
11 Ibid.
12 Ibid.
13 P.I.
14 Mr L. Harrison, 31 July 1992, at the Press Conference in Liverpool to launch the

new edition of *A Titanic Myth* by Leslie Harrison.
15 P.I. from The Rt. Hon. C. Parkinson, November 1990.
16 *The Sunday Telegraph*, 15 July 1990.
17 *The Daily Telegraph*, 16 July 1990.
18 *The Discovery of the Titanic* (Hodder & Stoughton, 1987), p. 200.
19 *The Arizona Republic*, 11 July 1990.
20 *The Daily Telegraph*, 9 July 1990, p. 3.
21 *The Times* (London), 24 February 1992.
22 *The Daily Telegraph*, 24 February 1992.
23 *The Sunday Times*, 1 March 1992.
24 Report Reappraisal, p. 7.
25 Ibid. p. 11.
26 Mr. L. Harrison, 31

July, 1992.
27 Report Reappraisal, p. 17.
28 Ibid. p. 10.
29 B 8693-8715 with emphasis on B 8698.
30 Report Reappraisal, p. 11.
31 *The Times* (London), 24 February 1992.
32 Mr L. Harrison, 31 July 1992.
33 *The Daily Post*, 3 April 1992.
34 *The Times* (London), 3 April 1992.
35 Ibid.
36 *The Daily Telegraph*, 3 April 1992.
37 P.I. From Stanley T. Lord, 1 May 1992.
38 *THS Commutator*, Supplement, June 1992.
39 Mr L. Harrison, 31 July 1992.
40 *Tristram Shandy*, Laurence Sterne, (1760) Chapter 17.

Postscript

The manuscript of *The Ship That Stood Still* had been with Leslie Reade for more than 15 years until his death in January 1989.

In his 85-year life Leslie Reade was a barrister, author and playwright. He was born in South Africa in 1904 and was educated in England and America. In 1925 he graduated from Oxford University where he had read English — and from where he had learned to love London, travelling up with his friends, "to spend an evening of listening to good English and Lloyd George in Parliament." He read for the Bar in London and soon after being called to the Bar began his literary career, writing for radio and periodicals. In the 1930s he published against the rise of Nazism in Germany, which brought him almost instantly on to Hitler's death list. During the Second World War he served his country in the army and was with the forces that fought in Germany. After the war he turned again to writing for the stage, radio and, in England and America, for television.

Leslie Reade found the invention of wireless almost magical and occupied himself with this for much of his spare time. Ocean-going liners were also an abiding interest, but it was the story of the *Titanic* and the involvement of the *Californian* in the disaster that fascinated him from boyhood until the end of his life.

For more than ten years he had researched and worked on the manuscript of *The Ship That Stood Still* and it was known to exist by a number of *Titanic* scholars and supporters of Captain Lord alike.

When in 1975 the book was in the final stages of production, typeset, corrected and indexed, Mr Leslie Harrison, then the General Secretary of the Mercantile Marine Service Association, withdrew his permission to use the information he had unconditionally supplied 11 years earlier.

In the campaign for Captain Lord, this seemed the best and most successful move that had ever been made by any of his supporters; it stopped the production process of the book instantly. It proved, however, to be a pyrrhic victory. For had *The Ship That Stood Still* been unobstructively published as planned in 1975 the supporters of Captain Lord would have had the best and most authoritative account of the incident they could have wished for; the solution of the *Titanic–Californian* mystery. They may also have been spared the humiliation and the disappointment of the results of the 1990-1992 reappraisal.

Leslie Reade was disheartened by the unexpected vetoes of those who were now his opponents. But he was not discouraged and he rewrote the parts of his manuscript that he could no longer use; there was ample similar material available from other sources.

By this time, however, a whole new factor had, quite naturally, started to influence the progress of things — *time*. Leslie was ageing and his health began to fail him. He was now in his 70s, but his sharp, Oxford-trained mind had not left him for a moment. He knew exactly what he wanted for his work, what had to be done and how to include and address the new developments in the campaign for Captain Lord. In the many years that I knew Leslie, we almost always found time to discuss these developments. So when, in 1989, I was asked to recover the manuscript and the source material for the book from Leslie's characteristic Victorian flat in the heart of London, and I read the last changes and additions he had made to it, it was clear that *The Ship That Stood Still* was as much a *tour de force* as it had always been.

With the approval of Leslie's widow, who had worked along with him on the book for all those years, a final update and editing of the manuscript was undertaken to cover the last years up to the present.

From the many conversations I had with Leslie, and being familiar with the unpublished work from the beginning, I felt I knew what he wanted for his work. Leslie's specific *Californian* sources, supplemented with some of my own material, gave the unique opportunity to complete and broaden the work, including the results of the 1990–1992 reappraisal that the supporters of Captain Lord had so jubilantly welcomed after more than 30 years of hard (and given the conclusions of the reappraisal) senseless campaigning.

As editor of the work of a close friend, there could be no other choice than to be certain that every piece of additional information, every sentence, changed or removed from the original, had to be handled in the spirit that Leslie Reade would have wanted. Most of these additions and changes we had repeatedly discussed personally. With the others, I was simply on my own. Still, this book tells in its own unique spirit, I believe, what Leslie Reade had always wanted his readers to know about that strange and bizarre mystery of *The Ship That Stood Still*.

Edward P. de Groot (Editor)
Hilversum, February 1993

Maritime matters for the non-mariner

Abaft: Towards the stern; opposite of "forward of".

Abaft the beam: An object is said to be, when it is behind a horizontal line at right angles to the ship's fore and aft (lengthwise) line.

Abeam: An object that is about at right angles to the middle of the ship.

Alleyway: Passageway, giving access to cabins or other parts of a ship, which on land would be called a corridor.

Bearing: The direction in which an object lies from the observer, taken by compass.

Compass deviation: Error of magnetic compass, i.e. the amount in degrees by which the needle points one side or the other of magnetic north. Deviation is plus, if compass points east of magnetic north; minus, if it points west of it. Deviation of the compass is caused by iron or steel in the ship's construction.

Compass variation: The angle between the magnetic and true meridian. It must be taken into the reckoning to get the true bearing or course.

Compass error: Deviation + variation. It is the angle between the direction of the compass needle and the true meridian.

Dead reckoning: Estimated calculation of ship's position (see 'Fix') since last position obtained. The calculation is based on mean of courses steered and distance by log, making allowances for the set of any current and other things. It is approximate, and seamen say a DR position may be wrong by a considerable distance. 'Dead' is said — unconvincingly — to be a corruption of 'deduced'.

Down to her marks: A ship is said to be in this condition when sufficient cargo is loaded to depress her to one or other of her loadlines (see 'Loadline').

Extra Master's Certificate: An optional certificate, being the highest obtainable of competency, awarded to a master after passing a difficult examination.

Fix: Ship's position obtained by observations of sun or stars, or of terrestrial objects, or by combination of both. Usual method of getting exact position when sun or stars visible — contrast with DR.

Freeboard: Vertical distance between loadline, measured on a ship's side, and the upper side of the freeboard deck; that is, the height of the upper deck at midships above the waterline at which the ship floats.

Gross tons: The commonest method of expressing the 'size' of merchant ships. It is *not* a measurement of weight, but of capacity, or the total internal volume of a vessel. It represents the number of units of 100 cubic feet under the tonnage deck, plus all the enclosed spaces above it. ('Tonnage' was originally a duty payable on tons, or 'tuns', of wine). The 'tonnage deck' in ships with less than three decks is the upper deck; in other ships, it is, counting from below, the second deck extending continuously fore and aft. *Gross register tons* is obtained from gross tonnage, excluding various spaces, such as engine rooms, crew's (but not passengers') quarters, store rooms, etc. Most dues are levied on register tonnage. Different nations have different rules for permissible deductions from gross tonnage, so a ship may have a different register tonnage in different ports. Gross and register tonnage may be 'fiddled' for various purposes such as prestige. So, a few years after World War I, when the *Leviathan's* owners wanted to call her "the largest ship in the world", she was remeasured, and her gross tonnage increased, to make her seem larger than the *Majestic*. Dues went up also, and, later, the *Leviathan's* g.t. was substantially, and quietly, reduced. Warships are measured by *displacement,* which is the actual weight of the vessel, including stores crew etc. It is usually larger than g.t., thus, the *Titanic* was 46,328 gross tons and 52,310 displacement.

Gulf Stream: A warm current in the North Atlantic. Its speed in the Gulf of Mexico may be as high as four nautical miles per hour, but farther north, in the ocean, it is only about 10–15 miles per day. The Gulf Stream now, among oceanographers, and others, is regarded as ending south of Newfoundland, and the continuing current is called the "North Atlantic Drift".

Heading: The direction in which the ship's bow is pointing.

Hove to: Lying stopped, with the ship's head pointing to the wind, and her engines working to keep her in that position. As the *Californian's* engines were not moving, she was drifting, strictly speaking, not 'hove to'.

Hull down: Description of a ship sighted so far away that her hull is beneath the horizon and can't be seen; only her superstructure, masts and funnels, etc. are visible.

Knot: A unit of speed. A knot is the equivalent of a nautical mile per hour, a nautical mile being 6,080 ft. Although during the course of this story even seamen have spoken of so many "knots per hour", strictly, 'per hour' is tautological.

Loadline: Marks on the ship's side, which indicate depths to which she may be loaded in different waters at different seasons.

Log: An instrument for ascertaining the ship's speed and distance run.

Log (book): The ship's journal. The ship's performance, her speed, courses, distance run, weather, incidents (such as sighting of other ships, and, certainly, any signals), etc., are entered. The law requires the master to enter certain matters. There are several logs: the *Official Log,* containing names of crew, their pay, scale of rations, data of passage, cargo, record of boat drill, etc.; *Engine Room Log, Scrap Log, Chief Officer's Log,* into which are copied by him the entries in the *Deck Log* made during each watch.

Masthead light: White light on the foremast, and, in larger ships, another 15 feet higher up on the mainmast as well. The light must show unbroken over an arc of the horizon of 20 points (an arc of 225°), visible from right ahead to two points abaft of beam on either side. Visible at least five miles.

North Atlantic tracks: Seasonal routes used since 1891 by agreement among the principal steamship companies for safety reasons — to avoid collision, ice, fishing boats on the Grand Banks of Newfoundland. There are separate east- and west-bound tracks, and special tracks for abnormal ice conditions. Tracks were altered after the *Titanic.*

"Not Under Command" **(or,** *"Not Under Control"***):** Said of a ship that is disabled or unmanageable for any reason, such as breakdown of her steering gear, engines, etc. The *Californian* was not in this condition.

Points of compass: There are 32, starting at north and going clockwise back to north. Each point consists of 11°15'. Modern ships, using the gyro compass, steer courses expressed merely in degrees.

Port: The left side of the ship, when facing the bow.

Quarter: The section of the ship's side towards the stern, literally, 45° abaft the beam.

Quartermaster: A rating promoted from Able Bodied Seaman (AB). His duties as quartermaster are to steer the ship. After his turn or 'trick' is over, he may do routine work, maintenance, messenger service or signalling while acting as stand-by QM (the usual abbreviation for the rank). In port, the QM is on duty at the gangway.

Run her way off: The time and distance between the stopping of a ship's engines and the stopping of the ship herself, due to that property of matter described in physics as 'inertia'.

Sidelights: Lights shown by ships under way: red on the port side, green on the starboard — to be seen right ahead to two points abaft the beam on either side. As each point is 11°15', or 11¼°, each sidelight has an arc of 112½°, and must be visible for a minimum of two miles.

Slip: The difference between the theoretical advance of the ship by the revolution of her propellers and her actual advance. This difference is expressed as a percentage. Slip is said to be caused by the propeller rotating in a yielding medium. *Positive* slip: when the actual advance is less than the theoretical; *negative* slip: when the actual advance is more than the theoretical, which may be caused by a following sea.

Starboard: The right side of the ship, when facing the bow.

Stern Light: White light at the stern, placed as nearly as possible on the same level as the sidelights. It must cover an arc of 12 points, or 135°, and be visible for a minimum of one mile. It is a warning to overtaking vessels.

Tramp: A cargo ship that carries any freight and goes anywhere that is profitable: in other words, a ship that is not restricted to a regular run or to one type of cargo. The *Californian,* although equipped for Leyland's Boston passenger-cargo service, was often used as a tramp.

Signals of distress

The international code for distress signals prevailing in 1912 was as follows:

SIGNALS OF DISTRESS

WHEN A VESSEL IS IN DISTRESS and requires assistance from other vessels or from the shore, the following shall be the signals to be used or displayed by her, either together or separately:*

IN THE DAYTIME
(1) A gun or other explosive signal fired at intervals of about a minute;
(2) The international code signal of distress indicated by NC;
(3) The distant signal, consisting of square flag, having either above or below it a ball or anything resembling a ball;
(4) The distant signal, consisting of a cone, point upward, having either above it or below it, a ball or anything resembling a ball;
(5) A continuous sounding with any fog-signal apparatus.

AT NIGHT
(1) A gun or other explosive signal fired at intervals of about a minute;
(2) Flames on the vessel (as from a burning tar barrel, oil barrel, etc.);
(3) Rockets or shells, throwing stars of any colour or description, used one at a time at short intervals;
(4) A continuous sounding with any fog-signal apparatus.

* This is interpreted by Mr Leslie Harrison as an order of priority in which the signals were to be used, i.e. that at night rockets were third in order of priority.

Appendix C

Affidavit of Captain Stanley Lord

I went to sea in 1891 as a cadet in the barque *Naiad* owned by Messrs J.B. Walmsley. After obtaining my second mate's certificate of competency I served as second officer in the barque *Lurlei*. In February, 1901, I passed for master and three months later obtained my extra master's certificate.

I had entered the service of the West India and Pacific Steam Navigation Company in 1897. This company was bought by the Leyland Line in 1900 and I continued in their service, being appointed to command in 1906 at the age of 29.

In April, 1912, I was in command of the liner *Californian,* having sailed from London for Boston, U.S.A. on 5th April. On 13th April, noon latitude by observation was 43° 23' North: on 14th April, the noon position by observation was 42° 05' N., 47° 25' W., and course was altered to North 61° West (magnetic) to make due West (true).[*] I steered this course to make longitude 51° West in latitude 42° North on account of ice reports which had been received *(Exhibits A and B)*.[§]

At 5 p.m. on 14th April, two observations of the sun taken by the Second Officer, Mr. H. Stone, to check the longitude were reported to me. These gave a run of 60 miles since noon, which was much ahead of Dead Reckoning. Another observation which I caused to be taken at 5.30 p.m. gave 64 miles since noon.

At 6.30 p.m. we passed three icebergs five miles south of the ship. These I caused to be reported at 7.30 p.m. by wireless to the S.S. *Antillian,* the message being as follows: *"6.30 p.m. apparent ship's time, latitude 42° 5' N., longitude 49° 9' W., three bergs five miles southwards of us regards Lord."* A little later I was informed that a routine exchange of signals with the *Titanic* showed that she had also received the message sent to the *Antillian.* These would appear to have been the same icebergs sighted and reported by wireless during the day by the *Parisian* in position 41° 55' N., 49° 14' W. *(Exhibit C).*

At 7.30 p.m. the Chief Officer, Mr. G.F. Stewart, reported to me a latitude by Pole Star of 42° 5½' N. This with the previous observation for longitude gave me proof that the current was setting to W.N.W. at about one knot.

At 8 p.m. I doubled the lookouts, there being a man in the crow's nest and another on the focs'le head.

At 8.5 p.m. I took charge on the bridge myself, the Third Officer, Mr. C.V. Groves, also being on duty. The weather was calm, clear and starry.

---

[*] Before the introduction in about 1914 of the gyroscopic compass, courses were stated in degrees from north or south. So North 61° West would now be 299°.

[§] All exhibits appear in 'The "Californian" Incident', published by The Mercantile Marine Service Association, March 1962. Only those with a [+] appear in this book.

At 10.15 p.m. I observed a brightening along the western horizon. After watching this carefully for a few minutes I concluded that it was caused by ice. At 10.21 I personally rang the engine-room telegraph to full speed astern and ordered the helm hard aport. As these orders came into effect the lookout men reported ice ahead. Under the influence of the helm and propeller going astern the ship swung round to E.N.E. by compass (N.E. true).

The ship was then stopped surrounded by loose ice and from one-quarter to half-a-mile from the edge of a low ice field. As I could not see any clear place to go through I decided to remain stopped until daylight. Allowing S.89.W (true) 120 miles from my noon position, and also taking into account the latitude by Pole Star at 7.30 p.m., I calculated my position as being 42° 5' N., 50° 7' W.

At 10.30 p.m. as I was leaving the bridge, I pointed out to the Third Officer what I thought was a light to the eastward which he said he thought was a star.

I went down to the saloon deck and sent for the Chief Engineer. I notified him that I intended to remain stopped until daylight but he was to keep main steam handy in case we commenced to bump against the ice.

I pointed out to him the steamer I had previously seen approaching from the eastward and southward of us and about 10.55 p.m. we went to the wireless room. We met the wireless operator coming out and pointing out the vessel to him I asked him what ships he had. He replied: "Only the *Titanic*," I thereupon remarked, judging from what I could see of the approaching vessel, which appeared to be a vessel of no great size and comparable with our own: "That isn't the *Titanic*." I told him to notify the *Titanic* that we were stopped and surrounded by ice in the position I had calculated, and he left at once to do so.

Later I noticed the green (starboard) light of the approaching vessel, also a few deck lights in addition to the masthead light previously seen.

At 11.30 p.m. I noticed that the other steamer was stopped about five miles off, also that the Third Officer was morsing him. I continued watching and noticed that she didn't reply.

At 11.45 p.m. I went on to the bridge, casually noticed the other vessel, and commented to the Third Officer that she had stopped and wouldn't reply to our Morse signals. He answered in the affirmative.

At ten minutes after midnight, it now being 15th April, the Second Officer came on to the saloon deck. I drew his attention to the fact that we were stopped and surrounded by ice and that I intended to remain stopped until daylight. I pointed out the other steamer to him, told him that she was stopped and that he was to watch her and let me know if we drifted any closer to her. He then went on to the bridge to relieve the Third Officer, and I went into the chart-room.

I sat there reading and smoking until 0.40 a.m. when I whistled up to the bridge through the speaking tube and asked the Second Officer if the other ship was any nearer. He replied that she was just the same and I told him to let me know if he wanted anything as I was going to lie down on the chartroom settee. I then did so, being fully dressed with boots on, etc., and with the electric light on. I left the watch on deck to the Second Officer with every confidence, as he was the holder of a British Board of Trade first mate's certificate of competency (foreign going) and my standing orders, which were well known to every officer, stated categorically that I was to be called at once in all cases of doubt.

At about 1.15 a.m. the Second Officer whistled down to say that the other steamer was altering her bearing to the south-west and had fired a white rocket. I asked him whether it was a company's signal and he replied that he didn't know. I thereupon instructed him to call her up, find out what ship she was, and send the apprentice, James Gibson, down to report to me.

I then lay down again in the chart room, being somewhat relieved in my mind at the news that the other ship was under way and removing herself from her earlier relatively close proximity. For some time I heard the clicking of the Morse key, and after concluding that the Second Officer had succeeded in communicating with the other ship, I fell asleep.

Between 1.30 a.m. and 4.30 a.m. I have a recollection of Gibson opening the chart room door and closing it immediately. I said: "What is it?" but he did not reply.

At 4.30 a.m. the Chief Officer called me and reported that it was breaking day and the steamer which had fired the rocket was still to the southward. I replied: "Yes, the Second Mate said something about a rocket."

I then went on to the bridge and was for some little time undecided as to the advisability of pushing through the ice or turning round to look for a clearer passage to the south-east. However, as daylight came in I could see clear water to the west of the icefield so put the engines on stand-by at about 5.15 a.m.

About this time the Chief Officer remarked that the steamer bearing SSE from us was a four-master with a yellow funnel and asked me whether I intended going to have a look at her. When I asked him why, he replied that she might have lost her rudder. I said: "She hasn't any signals up, has she?" He replied that she had not, but that the Second Officer had said that she had fired several rockets during his watch. I told him to call the Wireless Operator and see what ship it was. He did so but fifteen or twenty minutes later came back and reported that the *Titanic* had struck an iceberg and was sinking. Some delay was then experienced before we received an authoritative message giving the estimated position of the disaster but about 6 a.m. the following signal from the *Virginian (Exhibit D)* was handed to me: "'*Titanic struck berg wants assistance urgent ship sinking passengers in boats his position lat. 41. 46', long. 50. 14', Gamble, Commander.*'"

This position I calculated to be about S.16.W., 19 1/2 miles from our own estimated position. I immediately got under way and proceeded as quickly as possible on course between S. and S.W., pushing through about two to three miles of field ice. A lookout man was pulled in a basket to the main truck, given a pair of binoculars and instructed to look out for the *Titanic*.

At 6.30 a.m. I cleared the field ice and proceeded at full speed (70 revolutions). At 7.30 a.m. approximately, we passed the *Mount Temple* stopped in the reported position of the disaster. As there was no sign of any wreckage I proceeded further south, shortly afterwards passing a ship having a pink funnel and two masts, bound north, which turned out to be the *Almerian*.

A little later, I sighted a four-masted steamer to the SSE of us on the east side of the ice field, and received a verbal message from the Wireless Operator, that the *Carpathia* was at the scene of the disaster. I steered to the south until the steamer was nearly abeam when I altered course and proceeded through the icefield at full speed, making for the other steamer. She proved to be *Carpathia* and I stopped alongside her at about 8.30 a.m. Messages were exchanged regarding the disaster and subsequent rescue operations.

At about 9.10 a.m. the *Carpathia* set course for New York and I continued the search for survivors, the ship steaming at full speed with the Second Officer and a lookout man in the crow's nest. While carrying out this search, I saw the smoke of several steamers on the horizon in different directions. We passed about six wooden lifeboats afloat, one capsized in the wreckage; with the exception of two small trunks in a collapsible boat, the others appeared to be empty.

At about 11.20 a.m. I abandoned the search and proceeded due west (true) through the ice, clearing same about 11.50 a.m. The *Mount Temple* was then in sight a considerable distance to the southwest of us and heading to the westward.

The noon position was 41. 33'N:, 50. 09'W.; the latitude was taken under the most favourable conditions by the three officers and reported to me. I did not personally take an observation this day. From this observation I placed the wreckage in position 41. 33'N., 50. 01'W., being about S.S.E, 33 miles, from the position in which the *Californian* had stopped at 10.21 p.m. the previous evening.

I later called for written reports on the events of the night from the Second Officer and Apprentice *(Exhibits E and F)* [*see* Appendix D]. In amplifying his report, the Second Officer stated that the rockets he saw did not appear to be distress rockets, as they did not go any higher than the other steamer's masthead light nor were any detonations heard which would have been the case under the prevailing conditions had explosive distress signals been fired by a ship so close at hand. In addition, the ship altered her bearings from S.S.E. at 0.50 a.m. to S.W.1/2.W. at 2.10 a.m.; assuming her to have been five miles from the *Californian* when she stopped at 11.30 p.m., the distance she must have steamed to alter her bearing by this amount I calculate to have been at least eight miles.

While on passage to Boston, wireless messages about the disaster were received from Captain Rostron of the *Carpathia (Exhibit G);* the American newspapers "New York American" "Boston Globe," "Boston American" and "Boston Post" *(Exhibits H+, I, J+ and K+);* a passenger in the *Olympic* called Wick *(Exhibit L+);* and the Leyland Line *(Exhibits M and N+).**

After our arrival at Boston at 4 a.m. on 19th April, I was summoned with the Radio Officer to appear before the United States Congressional Inquiry in Washington. I gave my evidence there in accordance with the above facts. Subsequently I never had an opportunity to read a transcript of the proceedings or findings of this Inquiry, nor was the matter referred to by those I met on subsequent visits to American ports.

After the return of the *Californian* to Liverpool, I reported to the Wreck Commissioner and to the Marine Superintendent of the Leyland Line, Captain Fry. While in the latter's office, Mr. Groves, the Third Officer, volunteered the opinion that the ship seen from the *Californian* on the night of 14th April was the *Titanic*. This was the first occasion I had heard him make such a statement and I duly commented to this effect to the Marine Superintendent.

I was summoned by telegram to appear before the British Court of Inquiry in London, on 14th May and travelled down from Liverpool the previous evening. When I arrived in Court, Mr. Roberts, manager of the Leyland Line, introduced me to Mr. Dunlop and told me he was watching the proceedings on behalf of the owners and officers of the *Californian*. Apart from the questions asked by Mr. Dunlop when I was in the witness box, I had no further conversation with him nor at any time was I afforded an opportunity to discuss the proceedings with him or to suggest that navigational and other technical facts might be brought out which would verify the truth of the evidence which I had given.

Had I at any time been clearly warned — as I consider I should have been — that adverse findings in respect of the *Californian* were envisaged, I would have taken all possible steps during the Inquiry to call evidence to prove beyond doubt:

(a) That the "Californian" was completely stopped, with full electric navigation and deck lights burning, from 10.21 p.m. to 6 a.m. Additional evidence to prove this conclusively could have been provided by the production of the engine-room log books covering that period and by the testimony of the Chief Engineer and those engineer officers who kept watch during the night.

* For these messages, see Chapter 10.

If the Court could have been satisfied that the *Californian* was indeed stopped all night, then inevitably they would have had to conclude:

(i) that the *Californian* must have been beyond visual range of the actual position of the disaster, for in perfect visibility no other ship's lights were seen by the two lookout men and the two officers of the watch on the *Titanic* either before or immediately after she struck the iceberg, nor was the *Californian* in sight of the survivors as day broke. Additionally, none of the green flares burnt in the *Titanic's* boats which were seen at extreme range from the *Carpathia* were seen from the *Californian*.

(ii) that the *Californian* could not have been the ship later sighted from the *Titanic* which led to the firing of rockets, for this ship was clearly seen to be under way; to approach from a hull-down position; to turn; and to recede.

(b) That from the navigational evidence the "Californian" must have been at least 25 miles from the position of the disaster. Additional proof could have been supplied from the engine-room log books to show how far she steamed from the time of getting under way at 6 a.m. to reaching the wreckage at 8.30; in addition, further detailed consideration should have been given to the relative movements, positions and astronomical observations of the *Californian, Carpathia, Mount Temple* and *Almerian* from before noon on the 14th to the evening of the 15th April in an endeavour to fix as accurately as possible the *actual* as distinct from the *estimated* position in which the wreckage and survivors were found. A further point to which the Court gave no consideration was the fact that the area in which the *Californian* lay stopped all night was covered with field ice extending as far as the eye could see; the area in which the *Carpathia* found the *Titanic's* lifeboats contained very many large icebergs.

If the Court could have been satisfied that during the night the *Californian* was indeed at least 25 miles from the scene of the disaster, they would have had to conclude that even if the distant rocket signals beyond the nearby ship which were apparently seen from the *Californian* had been correctly identified as distress signals, and news of the disaster confirmed by wireless at the earliest possible moment, it would still have been quite impossible for us to have rendered any useful service, for bearing in mind the time taken to reach the wreckage in daylight, under the most favourable conditions, we could not have reached the survivors before the *Carpathia* did.

Finally, I would have submitted for the court's consideration the following two important points:

(a) That had I or the Third Officer any reason to conclude that the ship seen approaching from 10.30 p.m. onwards was a passenger ship steaming towards an icefield at 21 knots, then instinctively as practical seamen either one of us would have take immediate action to warn her that she was standing into danger.

(b) That it was perfectly reasonable for the Second Officer to decide that no emergency action was called for when a ship which had been so close to the *Californian* as to cause concern, and which had completely failed to respond to persistent attempt to call her up by Morse light, got under way and passed out of sight after substantially altering her bearing. This positive action was more than sufficient to nullify any previous concern which might have been created by her apparently making use of confusing rocket signals of low power reaching only to mast height, and lacking any explosive content or detonation such as was customarily associated with a distress rocket and which should have been perfectly audible in the calm conditions then obtaining.

I was also in Court on 15th May. I clearly recall that when Lord Mersey, the President, pressed Mr. Groves, the Third Officer, to express his opinion that the ship seen from the *Californian* was the *Titanic*, Lord Mersey commented that this was also his opinion — a comment which does not appear in the official record of proceedings.

I returned to Liverpool on the evening of 15th May, being due to sail in the *Californian* on 18th. However, after my return home I was verbally informed by the Marine Superintendent that I was to be relieved and I accordingly removed my gear from the ship.

I first read the findings of the Court of Inquiry in the press and while naturally not at all pleased at the references to myself, I was not unduly concerned as I was confident that matters would soon be put right. I immediately approached the Mercantile Marine Service Association, of which I was a member, and a letter putting my side of the case was published in the September, 1912, issue of the Association's magazine, "The Reporter" *(Exhibit O)*.

At a later stage, a Mr. A.M. Foweraker, of Carbis Bay, a gentleman who I never met, but who took a great interest in my case, supplied a series of detailed analyses of the evidence which were published in the "Reporter" *(Exhibits P and Q)* and also in the Nautical Magazine under the title of *"A Miscarriage of Justice"* (April, May and June issues, 1913).

Letters were addressed to the Board of Trade both by the M.M.S.A. and by myself *(Exhibit S+)** requesting a rehearing of that part of the Inquiry relating to the Californian. This request was consistently refused. The M.M.S.A. also sent a letter to the Attorney-General (Sir Rufus Isaacs) requesting an explanation of the comment in his closing address that *"perhaps it would not be wise to speculate on the reason which prevented the Captain of the 'Californian' from coming out of the chart room"* on receiving the Second Officer's message at 1.15. This obvious reflection on my sobriety I greatly resented, for it was my invariable practice to refrain from taking alcohol in any form while at sea, quite apart from the fact that no previous reference to such a possibility had been made during the course of the Inquiry. The only reply received was that Sir Rufus was on holiday and must not be troubled with correspondence.

I received a letter dated 6th August, 1912 *(Exhibit R+)§* from a Mr. Baker, who had served in the *Mount Temple* on her return voyage from Quebec. This appeared to indicate that she was the ship seen to approach and recede from the *Titanic*. Although this letter was brought to the attention of the Board of Trade *(Exhibit T)*, no action was taken for the reasons given in the department's letters of 29th August and 4th September, 1912 *(Exhibit U and V)*. Through Mr. Baker, I met Mr. Notley, the officer referred to in Mr. Baker's letters who had been taken out of the *Mount Temple*. He confirmed that he would give his evidence if called upon to do so, but could not volunteer information because of the adverse effect this might have upon his future employment — a conclusion with which I quite agreed.

I also corresponded with others whose evidence and opinion might prove of assistance to me and received letters from Captain Rostron of the *Carpathia (Exhibits W+ and X);†* Mr. C.H. Lightoller (Second Officer of the *Titanic*) *(Exhibit Y and Z);* and Captain C.A. Bartlett, Marine Superintendent of the White Star Line *(Exhibit AA)*.

Initially, I had been assured by the Liverpool Management of the Leyland Line that I would be reappointed to the *Californian*. However, I was later told privately by Mr. Gordon, Private Secretary to Mr. Roper (Head of the Liverpool

---

* See Chapter 17. Letter of Captain Lord of 10 August to B.D.T.

§ See Chapter 17.

† See Chapter 17.

office of the Leyland Line), that one of the London directors, a Mr. Matheson, K.C., had threatened to resign if I were permitted to remain in the company, and on August 13th I was told by the Marine Superintendent that the company could not give me another ship. I then saw Mr. Roper, who said that it was most unfortunate but the matter was out of his hands and public opinion was against me. I was therefore compelled to resign, up to which time I had been retained on full sea pay and bonus.

I continued my endeavours to obtain what I considered to be the justice due to me but without success, although I personally visited the House of Commons on 23rd October, 1912, and engaged in correspondence with the Board of Trade during 1913 *(Exhibits BB, CC, and DD)*.

Towards the end of 1912, I was approached *(Exhibits EE, 1 and 2+)** by Mr. (later Sir) John Latta of Nitrate Producers Steam Ship Co.Ltd. (Lawther, Latta & Co.), who had apparently been approached on my behalf by a Mr. Frank Strachan, United States agent for the Leyland Line, who had throughout done everything possible to assist me. After a visit to London to meet Mr. Latta, I was offered an immediate command with the company and entered their service in February, 1913. I served at sea throughout the First World War, and as the aftermath of the *Titanic* Inquiry in those days was not such as to affect me personally or professionally in any way, I decided to let the matter drop.

I continued to serve in Lawther Latta's until ill-health compelled me to retire in March, 1927. Sir John Latta's opinion of my service as a shipmaster is given in the reference I received from the Company *(Exhibits FF, 1, 2 and 3+)*.[§]

After my retirement, I was unaware of any adverse reference to the *Californian* in respect of the *Titanic* disaster, as I have never been a filmgoer and was not attracted towards any books on the subject. Latterly, my eyesight also began to deteriorate and the amount of reading I could do was consequently considerably curtailed. However, I noted some extracts from a book called *A Night to Remember* in the Liverpool evening newspaper, "Liverpool Echo", although the brief extracts which I read — which did not contain any reference to the *Californian* — did not impress me.

In the early summer of 1958, however, I became aware that a film also called *A Night to Remember* apparently gave great prominence to the allegation that the *Californian* stood by in close proximity to the sinking *Titanic*. I therefore personally called on Mr. W.L.S. Harrison, General Secretary of the Mercantile Marine Service Association, of which organisation I had remained a member without break from 1897.

Acting on my behalf, Mr. Harrison entered into correspondence with the producers of the film, the publishers of the book and later the author, asking for them to give consideration of my side of the story. However, those concerned maintained that the British Inquiry findings were authoritative and provided sufficient justification for the references to the *Californian* in their publications.

Being desirous of avoiding undue publicity, which owning to my present age and failing health would undoubtedly have serious effects, I am making this sworn statement as a final truthful and authoritative record of what occurred when I was in command of the *Californian* on the night of 14th April, 1912.

SWORN by the above-mentioned deponent Stanley Lord at 13 Kirkway, Wallasey, in the County of Chester, on this twenty-fifth day of June, 1959, before me, Herbert M. Allen, Notary Public.

(Signed) STANLEY LORD

*   See Chapter 17.

§   See Chapter 17.

Secret statements of Stone and Gibson

S.S. "Californian",
At Sea.
(18 April, 1912)

Captain Lord,
Dear Sir,
At your request I make the following report of the incidents witnessed by me during my Watch on the Bridge of this Steamer from midnight April 14th - 4.a.m. of the 15th.

On going up to the bridge I was stopped by yourself at the wheelhouse door, and you gave me verbal orders for the Watch. You showed me a steamer a little abaft of our Star-beam and informed me she was stopped. You also showed me the loose field ice all around the ship and a dense icefield to the southward. You told me to watch the other steamer and report if she came any nearer and that you were going to lie down on the chartroom settee. I went on the bridge about 8 minutes past 12, and took over the Watch from the Third Officer, Mr. Groves, who also pointed out ice and steamer and said our head was E.N.E. and we were swinging. On looking at the compass I saw this was correct and observed the other steamer S.S.E. dead abeam and showing one masthead light, her red side-light and one or two small indistinct lights around the deck which looked like portholes or open doors. I judged her to be a small tramp steamer and about five miles distant. The Third Officer then left the bridge and I at once called the steamer up but got no reply. Gibson, the Apprentice, then came up with the coffee at about 12.15. I told him I had called the steamer up and the result. He then went to the tapper with the same result. Gibson thought at first he was answering, but it was only his masthead lamps flickering a little. I then sent Gibson by your orders to get the gear all ready for streaming a new log line when we got under weigh again. At 12.35 you whistled up the speaking tube and asked if the other steamer had moved. I replied "No" and that she was on the same bearing and also reported I had called him up and the result. At about 12.45, I observed a flash of light in the sky just above that steamer. I thought nothing of it as there were several shooting stars about, the night being fine and clear with light airs and calms. Shortly after I observed another distinctly over the steamer which I made out to be a white rocket though I observed no flash on the deck or any indication that it had come from that steamer in fact, it appeared to come from a good distance beyond her. Between then and about 1.15 I observed three more the same as before, and all white in colour. I, at once, whistled down the speaking tube and you came from the chartroom into your own room and answered. I reported seeing these lights in the sky in the direction of the other steamer which appeared to me to be white rockets. You then gave me orders to call her up with the Morse lamp and try and get some information from her. You also asked me if they were private signals and I replied "I do not know but they were all white." You then said: "When you get an answer let me know by Gibson." Gibson and I observed three more at intervals and kept calling them up on our Morse lamps but got no reply whatsoever. The other steamer meanwhile had shut in her red side light and showed us her stern light and her masthead's glow was just visible. I observed the steamer to be steaming away to the S.W. and altering her bearing fast. We were also swinging slowly all the time through S. and at 1.50 were heading about W.S.W. and the other steamer bearing S.W. x W. At 2.a.m. the vessel was steaming away fast and only just her stern light was visible and bearing S.W.½ W. I sent Gibson down to you and told him to wake you and tell you we had seen altogether eight white rockets and that the steamer had gone out of sight to the S.W. Also that we were heading W.S.W. When he came back he reported he had told you we had called him up repeatedly and got no answer, and you replied: "All right, are you sure there were no colours in them," and Gibson replied: "No, they were all white." At 2.45 I again whistled down again and told you we had seen no more lights and that the steamer had steamed away to the S.W. and was now out of sight, also that the rockets were all white and had no colours whatever.

We saw nothing further until about 3.20 when we thought we observed two faint lights in the sky about S.S.W. and a little distance apart. At 3.40 I sent Gibson down to see all was ready for me to prepare the new log at eight bells. The Chief Officer, Mr. Stewart, came on the bridge at 4 a.m. and I gave him a full report of what I had seen and my reports and replies from you, and pointed out where I thought I had observed these faint lights at 3.20. He picked up the binoculars and said after a few moments: "There she is then, she's all right, she is a four-master." I said "Then that isn't the steamer I saw first," took up the glasses and just made out a four-masted steamer with two masthead lights a little abaft our port beam, and bearing about S., we were heading about W.N.W. Mr. Stewart then took over the Watch and I went off the bridge.

Yours respectfully,
(Signed) *Herbert Stone*
Second Officer.

Thursday,
April 18th, 1912.

Captain Lord,
Dear Sir,
In compliance with your wishes, I hereby make the following statement as to what I saw on the morning of April 15th, 1911 [*sic*]:

It being my watch on deck from 12 o'clock, I went on the bridge at about 15 minutes after twelve and saw that the ship was stopped and that she was surrounded with light field ice and thick field-ice to the Southward. While the Second Officer and I were having coffee, a few minutes later, I asked him if there were any more ships around us. He said that there was one on the Starboard beam, and looking over the weather-cloth, I saw a white light flickering, which I took to be a Morse light calling us up. I then went over to the key-board and gave one long flash in answer, and still seeing this light flickering. I gave her the calling up sign. The light on the other ship, however, was still the same, so I looked at her through the binoculars and found that it was her masthead light flickering. I also observed her port sidelight and a faint glare of lights on her after-deck. I then went over to the Second Officer and remarked that she looked like a tramp steamer. He said that most probably she was, and was burning oil lights. This ship was then right abeam. At about 25 minutes after twelve I went down off the bridge to get a new log out and not being able to find it, I went on the bridge again to see if the Second Officer knew anything about it. I then noticed that this other ship was about one point and a half before the beam. I then went down again and was down until about five minutes to one. Arriving on the bridge again at that time, the Second Officer told me that the other ship, which was then about $3\frac{1}{2}$ points on the Starboard bow, had fired five rockets and he also remarked that after seeing the second one to make sure that he was not mistaken, he had told the Captain, through the speaking tube, and that the Captain had told him to watch her and keep calling her up on the Morse light. I then watched her for some time and then went over to the key-board and called her up continuously for about three minutes. I then got the binoculars and had just got them focussed on the vessel when I observed a white flash apparently on her deck, followed by a faint streak towards the sky which then burst into white stars. Nothing then happened until the other ship was about two points on the Starboard bow when she fired another rocket. Shortly after that I observed that her sidelight had disappeared but her masthead light was just visible, and the Second Officer remarked after taking another bearing of her, that she was slowly steering away towards the S.W. Between one point on the Starboard bow and one point on the Port bow I called her up on the Morse lamp but received no answer. When about one point on the Port bow she fired another rocket which like the others burst into white stars. Just after two o'clock she was then about two points on the Port bow, she disappeared from sight and nothing was seen of her again. The Second Officer then said, "Call the Captain and tell him that the ship has disappeared in the S.W., that we are heading W.S.W. and that altogether she has fired eight rockets." I then went down below to the chartroom and called the Captain and told him and he asked me if there were any colours in the rockets. I told him that they were all white. He then asked me what time it was and I went on the bridge and told the Second Officer what the Captain had said. At about 2.45 he whistled down to the Captain again but I did not hear what was said. At about 3.20 looking over the weather-cloth, I observed a rocket about two points before the beam (Port), which I reported to the Second Officer. About three minutes later I saw another rocket right abeam which was followed later by another one about two points before the beam. I saw nothing else and when one bell went, I went below to get the log gear ready for the Second Officer at eight bells.

Yours respectfully,
(Signed) *James Gibson,*
Apprentice.

Maps of the icefield in which the *Titanic* sank

I

Captain Knapp's Chart "*Titanic* — Ice Barrier - Near-by ships" and explanation.

Senator SMITH. Captain, can you think of anything else that you desire to say that will tend to throw any light upon the inquiry being made by the committee into the causes leading up to this wreck, and subsequent events, including any memorandum or data bearing upon the position of the steamship *Californian* on the night of this accident?

Capt. KNAPP. I desire to submit the following "Memorandum on chart", marked "*Titanic* - Ice Barrier - Near-by ships, which is explanatory of Chart No. 2, which I have introduced in evidence.

The memorandum referred to is as follows:

HYDROGRAPHIC OFFICE,
Washington, D.C., May 14, 1912.

MEMORANDUM ON CHART
"TITANIC" – ICE BARRIER – NEAR-BY SHIPS.
6————-.

The chart bearing the above heading shows the ice barrier into which the *Titanic* undoubtedly steamed. The ice as shown on this chart, it will be noted, is grouped in one barrier, and not shown scattered as on the chart headed "Ice as reported near *Titanic*". From all the evidence before the Hydrographic Office — that is, the hearings before the Senate committee and the various reports made by steamers of ice in the locality in question — the Hydrographic Office deems that the ice barrier was, to all intents and purposes, as shown on this chart. Copies of the above-mentioned ice reports are forwarded herewith. There may have been, and probably were, other ice fields or bergs in this general locality, but they are not shown on the chart, as it is desired to bring out clearly, without other confusing details, the barrier into which the *Titanic* steamed.

An inspection of this chart will show that the *Mount Temple* ran into the southwestern end of this ice field at 12.55 a.m. (New York time), April 15. Thereafter to have reached the *Titanic* it would have been necessary for the *Mount Temple* to have steamed around the southern end of this ice barrier, and around it to the northward and eastward over 30 miles. As her highest speed does not exceed 13 knots (Lloyds Register) she could not have reached the scene of the *Titanic* disaster earlier than 3.15 a.m. (New York time) of that morning, or about 2 hours and

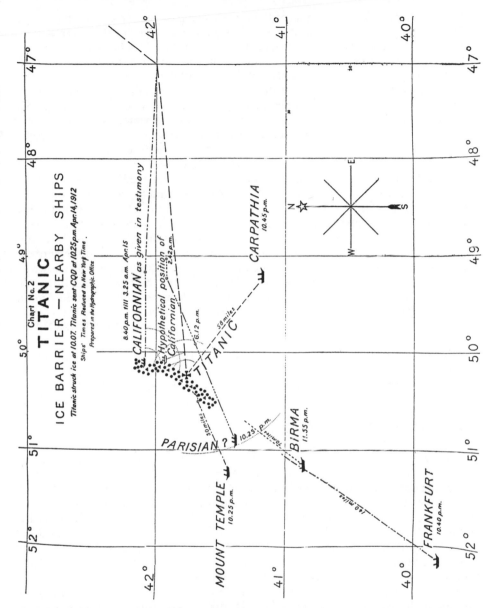

**Map I. Chart prepared by Captain John J. Knapp, US Navy: "TITANIC" —
ICE BARRIER AND NEARBY SHIPS" (US Navy)**

18 minutes after the *Titanic* sank (12.57 a.m., New York time).

A further inspection of this chart shows the *Californian* as located by the master thereof.

A still further inspection of the chart will show certain arcs of circles, shown in dotted lines drawn from the following centers: The position of the *Californian*, the position of the *Titanic*, the "hypothetical" position of the *Californian*. These arcs are drawn to represent the following: The radii of the arcs drawn about the *Titanic* as a center and the *Californian* as a center are identical, the larger radius being 16 miles and the smaller radius being 7 miles. Sixteen miles represents the distance at which the side lights of the *Titanic* could be seen from one standing on the *Californian* at the height of the latter ship's side lights, or the reverse, the 7 miles radius being the distance at which the side lights of the *Californian* would cease to be seen by a person from a boat in the water. A further reference to the chart will show, midway between the plotted positions of the *Californian* and *Titanic*, a plotted "hypothetical position of the *Californian.*" With the hypothesis that the *Californian* was in this plotted position, a dotted line is drawn on a bearing SSE. given by the master of the *Californian* as the bearing in which he sighted a large steamer. This dotted line is drawn to intersect the track of the *Titanic*. A line parallel thereto is drawn to also intersect the track of the *Titanic* at a point at which the *Titanic* appears to have been seen at 10.06 p.m., New York time, April 14 - at 11.56 p.m. of that date by the *Californian's* time — at which time the large steamer is testified to have been by Ernest Gill, of the *Californian* and the testimony of Ernest Gill of that ship will fix the *Californian's* position near or about the hypothetical position shown on the chart, if the lights seen on that ship were those of the *Titanic*.

A still further inspection of the chart will show that the *Californian*, if located in the position given by the master thereof, could have reached the scene of the disaster in about two hours, and, if located in the hypothetical position shown on the chart, the *Californian* certainly could have reached the *Titanic* in a little over an hour after she struck. The evidence taken in the hearings shows that the *Titanic* floated for two and a half hours after she struck the barrier.

JOHN J. KNAPP.

I invited especial attention to that part of the memorandum referring to the hypothetical position of the *Californian*, as shown on that chart, and, in connection therewith, it is desirable to explain that the arcs of circles drawn about the position of the steamship *Titanic* and about the position of the steamship *Californian* were drawn to graphically illustrate the testimony of certain witnesses before your committee.

Senator SMITH. What do these arcs indicate?

Capt. KNAPP. The outer arc around each ship is drawn with a radius of 16 miles, which is approximately the farthest distance at which the curvature of the earth would have permitted the side lights of the *Titanic* to be seen by a person at the height of the side lights of the *Californian*. The inner circle around each ship is drawn with a radius of 7 miles. This is approximately the distance after reaching which the curvature of the earth would have shut out the side lights of the *Californian* from the view of one in a lifeboat in the water. It appears, therefore, that if the *Titanic's* position at the time of the accident was as fixed by the testimony and if it was the side light of the *Californian* that was seen from the boat deck of the *Titanic*, the *Californian* was somewhere inside of the arc of the 16-mile circle drawn about the *Titanic*. It further appears that if the above hypothesis be correct, and if the side light of the other steamer could not be seen, as is testified to, from one of the lifeboats of the *Titanic* after being lowered, the *Californian* was somewhere outside of the circle with the 7-mile radius drawn about the *Titanic*.

In the case of the *Californian*, if the steamer which in the testimony given by members of the crew of the *Californian*, including the captain and the donkey engineman and others, is said to have been seen by them, was the *Titanic*, she must have been somewhere inside of the circle with the 16-mile radius drawn around the *Californian*. If that be the case, as the *Californian's* side light was shut out by the curvature of the earth from the view of anyone in a lifeboat of the *Titanic* after being lowered into the water, then the *Titanic* must have been outside of the circle drawn with the 7-mile radius around the *Californian*.

Further reference to this chart will show plotted a hypothetical position of the *Californian*. On the hypothesis that the *Californian* was in this position, a dotted line is drawn on the chart on the bearing given by the captain of the *Californian* as that on which the steamer was sighted. This bearing is drawn on the chart to intersect the track of the *Titanic*. Another dotted line is drawn parallel thereto from a point on the course of the *Titanic* where she apparently was at 10.06 p.m., New York time, April 14, that being 11.56 p.m. of that date of the *Californian's* time, at which Ernest Gill, a member of the crew of the *Californian,* in his testimony before your committee, stated that the large steamer was seen by him. If the *Californian* was in the hypothetical position shown on the chart, the *Titanic* could have been seen by the officers and crew of the *Californian* at the time mentioned.

Senator SMITH. Captain, are you able to state to the committee whether there was any vessel between the position of the *Titanic* just preceding and following the accident and the position of the *Californian* at that time?

Capt. KNAPP. From being present at hearings before your committee and from reading the printed testimony of witnesses examined by the committee I am led to the conclusion that if there was any vessel between the *Californian* and the *Titanic* at the time referred to she does not seem to have been seen by any of the ships near there on the following morning, nor have there been any reports submitted to the Hydrographic Office which would indicate that there was any such steamer in that locality. The evidence does not indicate to me that there was any such third steamer in those waters, especially in view of the fact that no such steamer was seen by other steamers or by those in the lifeboats the following morning, and as the ice barrier, from all reports, between the reported position of the *Californian* and that of the *Titanic* was impassable to a vessel proceeding to the westward, and there is no testimony to show that if such a steamer was between the *Californian* and the *Titanic* she proceeded to the eastward, the captain of the *Californian,* having testified that he last saw the said steamer proceeding to the westward and being on a bearing to the westward of the *Californian*. Nothing appears in the testimony to show that the steamer so seen reversed its course and proceeded to the eastward.

Senator SMITH. Captain, it appears from the testimony that there are established, by mutual agreement between the steamship lines, certain fixed courses, tracks, or lanes across the north Atlantic, and that the steamship companies order their captains to follow these tracks. Has the captain of a ship any discretion in this matter which would enable him to depart from the given track or course to avoid danger?

Capt. KNAPP. It is, of course, understood by all seafaring people, and, in fact, it should be understood by the public generally, that the trans-Atlantic steamers in following certain tracks in crossing the ocean are not supposed to adhere rigidly to those tracks when good seamanship dictates that they diverge therefrom. A seaman is supposed always to handle and navigate a ship in a seamanlike manner, and no hard and fast, rigid rules are laid down that require him to do otherwise. The following is from the International Rules, enacted by the Senate and House of Representatives of the United States:

Art. 29. Nothing in these rules shall exonerate any vessel, or the owner or master or crew thereof, from the consequences of any neglect to carry lights or signals, or of any neglect to keep a proper lookout, or of the neglect of any precaution which may be required by the ordinary practice of seamen, or by the special circumstances of the case.

This rule affirms a sea maxim that a captain must, in an emergency, handle or navigate his ship in a seamanlike manner.
Witness excused.
[Senator Smith thereupon entered in the record a memorandum from Capt. Knapp regarding the drift of ice on and near the Grand Banks, submitted by the Hydrographic Office, May 13, 1912. This memorandum is omitted here as its bearing on the *Californian* is remote.]

II

The sketch of the *Birma,* as prepared by Captain Stupling of the SS *Birma's*

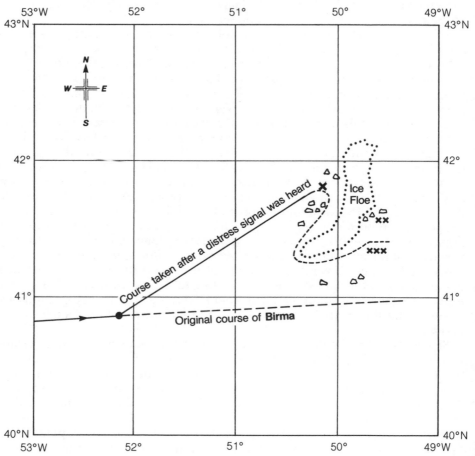

✗ **Titanic's** given position

✗✗ **Carpathia** picking up boats

✗✗✗ **Birma** observing **Carpathia**

⌂ Iceberg

- - - - **Birma's** track through and around the ice to **Carpathia**

Map II. Sketch, as prepared by Captain Stupling of the SS *Birma*
Track of the Birma *after receiving the distress signal. A diagram similar to this one was published in* The Daily Telegraph *on 25 April 1912. It is here presented with some minor corrections taken from Captain Stupling's original chart.*

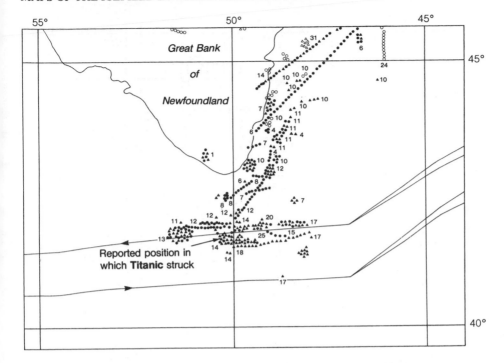

Map III. Detail of map prepared for US District Court, New York
The map is dated 25 June 1915 and lists icebergs and icefields for March and April 1912. The ▲ represent icebergs, the dots the icefields and on this section of the map are all for April. The numbers represent the date of sighting.

dash to the scene of the disaster, the morning of 15 April and the icefield, taken at seven a.m. First published 25 April 1912, by *The Daily Telegraph*. [See also Map II.]

III

Detail of map prepared for US District Court, New York, 25 June 1915; of icebergs and icefield for March and April 1912. The ▲ represent icebergs, the dots the icefield and on this section of the map are all for April. The numbers represent the date of sighting.

Independently these three charts clearly show the ice field in a north-east to south-west direction with the *Titanic's* position on the eastern side of the ice field, where it logically should be.

These three independently made maps are not regarded as favourite products of professional charting by the friends of Captain Lord. Their favourite map is actually another sketch and represented here as No. IV.

IV

Sketch, used mainly by the supporters of Captain Lord and often accepted by the media as the only map available, whatever their feelings or sympathies in the case.

It was first published in January 1913 by Captain John D'Arcy Morton in his article 'Pushed under the Wheels of a Juggernaut' for the MMSA's monthly *Reporter* and republished in March 1962, by the MMSA in 'The "Californian" Incident', with a Foreword by Leslie Harrison.

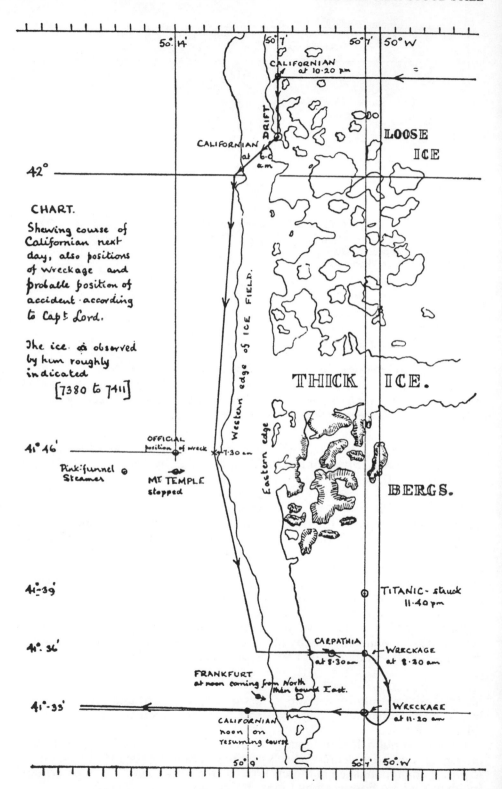

Map IV. Sketch used mainly by Captain Lord's legion
Attributed to Mr A.M. Foweraker, it was Captain Lord who provided its basis on 25 April 1912.

The sketch is attributed to Mr A.M. Foweraker, but its basis is the rough sketch that Captain Lord made in his own defence on 25 April, after Gill's story had been published in the *Boston American* and Lord realized, that "there would be an enquiry over it".

Since 1962 the sketch has been used in various subsequent accounts of the disaster, all in defence of Captain Lord; *THS* * *Commutator,* September 1964; U.S. Naval Institute Proceedings, March 1968, p. 66; *Sea Classics,* July 1970, p. 43, also No. 9, 1985, p. 75; *The Daily Telegraph,* 16 July 1990, p. 32 — here also used to give the track of the *Birma*.

Two imaginary features in the sketch stand out:

First — the direction of the icefield on the sketch, which is almost directly north-south, and thus placing the *Titanic's* CQD position to the west of the icefield, whereas she undeniably sank east of the field and on the same side where the *Californian* had been during the night.

Second — the curious 'fence' of "THICK ICE" that stretches in a right west-east direction directly from the field to the east. It lies comfortably between the *Californian* and the *Titanic,* effectively building a barrier of ice between the two ships. However, there is no substantial evidence to support its existence.

* TITANIC HISTORICAL SOCIETY; formally the TITANIC ENTHUSIASTS of AMERICA and the first *Titanic* club, established 1963. Today the world knows some seven of these amateur historical TITANIC clubs. Most, if not all, form the rearguard of Captain Lord's defence.

The *Mount Temple*

The following is the latter part of an opinion by Sir R. Ellis Cunliffe, the solicitor to the Board of Trade. The first part was his opinion on the censure of Captain Lord and the reasons for it. His comments on the *Mount Temple* are reproduced here with the punctuation (or lack of it) as in the original. The reference for the original document is [MT 9/920/6] M 31921.

". . . Now as regards the "MOUNT TEMPLE" it apparently is suggested by Captain Lord that the "MOUNT TEMPLE" was the ship whose lights were seen by the "TITANIC" and so far as I can gather that the "MOUNT TEMPLE" was between the "CALIFORNIAN" and the "TITANIC" on the night of the 14th or at all events in the morning of the 15th April. Further that the "MOUNT TEMPLE" was equally to blame for not getting fast enough to the assistance of the "TITANIC." What help Captain Lord will get from the mere contention that there was something blameworthy on the part of the Captain of the "MOUNT TEMPLE" I cannot at present see. According to the evidence of the Captain of the "MOUNT TEMPLE" and that of the Marconi operator on board her, the "MOUNT TEMPLE" on the night of the disaster was steaming West on a course to the South of that of the "TITANIC's" and was 49 miles distant from the "TITANIC" when she first heard her call for assistance, that would be 49 miles to the South and West of the "TITANIC".

According to the evidence given in America the "MOUNT TEMPLE" was in longitude 51° 14' W. latitude 41° 25' North when she heard the "TITANIC's" call, and at 3.25 a.m. arrived within about 14 miles from the spot where the "TITANIC" sank at 2.25 a.m. and stopped there because of ice in her way. It is also asserted by the Captain that from the time he turned his boat round to go to the assistance of the "TITANIC" he went as fast as he could until stopped by the ice.

Now unless the evidence of the Captain of the "MOUNT TEMPLE" and that of the Marconi operator on board her is a tissue of lies, and I must say that the evidence given by them in England, was in effect the same as that given by them in America, it would be utterly impossible for the "MOUNT TEMPLE" at any time while the "CALIFORNIAN" had in sight the vessel that she saw sending up rockets, to have been between the "CALIFORNIAN" and that vessel, and this is borne out by a chart or plan which was drawn out by the Captain of the "CALIFORNIAN" when he arrived in Boston, for by it he shows where his ship was stopped during the night and shows the course he took after he heard of the "TITANIC's" disaster to get round to her wreckage and it will be seen that about 6.30 a.m. he passed the "MOUNT TEMPLE" stopped to the West of where he eventually found wreckage from the "TITANIC". In the plan in question he shows a vessel to the North of the place where wreckage was seen and Captain Lord might possibly claim that that was the vessel that he saw on the night and not the "TITANIC". He was not able to state the name of the vessel, but that there was such a vessel there when day broke on the 15th April is corroborated by Captain Rostron of the "CARPATHIA" who states that at 8 p.m. on the morning of April 15th he saw two steamers to Northwards of where he was and that neither was the "CALIFORNIAN" and that he saw the masthead lights of another steamer between his ship and the "TITANIC'S" at about 3.15 a.m. but when these ships got into these positions there is no evidence to show. One would have thought that Captain Lord would, when on the spot have been anxious to satisfy himself on the question of the identity of this vessel and the best thing he could have done would have been to speak to her, but this he did not do. If the wreckage from the "TITANIC" drifted South from the place where the "TITANIC" sank, as appears to be the case, the spot at which the "MOUNT TEMPLE" stopped (and apparently she did not stop on her N.E. run until about 3.30) would be almost to the immediate West of the place where the "TITANIC" struck and the "MOUNT TEMPLE" would assuming she is properly placed in the plan be as far away from the "CALIFORNIAN" as the "TITANIC" was, and not heading West as the vessel was which the "CALIFOR- NIAN" saw, for the "MOUNT TEMPLE" had come back on her tracks on a N.E. course. Moreover if a vessel had been between the "CALIFORNIAN" and the "TITANIC" on the night of the disaster then assuming she was the vessel with a yellow funnel and 4 masts shown on Captain Lord's plan she cannot have been the "MOUNT TEMPLE" and would probably have easily been seen by those on board the "TITANIC" if she had been there during the night.

Now as I have stated before whatever may be said against the Captain of the "MOUNT TEMPLE" by those on board, and there are rumours that people on board seemed to think that at some time she saw lights (probably the flares from the boats in the water) and that she did not do all she could to get to the "TITANIC" as I am not able to agree that the vessel that the "CALIFORNIAN" saw was the "MOUNT TEMPLE" whether the Captain of the "MOUNT TEMPLE" did or omit- ted to do something that he ought not to have done or should have done (and according to his evidence and that of the Marconi operator, he did everything he could) may be a matter for further inquiry, but so far as I can see does not help Captain Lord.

There was I notice from the remarks made by Counsel for Captain Lord a sugges- tion that he might have mistaken the place where the "MOUNT TEMPLE" was stopped but no evidence was given to correct the plan put in.

As regards the Captain of the "MOUNT TEMPLE" those on board must have known full well what evidence he and his Marconi operator gave in America, and must have guessed that he and the Marconi operator would he called again as witnesses at the "TITANIC" Inquiry in England and if there were any allegations which persons on board desired to make against the Captain or any evidence which they thought ought to be before the Court in England they clearly ought to have volunteered to come forward as witnesses on the subject. There was nothing in the papers before the Board of Trade to suggest that the Captain of the "MOUNT TEMPLE" had omitted to do anything that he ought to have done. If the "MOUNT TEMPLE" could have been the ship which the "CALIFORNIAN" saw on the night of the disaster, I think the Owners of the Leyland Line should have produced evidence to this effect, and if they have reason to suppose that the Captain of the "MOUNT TEMPLE" has not told the truth, the Owners could produce this evidence. The Leyland Company's shares are owned by the combine who own the greater number of the White Star Line shares and they would be anxious to get at the truth.

It seems to me that it is for Captain Lord to obtain evidence from any source to show why the findings of the Court are wrong so far as he is concerned; it is not enough to suggest that someone else may also have been guilty of conduct that was blameworthy.

We have already told the Solicitors to the Leyland Line that if they will forward any statements from persons who contradict the evidence of the Captain of the "MOUNT TEMPLE" they will be carefully considered, but whether this would help Captain Lord is as I have said very doubtful and even assuming such evidence to be forthcoming I should have to lay the further facts as disclosed before the Counsel who conducted the Inquiry on behalf of the Board of Trade to know whether under the circumstances any further action is necessary on the part of the Board.

The evidence given by witnesses on board the "CALIFORNIAN" both in America and England, the evidence of Captain Rostron of the "CARPATHIA", the speech of Mr. Dunlop Counsel for Captain Lord at the Inquiry in England and the Attorney General's speech on the subject of the "CALIFORNIAN" are all of interest on the point under consideration, while the evidence in America and England of the Captain of the "MOUNT TEMPLE" and his Marconi operator deal with the matter from their standpoint.

The findings of the Court of Inquiry in America and of the Court of Inquiry in England show the view of Captain Lord's conduct taken by each Court.

I forward the Log of the "CALIFORNIAN" and the plan and notes prepared by Captain Lord, which should be taken great care of and should be returned.

I have thought it right to deal with this matter somewhat fully."

(Signed) REC 6/11/12

The man in the coal basket

The August 1968 issue of the US Naval Institute *Proceedings* contained a letter from Mr Leslie Harrison, which included the following passage:

> "One of the witnesses from the Californian still available today is Benjamin Kirk, who had the distinction of being hoisted in the coal basket to the main truck at 6 a.m. with instructions to look for the Titanic. If the Californian was visible from bridge level in the Carpathia, Kirk would certainly have seen the Carpathia from the Californian's main truck. Nothing was in sight, however."

This was an interesting and important statement. Although part of an otherwise typical letter, here, for the first time, was a simple statement by Captain Lord's supporters that a named member of the crew of the *Californian* was alive and still "available", presumably to give evidence. A check showed that Mr Kirk, a Liverpool man, had in fact been an AB in the *Californian* on her controversial voyage. He was then 22 years old, and had served in the Royal Naval Reserve. If it was really true he had seen nothing from the coal basket about six o'clock that morning, it would be important to find out — apart from his not seeing the *Titanic,* which, of course, had sunk hours earlier — why he had failed to see the four-masted steamer, which Stewart had discovered at 4 a.m. Apart from this, any opportunity of speaking to a member of the crew, who was an addition to the familiar roster of *Californian* witnesses, and who had no obvious partisan interest to colour his story, was something not to be missed. At the very least, his recollections would be something to compare with the mass of contemporary evidence from the *Carpathia* and elsewhere (*cf.* Chapters 8, 9, 20) which proved that the *Californian* was in sight of the rescue ship certainly by six o'clock, and actually long before. On the face of it, Mr Kirk's story seemed to be a contradiction of the MMSA's theory of "simultaneous mutual sighting" between ships.

Although Mr Kirk was said to be "still available", previous experience gave no ground for believing that he might be "available" for a talk with the writer; and there was no guarantee that a letter addressed to him in care of the MMSA would reach him. Necessarily, therefore, an independent search had once more to be undertaken. After encountering even more difficulties than those described in earlier searches, and several months later, the Social Security authorities in the North of England stated they believed they had traced an account referring to Mr Kirk. They, of course, refused to disclose his address, but undertook to forward one sealed letter to him. A letter requesting a short interview anywhere to suit Mr Kirk's convenience was dispatched.

Some weeks later, the self-addressed envelope sent with the letter was returned to the writer. Inside was a typed postcard, without address or signature, and reading as follows:

"7 February, 1969.
Mr. Benjamin Kirk thanks Mr. Reade for his approach but greatly regrets that owing to his present state of health he is not able to become involved in any discussions relating to the Californian."

The following month, March 1969, was distinguished in maritime circles by the publication of Geoffrey Marcus's book, *The Maiden Voyage*. Author and book were promptly and fiercely attacked by the Californians for his account of the incident, and for certain comments about Captain Lord. Fortunately, Mr Kirk's health recovered sufficiently for him to join in this discussion, and the November 1969, issue of *The Nautical Magazine* contained the following letter over his signature:

"Sir — I have read Chapter 18 ('The Row about the *Californian*') from the book The Maiden Voyage, by G.J. Marcus, and in particular the references to Captain Stanley Lord on pages 280, 282 and 283. I do not agree with these passages, having always found Captain Lord very understanding and a good master to serve under.

I was doing a second trip in the *Californian* as AB and was on look-out when she stopped in field ice. I came on watch again at four in the morning. There were no icebergs in sight. Later the Chief Officer asked me to go up in a coal basket, shackled to a mainmast stay and hoisted by a gantline, to look for survivors or wreckage or boats from the *Titanic*. I could see nothing. I remember very plainly first seeing the *Mount Temple* on the port bow and then the *Carpathia*. There were no boats or wreckage in the water, which was calm, but the *Carpathia* had boats on her foredeck. She steamed away and I came down.

When the *Californian* docked in Liverpool no one questioned me about what had happened. I did not go down to the inquiry. — Yours, etc. B. KIRK."

This letter contains much of interest and a good deal that is ambiguous. If his statement: "I could see nothing", refers only to 'survivors, wreckage or boats', it is clearly true; but if Mr Kirk meant he could see no ship sight when he was hoisted to the main truck, it would have been interesting, as well as important, to have tried to reconcile his 57-year-old memory with the contemporary evidence of Captain Moore, Groves, and at least four officers of the *Carpathia,* Bisset, Dean, Rees and Barnish, as well as the Steward Barker. Mr Kirk seemed to have regretted he was not questioned in 1912, but he could have been assured, if he had wished, of being cross-examined in 1969 much more thoroughly than would have been possible in 1912. Mr Kirk was 78 years old, and still a resident of the seamen's colony already mentioned. This was owned, incidentally, by the MMSA and the head of it, the "Captain", as he was called, was "one time Chief Officer W.L.S. Harrison."

Appendix H

Evans, Gibson and Groves afterwards

The careers of Captain Lord, Chief Officer Stewart and Second Officer Stone after the *Californian* are described in the text. Here is some information about the later lives of Wireless Operator Evans, Apprentice Gibson, and Third Officer Groves.

Cyril Furmston Evans. This modest young man served in both World Wars, and spent the whole of his adult life in the employment of the Marconi Company — Telecommunicators Cable and Wireless Ltd. For family reasons, he incorporated one of his Christian names into his surname, and so after 1924 became Cyril Furmston Furmston-Evans. He retired in 1957 as a Manager Engineer, and died very suddenly in July 1959 of a coronary thrombosis, leaving a widow.

James Gibson, who unintentionally clinched the case against the *Californian,* attained his Second Mate's certificate. He left Leyland's for the Cunard Line, where he served for many years in the old *Curmania* — victor in the historic duel with the *Cap Trafalgar* in World War I — and in the *Scythia.* Later, he joined the Holt Line, and made voyages to West Africa. He served under the Holt house flag in the Second World War. When ill health compelled him to leave the sea, he became a shore relief officer at Liverpool. He died in 1963, having been, in the words of his wife, "a seafaring man for some 46 years".

Charles Victor Groves. Having obtained his extra master's certificate, Groves served in submarines in World War I. In January 1916 his boat, E 17, ran ashore on Den Helder on the Dutch coast. The crew were rescued by Dutch seamen and taken to Holland, where they spent the rest of the war in internment. Groves, going back and forth between Holland and England, was allowed to spend no less than 14 months on parole in England until the war ended. The nature of his confinement can otherwise be guessed from the fact that on one occasion when his brother met him at Euston Station on arrival from his internment, Groves was accompanied by four huge and heavy trunks.

"My God!" the brother exclaimed, "What have you got there?"

"Coal," said Groves, the "prisoner", having brought what relief he could, with the permission of his gaolers, to his wintry and fuel-short England.

Easy-going as his internment was, Groves, who was ever active mentally, used the time he actually spent in Holland to make himself fluent in Dutch.

He had been married by 1914. After the end of the war, he joined W.A. Suter's Sheaf Line, and ultimately became their Marine Superintendent at Newcastle upon Tyne, and their most trusted adviser as well. As a commander at sea, Groves had a remarkably wide and agreeable reputation in many parts of the world as always having a happy ship.

Apart from Masonry, Groves had a wide variety of interests connected with the sea, both before and after his retirement, which took place about 1938. For many years he edited Reed's 'Distance Tables', and did much valuable work for Trinity House and the Royal Geographical Society, including a survey of Christmas Island, long before it attained world notoriety as the setting of a nuclear explosion. Concerned particularly with the status of British seamen, possibly the work closest to his heart was the Seafarers' Education Service. He was an enthusiastic member of the joint scholarship committee of the S.E.S. and the Royal Society of Arts, the object of which was to encourage deck boys and young seamen to study for navigating officers' certificates. One of his close friends was Rear Admiral Charles Edward Lynes, RN, who was said to be the only man, in modern times at least, who attained flag rank in the British navy "through the hawse hole", that is, from the lower deck.

In the Second World War, although he was retired, Groves, having long been in the RNR, served with the Admiralty at Southend, where he was attached to the Defensive Armament of Merchant Ships section. Groves was a well-known admiralty assessor, and as such took part in some 25 inquiries and other legal proceedings. Among them was the inquiry in Belfast in 1953 into the *Princess Victoria* disaster. Perhaps because of a memory of 1912, but certainly as an expression of his own compassionate nature, Groves, as an assessor, became known and respected for his merciful decisions. He had nonetheless a judicial mind, and as his unchanged story about the *Californian* and the *Titanic* proved, the mental and moral toughness to stick to an unpopular point of view, when convinced he was right. The late Emeritus Professor A.M. Robb, one-time assistant to Sir John Biles, who later filled with great distinction Biles's old chair of Naval Architecture at Glasgow University, sat as a fellow assessor with Groves at two wreck inquiries, one of which was into the loss of the *Princess Victoria*. Asked for his opinion of Groves's judgement on the *Californian,* which was so savagely criticized, and indeed derided, by Captain Lord's friends, Professor Robb gave an interesting answer: ". . . Captain Groves and I were in sincere disagreement almost from the start. Nevertheless I should have no difficulty in accepting his story of events on the 'Californian' at the time of the 'Titanic' tragedy." Captain W.R. Chaplin, CBE, wrote after Groves's death: "Rather shy and unassuming, few knew him well, but those who did admired him greatly for his sound judgement and readiness to weigh up opposing opinions on any subject under discussion."

As it was, he had a life of considerable achievement, and, following a rapid decline in health, he died on 4 September 1961.

Captain Lord's voyages as a Leyland Commander

Ship	Official Number	Capacity in which served	Date & place service began	Date & place service ended
Antillian	109493	Chief Mate	27.12.05 Hull	28. 2.06 L'pool
"	"	Master	8. 3.06 L'pool	24. 5.06 "
Louisianian	99322	"	24. 7.06 "	10.10.06 "
"	"	"	11.10.06 "	11.12.06 "
"	"	"	18.12.06 "	9. 3.07 "
"	"	"	14. 3.07 "	17. 3.07 "
"	"	"	21. 3.07 "	28. 5.07 "
"	"	"	12. 6.07 "	1. 9.07 "
"	"	"	10. 9.07 "	20.11.07 "
"	"	"	26.11.07 "	25. 1.08 "
"	"	"	30. 1.08 "	4. 4.08 "
"	"	"	30. 4.08 "	30. 6.08 "
"	"	"	1. 7.08 "	21. 9.08 "
"	"	"	5.10.08 "	30.11.08 "
"	"	"	1.12.08 "	4. 2.09 "
"	"	"	25. 2.09 "	5. 5.09 "
"	"	"	7. 5.09 "	14. 7.09 "
"	"	"	4. 8.09 "	6.10.09 "
William Cliff	93807	"	22.11.09 "	27. 1.10 "
"	"	"	7. 2.10 "	1. 5.10 "
"	"	"	31. 5.10 "	7. 8.10 "
"	"	"	15. 8.10 "	20.10.10 "
"	"	"	31.10.10 "	24.12.10 "
Californian	115243	"	27. 3.11 "	13. 6.11Am'dm
"	"	"	26. 6.11 Am'dm	5.10.11 B'hvn
"	"	"	5.10.11 B'hvn	22.11.11 L'pool
"	"	"	23.11.11 L'pool	15. 1.12 "
"	"	"	21. 1.12 "	30. 3.12 L'don
"	"	"	5. 4.12 L'don	10. 5.12 L'pool

(N.B. The above table is the result of a special search of the records at the General Register and Record Office of Shipping and Seamen, Cardiff.)

Am'dm = Amsterdam; B'hvn = Bremerhaven; L'don = London; L'pool = Liverpool

Crew of the *Californian*

Name	Age	Birthplace	Capacity	Wages per calendar month
Stanley Lord	35	Bolton		£20 per month, plus annual bonus of £50
G.F. Stewart	24	Liverpool	Chief Mate	£13
H. Stone	24	Devon	1st Mate	£ 9.10
C.V. Groves	24	Cambs.	2nd Mate	£ 8.10
W.F. McGregor	41	Liverpool	Carpenter	£ 7
Eppo. Dick	32	Liverpool	Bos'un	£ 6.10
S. Brennan	40	Liverpool	Bos'un's Mate	£ 5.10
R. Jones	60	Conway	Lamptrimmer & AB	£ 5.5
Louis Carswell	45	Greenock	Q'master & AB	£ 5.5
John Dalziel	35	Shetland	Q'master & AB	£ 5.5
J. Clapham	45	London	Q'master & AB	£ 5.5
Chas. Le Comes	43	Jersey	Q'master & AB	£ 5.5
William Ross	26	Everton	AB	£ 5
G. Jacob	19	Leeds	AB	£ 5
J. Ashton	21	Waterloo Liverpool	AB	£ 5
M. Ballantyne	49	Glasgow	AB	£ 5
W. Haydon	38	London	AB	£ 5
J. Lushey	56	W. Ham	AB	£ 5
B. Kirk	22	Liverpool	AB	£ 5
J. Onsworth	18	London	OS	£ 2.10
Harry Lawes	17	Plaistow	Deck Boy	£ 1.10
W.S.A. Mahan	37	Greenock	1st Eng.	£17
J.C. Evans	31	Bangor	2nd Eng.	£13
Jas. Fyfe	33	Birkenhead	3rd Eng.	£11
F.R. Hooton	23	Liverpool	4th Eng.	£ 9
John Sintich	51	Austria	Donkeyman	£ 7
O. Hoffmann*	32	Germany	Asst. Donkeyman	
Ernest Gill***	26	Sheffield	Fireman	£ 5.10
J. Zander	62	Germany	Storekeeper	£ 5.15
Geo. Glenn	23	Liverpool	Fireman	£ 5.10

Name	Age	Birthplace	Capacity	Wages per calendar month
W.H. Parry	30	Greenwich	Fireman	£ 5.10
W. Thomas	46	Jersey	Greaser	£ 5.15
T. Button	31	London	Fireman	£ 5.10
W. Kennerdale**	43	Liverpool	Fireman	£ 5.10
D. Donovan	42	London	Fireman	£ 5.10
W. Brennan*	52	Woolwich	Fireman	
H. Gerworski***	42	Germany	Fireman	£ 6.10
T. White*	20	London	Trimmer	
B. Murray	29	London	Fireman	£ 5.10
G. Melville	20	London	Trimmer	£ 5
C. Jessop	29	London	Fireman	£ 5.10
Wm. Hughes	35	Liverpool	Chief Steward	£ 7.10
S. Beal	29	Brighton	2nd Steward	£ 3.10
A.F. Bartmann	26	Amsterdam	3rd Steward	£ 3.10
C. Wilson*	32	London	Mess Room Steward	
P.W. Janssen	42	Holland	Ship's Cook	£ 6.10
Hy. J. Burlingham	41	Worcester	2nd Cook & Baker	£ 4.10
C.F. Evans	20	Croydon	Telegraphist	1/- per month (This was a nominal sum as his proper wages, £4 per month, were paid by Marconi.)

Substitutes

Name	Age	Birthplace	Capacity	Wages per calendar month
W. Ward	38	London	Fireman	£ 5.10
A. Homans	20	London	Trimmer	£ 5
W. Willis	20	Poplar E.	Trimmer	£ 5
W. Burke~	43	Liverpool	Fireman	£ 5.10
Albert Roberts~	26	Swansea	Fireman	£ 5.10

APPRENTICE	YEAR OF BIRTH	BIRTHPLACE	REGISTRY OF INDENTURE
James Gibson	1892	Southport	25.11.08 London (date of (place of signing) signing)

*   Failed to join
**   Died at Boston, Mass., 24. 4.12
*** Promoted to Asst. Donkeyman
~   Joined at Boston, Mass.
(The above is based on the Official Log and some P.I.)

Private night signals of steamship companies: transatlantic lines

LINE	SIGNAL	WHERE USED	DATE REGISTERED
Allan Line	1. Three rockets—blue, white, red—for mail steamers from Montreal, St John, N.B. & to Liverpool. 2. Three blue lights in a triangle for steamers bound to Glasgow direct. 3. Three blue lights in a triangle, followed by a blue light for steamers from New York to Glasgow calling at Moville.	Only in passing N of Ireland Signal Station (not used on high seas).	22 January 1903
		"	
American Line	Blue light forward; red light on bridge; blue light aft simultaneously.	Anywhere within British jurisdiction & on the high seas.	28 December 1894
Anchor Line	Red light & white light exhibited alternately from some conspicuous part of the ship; red light to be so exhibited as not to be mistaken for red sidelight.	On & near coasts of UK & on high seas.	4 December 1873
Atlantic Transport Line	Roman Candle throwing six balls of following colours: 1 green, 1 white & 1 red, to be repeated once in the same order.	Anywhere within British jurisdiction & on high seas.	20 October 1888
Canadian Pacific	Red pyrotechnic light near bow, yellow pyro. light amidships, & red pyro. light near stern, all burned simultaneously, to be followed by a blue light for steamers	Within British jurisdiction & on high seas.	5 April 1903

LINE	SIGNAL	WHERE USED	DATE REGISTERED
	crossing to Liverpool when signalling off Ireland.	"	
CGT French Line	Three Costan lights, blue, white & red, burned simultaneously at the fore, middle & after parts of the vessel respectively.		26 February 1890
Cunard Line	1. A blue light and two rockets bursting into golden stars, fired in quick succession.	Off Brow Head in the County of Cork, and off Queenstown Harbour in the County of Cork.	12 June 1874
	2. A blue light and two Roman Candles, each throwing out six blue balls to a height not exceeding 150 feet, and fired in quick succession.	Anywhere within British jurisdiction, and on the high seas.	12 June 1874
Furness-Withy	Green-red light on bridge followed by another immediately.		
Hamburg-Amerika HAPAG	Three Roman Candles burned in immediate succession at the stern of the vessel, each Roman Candle throwing to a ht. not exceeding 50 feet 7 stars in the following order of colour: white, red, blue, white, red, blue, white. (& other combinations on different routes, e.g. Hamburg—New York & Genoa—NY two pyro. lights [sic] red, white, blue.) Calling at Southampton: two pyro. lights [sic] —red, white, blue followed by a red light. The line had 17 different signals.	Off Scilly etc. and on high seas.	31 March 1874
Italian Royal Mail Steamship Company	Costan pyro. light showing colours, red, green, white, red in quick succession.	Within British jurisdiction & on high seas.	22 June 1901
F Leyland & Co	Three red pyro. lights burned singly but in quick succession.	Off Scillys, off Holyhead, at mouth of Mersey & on high seas.	20 November 1873

LINE	SIGNAL	WHERE USED	DATE REGISTERED
Manchester Liners	Three Roman Candles, 1 forward, 1 amidships, 1 aft, burned simultaneously, each throwing 3 green stars, followed by 1 red star to a ht. not exceeding 50 feet.	Anywhere within British jurisdiction & on high seas.	18 August 1898
Netherlands American Steam Navigation Co (Holland—America)	One green pyro. light from forecastle, 1 white pyro. light from bridge, 1 green pyro. light from poop—3 lights to be shown at same moment.	"	28 November 1888
NDL North German Lloyd	Two pyro. lights simultaneously, each of which changes from light 'commonly known as blue to a red light'.	"	22 February 1890
Red Star Line (SA de Navigation Belge-Américaine)	Three red lights simultaneously, 1 forward, 1 on bridge, 1 aft—Antwerp—NY service.	On or near coasts of UK (not on high seas).	18 February 1876
Scandinavian American (Forenede Dampskibs-Selskab, Copenhagen)	Two lights, first beginning with white, finishing with red; second beginning with red & finishing with white.		
White Star Line	Green pyro. light, followed by rocket throwing 2 green stars, rocket being followed by another green pyro. light. (For NY mail & passenger steamers, calling at Queenstown homewards.)	Off Brow Head, off Old Head of Kinsale & off Queenstown Harbour.	20 November 1903
	Ditto. (General): Two green pyro. lights, exhibited simultaneously.	Anywhere within British jurisdiction and on highseas, except as stated below (applies to Boston ships, cargo ships, etc.)	

Index

A Bibliography

The story:
"HEARINGS". US Senate, 62d Congress, 2d Session, Document No. 726.
"PROCEEDINGS". Cd. 6352 – 1912.
RMS "TITANIC" Reappraisal of Evidence Relating to SS "CALIFORNIAN". 1992.

The men:
F. LAWRENCE BABCOCK. *Spanning the Atlantic, A History of the Cunard S.S. Co.,* Knopf, 1931. (A very good book, not so well known as it deserves, and with an excellent bibliography.)
BERNAR HULDERMANN. *Albert Ballin,* Oldenburg, Berlin, 1922.
JACK LONDON (JOHN GRIFFITH LONDON). *The People of the Abyss* Life of London dockers 1903, Ibister & Co. Ltd., London.

The ships:
JOHN MALCOLM BRINNIN. *The Sway of the Grand Saloon,* Macmillan, 1971.
CRAIG J.M. CARTER. 'Sixty Years of the Leyland Line' (*Sea Breezes,* Vol. 16, July-December 1953).
HERBERT B. MASON, Editor, *Encyclopaedia of Ships and Shipping,* Shipping Encyclopaedia, London, 1908 (out of date, interesting and beautifully suited for 1912).
JOHN MAXTONE-GRAHAM. *The Only Way to Cross,* Foreword by Walter Lord, Macmillan, 1972, Patrick Stephens 1983.

The Press:
The Liverpool Courier, April-June 1912, *The New York Times,* April-June 1912.

Captain Lord's legion's favourite literature:
PETER PADFIELD. *The* Titanic *and the* Californian, Hodder & Stoughton, 1965 (a statement of a case for Captain Lord).
LESLIE HARRISON. *A* Titanic *Myth — The* Californian *Incident,* William Kimber 1986 and The Self-Publishing Association 1992 (a biography of Captain Lord and, as Padfield, a statement of a case in favour of him. The 1992 edition also contains an Epilogue with Mr Harrison's comments on the 1990-1992 Reappraisal).